DIG
WW2

JEAN HOOD

DIG
WW2

REDISCOVERING THE GREAT
WARTIME BATTLES

CONWAY

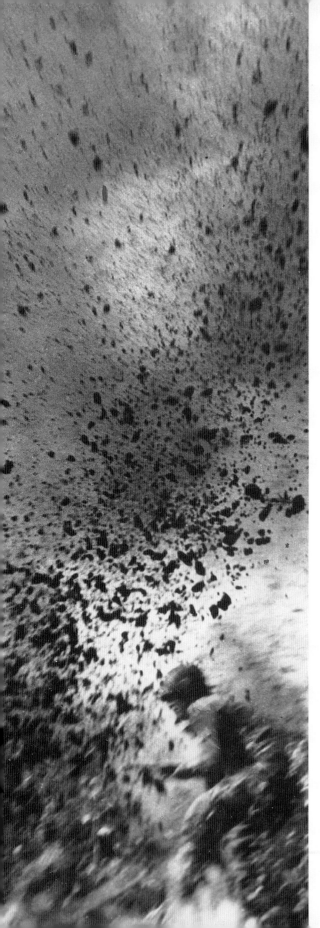

'For Lesley'

Text © Jean Hood, 2012
Volume © Conway, 2012

First published in Great Britain in 2012 by
Conway
An imprint of Anova Books Ltd
10 Southcombe Street
London W14 0RA
www.conwaypublishing.com

Produced in association with
360 Production
58 Davies Street
London, W1K 5JF
www.360production.com

A catalogue record for this book is available from the
British Library.

10 9 8 7 6 5 4 3 2 1

ISBN 9781844861507

Project Editor: Alison Moss
Edited by Christopher Westhorp
Picture research by Jennifer Veall
Design by Georgina Hewitt and Anna Matos Melgaco

Printed and bound by L.E.G.O. s.p.a., Italy

940.54

CONTENTS

INTRODUCTION

I have studied battles for a decade but focussing on the archaeology allowed me to break these encounters down into seconds. By plotting all the finds, we have been able to forensically reconstruct the course of some of the most important moments of World War Two.

Dan Snow

Still within living memory, the Second World War continues to fascinate each new generation, thanks to feature films, documentaries, newspaper articles and museum exhibitions, as well as through books and websites produced by veterans, historians and dedicated enthusiasts – not forgetting the dignified ceremonies of remembrance held annually around the world. The official archive of contemporary files, newsreels, photographs and radio broadcasts is vast. With so much information not just available but increasingly accessible, archaeology might seem unnecessary: a tool for reconstructing events and lives from a more distant and poorly recorded past.

Nothing could be further from the truth. As Dan Snow demonstrates in *Dig WW2*, the painstaking investigation of a site, as opposed to the mere plundering of wartime relics for 'trophies' or for commercial gain, has much to add to the recorded events of 1939–1945. The official files had to leave many questions unanswered, either because nobody was in a position to answer them at the time or because the war had moved on. More than half a century later the discovery of, for example, Spitfire wreckage in France may at last solve the mystery of why that aircraft crashed, thus writing a tiny footnote in history and completing an unfinished chapter in the memory of a family and a squadron. Developments in deep-diving techniques, and the increasing sophistication of submersibles, have begun to reveal the fates of surface ships and submarines that went down with all hands or in uncertain circumstances.

Dig WW2 also brings to life the visible but neglected legacy of the war in one part of the United Kingdom. Why is there a pillbox by the canal at Portna? What is the significance of the rotting wooden posts in the river at Lisahally or the iron ring in the slipway at Castle Archdale on the shores of Lough Erne? The answer is that they are all evidence of a time when Northern Ireland became not just important to the Allied war effort but vital to the conduct of the Battle of the Atlantic, a time when the accents of Ulster mingled with those of Allied countries as far away as New Zealand, Canada and Poland. This book goes further, looking at the defence of the whole of the United Kingdom, as well as exploring in greater depth the stories told in the television series and including others that deserve to be told, such as the shooting down of a Messerschmitt Bf 109 over Essex in 1940.

None of the tangible evidence, whether visible or unearthed, would be so engrossing without the human

dimension. The astonishing sight of Sherman tanks strewn around the seabed becomes the poignant narrative of a U-boat attack on a converted whaling ship and the rescue vessel that went to her aid, seen through the eyes of those who were there. A visit to a 'doodlebug' launch site in France leads on to the pilots who risked, and gave, their lives to bring the V1 rockets down before they could hit London. A soggy piece of leather proves to be a pilot's helmet. This was an essential piece of flying kit: issued to a particular man, grabbed whenever the call to scramble came through, a witness to every mission he flew, pulled off, damp with sweat, as he climbed out of the aircraft after returning safely – and finally left in the cockpit on the day he bailed out. It is as remarkable as the gun from the same aircraft that was restored to firing condition after 70 years in an Irish bog.

A regimental diary may tell us that a particular unit attacked the Hitler Line south of Rome, but empty German machine gun cartridges and the broken remains of a Canadian helmet in front of a fortification are sobering evidence of the bitter fighting in the final assault on one specific position out of many that faced the 1st Canadian Infantry Division and the tank squadrons supporting them. They represent instants in time, usually too small to have been recorded individually, and they are intensely visceral. To stare through the embrasure of a bunker at the English Channel, as tens of thousands of Germans did on D-Day, is a first step towards putting oneself into the shoes of someone who watched the approaching Allied armada and wondered what the day held. When added to the surrounding archive of memories, images and documents these visual and tactile experiences speak directly to us, providing a new dimension and helping us to an emotional as well an intellectual understanding. The past becomes as substantial and as real as the present.

ABOVE: Careful archaeology reveals the fragile remains of a helmet belonging to one of Canadian 1st Infantry Brigade during their assault on the left side of the Hitler Line in May 1944.

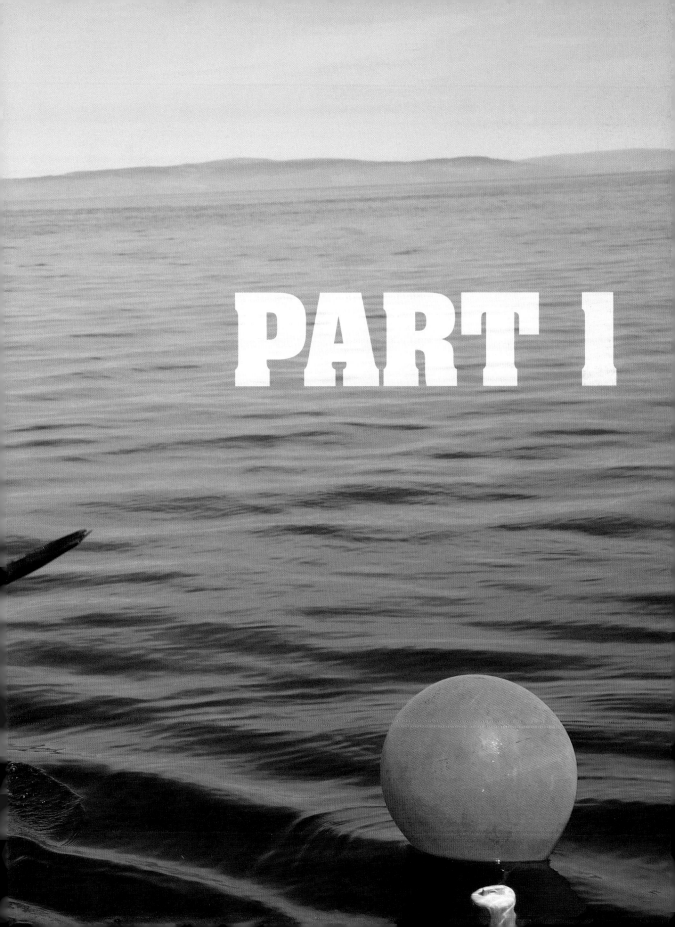

PART I

IN PERIL ON THE SEA

After the declaration of war on 3 September 1939, nothing much happened until the spring of 1940 when Germany unleashed its armies against Norway, the Netherlands, Belgium, Luxembourg and France.

Try telling that to anyone who served at that time in the Royal Navy, the Merchant Navy and RAF Coastal Command, or, for that matter, Germany's Kriegsmarine, and the politest response will be a sigh. They have no memory of what became known as the 'Phoney War'. Their war began the instant it was declared, and within hours the U-boats had chalked up their first success when Oberleutnant Fritz Julius Lemp, commanding *U-30*, sank the Anchor-Donaldson liner *Athenia*, with the loss of 118 lives. On 17 September the aircraft carrier HMS *Courageous* was torpedoed by *U-29*, and on 3 November 1939 HMS *Rawalpindi* became the first of 15 armed merchant cruisers to be sunk when she had the misfortune to encounter the German battleships *Scharnhorst* and *Gneisenau* while on patrol off Iceland. The Battle of the Atlantic was a tonnage war in which the Allies fought to neutralize Germany's naval forces before German submarines and surface raiders could strangle vital supply lines by sinking Allied merchant ships faster than they could be replaced. Prime Minister Winston Churchill was in no doubt of this, telling the House of Commons on 27 January 1942: 'But for the Merchant Navy who bring us the food and munitions of war, Britain would be in a parlous state and indeed, without them, the Army, Navy and Air Force could not operate.'

After the First World War Germany had been forbidden to construct submarines, but a covert building and crew-training programme was nevertheless well established before Hitler repudiated the Treaty of Versailles and began to expand the navy. During the inter-war years Karl Dönitz, himself a submarine commander from that earlier conflict, and since January 1936 in charge of Germany's U-boat arm, had promoted the idea of using groups of submarines offensively to hunt individual ships and convoys.

The submarines of each group would conduct independent patrols in their assigned areas until the first of them spotted a convoy. Breaking off patrol, this boat would report the sighting to FdU.[1] While other boats of the group, and any others operating at sufficiently close range, were being vectored in, the first boat would maintain contact with the convoy, running submerged by day and on the surface by night. When sufficient submarines were in place, the attack could commence. The German name for this was *rudeltaktik* ('pack tactic'), which became better known in English as 'wolfpack', and the attacks generally took place at night when it was far harder for lookouts to spot the prowling enemy on the surface. In fact, although they were called submarines, the U-boats operated more like torpedo boats with diving capability. Diesel

OPPOSITE: Convoys zig-zagged to make an attack more difficult for U-boats. In their columns, this Atlantic convoy steams on the port tack.

TOP: First casualty: her bows underwater, the *Athenia* lists to starboard.

ABOVE: Shocked survivors of the *Athenia* disembark from the Norwegian ship MS *Knute Nelson* at Galway, Ireland.

ABOVE: In May 1935 the Reichsmarine was renamed the Kriegsmarine. Here the new flag is hoisted aboard a group of newly commissioned U-boats.

engines powered the U-boats on the surface and recharged their batteries; when they dived, the engines were shut down and the batteries took over, but both speed and range were heavily curtailed. It proved to be a frighteningly successful tactic, but it could not be implemented immediately.

Dönitz had calculated that he needed 300 U-boats in order to starve the French and British out of any war: 100 would be on patrol, a further 100 on passage between the patrol area and the submarine bases, and the remaining third in dock for maintenance and repair while the crew enjoyed some leave. Unfortunately for him, the war broke out some four years too early, when he had only 57 U-boats at his disposal, of which only 24 were suitable for the task, effectively giving him only eight on offensive patrol at any one time at the start of the war.

However, Dönitz was not alone in finding his forces inadequate. The Royal Navy was gravely short of ships with which to defend Britain's convoys, and had to resort to arming merchantmen.

ARMED MERCHANT CRUISERS

The 50 passenger ships that were requisitioned in 1939 and 1940 by Britain's Admiralty for conversion into armed merchant cruisers (AMC) ranged in size from the 22,575 grt (gross registered tonnage) *Queen of Bermuda* to the 6,500 grt *Bulolo*. In addition, the navies of Canada, Australia and New Zealand requisitioned three, two and one AMCs respectively. An AMC's main armament consisted of between six and eight 6-inch guns: outdated and feeble firepower with which to oppose a German raider. Only three of the AMCs had a firing range exceeding 15,500 yards (14,175 metres), far less than that of even the *secondary* armament of a German battleship. Before she was sunk, *Rawalpindi* managed to hit the *Scharnhorst*, but the shell inflicted only minimal damage. AMCs did not possess the armour associated with warships of their size, and with the best of them capable of around 16 knots, they lacked speed. Flying the Royal Navy's White Ensign rather than the Merchant Navy's famous Red Ensign, or 'Red Duster', and designated HMS, AMCs were mainly used as auxiliary warships for patrols and convoy escort duties, and they paid a high price. Three were torpedoed in the 10 days from 16 June 1940, and a further 4 in a period of 30 days later the same year.

On 3 November 1940 HMS *Patroclus* and HMS *Laurentic* were both torpedoed by *U-99* after responding to a distress call by the submarine's first victim of the day, the refrigerated cargo ship *Casanare*. It took seven torpedoes to sink *Patroclus*, because the process of conversion to AMC had included the packing of the 'tween decks with empty oil drums to improve buoyancy in the event of being torpedoed. The following day, HMS *Jervis Bay* was sunk by the pocket battleship *Admiral Scheer*, for which she was no match, and on 2 December *U-99* disposed of HMS *Forfar*[2] 500 nautical miles (925 kilometres) west of Ireland. In all, of the 15 ships sunk while operating as AMCs, 10 were hit by submarines.

After 1942 most of the surviving AMCs were decommissioned as warships but not released from the war effort. Some joined the existing fleet of famous passenger ships requisitioned as troopships, and, with the exception of the unfortunate *Laconia*, survived the war. Those that continued under the White Ensign did so in the roles of depot, anti-aircraft, HQ or repair ship, Landing Craft Infantry (LCI), or in the single case of HMS *Pretoria Castle*, escort aircraft carrier.

HMS TRANSYLVANIA

For 14 years, Anchor Line's *Transylvania* provided a service from Glasgow to New York via Moville, Donegal. Built on the Clyde by Fairfield's, the 16,923 grt liner had been launched on 11 March 1925, with accommodation for 279 First Class, 344 Second Class and 800 Third Class passengers. Her acknowledged beauty was partly down to her sleek hull and elegant proportions but also to the rake of her two masts and three funnels, two of which were dummies and constructed purely for aesthetic reasons. At just over 552 feet (168 metres) long, she was powered by six steam turbines driving twin screws that gave her a speed of 16 knots, later upgraded to 17.

Her merchant career was marked by just two incidents, the first during a hurricane in late November 1928 when she responded to a distress call from the German cargo ship *Herrenwijk* some 560 nautical miles (1,040 kilometres) off Ireland. The height of the waves and strength of the wind precluded the launching of any lifeboats, but the 6,345 grt Danish ship *Estonia* also arrived and by working on the sheltered lee side of *Transylvania* rescued some of the crew before the conditions deteriorated further and the freighter sank.

ABOVE: The transatlantic liner *Transylvania* nearing completion at Scott's Yard, Greenock, Scotland.

The following year *Transylvania* had her own difficulties, grounding on the La Coeque rocks off Cherbourg in fog and having to return to the Clyde for repairs. Like most liners she underwent refits to remodel the passenger accommodation, and on 7 September 1939 she was requisitioned by the Admiralty as an AMC. Now with only one funnel, HMS *Transylvania* joined the 10th Cruiser Squadron, which patrolled the Denmark Straits to enforce the blockade of Germany, and under the command of Captain Francis Miles, OBE, RN, she successfully intercepted three German merchant ships.

On 9 August 1940 at around noon *Transylvania* sailed from Greenock on her eleventh patrol. Coincidentally, *U-56* was coming towards the end of her eleventh patrol, and Oberleutnant Otto Harms, her commander on five previous patrols, finally had something to show for his efforts: the sinking on 5 August of Elder Dempster Lines' 5,408 grt *Boma*, part of convoy OB 193. This was at a time when Harms' fellow captains – and rivals – such as Lemp, Schepke and Kretschmer were sinking Allied ships with impunity and winning the Knight's Cross. *U-56* had just moved to the French Atlantic base of Lorient, and at last luck was on her side.

At one minute past midnight, as the watch was about to hand over, *Transylvania* was steering a zig-zag course, her degaussing equipment operating to protect her against magnetic mines. Her crew were well aware of the even greater danger from German submarines, and her officer of the watch, Lieutenant John Wilson Tone, testified that:

'… we had one man in the crows nest, two men not only on the forecastle head but two on each side abaft the blast screens for P2 and S2 guns, two men in each wing of the bridge, the control part on the upper bridge and one man each side of the boat deck aft of the store shell guns crews'.[3] [All were equipped with binoculars.] 'I was on the starboard side of the bridge at the time and felt a heavy vibration of the ship. I had my binoculars to my eyes at the time, looking at some trawlers [sic] lights nearly ahead. I turned and saw just forward of the funnel a heavy column of what I presumed spray obscuring the horizon. I ran through the wheelhouse to the port side, looked aft and immediately assumed we had been struck.'

Harms had spotted the AMC at 23:45 and stopped; she was approaching at speed, a big ship with a long, high superstructure, and a raked bow and funnel. He fired from nearly 550 yards (500 metres) and counted the running time – 45½ seconds later came the flash and the sound of the detonation.

Captain Miles had only just turned in for the night and was still awake when the explosion burst on the port side. His gut instinct assessed it as a 'double shock': two hits, though the U-boat's war diary specified one. On reaching the bridge he was joined by Tone, who had just switched on the automatic alarms and greeted him with: 'I believe they have got us, Sir.'

Down among the engines, Engineer Lieutenant Thomas Phillips, RNR, felt the attack more strongly:

'There was a terrific explosion and a great deal of vibration … and I thought to myself she has got it on the port side and there may be damage to the port engine and I had better shut her off. I sent them [the engine room crew] upstairs. By the time we got there the relief engineer had pulled the cord acting the emergency cut out of the main engines. I did not see any water in the engine room at that period but the relieving engineer said that he saw water coming in the port side as if from the gland in the bulkhead of the port engine shaft, spraying over the generator.'[4]

Four minutes after the detonation the electric lights failed, and for the quarter of an hour that elapsed until the emergency lighting came on everyone used torches and oil lamps.

Jack Hider, who joined the ship early in the war as a signalman/coder, retained vivid memories of the time:

'… that evening I had just completed the First Watch with W/T Officer McDonald and was handing over to Signalman Coder Lee when there was a bang which sounded to be immediately below us. We jumped but, instinctively, knew what it was. The bridge immediately phoned for a torpedo message to go out. (Have been torpedoed on port side. Position ———— Time 0001) (A few miles North-West of Bloody Foreland off the North coast of Ireland). We were calm although a bit shaky. A second signal was sent – "My 0001. Correct position ———— - Time 0011". This was followed immediately by a further signal – "My 0001. Torpedoed in Engine Room. Cannot steam Time 0012". We packed books and corrected messages. Leech, the third signalman, came up. The emergency lights were not working. At this time we were not sure whether it was a mine or torpedo and then we sent a further message saying "Have been torpedoed or struck by a mine. Am not sure which. Time 0036". Soon after 0100 I went down to collect some of my gear. What a mess. When I came back Lee went down. Signalmen Page, Miller, Leech, Halliday, Middleton were all below. It was very hot. Some of the Stokers were singing and playing a gramophone.'

Harms saw the torches and the lamplight catching on the thickening pall of smoke. *Transylvania* was stopped and down by the stern. There was activity around the lifeboats. If he had had any torpedoes left he would have administered the *coup de grâce*. With the sea state and the visibility against him, and needing to recharge his batteries, he headed south, back to Lorient.[5]

Almost two hours after the torpedo hit, Hider had found no cause for serious concern. Like *Rawalpindi*, *Transylvania* was packed with empty oil drums for buoyancy.

'0143 – All's well. Lieut. Shaw, the First Lieut. says we should keep afloat for 24 hours so, with nothing else to do we sat or stood about chatting. I went down again to fetch some more gear. What a mess there was. I then returned to the Coding Office. An aircraft arrived on the scene at 0316, followed by the destroyers ACHATES, FORTUNE and ANTELOPE.

At 0324 another message was sent saying "Ship sinking slowly. Wind and sea increasing." Lieut. Tone (Signals Officer) phoned to say that Mr. MacDonald (First W/T Operator) and one Signalman Coder were to stay until message was sent and the remainder to go to their boats. As senior Signalman I sent Signalmen Leech and Lee and Third W/T Operator Cornish to their Boat Stations. Lee went but Leech wouldn't go for a bit until I had to order him to go (pulling that extra week's rank for the one and only time). Cornish wouldn't go either at

first. MacDonald had a bit of difficulty in getting the message out due to not enough power. Receiving stations were checking certain groups when Tone came and ordered all of us out of the Office. We locked the safes and had a final look round and left the Office for the last time about 0350. We then went along to P 1 Lifeboat. By now the poor old TRANS had a heavy list to port. P1 was just getting away and they had enough already so we asked them to have a boat sent back for us. We then went up top and, being the only signalman left aboard by then I sent a signal to the destroyer saying "Please send boat back. About 20 still on board". I had to use only the flashlight that I had been carrying. The Carley Floats were then lowered and some got away in them. The remainder of us went up on the bridge and the Skipper wanted to know why I was still aboard. Although I was a non-smoker I stood and sat on fo'c's'le smoking one of Lieut. Tone's cigars and drinking gin. Everybody was happy. I then spotted a cutter coming alongside. Due to the seas it missed S 1 Falls but got to S 2. We were then all able to go down the lifelines or Jacob's ladder into the waiting lifeboat and, with luck, several of us didn't even get our shoes wet. The last eight in order were Able Seaman Ironmonger, P. O. Agate, myself, Hay (Midshipman), MacDonald (Chief W/T Operator), Lieut. Tone (Signals Officer), Lieut. Shaw (First Lieutenant or Jimmy the One) and last of all Captain Miles R.N.R. We pulled away from the ship's side at 0435. Lieut. Tone and I rowed together for a bit after throwing away a cracked oar. Then he took over – since I was merely a Signalman he no doubt figured I was not much help with an oar. Although it was barely dawn I aimed my camera in the direction of the old TRANS when she was up and down but it was still too dark. She slipped out of sight at 0450. By this time there was quite a heavy sea running but we made it over to the Destroyer which was very appropriately named H.M.S. FORTUNE. I was signalling all the time with a lamp lent to me by R.N.V.R. Subbie Bailey. We came alongside the destroyer and I got out when it was my turn. As I waited for a big wave I was able to grasp the top of the hand rail first shot so was soon inboard once again being able to keep my shoes dry. Then I looked at where

the TRANS had been and said "There goes my brand new tiddly 32/6 [£1.62.5p] suit never used."'

The torpedoing claimed no lives: as Hider explains, the deaths all occurred as the ship was being abandoned:

'The Gunner was crushed between his boat and the destroyer and then had his arm cut off by the blades of the propeller. Chief Norgate (from the Bank in Cheapside, City of London) went between the boat and the destroyer and although they got hold of him he had too many clothes on so they could not lift him out. Many were tipped out when they left the TRANS, climbed aboard another lifeboat and then were tipped out alongside the destroyer. In one case a

BELOW: Divers investigate two of the bridge telegraphs still bolted on the wreck of the *Transylvania*.

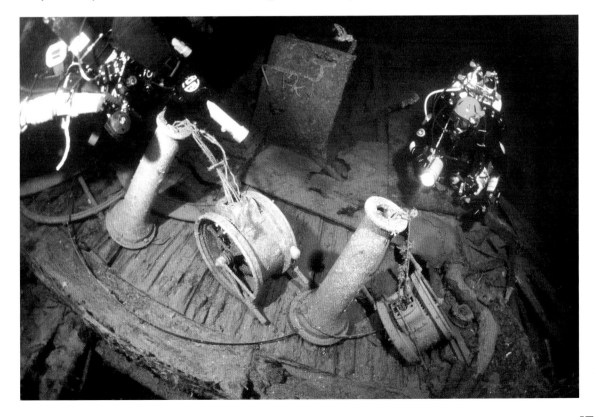

wave lifted the boat off the falls but left the stern hanging so that quite a number fell into the sea. My proper boat was one which capsized. Sea. Kellagher was the only one lost in our Mess (No. 16). There were about forty [36] lost and over 300 survivors. No one was lost at the time we were hit. One lifeboat was slipped early with only five men aboard and they were not seen again. The rest of those assigned to the boat crowded into the next lifeboat but being overloaded it capsized. A third lifeboat was over loaded and capsized alongside one of the destroyers and several were lost including one officer who was crushed between the lifeboat and the destroyer (possibly Chief Norgate mentioned above).'[6]

Hider's conscientiousness in sticking to his post to the very end was in marked contrast to that of others. The enquiry approved the efforts of Captain Miles and his executive officer, but severely criticized several of the engineer officers for putting their safety ahead of their duty and abandoning the engine room too soon. Only one, Lieutenant Commander (E) Young, was found to have carried out his duties completely satisfactorily; indeed, Captain Miles told the inquiry that he was the only engineer who was 'any use' to him. Although it was conceded that Phillips might not have been able to prevent the flooding that eventually sank the ship, Admiral Spooner, Rear-Admiral Commanding Northern Patrol, recommended that he and two others should not serve again in any Royal Navy ship.[7]

Otto Harms went on to command *U-464*, one of the Kriegsmarine's 'milk-cows' – a Type XIV, which carried no torpedoes but acted as a support boat to replenish other submarines. Spotted southeast of Iceland on 20 August 1942 by a long-range Consolidated PBY Catalina aircraft, *U-464* was sunk on her first war patrol with the loss of two of her crew. Harms spent the remainder of the war as a prisoner of war (POW). *U-56* was lost at her base in Kiel during an air raid in April 1945, with the loss of six of her crew of 19.

The wreck of the *Transylvania* lies upright at a depth of 425 feet (130 metres), some 36 nautical miles (66 kilometres) northwest of Malin Head. On a good day – and good days are not available to order in the North Atlantic – visibility is superb. That visibility and the condition of the ship make *Transylvania* a popular attraction for qualified and properly equipped divers.

THE CONVOY SYSTEM

There was nothing new about the convoy system: for centuries it was the most cost-effective way of protecting merchant ships against pirates or wartime enemies, and in the First World War it proved to be the only successful defence against the German U-boats. At the outbreak of the Second World War, the system was again put into operation. It saved lives and cargoes, but as Able Seaman Reg Mason, who had served in corvettes, said: 'It was the merchant ships that really got it rough. I mean, they didn't stand much of a chance when they got torpedoed, particularly on the way up with all the cargo that they carried....'

Each of the many routes – and those in use varied during the conflict

– had its own code letters: HX represented Halifax and was applied to convoys leaving from Halifax, Nova Scotia, bound for the UK (later in the war HX also embraced convoys from New York). HG was the route from Gibraltar to the UK, and ON(F) represented convoys of fast ships to North America. Each convoy on a route was numbered consecutively, giving every single convoy a unique alpha-numeric designation, of which PQ 17, ONS 5, HX 84 are perhaps best known. A handful of convoys were of such critical importance that they were planned as operations and best known by that name: nobody remembers convoy WS.5.21.S as anything other than Operation Pedestal, the convoy that saved Malta in the summer of 1942.

At the start of the war the Royal Navy escorted an outgoing convoy beyond the range of the U-boats, then picked up an incoming convoy and escorted it home. Coastal Command provided air cover. The Royal Canadian Navy (RCN) gave escort on the other side. After June 1940 and the occupation of France's long Atlantic coastline, the Germans established submarine flotilla bases at Brest, St. Nazaire, Lorient and La Pallice/La Rochelle, as well as at Bordeaux, which was shared with the Italians. This gave the U-boats a greatly increased range, well beyond that of Coastal Command aircraft. The transatlantic convoy route was therefore shifted further to the north, and instead of coming into Plymouth through the South Western Approaches, convoys were routed to and from Liverpool, round the north coast of Ireland.

The Royal Navy and the RCN had to find a way of establishing close escort for the whole voyage. Escort ships had been in short supply, but they increased in number after the USA – still neutral – agreed to supply Britain with 50 obsolete destroyers. The Flower class corvettes came into service around this time, followed by the River class frigates that were highly specialized and designed for Atlantic conditions. In addition, the RCN began a rapid expansion. Each escort group was commanded by a senior officer whose task was to bring the convoy home safely and on time.

As a supply officer in destroyers with the Royal Navy, John Cumming had witnessed:

'... an oil tanker going up, and the sea covered in this thick, black oil and men swimming through it and we couldn't stop to rescue them. As a matter of fact, it's one of the worst memories I have, of ploughing your way through men who were already swimming in this black oil and the ship just … the destroyer just ploughed its way through to get back to the convoys. So you're leaving folk to drown, as it were; there was nothing you could do about it. A bit harrowing.'

Close protection was achieved by stationing the escorts ahead, astern and on the port and starboard flanks of the convoy. The Commander-in-Chief (C-in-C) Western Approaches, Admiral – later Sir – Max Horton GCB, DSO**, instituted support groups that could work with one or more convoys as and when needed, and this led to the

ABOVE: A Town class destroyer launches an attack with depth charges on a suspected U-boat target.

such as the Hedgehog, which threw a shower of 24 contact bombs, and the Squid, which threw just three – each capable of breaching a submarine's pressure hull.

Reg Mason saw the results: 'We could have a full pattern of depth charges and for all those exploding at the one time maybe 100 feet or 150 feet down below, so the next thing you knew was the water spouts just shooting up. And if you made contact and actually had damaged a U-boat, the U-boat would just come up like that and then straight down. If that happened they were just lost with all hands. I've seen that happen once or twice.'

For the first half of the war, the lack of complete air cover presented a serious problem. Neither the RAF nor the Royal Canadian Air Force (RCAF) possessed aircraft with a range sufficient to escort convoys to the halfway point in the crossing of the Atlantic. Not even the entry of the USA could close up the large hole in the middle of the ocean known as the Atlantic Gap. The Royal Navy had too few aircraft carriers to spare any for routine convoy work, but the first escort carrier, a converted German liner, entered service in September 1941 as HMS *Audacity*, and in the three months of service that preceded her sinking she proved her worth. A number of tankers and bulk carriers were later fitted with a rudimentary flight deck and, in addition to carrying cargo, embarked a flight of Fleet Air Arm (FAA) or RAF aircraft. These were the MAC (merchant aircraft carrier) ships and CAM (catapult armed merchant) ships or 'Catafighters'. The main difference was that the aircraft on a CAM ship, usually a single Hawker Sea Hurricane, was fired off only in

formation of several highly successful hunter-killer groups.

The escorts' first anti-submarine weapons were ASDIC, better known today as sonar (for detecting submerged submarines), and depth charges, which were detonated at set depths by water pressure. These were gradually joined by HF/DF, in which triangulation was used to pinpoint a U-boat transmitting signals, and by radar, which detected a submarine on the surface. The simple depth charge was not replaced but after 1942 additional developments came into the arsenal, emergency because it could not land on again and so had to ditch near the convoy, while the Fairey Swordfish on the MAC ships were able to land on and could therefore fly patrols. Small purpose-built escort carriers went into production but they were not available in any numbers for the Battle of the Atlantic until 1944. A major help was the American-built Consolidated B-24 Liberator, a long-range bomber particularly well suited to taking on a well-armed submarine, and it helped produce an ace pilot (see overleaf).

One of the biggest contributions to convoy safety was the capture in May 1941 of *U-110* and the Enigma coding machine that was on board, enabling the Cypher School at Bletchley Park to decrypt intercepted U-boat messages, which meant convoys could be routed away from danger zones. Less easy to quantify is the personal contribution of individuals such as Admiral Horton (a poacher turned gamekeeper in that he brought to his job the insight of a successful submarine commander), his predecessor Admiral Sir Percy Noble and the clutch of escort group commanders who all built upon a combination of experience and intuition to revolutionize the convoy system.

COASTAL COMMAND AND THE WAR IN THE ATLANTIC

As Dan states in *Dig WW2*: 'At the height of the Battle of the Atlantic an Allied merchant ship was being sunk every four hours, which is why the protective cover of Coastal Command was to become so important. But in order for those aircraft to reach deep

into the Atlantic they needed airfields as far west as they could get.'

Coastal Command began the war badly placed to perform its vital role of protecting shipping. It had insufficient crews, too many old and unsuitable aircraft, too few depth charges, and no lights to illuminate the surface of the sea and catch surfaced U-boats charging their batteries after dark. The rudimentary airborne radar introduced at the end of 1939 to detect surfaced U-boats was not discriminating enough and aircraft altimeters were inadequate for the successful dropping of depth charges, which if released at too high an altitude would be smashed on impact with the water.

In addition, the further pilots had to fly to their patrol zones, the less time they could spend over the convoys or looking for U-boats before reaching PLE ('prudent limit of endurance') and having to return to base. In the first five months of the war, Coastal Command could claim only a half share of one submarine kill, that of *U-55*. The situation became acute after June 1940 as U-boat numbers increased and the

ABOVE: Catafighter: a Hurricane on the launch ramp of a CAM ship in August 1942.

'HAWKEYES'

In the air war the term 'ace' tends to be associated with fighter pilots, but as far as the U-boats were concerned there was no more dangerous foe than Ulsterman Squadron Leader Terence Bulloch DSO* DFC, nicknamed 'Hawkeyes' because of his exceptional ability to spot them. He was officially credited with sinking four U-boats and severely damaging a further two, a remarkable achievement given the difficulty of the task:

'First of all they were a very small target and we didn't really know the exact location of them. You could pick out the U-boat itself or track its making like a ship. Low cloud was the main thing that we liked; you could fly in and out of low cloud on the approach. The U-boat couldn't spot you until you were very close to it. You had to manoeuvre your aircraft, get it into position where you could attack it. When we actually attacked them we were flying down at 50ft above the sea – running in and dropping depth charges. They worked very well. They were quite lethal, but you had to get very close, within 10ft of the U-boat hull to be lethal.'

Bulloch joined the RAF just before the war, and given a choice between Bomber Command and Coastal Command he chose the latter, flying Avro Ansons from RAF Bircham Newton in Norfolk. During an exercise with the Royal Navy he dived down on the battleship HMS *Nelson* and dropped a marker on her foredeck, earning himself an official reprimand and promotion to Flying Officer.

In 1940 he converted to the modern Lockheed Hudson, and soon tasted success against Heinkel He 115 floatplanes, for which he was awarded the DFC. At the very end of 1940 he volunteered for a secret

OPPOSITE: Attack from the air. An RCAF Sunderland of Coastal Command attacks a surfaced U-boat with depth charges and machine gun fire. The photograph demonstrates the excellent visibility enjoyed by the flying boat's crew.

ABOVE: Heroes of the Battle of the Atlantic: Squadron Leader Terry 'Hawkeyes' Bulloch (left) and Lieutenant Commander David Balme. The latter led the party from HMS *Bulldog* that boarded *U-110* in 1941 and captured her Enigma cypher machine together with vital documents. The trophy he holds is the cap of *U-110*'s commander, Fritz-Julius Lemp, who was shot while attempting to reboard his U-boat.

mission, which turned out to be a trip to Los Angeles as a 'civilian test pilot' to 'buy' a Boeing B-17 Flying Fortress on behalf of the 'British Purchasing Unit'. The USA was still neutral; the Lend–Lease agreement had not yet been signed; officially, the US Army Air Corps (USAAC) could only train civilian pilots. Training complete, he signed for his B-17 and flew across America in four stages to reach Canada – his insurance did not cover night flights or bad weather. Back in uniform, and with the aircraft now sporting the RAF roundel, he took off from Gandar, Newfoundland, and accomplished the first transatlantic flight of a B-17 in a record-breaking 8 hours 24 minutes, averaging 245 miles (390 kilometres) per hour .

During his period as a transatlantic ferry pilot, he brought the first B-24 Liberators across the Atlantic. When the Franco–German armistice was signed, the Americans had been building Liberator bombers for the French Air Force. The RAF took over the order, specified some modifications and handed the aircraft to 120 Squadron, which was split between Nutts Corner near Belfast and Allied-occupied Iceland. By now a Squadron Leader with 120 Squadron, Bulloch was about to close the Atlantic Gap.

On 30 November 1942, two convoys left Halifax, HX 217 and the slower SC 111. Twenty-two U-boats gathered for the attack on HX 217 in the Gap, just as Squadron Leader Bulloch and his crew located it. During a 17-hour patrol, Bulloch spotted and attacked eight U-boats – a record for one sortie. He was relieved as planned by Squadron Leader Desmond Isted, who attacked a further five. Two U-boats are known to have been sunk, one at least by Bulloch. HX 217 lost only two ships, and the whole of SC 111 arrived safely. Bulloch received the Bar to his DFC. After the war he joined BOAC as a civilian pilot.

RIGHT: Aerial view of RAF Limavady, 1943–44, showing the perimeter and the layout of the runways.

Germans gained their Atlantic bases, thus extending U-boat range. An area of critical concern was the Western Approaches, the air defence of which fell to 15 Group, Coastal Command.

The initial limitations were gradually overcome with more suitable aircraft and improved technology, and the establishment of new airfields in Northern Ireland increased the westerly range of all aircraft, not just the Vickers Wellington and Armstrong Whitworth Whitley bombers and the Short Sunderland and Catalina flying boats that soon made up the bulk of 15 Group's strength. Northern Ireland, so important to the naval defence of convoys, now became an invaluable resource for the RAF and the Fleet Air Arm once transatlantic convoys were routed round the north coast of Ireland.

RAF LIMAVADY

Shattered glass and broken window frames, ivy climbing the walls, weeds forcing their way through the concrete runways and water seeping into the command bunker: Limavady is a mere shadow of its former glory as one of the most important RAF stations in Britain after the Luftwaffe had abandoned the Battle of Britain. Silence throbs in the cavernous hanger in which the ground crew once worked round the clock in noisy echoes to keep the Wellingtons and Whitleys operational.

Limavady was the first of 20 airfields

ABOVE: The derelict control tower at RAF Limavady.

built in Northern Ireland during the war and one of four constructed on the northern coast. When it was officially opened on 1 December 1940, with a single flight of 502 Squadron on station, Station Headquarters Office was located in the village's main street at Red Pillar House, one of several buildings requisitioned to house the first three officers and 141 airmen. Soon the rest of 502 Squadron arrived – the first operational squadron to be equipped with air-to-surface vessel (ASV) radar – along with detachments from 221 and 224 Squadrons, flying Whitleys, Wellingtons and Hudsons respectively. In one year, the pilots notched up over 25,000 flying hours. They flew long patrols round the clock, escorting individual ships and convoys, spotting survivors in lifeboats or in the water, and carrying out anti-submarine

(A/S) sweeps. Surfaced U-boats were attacked and either destroyed or forced to dive; the position was recorded not just in the log but also by dropping a sea-marker to leave a visible indication.

On 2 May 1941 Pilot Officer Atkinson of 224 Squadron took off in a Hudson at 12:46 to provide protection for Convoy SL 71S. Three-quarters of an hour later the crew sighted a convoy, which consisted of some 16 merchant ships and three escorts on an easterly course, not the one they were looking for.[8] Atkinson continued west until 14:45 when he began a low level 'creeping line search'. At 15:12, when at 1,200 feet (366 metres) in position 55°57´ N 13°33´ W:

'... we sighted an object which appeared to be a lifeboat burning a smoke candle. On closing with it identifying it as a U Boat on the surface. Co [course] 060 T [True]. Speed 5 Knots. Smoke appeared to be coming from conning tower. Began to dive to attack and the U Boat immediately submerged and turned to port about 15 degrees. Dropped stick of 3 D.C.s [depth charges] (250 lbs) spaced at 30ft intervals and set to explode at a depth of 100ft from a height of 150ft. speed 125 knots. All three D/Cs explodes straddling the peak of the wake. The third was 30 ft behind the second one. Dropped sea marker on oil patches formed by D/Cs and circled. Saw no wreckage until 15 minutes later when 2 round pieces of timber appeared floating on the surface. They might have been pieces of a mast.

1605 Left posn [position] of U Boat and resumed search for convoy.'

Atkinson never did find the convoy. Although he had not sunk the U-boat, he had forced it to dive and so disrupted its attack. Later in the war the tactic of 'scarecrow' gave way to that of destruction.

When a convoy was hit within range of Coastal Command, liaison and cooperation were important. On 15 September 1941 Pilot Officer Rumsey and the crew of Whitley J/502 were tasked with assisting the 7,321 grt *Vinga*. The Norwegian tanker, a veteran of the convoys, had left the Clyde on 13 September and joined OS 6. Her destination was Trinidad, but engine trouble made it impossible for her to keep up, and on the morning of 15 September she was a sitting duck for the unidentified German bomber that made four attacks with gunfire and bombs. *Vinga*'s radio operator managed to send out an SOS message before the survivors abandoned ship in the two lifeboats.

Rumsey took off from Limavady at 07:35, subsequently reporting:

'1012 sighted Norwegian M/V Vinga. Burning amidships and with large hole, probably bomb hole where bridge had been amidships, and flames showing approximately 30 survivors in two lifeboats who later got into one – the other sinking – one survivor in the water about one mile away – A/C circled lifeboat and signalled to pick up single survivor – A/C circled single survivor and dropped small dinghy and smoke float [.] survivor later picked up by lifeboat. Directed I42 to lifeboat which drew alongside and picked up survivors – I42 then closed with the Vinga and immediately turned hoses

upon the fire – in position 5802N. 1320W.
1355 relieved by O/502
1633 Landed base.'[9]

According to subsequent reports, none of the men in the lifeboat understood Morse code, but the behaviour of the Whitley in dropping the dinghy and then circling it led them to investigate and rescue the pumpman. The convoy escort directed to their assistance was the old destroyer HMS *Campbeltown*, ex-USS *Buchanan*, which later entered the Royal Navy's pantheon of glory when, stuffed with explosives, she was blown up at the gates of the Normandie dry dock at St. Nazaire on 28 April 1942, thus depriving the Germans of an Atlantic dock capable of repairing its capital ships.

The *Vinga* was towed to the Clyde where she was repaired. She returned to service and survived the war.

Limavady's temporary huts and requisitioned buildings gave way to hangars, a modern control tower, two additional runways, accommodation and ancillary buildings.

From 1942 to 1944 the airfield became an operational training unit (OTU) for bomber crews, though the high ground that surrounded it on three sides, coupled with the weather conditions, made take off and landing very difficult, even for experienced crews, and led to several fatal crashes. The local mountain, Benevenagh, gained the grim nickname 'Ben Twitch' – 'twitch' being the RAF term for the body tremors caused by operational stress.

Limavady returned to operational status in 1944 but closed on the same day that the Japanese surrendered – 15 August 1945. In the 1950s Limavady was used for training FAA pilots in deck landing.

ABOVE: Dominating the landscape of Co. Derry, Benevenagh rises like a cliff, a hazard to pilots in poor visibility and responsible for several fatalities.

THE BUNKER, THE SIMULATOR AND THE GREMLIN

RAF stations had an airfield battle HQ from which senior officers could direct resistance in the event of a German assault, and Limavady's is a rare survivor. The small bunker – described by *Dig WW2*'s aviation historian Jonny McNee as 'bijou … and it's water-filled as well. Lovely!' – is fitted with two embrasures, thus covering both sides of the site, and each has its Vickers machine gun mounting still in place.

Limavady's facilities expanded to include a hemispherical gun trainer dome, an early form of simulator for land-based anti-aircraft gunners. A gun was set up inside the building, film of enemy aircraft in flight was projected all over the pale walls, and the trainee gunner fired a beam of light at his targets. An instructor observed and scored the performance. There are several other surviving domes in Britain, including those at Langam, Wyton, and Mildenhall.

A piece of graffiti on an inside wall at Limavady depicts the Coastal Command gremlin, complete with umbrella, a wry reference to the Irish weather. Rather than having any folkloric origin, the idea of a malignant or mischievous creature causing problems to aircraft entered RAF slang in the 1920s as an explanation for unexpected mechanical malfunctions and gave rise to the expression 'a gremlin in the works'. The term was picked up by American pilots and further popularized during the war by Roald Dahl's book *The Gremlins* and by Warner Brothers' 'Falling Hare', a Bugs Bunny cartoon.

BELOW: A very secret bunker: Dan squeezes into the command bunker at RAF Limavady.

RAF EGLINTON

Now that the site has been redeveloped as City of Derry Airport, little remains of RAF Eglinton, which opened in 1941 as the fighter station to defend Derry (Londonderry) and provide protection for convoys. It was transferred to the Royal Navy in May 1943 to become HMS *Gannet* and RNAS Eglinton, as well as home to an anti-submarine warfare school. A glimpse of the station's operational past comes from a letter written in June 1945 by a young visual signaller in the Women's Royal Naval Service (WRNS), Stephanie Batstone:

'Dear Mum
Well here we are, and I'm afraid there is no getting away from the fact that it is pure, undiluted HELL. In fact I don't think anything could possibly be worse….

The camp is several miles from the station in the mostly very desolate country – no villages or even houses or farms. There are actually several camps – incredibly large and bewildering. About 400 WRNS, and masses of Navy, RAF, FAA, WAAF, Royal Marines and other odd bods. And altogether frightful. It never stops raining – just a continuous, hopeless, persistent, penetrating downpour. Everybody is intensely miserable – apparently after about two years here you acquire a sort of stupor of resignation.

Blankets, by the way, are ex WAAF [Women's Auxiliary Air Force] ones, and instead of being beautiful white ones like our naval blankets they are either grey or black. Perhaps just as well so that you can't see how dirty they are.

ABOVE: The gun trainer dome at Limavady.

BELOW: The Limavady gremlin, holding his umbrella.

The cabin is the most awful thing of all – an enormous barn of a place, filthy dirty, with 17 double bunks – 34 WRNS in it. You can't ignore the noise – it seems to go on all night … none of us have any drawers to put things in so we haven't even unpacked yet.

But perhaps the most awful thing is that there is no V/S [visual signalling] here. Most people don't even know what it is.…'[10]

Batstone's misery at having to do office work, compounded by the absence of bathplugs, having to wash in a mixture of steam and brown water, and being obliged to sleep with fleas and beetles, ended three months later when her wartime service finished.

FLYING ON WATER: RAF CASTLE ARCHDALE

The sinking of HMS *Hood* by the *Bismarck* on 24 May 1941 prompted the aghast Royal Navy to throw every resource into destroying the brand new German battleship. The engagement, which also involved HMS *Prince of Wales* and the German cruiser *Prinz Eugen*, took place in the Denmark Strait, a 300-mile (480-kilometre) navigational passage between Greenland and Iceland that leads south into the Atlantic. Damaged by two shells from *Prince of Wales*'s 14-inch guns, *Bismarck* headed for Brest. Swordfish torpedo-bomber biplanes from HMS *Victorious* found her, but were unable to inflict any damage, and the capital ships of the Home Fleet were not fast enough to catch her. While the cruisers HM Ships *Suffolk*

and HMS *Norfolk* shadowed her, Force H, based at Gibraltar, was ordered to intercept the *Bismarck* and slow her progress.

However, the cruisers lost contact, and but for a seaplane based at RAF Castle Archdale on Lough Erne, *Bismarck* might have made good her escape. Long-range aircraft had joined the hunt, flying extended patrols in dreadful weather. At 03:00 on 26 May a Catalina flying boat from 209 Squadron RAF, captained by Pilot Officer Denis Briggs, took off from Lough Erne. Visibility in the patrol area was 3 miles (5 kilometres) at an altitude of 800 feet (245 metres), 8 miles (13 kilometres) close to the surface. The squadron had just moved from Scotland to Castle Archdale and converted to the excellent US-built Catalina. The US Navy sent its personnel to help train the squadron, and the man at the controls when the battleship was sighted was Ensign Leonard B. Smith USNR (United States Navy Reserve):

'We started leg EG of area at 1000 and at 1010 I sighted what was first believed to be Bismarck, bearing 345 at 8 miles. Definite recognition was impossible at the time due to visibility. I immediately took control from "George" (automatic pilot); started slow climbing turn to starboard, keeping ship sited to Port, while the British officer went aft to prepare contact report. My plan was to take cover in the clouds, get close to the ship as possible, making definite recognition and then shadow the ship from best point of vantage. Upon reaching 2000´ we broke out of a cloud formation and were met by a

terrific anti-aircraft barrage from our starboard quarter.

Immediately jettisoned the depth charges and started violent evasive action which consisted of full speed, climbing and "S" turns. The British officer went aft again to send the contact report. When making an "S" turn I could see the ship was a BB and was the Bismarck, which had made a 90 starboard turn from its original course, (This was evident from wake made by his manoeuvring), and was firing broadsides at us. The A.A. fire lasted until we were out of range and into the clouds. It was very intense and were it not for evasive action we would have been shot down. The barrage was so close that it shook the aircraft considerably (one man was knocked from his bunk) and the noise of the burst could be heard above the propeller and engine noise. Numerous bursts were observed at close quarters and small fragments of shrapnel could be heard hitting the plane. The fitter came forward to pilots compartment saying we were full of holes. As soon as we were well clear of Bismarck we investigated the damage, which consisted of a hole in after port hull (about 2″ in diameter) and one in bottom hull directly below instrument panel (about 1″ in diameter). No other damage was visible at the time. I made short flight test (several turns, checked engines, etc) and finding everything satisfactory returned to area to resume shadow of Bismarck.'[11]

A second Catalina, from 210 Squadron at Oban, picked up the report of the *Bismarck* and now took over the job of radioing her movements, so at 14:45 hours Briggs and his crew were able to break off patrol to begin the long flight back to base, landing on the Lough Erne at 21:30 after 18 hours in the air. Based on the Catalina information, Swordfish from HMS *Ark Royal* located the battleship and a torpedo wrecked her steering gear, leaving her helpless. She was sunk 300 nautical miles (555 kilometres) off Ushant the following morning by HM Ships *Rodney* and *King George V*.

LEFT: A pair of Sunderland Flying Boats moored on Lough Erne.

To avoid compromising US neutrality, Smith's name was kept out of the media, and it was Pilot Officer Dennis Briggs RAF who was interviewed by the BBC.

With a body shaped like the hull of a boat, and superb visibility for the observers, as well as depth charges and an extended range, the Catalina was completely fit for purpose. Ted Jones, who became the captain of a Catalina at the age of just 20, flew 55 anti-submarine patrols: 'They flew like an old cow, but they were a lovely aircraft. They were built like a tank, solid, you know, but a bit heavy on the controls. We had a marvellous automatic pilot because we went up for 18-hour patrols and it wouldn't have been possible to fly one for that time.'

The Sunderland squadrons at Lough Erne – 201, 422 and 423 – did sterling A/S work throughout the life of the base, sinking seven and damaging five U-boats between them. A vivid report, dated 12 October 1943, of the attack on *U-610* four days earlier was submitted by Wing Commander J.R. Frizzle of 423 Squadron:

'… As F/O [Flight Officer] Russell took over control, we were at 500 feet, and not more than 700 yards on the U/Boat's port beam. I stood between the two pilots to watch the proceedings as F/O Russell partially closed the throttle and dove at a fairly steep angle because of our proximity to the U/Boat. I checked the position of the D.C. fusing switches and circuit lights and then watched the fire from the U/Boat and from our forward guns. I noted that fire from the U/Boat all appeared to be going well below the aircraft, but I was not sure where the fire was coming from. I did not observe any personnel on the U/Boat's deck though it made no effort to submerge. Our own fire from the .5 gun appeared very accurate and apparent direct hits were ricocheting in all directions.

The aircraft passed over the U/Boat at approximately one hundred feet and as we climbed with a fairly steep turn to port the galley advised that only 3 D.C.s had dropped. The second pilot got out of his seat and reset the D.C. Distributor, and we turned in for a second attack. However, as we approached for a second attack there was no submarine visible. There was in place 15 or more Jerries who appeared to be looking up at the aircraft, and a considerable amount of debris floating around. The D.C.s were therefore not dropped. My instantaneous reaction at the time was that the submarine had been definitely destroyed….'[12]

Sergeant Chuck Singer was the gunner in the mid upper tower of the much bigger Sunderland flying boat: 'For the first five or six hours it's very interesting and then after that you start … your eyes start getting sore and … you imagine things. You'd say, that's an aircraft and later on you find out it's just a flock of gulls or something, you know. But you had to be on the ball every second…. But it didn't bother us. We were too young. Nothing can happen when you're 19, can it?'

The involvement of Ensign Smith in the sinking of the *Bismarck* was not the only neutrality secret that had to be

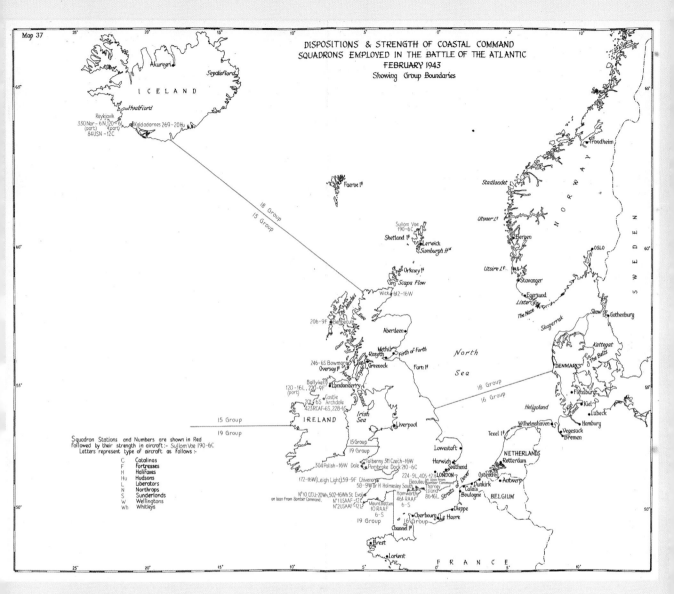

Map 37

DISPOSITIONS & STRENGTH OF COASTAL COMMAND
SQUADRONS EMPLOYED IN THE BATTLE OF THE ATLANTIC
FEBRUARY 1943
Showing Group Boundaries

ICELAND

Akureyri

Seydisfiord

Hvalfiord

Reykjavik
330 Nor - 6 N, 120 - 6L
(part)   (part)
84 USN - 12 C   Kaldadarnes 269 - 20 Hu

18 Group
15 Group

Faeroe Iª

NORWAY

Stadlandet

Trondheim

Sullom Voe
190 - 6 C
Shetland Iª   Lerwick
                   Sumburgh Hª

Utvaer Lª

Bergen

OSLO

Utsire Lª

Stavanger

Orkney Iª
Scapa Flow

Egersund
Lister Cª
The Naze

Wick 612 - 16 W

The Minch

SWEDEN

Skaw Pª Gothenburg

Skagerrak

206 - 9 F Stornoway

Aberdeen

North
Sea

Methil
Rosyth   Firth of Forth
                Farn Iª

Kattegat
The Belts

DENMARK

Flensburg

Kiel
Lübeck

246 - 6 S Bowmore
Oversay Iª

Greenock

18 Group
16 Group

Heligoland

Ballykelly
120 - 16 L, 220 - 9 F   Londonderry
(part)
201 - 6 S Castle
           Archdale
423 RCAF - 6 S, 228 - 6 S

15 Group
19 Group

IRELAND

Irish
Sea

Liverpool

Wilhelmshaven
Vegesack
Bremen

Texel Iª

Hamburg

NETHERLANDS
Rotterdam

15 Group
19 Group

Lowestoft

Squadron Stations and Numbers are shown in Red
followed by their strength in aircraft:- Sullom Voe 190 - 6 C
Letters represent type of aircraft as follows :-

C   Catalinas
F   Fortresses
H   Halifaxes
Hu   Hudsons
L   Liberators
N   Northrops
S   Sunderlands
W   Wellingtons
Wh   Whitleys

Talbenny 311 Czech - 16 W
304 Polish - 16 W Dale   Pembroke Dock 210 - 6 C

Harwich   Southend

LONDON

Ostend

BELGIUM

172 - 16 W (Leigh Light) 59 - 9 F Chivenor
58 - 9 W or H Holmsley South
Nº 10 O.T.U - 20 Wh, 502 - 16 Wh St. Eval
on loan from Bomber Command.
Nº 1 USAAF - 12 L
Nº 2 USAAF - 12 L   Mountbatten
                     10 RAAF
                     6 - S
19 Group

224 - 9 L, 405 - 12 L
on loan from
Bomber Command
Beaulieu
Thorney
Island
Hamworthy
461 RAAF   86 - 16 L
6 - S

Dover
Calais
Boulogne

Cherbourg Le Havre
16 Group
Dieppe

Channel Iª

FRANCE

Brest

Lorient

ABOVE: RAF Coastal Command
squadrons were organized into
regional groupings. 15 Group,
which included squadrons based
on Lough Erne, patrolled the
northern half of the Irish Sea and
the North Western Approaches.

downplayed. Some 10 miles (16 kilometres) northwest from Eniskillen, Castle Archdale and the nearby RAF Killadeas, home to the Catalinas of 131 Operational Training Unit, were the most westerly RAF bases in Britain. But between the bases and the Atlantic lay the thin strip of sovereign Eire territory known as the Donegal Corridor. The only way out for the RAF flying boats lay north and up Lough Foyle. The government of Eire came to a secret agreement with the British to allow RAF aircraft to fly over that strip, giving them a direct route west and increasing the time they could spend at sea (see also page 155).

Closed a decade or so after the war, Castle Archdale is now a country park and marina. The huts, hangars and refuelling pontoons have gone, but the slipway survives, complete with an aircraft anchoring ring set into the concrete, and some of the buildings remain, including the filter house that purified the lough water, an air raid shelter, and the operations building that now serves as a shop and restaurant. Killadeas was taken over by Lough Erne

Yacht Club. Like Limavady, Eglinton and the other Northern Ireland airfields the two bases played a vital role in the Battle of the Atlantic, in which the RAF and the Royal Navy cooperated to take on and defeat the menace of the U-boats.

CLUNTOE

The official opening of the air base at Cluntoe took place on 5 October 1942, well before it could be deemed operational. The personnel were accommodated in Nissen huts; water was drawn from nearby Lough Neagh and dispensed from a trailer; and electricity came from a generator. Only 2,000 yards (1,830 metres) of runway had been constructed and owing to 'frequent change in plans' only 10 percent of the technical site was complete. For a time the base was to be used only as an emergency landing ground for aircraft in difficulties and during bad visibility the following March it proved a lifesaver for a Bristol Beaufort from an OTU, which had run short of fuel and located the runway through the low cloud by mistaking garbage fires for beacons. A Gloster Gladiator landed in zero visibility, and in May a Curtiss Tomahawk put down with engine trouble.

By that time, and despite 'wilful damage on the part of civilian workmen with a view to theft of light fixtures and switches', the base was almost ready to be handed over to the United States Army Air Force (USAAF). The transfer took place on 30 August 1943, and for the next 14 months the skies reverberated to the roar of the B-17 Flying Fortresses and, from February 1944, B-24 Liberators.

Cluntoe acted as a Combat Crew Replacement Center where American bomber crews were trained – with the exception of the gunners who were sent off to the gunnery schools at Greencastle. So busy was the site that in July 1944 a total of 330 heavy bomber crews left Cluntoe/Greencastle ready to become operational.[13] During training, thousands of miles from home and no doubt well aware of the hazardous missions over occupied Europe that lay ahead, it is little wonder that some of them grasped the chance to take a boat out to Ram's Island, a forested strip of land in the shape of a seahorse, close to the western shore.

Walking through the trees, Dan empathized with the servicemen: 'It must have been a little paradise for them away from the sounds and smells of the vast military enterprise. And they showed their appreciation by carving their names into these trees and they're still here today. There's more hearts on these trees … a big "1944". "NJK, 1944" leaves his mark. This is obviously where the guys came. There's a lot of graffiti. Here's the best one yet: "NNP USA 44". There's a direct link with those servicemen who were here.'

BELOW: Almost 70 years later, the initials of US servicemen carved into the trees on Ram's Island live on.

U-155 – THE STORY OF A SUBMARINE

On 23 August 1941 a new U-boat was commissioned at Bremerhaven. By now the German shipyards were turning out submarines like sausages, but the entry into service of each boat was a moment for ceremony and celebration, and in the spring of 1941 the U-boat arm of the Kriegsmarine had cause for high spirits. Despite the recent death or capture of several of their first generation of aces, a loss that probably had a greater long-term effect than was realized at the time, the graph of Allied merchant tonnage sunk was heading steeply and satisfactorily upwards.

For Korvettenkapitän Adolf Cornelius Piening, the day was a milestone in his career: his first command. He had transferred from the surface navy in 1940 and as part of his training had made one patrol in *U-48* under Kapitänleutnant 'Vaddi' (Daddy) Schultze, a decorated commander famous for sinking the British cargo ship *Firby* and then sending Churchill a message in English that gave the position of the sinking and requested him to rescue the crew in their lifeboats.

After a training period at Stettin with the 4th Flotilla, Piening and *U-155* sailed from Kiel on 7 February 1942 on their first war patrol. Fifteen days later, while cruising off Greenland's Cape Farewell they encountered convoy ONS 67 bound for Canada, and fired a spread of three torpedoes, all of which were heard to explode. Two ships were sunk: the Norwegian *Sama*, loaded

with china clay, and the British tanker *Adellen*, in ballast. The *Sama* lost 19 crew out of 39, while 36 of the tanker's crew were killed. That particular convoy was also badly mauled by *U-558*, *U-158* and *U-587*, with six ships sunk and another damaged.

Piening's third success during his patrol was a mistake: he torpedoed the neutral Brazilian *Arabutan* off Cape Hatteras on 7 March, killing one of her crew. Several similar incidents during that year, resulting in more than a thousand casualties, induced Brazil to join the Allies in August.

U-155 returned not to Kiel but to Lorient in Occupied France, where she joined the 10th Flotilla and from where she set off for her second war patrol. Operating in the waters off Venezuela she preyed mostly on unescorted vessels of various nationalities, the largest of them the fully laden British tanker *San Victorio* that was on her maiden voyage for owners Eagle Oil & Shipping. A single survivor was picked up by the USS *Turquoise*, an armed yacht that patrolled those waters and also rescued survivors from Piening's next victim, the American cargo ship *Challenge*. In a patrol lasting 52 days from 24 April, *U-155* sank seven ships amounting to 32,392 grt.

Piening's greatest contribution to the war effort came with his third patrol, when, in the fortnight leading up to 10 August, *U-155* destroyed more than 43,000 tons of shipping. The ten victims ranged from the tiny Dutch ships *Draco* and *Strabo*, sunk by gunfire after their crews had been allowed to take to the lifeboats, to the *Empire Arnold* and another Eagle Oil & Shipping tanker, the *San Emiliano*.

The 7,045 grt *Empire Arnold* was a new ship, completed in May 1942. Owned by the Ministry of War Transport, she was managed on their behalf by Sir R. Ropner & Co. Ltd and registered at Hartlepool. She arrived at Boston in ballast on 12 August 1942, but instead of loading she was sent to Bethlehem Steel's shipyard at Staten Island where her holds were lined with wood. That pointed towards an explosive cargo: steel holds can create sparks. Ten thousand tons of tanks, trucks, aircraft and crates of material for the North Africa campaign came aboard, until, according to the memory of the 19-year-old radio operator Norman Watts, the ship was so heavily laden that her load line was submerged.

Although she left in convoy to sail on a route passing Key West and Trinidad, *Empire Arnold* was dispersed on 3 August to head for Alexandria via Suez. Routing Egypt-bound ships via South Africa was no guarantee of their safety, but taking the Mediterranean route though the Strait of Gibraltar at this period was tantamount to suicide. Even with an escort that included a battleship, four aircraft carriers, plus cruisers, destroyers and submarine screens, the merchant ships of Operation Pedestal were badly hit by Axis submarines, aircraft and E-boats at this very same time.

Watts recalled receiving an Admiralty message warning all British merchant ships in the area that a ship had been sunk by a U-boat. The incident had occurred north of *Empire Arnold*'s route, but: 'As the skipper said to me when I gave him the message, "If she goes this way…".'

At 10:30 on the night of 4 August, with *Empire Arnold* some 500 nautical miles (925 kilometres) from Trinidad, steering a zig-zag course at around 10 knots, Watts was off duty and washing his clothes on deck when the first torpedo from *U-155* hit the engine room. He heard the screams and the frantic efforts of those trying to get out through the doors.

'Everybody below was trapped. The watch below in the forecastle couldn't get out. Nobody in the engine room was alive. We came to a halt. We didn't take long to lose way because we were bucking a 3 or 4 knot current coming off the north coast of the South American continent, and the siren was sounding and everybody went for their lives. There was no question of sending a radio message: it was all too late…. There were about two boats, not two boat*loads*, got away. By then I was in the sea, and another torpedo hit us five minutes later, right into the Number Two hold, and, and the ship blew to kingdom come. … If you've seen films of Hiroshima, that's how the Empire Arnold went up. And the tanks, the diesel locomotives for the Egyptian railway that we were carrying, and bomber fuselages, Grant tanks, were tossed into the air like toys. … And the ocean was covered with debris: debris of every description, and also a few people. A few voices were calling out and screaming out. …

I can't remember a great deal except for being very frightened and cold and wet, even though the water was very warm. … and I heard the noise of an engine … A conning tower came up, water spilling off it, and there was this thudding of an engine.'

Propaganda had demonized U-boat crews as ruthless killers who would machine-gun survivors in the water. On only one occasion were they found to have done so; and a Royal Navy commander had committed the same crime. Watts watched anxiously as the submarine made a sweep of the area, the crew using boat-hooks to collect pieces of paper as if trying to work out what the ship had been carrying.

'It then slowed down tremendously … and I saw members of the crew bending over and pulling people out of the water, as I was pulled out myself. This was the U-155.

We were lined up on deck in the rags that we survived in and we were given glasses of water. First of all we were interrogated: what was your nationality? We said "British" and he said "Not *British:* English, Irish, Scots or Welsh?" … There was one lad from the Isle of Man, who said "I'm a Manxman". "What is that?" was the reply.'[14]

The bosun was handed a packet of German cigarettes. He put the carton in his pocket and gave the cigarettes to the men. Adolf Piening apologized for the sinking as attested by Watts and others. He then put them into two lifeboats. 'He survived the war, I'm glad to say,' Watts said. 'He was a gentleman. He behaved correctly. He had no room, he had no food.'

Standing orders stated that U-boats should try to take prisoner the

master/captain and chief engineer of their victims. Chief Engineer George Cassie had been killed when the torpedo that struck the engine room brought down the smokestack, but the injured Captain Tate was one of those brought onto *U-155*'s casing, and kept aboard. He was taken to hospital in Brest before being transferred to a POW camp, and his experience aboard the submarine was sufficiently

good that, post war, he attended *U-155*'s crew reunions. Piening already had on board another wounded captain: Christian Evensen of the Norwegian cargo ship *Bill*, which *U-155* had sunk on 29 July.

Evensen was not as fortunate as Tate and died in a German hospital at Rennes from the effects of inhaling chlorine gas, a perennial hazard on submarines.[15]

The two lifeboats kept company for five days before bad weather parted them. Watts's boat was commanded by the second mate, Percy Walton Barton, who, armed with the directions given by Piening, successfully kept a following wind until they were spotted on 11 August by an aircraft that diverted the Canadian merchant ship *Lawrendoc* to their assistance. They were disembarked at Georgetown, British Guiana, on 12 August, two days before the Norwegian ship *Dalvangen* landed the occupants of the second boat commanded by Richard Thomson, the first mate. Both men received commendations.

The only trouble Piening experienced was an aircraft attack on 19 August that caught the boat on the surface and killed one of his crew. He returned to base on 15 September, having already been notified by radio that his achievements had earned him the Knight's Cross. While his fourth patrol was leaner – three ships sunk and one damaged – it included a very valuable warship.

In October 1942, as Allied troops prepared to make their amphibious invasion of North Africa, codenamed Operation Torch, the escort carrier HMS *Avenger*, with three Swordfish biplane torpedo-bombers and a dozen Sea Hurricane fighters, was one of two carriers providing air cover for the landings at the Vichy French stronghold of Algiers. However, the Vichy forces quickly surrendered and *Avenger* was soon ordered home via Gibraltar, where she joined convoy MFK 1(Y) ready for the voyage to the Clyde.

News of the convoy could not be kept secret. A message went out to all U-boats in the area: '… on 14 November at 1800 a convoy comprising one aircraft carrier, two auxiliary cruisers, two destroyers, two corvettes and five large transports put to sea in the Atlantic.' In fact, there were two aircraft carriers: the other was the elderly HMS *Argus*. Among the boats to pick up the signal that same evening was *U-155*, now operating as part of the Westwall group, a powerful 20-strong wolfpack massing west of Gibraltar.

U-564 spotted the target and made a signal to that effect to alert the other boats, which Piening received at 19:20 Berlin Time on the 14th. Intermittent showers hampered visibility but at 02:55 [01:55 GMT] he discerned the shadows of two destroyers 80 degrees astern. They were travelling at 15–20 knots and zig-zagging on a roughly westerly course at a distance of approximately 3,300 yards (3,000 metres). By 03:45 [02:45 GMT] he had a good view of the prey: 'Convoy bearing 75 degrees in view, 8 large shadows, in wide formation (overlapping columns). Speed 15 knots. Two escorts on intended attack side.'

The convoy was steering 270 degrees in four columns spaced 5 cables – just over 1,000 yards (915 metres) – apart. Spacing within each in the column was supposed to be 2 cables but the commanding officer of HMS *Ulster Monarch* stated that they were 'by no means closed up to their proper distances' and the gap was more like 4

or 5 cables. *U-155* was off the port side of the convoy; HMS *Avenger* was in the middle of the second column.

Overlapping columns made good targets, and everything was propitious for the submarine that was now just under 1,100 yards (1,000 metres) away. Then at 04:05 (03:05 GMT] Piening observed 'leading escort using its searchlight, firing machine guns outwards and throwing depth-charges'. The radio direction finding (RDF) equipment of the escort ship HMS *Wrestler*'s had detected a U-boat, and she was taking action. A message should have been passed to the rest of the convoy, but it was never sent due to a 'communications failure'. The convoy was ordered to turn 45 degrees to starboard, away from the threat. Piening now found his firing distance rapidly increasing from less than 1,100 to 2,735 yards (1,000–2,500 metres).

Closing to 1,640 yards (1,500 metres) he fired a spread of four torpedoes and then a further pair. Hardly were the torpedoes running

ABOVE: Instituted in 1939, the coveted Knight's Cross was awarded to 144 men from the U-boat arm, mostly submarine commanders. Three higher grades existed, the highest being the Knight's Cross with Oak Leaves, Crossed Swords and Diamonds. Of the 27 awarded to the German armed services, two were won by U-boat commanders.

USS *Almaack* cargo ship	*Ettrick* troopship	*Samuel Chase* commodore's ship	*Letitia* troopship
Orbita troopship	HMS *Avenger* escort carrier	HMS *Argus* aircraft carrier	*Dempo* Dutch troopship
HMS *Ulster Monarch* Landing Ship Infantry (LSI)	*Macharda* cargo ship		

LEFT: The disposition of ships within the convoy, excluding escorts.

than he saw a second escort turn on its searchlights. The scene was becoming unhealthy. Time to crash-dive and listen underwater.

The cargo ship *Macharda* claimed to be 2 cables behind HMS *Avenger*:

'… on the turn explosions were heard in the direction of ALMAACK and ETTRICK then AVENGER was hit on the port side admidships. There was a high column of water then a second explosion a few seconds later and the midship section was blown right out and the vessel collapsed in the middle [.] she was immediately enveloped in flame of a dull red colour which rose to a great height then the bow and stern rose in the air and sank very quickly [;] the bow disappeared first. A buoy with light attached was seen floating after the stern sank and snowflakes were fired from all the ships. Men were seen jumping through the flames into the sea and others sliding down the flight deck into the flames. From the time the vessel was hit until the time she disappeared was about two minutes.'[16]

Ettrick sank five hours later; *Almaack* was badly damaged but stayed afloat and was towed to Gibraltar for repair. Casualties on those two ships were light, but the torpedo that struck *Avenger* hit the bomb room, and a mere 12 men out of a complement of well over 500 survived.

Avenger's explosion caused serious anxiety among the officers of other escort carriers about the design of their ships. To dampen dangerous speculation and restore confidence, the Admiralty published the findings of its inquiry, which was that: 'HMS *Avenger* was struck by a torpedo at about 75 frame on the port side and this caused the bomb room to explode. More than one torpedo hit is considered unlikely.' As a result, modifications to and around the bomb room were made on her sister-ships, and bomb storage was confined to the centre of the ship, away from the vulnerable sides.[17]

Life now became more difficult for *U-155*. Her fifth patrol began on 8 February 1943 and netted just two ships with a combined tonnage of less than 8,000 tons; the next two were barren. Air attacks on U-boats were increasing, and five of *U-155*'s crew were injured by gunfire from de Havilland Mosquitoes during June. With Allied escorts highly active in the Bay of Biscay, Piening advocated a new route for submarines on passage in that area. Instead of taking the shortest route across the Bay, he recommended hugging the coastline, which was at the limits of Allied aircraft. The tactic worked until the Allies caught on and deployed their hunter-killer groups further east.

Piening commanded *U-155* for the eighth and last time in September 1943. It was an exceptionally long patrol of 103 days, but *U-155* sank only one vessel: the Norwegian cargo ship *Siranger* was torpedoed off the coast of northern Brazil on 24 October. Nobody was killed, and although Dönitz had issued the so-called *Laconia* Order that forbade U-boat commanders from rendering assistance to the survivors of U-boat attacks, Piening took the injured third mate, Otto Friis Hansen, into the submarine, where the doctor aboard operated on his arm.

A few weeks later it was *U-155*'s turn to suffer when she was bombed by aircraft. Badly damaged, she crash-dived and successfully reached Lorient on New Year's Day. Her captain remained ashore as commander of the 7th Flotilla, and Oberleutnant Johannes Rudolph took command of *U-155* for one single and uneventful patrol, *U-155*'s longest, of 105 days.

U-155's career sums up the U-boat war. The diminishing successes of the second half of the Battle of the Atlantic were coupled with an escalation of the number of U-boats sunk and men lost. The U-boat was far from invulnerable. When one was sunk she often went down with all hands, either to be crushed by the water pressure as she fell far below the maximum depth her hull could bear, or to sit helplessly on the bottom in shallower water while the crew used up the last breaths of oxygen or made desperate attempts to use their escape apparatus. The result was that increasingly young and inexperienced officers gained commands – when Oberleutnant Ludwig-Ferdinand von Friedeburg briefly took over *U-155* on 15 August 1944 at the age of 20 years 3 months he was the youngest officer to command a submarine.

Now attached to the 33rd Flotilla, *U-155* sailed from Lorient on 9 September, the very last U-boat to evacuate the French base that had proved so useful. She swept up towards Greenland, down the North Sea and safely into her new base at Flensburg. She had just one sting left to deliver. As the European war came towards its end, *U-155* under the command of Oberleutnant zur See Friedrich Altmaier was on passage to Norway. Allied bombers, escorted by fighters, were still mounting heavy raids on German cities, and on 4 May *U-155* was one of three boats to attract the interest of North American P-51 Mustang fighters from 126 Squadron RAF as they escorted North Coates Strike Wing. *U-155*'s deck gun opened up and hit the aircraft of Squadron Leader Arne Austeen, which crashed into the sea, killing the Norwegian ace just one day before *U-155* surrendered at Baring Bay, Denmark, and four days before Germany, too, admitted defeat. The submarine that had sunk 26 Allied ships was to be scuttled by the Allies as part of Operation Deadlight (see pages 63–68).

ABOVE: The fate of many U-boats: *U-625* was sunk on 10 March 1944 west of Ireland by Short Sunderland Mark III, EK591 'U' from 422 Squadron, RCAF, based at RAF St Angelo on Lough Erne. Depth charges straddled the submarine and exploded around the stern; the aircraft's rear gunner attacked the bows and conning tower. As the submarine slowly went down, the crew took to their dinghies – but were drowned in a storm.

1

2

3

THE WRECK OF U-155

1: Looking forward from the conning tower.

2: The four bow torpedo tubes.

3: The beam from the torch spotlights a gun mounting; all deck guns were removed before submarines were sunk during Operation Deadlight. Note that the diver is carrying spare cylinders to allow him to maximize his time on the wreck.

U-155 is a superb but challenging dive. Not only is she in exceptional condition for a submarine that has spent more than 65 years sitting on the seabed, but on a good day the waters off Malin Head are so clear that even at more than 230 feet (70 metres) beneath the surface the ambient light provides perfect visibility. The beams from the divers' torches as they glide around are required only for peering into nooks and crannies. At that depth, the natural colours fade, especially the reds, and the submarine appears green.

The light and the availability of high-quality, wide-angle lenses make it possible to see the full extent of the boat, which enhances the beauty of the experience. The Type IXC U-boat was designed with a pressure hull around which was fitted a lighter steel hull to protect the external tanks and fittings. The casing was not designed to withstand pressure, so the vents allow the water to flow freely through, and pollock swim in and out. On one famous occasion in 1942, two British submariners won the Victoria Cross after crawling between the casing and pressure hull of their own boat, HMS *Thrasher*, to remove and jettison German bombs that had penetrated the casing but failed to explode.

A combination of degraded steel, silt and shells encrust the conning tower and the 'wintergarden' built aft of it. This was where the submarine's anti-aircraft guns – removed before scuttling – were mounted. The upper and lower conning tower hatches were left open to ensure she sank. Towards the stern, the long propeller shafts emerge from the hull. The only obvious damage is the loss of the four forward torpedo tubes and hydroplanes, but even this large piece lies beside the submarine, inviting investigation.

Until the 1990s diving on a wreck at this kind of depth using basic compressed air would have been dangerous due to nitrogen poisoning caused by breathing air at great depth.

Now, professional divers such as Rich Stevenson, who led the *Dig WW2* dives, are regularly working at 245 feet (75 metres) and beyond thanks to rebreathers, trimix and heliox.

Divers breathing compressed air simply inhale the air, and then exhale into the water. They can do this until the cylinder is empty, by which time they need to be safely at the surface. From a diver's point of view, breathing is a very inefficient use of oxygen. During inhalation, the lungs exchange oxygen for waste carbon dioxide, but they absorb less than a quarter of the oxygen in the air, so exhaled air contains around 17 percent oxygen. Moreover, the stream of bubbles can disturb the area on which underwater archaeologists are working, or betray the presence of military divers on covert operations. A closed rebreather system is a self-contained unit that allows the diver to exhale the air into a counter-lung and, when the oxygen content becomes depleted, the rebreather replenishes it with oxygen from a separate tank.

In fact, divers working at the depth of *U-155* do not breathe normal air but heliox (a helium and oxygen mix) or trimix (a nitrogen, oxygen and helium mix). Both avoid oxygen poisoning and nitrogen narcosis; the latter affects the diver rather like alcohol, but the effects are quickly reversed by ascending. Stevenson used trimix for the *U-155* dive.

Fully trained divers can stay down for much longer using rebreathers, but must maintain discipline on the ascent, rising no more than 33 feet (10 metres) per minute in order to avoid painful and potentially fatal decompression sickness: the bends.

In addition to a wet or dry suit the dive team wore buoyancy control devices – effectively an inflatable gilet that enables the diver to achieve neutral buoyancy and to which the rebreather is attached. Once on the scene the team used DPVs (diver propulsion vehicles) to move around the wreck. These are battery-powered, handheld units that tow the diver, because exploring a 260-feet-plus (80-metre) long wreck such as *U-155* is tiring.

Stevenson began filming *U-155* from the stern, using a Canon 5D Mark II DSLR still camera with video capability, running in High Definition at 24 frames per second. This is a standard camera, protected by a special waterproof housing capable of withstanding the pressure that exists at such depths.

STARS AND STRIPES IN DERRY

With so much shipping routed through the North Western Approaches, and Liverpool a prime target for the Luftwaffe, Derry gained in importance during the war. At the end of 1940, the Admiralty was in negotiations with Belfast shipbuilders Harland and Wolff to expand facilities:

'The necessity for the immediate setting into operation of the repair facilities at Londonderry cannot be too highly stressed. Even now, with the winter only just commencing, it is becoming increasingly difficult to arrange for the immediate taking in hand of repairs to destroyers, escort vessels etc. ... Detailed proposals should also be forwarded for the additional machinery, the dockside crane and also for the lengthening of the dock to enable it to take Town class destroyers.'[18]

Ebrington Barracks became the Royal Navy's shore base, commissioned as HMS *Ferret*, and Harland and Wolff workers were employed at the naval ship repair facility at Derry's former Pennyburn Shipyard. A large quay was built on the Foyle at Lisahally where the water was around 18 feet (5 metres)

BELOW: The rotting pillars of the jetty at Lisahally, constructed to accommodate convoy escorts during the Battle of the Atlantic.

deep; 2,300 feet (700 metres) long and connected to the shore by three piers, it was serviced by a narrow gauge railway.

By April 1941, the port had become the main base for the transatlantic convoy escorts, with anything up to 65 in harbour at any one time and thousands of British and Canadian naval personnel in the city, as well as a seasoning of Free forces. They were soon joined by the Americans who established a naval base there as part of the Destroyers for Bases Agreement signed in September 1940.

In June 1941 a large group of US 'technicians' arrived in Derry. Within six months there were more than 700 of them, all ostensibly civilians – an advance guard to establish a US facility as part of the September agreement by which 50 elderly destroyers were given to Britain in return for bases around the world, of which Derry was the first. These vessels became the Town class. The civilian nature of the Americans' work was stressed until after Pearl Harbor in December 1941, when the new base was almost complete. Among the facilities was a naval communications station that functioned until 1977.

The arrival en masse of the Americans had a major impact on the city, and was resented by a significant proportion of the local men who soon discovered that the Derry girls were falling for the well-paid newcomers, black and white, with their gifts of chocolate, chewing gum and stockings. Children who had become used to rationing were thrilled by the handfuls of sweets liberally dished out. With so much naval activity to support, Derry had full employment, and despite its vital strategic importance it was spared the bombs that hit Belfast, Liverpool and other major ports. Just two parachute mines were dropped on the city, one of which killed 15 people living on the Messines Park housing estate.

SO NEAR YET SO FAR – EMPIRE HERITAGE

By the end of August 1944, and with their army being pushed back towards their own borders following the Normandy landings, the Germans had lost any realistic hope of winning the war. They had been defeated in the East by the Soviets at Stalingrad; and in North Africa by the British and Americans; their European ally, Italy, had signed an armistice; and the US Navy was inexorably destroying Japanese air power in the Pacific. Tactical and technical advances in Allied A/S warfare had all but emasculated the U-boats since May 1943 and the epic battle for convoy ONS 5 when four wolfpacks, with a total of 56 U-boats, had mounted a fierce attack on a single convoy and, while sinking a dozen ships, had taken heavy losses at the hands of a skilled and determined escort.

Despite the cumulative effect of such reverses, Hitler was no more minded to raise the white flag than Churchill had been in the summer of 1940, and he would continue the submarine war against the convoys that brought vital supplies of equipment, food and fuel to Britain to maintain the Allied land offensive in Europe. Prior to D-Day, the U-boats had been withdrawn from the convoy routes in order to oppose the amphibious landings that the Germans knew to be imminent. Now they were being sent once more to do what they had done best, and with their newest defence, the snorkel, increasingly available.

At its simplest, the submarine's snorkel was a tube that, provided its top remained above the surface, allowed the diesels to draw fresh air while submerged. The snorkel did not offer immunity from detection; the feather-like wake created by snorkels could be spotted by day; nor did it improve underwater speed – anything above 6 knots could tear it off, but it did allow a boat to recharge batteries just under the surface, safe from detection by radar. In the second half of 1943 the Germans began to retro-fit them to their Atlantic submarines.

With or without snorkels, it was a difficult time for submarine crews. Increasingly convoys were getting through unscathed, and during the first six months of 1944 only 121 ships had been sunk or damaged by U-boats: fewer than in an average month in 1942, and fewer than the number of U-boats sunk in the same period.

Nonetheless, there were still opportunities for a cool-headed commander such as the 29-year-old aristocrat Kapitänleutnant Hartmut Graf von Matuschka, Freiherr von Toppolczan und Spätgen, commander of *U-482*, a boat fitted with a snorkel and based at Bergen, home to the 11th Flotilla in Occupied Norway. On 16 August von Matuschka sailed on his first war patrol in *U-482*.

As *U-482* reached the waters off the north coast of Ireland, a big convoy was forming on the opposite side of the Atlantic, an amalgamation of three convoys from Sydney, Halifax and New York. They were drawn up in 14 columns, each containing between six and nine ships, creating a rectangle 7 nautical miles (13 kilometres) wide and 3 nautical miles (5.5 kilometres) deep, their escorts protectively positioned around them. In fifth place in the ninth column, with four vessels ahead and three astern, steamed the *Empire Heritage*, a large former whaling factory ship which had been converted into an oil tanker. Her crew of 69 was augmented by two convoy signalmen, to handle the extra traffic that convoy procedures generated, four British Army personnel and 11 DEMS (Defensively Equipped Merchant Ship) gunners to man the 4-inch gun, the 12-pounder and the six Oerlikons that she carried for protection. In addition, she was repatriating 73 passengers, almost all of them 'distressed seamen' rescued from sunken merchant ships.

Empire Heritage was more than just a tanker; she had much in common with a modern car ferry. Her factory deck was ideal for transporting cargo such as tanks and even aircraft, and without a whale-processing workforce on board she had surplus accommodation that was suitable for passengers. On 25 August, under the command of James Campbell Jamieson, she left New York as part of convoy HX 305 with a 2,000-ton deck cargo that included dump trucks and Sherman tanks, as well as her oil.

Five days after HX 305 sailed, von Matuschka struck lucky, picking off the 10,448 grt American tanker *Jacksonville* just north of Malin Head. She was part of convoy CU 36 from New York and carried over 140,000 barrels of oil, with

a crew of 49, plus 29 armed guards. Von Matuschka chose the moment when the convoy split and the *Jacksonville* was the last ship in the single column that peeled away for Loch Ewe while the rest of the convoy continued to Liverpool. Fired into the tanker's starboard side, the first torpedo set the cargo ablaze; the second broke her back. With the ship and surrounding water on fire, only two of her complement were saved.

The escorts hunted in vain for *U-482*. Not only did they fail to detect her, but, the following day and north of Tory Island off the Donegal coast, von Matuschka succeeded in torpedoing HMS *Hurst Castle*, one of the Castle class corvettes belonging to Escort

Group B – 17 of the corvette's 124 crew members died.

Von Matuschka headed further to the northwest and encountered the huge outward bound convoy ON 251, which had left Liverpool on 1 September. Ten minutes after midnight on 3 September he put a torpedo into the Norwegian ship *Fjordheim*, loaded with 4,000 tons of anthracite from Swansea. Three men on watch were killed by the explosion; 32 got away in the lifeboats and three were rescued from the water.

It was shaping up to be the kind of successful patrol enjoyed by the legendary U-boat commanders of the earlier years of the war, and *U-482* was not yet out of torpedoes.

ABOVE: A U-boat running submerged, using her snorkel to provide air to the diesels. Note, however, the tell-tale wake. The first snorkels were hinged, and when not in use could be lowered to the decks. The snorkel seen here, forward of the periscopes, is the telescopic design fitted to Type XXI U-boats.

ABOVE: A convoy assembles in Bedford Basin, Halifax, Nova Scotia in 1941, ready for the dangerous transatlantic voyage.

Meanwhile, the voyage of HX 305 progressed uneventfully: the convoy encountered nothing worse than a little fog early on. It was protected by Escort Group C.5 ('C' indicated Canadian) commanded from HMCS *Dunver* by Senior Officer Escort Group, Acting Commander George Stephen OBE, DSC. Stephen was experienced, but in July, following the tragic sinking by friendly fire of the Free French submarine *La Perle*, he had been reprimanded over his failure to exercise proper command of the escort, and communications aboard *Dunver* were pronounced poor.

Despite the dramatic decline in sinkings, no convoy took its security for granted. From June onwards, the Admiralty had repeatedly warned escorts of a change of U-boat tactics in the comparatively shallow waters of the North Channel: if spotted, they were likely to dive and lie stopped on the bottom, head to tide, making ASDIC detection difficult. Escorts, therefore, were to use echo soundings and remember that depth charging could damage a snorkel, forcing the submarine to charge her batteries on the surface and open herself to air attack. On 1 August C-in-C Portsmouth wrote:

'… the following action is to be taken if a U-boat is sighted or reveals her presence by attacking shipping.
(A) Deliver an immediate counter attack. This is to be by eye if Asdic contact is not established immediately.
(B) On completion, if still without Asdic contact, plaster the area liberally with depth charges on the assumption that the U-boat will bottom close to her diving or attacking position.'[19]

The Admiralty had sent two signals warning HX 305 it was heading into an area of submarine activity (one as a consequence of the sinking of the *Fjordheim*), and according to the commanding officer of HMCS *Long Branch*, Lieutenant Commander Rendell Johnson, the escorts received a daily 'U-boat situation report', which made him, at least, consider the strong possibility of an attack.

Meanwhile *U-482* was quietly patrolling those same well-stocked hunting grounds. On 7 September a tempting target appeared in the periscope, the 20,000 grt Dutch ship *Oranje*, but von Matuschka recognized her as a hospital ship and left her well alone. The submarine had carried out most of her patrol using her snorkel, but her commander was now becoming concerned about the intensity of Allied A/S patrols in the North Channel.

By this time the convoy was off the Donegal coast in the North Western Approaches and steaming into the area where HMS *Hurst Castle* and *Jacksonville* had met their ends. Its protection had by now been increased by the arrival of a support group, Escort Group 5 (not to be confused with 5.C), the ships of which were in line abreast, forming a wide screen 5 nautical miles (9 kilometres) ahead of the convoy. The ships of the close escort surrounded the convoy using ASDIC, radar and HF/DF to detect any lurking U-boats. Some of the escorts were towing CAT (Canadian Anti-Acoustic Torpedo) gear to deflect acoustic torpedoes away from the ships' propellers.

That night Stephen sent the escorts a 'signal of night intention' codenamed Pineapple[20] Dark, in case of attack. This was one of several standard responses to different types of attack, and was chosen on the basis that any attack would be made by more than one U-boat, though a wolfpack attack was now highly unlikely. The purpose was to create an opportunity to hunt the attacker while simultaneously forcing other U-boats to stay down, and its execution required the escorts to proceed for 30 minutes in wide zig-zags to maximize their ASDIC coverage. Pineapple also commanded specified escorts to fire starshells towards the direction of attack – not the convoy – to illuminate or thwart one or more additional attackers. Pineapple Dark, however, was to be executed without starshells.

Stephen was also preparing for the moment, scheduled for 04:30 GMT, when the Lock Ewe section would detach. At 22:59, the convoy's rescue ship, *Pinto*, was using her HF/DF equipment when she got a second class contact bearing 52 degrees: a submarine drying out its aerials some 30 nautical miles (55 kilometres) away. The message was passed to Stephen but he did not consider it definite and so did not forward it.

Shortly before 02:00[21] GMT on the 8th *U-482* detected the convoy with her hydrophones. It began to pass over her. Von Matuschka sent the crew to combat stations and ordered periscope depth in order to see what he was dealing with. Through the clouds the moon glimmered, and he was inside the convoy with enough light to launch his attack submerged. Although he made no record of why he chose one ship over another, and did not recognize *Empire Heritage* as a tanker, she must have stood out as the obvious victim among the ships that he could see. At 05:51 [03:51 GMT] he gave the order to fire No. 3 tube, angled to hit the ship amidships.

The torpedo hit the starboard side of the tanker after 42 seconds and detonated as it smashed into No. 8 tank. Seconds later the fuel exploded, but von Matuschka could not see the results of his handiwork. To make sure that *Empire Heritage* could not limp home, he fired a second 'eel' four minutes later from No. 1 tube, but not having heard it detonate he concluded that it had missed: 'My mistake' he wrote, blaming himself for setting the wrong speed. More likely, as the evidence of the survivors suggests, *Empire Heritage* had sunk in the four-minute interval

BELOW: *Empire Heritage* as she would have looked at the time of her loss.

between shots. It is possible, though not proven, that the ship may have had an inherent weakness dating back to the time when she was welded back together in 1941 after striking a mine and splitting in two.

The speed of the sinking and the fact that it happened at night left many of *Empire Heritage*'s crew and passengers trapped. The lucky ones were those who, like the chief mate J.C. Gibson, got on deck quickly:

'I jumped out of bed, slipped on some clothes and my lifejacket, and hurried on deck, arriving there approximately two minutes after the explosion. I noticed that the fore deck was completely awash, and the next moment I was lifted off my feet and washed overboard. I did not have time to fasten the tapes of my life jacket before taking to the water and on surfacing I grabbed a buoyancy tank which had broken away from a lifeboat. I was just in time to see the funnel of the ship disappearing, approximately three minutes after the explosion.

I eventually drifted alongside a raft which had floated clear, and scrambled on to it. There were already five men on it, all of whom had been in the water and were covered with fuel oil.'[22]

Rush Webb was a US Navy signalman, serving on the *Martin Van Buren*, which was sailing on the starboard side of *Empire Heritage*.

'Most of us assumed the submarine war was about over and I had removed my outer clothes for the first time during the war while at sea when I turned in that night. Upon hearing the explosion I dressed and ran to the bridge and the Captain told me to break out my Aldis lamp and notify the Commodore of the convoy. We assumed it was a torpedo and not a mine. I could see the superstructure of the ship directly ahead of ours in our column and I aimed my Aldis lamp there and beat out a series of SSSSSs in Morse code which was the signal for a submarine attack. After about ten minutes or so, our Radio Operator appeared on the bridge and told us a ship had broken radio silence and got a wireless message off and the captain told me to discontinue my signalling.

It was at that point I turned and looked in the direction of the stricken ship for the first time and saw a light appearing above the surface of the water, and I assumed it to be the *Heritage* trying to launch lifeboats. Actually the *Heritage* may have already capsized and the light may have come from the lights on the life jackets of survivors in the water. We could not see or hear any utterances from the survivors. Merchant ships were instructed not to stop for survivors.'[23]

Von Matuschka launched a third torpedo, this time acoustic, from No. 4 tube, still unaware that his victim was gone. After two minutes seven seconds it detonated. He turned to line up a stern shot, but he had lost his firing position and the convoy had passed.

Some aboard HCMS *Dunver* saw red flashes rising to a height of 70 feet (21 metres), but this was not reported higher up the chain of command than to the second officer of the watch. It was the refrigerated merchant ship *Jamaica Planter* that signalled the loss of the ship, a prompt act for which she would afterwards be congratulated by the Admiralty. In response, Commander Stephen ordered the escorts to commence Pineapple Dark. The convoy proceeded as if the incident had never occurred. The rescue ship, *Pinto*, dropped back to pick up survivors. She was specially equipped for her role, with boats, an operating theatre, and accommodation and clothing for 150 survivors. She was to be joined by one of the escorts, the armed trawler HMCS *Northern Wave*.

Gibson and his fellow survivors spent around half an hour on their raft. *Empire Heritage*'s fourth officer, R.P. Tweedy, had quickly moved to rig the weather-screens on his own liferaft in order to protect its soaked and shocked occupants from the wind-chill before jumping onto another to do the same. Then the *Pinto* picked her way through the floating oil and wreckage and began picking up survivors.

U-482 hung around. Through the periscope von Matuschka observed *Pinto* and failed to recognize her as a rescue ship. Instead, as he recorded in his war diary, he decided that she was a damaged 5,000 grt tanker and must therefore be the victim of his third torpedo. Time to get into position to finish her off.

'I miscalculate and pass very close to its bow and to liferafts a few metres away where torches are being used, as on the tanker itself. Additional proof, along with the unmistakable sounds

of sinking, that a steamer has gone down.'

Gibson and others spotted 8 feet (2-metres plus) of periscope 'passing close across the *Pinto*'s bows from starboard to port, and also heard her engines. This submarine came from the direction off the land, steering approximately N.N.W. at roughly 10 knots. A few seconds later the periscope disappeared'.[24] She was seen, too, from *Pinto*, and on receiving a signal 'periscope port' *Northern Wave* went in pursuit.

Von Matuschka must have had nerves of steel as he fired from No. 5 (stern) tube. He recorded that the torpedo hit the starboard side amidships, sending up 'black columns' as high as the *Pinto*'s masts. He turned the periscope for an all-round look and spotted a trawler. By the time he had swung back to the subject of his attack: 'nothing more of the tanker to be seen'. The rescue ship had sunk in 90 seconds, taking with her many of her crew and some from that of *Empire Heritage*. Survivors climbed aboard the rafts that had been gathering around *Pinto*.

Northern Wave was in the impossible position of being the only ship in the immediate area to hunt the submarine and rescue the survivors. She chose the rescue role, because had she thrown depth charges or moved at any speed through the water even more men would have died. Inexplicably, several of the crew of *Northern Wave* stated that while they were pulling out survivors not only was a torpedo fired at them but that a periscope wake was seen and their ship ran over what they believed to be the submarine. But no

other U-boat was in the area, and *U-482*, satisfied with her morning's work, had prudently withdrawn. On board *Northern Wave*, the *Pinto*'s doctor, still in his soaking clothes, set what Gibson described as 'a magnificent example by his cool and efficient conduct', working without a break to treat the injured.

Casualty figures for *Empire Heritage* are slightly contradictory, but probably 110 out of 159, including her master, James Campbell Jamieson, were lost. Aboard *Pinto*, 21 out of 59 died.

The Court of Inquiry had little to say about the sinking of *Empire Heritage*, concentrating instead on what happened afterwards. Shepherd bore the brunt of the blame for negligence, poor communications and for ordering Pineapple rather than Banana – the latter being a response designed to hunt a single U-boat. Von Matuschka, by contrast, was warmly congratulated by Grossadmiral Dönitz, and decorated as an inspiration to other commanders – but *Pinto* was his last victim. *U-482* failed to return from her next, barren, patrol. Despite several explanations and dates for her loss, it is now accepted that she was the submarine sunk by HMS *Ascension* on 25 November about 120 nautical miles (220 kilometres) north of Faraid Head, Sutherland.

ABOVE: HM Trawler *Northern Wave*, convoy escort.

1

2

EMPIRE HERITAGE AND HER CARGO

1: A Sherman tank lies upside down. The track has come off on the right-hand side, exposing the wheels.

2: An incredible sight: a diver swims through the 'Sherman graveyard'.

Now lying some 230 feet (70 metres) down off Malin Head, *Empire Heritage* offers one of the strangest experiences to be found in any waters for experienced divers. The ship itself was badly damaged in the sinking, and now lies completely collapsed and broken, making it a hard wreck to move around. It is possible to recognize features such as the huge propeller with blades each taller than a man, the tall derricks, and the huge boilers that have broken away, but not to assess the damage inflicted by von Matuschka. In any case, the real lure for divers is not the ship but the extraordinary sight of her cargo lying across the seabed. Viewed without any clue as to scale, it is as if someone has dropped a box of die-cast Sherman tanks and other military vessels. Some of the tanks are upright, others lie on their sides; some have their tracks in place; a few have their hatches open, inviting exploration. There are tyres that look as pristine as the day they were manufactured.

One awestruck diver described what he had seen as: 'The remains of the ship and a jumble of Sherman tanks piled on one another – scattered, like the hand of God just picked them up and placed them in random order.'

Originally named *Tafelberg*, *Empire Heritage* had been constructed at Newcastle-upon-Tyne by Sir W.G. Armstrong, Whitworth & Co Ltd for the Kerguelen Sealing & Whaling Co. Ltd that was based in Cape Town, and at the time of her completion in 1930 she was the largest factory ship in the world. Her design reflected the requirements of her trade: a stern slipway between the funnels up which the whales were winched, to be cut up on the plan deck beneath the towering 50-feet (15-metre) derricks located amidships. Underneath, on the

RIGHT: A dramatic photograph of the future *Empire Heritage* in two sections after breaking apart in 1941.

factory deck, 34 meat-and-bone digesters and 18 blubber digesters[25] had once processed the raw commodities, storing the extracted oil in tanks capable of holding 16,000 tons of oil. The bridge and crew accommodation were situated well forward.

Tafelberg was just one of many such factory ships requisitioned during the Second World War and converted into oil tankers. Many fell victim to attack: their size and shape marked them out as important. *Tafelberg* was unlucky: she hit a mine in the Bristol Channel on 28 February 1941 and broke in two after striking a sandbank while under tow. The insurers wrote her off as a total loss, but such ships were valuable in wartime, so the Ministry of War Transport acquired the two parts, had them welded back together, and appointed Christian Salvesen & Co. to manage her. In March 1943 she resumed her war service under the name *Empire Heritage*. For the most part she shuttled safely across the North Atlantic, but from late 1943 until April 1944 she was be found at Aden, Suez and even Bombay before returning to the Atlantic convoys. On 8 September 1944 she finally met her end when she was torpedoed by *U-482*.

ABOVE: This tank came to rest in an upright position and its gun turret remains intact.

THE U-BOAT THAT CAME TOO LATE

Even in 1939 the Germans knew that their submarine technology was old, but the real problem at the start of the war was not the wrong type of boat but the insufficiency of ocean-going U-boats of *any* type, although production rapidly increased and built up the numbers of Type VIIs and Type IXs. The cracks appeared in 1942. Although this was the most successful year for the U-boats in terms of tonnage sunk, they took losses that finally convinced BdU that Allied escorts and aircraft were using radar that rendered a surfaced U-boat as visible as a cruise liner in peacetime. If the Kriegsmarine was to regain the initiative, it needed a true submarine, and quickly.

Germany had the technology to achieve the powerful, air-independent propulsion system essential for underwater speed and endurance. In 1939 work had begun on V80, a scaled-down prototype of a Walter boat (named after the engine designer Hellmuth Walter), which used a closed-cycle engine fuelled by perhydrol, a concentrated form of the highly reactive chemical hydrogen peroxide. Walter conceived a double hull, formed of two superimposed horizontal cylinders creating an '8'-shape, with the smaller-diameter lower cylinder devoted to the large quantities of perhydrol that would have to be carried. V80 achieved the staggering speed of 23 knots submerged, and two full-size boats were ordered, but the problems and dangers associated with using perhydrol, and the lack of time to resolve the issues, led to the scrapping of both boats before completion.[26]

The Type XXI, or Elektro Boat, emerged during a conference at the end of 1942. It was based on Walter's double hull design but with the lower compartment full of high-capacity, super-light batteries, trebling the power available. At 1,620 tons surfaced, the Type XXI was far larger than any other German submarine type, but the batteries gave full speed at 17 knots for an hour, more than adequate for an attack or an escape. Reduce that to a sedate 5 knots, and the battery charge would last five days, making transit safer in dangerous waters. When silence was essential, the boat could run on a 225-horsepower electric motor at 3.5 knots. Recharging on diesels for three or four hours a night, which could be done while snorkelling, was sufficient to keep the batteries full, and incorporated into the design were radar detectors and hydraulically assisted torpedo loading re-gear. For the first

BELOW: A schematic view of the Type XXI U-boat, Germany's first true submarine,

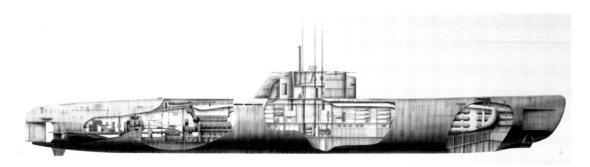

RIGHT: Admiral Karl Dönitz (centre) examines charts with Kapitänleutnant Adalbert Schnee (left) and Kapitän Zur See Eberhard Godt in 1942.

time U-boat crews would enjoy a luxury previously found only on US submarines – freezers.

The building programme was ambitious and bedevilled by problems. Almost 400 Type XXIs were planned, but when the war ended only 118 had been commissioned, of which just one, *U-2511* commanded by the 32-year-old Korvettenkapitän Adalbert Schnee, was fully operational. One reason for this failure to bring the Type XXI into combat was the long training period that was required and which took place in the Baltic. Schnee's training was interrupted in late January 1945 by the Kriegsmarine's desperate need to evacuate tens of thousands of wounded soldiers and German civilians flooding into towns around the Bay of Danzig before the area fell to Stalin's forces.

During Operation Hannibal, German ships, including around 40 U-boats, embarked more than 250,000 people, mostly civilians, but some technical, military and Gestapo personnel. Soviet submarines were active in the area and on the night of 30 January, off the Stolpe Bank, *S-13* torpedoed the *Wilhelm Gustloff*, which had left Gotenhafen (Gdynia) that morning with at least 8,000[27] people aboard. *U-2511* had sailed the same day from Danzig with refugees and was travelling submerged. She surfaced to pick up some of the *Gustloff*'s survivors. At the risk of his life, Oberleutnant zur See Horst Willner of *U-3505* smuggled his wife aboard in seaman's clothes and hid his baby daughter in a bag. From Danzig, he then called at Gotenhafen to embark more than 100 women and children.[28] The evacuation by sea went on until the end of the war, and the sinking of just three liners, *Wilhelm Gustloff*, *General von Streuben* and *Goya*, accounted for approximately 18,000 deaths.

U-2511 left Kiel for the Norwegian base of Horten on 17 March 1945, and from there she moved to Bergen. Her single war patrol began on 3 May when she sailed from Bergen, out through the fjords, heading into the Atlantic. Schnee and his crew had confidence in their submarine and she did not disappoint. When their ASDIC picked up the presence of enemy warships Schnee ordered 16 knots, turned away and raced on the opposite course to the hunters. Similar situations presented themselves and *U-2511* escaped every time without being depth charged. Knowing they had been picked up by ASDIC no longer induced fear: they knew they could get away.

On 4 May, Dönitz, who had been Führer since Hitler's suicide on 30 April, ordered the U-boats to end hostilities and return to their bases.

Some commanders thought it was a trick, but Schnee was one who obeyed and turned back for Bergen to surrender. What happened then is still as controversial as it was when Schnee and the officers of HMS *Norfolk* apparently pored over each other's logbooks a few days later.

The message to return was only a few hours old when *U-2511*'s ASDIC operator picked up the sound of a propeller. Schnee came to periscope depth and observed several destroyers[29] and a cruiser of the *Suffolk* class just 655 yards (600 metres) away and evidently unaware of the submarine's presence. This was as good as point-blank range, and having shared the periscope view with the engineer officer and the officer of the watch, Schnee gave orders to dive. *U-2511* passed under the British ships and returned the following day to Bergen. HMS *Norfolk* arrived on the 8th and officially liberated the city. Her officers showed understandable interest in *U-2511*, and Schnee told them that

their cruiser had been a sitting duck. By his account, their initial disbelief in his story ended when the cruiser's logbook and the submarine's war diary were brought together and compared. Unfortunately, the war diary subsequently disappeared, and it is now impossible to verify or disprove the story.

OPERATION DEADLIGHT

At the end of the First World War, the Germans famously scuttled their High Seas Fleet at Scapa Flow to prevent its dispersal to Allied navies. Less well known outside wreck-diving circles is the Second World War U-Boat graveyard in the waters between Scotland and Northern Ireland.

German submarines which surrendered at the end of the war were ordered to Britain for disposal. Lieutenant Frank Lang RNVR, who was serving aboard the minesweeper HMS *Lioness*, was sent to meet two of

LEFT: The end of the war for a Type VII U-boat, brought to Lisahally to surrender. British and German personnel stand on the bridge.

them and escort them into Loch Ryan on the west coast of Scotland. Eight of his crew of 11 were armed either with a Lanchester submachine gun or a revolver; he carried both, plus a couple of hand grenades to be on the safe side.

'Each member had full instructions as to what to do when we boarded. We had a few practice runs before we reached the contact area.

We had to rendezvous with two U-boats, they were on the surface flying the black surrender flag. Roger signalled them to form up on our starboard beam and without any trouble we sailed into Loch Ryan, where we tied up alongside the wall. The U-boats secured on the other side of the loch. There were about half a dozen others. Later that day a few more came in under escort. The place was cluttered up with U-boats.'[30]

Another who was involved in those tense days, during which 156 boats surrendered in various ports in Britain, Europe and as far afield as Argentina, was Able Seaman Tex Beasley, RN:

'We went out in early May to meet up with the U-boats that were surrendering. Behind them were many many other U-boats, I don't know how many but quite a few, so the Skipper said, "Right, you're in action now, over." So we jumped from our boat onto the U-boat and I said to who I presumed was the Commander: "Guten Morgen, sprechen Sie Englisch?" He said, "Yes, rather well, I think." The other guy that came up had an American

accent but with a German-American accent – you know what I mean? That sort of thing. And he said, "What would you do," he said, "if I just did a crash dive?" I said, "I'd shoot you right between the eyes."'

The USSR, USA and Britain agreed to retain up to 30 boats and divide them equally, primarily for study. Most (116) of the remainder were to be sunk in Operation Deadlight. Of these, 86 were held at Loch Ryan, and 30 at Lisahally where, from the deck of the destroyer HMS *Offa*, Sub-Lieutenant, later Commander, David Hamilton saw them moored 'in trots' – rows – along the long quay that had once been the home of the convoy escorts. Arrangements were made to take advantage of any good weather within the scheduled disposal period to provide the Fleet Air Arm and Coastal Command with air practice, the Third Submarine Flotilla with torpedo testing opportunities, and the Royal Navy's A/S ships with the chance to evaluate the operational effectiveness of the triple-barrelled anti-submarine mortar known as the Squid. Most, however, were to be sunk by scuttling charges:

'If the weather is suitable for boarding, the method of scuttling will be by safety fuse, charges being placed so as to collapse the bow and stern torpedo tubes and also blow certain hatches. If the weather is unsuitable for boarding, the scuttling charges will be fired electrically. Should both these methods fail, the towing vessel is to sink the U-boat.'[31]

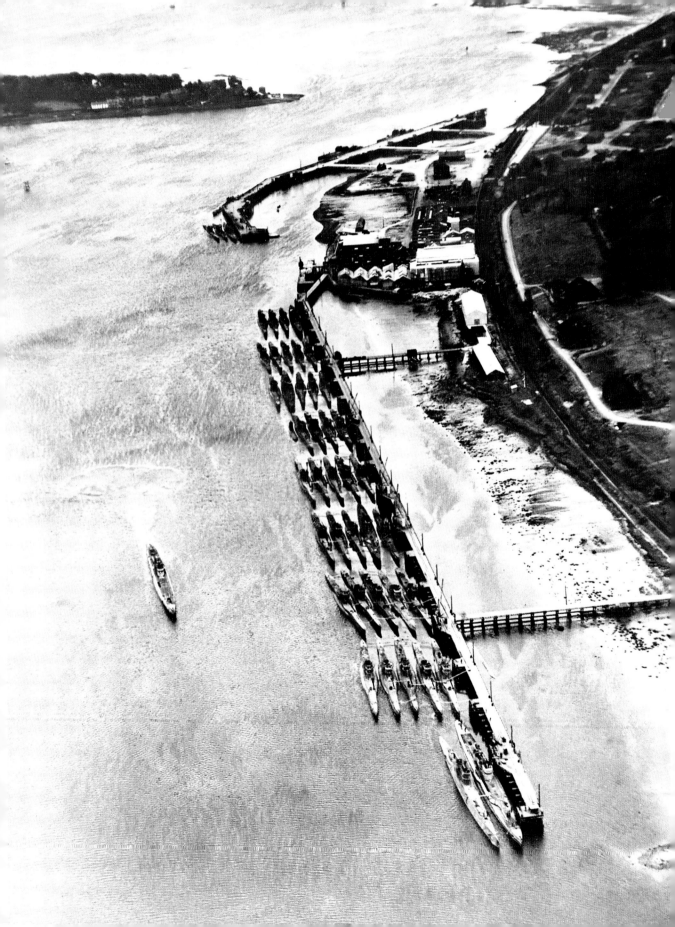

RIGHT: Operation Deadlight
in progress, as a Type XXIII
Elektro Boat is towed from
Lisahally through Lough Foyle.

Security was intended to be tight, as journalists and foreign observers, particularly Soviet, were to be present. The Squid mortar was not to be used within sight of press or observers. The operation took place in the depths of the 1945/46 winter and, as Hamilton points out:

> 'Weather in that part of the world was not particularly friendly and the initial idea of towing the boats out with a small demolition crew on board, who would set the charges and then be picked up by the destroyer's motor cutter, was abandoned The other problem was that the towing speed was not much more than 4 knots, which, in a roughish sea, meant that we often did not have steerage way. A trip of 100 miles northwest at 2 knots was tedious, to say the least. Anyway, the first U- boat we towed was sunk by the first salvo we fired from the 4.7 inch guns, the gunnery officer [G.O.] was beside himself with delight The

second one out took about 10 salvoes and the third, a small four-man submarine, was never hit and sank itself in disgust. The G.O. hid somewhere in shame. Quite a lot of the boats broke adrift and sank anyway.'[32]

His experience was reflected in the official narrative. On the first day of operations from Lisahally most of the U-boats had to be sunk by gunfire from the Polish destroyer *Piorun* – an indefatigable vessel that had recklessly taken on the *Bismarck* earlier in its service and whose crews would have found special satisfaction in their work. The following day was no better and on New Year's Eve HMS *Pytchley* managed to lose her U-boat entirely. The seventh and final 'lift' from Lisahally took place on 7 January 1946, and among the failures of that day was the forced sinking by gunfire of Schnee's Type XXI, *U-2511*, in position 55°37´ N 07°49´ W.

Among the most interesting submarines towed out from Lisahally was *U-2336*. The Type XXIII was a small coastal version of the Type XXI Elektro Boat, constructed so it could, if necessary, be transported in short sections by railway truck to destinations such as the Black Sea. By the end of the war, six Type XXIIIs had carried out operational patrols, sinking five Allied ships. *U-2336* had the dubious distinction of sinking the last two ships in the war against Germany when it torpedoed *Avondale Park* and *Sneland 1* off Dunbar on 7 May 1945 – the penultimate day of the war.

The Loch Ryan tows, which had begun on 25 November, had their own fair share of failures, with tows breaking, boats foundering, and weather too bad for air practice. On 16 December *U-1009* was 'Sunk by gunfire owing to Acute Case of stomach trouble'.[33]

Clustered most thickly in the clear sea off Malin Head in depths from 150 to 600 feet (45–180 metres), the sunken U-boats lie along a 200-nautical-mile (370-kilometre) line stretching roughly northwest from Loch Ryan, through the North Channel and out into the same North Western Approaches in which they once stalked the merchant convoys and caused Churchill to admit

BELOW: The wreck of *U-2511*. Pieces of casing have broken away from her stern, obscuring the view of the starboard propeller which now sticks up at a strange angle.

that 'the only thing that ever really frightened me during the war was the U-boat peril'.

DIVING U-2511

Beautiful in the green light, the elegant, form of *U-2511* lies over on her port side. Fish flicker around the fragile casing pierced like filigree and torn by the peacetime shell that sunk her. Although her conning tower and snorkel are thickened by encrustation, they seem otherwise perfect. It is a fitting grave for Germany's first true submarine, but as Dan commented after watching the footage brought up by the dive team: 'I was overwhelmed by the fact that 70 years ago it was a potentially decisive weapon. If more of those U-boats had been produced earlier in the war it could have radically altered the outcome of the fighting.'

THE SURVIVORS

A few U-boats survived the cull. Most of those reserved by the Allies were eventually broken up. There are memories of half a dozen U-boats (*U-712*, *U-953*, *U-1108*, *U-1171*, *U-2348* and *U-3017*) remaining at Lisahally until the Royal Navy, which had never made any use of them for experimentation or target practice, finally sold them for scrap in April 1949. *U-505* had been captured by the US Navy, and it demanded her exemption from Deadlight, as a result of which she became a war memorial and visitor attraction in Chicago. Scuttled by her crew near Flensburg, the Type XXI *U-2540* was raised by the Germans in 1957, recommissioned as

the *Wilhelm Bauer* for research and then taken over by the Deutsches Schiffahrtsmuseum, which has restored her as a Second World War submarine. *U-995* was given in reparations to the Norwegian Navy, and when she became obsolete the Norwegians handed her back to Germany. Today she sits at Laboe on the eastern shore of the Kieleförde, not far from the memorial to the U-boat dead of two world wars. The trio would have been the only full-size Second World War boats now above the sea bottom, but for the mysterious decision of one captain to avoid surrender in 1945.

U-534

U-534 and her only commander, Kapitänleutnant Herbert Nollau, had had a very quiet war, from her commissioning in December 1942 until her loss on 5 May 1945. The Type IXC/40 made just two full war patrols, in which the solitary achievement was the shooting down of a Wellington from 172 Squadron RAF on 27 August 1944,[34] and much of the work had been meteorological. Although that work had been vital to the Germans in their attempts to predict when the Allies would launch their invasion of Europe, it did not earn awards for gallantry. On 3 May, with Hitler dead and his nominated successor, Dönitz, just a few days from accepting the Allied demand of unconditional surrender, *U-534* became the last submarine to sail from the great U-boat base at Kiel, out through the Kieler Förde and north into the Kattegat, the thin stretch of sea between the Jutland Peninsula and Sweden that leads via the Skagerrak into the North Sea. Off Copenhagen she bottomed, and there her commander received the order to return and surrender. But he ignored it.

On 5 May, in company with two Type XXIs, *U-534* continued up the heavily patrolled Kattegat; none of the boats displaying the black[35] flag of surrender. Why 26-year-old Nollau acted as he did will never be known: he disclosed nothing to his crew at the time and committed suicide some 20 years later without ever having given an explanation.

The three submarines were detected that same day, proceeding on the surface in staggered line ahead, and Liberators from two Coastal Command squadrons were sent to intercept them. The first to attack was 'E for Edward' from 547 Squadron.[36] *U-534* was powerfully equipped with six anti-aircraft guns to deal with such attacks and opened fire while the fast Type XXIs dived to take advantage of their underwater speed. With his wing shot off, 'E for Edward' went down, and only one of the crew survived.

'G for George' made its first run, dropping six depth charges, all of which overshot and earned bomb-aimer Neville Baker some choice words from the pilot, Warrant Officer John D. Nichol. Baker prepared four bombs for the second run, keeping a final pair in reserve. They were not

BELOW: The Type IX submarine *U-505* arrives at Chicago in 1954 to begin a new life as an exhibit in the city's Museum of Science and Industry.

ABOVE: Looking into the engine room of *U-534* now that the submarine has been cut into four glass-ended sections and stabilized to prevent further deterioration. At the far end, daylight can be seen and beyond that is the next section.

survived the ascent, two of whom later died from exposure, but the fifth forgot the cardinal rule of breathing out while ascending and died from lung expansion. Nichol was awarded the DFC.

Later the questions began. Why did she run? Was she carrying Nazi gold and diamonds? Had senior Nazis been using her in an attempt to flee the advancing Allies? Was it significant that her radio operator was Argentinian? Why did she leave Kiel only half full of fuel and then have to scrounge diesel from other submarines?

In 1986 wreck-hunter Aage Jensen found *U-534* 12 nautical miles (22 kilometres) northeast of Anholt island, but investigating her on the seabed was impossible. With finance from Danish publishing magnate Karsten Ree, Jensen set about raising *U-534*, and after years of delay caused by political objection and safety and environmental arguments the operation got underway in the summer of 1993, watched by former members of both her crew and that of 'G for George'.

Tons of mud had to be removed from over and around her before a huge steel sling could be manoeuvred under her hull amidships. Because she lay in a deep crevasse it was decided to make the lift in two stages, the first to pull her free of the mud and drag her into shallower water, the second to bring her up into the light. Bad weather hampered the work: 11 of the allotted 30 days were lost, but on 23 August the clock began to run backwards for the eight veteran submariners and the four former crew of the Liberator, all staring intently at the grey water as the slender, corroded barrel of a submarine's anti-aircraft gun broke

needed: the first depth charge hit the casing, rolled off and exploded at the set depth below the submarine, punching a hole in the starboard side above the propeller shaft and breaching the pressure hull. As *U-534* began to fill and sink, Nollau and most of his young crew hastily scrambled out, but five men went down with the submarine, trapped in the forward torpedo room. *U-534* settled on the seabed nearly 220 feet (67 metres) down, and, using their breathing apparatus, the five men were able to escape through the hatch. Four

the surface. Then came the broken bridge and the conning tower, and as the huge floating crane painstakingly wound in the steel hawsers of the sling beneath the rusting hull, *U-534* slowly resurfaced, rose higher – then hung expectantly in the air.

The torpedoes and other ordnance were removed and detonated at sea, while *U-534* was taken to dry dock to begin the task of removing hundreds of tons of silt and water before she could be explored.

There were no remains of dead Nazis, nor any gold, just a perfect time capsule, with hundreds of artefacts in unexpectedly good condition. Paper items, including a copy of the 1941 *Die Handelsflotten der Welt*, which the crew used to identify and cross off their merchant victims, were put into deep freeze, desalinated and very carefully dried and separated.

U-534 went on display at Birkenhead, on the opposite shore of the River Mersey to Liverpool – the city that in 1941 had became home to Western Approaches Command, from where the convoys and their defence were planned. While *U-534* was based at the Historic Ships Museum visitors were able to climb down into the hull and walk past the rusty pipes, handwheels and diesels – an unsettling but moving experience. When in 2006 the museum was forced to close due to redevelopment of the site, *U-534* was moved to Mersey Travel's Woodside Ferry Terminal, further along the river, where she is displayed in four sections, and where her artefacts can be seen in a purpose-built museum.

ABOVE: Imposing and yet rather sad as the weather takes a toll of her rusting hull and superstructure, *U-534* awaits her fate after the closure of the Historic Ships Museum at Birkenhead.

71

PART 2

THE AIR WAR

As war approached, the RAF was ill-prepared in all departments. In 1938, Fighter Command had possessed five squadrons equipped with the Hawker Hurricane and one with the Supermarine Spitfire, with pilots for the latter still in training. Its remaining strength lay in obsolete biplanes that were no match for a Luftwaffe that had been building up its capability for a decade. The best aircraft in the hands of Bomber Command at the start of the war were the Whitley, a plodding aircraft that would do far better service with Coastal Command, and the Wellington, which was vulnerable to fighters, though its geodesic construction allowed it to absorb punishment that would have downed many another aircraft.

Although the 'Phoney War' consisted primarily of dropping propaganda leaflets and attacking German naval ships in port, Bomber Command's lack of suitable aircraft resulted in unacceptable losses among crews at the hands of German fighters and anti-aircraft guns. On 14 December 1939 five out of 12 Wellingtons were lost on patrol over the North Sea. Four days later 12 out of 22 were shot down by German fighters. If Bomber Command had possessed greater resources, and Fighter Command sufficient modern aircraft to provide cover, the valiant attempt to stop the German advance into France at Sedan in May 1940 might not have ended so badly. As it was the fighters were outnumbered 3:1 and about 60 percent of bombers were lost.

The Luftwaffe was in every respect stronger at the beginning, but as was the case in the other services, a rapid period of catch-up took place. British aircraft production and development accelerated until it overtook the Luftwaffe. Pilot training increased, but it was a slow process, and when the Battle of Britain began in July 1940, the RAF needed airmen from wherever it could find them.

It may well have taken the 1968 film *The Battle of Britain* to inform the wider British public that while that campaign was a triumph for the RAF (not forgetting the Fleet Air Arm pilots involved) it was not an exclusively British victory. Churchill's 'Few' included more than a few pilots of other nationalities – 595, in fact: primarily Poles, New Zealanders, Canadians and Czechs, but with a sprinkling of others including Australians, Belgians, Free French, Irish – not to mention nine Americans who defied their own country's laws in order to fight, becoming the vanguard for many others.

THE EAGLE SQUADRONS

'We of Fighter Command', said Air Chief Marshal Sir William Sholto Douglas KCB, MC, DFC standing on the parade ground at RAF Debden and surveying the men drawn up in their ranks before him, 'deeply regret this parting, for in the course of the past eighteen months, we have seen the stuff of which you are made, and we could not ask for better companions with

ABOVE: Olympic gold medallist William Fiske exchanged the thrills and dangers of piloting a bobsleigh in the Olympics for taking on the Luftwaffe in a Hurricane during the Battle of Britain.

Eagle Squadrons: American units within the RAF that were composed of volunteers who came to fight for Britain *before* the USA had entered the war. By the time of the ceremony the USA had been irrevocably committed to the war for almost ten months; it was time for them to exchange their RAF uniforms for those of USAAF.[1]

Joining the armed forces of another country is at best a risky business, irrespective of the dangers posed by the enemy. The Free French, Poles, Dutch, Czechs, Norwegians and others left their families vulnerable to reprisals and, because they could not send home their wages, poverty. The first American fliers and sailors who volunteered in 1940 imperilled their citizenship, and all that went with it, because of the USA's Citizenship Act of 1907 and the inter-war Neutrality Acts, the last of which was passed as late as 1939. A presidential proclamation in the same year made it illegal to recruit Americans on American soil for service in another nation's armed services, and barred American citizens from travelling abroad to join foreign forces.

The threat of draconian penalties did not stop them. Some pretended to be Canadian or simply travelled to England via Canada. There were also Americans living in Britain, such as Flight Lieutenant James 'Jimmy' Davies DFC who had joined the RAF three years before the war and was an experienced Hurricane pilot with 79 Squadron. Killed in action in June 1940 he had already been credited with six outright kills and two shared kills.

The wealthy William Lindsley Fiske, a bobsleigh champion who had won Olympic gold in 1928 and 1932 (he

whom to see this fight through to a finish. … You joined us readily and of your own free will when our need was greatest. … There are those of your number who are not here today – those sons of the United States who were first to give their lives for their country. We of the RAF, no less than yourselves, will always remember them with pride.'

The occasion, on 29 September 1942, was the deactivation of the three declined to compete at the 1936 Berlin Olympics), was another who wangled his way into the RAF in time to fight in the Battle of Britain as a member of 601 Squadron. At the time, 601 was nicknamed the 'Millionaire's Squadron' because it had been founded by wealthy young men at the exclusive White's club in London, and it doubtless helped create the myth that RAF pilots were all educated at public schools when in fact the figure was well under 10 percent. Suffering from burns, Fiske nursed his damaged Hurricane back from a sortie on 16 August but subsequently died from surgical shock. Although he was neither the first American to die in the battle, nor the most successful American fighter pilot, he was posthumously honoured with a plaque in St. Paul's Cathedral.

Davies and Fiske served and died too early to have been part of the Eagle Squadrons, which were the work primarily of the wealthy US-born Charles Sweeny who had grown up in Britain and was working in London. The squadrons had a precedent in the form of the Lafayette Escadrille, an American squadron that, with the tacit approval of the US Government fought with the French during the First World War.

Sweeny began his recruitment secretly, routing his protégés through Canada and financing the operation himself or through donations, even before he had consulted the British. His work was significantly assisted by aviation artist Clayton Knight. In June 1940 Sweeny put his proposal to Minister of Production Lord Beaverbrook and on 2 July the Air Council agreed the formation of what became 71 Squadron, the first Eagle Squadron. The name derived from the shoulder flash that Sweeny designed himself, based on the eagle insignia on a US passport. On seeing it, his father suggested the new units be called Eagle Squadrons.

There was no shortage of volunteers. They may have detested the idea of Nazism but what really motivated them was the opportunity to become qualified and experienced fighter pilots by the time the US entered the war – which, they were convinced, would happen sooner rather than later. Not only would they avoid the stiff competition for every place in USAAF but they would fly the world's best fighter then in service.

After the Fall of France, the USA became more lax in enforcing the bars to enlistment, and the vexed question of the Citizenship Act of 1907 was circumvented by Knight's solution of having the pilots swear to obey their commanders rather than take any oath of allegiance to the British Crown. If the US State Department did not – could not – approve, neither did it make any overtly hostile counter move.

It was not until the spring of 1941 before the first Eagles became combat-ready and supplied with enough aircraft to be declared fully operational, but when they did they performed sterling service into the third quarter of 1942. After the USA entered the war, USAAF proposed not only to disband them but to scatter them throughout the air force. Only the pilots' threat to

ABOVE: The badge of the Eagle Squadrons. The eagle holds a sprig of laurel and five arrows.

ABOVE: Group Captain Charles Sweeny (right), Honorary Commanding Officer of the Eagle Squadrons with the C.O. of the training station.

remain with the RAF secured an agreement that their squadrons be transferred intact. Some pilots, allegedly not wanting to take the risk of failing the USAAF medical with its stricter eyesight and age requirements, remained with the RAF, despite the much lower wages.

ON THE WRONG SIDE OF THE BORDER

One of the most experienced of the would-be Eagles was 22-year-old Roland L. Wolfe from Nebraska, who had logged almost 1,000 hours since getting his commercial pilot's licence

in 1940 and was itching to fly what American pilots called a 'hot-rod' aircraft. By the time he joined up in 1941 the RAF had temporary training facilities at Love Field, Dallas, while the purpose-built Terrell facility was under construction. Having completed his training in May, Wolfe travelled to England via Canada and, after a delay caused by an influx of pilots, was posted to 56 Operational Training Unit (OTU) at Sutton to be turned into a combat-ready Hurricane pilot. On 25 August 1941 he became part of 133 Eagle Squadron at Duxford, carrying out North Sea sweeps and practising manoeuvres.

Unfortunately for 133 Squadron, the early autumn was marred by several accidents and they were sent off to RAF Eglinton in Northern Ireland for additional training and conversion to the Spitfire Mark IIa. Some travelled by land and sea; the remainder, including Wolfe, flew by stages. After refuelling for the first time near Chester, the pilots were scheduled to make a second refuelling stop at RAF bases on the Isle of Man, but in the atrocious weather and poor visibility – so bad that two pilots turned back – four aircraft, including that of Flight Commander Andrew B. Mamedoff, crashed on the island in separate and fatal incidents.

From Eglinton the squadron flew the vital but often boring patrols to protect the incoming and outgoing North Atlantic convoys; on 14 November they carried out five such patrols, each flown by two pilots. New pilots replaced the dead, but still fatalities occurred: two in a week. Then, on 30 November 1941, Wolfe took off at 10:30 in P8074, notable for the words 'Garfield Weston No. 1' written in yellow letters down the side of the cockpit.

Willard Garfield Weston represented the parliamentary seat of Macclesfield during the Second World War, but more importantly he was a Canadian millionaire who had made a fortune from his transatlantic biscuit empire. Disturbed by RAF fighter losses on one particularly bad day during the Battle of Britain he donated £100,000, financing the construction of 20 Spitfires of which Wolfe's was the first.

Like that of so many aircraft during the war, the life of P8074 was to be brief. Built at Castle Bromwich, the Mark IIa was allocated via 37 Maintenance Unit to 222 Squadron in March 1941, and less than a month later it was hit by machine gun fire from a Junkers Ju 88. In June 1941 P8074 was transferred to 501 Squadron, where it again suffered damage, and at the end of October it was allocated to 133 Eagle Squadron.

Not far from Eglinton, on his way home in the grey mists of early winter, Wolfe found himself in trouble when his engine began to overheat, threatening to seize up. Accepting the inevitable, he removed his helmet, goggles and throat microphone and radioed that he was 'going over the side'. Then he undid the straps of his harness and bailed out. The incident

ABOVE: 71 Eagle Squadron pilots Andrew B. Mamedoff (left), Vernon 'Shorty' Keogh and Eugene Q. Tobin checking details with the Adjutant. The photograph probably reflects the founding of the squadron on 20 September 1940 at RAF Church Fenton, as they were the first three pilots to report. All were killed between February and October 1941, Tobin in action, the other two in accidents.

ABOVE: Bud Wolfe's Identity Card.

was witnessed by local people, including Mick Harkin: 'The only thing I remember was we were at Mass in Ballinacrae and before we went in to church this plane was hovering around and we were all looking at her and we thought she was in trouble. And after some time, I don't know how long, the man bailed out, the pilot bailed out.'

At 13:40, seven aircraft from the squadron took off to look for him, returning from their unsuccessful search at 14:50. Squadron Leader, later Wing Commander, Eric Thomas DSO, DFC* led a second search over land and sea, but found no trace.

P8074 had crashed deep into a bog near Moneydarragh on County Donegal's Inishowen Peninsula, west of Lough Foyle and north of Derry (Londonderry). Wolfe had landed safely around 10 miles (16 kilometres) from Eglinton – but just on the wrong side of the border between Northern Ireland and Eire (the Republic of Ireland).

Eire was neutral, and its citizens were not of one mind when it came to the war. Support for Germany was limited, and only a handful of Irish citizens appear to have actively served in German units. Over 40,000, by contrast, joined British forces, setting aside their struggle against centuries of British rule that had ended only in 1921 with the founding of the Irish Free State. The vast majority, however, supported their government's position of neutrality – and while that included measures favourable to the Allies (including blackouts in coastal towns to prevent the Luftwaffe pilots fixing their positions, passing on submarine reports and not objecting to the military use of the disputed waters of Lough Foyle) it also meant the internment of Allied and Axis naval and aviation personnel found within their territory.

A 'CUSHY' PRISON

Wolfe's hopes of returning to Eglinton were dashed when he was taken south to the Curragh in County Kildare where the Irish had constructed an internment camp on the edge of an army barracks. With its wooden huts, rolls of barbed wire, gun posts at each corner, armed guards, and inner and outer perimeter fence it looked a typical POW camp. Its internees soon found out that the reality was considerably different.

Firstly, the rectangular camp was divided by a tall wire fence into two compounds: one Allied, one German. Flying Officer John Holgate of 252 Squadron, who was interned along with F/O Hugh Verity in May 1941 after crash-landing their Bristol Beaufighter, recalled that the Germans celebrated the news of the sinking of HMS *Hood* by singing their national anthem all night. A few days later the Allies rejoiced noisily at the Royal Navy's destruction of the *Bismarck*.

Secondly, the conditions were vastly superior to any POW camp. Holgate and Verity arrived to find their RAF comrades welcoming them with an all-night party lubricated by cheap alcohol supplied by the embassies of Allied countries: whisky at 7/- and gin at 6/- a bottle. Guinness was free. The following year, Flight Lieutenant Bobby Keefer RCAF was shown the bar and permitted to set up a tab until his pay began to come through. Food was plentiful – and so, after a fashion, was freedom.

Parole was available to officers – German and Allied – for three hours in the morning and afternoon, plus a further four and a half hours in the evening. A full day's parole would be granted once a month for a trip to Dublin, and married internees could bring their wives to Ireland and spend three nights per week living off-camp with them. (Sergeant pilots, however, were NCOs and, until the Air Ministry in London accorded them honorary officer status, were not considered to have any honour to pledge as surety for their return.)

To obtain parole, a slip giving the time of departure and the agreed return was signed by the internee and parole officer. On return, the slip was taken out of the drawer in which it was kept and then cancelled.

Some prisoners thought that accepting parole contradicted the duty to try to escape. The Air Ministry clarified the situation, instructing detainees that they were not allowed to give their parole in the usual sense of making an overall promise not to escape or take up arms again – but that

they could give it for specific periods and purposes.

'(ii) Examples of the purposes for which the undertaking mentioned above may be given are for exercise, recreation and medical treatment, provided that the undertaking is clearly limited to the period of temporary release.'[2]

Only civilian clothes could be worn outside the camp, so internees borrowed clothes for their first visit to Dublin, where they could have themselves kitted out, if not as officers then certainly as gentlemen, and with a 10 percent discount for the RAF. They were then able to pass the time playing golf, riding to hounds and dining out – even with off-duty squadron friends from across the border – while simultaneously planning honourable escapes in the traditional manner of tunnelling under or climbing over the wire. The acquisition of escape material such as maps or wire-cutters while out on parole was forbidden, but one new arrival turned up still carrying his navigation bag, and the guards failed to recognize what it was. Outside help came from packets of Churchman's cigarettes, which obligingly contained collectible cards from which a map of Ireland could be built up.

Verity[3] and Holgate spent less than two months at the Curragh before they escaped in an acceptable fashion. Two fliers returned from parole, one pretending to be drunk. The guard was called, and when he appeared he was promptly trussed up. Wire-cutters dealt with the fences and the detainees were soon out. The guards fired – but, incredibly, they had not been issued with live rounds. Using false papers and taking advantage of heavier than usual traffic because it was Derby Day, Verity and Holgate crossed the border by train.

A MATTER OF HONOUR

Wolfe was no more willing than the British pair to twiddle his thumbs for the duration of the conflict. On 2 December 1941, a couple of days after his arrival, he wrote to the Irish Taoiseach (Prime Minister) Éamon de Valera, asking to be repatriated, and promising '… not to take up arms again against any of the axis powers. I was a member of the Eagle Squadron whose members do not swear allegiance to the King or his Country. They are, more or less, just working for hire.'[4]

While waiting for a reply Wolfe put into practice an idea that hinged on the parole officer's being off-site when he himself returned at 22:30 from dining with a squadron friend in the nearby town of Naas. He entered the guard

RIGHT: One of the buildings housing POWs at Curragh camp, as it appears today.

BELOW: The gate to what was once the parole hut at the Curragh POW Camp, through which Bud Wolfe walked to freedom.

hut, helped himself to the stamp and cancelled his pass. Then he took another, signed it and went out again, telling the guards he was going for a drink. Now he pretended he had forgotten his gloves. Having gone back for them, he slipped into the hut and cancelled his pass, which he then left. Technically, he was no longer on parole. As he walked back to the gate he calculated, correctly, that the guards would be less punctilious than Fitzgerald, the parole officer, and not ask to see the pass again.

By his reasoning he had left the camp without having given his parole. The following day he returned to RAF Eglinton.

Wolfe had expected a warm welcome. Instead, the RAF returned him to the Curragh on the basis that his escape had been obtained by underhand, even dishonourable, means. Among the non-British aircrew there was some ill feeling about his

treatment: whatever diplomatic and political niceties existed between the governments of Eire and Britain surely could not apply to them, but the RAF, in which they were serving officers, remained adamant. It was not a mere quibble about honour; the British were simply anxious to avoid a diplomatic incident that might jeopardize the not inconsiderable help they were getting from their neutral neighbour.

Wolfe's earlier written request for repatriation to the USA was refused, and he remained at the camp until it was closed in 1943 and the internees were allowed to return to active service.

Wolfe joined 336th Fighter Squadron of the 4th Fighter Group of the US Eighth Air Force. He survived the war and continued his career as a fighter pilot, flying North American F-86 Sabres in Korea and Republic F-105 Thunderchiefs in Vietnam, rising to the rank of lieutenant colonel after a career of 28 years.

ABOVE: Second from the left, Captain 'Bud' Roland Wolfe relaxes outside 82nd Fighter Squadron's ready room at Duxford in 1944. Wolfe had transferred to the US 8th Army Air Force in 1943.

MARK IIa – THE DONEGAL SPITFIRE

1: The pit is dug with stepped sides to prevent the walls collapsing. Early finds confirm that this is the crash site.
2: Unbuckled by the impact, the first of the Browning machine guns is pulled out.
3: Some of the .303 ammunition caps.

Although the crash was well known, and many local people had visited the site in 1941 to help themselves to souvenirs before the RAF made a token attempt at salvage, the bog had closed over the Spitfire and grass had healed the ugly wound on the moorland slope. Aviation archaeologist Jonny McNee joined forces with the *Dig WW2* team in order to see what could be learned and recovered from the site.

The area was scanned with ground penetrating radar (GPR) but no trace was found. Only as the dispirited team were returning to their vehicles in the deteriorating light of a wet summer's evening did the machine record an unmistakeable contact. It was too late to do anything: the dig had to wait for the following morning.

Wet, deep and spongy, and described by aviation expert Steve Vizard as 'like a blancmange', peat bogs can be extremely dangerous. Setting up a 20-ton excavator was difficult, and the load had to be spread over as wide an area as possible using bog mats made of large railway sleepers. The worst fear concerned the depth of the pit that might have to be dug. The deeper the pit, the greater the risk of the soft sides collapsing, pulling down with them the excavator and its driver. Another possibility was that the hole might simply fill with water like a sump. As the first scoops were removed, brownish water did flow in, but below that the peat was firmer.

During the morning, the first remains were found; whatever the bog had swallowed, it had refrained from digesting. Excitement rose, prompting Dan to exclaim: 'Every single scoop is like opening a Christmas present. … You've no idea what you're going to find. No idea of what it uncovers.'

Work with the digger gave way to hand excavation, and one by one five long Browning .303-inch machine guns emerged, along with a case of ammunition belts, the rounds gleaming as if new. A sixth would follow. All had to be handed over to experts from the Irish Defence Forces for deactivation, to make them safe for subsequent exhibition at Derry's Tower Museum.

Despite the fact that the aircraft had gone down at well over 300 miles per hour (480 kilometres per hour), the guns were remarkably well preserved, for which a fortuitous combination of three factors was responsible. Firstly, the soft damp bog had been kind to the aircraft, allowing it to decelerate far more gently than an impact directly onto rock or clay. Secondly, though 70 years had passed since it was spilt, aviation fuel still saturated the ground, coating and protecting the wreckage and filling the damp air with an unmistakeable odour as it was finally exposed. Thirdly, below the peat was a layer of clay which, being anaerobic, helped to keep out the oxygen that facilitates corrosion.

As the day wore on and the rain set in, the team reached the remains of the cockpit, and that yielded unexpected finds. Gauges, large pieces of cockpit armour plating, and even the pilot's cushion were brought out. A delighted Jonny McNee unfolded a piece of a side panel with part of the phrase 'Garfield Weston No. 1' still legible in yellow paint – proof, if needed, that this was the first of the presentation aircraft.

The best was yet to come. Dan found himself holding 'Bud' Wolfe's cockpit harness strap: 'This is my favourite find so far, I think: this is one of the harnesses from the cockpit and Bud Wolfe would have pulled this bit here seconds before he ejected – absolutely incredible.'

That, however, was before the discovery of a soggy leather helmet rapidly left him almost bereft of speech. 'That's extraordinary. This is something I never believed that we would find: "Bud" Wolfe's original flying helmet, worn by him on that sortie, still attached to the original oxygen mask, survived underground for 70 years, removed by him just before he bailed out. Just speechless.'

With it was a first aid kit, and the most precious, fragile survivor of all, Wolfe's flying logbook: both left where he had placed them.

Filming the dig required cameraman Mark McCauley to use the techniques of both cinematographer and photojournalist:

'One is, always being ready to capture something when it happens, and concentrating all day on the experts and being with Dan, and the other is shooting beautiful landscapes that can set the scene. The light was absolutely beautiful, and it was on a lovely hill rolling down towards the sea in Donegal, Ireland. We went out with all the equipment. They spent three hours, and from my point of view the light got worse and worse and worse, and then it started to rain, and they'd almost given up, and then they decided, "Okay, we'll just walk back to the cars and we'll do the detecting on a line, just as we go back". And we could have said, "Well, okay, it's probably not going to find anything", but we stuck with it, and we filmed them on the way back – and they found it at the last minute. The light was terrible, but that's the compromise: it's not about the light, it's about finding the thing.'

The excavation of the aircraft had two totally unforeseen sequels.

When news reached Canadian billionaire Galen Weston, son of the man whose donation had financed its construction 70 years earlier, he at once offered a substantial donation to fund the conservation of Wolfe's personal effects, and also for a case to display some of the artefacts at Tower Museum. Once conserved, the logbook and helmet will be given to Wolfe's two daughters, but P8074's tail wheel will go on permanent display at City of Derry Airport, the civil aviation facility built on the site of RAF Eglinton from where the Spitfire took off for the last time on 30 November 1941.

Lieutenant Colonel Dave Sexton, ordnance technical officer, considered the condition of the six machine guns he was to deactivate and began to wonder whether it would be feasible to restore one to firing condition. Taking the best-preserved components from the guns and making a few repairs, he and his team

4: Bud Wolfe's helmet.

5: Wolfe's flying logbook; against the odds, it survived.

6: Leaking aviation fuel helped to preserve the remains of the aircraft.

7: The red and white paint of the RAF roundel emerges as the crumpled piece of fuselage is opened.

8: The remains of the pilot's oxygen mask.

INSTRUCTIONS FOR USE.

GENERAL.

700 may be used for any period specified by Uni...

full.

is to be completed in ink or indelible pencil...

aeroplane...

CAPACITY
SPACE 1·75 G...
TAL CAPACITY 7·55 GAL.

lister

4

5

6

7

8

ABOVE: Mounted on a modern tripod, the Browning machine gun is ready to fire for the first time in 70 years.

were able to assemble a completely authentic Browning. The only question was: would it fire? Dan provided the answer in November 2011.

To reduce the risk he fired it remotely, from the protection of a trench in case the barrel blew. Modern .303-inch bullets were used as they were less likely to jam. Turning the handle of the remote mechanism, he was rewarded by a staccato roar; fire burst from the muzzle and spent shells cascaded out of the breech. In 15 seconds, 300 rounds were gone. That represented the total firing time for a Spitfire in combat before it had to return for rearming.

Dan summed up the dig:

'When you come to a hillside like this and dig these objects out of the ground: the straps that held the terrified pilot into his cockpit as his plane failed; engine that overheated and forced him to bail out, those things take you back to a moment in time. They allow you to touch the past, they allow you to smell the past, even though that event happened 70 years ago.'

THE 'ONE MAN AIR FORCE'

In 1949 the former Eagle Squadron pilot Dominic Salvatore Gentile replied to a request asking about his experience as a fighter pilot by describing his first two successes. They were gained while flying a Spitfire during the 1942 Dieppe Raid, in which a Canadian–British force attempted an amphibious landing at Dieppe – not as the prelude to an immediate invasion but to test the German defences. The operation was a disaster, but the experience gained was of material value when planning the North Africa landings and D-Day.

'The F.W. 190 [Focke-Wulf Fw 190], which I got on this occasion, had just finished shooting down one of our spitfires when I jumped him. He started to roll for the deck immediately and I followed him, clobbering the F.W. 190 at about 3000 feet, at which time he rolled over lazily and slowly and hit the beach where the Commandos were coming in.

After I had gotten the F.W. 190 a J.U. 88 started to dive bomb the troops on the ground – I managed to

ABOVE: Former Eagle Squadron pilot, Captain Gentile, receives his DSC from General Dwight Eisenhower in April 1944.

get on his tail and started to clobber him. The J.U. 88 jettisoned its bombs in the Chanel [sic, the Channel] and missed its target. I closed in and got one engine burning – the aircraft finally exploded and crashed inland. These were my first two victories.

At the time of combat I didn't think too much about my feelings but upon returning home and being relaxed you can look back on all the things you did and didn't do and see the reason behind each move. While the fight is on, your mind feels empty and feels as if the flesh of it is sitting in your head bunched up like muscle and quivering there. The hardest pressure on a fighter pilot … when under attack is because the brains of a pilot have a dissolved effect and becomes just dishwater in their heads so pilots usually freeze to their stick and straighten out and run right into their graves like men stricken blind who run screaming off a cliff.'[5]

Born in Ohio of Italian descent, Gentile served with 133 Eagle Squadron until September 1942 when he transferred to USAAF as a member of 336 Fighter Squadron, 4th Fighter Group. Between 16 December 1943 and 8 April 1944 he destroyed 28 German aircraft, 22 of them in the air, becoming one of USAAF's top pilots.

General Dwight D. Eisenhower called him a 'one man Air Force'; to President Franklin D. Roosevelt he was 'Captain Courageous'. Gentile was only 31 when he was killed in 1951 during a routine training flight in a Lockheed T-33 Shooting Star. The aircraft went out of control, but when the sergeant who was with him froze in terror and could not activate his ejection gear, Gentile sacrificed his own chance of ejection and made a valiant but doomed attempt to land the plane at Andrews Air Force Base, Maryland.

MESSERSCHMITT DOWN

The official end of the Battle of Britain came on 31 October 1940, when major daylight attacks by Luftwaffe bombers ceased, but if its purpose was to dissuade Hitler from invading Britain, then arguably it ended on 17 September when he postponed Operation Sealion indefinitely.

Daylight bombing raids did not stop. On 15 November a 29-year-old Feldwebel (Staff Sergeant) named Otto Jaros climbed into the cockpit of Yellow 9, a Messerschmitt Bf 109, works number 6353, and took off for a raid over southeast England. Flying in formation with him were eight fellow pilots from 3 Staffel, 1 Gruppe, Jagdgeschwader 26 (3 Squadron, Group 1, Fighter Wing 26). With their distinctive yellow noses, the 109s of JG26 were a familiar and ominous sight in English skies and even if their claim to have shot down almost four times as many aircraft as they lost in the Battle of Britain cannot be verified, they were undoubtedly an elite force.

Nine Hurricanes of 605 Squadron RAF had left Croydon at 12:53 on a routine patrol of the Biggin Hill line in company with 501 Squadron, and apart from a towering storm cloud, the weather was fine and clear. The redoubtable Flight Lieutenant Christopher 'Bunny' Currant DFC flew Red 1, with Sergeant Eric Wright as Red 2. Both were Battle of Britain veterans, and while Wright could

were often given commissions and Wright was to be one who progressed to high rank.

They had not been airborne for long before Control alerted them to the presence of 'bandits' to the east. At 27,500 feet (8,380 metres) they spotted the Messerschmitts flying at around 20,000 feet (6,100 metres), heading east along the Thames, each with a 250-pound (113-kilogram) bomb strapped beneath the fuselage.[6] Once the attack commenced the German pilots jettisoned their bombs.

'The squadron went into line astern. "A" Flight leading, did a half roll and dived straight down onto the Me/109's which were in rather straggling formation. Red 1 dived upon the leading right hand Me.109 getting in a 2 ring deflection shot from 350 yards. The enemy aircraft then turned slowly right, Red 2 giving it another 2 second burst on its starboard quarter from 350 yards. The enemy aircraft pulled up in front of him, thus enabling Red 1 to get in behind and give a continuous burst from 200 yards, bits flew off it and black and white smoke came from it. In this neighbourhood there was a large storm cloud from 1,500 feet up to 15,000 feet, and as the enemy aircraft entered this, it was on its back with its port wing on fire. Red 1 then lost sight of it over the mouth of the River Medway. Red 2 followed in, diving upon the leader of the last vic[7] of Me.109's giving a 2 second 2 ring deflection shot closing to 100 yards. The enemy aircraft turned left, and Red 2 gave it a 1 ring 2 second deflection shot on its port quarter

not equal Currant's combat victories, he had chalked up at least five aircraft destroyed and a further six damaged.

A sergeant pilot like Wright was an NCO; he flew alongside commissioned pilots while earning rather less, he was not permitted to enter the officers' mess, and he was eligible for the Distinguished Flying Medal (DFM) rather than the Distinguished Flying Cross (DFC). One small consolation of being an NCO, however, was that a sergeant pilot did not have to bear the cost of his uniform. Sergeant pilots from 50 yards. The enemy aircraft then turned slowly right, Red 2 giving it another 2 second burst on its starboard quarter from 100 yards. This put the enemy aircraft into a spin from which it recovered at 10,000 feet, so Red 2 fired a further 3 second burst from astern above.'[8]

After Wright's last attack, Otto Jaros had little choice but to bail out, watched from the ground by 12-year-old Orsett schoolboy Bob Robinson and his elder sister, Betty. Seeing the Messerschmitt plummeting down towards the nearby village of Horndon on the Hill, Bob decided to give afternoon school a miss and look for the crash-site instead.

As Jaros descended on his parachute one of his flying boots fell off and was picked up by a farmer who kept it for more than 30 years before throwing it away. Unbeknown to the young German, he was over the small Essex town of Laindon where, during the inter-war years, families living in London had bought little plots of cheap farmland. They built small bungalows to which they could escape by train at weekends, though there were no roads, no running water and no electricity. During the Blitz, the Plotlands, as they were called, were safer than the East End, and by the end of the war some 25,000 people, many bombed out of their London homes, were living there in a thriving community. They had no reason to like the Luftwaffe, and 10 days earlier a nervous member of the local Home Guard had fired – unsuccessfully – at Feldwebel Johan Illner after he bailed out of his Bf 109 over Laindon. Illner had been saved from local anger by the intervention of a feisty woman who took the view that although he was a German he was also someone's son.

Jaros, who was a husband and father as well as someone's son, landed unhurt in a small yard behind a shop and lay there for some time. A few locals looked over the high walls and gave him verbal abuse but he was not threatened, and eventually the police arrived and took him to a cell at the police station, where a policeman's wife gave him a large mug of strong tea and some bread and jam. 'For you', they said, 'the war is over.' The following morning he was provided with a pair of plimsolls and later taken away to spend the rest of the war as a POW. It was Christmas 1946 before he was released to return home to the shattered remains of Munich and be reunited with his wife, Hildegard, and the daughter he had last seen as a tiny baby.

Coincidentally, the man who shot him down also ended the war as a POW. The squadron returned in triumph to Croydon. Bunny Currant had another kill to his name, Yellow 1 and Yellow 2 claimed one apiece, and Yellow 3 had a 'probable'; 21-year-old Wright was awarded the DFM, with the citation, 'This airman has displayed fine qualities of leadership, skill and courage. His sound tactics and efficiency have enabled him to destroy at least six enemy aircraft'.[9] His commission came through in December.

At the end of 1941 Wright was posted to the Far East with 232 Squadron, taking command after the commanding officer was killed in February 1942. In Java, Wright reformed 605 Squadron, but all the personnel were captured by the

Japanese after evacuation plans failed. Following his release in 1945, he accepted a permanent commission and enjoyed a successful post-war career, retiring as Air Marshal Wright.

Otto Jaros might have remained a mere line in the history of the Second World War had not David Campbell, the son of Betty Campbell, née Robinson, coincidentally become interested in Second World War aviation archaeology. Betty then told him how she and her brother Bob had watched an aircraft come down. Bob suffered a heart attack before he could show his nephew the exact crash-site, but the following year he took him to the field, and, with the support of the landowner, the dig took place over five days in September 1973. David Campell and fellow enthusiast Roger Pickett recovered a large amount of Messerschmitt Bf 109, works number 6353. While engines tend to survive reasonably well, to find the rudder, propeller blades and bomb rack in good condition was a cause for celebration.

What of the pilot? Campbell was keen to learn whether Jaros was still alive, and went to the German authorities:

'... who contacted Otto and gave him my address but gave him no indication as why I wanted to make contact. A letter arrived from Otto in April 1974, with his address and a telephone number, asking why we would like to make contact.

I was working at the local technical college and asked one of my colleagues in the language department to speak with him and explain the reason why we wished to contact him.

After a short silence on the other end of the 'phone a very excited Otto Jaros wanted all the details of his aircraft and what had happened to it.'

In August 1974 Jaros and his wife travelled to Essex to be reunited with the remains of the aircraft, which at that time were still at Campbell's home. Often in the morning before breakfast

RIGHT: In the shelter of the wing of his Me. 109, Feldwebel Otto Jaros brings his logbook up to date or writes home to his family in Munich.

he would go down the garden to contemplate it, and up until his death in 1996 he enjoyed a warm friendship with two generations of the Campbells. By that time David Campbell had formed his association with the Lashenden Air Warfare Museum at Headcorn Aerodrome near Maidstone, and the remains of 6353 were passed to their care. During the 1980s, Roger Pickett, who had founded the Thameside Aviation Museum, carried out a final excavation and rescued additional artefacts, now at the museum in Coalhouse Fort, East Tilbury, Essex.

The Hawker Hurricane was a stalwart of the RAF in the early part of the war. It was the first fighter to crack the 300 miles (480 kilometres) per hour barrier, and if it was slower than the Messerschmitt Bf 109, it could out-turn it. Like the biplanes of the day, it had a fabric-covered frame for the fuselage, which made it easy to repair but gave it no protection against fire; the wings were skinned with duraluminium. Although it has been overshadowed in the public's imagination by the Spitfire, the Hurricane served in many theatres of the war and in the Battle of Britain it shot down more enemy aircraft than any other type.

Although Fighter Command's primary task was to destroy enemy aircraft, squadrons were sometimes called in to assist with convoy protection. When *Dig WW2* investigated a Spitfire crash involving a pilot of Fighter Command a fascinating career emerged.

ABOVE: Re-arming a Spitfire in 1940.

MARK Vb – THE CREWKERNE SPITFIRE

1: Townsend Cemetery.
2: A short prayer from Mr David Cuthbertson, representing the Church, before the dig begins.
3: Members of Marches Aviation Society and the production team.
4: Oxidized aluminium: the first trace of Spitfire.
5: Using a ferrous metal detector to pinpoint the location of the engine.
6: First close-up look at the back of the engine.
7: With great precision the operator of the digger gathers up the engine.
8: Dan considers the force of the impact that bent and split the engine.
9: Scraping away clay.
10: Part of the reduction gearing begins to emerge.
11: Part of the propeller boss that took the full force of the crash.
12: The partial remains of the magneto.

12 March 1942, 13:00 hours. A young Canadian pilot is flying above the cloud over Somerset. He has no idea where he is, and his fuel gauge is now registering 0. When the Merlin 45 engine fails, his Spitfire will quite literally fall out of the sky. Below him lies Townsend Cemetery on the edge of the small market town of Crewkerne, gently sloping down to the hedge that now separates it from land farmed by the family of George Thomas. The hedge was not there in 1942 when George was 19.

'A footpath went right along the field, here. Somewhere along here there was a little kissing gate. I was down in the lane, just down there. I didn't see anything – all I heard was one heck of a *whoooosh*, and I looked up and just saw the tail of it go down. Our carter's daughter was there and it frightened her to death. She was nearer than I was. I got her home. A lot of people came up, taking souvenirs. There was nothing much to see when I came up, but there were about 20 RAF lads digging the hole. We knew [the pilot] had baled out.'[10]

The Spitfire had come down in an unused corner of the graveyard, and the RAF swiftly retrieved what they could, which, given the nature of the crash, would primarily have been the guns and any ammunition. The crater was filled in, the grass grew back, and the site automatically gained official protection as both a military wreck-site and, in this case, consecrated ground. *Dig WW2* sought permission to investigate the site not only from the Ministry of Defence, the owners of military aviation wrecks on British soil, irrespective of whether or not human remains might be present, but also from the Church of England in the person of the Bishop of Bath and Wells.

The early finds from just a few feet down comprised only scraps, mostly of badly corroded metal, including a piece of a fuse box, a small gauge and bits of the seat. Everything was jumbled up, inviting the suspicion that when the RAF had finished their work in 1942 they just threw the rubbish into the hole. Fragments of oxidized aluminium from the wings and fuselage appeared as a blueish-white powder, colloquially known as 'Daz', from its resemblance to the soap powder.

The focus was now on finding the engine. It was becoming evident that the Spitfire had come down, if not vertically, then at a very steep angle, punching into the heavy Somerset clay. Such crashes tend to concertina the fuselage and 'suck' everything into the hole created by the engine, reducing the aircraft to a compressed mass rather than scattering debris across a wide area. The experts calculated that the engine would have penetrated to 15 feet (4.5 metres).

The further down the team dug, the less oxidization had taken place; the finds were still small, but now identifiable. Two metallic plates were recovered, both clearly legible, one – bearing the magic word 'Spitfire' – from the oil cooler, the other from an instruction data plate on the starter drive unit.

Then at 12 feet (3.5 metres) down, with the soil showing the dark stains of disturbance and the magnetometer indicating the presence of one concentrated area of ferrous metal, the excavator clanged against something solid: the back of the engine, proving that the Spitfire had indeed hit the ground vertically. Further digging revealed a layer of rock at 15 feet (4.5 metres), which had stopped the engine dead.

When brought up, the Merlin 45 was graphic proof of the force of the impact: split almost in two, and with the heavy crankshaft bent back on itself. There was no difficulty in identifying the reduction gearing and air exhaust; some of the wires were still in place. Most impressive, despite being plastered with thick clay, was the propeller boss. Although the wooden blades would have been smashed to splinters before they rotted away, a few fibres of wood survived, attached to the boss. Mark Vb Spitfires were fitted with propellers made either of metal or Rotol's 'Jablo': laminated and compressed Canadian birch.

No trace was found of the serial number, but the Spitfire was noted in the operations records book (ORB) of 602 Squadron[11] as AD189, from which it was identified as a Mark Vb built at Castle Bromwich Aircraft Factory, fitted with a Merlin 45 engine and sent to No. 9 Maintenance Unit – RAF Cosford – on 6 October 1941 for dispersal before being assigned to 602 Squadron on 13 October 1941.[12] On 12 March the pilot who bailed out was Sergeant Frederick David Schofield, known to his friends as Dave or, because of his hair colour, Red.

ABOVE: Eyewitness George Thomas shares his memories of the crash with Dan.
RIGHT: Dan and the team demonstrate how far the engine drove into the Somerset clay.

CANADIAN IN THE COCKPIT

The son of a distinguished architect Frederick Schofield was born in Winnipeg in 1921 and grew up in Montreal. After being accepted for pilot training under the Empire Air Training Scheme (EATS) in September 1940, he gave up his engineering studies at McGill University. Although Commonwealth pilots were routinely serving as RAF officers before the outbreak of war, additional aircrew were urgently needed, and EATS was set up to train new recruits to a common standard in Australia, New Zealand, Canada and – later – South Africa and Southern Rhodesia. Schofield went solo in December 1940, gained his wings at Ottowa in March 1941 and was posted as a sergeant pilot to England in April.

After six weeks at 55 OTU, RAF Usworth, County Durham, Schofield was assessed as 'Average' and posted on 15 July to 132 Squadron at Peterhead. Here he had his first encounter with a Spitfire. 'Nifty machine. Bags of power. Best yet!!' he recorded enthusiastically in his logbook. Of his first significant operation, a convoy patrol on 15 August, he wrote simply 'Wahoo!'

Four days later life became more dangerous: he was sent to 485 Squadron at Redhill. Although the Battle of Britain had been won comprehensively the previous summer, there was no respite for the RAF, whose fighter pilots found themselves in a similar position to that in which the Luftwaffe had been: having to cross the sea and take the fight to the enemy in a foreign country. The RAF pilots flew a variety of offensive operations codenamed: 'circus', providing fighter protection to bombers for the purpose of engaging enemy fighters in combat – effectively, the bombers were bait; 'ramrod', escorting bombers on missions to destroy targets; 'rhubarb', attacks on targets of opportunity; 'rodeo', fighter sweeps over enemy territory; and 'sweep', clearing the enemy from the sky.

Now flying a Spitfire Vb – 'much impressed' Schofield flew in a fighter sweep to St. Omer, evading two Messerschmitt Bf 109s attempting to shoot him down, followed by a circus to St. Omer. The posting lasted until the end of November, when he was sent to RAF Kenley, home of 602 Squadron, a New Zealand unit in which Schofield was one of just two Canadians. His assessment had improved: he was now graded 'Above Average. A good squadron pilot'.

The commander of 602 was Squadron Leader Alan Deere DFC*, a future Air Commodore, who was shortly succeeded by Dermot 'Paddy' Finucane.[13] If Deere was an admired ace, Finucane was well on the way to the status of a legend. By the time of his death in action on 15 July 1942, aged only 21, he had just become the RAF's youngest Wing Commander, been credited with 26 individual kills, won the DSO and been awarded two bars to his DFC.

Finucane became an inspiration to Schofield, who admired his coolness in the heat of combat. It was something he himself needed on 12 March 1942 when 'A' flight was called to provide continuous protection to a torpedoed convoy escort proceeding to Portsmouth under tow.[14] Together with

Flight Lieutenant Lane, Schofield took off from RAF Kenley at 11:55, and, according to the ORB: 'F/Lt Lane located convoy south of Brighton but Schofield had his finger stuck[15] and lost his way home, climbed above cloud.' At 13:00 hours he was a mile from Crewkerne, out of fuel. Prudently he bailed out in advance of disaster and landed safely, suffering no more than

slight shock; his plane began the vertical dive that ended in the clay at Townsend Cemetery. He was quickly back in the air, and 16 days later he damaged an F.W 190 in combat; the film shot by the camera fitted to his Spitfire's wing is preserved in the Imperial War Museum, London.

Schofield said goodbye to 602 Squadron a month later when he

LEFT: Royal Canadian Air Force Spitfire pilot Frederick D. Schofield.

joined 601, which was no longer the 'Millionaire's Squadron'. The 9th of May found him on the deck of the aircraft carrier USS *Wasp*, strapped into the cockpit of his Spitfire and preparing to take off for Malta. From mid-1940 to 1943 the Mediterranean was a graveyard for ships, men and aircraft. Attacks by German and Italian fighters, dive-bombers, E-boats and submarines harassed – and sometimes decimated – the Allied convoys sent to supply North Africa and the vital stronghold of Malta. RAF squadrons defending the small island were regularly reduced to a handful of serviceable aircraft and had to be resupplied. In April, 46 Spitfires, flown off the USS *Wasp*, had reached Malta; four days later, only six remained. Once again *Wasp* was asked to embark fighters, this time for the hastily organized Operation Bowery.[16] Pilots flew to Renfrew, near Glasgow, where they were issued with tropical kit; 47 Mark Vc Spitfires, drained of fuel but carrying the additional weight of a jar of mosquito repellent and a sandfly net, were then taken by road to be loaded aboard the American carrier. After refuelling at Gibraltar, *Wasp* rendezvoused with HMS *Eagle*, laden with 17 Spitfires from Gibraltar, and the heavily defended convoy headed at 26 knots to within flying range of the island.

Wasp turned into the wind and went full ahead to give the pilots the best chance of a successful take off. These were RAF pilots, unused to the unforgiving nature of aircraft carrier take offs that were routine, but still hazardous, to the FAA.[17] Second in line on the deck, Schofield watched his friend, Sergeant R.D. Sherrington RAFVR accelerate down the flight deck. Flaps insufficiently adjusted, the Spitfire failed to get airborne; it crashed into the sea and the carrier thundered at full speed over man and machine.

As in combat, there was no time to adjust to the loss of a friend; Schofield made a successful take off and reached Malta where he flew for three weeks, getting a hole in his 'kite', before travelling by Wellington bomber to the Middle East.

This was to be Schofield's most concentrated period; 601 assumed a nomadic existence, moving from one primitive landing ground to another and dogfighting their way across Egypt, Libya and Tunisia as dictated by the flow of the desert war. On 21 August the squadron shifted from RAF Helwan to Landing Ground 154. Next day '10 Spitfires took off on an offensive patrol, intercepted and attacked the enemy S.W. of BURG EL ARAB. P/O SEWELL fired and observed strikes on ME. 109. F/Sgt Schofield was seen to attack ME.109 from below'.[18] Schofield wrote in his log: '… Engine cut – shot up by 109. Squirted at 109. Percy [F/O William Richard Percival Sewell RCAF] saw it spinning down.' During four attacks by the German fighter, shrapnel ripped into Schofield's left side but he managed to crash-land his damaged aircraft at Burg el Arab near Alexandria and was carted off to hospital. Six days later, still with shrapnel in his leg, he was discharged fit to fly.

He was back in the air on 2 September for a sweep when he was attacked by four 109s. This time he was not so lucky: 'Another fairly successful day, marred by the loss of one Spitfire

BR.188 by enemy action, the pilot CAN.77188. F/SGT SCHOFIELD baled out. Pilot is presumed missing.' The following day the squadron received a signal from the New Zealand Division with better news: Schofield 'suffering from burns had been evacuated through medical channels and that the plane was an overall loss'.

When Schofield had bailed out of his burning aircraft his clothes were ablaze. It was mid-December before he was discharged from hospital after treatment that included skin grafts for second-degree burns to the arms, legs and face, but he was soon back with the squadron and in January 1943 he flew a familiarization trip, which he described as 'quite interesting'. The following month he was promoted to Warrant Officer. When the squadron was scrambled at its Gabes Main airstrip on 7 April 1943 he went into action against 109s and 88s and shared a Dornier Do 217 with Flight Lieutenant Nicholls (who inflicted the initial damage and Schofield finished it off), while Sewell claimed one definite kill and one probable. Canadian Press interviewed him shortly afterwards and quoted him in an article that appeared in the *Hamilton Spectator*: '"I went for the Dornier as it dived away and got in a burst at short range," said Schofield. "At 4,000 feet it burst into flames and went into the sea."'[19]

At the end of May, by which time the squadron had turned its attention towards Italy, Schofield returned to England for a year as an instructor, and on 29 October he gained his commission as a pilot officer. He became operational again in May 1944, joining 19 Squadron, which had equipped with the P-51 Mustang III armed reconnaissance dive-bomber (although in 1938 it had been the first squadron to fly the Spitfire). Schofield flew over France on D-Day -1 to bomb a petrol dump near Paris, and in the days after the invasion participated in armed reconnaissance over the Argenton area. Flight Lieutenant Ken 'Paddy' French was engaged on similar missions:

'There were Spitfires roaming all over northern France. The French people were warned time and time again: keep off the roads during daylight hours. The Germans spent all day under cover hiding in woods and things … sometimes an odd vehicle might come out and it was soon to be pounced upon. It'd be shot up. The army might ask you to shoot up anything, trains or anything like that. I mean, sometimes we were dive-bombing these railway marshalling yards and things like that to upset their communications.'

ABOVE: Like every serviceman, Schofield carried his ID – or 'dog' tags. Two tags, joined together, were issued so that if the wearer were killed, one could be taken for administrative purposes and the other would remain with the body so it could be identified for burial.

Schofield's luck went AWOL once more when, during the afternoon of 20 June, the squadron launched a dive-bombing attack on the railway marshalling yards at Rambouillet on the outskirts of Paris in order disrupt German troop and equipment movements:

'Whilst approaching Dreux aerodrome 16 F.W. 190s were sighted slightly above. Bombs were jettisoned and the squadron climbed hard until well above the F/A. Green section were the first to attack, closely followed by Tonic and White, and a first class dog fight developed, which cost the Hun 2 destroyed, 1 Probable and 5 damaged for the loss of P/O Schofield, who was last seen going down on fire and must be presumed killed.'[20]

Squadron Leader W.M.C. Gilmour DSO, DFM went on to describe the incident two days later :

'FDS was flying White 2 when the Squadron engaged about 16 FW 190s over Dreux, France at 12,000 feet. In a general melee and dog-fight everyone got separated and about five minutes after the commencement of the fight a Mustang III was seen going straight down with flames pouring out of both wing roots. The aircraft was not watched for long and the pilot was not seen to bale out.'[21]

The Canadian newspapers included Schofield in their list of casualties, but although his squadron comrades had not seen him bail out, the Germans had, and he was in no mood to be taken prisoner:

'We encountered 12 F.W. 190s over the N.W. corner of Foret d'Ivry. I was attacked from astern. The aircraft caught fire, and I baled out, landing in the wood.

I hid my parachute and [illegible] under bushes then started walking in a westerly direction. I spent the night in a field of oats on the outskirts of Neuville. The next morning (21 June) I contacted a farmer working in the field. He brought me to his farmhouse and gave me civilian clothes. He then told me to continue west, avoiding St. Andre and to keep south of Conches. By nightfall I reached the outskirts of Angerville la Campagne where I contacted a farm labourer. He took me to a barn where I spent the next two nights. On 23 June he brought me into a café in Angerville, where I was introduced to a member of the resistance movement.'[22]

Schofield was moved to Sacquenville and issued with false papers describing him as a farm labourer. For two

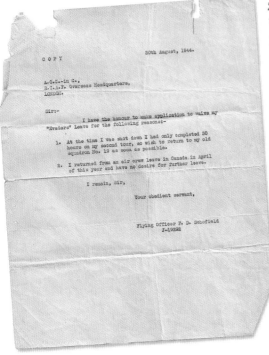

BELOW: Schofield's request on 30 August 1944 to forgo the period of leave given to those who escaped from the enemy.

months, while working on local farms, he kept up that assumed identity. On 21 August, a day before American troops entered the town, he was taken to Brosville, from where he was collected by the RAF and sent on evader's leave. Anxious to get back in the air, he appealed, in vain, against the decision.

By the time he returned on 5 October, the squadron was back in England and coming to the end of a stint at RAF Matlaske, escorting bombers into Germany.

'Flap and bother and what have you', ran the squadron ORB on 14 October. 'The powers that be suddenly produced another show just to facilitate our move. After a mad rush of packing and briefing and breakfast (for some) the Sqdn was airborne at 0745hrs to escort a thousand Lancs and Halifaxes to Duisberg. … Hopes ran high (or low!!) when "jet jobs" were reported but unfortunately (or fortunately) they turned out to be friendly Mosquitoes. … Andrews Field, though not quite Utopia, seems to be a great improvement on Matlaske. Larger mess, better billets, magnificent airfield, W.A.A.F.'s (not yet in evidence!!!) but darned awful food.'

Schofield remained with 19 Squadron until the end of the war, first at Andrews Field (Essex), then Peterhead and finally Acklington, mostly escorting Mosquito bombers on long-range escort operations, which were no less eventful than during his previous years in the RAF. Throughout his service his logbook lists the names of the comrades who were killed, whether it was being 'clobbered by light

flak (16 holes)' or watching as 'Robbie piled into a hill'. 'A hell of a lot of water in the North Sea', he wrote feelingly in February 1945.

Following his 'Completion of Voluntary Service in an Emergency', Schofield left the RCAF at the end of the war and returned to his native Canada to continue his education. He qualified as an accountant and built a career in finance, eventually being transferred to New York where he and his family settled. The scars from the burns to his face soon faded away but not those on his legs and body, and the last few years of his life were marred by painful circulation problems that doctors ascribed to the failure to remove all the shrapnel from his leg in 1942. Glamorous though his career as a fighter pilot may seem, the reality for those who served through the war was very different. Frederick Schofield was left with mental as well as physical scars, and he spoke very little about the war. He died in New York in 2003.

The propeller boss recovered by *Dig WW2* is being prepared for exhibition at the Crewkerne and District Museum; the engine is now on display at Fort Perch Rock Aviation Archaeology Museum at New Brighton on the River Mersey.

ABOVE: Identity card forged in 1944 by the French Resistance for Frederick Schofield, stating him to be a blue-eyed, red-haired agricultural worker by the name of Michel Paul Emile Davy whose nose was of normal size.

RAF KENLEY: HOME TO MANY OF THE 'FEW'

Opened in 1917 and close to Croydon, Surrey, RAF Kenley, where Schofield joined 602 Squadron, became a household name during the Battle of Britain. Hornchurch, Biggin Hill, Croydon and Kenley were just four of the airfields in the southeast of England from which fighter squadrons were routinely scrambled to engage the Luftwaffe in the desperate summer of 1940. Kenley's importance was only emphasized on 18 August 1940 when German bombers launched a devastating attack that damaged the runways, wrecked hangers and destroyed or badly damaged a number of aircraft.

On 12 February 1942 Group Captain F.V. Beamish and Wing Commander Boyd took off from Kenley on Channel patrol and spotted two heavily escorted German battleships, the *Scharnhorst* and *Gneisenau*, which had broken out of Brest and were racing through the Channel towards their German bases. Kenley Wing was scrambled to attack the fighters but failed to disrupt what became known as 'The Channel Dash'.

Fighter Command remained at Kenley until 1959, and today the only aircraft allowed to fly from the aerodrome are gliders. Although many of the buildings, including the control tower, have been demolished, and some of the land has been used for housing, Kenley is considered the best preserved of all the Second World War airfields. The officers' mess and the headquarters have been given Listed Building status, the perimeter fence and runways are intact, and a number of the defensive features are still in place, including 11 of the 12 blast pens. These were large, open, E-shaped concrete

structures covered with earth; any aircraft parked in the shelter of their walls were defended against the blast from bombs exploding nearby, though not from those landing inside the protected area. The pens also served as air raid shelters. Another interesting survivor is the range where the pilots tested and emptied their fighters' guns, the marks still clearly visible in the wall.

In 1952 scenes from the Battle of Britain film *Angels One-Five* were shot at Kenley, and three years later the cameras returned to film the airfield scenes in *Reach For The Sky*, the story of RAF ace Douglas Bader.

Few decommissioned airfields have fared as well as Kenley: Hornchurch, for example, was partially lost to housing and gravel; Driffield, like Limavady, is a derelict, decaying shell. However, all across the country there are visible relics of a time when Britain's survival depended on the RAF and when Allied air power based in Britain made a vital contribution to the final victory in Europe.

THE FORTRESS OF LOUGH FOYLE

There is a long tradition of giving names and ascribing human qualities to machines, primarily ships, locomotives, cars and aircraft. This anthropomorphism creates a sense of comradeship, particularly in situations where there appears to be a critical level of mutual dependence. During the Second World War, the most famous American bomber was the B-17, popularly known as the Flying Fortress. The name was conferred on it by a reporter present at the unveiling ceremony, who, impressed by its gun turrets and bomb-carrying capability, remarked that it looked like a flying fortress. B-17 crews gave names to their individual aircraft, such as *Liberty Belle*, *I'll Get By*, *Sally B* and, most famously, *Memphis Belle* – and frequently painted the nose cone to complement the name. The B-17 that bore the serial number 41-24516 for its short life was named by its crew *the Meltin' Pot* – an allusion to the name of its pilot, Captain William Curtis Melton and to the composition of its crew, who exemplified the concept of the USA as the 'melting pot of Europe'.

The Meltin' Pot was the lead aircraft of the 368th Squadron, 306th Bombardment Group (Heavy). Activated on 1 March 1942, it was scheduled to move to Thurleigh Airfield, England, during August and September 1942 to join the Eighth Air Force. Once established, the highly active group proved effective over Occupied Europe and Germany, bombing strategic targets and supporting troops at D-Day and for the remainder of the war.

But first the aircraft had to get to Britain, and transatlantic flight was nowhere near as routine in the 1940s as

ABOVE: This B-17F Flying Fortress, B-17G-85-DL, serial 44-83546, played the part of the eponymous heroine of the film *Memphis Belle*, with replica nose cone art copied from the original aircraft and modifications that allowed it to pass for a B-17F.

OPPOSITE: Actor Kenneth Moore strolls past a line of spitfires at RAF Kenley, where *Reach For The Sky* was filmed.

it is today. Unpredictable weather over the ocean, more rudimentary navigation and restricted range were the three prime difficulties, and, if technical problems were encountered, the crew's options were very limited. The alternative – dismantling aircraft and shipping them in crates – was an unattractive option, given both the vulnerability of convoys to submarine attacks and the amount of space such huge machines would take up. Fortunately, it was a problem the RAF had confronted in 1940, when it first began to take delivery of aircraft built in Canada and the USA, which it solved by establishing a ferry service that at first used RAF pilots such as Terry Bulloch, and then civilian pilots.

USAAF quickly established similar procedures under the name of Ferrying Command (later Air Transport Command, ATC), operating not only across the North Atlantic but into the Pacific theatre of operations. With the northern route crowded, ATC established more southerly routes, with refuelling stops in Florida, Trinidad,

British Guiana, Dakar and Marrakech, using RAF Valley and RAF St. Mawgan as the destination. Like the RAF, ATC used civilian pilots, with both air and ground crews going by sea, but some aircraft were flown by their own crews. *The Meltin' Pot* was one such, and would be taking the Gander route to Prestwick.

The crew first came together in July 1942 and were sent to Alomogordo in New Mexico for bombing training. Melton, who was 22 and an engineering graduate, had qualified as a pilot in February 1941 and had test-flown many aircraft after repair to check that they were airworthy. His co-pilot was Second Lieutenant Alexander Kramarinko, of Russian parentage, while the navigator was First Lieutenant Charles L. Grimes, nicknamed 'Pappy' because he was the oldest. The fourth commissioned officer, Second Lieutenant Robert T. Levy came from a rich Jewish family. The five staff sergeants, William L. Cherry, Malone E. Snover, Gilbert G. Shoemaker, Ernest P. Garland and Leland G. Kessler were the engineer, radio operator and gunners respectively. Kessler was a gifted artist and responsible for customizing a number of nose cones.

Training complete they returned to Westover, Massachusetts, awaiting orders. On 10 September at 08:25 Melton took off for Gander. In addition to the nine crew, the aircraft carried two passengers and as much essential equipment as could be accommodated, given the weight restrictions imposed to improve fuel economy. The term 'essential equipment' was stretched thinly to include Levy's case of Bourbon whiskey, Grimes's record player and his collection of more than a hundred 78rpm records of Tommy Dorsey's orchestra in which he had played sax, together with large quantities of cigarettes, candy and toiletries. They must have known that life under rationing would be grim.

The aircraft landed at the remote Canadian air station for refuelling; instead of bombs, *the Meltin' Pot* was to carry additional fuel tanks in the bomb bays, and it would be taking off for Britain the following night. There was anxiety among all the crews about the long flight, augmented by the unexplained loss[23] of one of the 423rd Squadron's Fortresses the previous week and by rumours of sabotage.

Before the crew climbed aboard ready for take off at 21:30 the wealthy Levy came back with a pile of genuine Parkas, one for each of the crew.

For two hours all went well, until around 23:30 the de-icers failed and the wings began to freeze up. Melton increased altitude and eventually found a warm air current to disperse the ice, allowing them to descend into what became wet conditions, but within 20 minutes No. 2 engine was overheating and emitting sparks from the nacelle. The decision was taken to 'feather' it (jargon for shutting it down) – the aircraft could fly on three engines at the cost of worse fuel consumption.

Forty minutes later, No. 3 engine was running hot and spewing out flames – there was no choice but to shut it down. An attempt to restart No. 2 failed when that, too, caught fire. The only consolation was that the faults had occurred in the two inboard engines (those closest to the fuselage). *The*

Meltin' Pot continued steadily on her two outboard engines, though they were running hotter than usual with the strain; but there was real fear – if not in the cockpit, then certainly behind it, where Levy's Bourbon was opened. Orders to throw out all non-essential cargo seem to have been ignored.

They finally sighted Ireland but had no wish to land in Eire and be interned. While Kessler began transferring fuel from the dead to the working engines, the captain headed for Northern Ireland.

The aircraft was losing height rapidly and Melton ordered the crew to prepare for ditching. No. 1 engine gave up. Through the Perspex windscreen the water rushed to meet him. In a few seconds the plane would hit the water and shatter itself to pieces.

Tail down, *the Meltin' Pot* confounded all the fears of the crew, skidded onto Lough Foyle and floated as the shaken crew picked themselves up and prepared to evacuate. Under normal circumstances, a Flying Fortress might be able to float for 30 seconds, but *the Meltin' Pot* had the advantage of empty fuel tanks in her bomb bays. Like the oil drums stuffed into HMS *Transylvania* specifically for that purpose, they provided buoyancy and so gave the aircraft an extra four minutes.

Kessler panicked and jumped out into the swift current of the choppy lough; the other 10 people evacuated safely into two yellow inflatables, which were gathered by the wind and tide.

As the Flying Fortress crash-landed on the water, Mrs Nellie Benson and her daughter Elizabeth were just casting off in the former's 12-feet (3.5-metre) dinghy, *Redwing*. Nellie, the wife of the vicar of Lower Moville, was an accomplished yachtswoman in her fifties and did not let her heart condition interfere with her love of the sport, nor was she about to be beaten by a 7-knot outgoing tide. Elizabeth never forgot that Saturday:

'It was a lovely day with a spanking breeze and my mother said, "Let's go for a sail", so we went out and we heard this terrible noise and looked up and to our horror we saw this huge plane, and it obviously was going to crash, it was diving down. The sudden knowledge that it was going to crash I still remember vividly and the fright I suppose I felt for the people in it.'

By the time the women had left Greencastle Harbour they could see that *the Meltin' Pot* was sinking. Four men had got into one yellow inflatable, another six into a second. There was no sight of Kessler drifting in his life jacket. The Bensons made for the liferaft with the four men on board.

'So we sailed, and when we got there my mother was able to bear down on it. We grabbed it and I made it fast alongside. And men … well the men didn't say anything. I said, rather quavery-voiced, "You're all safe now". So we just held on. I think they must have been in shock in the boat. Well it must have been a terrible trauma for them and they didn't say a word. I often wondered if they thought I was speaking Irish or what on earth they thought because I did say you're all right, but there was no reaction.'

Redwing began to tow the raft, and the Bensons were soon relieved to see HMS *Sir Gareth* coming from Derry towards them. The ditching had been spotted from the nearby control tower and the minesweeper diverted to assist. Apart from Kessler who had cracked his ribs, the rest of the crew was unhurt. An American officer later visited the Bensons but failed to offer a word of thanks.

Only three of *the Meltin' Pot*'s crew survived the war: Melton, Kessler and Kramarinko. Grimes was killed in a raid on the U-boat base at La Pallice on 18 November 1943, Levy in January 1943. Kessler's four fellow staff sergeants died together when their aircraft was shot down by anti-aircraft fire two months later, and Kessler would have been with them had he not been ill. Kessler bailed out in May 1943 after his aircraft was shot up over Wilhelmshaven and spent the remainder of the war as a POW, while Kramarinko was shot down over Belgium in 1943 and arrested after eight

days on the run. He, too, ended the war as a POW.

Flying on fewer than the recommended number of engines was a perennial problem for pilots. Shortly before VE Day (7 May 1945), Australian pilot – and international cricketer – Flight Lieutenant Reg Ellis and his crew of 463 Squadron were part of a 1,000-bomber raid over Germany; 900 went to Berlin, but 100 were detached to bomb the town of Merseburg. Heavy flak and a fighter attack left Ellis with half his scalp, an engineer badly wounded in the shoulder, and an Avro Lancaster with both port engines dead and only the starboard outer working properly. Despite the blood streaming down his face, Ellis regained control of the aircraft and nursed it for more than 650 miles (1,040 kilometres) as the crow flies, before diverting to the USAAF base at Rennes in Brittany where he managed a successful landing and

ABOVE: A B-17 Flying Fortress on its way to England.

an American doctor put almost a hundred stitches into his scalp.

Divers from the local Inishowen Sub-Aqua Club found *the Meltin' Pot* in August 2001 after three months of searching. It lay on its back at a depth of 70 feet (21 metres) among mussel beds. They were very cautious during their initial explorations, knowing only at the time that four people had been rescued and fearing that human remains might be in the wreckage. A second cause for concern was the amount of ammunition that might be on board: although the plane carried no bombs, it contained 100 pounds (45 kilograms) of ammunition for each gun. Among the artefacts they found were personal items: the – empty – bottle of whiskey, aftershave and an electric razor.

The focus then changed from recovering artefacts to discovering whether any of the crew on that fateful flight were still alive. Seamus Carey, founder of the club, tracked down Lee Kessler and Curtis Melton. Although Kessler died before he could visit the club and see the salvaged items, Melton was able to make the journey and be reunited with Elizabeth Benson (now Ferguson) who had sailed to the rescue some 60 years earlier.

'What's so astonishing about this crash,' said Dan, 'is that nowadays that would be a momentous, life-changing event for anyone, but for these crewmen it was just another terrifying event that they had to endure during their wartime service. Just days after this crash they were out flying combat missions … In the tumultuous wartime service of these men this crash barely gets a passing mention.'

THE SPITFIRE THAT 'SQUASHED THE ENEMY'

The words Merlin and Spitfire are so firmly associated with one another that it is hard to imagine any other engine powering the iconic fighter. However, in 1943 the Rolls-Royce Griffon supplanted the Merlin in several types of Spitfire.[24] Many modifications to the Spitfire were made during the course of the war to improve overall performance or equip it for specialized roles, and the Mark XII was a very successful development, of which just 100 were made. With clipped wings, a Rolls-Royce Griffon Mark III or Mark IV[25] engine, and a powerful armament in the shape of four .303-inch machine guns and two 20-millimetre cannon, it was a highly manoeuvrable, low-level fighter designed to take on the Focke-Wulf Fw 190. With hindsight, the 'low-altitude' engine's name appears ironic given that in 1975 a Rüppell's griffon vulture reached an altitude of almost 38,000 feet (11,580 metres) before being sucked into an aircraft's jet engine.

The first unit to fly the Mark XII operationally was 41 Squadron, in April 1943, followed a month later by 91 Squadron. In June the two came together at RAF Tangmere's satellite airfield at Westhampnett, becoming the Tangmere Spitfire XXII Wing, part of 11 Wing. Both were international in their composition, especially 41 Squadron, which in the course of the war comprised fliers from countries as diverse as Uruguay and Austria alongside the obligatory British, Canadians and New Zealanders. It had once included Dutch officer Flight Lieutenant Bram van der Stok who, after being shot down in April 1942 and

imprisoned in Stalag Luft III, became one of just three airmen to succeed in what later became known to film-goers as *The Great Escape*. On his return he was posted to 91 Squadron.

The ebullient entries in the two squadrons' operations record books and diaries testify equally to the pilots' morale and to their success rate. Whether fighting off German raids on the south coast, flying ramrods in support of bombers attacking German airfields in France, or finding targets of opportunity – rhubarbs – they proved more than equal to the task; 41 Squadron had been in almost continuous combat since the start of the Battle of Britain and had suffered heavy losses, but now they relished cheaper victories. A 91 Squadron diary entry, dated 25 May 1943, when they were still based at RAF Hawkinge, reveals delight at their new aircraft:

'We got the Huns tonight – five of them, all in the drink. It was a grand occasion for 91 Squadron, and this entry ought to be typed in red. … the C/O, with Johnny Round as his No. 2 and F/O Maridor and P/O Davy Nos. 3 and 4, went on a low patrol off Dungeness area at 21.25 hrs. They were not out long and came into land at 21.50 hrs. This was where the fun started, for about 12 F.W. 190's came in with the intention of dealing a shrewd blow at Folkestone at about this time. The C.O. and Johnny had landed and just taxied to dispersal when the greens were fired, so whipped off again smartly, while Maridor and Davy, who were circling to land, went "through the gate" to Folkestone. There were guttural cries of "Alarm!" "Alarm" from the surprised Huns, who broke away and ran for home, dropping their bombs in the sea, except for one which fell in a bathing pool and injured one person. The XII's had the legs of the 190's, and having flown through a lively A.A. barrage, smacked down

ABOVE: Brothers in arms, but only one would return from the war: Fred Heninger (right) and elder brother Ray .

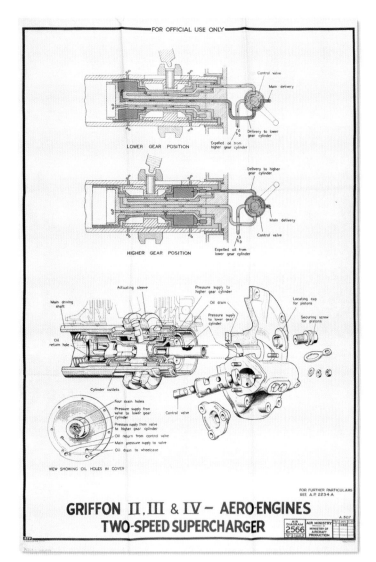

Control valve

Main delivery

LOWER GEAR POSITION

Delivery to lower gear cylinder

Expelled oil from higher gear cylinder

Delivery to higher gear cylinder

Main delivery

Control valve

HIGHER GEAR POSITION

Expelled oil from lower gear cylinder

Actuating sleeve

Pressure supply to higher gear cylinder

Oil drain

Main driving shaft

Pressure supply to lower gear cylinder

Locating cap for pistons

Securing screw for pistons

Oil return hole

Cylinder outlets

Four drain holes

Pressure supply from valve to lower gear cylinder

Pressure supply from valve to higher gear cylinder

Control valve

Oil return from control valve

Main pressure supply to valve

Oil drain to wheelcase

VIEW SHOWING OIL HOLES IN COVER

FOR FURTHER PARTICULARS SEE A.P 2234 A

GRIFFON II, III & IV – AERO-ENGINES
TWO-SPEED SUPERCHARGER

A.807

AIR DIAGRAM 2566

AIR MINISTRY MINISTRY OF AIRCRAFT PRODUCTION

ABOVE: Schematic and cutaway drawings of one part of the Rolls Royce Griffon engine.

angle. No opposition at all'. The Luftwaffe obligingly came to the rescue, and the squadron was able to report, 'We are kept busy now, much to the delight of the pilots'. During the escort of 72 Martin B-26 Marauder bombers to Beauvais they encountered 10 Fw 190s: 'Spitfires V, IX and XII closed in from every direction, and a most glorious dog fight ensued, during which the wing destroyed 5 FW. 190s with 2 probables and 1 damaged.'[27]

In September 1943, 91 Squadron became the most successful squadron of 11 Group, no small achievement given the competition. But life for the RAF fighter pilots was no uninterrupted celebration. Flying Officer Geoffrey Bond was killed that month, one of six pilots lost during the year. On 6 December, with cloud at 6,000 feet (1,830 metres), 91 Squadron took off at 11:10 to practise tactics and formation:

'While in the Horsham area Red 2 (F/O Thomas) collided with Yellow 2 (F/O H F Heninger) and both aircraft spun down. This happened about 9000 ft in good conditions above cloud. Fred Heninger baled out and landed close to Horsham quite safely, being well received at a nearby farmhouse and given the odd shot of brandy. Thomas, however, bought it, and crashed in his A/c just to the East of Horsham. Fred was back in the Mess after lunch, being brought back by Army truck, and could give no reason for what had happened. He was promptly seized on by Doc Pattrick and clapped into sick quarters, emerging in a day or so....'[28]

five of them, two falling to the C/O, one to each of the others. Matt and Kyn, who had been scrambled, saw some of this, but didn't get a chance to have a crack at anything themselves, while F/O Bond ... saw a 190 go straight in near Gris Nez. It turned out that this must have been the one that Davy engaged, which was disappointing for Bond....'[26]

In August, 41 Squadron were complaining that a ramrod to Poix Airfield had been 'very tame from our

A couple of weeks later Fred, a Canadian from Calgary, was shooting for the squadron in a match against their rivals from 41 Squadron. Also in the team was the man who had been most relieved by the 22-year-old's narrow escape: his elder brother, Ray. Determined to fly for the RAF, the pair had joined up on the same day in 1941, trained together and gained their commissions at the same time. Both became pilots in 91 Squadron, with the proviso that they should not fly on the same operations.

On 6 January 1944 Fred was flying EN223 on a ramrod covering bombers on a mission to the Rouen area – almost certainly attacking the V1 launch sites known to be under construction in that area: 'We got close to some Huns but couldn't see them – they must have been away up in the very bright sun. Freddy Schade had to turn back as his engine wasn't too good, and Fred kept him company. Fred himself had engine trouble after this and had to bale out. This was tough luck.'[29]

It was worse than tough luck. Fred got out of the Spitfire, but as his parachute deployed the strings became caught round the tail. The aircraft plunged to the ground southeast of the Normandy coastal town of St. Valery-en-Caux, dragging him with it. His body was recovered and buried at Grandcourt War Cemetery, southeast of Dieppe. His brother took his loss badly.

On 13 June the diary of 91 Squadron recorded: 'Great excitement was caused by a pilotless aircraft coming over at dawn and exploding violently near the drome. It turned out to be Hitler's secret weapon, which incidentally we had known about for the last 10 months….'

Four days later, the squadron added a new task to its job specification: chasing 'divers': flying bombs.

BELOW: Dan and Jonny McNee approaching Grandcourt War Cemetery where Fred Heninger is buried.

MARK XII – THE DIEPPE SPITFIRE

1: Dan with the remains of Heninger's Spitfire. As it hit the ground at terminal velocity the aircraft concertinaed in on itself, to create a mangled mass of smashed metal buried 20 feet (6 metres) beneath the surface.

2: The Griffon engine that cost Heninger his life.

3: The tail wheel, still with air in the tyre.

What happened to Heninger's Spitfire to make it crash? There were enemy aircraft in the vicinity, but probably not close enough to have hit the aircraft, though a claim was made. Freddie Schade reported seeing puffs of black smoke coming from EN223's engine, suggesting engine or fuel problems, and the only chance of learning the truth was to examine what was left of the aircraft. *Dig WW2* were off to France.

Laurent Viton, a French postman with a passion for listing and honouring every Allied airman killed in his local area, knew the location of the crash-site: a field near the Normandy village of Le Mesnil-Durdent, and the metal detectors quickly homed in on the exact spot to dig. From just a few feet below the surface the first pieces of fuselage emerged, one bearing traces of the red and blue circles from the RAF roundel. The cockpit door was recovered. Dan stared at the instruction that was still legible, a reminder that Heninger would have seen every time he climbed into the cockpit: 'That is magic. *"Make sure door is locked before flight".*'

One find in surprisingly recognizable condition was the Spitfire's G45 camera, which would have been mounted in the wings close to the guns in order to obtain a gun's-eye view of attacks on enemy aircraft that could later be shown to pilots as part of their training. For Dan it was 'like finding the black box'. Aviation archaeologist Steve Vizard examined it with him and commented that the lens was almost intact. 'The rest of it's obviously in a pretty sad state but that's the actual film cassette. Send it off to Kodak and see what they can do.'

Equally impressive was the tail wheel; and the cockpit, though heavily compressed, had all its instrumentation.

The main attention was centred on the engine, which came out intact. The moment it was exposed, aviation archaeologist Jeff Carless knew why the aircraft had crashed: 'Engine failure. We know that for certain now. Now we've lifted the engine up we can see it's thrown a con rod off the crank. … It's a classical sign of losing a big end bearing failure, and it's thrown through the crank case. That happened when the engine was running. That wasn't the result of hitting the ground.'

Following Viton's agreement with the mayor of Le Mesnil-Durdent, whose father witnessed the crash, Heninger's engine is to be displayed in the community's town hall. Dan went to Grandcourt to see his grave: 'The amazing thing about that dig for me was that when you come here and just look at a headstone you don't really think about the circumstances under which they died, really, but seeing that twisted metal, that compacted, shattered wreck, I'll never quite look at a fighter pilot's tomb in the same way again.'

DESIGN DEFECT OR MECHANICAL FAILURE?

Give a pilot a new type of aircraft and his natural reaction will be to fly it to its limits and squeeze every advantage out of it. The Mark XII Spitfires with their Griffon engines had worked hard for 41 Squadron and 91 Squadron for over seven months without any design faults or systematic manufacturing defects showing up, and although EN223 had been sent to 91 Squadron only on 20 November 1943, it was one of the earlier Mark XIIs to have been produced. A detailed article on the engine in the specialist aviation magazine *Flight*, dated 20 September 1945, had only praise for the design and performance of the Griffon, declaring that the Mark XII Spitfire 'effectively squashed the enemy'.

Heninger had probably just been unlucky; or maybe production pressures meant that his particular engine had not been subjected to sufficient levels of factory testing.

The lack of incidents involving the Griffon contrasts with the problems associated with the early Merlin which, unlike the fuel-injected engines of the German fighters, had an SU carburettor that was prone to cutting out if the aircraft was put into a negative G manoeuvre – pitch the nose hard down, as pilots would usually have to do in a dogfight, and the fuel ceased flowing into the engine. At best the aircraft lost power in a critical situation and the enemy escaped; at worst, either the enemy took advantage of the situation or the engine died. The problem was ameliorated simply and cheaply by aviation engineer Beatrice 'Tilly' Shilling who designed a fuel restrictor consisting of a metal disc with a hole in it. Grateful, if irreverent, pilots christened it the 'Tilly orifice' or 'Miss Shilling's orifice' in her honour.

Upgrades of tried and tested engines could introduce problems. A FAA squadron that converted from the much-appreciated Grumman TBF/TBM Avenger I to the Avenger II in 1945 suddenly found themselves unexpectedly losing power in the landing circuit, and aircraft were actually lost. The problem was finally traced to something as trivial as the spark plugs.

FLYING BOMBS AND ROCKETS

The British called it the Flying Bomb, Doodlebug or Buzz bomb, and from the night of the 12/13 June 1944 it caused terror, death, injury and destruction in and around London. More than 9,000 were fired towards the British capital from launch sites in the Pas de Calais.

Germany had begun the flying bomb programme before the war with the aim of developing a pilotless aircraft, but in 1942 the concept of the V1 took shape and a prototype of the Fieseler Fi 103 was tested that December, not on a launch pad but by being air dropped from a Focke-Wulf Fw 200. Developed and built by Fieseler at Peenemünde Airfield on Germany's Baltic Sea coast, some 20 miles (32 kilometres) from the Polish border, the V1 looked rather like a small aeroplane with stubby, almost rectangular wings. Its fuselage measured just over 27 feet (8 metres) and it had a wingspan of more than 17 feet (5 metres) – but that was where the resemblance to an aircraft ended. The fuselage was little more than a 1,895-pound (860-kilogram) warhead, packed with Amatol-39 high-explosive, and instead of having an engine driving one or more propellers it was powered by a pulse jet engine mounted above the rear of the fuselage. An autopilot and gyrocompass replaced the human element.

The V1 was most commonly launched from the ground, up a concrete ramp, which had to be angled towards the target and sited within 150 miles (240 kilometres) of it. Once launched, the bomb buzzed along at up to 400 miles (640 kilometres) per hour until the odometer calculated that it was on target, whereupon the V1 began to dive. Starved of fuel, the engine cut out and those on the ground who had heard the distinctive approach now had no idea where it would land until the

explosion occurred. (Paradoxically, the cutting out of the engine, which caused so much dread, was in fact a defect that the Germans eventually remedied.) The V1 could be launched by day or by night, and unlike aircraft it was unaffected by bad weather. Spitfire pilot Flight Lieutenant Ken 'Paddy' French, who tried to chase one, recalled the unmistakeable sound: '... a sort of chug chug chug noise, so even if you couldn't see it, you heard it, you knew it was a flying bomb and not an aeroplane.'

Rumours that the Germans were developing something like a winged bomb had reached British Intelligence as early as 1942 but it was not information that could be acted upon. The opportunity would come in 1943, thanks to one of the bravest and most resourceful members of the French Resistance: Michel Hollard, founder and head of the group Réseau Agir.

BELOW: The German censor has removed any background detail that might identify this V1 launch site. The bomb on the left has been placed on a trolley and will be taken to the Richthaus where the course will be set. That on the right is being secured on a bogie for movement around the site.

THE MAN WHO SAVED LONDON

As the Germans closed in on the French capital in 1940, engineer Michel Hollard, a decorated hero of the First World War, decided to fight on in his own way by passing information to the British. He travelled at great risk to neutral Switzerland to offer his services as an agent, only to receive a lukewarm welcome at the British Embassy in Berne. Undeterred, he promised to return.

In the meantime, the sceptical and understandably wary British did their homework and thoroughly vetted him: his second welcome was cordial and his help accepted. In the course of the war he made an incredible 96 further trips into Switzerland to hand over information gathered by himself and the network of agents he gradually built up: the Réseau Agir. The information proved extremely valuable and led, for example, to the bombing of Abbeville and the docks at Marseilles. Such was his accrued credit that when he arrived in August 1943 with what looked to be vague information on suspicious construction activity near Rouen, his intelligence was passed on to London and taken seriously.

The information had begun with a report from one of his agents in Rouen who had overheard a conversation between two French contractors on the nature of their work for the Germans. Their words made no sense to the agent, himself an engineer, and he passed his suspicions to Hollard – who went to investigate.

Under the pretext of offering moral and religious books to workers, he obtained the locations of various sites around Auffay, and having found one that looked promising he gained access as a worker. Immediately he was struck by the sight of a short, newly constructed road, down the centre of which a row of wooden posts had been set. A string was stretched along the top of the posts, and it extended far beyond it. Each post had a metal disc set into the top. It dawned on Hollard that he had seen road surveyors using this technique. Careful not to betray what he was doing, he bent down and took a compass bearing.

Back in Paris that night he took out his map of the English Channel and laid his compass on it: 315° pointed straight to London. He took the information to Lausanne, to the contact assigned to him. As a result, he was asked to find more sites, and by the end of October he had identified a hundred sites, on a line roughly parallel to the Channel coast. But he had no idea of their purpose, other than that it must involve an attack on London, until one of his newer agents persuaded draughtsman André Comps to get a job on one of the sites. That site was Bois Carré, 10 miles (16 kilometres) from Abbeville. At appalling risk to his life, Comps copied the plans of the buildings – one of them a strangely curved tunnel – and concrete strips, before finally purloining the plans of what was to go onto the strips of concrete: ramps with rails. Hollard took the information to Switzerland.

This was the information that London needed. By now they knew about Peenemünde and the flying bomb: the pieces of the jigsaw were resolving themselves into a picture of the threat that faced Britain.

Hollard continued to work for the British, but in February 1944 he was arrested by the Gestapo, tortured, imprisoned and, after D-Day, deported to the concentration camp of Neuengamme. He was subjected to a period of forced labour and brutality that killed many of the captives, until in April 1945 he was taken to Lübeck and herded aboard the *Thilbeck*. The rumour was that the prisoners would be sunk at sea.

French-speaking prisoners including Hollard were suddenly transferred without explanation to a ship bound for Sweden in an arrangement brokered by Count Bernadotte. Most of those left on the German ships were killed when the captains ignored RAF orders to surrender. At Neustandt anxious British officials demanded news of Hollard, 'the man who saved London', as Lieutenant General Sir Brian Horrocks KCB, KBE, DSO, MC described him. But Hollard was on his way to Sweden and was one of the first to be repatriated. He was awarded the DSO and the Croix de Guerre but refused all other reward for his work. He returned to engineering and died in 1993.

DESTROYING THE DOODLEBUGS

Hollard brought vital information to British intelligence in Switzerland in August 1943 (see opposite page). Days later his contact in Lausanne received a second visitor, this time from Luxembourg, carrying a message that a winged missile had been fired into the Baltic. Again in August, a Dane found a missile in the sand on the Danish island of Bornholm. He sketched it, and that drawing also made its way to London.

The reports came not long after information from Polish agents alerted the British to work going on at Peenemünde and led to RAF photo-reconnaissance. Further missions were flown to photograph sites in the Pas de Calais, and a comparison of the images proved beyond doubt that the sites were all part of the same plan. The top analyst was WAAF Constance Babington Smith, who picked out the dark elongated shape that looked rather like a railway ramp. The most striking building was a long, tunnel-like structure that ran straight until it curved at one end. From the air it had the shape of a ski lying on its side, and led to the sites being called 'ski sites'. The challenge was how to deal with them.

The first response was to attempt to destroy them by bombing. Peenemünde had been attacked as early as August 1943, with the loss of 41 bombers, and early in December strikes commenced against the 'ski sites' as part of Operation Crossbow. Some 96 targets were targeted, with priority given to those close to completion, and by March 1944 almost all had been either destroyed or to some extent damaged.

Nevertheless, because the Germans started building modified sites, omitting the easily identifiable 'ski'-shaped buildings, there were sufficient operational sites for the campaign to begin in June 1944. Sites were camouflaged to fool Spitfire pilots such as Flight Lieutenant Ken 'Paddy' French, who carried out dive-bombing raids and noted that: '… they would cut out a strip in the wood, cut down some trees, put the launching site into the wood, and then the rest of the trees: they pulled them together with strong wires so that looking down from above it still just looked like an ordinary wood.'

When the first bombs began to land in Britain, anti-aircraft guns were used against them, but the bombs were small, fast targets and they flew inconveniently in the space between the optimum altitude for engagement by the light anti-aircraft guns and that of the heavy anti-aircraft batteries. Although improvements in essential technologies such as fire control improved the success rate of the gunners, too many bombs got through and casualties mounted. One estimate calculated that, out of 8,617 bombs launched towards London, 2,340 had reached their target, killing 5,500 people and seriously injuring 16,000,[30] and at its peak a hundred bombs a day were being launched.

Churchill told Parliament on 3 April 1944: 'If the Germans imagine that the continuance of this present attack, which has cost them very dear in every branch of production, will have the slightest effect upon the course of the war or upon the resolve of the nation or upon the morale of the men, women

RIGHT: While examining a reconnaissance photograph of the top-secret facility at Peenemünde, Flight Officer Constance Babington Smith spotted a V1 on its launch ramp. Here she uses an enlargement of the photograph to brief a senior officer.

and children under fire they will only be making another of those psychological blunders for which they have so long been celebrated.... There is no question of diverting our strength from the extreme prosecution of the war, or of allowing this particular infliction to weaken in any way our energetic support of our Allies.'

Misinformation was a valuable tool in the fightback. Double agents reported bombs landing only in West London, encouraging the Germans to adjust the guidance system. These agents were so successful that the Germans believed them rather than the accurate information fed back by their own transmitting devices.

The RAF and the US Eighth Air Force were playing their parts, and the bombing of the Fieseler works at Kassel in October 1943 stopped the supply of V1s to Peenemünde for several months. Fighters were also used to attack the bombs in flight, though the only types fast enough to catch or stay with them were the Hawker Tempests, which fortuitously entered service in small numbers in January 1944 with 150 Wing; Mosquitoes; Spitfire Mark XIVs, with their Griffon engines; and P-51 Mustangs.

There were three ways of dealing with the V1s, none of them for the fainthearted. One was to use slipstream to send the bombs – called 'divers' by the RAF – spinning out of control. Captain J.P. Maridor, of 91 Squadron, who shared a kill on 5 July: 'Saw diver N. of Rye being attacked by a Mustang. Attack was made astern at 100 yds range saw strikes but one cannon jammed so closed into 50 yds and gave second burst. Diver went into slow turning dive so flew directly in front of diver and with slipstream caused it to spin in exploding in a field.'

The pilots of 91 Squadron, who had converted to the Mark XIV Spitfire, soon became experienced V1 chasers and invented the second technique, 'tipping':

'Collier's effort was a clear case of determination crowned at the last moment by success. He came across this particular "diver" just after it had crossed over Beachy and immediately gave chase. Getting within range he fired, with no apparent effect as it carried straight on. This peeved him somewhat, so he had another go, and in fact several other goes, but still

123

nothing happened, and what was worse, he ran clean out of ammo. By this time Ken was really swearing mad and was determined to do or die. He therefore formated with [flew in formation alongside] it and with his wing tipped it over. On his second attempt try [sic] down it went in a light spin, but it very nearly landed in the centre of a town. However it did no damage and F/O Collier thus brought into practice a new method of getting rid of these flying bombs.'[31]

Then there was the simple expedient of firing at it and risking a mid-air explosion that could destroy the attacking aircraft, too.

When Captain Jean Maridor was killed after firing at close range at a V1 heading straight for a military hospital, nobody who knew him doubted that he had taken a very deliberate decision. As an experienced pilot with 91 Squadron he had chased numerous flying bombs and destroyed 6½. On 3 August 1944, eight days before he was due to marry his English fiancée, Jean Lambourne, in Oxford, he had taken off from RAF Deanland at 12:15, and shortly afterwards spotted a 'diver' coming in over Rye. His first attack hit the bomb but failed to explode or bring it down; he tried again, pulling maximum power from the Griffon engine of his Mark XIV Spitfire, and closing to less than 50 yards (45 metres). After a burst from his cannons, the bomb exploded in front of him, but it ripped off his aircraft's wing. Maridor's Spitfire crashed close to the lake in the grounds of Benenden School in Kent, which, like many during the war, had been temporarily converted into a hospital.

As a small child growing up near Le Havre, Maridor had shown no heroic qualities. He was timid and easily distressed by noise, but when he was 4 years old, his parents took him to an air show and he became obsessed with aviation. His father paid for him to have a flight at the Bléville aerodrome, hoping it would cure him, but it had the opposite effect: the quiet boy dreamed of being a pilot, and as he grew up he spent all his spare time down at the aerodrome, helping to push the planes around.

On leaving school, Maridor – who as a boy had been terrified of men with beards – began to train as a barber; at the same time, encouraged by one of the pilots, he also took flying lessons, and he gained his basic licence in 1937 at the age of 16, making him France's youngest pilot. In 1939 he joined the Armée de l'Air, but in June 1940 he left France on the *Arandora Star* for England and joined the Forces Aériennes Françaises Libres.

In 1942 he was posted to 91 Squadron RAF, flying Spitfires for the first time alongside the Heninger brothers, and apart from a five-month posting to 615 Squadron he remained with 91 Squadron. Reserved yet passionately determined, Maridor reached the rank of captain, won the DFC and the Croix de Guerre with eight Palmes, and on 9 May 1943 General de Gaulle made him a Compagnon de la Liberation. At the time of his death his score stood at: 3½ aircraft destroyed, 2 probables and 3 damaged; 20 ships damaged or sunk; 6½ flying bombs brought down; and numerous ground targets attacked. After the war his body was repatriated to Le Havre. A piece of his aircraft is preserved at Benenden School.

For all their courage, enterprise and determination the RAF and the heavy anti-aircraft (HAA) gun crews could shoot down only a proportion of the V1s. The destruction was finally ended when the Allied advance that followed D-Day overran the sites and pushed the Germans back beyond striking range.

LEFT: French ace, Jean Maridor of 91 Squadron, with his arm in a sling after an incident involving a Canadian pilot in 1942.

BOIS CARRÉ LAUNCH SITE

The *Dig WW2* team found the buildings at Bois Carré surprisingly complete and it was possible to understand the operation of the whole site. The bombs arrived unassembled, and, with the exception of the wings, were put together in a large workshop.

The bombs were then transferred to the long 'ski' building, for storage. Dan walked into it and gazed around as Hollard's colleague, André Comps'

famous sketch map translated itself into bricks and mortar:

'This was the tunnel in which the V1 rockets were stored and you can see just how strong this casing is. You've got concrete blocks here, aggregate in the middle and then another set of concrete blocks; incredibly thick. The ceiling is … you can see the reinforcing rods there, this is reinforced concrete. They believed that these V1 rockets, of which there

BELOW: The annotated aerial reconnaissance image of the V1 launch site at Bois Carré, near Yvrenche, confirmed the construction of 'ski-sites' in the Pas de Calais and demonstrated how the Germans made use of small 'square woods' to hide their operations.

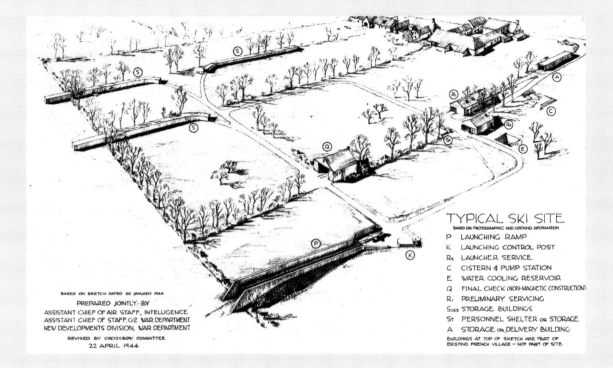

TYPICAL SKI SITE
BASED ON PHOTOGRAPHIC AND GROUND INFORMATION
P   LAUNCHING RAMP
K   LAUNCHING CONTROL POST
R₂   LAUNCHER SERVICE
C   CISTERN & PUMP STATION
E   WATER COOLING RESERVOIR
Q   FINAL CHECK (NON-MAGNETIC CONSTRUCTION)
R₁   PRELIMINARY SERVICING
Sₜₒ   STORAGE BUILDINGS
St   PERSONNEL SHELTER ᴏʀ STORAGE
A   STORAGE ᴏʀ DELIVERY BUILDING
BUILDINGS AT TOP OF SKETCH ARE PART OF
EXISTING FRENCH VILLAGE – NOT PART OF SITE.

BASED ON SKETCH DATED 20 JANUARY 1944
PREPARED JOINTLY BY
ASSISTANT CHIEF OF AIR STAFF, INTELLIGENCE
ASSISTANT CHIEF OF STAFF, G-2 WAR DEPARTMENT
NEW DEVELOPMENTS DIVISION, WAR DEPARTMENT
REVISED BY CROSSBOW COMMITTEE
22 APRIL 1944

ABOVE: The 'ski site' at Maisoncelle, based on a sketch dated 20 January 1944 and revised four months later.

could have been 20 in here at any one time, were war-winning weapons. No expense was spared to keep them safe. Interestingly, the Allies referred to this one as the "ski site", it's curved at the end there and it's very straight there and that's because any blast that went off at the entrance would be absorbed by this bend here and wouldn't set off a chain reaction of all the V1 rockets all the way down the tunnel and you can see that's 150 yards.'

Detonators were stored in a separate building to reduce the risk of disaster.

Most buildings included ferrous metals in their construction, even if it was only as door hinges. Dan moved on to another structure that was built without iron or steel: the Richthaus, in which the wings and detonator were fitted to the V1 and final adjustments made before launch.

'It was state of the art at the time but just before the rocket was fired they had to bring them in here and make sure that the guidance system was finely calibrated. If there were any ferrous materials near, the compass could be confused and the rockets could misfire and head off in the wrong direction. That's why there was no metal in this building at all. Even the door hinges were made out of wood. In fact you can see they've had to use almost Roman loadbearing concrete arches there because there was no metal reinforcing allowed.'

The V1 was launched on a 157-feet (48-metre) metal ramp, with a blast wall to protect it from bomb damage and offer some protection to the personnel, though they had a bunker to which they had to retreat. The steam catapult was powered by a high-pressure steam boiler in which hydrogen peroxide and potassium permanganate were mixed, engendering a violent reaction to create steam and water, leaving behind manganese oxide and a small amount of potassium as by-products. After each launch, the residues had to be washed off the ramp and out of the steam boiler using a high-pressure hose, requiring a building with a compressor and another to store soft water – hard water would leave limescale deposits.

Although the ramp is long gone, the blast wall remains, and Dan was able to replicate Michel Hollard's compass experiment.

'It's so striking, when you actually come here and see this V1 launch site, that this ramp is actually very inflexible. It's almost literally set in stone. You couldn't adjust it to fire at different targets. So this one is aimed at one particular spot and by looking at the compass we can work out where that is. That is 315 magnetic. So now we just place the compass down on the map. The arrow is where we are now. Let's see where 315 gets us … it places you directly pointing at London. This entire complex is designed to execute one very simple idea, and that is to send as much high explosives as possible that way towards London.'

THE REICHENBERG SUICIDE BOMB

Without a pilot, and at a time that predated sophisticated guidance systems, the V1 could not be used to target a specific building such as the Houses of Parliament or a military objective such as a capital ship. By the end of 1943, the idea of a piloted version had been mooted, and in 1944 Deutsches Forschungsinstitut für Segelfug designed the Fieseler Fi 103R, codenamed Reichenberg, with modifications that included ailerons, stick and rudder controls, and a cockpit forward of the overhead air intake that was fitted with basic instrumentation on a wooden panel.

Testing was carried out at Lanz, equidistant from Berlin and Hamburg, with the Reichenbergs released from Heinkel He 111s. After the first two prototype flights ended in fatal crashes, the test flying was given to Heinze Kensche and Hanna Reitsch. Both had near misses, including an incident in which Kensche lost a wing but managed to bail out.

While the Reichenberg went into production, recruiting volunteers for 5 Gruppe, Kampfegeschwader 200 began. The pilots quite literally signed away their lives, and the squadron became known as the 'Leonidas Staffel' – Leonidas being the king of ancient Sparta whose followers died to the last man at Thermopylae.

Before any pilots could be asked to sacrifice themselves, the project was cancelled for reasons that included Hitler's conviction that the war was not going so badly that such desperate tactics were needed and that the weapon was 'un-German'. The 175 or so Reichenbergs already completed were abandoned.

One was brought back to Britain in 1945 and exhibited at Farnborough that same year, along with other German aircraft. After that it was supposed to be

investigated by Bomb Disposal, but for the next 25 years it simply passed from one unit to another, deteriorating in the process. It broke its back and lost its original nose cone, the rear fuselage skinning needed replacing, the plywood of the wings had degraded, and the bottom of the cockpit had rusted through: it was destined for scrap, until rescued by Lashenden Air Warfare Museum in 1970.

At that time, expert restoration was technically and financially unfeasible; the museum could only stabilize the Reichenberg and carry out cosmetic work.

In 2007 Auktionshaus für Historische Technik, based near Munich, became interested in it while they were working on another example. The result was that amid frantic fundraising, Lashenden sent their machine to Germany for complete restoration. The work, which was completed at a cost of some £30,000, has brought the Fi 103R to as near flight status as possible. The cockpit has been restored with original instrumentation, the fuel and electrical systems are operational, and although the engine is in running order, the weapon must never fly.

TOP: Already a little battered, this Fi 103R-4 'Reichenberg' went on display at Farnborough in 1945. This is the weapon rescued and restored by Lashenden Air Warfare Museum.

ABOVE: The Fi 103R-4 'Reichenberg' in 1970 on its way to its new home at Lashenden.

PART 3

HOLDING THE FORT

Attack may well be the best form of defence, but after the First World War, and despite the rebirth of aggressive militarism in Hitler's Germany, there was little appetite in France and Britain for fighting another war, let alone starting one. This led to the policy of appeasement during the 1930s, from which Hitler concluded that just as Germany's occupation of Czechoslovakia had been rubber-stamped in Europe's corridors of power so would her invasion of Poland.

When it came to self protection, even in the new age of air power, Britain still derived considerable advantage from being an island, but France shared a long land border with Germany, and from 1930 the French Government set about constructing a massive steel and concrete defensive line in front of it, from Luxembourg to the Swiss border. The line was named after Minister of War André Maginot, who did not live to see its completion.

The Maginot Line was not conceived as a barrier on which a German army would break its teeth in futile and costly attacks, nor was it a continuous construction such as Hadrian's Wall; rather, it was a series of chunky concrete and steel emplacements designed to provide early warning of a sudden attack, give the French time to mobilize their own army, and redirect any German offensive. It was an impressive but expensive project that turned out to be a white elephant: a fortification for a past age. A second string of fortifications known as the Alpine Line covered the Franco-Italian border, and that fulfilled its purpose.

Unlike the later Atlantic Wall constructed by the Germans, and the coastal defences built by the British in 1940, the Maginot Line was far more than a 'crust'. It was divided along its length into 21 fortified sections, and had strength to a depth of at least 12 miles (20 kilometres). The primary structures within each sector were between one and four self-contained strong forts, or *ouvrages* ('works'), garrisoned by between 500 and 1,000 soldiers.

Each *ouvrage* was formed of six or more interconnected bunkers, surmounted by steel cupolas for guns, and equipped with power plants and railways. Concrete walls and roofs up to 10 feet (3 metres) thick protected against enemy bombs and artillery. Subordinate to the *ouvrages* were hundreds of blockhouses and, close to the border, control posts; all of it was linked by telephone. These structures, as well as lines of barbed wire, supplemented by roadblocks, stood in the way of invaders.

In May 1940, the Germans advanced to the Maginot Line, but this was merely a feint, as was the invasion of Belgium. The great architect of German tank warfare, General Heinz Guderian, was busy tearing up the French script by leading 1,500 tanks at breakneck speed through the mountainous forest of the Ardennes that the French had considered impassable by armoured divisions. On 13 May, four days after the offensive had begun, Guderian crossed the River

ABOVE: Anti-tank defences snaking along the Franco German border as part of the Maginot Line.

Meuse and began the thrust towards the Channel ports that drove the British and French armies onto the beaches of Dunkirk.

The Germans had constructed their equivalent of the Maginot Line along Germany's borders with France, Luxembourg, Belgium and the Netherlands just before the outbreak of the war, most of it parallel to the French line. It was not of the same complexity nor, for the most part, of equal strength, and it came into the war only in 1944, after D-Day, when the Allied troops were advancing to Germany. Hitler had referred to the line as 'the Westwall' in 1939, but the British regarded it as the successor to

the Siegfried Line of the First World War, hence the song that appeared in the same year:

'We're going to hang out the washing on the Siegfried Line.
Have you any dirty washing, mother dear?
We're gonna hang out the washing on the Siegfried Line

Cause the washing day is here.
Whether the weather may be wet or fine
We'll just rub along without a care.
We're going to hang out the washing on the Siegfried Line
If the Siegfried Line's still there.'[1]

Much of the Westwall was demolished after the war, but interest in it is now growing, and enthusiasts are visiting and recording what remains, from bunkers to the concrete 'dragon's teeth' tank-traps in the Eifel region. The French have also seen a growth of interest in the Maginot Line bunkers, some of which are now museums. Structures in both lines have also found new leases of life as varied as houses, a mushroom farm and a protected bat roost.

The Westwall project was to be dwarfed by the next German defensive building project, the Atlantic Wall, which took place during the war itself, but from 1939 until 1942, fears of an Allied invasion were well down the list of Hitler's priorities. Instead, it was in Britain and Northern Ireland where an urgent need for supplementary defences – technological, concrete and imaginative – was suddenly apparent. From Magilligan Point and Scapa Flow to Dover and St. Michael's Mount, the landscape is still speckled with the evidence of programmes of deception and defence that were put into operation before and during the war, accelerating dramatically during 1940 when the invasion threat was at its height. Although much of the construction work was dismantled either systematically or ad hoc in the post-war decades, and erosion has taken a toll – particularly of

ABOVE: A formidable triple casement along the Maginot Line with 75-millimetre guns protruding from the small embrasures.

the remaining crust of coastal fortifications – concrete pillboxes still squat in fields with dogged persistence, spigot mortar emplacements nestle in grass verges, winds scourge anti-tank defences, filigree transmitting towers scrape the skyline and the ghosts of moorland decoy sites reveal themselves in satellite images.

CHAIN HOME RADAR, THE COASTAL GUARDIAN

In 1935 the only early air raid warning system in the whole of Britain had consisted of a solitary concrete acoustic mirror sited on Romney Marshes. The answer to that glaring weakness in the nation's defences came as a by-product of experiments in VHF radio transmission by the Post Office, which in those days had responsibility for telegraphy and telephony. In 1931 the engineers had complained about interference from passing aircraft, and when the significance of this was realized, serious government work began. On 26 February 1935 the ability of radar to detect aircraft was proved in an experiment at Daventry. Almost immediately the government poured money into the creation of a chain of coastal radar stations around the country, including Northern Ireland, each one operating horizontally polarized radiation. During the war, operators became adept at counting enemy aircraft flying in close formation, a vital skill in estimating the strength of an enemy raid.

Very few of the masts remain, but it is not unusual to find the ancillary buildings that housed the generators, operators and all the equipment.

Millisle and Kilkeel both have good examples – stencilled on the Kilkeel building is the lingering warning: 'No admittance except to authorized personnel. Danger 3300 volts.'

By 1945 there were approximately 50 Chain Home (CH) stations, of which the 21 constructed between the Isle of Wight and the Orkney Islands shared the same distinctive characteristics: three or four steel transmitter towers, 360 feet (110 metres) high and 180 feet (55 metres) apart, each with three cantilever platforms; and four 240 feet (73-metre) high receiving towers that were made of wood, fitted with three antenna stacks and looked not unlike scaled-down versions of the Eiffel Tower. CH stations could pick up a German aircraft 80 miles (128 kilometres) away if it was flying at 10,000 feet (3,050 metres), dropping to 50 miles (80 kilometres) at 5,000 feet (1,525 metres). Later in the war they

OPPOSITE: The last Chain Home Radar transmitting mast at RAF Stenigot, near Louth, Lincolnshire, has survived because it is used for the Climbing Aptitude Test by the Army Careers Office, and is now a Grade II Listed Monument. On a clear day, the North Sea and the Humber Bridge can be seen.

BELOW: Using the Cathode Ray Tube, a radar operator at RAF Bawdsey Chain Home station, plots an aircraft in May 1945.

detected the approach of V2 rockets, making CH the world's first ballistic missile detection system by a decade – and by enabling the trajectory of a rocket to be plotted, the launch site could be identified, which allowed Bomber Command to destroy it.[2]

In 1938 it was realized that low-flying aircraft could slip 'under the radar' and consequent work on the problem led to the installation of Chain Home Low (CHL) radar, capable of detecting aircraft flying as low as 500 feet (150 metres) when 25 miles (40 kilometres) away. As the war progressed, the Germans worked out that by coming in at 100 feet (30 metres) – a task for a highly skilled pilot – they could thwart even CHL. The development of the cavity magnetron by John Randall and Dr Harry Boot gave rise to the Chain Home Extra Low (CHEL) that made it impossible for German pilots to avoid detection even at very low altitude.

In 1943, after the fear of invasion had faded and the home-based RAF and USAAF squadrons were on the offensive, radar operator Hilda Pearson reported for duty at Bawdsey Manor, a top-secret government research facility in Suffolk, on the east coast of England, where the first of the CH facilities had been constructed in 1936.

'The WAAF girls occupied the first floor of the Manor House, while the men lived in wooden huts in the grounds. We worked in the Receiver Block, a building with no windows and only one door, where the only people allowed in were the operators and mechanics with an Officer in charge. We worked in four shifts over 24 hours, with most of our free time being spent in having a meal and sleeping.

As far as I remember, the crew each time consisted of three operators, two mechanics and the Officer in charge. One operator would sit in front of the receiving screen wearing a headset and mouthpiece which was connected to the main Plotting Room at Fighter Command, and she would be reporting every movement that she saw on the screen using a special formula of words and symbols. Next to her sat another operator as assistant and backup. The third operator would be waiting her turn to take over. The Officer in charge was connected to Headquarters by telephone. The mechanics were kept busy doing mysterious things to the machinery, on which no speck of dust was allowed – between us we did all the cleaning of the room as no domestic staff was allowed in. This was a time when organized groups of bombers would leave East Anglian airfields for Germany, returning later in smaller straggling groups or single planes, some of which might be showing a special distress signal which we could pick up on our screen and an Air-Sea-Rescue unit would be notified of its position.'[3]

The value of the system cannot be overemphasized. Some post-war American historians have criticized it as primitive, but based on tried and tested technology it was ready in time for the war and it gave the squadrons of Fighter Command precious time in which to scramble and intercept the enemy.

ANTI-AIRCRAFT (A/A) BATTERIES

CH radar and courage, however, were not enough during the Blitz that began in the late summer of 1940. The heavy night-time bombing of Britain's cities is popularly portrayed as Hitler's attempt to break the country's resistance by terrorizing its citizens, but while that was undeniably a component, the primary targets were industrial, logistical and military sites. Top of the list were the aircraft factories and aerodromes that allowed the RAF to continue the Battle of Britain, and from early 1941 ports became particularly vulnerable. Only eight RAF squadrons were equipped with the airborne interception radar that was essential for fighting at night, and although the powerful Bristol Beaufighter, fitted with A1 Mark IV radar, was coming into service it was plagued by performance issues.

The task of bringing down the night-raiding German bombers fell to the heavy anti-aircraft batteries (HAA) and searchlights of the Royal Regiment of Artillery (RA), but a large number of guns and searchlights had been

BELOW: A female anti-aircraft gun crew marching past their 3.7-inch gun.

abandoned during the evacuation from France, and the procurement not just of replacements but of additional numbers proceeded slowly. The gun-laying radar that existed was inadequate to the task of tracking moving targets in dark skies, in addition to which the batteries were in action round the clock, leading to exhaustion among the men and wear to the gun barrels. Once a battery opened up, it became an unprotected target in its own right. Crews suffered casualties from both enemy action and from accidents, but they shot down 169½ night bombers between October 1940 and 12 May 1941 – three being shared with the RAF. How many they damaged and how many they dissuaded is an incalculable figure.

At the start of the war, Belfast was seen as being at very low risk of an attack, and had no protection, but when Northern Ireland found itself close to the heart of the war effort, 16 HAA sites were set up to protect the city. The approach to Derry (Londonderry) along Lough Foyle also became heavily defended, especially after American forces arrived.

HAA batteries were constructed to a generally consistent plan: a set of

BELOW: Looking for enemy aircraft. The women of the A.T.S. who served with A/A Batteries were known as Ack-Ack Girls.

sunken square or octagonal gun pits spaced around the perimeter of an arc or circle, each with its own set of built-in ammunition lockers. At the centre stood a command post, while ancillary buildings for radar, accommodation and stores, together with shelters and pillboxes for defence, were located in the vicinity.

The batteries, some with searchlight units attached, were manned not only by men from the RA but also by women from the Auxiliary Territorial Service (ATS). The first women began training in the spring of 1941, and eventually there were some all-female units. The most high-profile recruit was, from 1942, the Prime Minister's daughter Mary (later Lady) Soames; in January 1944 she was one of those helping to defend Britain from the V1 rockets, and in a letter to her father signed herself 'YOUR DOODLE GUNNER'. Elsie Lynch was a volunteer who quickly took to gunnery work:

'A gunsite consisted of about eighty personnel, male and female, gun crews, predictor operators, telephonists, clerks, cooks, orderlies, drivers and of course radar crews. … When the guns opened fire all hell was let loose, anything that was standing on barrack room shelves came tumbling down and even wearing our rubber earplugs did not deaden the sound. Unfortunately enemy air raids were nearly always in the middle of the night, the alarm bell would ring and "Action Stations" was the cry. We jumped out of bed pulling on battle dress over our pyjamas, grabbing tin hat and respirator and running a good way to the G.L. [gun-laying] set, or the transmitter whichever we were manning, if it was the transmitter we had first of all to start the diesel engine.'[4]

Irene Foxwell volunteered for war service and deliberately turned down administrative work in favour of becoming an Operator Fire Control with a gun battery in the early days of aircraft detection by radar. After training at Oswestry she served with batteries across the country, often in freezing winter conditions on the east coast.

'A profusion of aerials high on the cabin roof had to be cleaned, checked and greased – a stomach-churning experience if heights were not your forte! The massive diesel engine, the source of energy supply, had to be cranked manually, and at our first attempts we jumped back fearfully as it shuddered into life, like

BELOW: Exposed to the elements, a searchlight crew tries to pick up and track German aircraft, to enable the anti-aircraft batteries a target. Images of the long beams of light that swept the night skies over strategic targets have become a symbol of home front resistance.

some monster awakening from sleep. Very soon we became quite adept at this task and came to enjoy the cleaning and oiling necessary to keep it in pristine condition.

In essence the transmitter was a mini power station which transmitted signals from its huge aerials into space. It was on a turntable and when in operation had to be revolved continually through 360 degrees until a plane was actually being "followed" by the receiver, when instructions would be given to keep to a certain bearing. Revolving the transmitter cabin was done manually by each of the two operators in turn.

The cabin containing the receiving equipment was placed some distance away. Here the other four members of the team operated. Number One was in charge and when operational would be in telephone communication with the Officer in charge of the plotting-room situated underground at a Command Post. Number two was the range finder, Number three bearing and Number four elevation. This cabin was very cramped and once inside and seated, there was no room to move. In front of each operator was a small cathode-ray screen on which appeared a line of green light. This would be distorted upwards to a bleep each time a signal was picked up from planes in the vicinity. On the command to "follow" each operator lined up against the bleep, and kept it in alignment.

It seemed quite eerie at first, sitting in complete darkness apart from the glow from the tubes. In the case of range and elevation, keeping aligned was done by means of hand operated wheels, but the bearing operator sat astride a bearing column and had to revolve the whole cabin manually. Later, training complete, this came to be my task – I still have large biceps.

… After locating the plane, data was transmitted electrically along cables to the plotting table in the Command Post and thence to the gun dials. We soon mastered the mechanics but becoming proficient was a longer process.'[5]

To distinguish friendly aircraft, an 'identification friend or foe' (IFF) system was in place. Allied aircraft emitted a tiny beep for which the operators had to be on the alert when aircraft were picked up on their approach.

More than a thousand Heavy, Light and 'Z'[6] A/A sites were built, of which less than 200 remain; 60 are considered of national importance.

HOODWINKING THE HUN

Radar could warn of the approach of German aircraft; the RAF could attack them, but in the expectation that the Luftwaffe would succeed in dropping many of their bombs a great deal of creative thought went into how to deceive them into hitting the wrong target.

Proposals to build decoys that from the air would look like factories were rejected in 1940 on cost grounds: the Swinton Committee calculated that each dummy structure would cost £20,000–£30,000. An exception was made for four aircraft factories and

ABOVE: A boiling oil fire burned spectacularly, and was easily visible from the air. It could be set off manually or electrically.

two wireless telegraphy stations operated by the Air Ministry. In May 1940 the Civil Defence Committee approved an experiment in decoy lighting on the moors above Sheffield, simulating not just the glow of the city's massive Templeborough Rolling Mills but other potential targets including Chesterfield's railway marshalling yards:

'The northern site (corresponding to Sheffield) covers about four miles in length on the Bradfield and Foulerton [Fullerton] moors, and the southern (corresponding to Chesterfield) upwards of a mile on the Curbar moors. The relative positions of the two sites are closely similar to those of the originals, but the general line of the northern site is roughly NNE instead of NE as in the original. This and certain minor departures from the initial plan were necessitated by the extremely rough nature of the ground.

Details
The main features of the northern site comprise:
(a) a row of mimic furnaces spaced at intervals over a line 1000 yards in length, representing those at Templeborough.
(b) four railway marshalling yards, representing those at Rotherham, Grimesthorpe, Wicker and Queen Road.
(c) two stretches of factory roadway.

These features are sited in relative positions corresponding to the originals, except that the scale is only about two-thirds of the actual.

(a) consists of a total of twenty-four powerful flood-lights, with orange screens, projected obliquely on the ground, all direct light above the horizontal being cut off. By means of dimmers the glow produced will be brought quickly up to full intensity and then gradually switched off.

(b) and (c) are practically replicas of the originals.

The southern site comprises a marshalling yard (a replica of that at Chesterfield) and a factory road.

It is intended in both cases to give extension to the scheme by distributing some 120 hurricane lamps over suitable areas corresponding to Sheffield and Chesterfield. It has not hitherto been possible to operate these, except a few for testing purposes, because of the difficulty of extinguishing them quickly in the event of an air raid warning.

Preparations are well advanced for a number of oil fires on each site, to be started electrically from a distance if required....'[8]

The trial took place on 15 July. The following day Sir Thomas Gardiner, Joint Secretary at the Ministry of Home Security, received a memo:

'Lord Harlech [North-Eastern Regional Commissioner for Civil Defence] has just telephoned from Leeds to say that Brigadier Smythe who has just taken over command of a Brigade at Leeds to which is assigned the duty of guarding the reservoirs outside the City, has been into his office to report that last night by the order of Colonel Jacobs Larcombe, R.E.,[9] all the reservoir area was brilliantly lighted in order to attract enemy planes away from the City and induce them to bomb the reservoirs instead. This was done without any previous information being given to the Region or the higher military authorities, and Lord Harlech is extremely concerned as to the result of any such procedure. In his opinion if the reservoirs are bombed, the water will escape and cause a flood which will do immense damage in the city itself. Both he and the military authorities are completely opposed to the scheme and wish to know immediately on whose orders Colonel J. Larcombe is acting. All that is known at present is that Colonel Larcombe says he is acting on direct instructions from the Home Office.'[10]

Gardiner apologized for the communications failure, and passed on the Air Ministry's assurance that the dams could not be accidentally breached by an enemy bomb (as was subsequently proved to be true when the RAF began to make plans for attacking a certain set of dams on the Ruhr). The Commissioner, though mollified, voiced a new concern:

'But what I specially want your guidance on is, what can I say to the Civic Authorities, and eventually the public about this lit up dummy

OPPOSITE: Colonel Turner (front row, centre) and the staff of his secret department at the Air Ministry team who implemented his programme of decoy and deception.

THE DICTATOR OF DUMMIES

A career engineer who joined the Royal Engineers in 1900, Colonel Sir John Turner CB, DSO was chief engineer to the air force in India when he retired from the British Army in 1931 at the age of 50. For the next eight years he held the post of Director of Works and Buildings at the Air Ministry, overseeing the design and building of RAF stations at a time of great expansion, before retiring, or so he thought, in the summer of 1939. When in September the Air Council decided it needed a retired officer to take charge of its secret decoy airfield programme, Colonel Turner was, if not the first choice, at least an inspired one. A qualified pilot, he had drive, zeal and, above all, imagination.

Tenders for dummy aircraft were already being evaluated when Turner took up his post, and he was immediately impressed with the cost-effective Wellington produced by Sound City Films, based at Shepperton Studios. It was the beginning of a long and productive relationship that saw the techniques of the film studio translate into credible aircraft mock-ups. Crews detailed to man the decoy sites were taken to Shepperton to learn how to erect the aircraft, and given a welcoming speech written by Turner, explaining the

work, and enjoining them to absolute secrecy. By the end of the year his department was coordinating and implementing the national decoy strategy.

Not everyone was convinced. An unsigned minute,[7] probably from someone on the Ministry of Home Security's Camouflage Committee, complained that Turner, backed by the Air Ministry, had encroached on their work and recommended that the writer get involved with Turner's work on decoy factories 'because we are not at all sure he is going the cheapest way about it … I understand that he has put himself in the hands of the film trade, and I am not at all sure that they are the cheapest or the best people to produce this kind of work'.

From February 1944 until D-Day+6, Turner worked on the decoy lighting aspect of Operation Fortitude – a plan to convince the Germans of a build-up of troops in East Anglia ready for a landing in the Pas de Calais that would take place after those in Normandy. He retired at the end of the war, having ensured that the secret work begun by his department would be continued. He died in 1958 after devoting his retirement years to The Children's Society.

ABOVE: A group of raised braziers – basket fires – burn fiercely.

Sheffield? The moment it is lit up even experimentally it will become known and reported over a wide area. Anyone living high up in the top part of Sheffield will see it and report breaches of the blackout to the Police. The City will become full of rumour and some explanation must be given. … Mystery leads to talk and the exercise of the imagination. … In England you cannot keep secret anything so unsecret as lighting up an area of moorland near a great city….'[11]

Convinced by the success of airfield decoys, the Civil Defence Committee gave the go-ahead to construct more civil decoys, and, importantly, gave responsibility for coordination to Colonel Turner (see page 145). To

protect the civilian population, decoys were, as far as possible, to be sited in sparsely populated areas, with no main light or fire within 400 yards (365 metres) of a building, 800 yards (730 metres) of a village or three-quarters of a mile to a mile (1.2–1.6 kilometres) of a small town.

They were not to be sited near main railways lines and hospitals (particularly mental hospitals), standing crops should be avoided, and in cases of considerable risk to an occupied building, the occupants should be 'removed' and the building requisitioned.

The Sheffield decoy took hits, but Turner closed it in October 1940 because it was wrongly positioned: it was *north* of the city and, therefore, did not intercept the bombers' approach.

By then, many more civil decoys were operational or under construction, and Turner developed and refined the simple creosote fires first used on the airfields to protect cities.

The Germans possessed electronic navigation systems based in France to direct bombers. The first, Knickbein, was uncovered by the codebreakers at Bletchley Park and the RAF's 80 (Signals) Wing was thereafter able to jam it. Its sophisticated successor, the X-Gerät, used three radio beams to a) direct the pilot towards the target, b) indicate the point at which to commence the bombing run, and c) pinpoint the target. Bletchley uncovered that, too, but not quickly enough to save Coventry from the bombing raid that destroyed so much of the city on 14/15 June 1940. Turner responded by putting in place large civil fire decoys to protect large cities; the majority of them were in the Midlands but Clydeside, Humberside, Tyneside, London and the Bristol Channel were also covered. Called 'Starfish sites', they were commissioned in the first six months of 1941.

The creative minds of Sound City Films at Shepperton Studios were involved. Raised basket fires, like braziers, were set ablaze by flare cans of creosote, themselves electrically ignited. Coal fires, crib fires, boiling oil fires – into which bursts of water and oil flowed to create spectacular flames; all burned in a different way to give an overall realism. Firebreaks had to be dug around the sites and between fire groups.

The fires were lit only when the first bombers passed over, so that each

aircraft would assume one of their number had identified the target and started the bombing run, thus prompting them all to release their bombs. Several 'Starfish sites', notably the one at Portsmouth, fulfilled their purpose admirably; others were rarely or never hit.

After D-Day, the process of dismantling the sites began, and today the firebreaks that remain in place are often the only visible clue to a site. Those 'Starfish sites' whose shadows remain are usually to be found situated on undeveloped areas. Middlesbrough's Sneaton Moor 'Starfish' and the outlines of the experimental decoy marshalling yard on Curbar Moor are both visible from the air. Control buildings are more likely to have survived: sold or given by the Air Ministry to the landowners on whose property they stood.

ABOVE: A 'Starfish site' contained fires of different types, burning sawdust/scrap wood, oil and paraffin. This increased realism because different targets would burn in different ways in response to bombing.

ABOVE: The nailboard has been set up and Dan prepares to complete the circuit. Success: the decoy fire begins to burn as dusk comes down over Corrody.

THE DERRY DECOY

Two decoys for Derry were constructed just south of the city in 1942, at Glebetown, near Corrody, and at Lisglass, codenamed SF50(a) and SF50(b) respectively. Earlier that year, six had been set up to protect Belfast. The latter's 'Starfish sites' should have been built in 1941, in the wake of the bombing, but there were serious fears that the IRA would betray their existence to the Germans at the embassy in Dublin and possibly imperil the entire decoy programme. To conceal their purpose, the two Derry and six Belfast decoys were stated to be RAF ammunition dumps; they were heavily guarded and surrounded with barbed and Dannert concertina wire. During construction, lorries carrying bombs arrived quite openly – while the Starfish materials came in under cover. The fires were different to those elsewhere, mainly consisting of compacted greaseproof paper soaked in oils, and they were hidden from public view in fake huts. In February 1943, a mere three months after becoming operational, the two Derry sites fell victim to Air Ministry cuts that closed a number of sites in order to release staff for other duties, much to Turner's dismay.

Dan went to Glebetown with Irish historian Richard Doherty to see the site of the Derry decoy. All that remains is the bunker that housed the generator and acted as a bomb shelter for the crew. It is more exposed than it would have been during the war now that the protective earth has been stripped away, but the interior is solid and well preserved. As Richard Doherty explained: 'If you look at it in terms of the size of the city in proportion to any other city in the United Kingdom outside London, Derry is the most heavily defended one, which underlines its importance to the Royal Navy and the Allies generally in the Battle of the Atlantic.'

Outside, on the windswept slope above Derry, pyrotechnics expert Donal Neill from Pains Fireworks was preparing to show Dan just how easy it could be to set the whole slope ablaze to simulate a burning city, using technology that was available and might have been used in 1942. He filled a brazier with wood and peat, both available locally, drenched them in inflammable liquid, inserted a portfire type of fuze, and wired up a small ignition charge using standard two-core wire. He then ran the wire to a nailboard (in this case the 'nails' were modern plastic wire connectors) and wired one strand into the 'common' side of the board, which connected to one terminal of a battery. The other strand was wired to a single connector on the opposing side of the board. If more braziers had been set up, every wire would have been run to the board, with one strand from each wired into the common side and each of the other strands wired into its own individual connector. To start the fire, Dan took the wire attached to the other battery terminal and touched the individual connector, completing the circuit and initiating ignition of the charge. Almost immediately, the brazier began to blaze.

Had there been a number of braziers, the loose terminal wire would have been wiped down the whole line of connectors, setting off one charge after another.

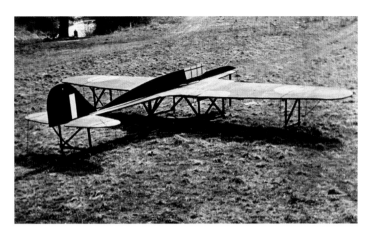

AIRFIELD DECOYS

The civil decoys and 'Starfish sites' were preceded by the use of decoys at airfields. Well before the war the protection of airfields had been seen as a particular concern, and the idea of creating dummy replicas of existing RAF stations was debated during the 1930s, but not until 1938 did the Air Ministry apply serious thought to the subject. It was quickly recognized that such decoys would not only be very expensive to build, but also that they would not be effective during daylight hours. An alternative solution to the problem of daylight raids lay in the policy of aircraft dispersal: spreading aircraft around their base, rather than parking them in groups, and creating satellite airfields, close to but not less than 5 miles (8 kilometres) from the parent base. Ideally these satellites were to be civil aerodromes, but as the growth in civil aviation had not produced sufficient of these, many would have to be created in fields and on other open ground.

Because the satellite stations would be very basic – hardly more than a dummy flare path and a few tents or

ABOVE: From the air it looked like a parked Spitfire, but the wings and fuselage of this dummy aircraft are as two-dimensional as those of a toy balsa-wood glider.

dummy huts for accommodation, equipment and communication – faking *those* would be comparatively simple, especially with the addition of a few dummy aircraft to increase verisimilitude.

There was considerable enthusiasm for night decoys because they could be sited almost anywhere and depended primarily on lighting to create the illusion of their 'parent' airfield. Night-lighting decoys were designated as 'Q lightings' but more usually referred to as 'Q sites', while day decoys were 'K sites'. Some fulfilled both roles and had dual designations.

R. Howlett, a young aircraft hand (ACH) general duties, had volunteered for a posting to RAF Mildenhall but was to be stationed at the nearby Cavenham decoy site (Q/K30a), which was 'to act as a magnet, for the bombs intended in our case for Mildenhall. … The word "suicide squad" was bandied around, without any real seriousness.'[12] Before his squad was sent to Suffolk, their first task was to learn how to assemble dummy aircraft: 'Our particular ones were Wellingtons – known as "Wimpey's". The wings, fusilage [fuselage] and tail-planes were all in sections and having been manoevred [sic] into position by a gang of strong men they were bolted together. The skeleton upon which they were built was made of tubular scaffolding. All this equipment was made at Shepperton film studios. It was quite an achievement, and accurate in all the details.'

The site proved to be a heath covered with gorse, holes, mounds and scrub, and while Howlett's unit were clearing the land and turning it into a plausible airfield they lived under tarpaulins hung from the trees. The dummy aircraft arrived and were assembled, covered in white linen and painted in wartime camouflage by the artistically talented. 'With the aid of a string and a pencil, the roundels were drawn. The tailplane marking and the identification letters also followed. It was obvious that the A.C.H was a very versatile animal.'[13]

With the flare path installed and a phone link from Mildenhall running to the dugout, the decoy was up and running by the end of April 1940:

'For several nights we were called upon to break the four minute mile to the shelter from our camp on the other side of the site. The drill was fairly simple. "Ops" would ring through and the operator on duty at our end would relay the message to the guard. He in turn would walk in, shout out "yellow warning". This was merely a standby. A few minutes later it would probably be "Red warning" – "Raiders imminent". It also meant within minutes the flare-path would be switched on, inviting any enemy aircraft in the vicinity ... to bomb the site. Upon the receipt of the latest information it was no use hanging around. The dress was pyjamas, greatcoat, boots unlaced, or gumboots, plus a rifle, gas mask and other sundry equipment.'[14]

Cavenham was bombed and strafed on several occasions, and two UXBs ('unexploded bomb') were reported to the Bomb Disposal Unit. On one occasion it experienced a very near miss:

'"Red" warnings during this time were coming through all the time. We became quite accustomed to piling down the shelter. There were chairs and a table there, with packs of cards and games to while away the hours of the night. No-one paid much attention to the noise of the aircraft overhead this night, it was quite customary for our aircraft to be going out on raids, at the same time that enemy aircraft were over this country. Some of the chaps were playing cards, and in a corner Fred Rednall, as studious as ever, was concentrating upon a game of draughts. Suddenly the chatter was stilled as the unmistakable crump of exploding bombs was heard. Looking back, I do not recall any fear or panic when it was realised that the nearest bomb was mere feet away. Coupled with this, was the smell of the bombs themselves, and the damp earth that had been disrupted. Immediately after the initial silence, noise broke out again, with everyone shouting in unison. Above it all, as impersonal as ever, came the voice of Fred Rednall calling, "I say you chaps, not so much noise, I can't concentrate on my game".'[15]

Night-lighting decoy fields were a worrying source of potential confusion to RAF pilots. Howlett's team had to fire Verey cartridges to dissuade a brace of de Havilland Tiger Moths from landing, and he recalled being roused by Rednall with the news that: '"A kite has just landed on the site. I think it's a Wimpy." There on the flare path was a Wellington, standing on its nose.' The bomber was repaired and, while

Howlett and his comrades watched in trepidation, the pilot made a successful take off. A similar incident involving a Wellington occurred at Nazeing Common, the 'Q site' protecting North Weald, but the damage was too great for on-site repair and the bomber had to be dismantled and carted away.

Colonel John Turner had noted a tendency for bombers to drop bombs on areas that were already on fire. He capitalized on this by creating decoy airfield fires in tins of creosote with flammable roofing felt hung above to create a realistic impression of what was to be categorized as a 'large sputtering fire'. These 'real' fires were sited at a number of decoy airfields, but not at Cavenham.

By the end of 1941 Cavenham was redundant and soon dismantled. Today the ground is farmland and betrays no evidence of its wartime activity. Most 'K' and 'Q' sites were intentionally insubstantial with little permanent construction, but among those of which some solid traces remain are the decoys at Maxey, Downholland Moss and Nazeing Common.

The success of the decoys varied. The day decoys were far less effective than the night ones, and evaluating how many bombs were deliberately dropped on those night decoy sites is impossible. Only bombs dropped on, or very close to, a site were counted, which immediately excludes any that were dropped in response to the sight of the decoy lights but which fell wide of the target. The Air Historical Branch calculated this at what it conceded to be a very conservative average of 5 percent.

All the above were designed to keep Britain safe from the threat of invasion

and in a position to continue the war. In May 1940 the government was forced to implement plans to counter the German invasion that would certainly follow any failure of the RAF to win the Battle of Britain and of the Royal Navy to maintain command of territorial waters. A large-scale amphibious assault could take place at any suitable spot along the south and east coasts of the British mainland, and there were additional fears that Hitler might consider a landing in Eire, which, if successful, would give him the further option of a west coast invasion.

DRAWING A LINE

'The immediate object is to divide England into several small fields surrounded by a hedge of anti-tank obstacles which is strong defensively,

OPPOSITE: In February 1945 the Secretary of State for Dominion Affairs, Lord Cranborne, set out the extensive military cooperation which Britain had received from Eire. This clearly contradicted the erroneous perception that the Government of Eire was pro-German.

using natural accidents of the ground where possible. Should Armoured Fighting Vehicles attack or airborne attacks break into the enclosures the policy will be to close the gate by blocking the crossing over the obstacles and to let in the "dogs" in the shape of armoured formations, or other troops, to round up the cattle.'[16]

Southern Command used this farming metaphor to describe the concept of the Stop Line. The existing combination of natural barriers and man-made obstructions, such as rivers, canals and railway cuttings, augmented by new fortifications, would pen invaders into well-defined areas, holding them up until regular troops could arrive to deal with them. The fortifications included a range of pillboxes, roadblocks, anti-tank trenches, spigot mortars and other types of gun emplacement. They were concentrated in the south and the east of England, which were considered the most likely landing sites, and there were concentric rings around London.

Stop Lines were set up by the Home Defence Executive, which was run by the C-in-C Home Forces Sir Edmund Ironside, until his replacement by General Brooke in July 1940, after which more emphasis was given to coastal defences and mobile forces. Whether the forces of the Volunteer Defence League (renamed the Home Guard in July 1940) could have used the Stop Lines to hold up a determined German invasion until professional troops arrived is a moot point.

The fear that German troops would land in Eire led to similar precautions being taken in Northern Ireland to those on the mainland, based around CH radar to give early warning and on Stop Lines to halt the enemy. From Newry in the south to Coleraine in the north, a line bisected the province vertically, following the course of the Newry Canal, Lough Neagh and the River Bann. To the east of that line the province was further divided in five loosely horizontal lines: Carnlough Bay to Lough Neagh; Larne to Antrim; Holywood through Belfast and along the River Lagan; Lough Neagh to Ardmillan; and Portadown to Dundrum. A separate defensive ring encircled Belfast, and Derry was also heavily protected.

The pillbox at Portna, near Kilrea, was part of the Newry to Coleraine stop line, and it commands an excellent view down the Bann Navigation, covering one of the five locks between Lough Neagh and the sea. It is remarkable not only for the biblical reference above one of the embrasures that reminded the guards to take their duties seriously, but also for the quality of its preservation: it still contains some of the wooden shelves and iron shutters; the door is intact, as is the gate into the small defensive courtyard in front of the door.

One form of defence exclusive to Northern Ireland among the home nations was the advance laying of explosive charges, primarily to demolish bridges over canals and rivers. The River Bann and the Newry Canal had a significant number of crossings that could have been blown up at a moment's notice, and the Craigavon Bridge in Derry was wired for destruction in the event of a German invasion from Donegal. Local rumour

However he went on to say that the problem I stated did exist and he would assure me that if the situation arose he would deal with it as a realist. The moment he was assured that aggression had taken place in serious form or was likely to take place in serious form beyond the capacity of local forces he would at once summon our assistance.

I said that provided we had that basic undertaking progress could be made in our plans and that next week I had hoped to have General Harrison in Dublin to establish the machinery of liaison. If we took the step of sparing equipment when our resources were so strained it was not difficult for him to draw his own inferences as to our attitude.

*   *   *   *   *   *   *   *

Yours, &c.,

J. L. MAFFEY.

P.S.—When this comes up again I will stress the need for the special equipment and have our men handling it if a sudden emergency arose in the near future.

J. L. M.

FACILITIES OBTAINED FROM THE GOVERNMENT OF EIRE DURING THE WAR

W.X. 101/92.   No. 50.

(Top Secret.)

[A note of these facilities formed the annex to a memorandum by the Secretary of State for Dominion Affairs dated the 21st February, 1945 (W.R. 208/177), on the position of Eire in connexion with the question of inviting neutrals to attend the San Francisco Conference.]

In general, the Eire Government were willing to accord the United Kingdom Government any facilities which would not be regarded as overtly prejudicing their attitude of neutrality. In particular, they: —

(a) agreed to the use of Lough Foyle by the United Kingdom for naval and air purposes. The ownership of the Lough was disputed, but the Eire authorities tacitly did not press their claim in the then conditions and also ignored any flying by United Kingdom aircraft over the Donegal shore of the Lough, which was necessary in certain wind conditions to enable flying-boats to take off from the Lough (see No. 90);

(b) agreed to the use by United Kingdom aircraft based on Lough Erne of a corridor over Eire territory and territorial waters for the purpose of flying out to the Atlantic;

(c) arranged for the immediate transmission to the United Kingdom Representative's Office in Dublin of reports of submarine activity received from their coast-watching service (see No. 91);

(d) arranged for the broadcasting of reports by their Air Observer Corps of aircraft sighted over or approaching Eire territory (this did not include United Kingdom aircraft using the corridor referred to in (b) above);

(e) arranged for the extinction of trade and business lighting in coastal towns where such lighting was alleged to afford a useful landmark for German aircraft;

(f) supplied the United Kingdom with meteorological reports;

(g) agreed to the use by United Kingdom ships and aircraft of two wireless direction-finding stations at Malin Head;

(h) supplied particulars of German crashed-aircraft and personnel crashed or washed ashore or arrested on land;

(i) arranged for staff talks on the question of co-operation against a possible German invasion of Eire, and close contact was maintained between the respective military authorities;

(j) interned all German fighting personnel reaching Eire, while, after protracted negotiations, Allied service personnel were allowed to depart freely and full assistance was given in recovering damaged aircraft;

(k) agreed either to return or at least intern any German prisoners who escaped from Northern Ireland across the border into Eire;

(l) throughout offered no objection to the departure from Eire of persons wishing to serve in the United Kingdom Forces nor to the journey on leave of such persons (in plain clothes) to and from Eire;

(m) exchanged information with United Kingdom security authorities regarding all aliens (including Germans) in Eire;

(n) agreed to the establishment of a Radar station in Eire for use against the latest form of submarine activity.

---

suggested, however, that the detonators were kept miles away in Antrim.

This preparation was not made without good reason. In 1940 there were two plans for the invasion of Ireland in existence. Plan Kathleen was drawn up by Liam Gaynor of the IRA and approved by the organization's acting chief of staff, Stephen Hayes. Its object was the German invasion of Northern Ireland on the Derry coast, supported by an IRA ground offensive beginning in County Leitrim, and its ultimate goal was the creation of a united Ireland. The plan was taken to Berlin in April 1940, where the Germans, who had expected rather better from the IRA, immediately recognized it as hopelessly naïve.

The Germans had their own plan: Operation Green – the invasion of Eire. This was a companion to Operation Sealion, though some historians point to the lack of secrecy surrounding it to make a case that it was less about invasion and more about scaring the British into wasting their scarce resources on countermeasures. Hitler's view was that any landing in Eire should not be a contested invasion but the result of an agreement with Eire, and Grossadmiral Raeder had no confidence that an amphibious invasion could be adequately supported to ensure its success. Like the IRA plan, it came to nothing, but the advantages to Germany of bases in Ireland to prosecute the Battle of the Atlantic and the invasion of Britain were too obvious to be ignored on either side of the Irish border.

As a result, in May 1940 the governments of Britain and Eire began joint work on Plan W, by which British forces would be invited into Eire to help oppose any German landing. The longstanding suspicions, dislike and differences between what were now two sovereign states, were largely put aside during what was generally known south of the border as 'The Emergency'.

The extent of the cooperation that the government of Eire extended to the Allies as a friendly neutral was catalogued by the Secretary of State for Dominion Affairs, Lord Cranborne, in his letter to the War Cabinet (see page 155).

PILLBOXES

From 1940, around 28,000 pillboxes were built to guard coasts, crossroads, bridges, railways, canals, reservoirs and other strategic sites. They fall into the category of 'hardened field defences', and were frequently integral elements of the numerous Stop Lines. Some of the coastal pillboxes have been undermined and eroded by wind and tides, but 6,000 or so are thought to have survived across Britain.

Designs varied, depending upon the location, the purpose and the calibre of weapon to be fired from them: from rifles via light machine guns to anti-tank 6-pounders. Some showed their full height, others were partially sunk so that their embrasures were close to the ground; on hillsides they might be set into the slope, staring over the valleys.

There were several standard types:

Type 22 – hexagonal with a door in one side and embrasures in the other five.
Type 23 – rectangular, 8 feet by 16 feet (2.5 metres by 5 metres) with one

half open to the sky for the operation of an A/A gun.

Type 24 – irregular hexagon; the most common type.

Type 25 – circular with three embrasures, this 8 feet (2.5 metres) in diameter version was made by pouring concrete into shuttering formed by two concentric rings of corrugated iron that gave it a horizontal rib pattern.

Type 26 – 10 feet (3 metres) square.

Type 27 – hexagonal or octagonal with an open central well for an A/A gun as well as outward facing embrasures.

Type 28 – 20 feet by 19 feet (6 metres by 5.8 metres), designed for a 2-pounder or a Hotchkiss 6-pounder anti-tank gun, with shellproof walls. This was in addition to the specialized Vickers machine gun emplacement, which contained a trapezoidal table.

A standard pillbox had bulletproof walls 12 inches (30 centimetres) thick. Most had an internal wall, often Y-shaped, with the open head of the 'Y' facing the door in order to hinder any attack and prevent ricochets. The embrasures were often stepped, so that if enemy fire hit the side of the opening the bullets would ricochet away. While the pillbox would be made locally, from concrete poured between wood or brickwork shuttering (the pattern left by wooden shuttering can often be seen imprinted on the ceiling), the embrasures were manufactured separately. There were regional variants of pillboxes and several specialized airfield designs such as the Pickett-Hamilton Fort and the very rare Tett Turret.

An unusual double pillbox exists at Magilligan Point, still guarding the narrow exit from Lough Foyle to the Atlantic. During the war it was backed

ABOVE: A coastal observation post at Shellness, Isle of Sheppey. Built with two levels, it overlooks the River Swale as it enters the Thames Estuary.

up by a pair of 6-inch naval guns, HAA batteries and searchlights, protecting the convoys and escorts entering and leaving the lough. Stepped one above the other, they command a 270-degree view down the lough and round the point.

During the war, pillboxes would have been camouflaged with earth, netting or by siting them in hedges. The survivors may sometimes be hard to spot because they are often overgrown or have been pressed into service as sheds or stores. Many, however, look forlorn and exposed as they stand in cultivated fields that were once deemed strategic locations from which to attack an invading German force.

The most unusual pillbox was one designed to defend an airfield from German parachutists. The enemy would have expected resistance from perimeter pillboxes and shelters but the sudden materialization of two or three stumpy cylinders in the middle of the airfield, gunfire spraying from the slits, would have taken them by surprise.

Such was the theory behind the Pickett-Hamilton Fort, warmly embraced by Churchill despite being one of the more bizarre defences to be put into production just before and during the early part of the war. Unfortunately, as the RAF rapidly realized, it was also among the most useless, but by 1942 when the project was brought to an end, 335 had been installed, at a cost of £240 each.

Architect Donald Hamilton conceived what the manufacturers, the New Kent Construction Company, called a 'disappearing pillbox', consisting of two reinforced concrete cylinders. The bottom cylinder, about the height of a medium-sized man, was set into a concrete base and buried to ground level; the upper section (the rising head) fitted snugly inside like a

OPPOSITE: This Type 24 pillbox on the Macclesfield Canal near Lyne Green was one element of GHQ Command Stop Line No. 6 that ran from Tamworth, Staffordshire, to a point 6 miles southeast of Manchester, via Trent Valley and the eastern side of Stoke-on-Trent, to Macclesfield and Stockport. It commanded the railway line and the bridge over the canal.

BELOW: Peering round a tree, this pillbox once defended the perimeter of RAF Bramcote. It is built of bricks and concrete, and the corner and central embrasures gave a good view of the airfield. The internal blast wall can be glimpsed through the right-hand embrasure.

ABOVE: A pillbox masquerading as a bus stop, one of a number of clever attempts at concealment. Some pillboxes were put up without authority, prompting Major General Majendie, commanding the 55th Division, to write: 'I am very much afraid we have gone pill-box mad, and losing all sense of proportion in siting defences … The countryside is covered with pill-boxes, many of which will never be occupied, many could never serve any useful purpose, and many face the wrong way.'

lid and was covered in green camouflage paint. When the rising head was fully retracted, the fort revealed only its circular roof, 9 feet (2.75 metres) in diameter, and that was flush to the ground so that aircraft could run over it, thus solving the problem of siting hardened field defences in areas of aircraft operation. The rising head was raised by a hydraulic ramrod that was operated either by hand or by using a compressed air bottle. When raised, it revealed two slits, one for each of the two machine gunners manning the fort. Various manufacturers were contracted to build what, inevitably, became known as the 'pop-up pillbox'. Most Pickett-Hamilton Forts conformed to this description, but RAF Worthy Down near Winchester is home to a four-man, counterbalance variant, of which only around 12 were built.

Ingenious as the idea was, the 'pop-up pillbox' had too many drawbacks. The forts were not strong enough to take the weight of bombers and their field of view was very low and purely horizontal, unless the entrance hatch was raised to give an unsatisfactory view of the sky. The forts would only fulfil their role if they could be manned before any invasion took place. Only light weapons and limited ammunition could be kept inside, and, being situated at ground level, the forts had an unpleasant habit of filling with water. That last defect ensured that, with one exception, surviving forts are badly corroded inside.

To enter a 'pop-up pillbox', you climb through a small metal hatch in the roof and down a few metal rungs onto a raised concrete platform that runs around the edge, leaving a central hole through which the ramrod sticks up. When the pillbox head is raised, the guards standing upright on the platform are able to look out and fire out of the slit; however, when it is retracted it is impossible to stand up.

RIGHT: The Pickett-Hamilton Fort with entrance hatch open and rising head extended to show the embrasure. The fort was taken out of the ground for preservation and display purposes at Lashenden Air Warfare Museum; the sandbags and grassy mound behind it demonstrate the depth to which it would have been planted. The window was added to allow visitors to see the interior.

RIGHT: A revolving Tett Turret still in place at Hornchurch, Essex, where much of the former RAF station is now a country park.

THE LASHENDEN 'POP-UP PILLBOX'

Lashenden Air Warfare Museum, sited at Headcorn Aerodrome, Kent, was very anxious to add a Pickett-Hamilton Fort to its collection and when aviation historian Robin Brooks discovered one that, against the odds, was dry inside, he realized that there was a possibility of restoring it to working order. The pillbox had been part of the defences of RAF Manston, and the operators of the site, Kent International Airport, were happy to donate it to Lashenden and allow the recovery to take place.

Excavating several tons of 60-year old concrete without damaging it was a specialized undertaking, and the museum turned to a locally based military unit: 36 Engineer Regiment of the Royal Engineers, which accepted the task as a useful exercise, and in March 2006 the preliminary surveying work concluded that it was achievable. With the regiment's commitments in Iraq taking precedence it was May before the engineers arrived on site with their heavy excavation equipment to dig through 10 feet (3 metres) of chalk to reach the concrete base of the structure. The good news was that, apart from one crack, the concrete was intact.

Now it was down to the civilian crane team. The first task was to lift out the 3-ton rising head. Slowly it came out, revealing not just the gun slits and the original camouflage but the three wheels on which the rising head ran up and down the inside of the outer cylinder. Then came the two sections of the outer cylinder. All that remained for the afternoon was the 5-ton base out of which projected the lifting equipment.

The base proved to be the most stubborn of the elements. In the end, shackles were attached to the steel ramrod and the structure came out intact, ready to join the rest of the fort on a low-loader bound for Lashenden. Although the lifting mechanism had seized up over the years, museum members David Wild and Barry Baker spent a year and a half restoring it to working order. To their surprise the air bottle was intact and the vertical storage cylinder still contained oil in pristine condition.

The museum then had to tackle the question of how to display the fort: whether to set it into the ground, as it would have appeared, or leave it exposed as an exhibit? Worried about long-term degradation of the outer cylinder were it to go back into the earth, the museum elected to leave the fort above ground, but with sandbags and earth heaped up to the top of the outer cylinder around two-thirds of the perimeter. A small window allows visitors to look inside, and the rising head can also be seen in action. However, given the age of the mechanism, and modern-day concerns about health and safety, the operation is carried out using a power pack rather than the hand pump or gas bottle.

1: Starting to unearth the Pickett-Hamilton Fort at RAF Manston. **2:** Taking stock.
3: Reaching the bottom; the concrete was in good condition. **4:** Attaching chains to the ramrod. **5:** Lifting the base.

ROADBLOCKS

Permanently blocking a road was rarely a viable option, so a compromise was made in the shape of semi-permanent obstacles, often consisting of hefty concrete cylinders or cubes. Steel barriers were created by siting a pair of such concrete blocks, one either side of the road, and each with a vertical slot into which a strong steel bar – usually a length of railway track or a reinforced steel joint – could be dropped. The blocks and cylinders can often still be found, lying abandoned next to rural bridges. 'Hairpins' and 'hedgehogs' required sockets in the road: the hairpin consisted of a piece of heavy steel bent 60 degrees, with each end inserted into a socket; the 'hedgehog' consisted of vertical steel bars dropped into sockets. All these roadblocks could have been dismantled by the invader and would at best have slowed the advance, at worst have left him vulnerable to attack from a covering gun emplacement.

Other obstacles to the movement of tanks took the form of simple trenches and concrete dragons' teeth (sometimes called 'pimples') in the shape of pyramids and frustrums.

SPIGOT MORTAR EMPLACEMENTS

Thousands of round-top cylinders with protruding steel pintles and made from reinforced concrete were distributed to the Home Guard between October 1941 and July 1942. They were designed to support a spigot mortar, and were known as spigot mortar emplacements.

The 29mm spigot mortar, nick-named the 'Blacker bombard' after its Irish designer Lieutenant Colonel Stewart Blacker, was a portable, muzzle-loading anti-tank weapon, a comparatively cheap and cheerful substitute for the 2-pounder guns, of which too many had been lost in France at the time of Dunkirk. The mortar was used on either a cruciform platform or the simple steel and concrete pivot, and each mortar was allotted four concrete emplacements which could be located close to strategic sites such as bridges. The emplacements were usually set

ABOVE: A concrete roadblock on a major road. These defences were removed after the war, but sockets for 'hairpins' and 'hedgehogs' can sometimes be spotted. A set of four exists on Richmond Hill, Macclesfield, where it crosses the canal and was part of Stop Line No.6.

into pits 3-feet (1-metre) deep, to conceal the three-man crew, with brick or concrete revetments and also ammunition lockers. There are examples at Coalhouse Fort, Tilbury, however, that were hidden behind sandbags.

Two types of projectiles were issued: one was anti-personnel, with a range of just under half a mile, and the other was anti-tank, effective at close range. However, the spigot mortar was not universally popular. The General Officer Commanding Home Forces Sir Alan Brooke KCB, DSO** thought it unsuitable for the defence of airfields, and RAF personnel, including the RAF Regiment, were not allowed to use it. The Home Guard's initial pleasure at being issued with a proper weapon did not last. 'It is', wrote Lieutenant Colonel Herbert, commanding 3 Battalion, Wiltshire Home Guard in November 1941, 'apparently now only for use against moving targets up to 75 100 yards. Charming for the Home Guard who have to load it, from the front in full view of the enemy 100 yards away.' Later in the month he lamented: '… I have no possible use for them; so they will merely add to the dumps of scrap iron already lying about in our Wiltshire villages.'[17]

A later variant of the 'Blacker bombard', the PIAT (Projector, Infantry, Anti Tank), was used to great effect in many theatres of the war, from Russia to Sicily and Arnhem. A PIAT attack on a field gun was one of several exploits that earned Company Sergeant Major (CSM) Stanley Hollis of the Green Howards the sole VC that was awarded on D-Day.

ALL AT SEA

'Two cement columns with a tray on the top with all the armament supposedly for firing at aircraft coming in to attack London'[18] was how William Bartholomew described Tongue Sand, one of seven forts erected in the Thames Estuary in 1942. 'The radar set was an RAF set … which had a big searchlight in the middle, but we never used it, and we had seats in front of these sets – there were two sets, and one gave the altitude and one gave the bearing.' The forts were also equipped with A/A guns, but according to Bartholomew, his commander on HM Fort Rough's Tower never fired at 'incomers' in case they retaliated by bombing the forts.

There were two totally different types of forts – naval and army. Tongue Sand and Rough's Tower, in which Bartholomew served between August 1942 and February 1943, were two of four Maunsell naval sea forts, the others being Knock John and Sunk Head. The sea forts were designed by civil engineer Guy Maunsell, who conceived the idea during the dark days of the Battle of Britain as a simple defensive measure against the Luftwaffe:

'It will be seen, therefore, that the manufacture of these Forts would proceed in four stages. The first stage would be the building of the Pontoon inside the cofferdam on the foreshore, the second stage would be the building of a citadel while the pontoon was afloat, moored alongside of a jetty in the Thames. The third stage would be the placing of the equipment on Board and the

OPPOSITE: Home Guard soldiers being trained to use the much-maligned Blacker Bombard spigot mortar. The weapon is mounted on an emplacement made of reinforced concrete and with a steel pintle on which it can swivel. A projectile protrudes from the muzzle of the mortar; the soldier on the right holds another.

final stages would be the towing of
the pontoon and sinking of it in the
position previously stated.'[19]

He estimated the cost for three forts at
£80,500, which included a profit for the
builders of £20,100.

The first to be completed was
commissioned as HM Fort Rough's
Tower on 8 February 1942 and towed
out the following day. It left Tilbury at
09:15 and at 16:45 was settling down
nicely some 7 miles (11 kilometres) off
the Suffolk coast. The pontoon that sat
on the seabed measured 152 feet (46
metres) long and 20 feet (6 metres)
deep, and the two hollow cylinders that
rose from it to support the deckslab

were 22 feet (7 metres) in diameter and
68 feet (20 metres) high. The deckslab –
which Bartholomew called the 'tray' –
acted as the lower gun deck and the
base for both the upper gun deck and
the reinforced concrete citadel, the
building that housed the galley and the
officers' mess. Each cylinder was
divided horizontally into rooms
accessed by internal ladders. One
contained, in ascending order, the
stores and magazine, the control
rooms, two levels of sleeping quarters
for the men, and the crew's mess. The
other accommodated the engine room,
a second magazine and stores, the
officers' sleeping quarters and the petty
officers' mess.

Although the four naval sea forts that
were constructed had a complement of
up to a hundred men, and did fire at
enemy aircraft, life was dull. The crew
alternated one month on and two
weeks off, so, with nowhere to go when
off duty, Bartholomew read a lot of
books during his time on board.

By 1950 the Royal Navy had lost
interest in the forts. The doors were
welded up, but the 3.7-inch A/A guns
were left behind. During the 1960s all
four forts were used at various times as
'pirate radio stations', illegally
broadcasting pop music. Three were
particularly attractive for this purpose
because they lay outside British waters.
All four remain, and since 1967 Rough's
Tower has been occupied as the
independent Principality of Sealand.

The three army forts looked very
different. Each was composed of seven
individual towers mounted on four
slightly splayed legs. Five of the towers
– four gun towers and one Bofors tower
– formed a semi-circle around a central

command tower, while the seventh, the searchlight tower, was at a slightly greater distance. Each satellite tower was connected to the command tower by a walkway. The towers were constructed from iron and steel, with ladder access from the sea. Three forts were built – The Nore, Shivering Sands and Red Sands – and all saw action. Today, only the last two remain, but during the 1960s they, too, became 'pirate radio stations'. With their walkways long rusted away the army forts stand derelict, oddly reminiscent of H.G. Wells' Martians or the AT-ATs from *Return of the Jedi*.

MILLISLE FARM

The defence of the United Kingdom was of critical concern to the many refugees from Hitler's Europe, especially the Jews who had experienced persecution and violence in Germany during the 1930s. Following the terror of Kristallnacht on 9/10 November 1938, when Nazis rampaged through the streets smashing Jewish-owned businesses and arresting, murdering and beating up Jews, the British Government agreed to take in Jewish children. As the Home Secretary Samuel Hoare put it: 'Here is a chance of taking the young generation of a great people, here is a chance of mitigating to some extent the terrible suffering of their parents and their friends.' Beginning on 1 December 1938 and ending on 1 September 1939, the *Kindertransport* scheme brought some 10,000 children, all aged under 17, to Britain.

The British scheme was officially organized, but individuals from Britain and other countries also rescued Jewish children, not just from Germany but also from Austria, Poland and Czechoslovakia. Many of the children had been sponsored by individual families – Jewish, Christian and Quaker – and had a home waiting for them; others were allocated places. The Jewish Association found a run-down farm at Millisle in County Down, Northern Ireland, and turned it into something similar to a *kibbutz*: a self-sufficient community for dozens of German, Austrian and Czech children. The accommodation was dilapidated and basic – wooden huts in a sloping field – but they turned it into a home, and if they could not always be happy, because they were missing and fearing for the families left behind, at least they could live. One of those children was Walter Kammerling, and he remembered his arrival:

'… everybody got a bottle of milk when we got on the farm. That I remember. It was rather refreshing. Though we lived, we joked together, whatever, we worked together, and we realised that though we lived together we didn't know anything about each other. It was almost like wounded animals licking their wounds.'

They went to school, worked on the farm and carried out their chores – and one night Kammerling saw the fires glowing over Belfast:

'I remember there was only once we were woken up at night because Belfast, I think, was bombed. And I remember people came out into the

169

ABOVE: Scenes of everyday life at Millisle for the young Jewish refugees. As Walter Kammerling remembers: 'The farm was a lifesaver, because where else would I be? It's the mere fact that I was there; that I had the facility to be there. Where else would I have been otherwise?'

corridor there and waited at night and we saw in the distance fires, etc. But life on the farm carried on. I loved the harvesting. I loved all the other stuff. I worked with animals. In the evening when we finished off, sometimes they had musical evenings. Maurice Silberstein, he was the carpenter actually, he selected records and records were played; it was marvellous.'

The buildings still stand, as run-down as when the first children arrived, but with a few reminders of those wartime days: a set of scales that were probably used in the kitchen, a piece of graffiti on a doorframe and a cobwebbed blackout blind fixed to a wooden frame that could slide into place under a skylight.

After the war, some of the children went home; others, their families murdered by the Nazis, remained and settled permanently in the country that was supposed to have been a temporary refuge.

The children were not the only foreigners in Britain. As well as the Allied service personnel of many nationalities, there were more than a thousand[20] POW camps for tens of thousands of Axis prisoners. Camp 60 on Lamb Holm left two enduring legacies on the Orkney Islands, one of which was of astonishing beauty and created in the most unlikely circumstances.

In 1939 the battleship HMS *Royal Oak* was torpedoed and sunk by a U-boat while at her moorings in the supposedly impregnable anchorage of Scapa Flow. To prevent any repetition of the feat the Admiralty ordered work to begin on what became known as the

Churchill Barriers, which closed off the channels between the islands with concrete blocks. The labour was provided by Italian POWs captured during the North Africa campaign, who, when they cited the Geneva Convention's ban on using POWs for war work, were told that they were building causeways to provide road access between the islands.

In 1943 Father P. Gioacchino Giacobazzi arrived at the camp as a padre and convinced the camp commander, Major Thomas Buckland, of the need for a Roman Catholic place of worship. Buckland ordered two huts, which, when set end to end, made a rudimentary chapel, and a group of prisoners led by Domenico Chiocchetti, a talented artist, began work to transform the

soulless tunnel. The interior was lined with plasterboard on which Chiocchetti began to create frescoes and trompe l'oeil paintings to create the illusion of carved brick and stone. Above the altar he painted a Madonna and Child, based on a small picture that he carried with him of Nicolò Barabino's painting 'The Madonna of the Olives'. Another POW, Guiseppe Palumbi, a skilled metalworker, made the elaborate wrought iron rood screen. Many of the fittings and religious objects were made out of the tins in which their meat arrived, but Buckland helped them to obtain an appropriate length of fabric for the altar cloth. The final element of the transformation was to construct an Italianate façade and portico, complete with belfry,

ABOVE: A renaissance dream on a Scottish island: the Italian Chapel on Lamb Holm.

ABOVE: While the chapel has been restored, Millisle has fallen further into disrepair. This is the sight that met Dan when he walked around the rooms.

Although the camp was demolished after the war, the chapel remained; Chiocchetti even stayed on to finish the work and subsequently returned to carry out restoration.

Glasgow's Kelvingrove Museum houses a remarkable wartime triptych painted on old flour bags in Quattrocento style by another Italian POW, Giuseppe Baldan. He was held in a camp in the Sudan, where the chapel was a mud hut, and when the camp was closed the paintings, collectively known as La Faruk Madonna, were given to the camp commander in recognition of his humanitarian regime.

FORTRESS EUROPE

After the Battle of Britain the threat of invasion evaporated as Hitler abandoned Operation Sealion and turned his attention to his ideological enemy, the USSR. Hitler believed that

for as long as Britain's only allies in arms were her colonies and dominions and the limited number of Free Polish, Czech, Dutch, Belgian, Yugoslav, Norwegian and French forces that had managed to evade his clutches, he could safely discount the possibility of an Allied invasion of western Europe. Even after the USA entered the war it was almost a year before it could be said – at least with the benefit of hindsight – that the fortunes of war were deserting the Axis powers. What did concern Hitler, however, was Britain's irritating habit of launching naval and commando raids along the coast of Occupied Europe, particularly Norway. Prior to the end of 1941 his plans for coastal defence had concentrated almost exclusively on the U-boat pens at his new French Atlantic bases because they were such obvious targets for Allied bombers. The coastal batteries along the Channel coast in the Pas de Calais area he had demanded in

July 1940 were less for defence and more to provide active support for the aborted Operation Sealion. On 14 December 1941 he issued a Führer directive, requiring a coastal defence chain in the style of the Westwall. Norway was the priority, with France in second place.

Two months later, commandos of the new British 1st Airborne Division carried out their maiden operation. Dropped close to the village of Bruneval, near Le Havre, they captured and brought back a Wurzburg transmitter – the very latest development in German radar. A new Führer directive (demanding greater priority for the fortifications) followed on 23 March, five days before the gates of the dry dock at St. Nazaire were blown up during Operation Chariot. This concentrated German engineering minds on the subject of how to protect the Reich's territorial gains using steel and concrete along a coastline that measured 2,400 miles (3,840 kilometres) from Spain to Norway – and to complete the project by May 1943. Hitler was convinced that no Allied invasion could occur before then, and that when it did happen the Allies would choose a seaport. He called a conference in August to thrash out the plans, this time a few days

BELOW: High-ranking German officers observe the strengthening of coastal defences at Dieppe. The Minister of Armaments and War Production, Albert Speer, stands on the right, face in profile.

Feuerbereit! Das Geschütz einer der zahlreichen Batterien, deren Reichweite einen Angriff schon auf hoher See zunichte machen

DER
ATLANTIK-WALL

ABOVE: A long-range coastal gun protrudes from its reinforced bunker to threaten shipping and deter invasion.

before the Allies launched the fiasco known as Operation Jubilee or the Dieppe Raid.

Both sides took different lessons from Dieppe. The Allies drew on the experience when they began planning the invasion of North Africa (Operation Torch) and northwestern Europe (Operation Overlord) – when they chose beaches rather than a seaport. Hitler took it as confirmation of the need for what became the Atlantic Wall.

This vast project, a disproportionate response to the small-scale raids, required millions of tons of concrete and steel and a huge workforce. Construction was carried out by the Todt Organization (set up by the late Fritz Todt, but headed by Albert Speer following the founder's death in

January), using unpaid, forced labour. In fact, obtaining the labour force was easier than securing sufficient construction materials to keep pace with the schedule.

The coastline was divided into *KVAs*[21] (coastal defence sectors), which were far closer together along the Channel coast – that being where the expected Allied invasion was most likely to occur – than the Atlantic, and strongest of all in the Pas de Calais. Certain seaports including Cherbourg and Calais were designated fortresses and their defences significantly upgraded. Existing French defences were incorporated where suitable.

Batteries under naval control were designated MAA (Marine Artillerie Abteilung) and had formidable firepower, with most of the guns ranging in calibre from 105 to 155 millimetre. Along the Channel coast that gun size increased significantly, and the Lindemann battery at Sangatte was composed of three 406-millimetre guns with 65-feet (20-metre) barrels, originally built for a class of battleship that was scrapped before construction. Depending on the projectile, each gun's range was 26–35 miles (41–56 kilometres) and they regularly fired across the Channel to hit Dover and the surrounding area. The three casemates of that one MAA were made using more than 1,800,000 cubic feet (51,000 cubic metres) of concrete. Several other naval batteries employed redundant warship guns measuring 380 millimetres (nearly 15 inches), including that of the French battleship *Jean-Bart*.

Army gun batteries filled in the gaps between the big naval defences; again concentrated along that stretch of the Channel coast from Bray-Dunes just east of Dunkirk to Berck Plage about 10 miles (16 kilometres) south of Le Touquet, known as the Iron Coast. The primary aim of the naval guns in the Atlantic Wall was to blow any invasion force out of the water long before it got close enough to decant troops and equipment; that of the army defences was to repulse an invasion that reached the beaches. Such were the competing demands for raw materials and manpower in all theatres of the war that construction was desultory for the first 12 months, leading the commander of the 15th Army, Hans von Salmuth, to liken the Atlantic Wall to a string with a few knots tied along its length.

By the autumn of 1943 it was clear that a major Allied amphibious landing in France was only a matter of time and tide. Convinced that it would occur in the spring of 1944, Hitler demanded priority for the Atlantic Wall. He was also concerned to defend the V-rocket bases. Needing an energetic and authoritative commander for the project, he turned to Generalfeldmarschall Erwin Rommel, the 'Desert Fox' of North Africa fame.

Rommel did not disappoint him, at least not as far as energy was concerned. More than a million tons of steel and 17 million tons of cement were poured into creating additional defences along the Normandy coast. Although forced French labour was used by the Todt Organization, Rommel insisted that the men be paid for their work.

Once again there was no wall in the literal sense, rather another chain of reinforced concrete strongpoints – *Widerstandsneste* ('resistance nests') – sited around 1,000 yards (915 metres) apart and consisting of a combination or network of pillboxes, shelters, casements, trenches and Tobrukstands[22] with walls 6-feet (1.8-metres) thick. Configured to provide overlapping fire, and with smaller fortifications in the gaps between them, the *Widerstandsneste* would ensure that no exit from any beach was out of sight or range. In areas vulnerable to Allied air attack, the casements had to be roofed to make them bombproof. Set wholly or partially into the ground, they showed little more than their embrasures to the sea.

By the time Hitler could be said to have finally achieved his European fortress, his empire was crumbling from below.

WIDERSTANDSNEST 31

Today the concrete pillboxes of the once fearsome *Widerstandsnest* 31 (WN 31, or Resistance Nest 31) to the west of the River Seulles at Courseulles-sur-Mer lie tumbled among the dunes. The paths that criss-cross the sparsely grassed ground lead visitors across the hidden roofs of buried emplacements and past concrete blisters that were once cupolas supporting a tank turret or a machine gun. Most of the damage is the result of coastal erosion over the past 70 years rather than the events of D-Day: not so much a comment on Hitler's hubris in proclaiming a 1,000-year Reich as a demonstration of the biblical parable of the foolish man who built his house upon the sand.

In 1944 this site, 160 yards (146 metres) wide and some 500 yards (457 metres) long, contained 27 known elements, of which around 15 were virtually bombproof gun emplacements, either casements containing big guns firing 75- or 50-millimetre shells or emplacements and Tobrukstands for machine guns and mortars. The assorted elements were connected by trenches to the other buildings. The ammunition stores and crew shelters were buried in the sand and accessible from ground level by descending steps.

After the troops had gone the fortifications were abandoned to the elements and then sealed up in the 1950s. The increase in battlefield tourism and family history research has turned *WN* 31 into a tourist attraction, but more significant to the French is its role as a physical link to a period in history that has left its mark on the psyche of those who lived through the Second World War and those who grew up in its shadow.

BELOW: The remains of *Widerstandsnest* 31 that lies west of Courseulles-sur-Mer.

1

2

3

4

THE ATLANTIC WALL BUNKER AT JUNO BEACH

1: Exposing the entrance to the bunker in the dune.
2: Dan discovers the entrance is blocked with sand.
3: Clearing some of the sand away.
4: Dan speculates on how much sand he will have to shovel himself.

It is easy to walk along Juno Beach and view the remains of the exposed casemates, but the positions buried among the dunes have been sealed since the 1950s, and it was one of those – a possible shelter located north of the Juno Beach Centre – that, with the consent of the authorities and the assistance of the museum curator, Dan and the team had the opportunity to investigate.

An excavator was used to dig down to the heavy boards covering what proved to be a flight of concrete stairs leading down to an entrance. Sand had partially filled the space, obliging Dan to dig his way to the bottom. At this point, the bomb disposal expert, Bill Shuttleworth of IDPL (International Defence Procurement & Logistics), went ahead with his gas detection equipment to check that the percentage of oxygen was adequate and make sure that nothing noxious had built up in the intervening period. The air proved to be fresh, but he remained on hand at all times in case any sealed spaces were uncovered, and to deal with any discarded ordnance that might turn up.

When Dan entered the bunker he was seeing it for the first time; he had carried out no preliminary reconnaissance. The challenge for cameraman Mark McCauley was how he might capture that moment of discovery and at the same time allow the viewers to share it from Dan's perspective. 'You're just lighting it as he's discovering it, so the last thing you want to do is to go and flood the place with big floodlights. As he walks along, you want to see the walls, and as he walks into a room it lights up.' To achieve that genuine immediacy, he bought two battery operated striplights, about a foot long, from an ordinary retail hardware shop and stuck them together, back to back, using strong Velcro. Dan was able to carry the light into the bunker, and whenever he held it up not only did he illuminate the spaces but also his own face.

Turning right, Dan was faced with what appeared to be a passage, leading away towards the beach, but partially blocked by sand. He scrambled up onto the sand, which left just a couple of feet of headroom and peered ahead and around, looking into corridors that led off from either side, and over the top into what appeared to be another passage. Preceded by Bill, he crawled further forwards, head scraping on the rusty iron beams supporting the wooden lining to the ceiling, until the bad news from the bomb disposal man: 'Okay, the wall's gone completely here.'

The right-hand wall was not just bulging inwards from the weight and stress of the unstable sand outside, it had split horizontally and could collapse at any time. It was too dangerous to continue, which was a disappointment because the passage clearly continued for some considerable distance towards the sea, very possibly linking up with the observation bunker overlooking the beach.

The main subterranean space consisted essentially of two solidly built rooms and passages, and it was clear that this complex did not conform to any of the standard constructions and was probably unique. Building a *Widerstandsnest* had much in common with designing a fitted kitchen: choose the appropriate number and type of standard units from what amounted to a catalogue and assemble them to create a functioning strongpoint. The tunnel complex, however, had to be custom-built to fit the site.

The ordinary open trenches that linked the elements of WN 31 were vulnerable to attack. By contrast this underground warren had given the Germans the capacity to move around in safety, reinforcing, resupplying or evacuating particular emplacements. During the naval bombardment, troops might well have used the tunnels in order to pull back temporarily from their forward positions in case a lucky shell came through an embrasure or a fighter strafed a trench. Once the assault began, defenders could go to ground and suddenly reappear behind attackers who thought they had successfully cleared out an emplacement. This was not in evidence at Courseulles, but the tactic was used elsewhere on D-Day. As Dan put it: '... the Germans always had a way of escaping a bunker that wasn't through the front door.'

The two rooms yielded nothing in the way of artefacts beyond a piece of metal that might have come from a Churchill tank and been thrown in after the battle, but clues as to the functions of the rooms were found on the walls: a recess that could have held a weapons rack; fixings for narrow bunk beds; a nail casually hammered in to make a hook. The ceilings still had their wood lining, suggesting that post-war the bunker had not been accessible to local people, who would have stripped out the wood to burn during the cold winters.

Of particular interest was a small aperture, blocked by corrugated iron but with evidence of a void beyond; this was almost certainly a secret exit such as had been found at other sites. It was located in the corner of the far room, the blastproof door to which had long gone but would have been made of 2-inch (50-millimetre) steel. Either side of the doorway were two small openings, that once would have been closed with steel plates and through which machine guns could have been fired to cover the escape of those inside in the event of enemies infiltrating the bunker. This type of complex could easily have been defended by a small section of a dozen men. As Dan noted:

'It would have been a lonely place, in many ways, to wait for the Allied invasion they knew was coming. You hear a fair bit about D-Day but you very rarely hear about the experience of the German soldiers that manned these fortifications. Having built them, they would have waited for months and months for the inevitable Allied assault, praying it would fall somewhere else on the French coast, I'm sure. And then in June the massive aerial bombardment followed by naval gunfire on an unprecedented scale as thousands of naval ships out to sea pounded this coast and the Germans faced this terrible choice between holding out, desperately fighting to the last man and almost certainly being killed by flamethrower or shell or surrendering early and maybe saving their skins.'

Local resident René Lemars from nearby Creully came down to the dig: 'As a boy I played around here and I even slept one night here in August during the school

5: The underground entrance.
6: One of the rooms. The black panel might have been used as a chalk-board; beneath it is a storage space.
7: A tunnel leading towards the forward observation bunker, but heavily blocked by sand.
8: The wooden lining to the ceiling can clearly be seen above Dan's head. He holds the double striplight that simultaneously illuminates his face and the scenes around him.

holiday a year or two after the landings and all that [the bunker] was filled in with debris, wrecks, metal bits, etc., but over there … I slept with two friends of mine. We slept under a small triangular cover used by German snipers, and we slept underneath it all night; it was very cold at 4:00am! That's the oldest memory that I have of those sites.'[23]

From the bunker Dan walked down one of the beach exits onto what is now a popular holiday beach but which on 6 June had been a killing field of barbed wire coils, crashing mortar shells and whining and spitting bullets. He stared out at a sea that had been dark with landing craft and a sky black with air support. Then he carried on a short distance to the remains of the casemate that became known as 'Cosy's Bunker' (see also pages 241–242). Above the side embrasure from which the heavy gun had once extended its muzzle to enfilade the beach and stop any troops getting up the narrow exit, the concrete blocks showed the effect of a massive impact. It was unlikely to have been the result of the aerial bombardment or the naval barrage that preceded the landings, which suggests that the damage was inflicted by a tank of the 1st Hussars, landing on Juno behind the infantry, a major blow in the breaching of the walls of Fortress Europe.

BELOW: Dan considers the events that took place on this peaceful beach almost 70 years ago.

PART 4

BREACHING THE WALLS

The war in North Africa had begun back in the summer of 1940 when the Italian army in Libya began an advance on Egypt, aiming to capture the Suez Canal and the oilfields of the Arabian Peninsula. After the Italians were halted by General Archibald Wavell's small army at Mersah Matruh and pushed back, Hitler dispatched troops under General Erwin Rommel to deal with the situation, and the conflict flowed back and forth across the desert, creating the legend of General Bernard Montgomery's 'Desert Rats' and Rommel's Afrika Korps. The decisive engagement took place at El Alamein over a three-week period beginning on 23 October 1942, and after the war Churchill was able to look back and say: 'Before Alamein we never had a victory, after Alamein we never had a defeat.'

The last days of the battle coincided with Operation Torch, in which an Allied force launched a successful assault on French North Africa, leading to a cautiously optimistic speech by Churchill on 10 November: 'This is not the end, it is not even the beginning of the end. But it is, perhaps, the end of the beginning.'

The Allies were now on the offensive. One regiment that made its mark in the closing months of the war in North Africa and the seemingly interminable Italian campaign was the North Irish Horse.

THE NORTH IRISH HORSE

Founded in 1902 as the North of Ireland Imperial Yeomanry and renamed the North Irish Horse (NIH) in 1908, the NIH was a cavalry regiment that recruited in the northern counties of what was then an Ireland united under British rule, and it harked back to the days when regiments were raised and patronized by wealthy aristocrats.

With little scope for cavalry in the trench fighting of the First World War, many NIH members fought with other regiments. One such was Acting Lieutenant Colonel Richard West, who was on secondment to the Tank Corps in 1918 when he was killed in action, adding a posthumous Victoria Cross to the Military Cross and DSO and Bar he had already won.

After the war the NIH faded to a paper regiment, until by 1934 its Honorary Colonel, Major Sir Ronald Ross Bt., MC was its only member. It was reconstituted as an armoured regiment in 1938 after the government woke up to reality and began to expand Britain's armed services. The NIH served on the Home Front until January 1943 when, equipped with new Churchill tanks (see page 189), it was posted to North Africa and thrown into action in northern Tunisia to help oppose a German Panzer attack heading for Béja. From then on, the NIH was regularly in action, and became famous as the first armoured regiment of the western Allies to destroy a German Tiger tank, taking out two on the same day in February 1943.

The crowning achievement of the NIH was the attack on a position known as Longstop Hill, made up of two summits: Djebel Ahmera and Djebel Rhar. The former was taken by

OPPOSITE: Tank support for the East Surrey Regiment from the North Irish Horse at the battle of Longstop Hill, Tunisia 1943.

BELOW: A Churchill tank of 'C' Squadron North Irish Horse gives a lift to men of the 3rd Battalion, 21st Infantry (Italian) in 1945. The NIH and their Churchills served for a year in the Italian Campaign.

FOLLOWING PAGES: Playing the tank commander: Dan in Nigel Montgomery's restored Churchill.

36th Infantry Brigade on 23 April, and three days later the NIH and the 5th Buffs – the Royal East Kent Regiment – were able to use the slopes as the starting point for their assault on Djebel Rhar to capture the German guns. Working closely together, the two units pressed steadily up the mountain, the tanks in echelon up the steep incline.

'At the head of the saddle between the Ahmera and the Rhar, Lt. Pope encountered another machine gun and mortar post, and finally a 75mm gun … after one round of 6pdr. and a burst of Besa the crew surrendered; Sgt O'Hare then tackled the ascent and on reaching the summit after a magnificent climb, took over 50 prisoners.'[1]

Among the prisoners was the German battalion commander, who told his captors: 'The Djebel Rhar is one of the strongest defensive positions that one could ever hope to occupy. I would have been prepared to hold it against a full-scale British infantry brigade attack. When it was apparent that tanks were being used over the high ground I knew that all was over.'[2]

The NIH joined the Italian Campaign just after Monte Cassino, and fought from the Hitler Line all the way to the end of the campaign in Italy in April 1945. Following many changes, particularly amalgamations of regiments, the NIH today forms 'B' Squadron of the Queen's Own Yeomanry, with barracks at Belfast.

THE CHURCHILL TANK

The first War Office specification for what would become the Churchill envisaged a tank capable of operating on a First World War battlefield of mud, craters and obstacles, but the prototype A20, designed by Harland and Wolff at Belfast, had hardly turned a track in 1940 before the disaster that led to Dunkirk rendered it obsolete. The tank would be too slow and ponderous to deal with the new reality: the possible invasion of Britain. The specification was changed and the design contract given to Vauxhall, which came up with the A22 Churchill tank. So urgent was the need that the tank was put into production at Luton in June 1941 without proper trials and with Vauxhall stating that teething troubles would be rectified in the field.

The tank had its supporters and detractors. The experience of Sergeant Gerry Chester of the NIH was overwhelmingly positive: 'The Churchill tank was the best British tank of World War Two, no question about it. We felt safe in it, which was important. It was a great tank to be aboard.'

Some complained it was slow – up to 8 miles (13 kilometres) per hour cross-country and 15 miles (24 kilometres) per hour on the road – but as the NIH proved, it could go where no other armour could follow. The regiment's success at Longstop Hill saved the Churchill from being taken out of production and gave the tank its reputation for excellent infantry support, where speed was not required. The heavy armour enabled it to withstand punishment, but its worst failing was its under-gunning, leaving it at a serious disadvantage when engaged by German Panthers and Tigers. During the war the turret gun was gradually upgraded from a risible 2-pounder, in the Mark I of June 1941, to a 75-millimetre gun by the time of the Mark VI in December 1943. The main hull armament was a 7.92-millimetre Besa machine gun capable of firing between 450 and 850 rounds per minute.

The five-man crew comprised the tank commander, the driver, the co-driver (who also fired the Besa and carried out useful tasks such as making the tea), the wireless operator and the gunner. Because the tank had to be a self-contained unit, the crew were multi-skilled and invariably willing to do what needed to be done, from maintenance to cooking. Chester's role as a driver/operator included taking charge of the radio and loading the heavy gun.

Churchill tanks have survived in several museum collections including the Tank Museum at Bovington. Three are in the hands of Nigel Montgomery, whose father served in the NIH, and who has lovingly restored one and is now working on the remaining two. He gave his Mark IV the chance to see what Dan was made of.

As tanks went, the Churchill was extremely roomy, thanks to its suspension system, though Dan was not convinced: 'I don't fancy trying to get out of here in a hurry. I'm not sure it's designed for a tall person.' Once in the drivers' seat he looked through the window, noting that 'unfortunately it's facing towards the enemy. You'd want this closed, wouldn't you'.

When the tank was in action the window was closed by a steel shutter and the driver then had to rely on the periscope that offered little more than a slit of vision. It made driving in darkness, dust or smoke very difficult.

Up in the turret, Dan enjoyed the commander's view, but recognized that it was a vulnerable position, an impression that remained with him as Nigel Montgomery took him cross-country: 'Being in this tank is really an assault on the senses: the sound and smell of the engine and being jolted around. It's like being at sea. And it's a strange feeling; on the one hand you feel very secure and protected but you also feel that you're in a lumbering, slow machine that would attract lots of enemy fire.'

When it went into action against the Hitler Line, that is precisely what it did do.

BREAKING THE HITLER LINE: FROM SICILY TO CASSINO

All roads lead to Rome, but the Eighth army advancing towards the Italian capital from the south of the country in the second half of 1943 was destined to be funnelled – by geology, weather and German contrivance – along one specific road: the Strade Statali 6 (SS6) that ran past Monte Cassino and through the Liri Valley. It was in this region that the Allies faced some of the toughest fighting of the war, culminating in the attack on the Hitler Line by the 1st Canadian Infantry Division and the armoured units supporting it.

The Italian campaign had begun with the successful invasion of Sicily on the night of 9/10 July 1943, leading swiftly to the overthrow of Mussolini on the 24th. On 3 September Marshal Badoglio signed an armistice with the Allies – the same day Allied forces landed on the Italian mainland. News of that armistice was announced five days later, by which time the German forces were seizing what Italian assets they could secure and Allied forces were pushing north from the 'foot' of Italy. Against stiff resistance, a third Allied force had established a beachhead further north at Salerno and was in a position to break out and take Naples. A popular uprising in that city forced out the Germans, and the Allies entered on 1 October.

Difficult as the campaign had been, it was to get much harder. The Apennine Mountains that divided the country vertically not only channelled traffic into corridors, but also engendered rivers that flowed either east into the Adriatic or west into the Tyrrhenian seas, slicing the corridors into chunks. The Germans were swift to establish a series of well-defended lateral stop lines south of Rome on which they could fall back, the first being the Volturno Line, based on the rivers Volturno and Biferno; then came the Barbara Line; the strongest, the Gustav Line, stretched from Ortona in the east to Minturno in the west. The Gustav Line's western edge was buttressed by the Bernhardt Line, and

BELOW: The medieval abbey of Monte Cassino, dominating the road to Rome. Erroneously believing the Germans to have occupied it, the Allies ordered it to be bombed. It was rebuilt after the war.

The British reorganized themselves and improved the ragged supply lines that had so nearly led to defeat. It was almost a month before they crossed the River Trigno to breach the Barbara Line. In the west the Americans also moved forwards, along a wider front, and the Germans decided to make a fighting retreat to the Bernhardt and Gustav lines. The slow pace of the Allied advance, hampered by steep hills and by foul weather that turned the low-lying ground into a morass, was precisely what the Germans needed in order to gain time to reinforce their primary defence line.

The Canadians, a major component of the British Eighth Army, took Ortona just before New Year after a week of savage house-to-house engagement that cost the lives of 1,372 soldiers from the Loyal Edmonton Regiment and the Seaforth Highlanders of Canada. By that time the winter weather had precluded any advance on Rome along the Strade Statali 5, the main road from Ortona, and the flooding of the Pontine Marshes by the Germans had limited the western coastal route. SS6 was all that was left, and it crossed the Gustav Line to enter the Liri Valley immediately below the monastery-topped heights of Monte Cassino.

In this brutal, winter landscape of rough, folded mountains, small towns, swollen waterways and valleys, the Allied advance stalled in front of the rivers Rapido and Garigliano that provided the natural defences of the Gustav Line. The Germans were thoroughly dug in on the heights with their artillery commanding the road.

should both be breached the defenders could retire to the Hitler Line, a short defence that crossed the Liri Valley some 7 miles (11 kilometres) up the SS6.

Units of the British Eighth Army's 78th Infantry Division crossed the Biferno near Termoli on 3 October, but found themselves unsupported and about to face the tanks of the 16th Panzer Division that were racing to oppose them. In the nick of time, the British engineers received their equipment and managed to construct a heavy-duty Bailey Bridge for the armour, and after stiff fighting the line was broken on the 6th. When the US Fifth Army, which included the British X Corps, pushed through the western half of the Volturno Line, Generalfeldmarschall Kesselring sanctioned a German withdrawal to the Barbara Line.

In this context, an amphibious landing was carried out on 22 January 1944 at Anzio, well behind the Gustav Line, aimed at catching the Germans off their guard, forcing them to take troops from the Gustav Line and trapping them between the two Allied armies. In the event, those who established the beachhead were forced to hold on for four months until events at Monte Cassino resolved themselves.

Between January and May four grim battles were fought on the heights around Cassino, until the whole area was a shattered ruin, the monastery all but destroyed by a huge Allied air strike. The final Allied attack, the first element of Operation Diadem, commenced on the night of 11/12 May.

The British Eighth Army – which included Canadian, Polish, Gurkha, Indian, New Zealand and co-belligerent Italian troops – would play the leading role in the Monte Cassino attack, while General Mark Clark's US Fifth Army and the French Expeditionary Corps, with its Algerian and Moroccan units, would begin to advance along a more westerly route, breaking the Gustav Line and crossing the Aurunci Mountains. Once Cassino was taken, the Eighth Army would move parallel to the Americans and French, but up the Liri Valley, pushing back the Germans, breaking the Hitler Line between Aquino and Pontecorvo, and securing SS6. The troops at Anzio would break out and cut off the German retreat. This coordinated triple-pronged attack would stretch German manpower and prevent Kesselring from sending any divisions away from Italy, a major consideration given that the Normandy landings were less than a month away.

ABOVE: Aerial view of the carpet bombing of Monte Cassino.

ON THE HITLER LINE

Monte Cassino fell to the Polish assault of 17 May and the Eighth Army, under General Sir Oliver Leese, duly advanced along the valley as the Germans carried out a fighting withdrawal to the Hitler Line.

In January, Hitler had ordered the name to be changed to the Sengerriegel (the Senger Line) – after General von Senger und Etterlin, the man responsible for its creation – to avoid the damage to his pride and to German morale that would follow if it were breached, but the Allies naturally continued to refer to 'the Hitler Line'. It commenced near Piedimonte on the lower slopes of Monte Cairo, passed through Aquino and Pontecorvo in the Liri Valley, where its defences were strongest, and climbed over the Aurunci Mountains to meet the Tyrrhenian Sea at Terracina, below Anzio.

The 78th Infantry Division hurried up to Aquino in the hope of taking it before the Germans could reinforce it with the defenders from Monte Cassino, but they came too late and were pushed back by the powerful guns sited in and around the town. Although the Germans were short of infantry and food they were well provided with weaponry and ammunition.

The 1st Canadian Corps, consisting of the 1st Canadian Infantry Division and the 5th Canadian (Armoured) Division, fought their way up to the Hitler Line through countryside that was attractive in peacetime, but which in war was frustrating and favoured the defenders, being:

'... undulating but very thickly wooded. Between the trees there was corn, still green and standing about 4ft high. The whole area was intersected with valleys, some fairly wide, and some more in the nature of ravines; all these valleys were wooded and, in addition, narrow sunken roads ran through the area. As a result, visibility was never more than 100 yds all round and generally only about 50 yds. The close country provided excellent possibilities for ambushing tks [tanks] and the valleys, useful covered approaches for enemy tks and SP [self-propelled] Guns. The corn provided good hiding places for the hunters, and snipers abounded in the trees....'[3]

During the approach to the line, map reading was: 'proving a very difficult job these days; there is such a mess of trails running in all directions, many of which are not on our maps. Movement is almost always along these narrow wooded trails and tracks, which present a terrific problem for an Army on the move and is an amazing sight to see. All rds [roads] are clogged with tpt [transport] and progress is slow.'[4]

BEHIND THE WIRE

Between Aquino and Pontecorvo the Hitler Line zig-zagged and kicked its way through the wooded belt along the road linking the two towns. It was constructed along a slight rise, enabling its defenders to command a thousand or so yards of land to the south. Both flanks were overlooked by high ground, ideal for enemy observation posts, and the approach was bounded by two rivers: the Liri on the left and the ravine of the Forme d'Aquino on the right.

Other gullies, also at right angles to the line, made lateral movement difficult for any attackers.

Almost the entire length of the line was guarded by an anti-tank minefield, itself enclosed within a double-apron barbed wire fence. A second minefield extended on either side of the road to Pontecorvo from Pignatore, and a third sat forward of the thick perimeter wire close to the ravine, covering one of the narrow approach tracks. Some of the Teller mines were buried, but most were visible. The wire took the form of double-strand or concertina barbed wire. Anti-tank ditches, anything up to 30 feet (9 metres) wide and 15 feet (4.5 metres) deep, partially flooded in some areas, had been created from craters.

The most troublesome of the fixed defences consisted of nine Mark V Panther tank turrets, mounted on concrete cupolas above standardized steel-reinforced pillboxes set into the ground. Their 75-millimetre guns had all the advantages of a 360-degree motorized traverse, and they were sited to cover the minefields and other anti-tank obstacles. They had a range of approximately 1,200 yards (nearly 1,100 metres), though gunners preferred to let the enemy close to 800 yards (730 metres), and the only way to destroy them was at comparatively close quarters. Each was defended by a pair of towed guns, sited 150–200 yards (135–180 metres) behind in echelon or on the flank, as well as by lighter

LEFT: Canadian forces advancing towards the Hitler Line.

A Canadian
infantryman examines one
of the Panzer turrets that
caused so many casualties
among the tanks.

weapons. Greater reliance, however, was placed on the towed guns, mostly of 75-millimetre calibre.

The self-propelled (SP) guns included 88-millimetre heavy anti-tank Hornets and 75-millimetre assault guns mounted on tank chassis or armoured half-tracks; out of some 62 anti-tank guns, around 26 were self-propelled and could be deployed to respond to the developing situation rather than covering obstacles and approaches.

Standard types of machine gun

emplacements, such as the Ringstand 58c, were made by pouring concrete over steel reinforcements; they had a 33-inch (84-centimetre) diameter opening with a steel traversing ring, and they could be linked to prefabricated steel shelters. Forward of the concrete emplacements were weapons pits and dugouts with covered approaches and steps down to rectangular rooms that were revetted with wood and covered in gravel to a depth of 3–5 feet (0.9–1.5 metres) to protect against air or artillery attack.

Add to this the 10-, 12-, 15- and 21-centimetre mortars, the five- or six-barrelled Nebelwerfer rocket-launchers (nicknamed 'Moaning Minnies' by the infantry on the receiving end), the snipers in the trees and a handful of tanks acting independently, and the Hitler Line defences were a formidable barrier – particularly at Aquino where they could target the unprotected right flank of their enemy, which turned out to be the unfortunate 2nd Canadian Infantry Brigade and, in particular, Princess Patricia's Canadian Light Infantry (PPCLI), familiarly known as the Patricias.

THE ATTACK ON PONTECORVO

The parallel French advance, on the south side of the River Liri, made progress to the high ground south of Pontecorvo, which they secured on 21 June. Canadian commanders began to hope that their own 1st Canadian Infantry Brigade would push through on the other side of the river and take the town, sparing the 2nd and 3rd brigades a potentially costly frontal assault.

The 48th Highlanders of Canada had begun the chase on the morning of 18 May, moving up the road parallel to the River Liri and taking a number of prisoners. The ground between themselves and the river was held by the 4th Princess Louise Dragoon Guards. The following day brought the 48th to higher ground overlooking the line, with the Hastings and Prince Edward Regiment – the 'Hasty Ps' – on their right, and some good recce work

by Sergeant Caldwell's platoon provided a clear picture of the German defences ahead.

The 48th held their position on 20 May and tried to get some rest despite the afternoon shelling that injured five men and killed one. Late on the 21st they were told they were to attack next morning. It was a hastily conceived operation – an unexpected change from the original plan, codenamed Chesterfield, which provided for a simultaneous attack by all three brigades – and their CO was most unhappy about it. The 48th were to break through and create a bridgehead, which the Royal Canadian Regiment (the Royal Canadians) would relieve, allowing the 48th to move forwards to the ridge. The Hasty Ps were then to cross the Hitler Line and move across the front of the 48th while the Royal Canadians would also advance. In the fourth phase, the leapfrogging would continue as a reorganized 48th advanced through the other two regiments.

In the short time from briefing to start, the sappers carried out what mine reconnaissance they could and tried to make gaps for the tanks; the infantry and their supporting tanks married up and 'netted' – tuned – their No. 18 short-wave radio sets as best they could.

Princess Louise's Dragoons began the action at 07:00 and initially had considerable success, destroying two German tanks and taking prisoners.

At 10:30 the 48th began to advance, with 'B' and 'D' companies in the lead, their tanks following until the consequences of the less-than-thorough overnight reconnaissance revealed themselves. Mines that had been missed exploded under tanks, and the infantry began to take casualties until they were forced to go to ground by the weight of machine gun fire. Battalion headquarters (HQ) took shelter by a German pillbox as the Nebelwerfers and mortars opened up, and overall progress was slow that afternoon. Two companies of the Royal Canadians came up before the light finally went, and the 48th dug in for the night under shell and rocket attack, waiting for dawn to bring them relief in the form of the Hasty Ps and the rest of the Royal Canadians.

By midnight senior commanders had fallen back on Plan A, Chesterfield: an attack on 23 May by the 2nd and 3rd brigades along the 5,000-yard (4,570-metre) front between Aquino on the right and Pontecorvo on the left to support a renewed attack by the 1st Brigade on Pontecorvo. The 78th Infantry Division would provide a feint to stop the Germans in Aquino shelling the Canadian right flank, and further to

the north the Poles would apply pressure on Piedimonte.

THE 2ND BRIGADE GOES IN

May 23rd dawned cool, with thick ground mist and poor visibility. Reveille at 04:00 for the Seaforths was followed by a cold breakfast. They had moved into position the previous evening and been joined by the men and tanks of 'B' Squadron, NIH. The Seaforths were veterans of hard combat in Italy; the NIH and their Churchill tanks had arrived in Naples from North Africa only a month earlier, but since early May they had been training near Foggia with the 1st Canadian Infantry Division. The NIH had also re-equipped two troops of each squadron with Sherman tanks.

The 2nd Brigade were to attack two battalions up and one in reserve. On the far right, 'A' and 'C' companies of the Patricias, with 'A' Squadron NIH, moved up to the start line alongside the Seaforths, leaving 'B' Company in reserve. H-Hour was 06:00, and 135 minutes had been allotted to the two battalions to secure the first objective, the Aquino to Pontecorvo road, codenamed Aboukir. The reserve battalion – the Loyal Edmonton Regiment, with the armoured support of 'B' and 'C' squadrons of the 51st Royal Tank Regiment (RTR) – were to advance behind them, arrive at the road by 08:15, pass through the Patricias and, together with the Seaforths, proceed to the second objective: the road from Pontecorvo to Castrocielo that crossed the SS6.

Towards the centre of the line, in the 3rd Brigade sector, the Carleton and York

BELOW: Troops take shelter in a pit or crater as German gunfire bursts from the treeline.

Regiment and their two squadrons of the 51st RTR were getting into position: they would attack with one battalion up, and when they reached Aboukir then the West Nova Scotia Regiment and their tank support, the Three Rivers Regiment, would come through.

On the maps, the distance between the start lines and the objectives was subdivided by reporting lines, designed to enable the battalion HQs to keep track by wireless of the progress up ahead.

At 05:45 the Allied artillery began firing at previously identified enemy positions. Twelve minutes later the front erupted as more than 780 guns, just about everything in the Allied artillery arsenal, opened up from behind the regiments to create a barrage along a 3,200-yard (2,926-metre) front, firing to a depth of 3,000 yards (2,743 metres). It was not the kind of softening-up barrage to kill and demoralize the enemy that proceeded the battles of the First World War; this was a creeping barrage, specifically organized to support the infantry and tanks that now began to move forwards closely behind it — 'leaning on the

barrage', in military jargon. Every five minutes it was lifted forwards by 100 yards (90 metres) to keep just ahead of the advancing troops.

'The steady pounding of guns, the roar of tks [tanks] moving fwd, and the marrying-up, made a terrific din, and set the pace for a somewhat hectic day. Major W. deN. Watson, MC, Comd A Coy, pushed off with a cheerful remark, "see you on the objective". Lt-Col R. C. Coleman, MC, Comd Loyal Edmonton Regt, was also seen wearing a soft hat, placidly smoking a pipe, and a happy smile on his face... The enemy's counter bty [battery] barrage was not long delayed, the wail of nebelwerfers, and a shower of 10 and 15cm arty [artillery] rained on the woods, adding to the noise and confusion.'[5]

The forward companies of the Patricias moved steadily through the woods, 'leaning on the barrage' and blinded by the smoke and dust; it was hard for the NIH to steer the tanks when visibility was so bad that the muzzle was barely

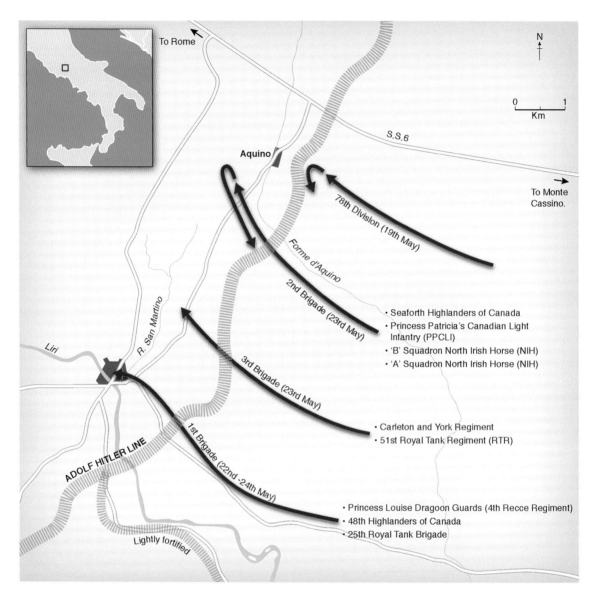

To Rome

Aquino

S.S.6

78th Division (19th May)

To Monte Cassino.

Forme d'Aquino

2nd Brigade (23rd May)

R. San Martino

Liri

3rd Brigade (23rd May)

1st Brigade (22nd -24th May)

ADOLF HITLER LINE

Lightly fortified

• Seaforth Highlanders of Canada
• Princess Patricia's Canadian Light
  Infantry (PPCLI)
• 'B' Squadron North Irish Horse (NIH)
• 'A' Squadron North Irish Horse (NIH)

• Carleton and York Regiment
• 51st Royal Tank Regiment (RTR)

• Princess Louise Dragoon Guards (4th Recce Regiment)
• 48th Highlanders of Canada
• 25th Royal Tank Brigade

0   1
Km

N

ABOVE: The opening attack on the Hitler Line by the three brigades of the 1st Canadian Infantry Division and their supporting tanks.

visible from the turret; many tanks were closed down with all hatches shut. By 06:20 they had achieved the first reporting line, codenamed January; February was reached at 07:10, by which time the German fire was intensifying. The feint by the 78th Infantry Division, designed to draw the fire of the Germans at Aquino, had failed to achieve its object, exposing the Patricias and the support squadron to

fierce artillery attack on their right flank, as well as across their front. To make matters worse, that allotted front measured less than 300 yards (274 metres). Effectively they were squeezed between the Seaforths and the edges of the gullies cut by the Forme d'Aquino. By the time they had reached the second reporting line, that distance had reduced to a mere 150 yards (137 metres) — far too narrow for tanks trying

PONTECORVO				AQUINO
1ST CANADIAN INFANTRY DIVISION				
1st Canadian Infantry Brigade:	3rd Canadian Infantry Brigade:		2nd Canadian Infantry Brigade:	
Princess Louise Dragoon Guards (4th Recce Regiment) 48th Highlanders of Canada	Carleton and York Regiment		Seaforth Highlanders of Canada	Princess Patricia's Canadian Light Infantry (PPCLI)
25th Royal Tank Brigade	Two squadrons of tanks from 51st Royal Tank Regiment (RTR)		'B' Squadron North Irish Horse (NIH)	'A' Squadron North Irish Horse (NIH)
RESERVE	RESERVE		RESERVE	
Hastings and Prince Edward's Regiment; Royal Canadian Regiment	West Nova Scotia Regiment		Loyal Edmonton Regiment	
142nd Royal Armoured Corps (RAC)	Three Rivers Regiment			
	Royal 22nd Regiment		'B' and 'C' squadrons 51st Royal Tank Regiment (RTR)	

to manoeuvre, and turning them into a neatly compressed target for the enemy on two sides.

The third reporting line – March – lay in the open cornfields, and it was here, around 07:40, that the tanks came under even more sustained and accurate fire from the SP and camouflaged Panther turret guns. At the same time, they entered a minefield that reconnaissance had failed to discover. The mines did not trouble infantry, but they halted the tanks of 'A' Squadron. One tank was blown up; a second stopped and was hit by a shell from an SP gun. Lieutenant Hunt, commanding No.5 Troop, was ordered to work out a safe route. In the dreadful visibility the troop leader's tank manoeuvred too close to the edge of a gully, and plunged over the side. Miraculously, it landed upside down on a plateau 50 feet (15 metres) below, bounced up and flipped 180 degrees back onto its tracks. The crew were bruised and badly shaken, but the driver, Davy Graham, had somehow turned off the engine during the fall.

ABOVE: The Allied order of battle for the attack on the Hitler Line along the road between Pontecorvo on the left and Aquino on the right.

After a swig of whisky all round they inspected their tank and discovered that it was in working order. Graham then pulled off an extraordinary feat of driving the tank down the ravine and finding a way back up to the top to rejoin the fray.

The Patricias advanced unsupported to the wire. Chaos ensued as communications broke down between infantry, tanks and HQ. All along the line German fire had taken out the radio sets and their operators; the battalion HQ in the woods was pinned down under heavy fire and taking casualties. Major Griffiths of the NIH went back on foot to the Patricias' HQ 'rather distressed, feeling his tanks had failed us. Actually, the tanks were doing everything possible to get fwd, and taking severe cas [casualties]'.[6]

Runners sent to make contact with 'A' and 'C' companies failed to return. Captain A.A. Campbell led 'B' Company forwards but could not get past the wire because of the withering fire. Caught at the wire and unsupported, the 'A' and 'C' companies were suffering heavy casualties.

The Seaforths had set off at the same time as the Patricias, and started to take casualties within the first 100 yards (90 metres) of the start. Two companies reached the barbed wire at 08:30, putting them just 300 yards (274 metres) from the road, but it was almost four hours of vicious fighting from one pillbox or emplacement to the next before the remnant managed to cross the German defences and gain the first objective. It was left to Major J.C. Allen and two wounded lieutenants – the rest of the officers were either dead or too badly injured to continue – to organize the one hundred men still capable of fighting on.

Casualties were also high among the tanks, as was trepidation; the NIH's Chester admitted candidly: 'When we first went into action, most of us – well I was – dead scared of what was going to happen, you know. I was 19, you know. There was so much gunfire and flames that we couldn't see because there was dust everywhere. Our visibility was estimated to be no more than 10 yards.'

Through the blinding clouds of dust, the SPs and Panther turrets kept up a merciless rate of well-aimed fire, creating a bewildering cacophony of carnage in which the snipers snapped silently from the trees. Tanks burst into flames; those crews fortunate enough to escape crouched in craters or sheltered behind burnt-out vehicles. The tanks of 'B' Squadron's commanding officer and his second-in-command were among five knocked out, the latter by a turret only 30 yards (27 metres) away. Chester was driving the commander's tank:

'We didn't see that Panther turret. We didn't see it and it was so close to us. We advanced through all the smoke and dust and then we got hit on the starboard side three times. Skipper gave the order to bail out. We got out. My driver was badly cut, almost in two, and he died. A further shot hit the turret which shot fragments of red hots all over, one of which seriously wounded the tank commander Gordon Russell. Took a large piece out of his skull and we thought he was going to die. He didn't, fortunately.'

Captain Christopher Munro Thomas, recce captain of his squadron, stepped up to take command of the 11 surviving tanks of 'B' and 'C' squadrons from the seriously wounded Major G.P. Russell, MC. Thomas was subsequently recommended for the Distinguished Service Order but was awarded the Military Cross. The citation reveals the achievement:

'… Early in the battle his sqn was involved in very heavy fighting in the course of which both his sqn leader and that of the flanking squadron were knocked out and out of 30 tanks in the area, he took comd and re-organised the remaining 11 fit ones. He did this on foot, under heavy fire in full view of the enemy. Having reorganised this force of 11 tanks, he carried out the original plans for the two squadrons and against all opposition fought his way to the objective, losing three more tanks on the way, to emplaced A.Tk [anti tank] guns at 100 yards range. In the course of this action he destroyed one Mk V PANTHER emplacement, one Mk IV Special, one 75mm A.Tk gun, one 20mm gun and over-ran a complete enemy inf strong point. The fact of his forces penetrating the enemy line was largely instrumental in the rolling up of the complete HITLER LINE. Whilst holding the objective his own tk and five others were destroyed. Despite this, Capt Thomas would NOT leave the objective until ordered to do so. …'

The courage displayed went through the ranks. The Military Medal – the equivalent of the Military Cross for 'other ranks' – was won by one of Thomas's depleted NIH command, Sergeant William John Maxwell. Thomas's composite squadron had reached the second objective at 12:00, but 45 minutes later had to withdraw

ABOVE: This painting is based on the photograph shown to Dan (see preceding page). It shows a *Panzerturm* blown off its mounting during the battle.

back through the line under heavy fire. Caught in a trap, they lost more tanks, including that commanded by Sergeant Maxwell:

'At 1300 hrs. his tank was hit by a heavy caliber anti-tank gun and put out of action. The area around the tank was being subjected to very heavy enemy shelling and mortaring. Sergeant Maxwell ordered his gunner to dismantle the Besa 7.92 mm machine-gun and to set it up in a fire position on the ground. When this had been done, Sergeant Maxwell ordered the rest of the crew to take cover in the tank while he continued to fire the Besa at the enemy. His action was instrumental in pinning down a complete enemy strong point. This so angered the enemy that a heavy mortar concentration was put down on his position as a result of which his Besa

was put out of action and he himself severely wounded. His devotion to duty has been an inspiration to the Regiment and courage cannot be over-recommended.'

Just four tanks made it back, and they were ordered to join the survivors of 'A' Squadron, which had also been ordered to fall back, in anticipation of a German counter-attack that never happened. Chester summarized the action: 'At the end of the day we had 15 tanks totally destroyed and were not recoverable. The ones which were damaged were recovered and came back to service. It was a tough day for the regiment – the toughest we'd had in either war. It was catastrophic as far as losses.'

As soon as the Patricias had moved off at 06:00, the companies of the Edmontons took their position, ready to advance alongside two squadrons of the 51st RTR. The start line was the road

objective codenamed Aboukir, where they were due at 08:15. 'Before we had moved 100 yards it was seen that the PPCLI were encountering opposition and the heavy enemy mortar and shell fire made going difficult as we were slowed down by their reserve company. The Bde pushed on through very heavy fire but the going was slow and it was quite evident that we would not reach our start line by 0815 hours.'[7]

At 07:30 that second phase was advanced to 08:45. Despite the shells, mortar rounds and machine gun bullets, the Edmontons pressed on through the rear of the Patricias who were trying to consolidate by a gully. The two companies could no longer move abreast but had to go one behind the other, and as 'A' Company came out into the cornfield they were 'subjected to a murderous fire of arty [artillery], mortar and MMG [Medium Machine Gun]. Enemy snipers were also extremely active, some of them being hidden in the lower branches of trees,' and shooting the troops from behind. Just 20 yards (18 metres) from the barbed wire, 'A' Company were forced to go to ground. They had many wounded, including their colonel, Rowan Coleman MC, who continued to direct operations, urging 'A' Company to stand up and get through the wire. An attempt was made, but faced with the intensity of the firing and the presence of anti-personnel S-mines the men were helpless. The S-mine, familiarly known to Allied troops as the 'Bouncing Betty', did not explode in the ground like an anti-tank mine but sprang into the air before detonating at around crotch height in a deadly hail of steel balls and shrapnel.

The regiment was out of radio and visual contact with the tanks, which were caught on the minefield for several hours until the sappers could clear a

ABOVE: That same view today, looking northwest towards Monte d'Oro, the mountain that dominates Pontecorvo.

207

path and so were unable to respond to appeals for support. Three immobilized tanks, however, were able to fire at the machine gun positions, until at around 11:00 'a Mark V Panther tank put in an appearance about 500 yards in front of "A" Coy and brought gun and MMG fire to bear on our tps [troops] also setting the 3 North Irish Horse tanks ablaze'.[8]

Two troops of the 51st RTR were ordered to get up to the objective to support the Seaforths. Major Griffiths, commanding 'A' Squadron NIH, told them it would be suicide to attempt it.[9] The NIH were having their own torrid time, as evidenced by the citation to the Bar to Griffith's MC:

'... 600 yards from the Start Line his squadron was held up by the obstacles and an extensive enemy minefield. Visibility was 10 yards and the squadron came under very heavy enemy shelling and mortaring which continued incessantly for 28 hours. Touch was lost with the infantry and a battle commenced with the powerful anti-tank defences. Major Griffith controlled this battle on foot despite the heavy enemy fire and besides accounting for several snipers himself, his tank destroyed two Mark V tanks (Panthers), two 75 m.m. anti-tank guns, one 88 m.m. anti-tank gun and inflicted severe casualties on the enemy infantry. Four of his Churchill tanks were destroyed in this action. As it was found impossible to by-pass the minefield and all attempts at gapping were unsuccessful, Major Griffith decided to consolidate his gains. To do this, he left the safety of his tank and for many hours on foot

and under intense fire, directed the forming of a strong point.'

All that the Edmontons knew was that the Seaforths had got two companies fighting for their lives on the objective and were in no more position to help than were the Patricias. Their only relief came after Major A.F. MacDonald called for smoke to be laid down on their right flank, to confuse the German guns at Aquino. Most of their communications had been maintained by officers and runners going back and forth under fire, and their casualties were grave. For 13 hours they suffered under the most concentrated gunfire the battalion had ever known.

Despite the loss of their tank support, the depleted Seaforths held their position on the Aquino to Pontecorvo road until 17:00 when three German tanks overran their position and forced them back. The Seaforths' regimental quartermaster brought dry clothing and hot food to brigade HQ for the exhausted survivors.

With a fighting strength of just 77, including officers, the Patricias drew back to the March reporting point, and 'C' Company of the Edmontons was sent to help cover their left flank for the night.

TAKING PONTECORVO

'Everyone realised that the Hitler Line was going to be tough to crack, but they also realised that this was going to be a history-making day for the 1st Inf Bde and especially the Hast & PER No one even doubted that the job couldn't and wouldn't be done.'[10]

The 1st Brigade were not part of Operation Chesterfield, but were to

continue their work in progress, knowing that the explosion of activity along the rest of the line would leave the Germans unable to transfer any additional troops to oppose them. On the very left of their front, the 48th with 142nd Regiment Royal Armoured Corps (RAC) advanced during the morning to high ground north of Pontecorvo and bore the early brunt of German shelling from the town. By 12:40 they were badly cut up; 'B' Company were so depleted they had to merge with 'A' Company, which had just come up behind them and whose commanding officer decided against trying to reach the objective because there was no tank support. A self-propelled gun was causing a lot of trouble. Major Clarke thought it advisable to wait until dark before sending the pioneers to capture it.

The Hasty Ps, together with their artillery, were ordered to make contact with the 48th and relieve the pressure on them.

After the regiment's pioneer corps had lifted a number of anti-tank mines from right under the enemy's nose, a reconnaissance was carried out to pinpoint enemy positions, and at 14:00 a platoon from 'D' Company began the attack that saw the regiment drive the Germans out of the town by 17:00, taking out the self-propelled gun that had hindered the 48th's advance. The writer of the regimental war diary was jubilant when he wrote up the results:

'In addition to the destruction of their line and their forced withdrawal, the enemy lost a great number in dead, numerous wounded and some 300 prisoners in this one sector. … The Tanks, returning to harbour after the battle, passed through the gap again and Major Austric's Tank hit a teller mine, throwing a track. The hatch cover came down and knocked the Major unconscious. He came too [sic] swearing lustily, to think that they had come through the action without a casualty and then he had to be knocked out by a hatch and have his tank knocked out by a stray mine.

'The Tank Squadron [from 142nd Regiment RAC] did an excellent job for us both in direct support and in indirect shoots. We are all very grateful to them for their splendid effort and co-operation.

'The Bn was overrun with German prisoners and everyone kept rooting them out of dug-outs and houses. … and in one bunch alone we sent 104 of Hitler's pets, the boys with which he was going to conquer the world.'[11]

THE PRICE OF VICTORY

Positioned in the centre, the 3rd Brigade also saw the day go to plan in terms of their specific objectives. The Carleton and Yorks set off with the barrage and reached their objective by 08:30, but failed take out the German guns. This left the squadrons of the 51st RTR in a vulnerable position on the raised ground of Campo Vicenzo, and facing an imminent battle of their own. To make matters worse they had encountered a minefield and quickly lost three tanks: 'The presence of this minefield forced what remained of the battalion to fight the battle out where it stood. Both Sqn Ldrs had been knocked out and R.H.Q. [Regimental Head Quarters] were under direct fire. However, the C.O. took over the centralised control of the remainder and they managed to engage and knock out all the enemy a/tk guns, tks and SP guns on their immediate front.'[12]

The bald details of the war diary disguised the cost to the regiment, which by 10:00 had caught up with the Carleton and Yorks on the road. Some of that cost was graphically illustrated in the memoir of Laurence Wilmot, chaplain of the West Nova Scotias, which was following up, ready to pass through the Carleton and Yorks. He recalled that a young tank officer, brought to the regimental aid post that shared premises with the West Nova Scotias' HQ, refused treatment until his injured crew were rescued. Wilmot got together a stretcher party and went out through the shrapnel and sniper fire. They dealt with several casualties en route and then:

'I went on alone and soon found the three men I was seeking, huddled in a shell hole. One had suffered a broken arm, another a broken leg, and the third had lost a lot of blood and was broken up internally. I dressed the wounds of the most serious case as carefully as possible but I could not bring him much relief. … His suffering from his internal injuries was so terrible that his crew members instructed me to administer morphine….'

Together with two walking wounded who chanced upon the scene, Wilmot used the door from an abandoned dugout to improvise a stretcher, but the seriously hurt trooper died just after being placed on it. 'The major fear of the other two wounded chaps was that the fuel tanks in the tank, not more than six feet away, would blow up from the fire that was now a blazing inferno. If that happened, they could be covered with flaming debris. Fortunately, when the explosion came, it blew out the other way and did not affect us.'

Having managed to get the wounded back to the aid post, and snatched a cup of tea, Wilmot went out with another stretcher party:

'The incoming shell emitted a terrible howl, which I thought was the music of the spheres for me. It was followed by a tremendous explosion that covered us with dust and smoke. I felt as though I had been hit on the head by a sledgehammer. The blow forced me to my knees. As I struggled to right myself, I called to the men behind me, "Are you all right?" while simultaneously feeling my head for wounds. Blood was spurting out the right side of my head and dripping from the inside of the helmet onto my shoulder and splashing onto my face. The men replied, "We're okay, but what about you, Padre?"

Realizing that if there was a hole in my head big enough for me to feel with my fingers I would not still be standing, I said, "Okay, but let's get out of here before they send another one," and led the way across the road and into the regimental aid post without further incident.

I later figured out that a piece of shrapnel penetrated my helmet just above the left temple, was deflected upwards by the tough steel of my tank helmet, cut the cord of the harness that fits it to the head, clipped off a handful of my hair, and passed out the upper right side of the helmet in two parts. Somehow, a small piece of metal, probably from the helmet, came down and nicked the top of my right ear, which was the source of the bleeding. I was deaf and had a severe ringing in my ears for some time afterwards.'[13]

The first company of the West Nova Scotias had achieved their objective in a mere 45 minutes with the support of the squadron from the Three Rivers Regiment that had taken over from the ruins of the 51st RTR. The remainder of the two regiments were coming up quickly to join them. General Chris Vokes decided that the brigade should capitalize on their achievements, despite the problems on the right. The second barrage of the day began, and, 'leaning' on it, the reserve – the Royal 22nd Regiment with two squadrons of the 12th Canadian Armoured Regiment – advanced so quickly that by the time the surprised Germans had initiated their own counter-barrage, the Canadians were through underneath it. At 18:00 they were on the Pontecorvo

ABOVE: A job well done: Private Slim Harrison of Princess Patricia's Canadian Light Infantry shakes hand with tank driver Jack Marlborough, serving with the Royal Tank Regiment.

road. The Germans managed a brief counter-attack and took prisoner a number of men from 'A' Company of the West Nova Scotias, only to march them right into the arms of their comrades in 'B' Company.

THE END OF THE LINE

Overnight resistance was still persistent. Pontecorvo was taken and the 5th Canadian (Armoured) Division were able to fight their way to the River Melfa. German forces at Aquino and Piedimonte stubbornly continued to hold out until evening on the 25th, their late retreat delaying, as planned, the Eighth Army's access to the main road for which they had fought. The situation in Aquino was particularly unkind to the Patricias, still exposed to flanking fire until what remained of the town was evacuated.

With the German withdrawal from the line, regiments could search for the wounded and recover and bury the dead. On the 25th there was good news for the Patricias:

'Maj. W. deN. Watson, MC, [PPCLI] was located in a shell hole near an 88mm gun. He had a wound in one arm and a piece of his helmet and schmeisser bullet lodged in his forehead, but was otherwise quite all right.'[14]

Later Major Watson was reported as saying that he had spent the battle lying under the muzzle of the gun, and every time it fired – and it was a very active gun – his body bounced a foot in the air.

The 2nd Brigade offered space in their cemetery for the bodies of the 32

officers and men of the NIH killed in the battle. The service was held on the 26th, with the pipe major of the Seaforths playing 'The Flowers of the Forest', and a salute fired by men of the three infantry regiments. The attachment between the Canadian infantry and the armoured regiments of the British 25th Tank Brigade had become strong. General Vokes gave the 25th the right to wear the Canadian emblem, the maple leaf; the brigade's commander, Brigadier J. Tetley, wrote to General Vokes: 'We ask nothing more that to fight with 1 Cdn Inf Div under your command, and will help to make Kesselring run faster and farther yet.'

This respect did not stop Tetley writing with some asperity in his report on the action:

'It still does not seem to be fully appreciated by the Inf that it is part of their job to seek out and destroy enemy A/Tk posns – on many occasions the Inf passed over dug-in A/Tk guns and left them to take on the tks following behind. The result of this was generally that the Inf were pinned to the ground by m/g [machine gun] fire, and the tks, being separated from them and unable to advance owing to A/Tk guns and minefields, were unable to assist.'[15]

Despite being organized in haste and subjected to late changes, the assault on the Hitler Line succeeded, at the cost of 513 Allied lives, mostly Canadian, and many more German. For the Patricias and the NIH the losses were the worst they had ever suffered in a single action. 'Was I feeling proud when I took part?' Chester asked rhetorically. 'In a way,

yes. In a way. Most of us thought during the war that the war was worthwhile, you know. It was a war we felt had to be won, and it was a right war. It was with inward pride that we fought a good battle and we won. As simple as that.'

The days immediately afterwards were congested and confused, but at the same time as the artillery had opened up on 23 May, so had the Allied guns at Anzio as the US VI Corps prepared to break out and link up with the Fifth Army under General Clark. Days of fierce fighting followed, pushing the Germans back. The commander of Allied forces in Italy, General Sir Harold R.L.G. Alexander, ordered General Clark to use the VI Corps to attack behind the German lines on the SS6 at Valmontone in order to cut off the German retreat, but Clark deliberately disobeyed the order. Instead, he led the American troops into Rome on 4 June, believing that the Americans, and they alone, deserved the glory of liberating the first European capital. His additional justification – that the VI

Corps did not have the strength to fight another battle after breaking out of Anzio and taking on the Germans at Cisterna – has divided opinion; his critics maintain that he allowed Kesselring to salvage more of his armies than would otherwise have been possible, so that the Italian campaign was greatly prolonged. In any case, the glory of entering the undefended capital of Italy was outshone 48 hours later by events on the French coast.

By February 1945, when they were withdrawn, 92,757 Canadian soldiers had fought in Italy, of whom more than a quarter became casualties – almost 6,000 of them killed.

'It is with great sorrow and regret that I see you and your famous Canadian Corps leaving my command. You have played a distinguished part in our victories in Italy, where you will leave behind a host of friends and admirers who will follow your future with the liveliest interest.'
(Field Marshal Alexander to General Foulkes, February 1945)

ABOVE: The Cassino War Cemetery where the British and Canadian dead of the Hitler Line were reburied together after the war.

THE HITLER LINE IN THE LIRI VALLEY

1: Dan and the team on the roof of the Ringstand.

2: The concrete emplacement for the *Panzerturm*. Little wonder such defences were hard to spot during reconnaissance.

Dan: 'Italy was brilliant. Basically you could trace the course of an assault on a German strongpoint.'

Dan and the team went out to the Liri Valley to work with members of the Associazione Linea Gustav, who, as well as carrying out painstaking research into the Gustav Line, have turned their attention to the Hitler Line. Researcher and battlefield expert Damiano Parravano, who liaised with *Dig WW2*, explained:

'We have recently conducted extensive research on the Hitler Line. The big problem for us is that there isn't as much information as for the other lines. We know that the first works were started in December 1943 and that they consisted of concrete emplacements, mine fields, anti-tank ditches, etc., but along the line there were also camouflaged objects, which were unrecognizable from the aerial imagery. Because the Hitler Line was in action for only a few days, from the 18th May until the 23rd–24th of May 1944, we don't have as many details – documents, footage or pictures – of the period prior to the fighting, as we do for the Gustav Line. Therefore, any new discoveries and knowledge make our work really important and interesting because they build on the historical facts and the more technical aspects of the war here. Our research won't change the general view of the Liri Valley's historiography, but it will improve our detailed knowledge.'

The first dig took place on the far left of the Hitler Line, near to the River Liri, the area where the 1st Brigade fought on 22/23 May. The Italians had identified a bunker 10 yards (9 metres) behind a low bank, heavily overgrown and probably untouched since the war. The site is on private land; the team have the full permission of the landowner and they keep its location secret. Their aim was to discover what type of fortification it was and whether it had seen action in the battle or simply been abandoned without a fight. Had the Canadians been given enough tank support to allow them to get close up and round the flank, using the low bank for cover?

First of all they investigated the approach, using a petrol strimmer to clear away the vegetation before scanning the ground with a conventional metal detector.

Almost immediately the detector began to bleep, and some work with the trowel brought up a quantity of Allied .303-inch casings lying just below the surface. Dan considered the implications.

'This is a casing of a bullet fired right here. We're 10 metres away now from this bunker. This is not long-range duelling. This is the final assault, putting down fire on that bunker, trying to kill the inhabitants or perhaps trying to get them to

3

4

5

3: A handful of standard .303 shell casings found close to the Ringstand.

4: Potentially grim evidence of the conflict: a Canadian helmet found close to the Ringstand.

5: Searching for the relics of war among the poppies of the Liri Valley: Damiano Parravano and Alberto Fontana of Associazone Linea Gustav carry out preliminary work on the Allied side of the Ringstand.

surrender. We've been looking here for two minutes max, and there are these cases coming out the ground every few seconds. This is evidence of a huge firefight.

This is a fight that would have lasted for no more than a few minutes 70 years ago. Absolutely extraordinary that archaeological material still remains of that split second in time, and yet here we have it.'

In the meantime, and still close to the surface, the metal detector had made another discovery. Working with great delicacy, the team revealed the rim of a helmet lying upside down. Using trowel and brush they gently removed the earth inside and eased the helmet out of the ground. Most of the crown was missing. It was definitely Canadian, and the man who had worn it could well have been a casualty, perhaps fatally injured, in the vicious final assault.

Close to where the helmet was found, the team turned up a machine gun bullet from a British tank, and around the exposed bunker, coils of rusty barbed wire were handled with due respect.

The bunker revealed itself as a Ringstand 58c, one of the most common types of hard fortification, also known as a Tobrukstand.

Previous flooding had eroded much of the earth behind the emplacement, completely exposing the entrance so Dan was easily able to enter from the rear. A short flight of steps led up from a small ante-room to the combat chamber. In 1944, the outside of the circular hole in the slightly domed ceiling would have been fitted with a steel ring on which a machine gun, operated from inside the combat chamber, traversed. Such an emplacement would have been manned by just two soldiers. Seen from the front, very little of the Ringstand would have protruded above the earth, less than today, and the slight ridge into which it was set gave it a formidable command of the fields that the Canadian infantry and their supporting armour had to cross. While Dan sat on the roof, the Italians handed up German machine gun rounds and portions of the ammunition belt.

Among the bullets found at the base of the bunker was a round that had clearly hit the front wall. Dan exclaimed:

'That is just extraordinary. While these German casings are from bullets going that way, this is what's coming back the other way. This is actually a bullet, a British Allied bullet, and it's been battered because it's hit this concrete wall. The concrete's done its job. And it's split and twisted this bullet into all sorts of different shapes. This is incoming fire. This is the proof we need. This is outgoing, this is incoming – no question.'

Parravano took Dan a little further east, to the site of a Panzer turret just like that which Gerry Chester and his Churchill tank crew had failed to see until they were only 30 yards (27 metres) away. It is long gone for scrap, but a photograph exists of it, barrel raised towards the sky in futile defiance while Canadian soldiers pose beside it.

As Dan approached the position from the front, he reflected that he was following the path of the troops in 1944: 'Walking across this fairly flat, wide open,

lush, Liri Valley the troops would have felt very, very exposed to the German
machine gunners just there. And of course they would have been cut down
instantly were it not for the fact that they weren't alone. They had the support of
their tanks. The tanks were behind them blasting high-explosive shells towards
those German positions, forcing the Germans to keep their heads down, and
there's shrapnel all over these fields – like these pieces of shell casing here. It
allowed the infantry to get nice and close to this German bunker.'

The Allied dead now lie in the beautifully tended graves of the cemetery below
Monte Cassino: 'After the battle the dead of the Canadians and the North Irish
Horse were buried alongside each other. This was entirely appropriate for men
who had fought and fallen together, men who had broken the Hitler line.'

WHY CALL IT D-DAY?

'D' is sometimes thought to stand for 'dis-embarkation' or 'departure' but it was just a convenient piece of alliteration, not an abbreviation. There were two strong reasons to avoid using the actual date. Firstly, if the operation were to remain secret, the fewer who knew the date, the better for security. Secondly, the planners had to work backwards and forwards from the date on which the troops were to land. Everything from air and naval support to troop movements, communications, food and ammunition supplies, and hospital facilities had to be precisely coordinated so that the operation began with everything in place and continued smoothly afterwards. Therefore, the days were referred to as D-Day–2, D-Day–1, D-Day, D-Day+1, D-Day+2, and so on. If, as was highly probable (in fact, it actually happened), the date of the invasion had to be changed, there was much less chance of people being confused as to whether a specific date referred to the original or the revised plan.

ABOVE: British troops disembark from landing craft on D-Day.

ORDERS TO SAIL

Even as Allied troops in Italy moved closer to Rome at the end of May, around 170,000 more began to gather at camps and bases along the south coast of England. The harbours seethed with transports and landing craft as Operation Neptune, the first part of Operation Overlord, approached. The biggest amphibious invasion ever carried out had been a year in the planning, under conditions of such high security that, despite the numbers of troops and administration personnel involved, very few people knew when and where it would take place until it was underway; training had been carried out using maps, photographs and models, all with bogus place-names. Major (later Major General) Tony Younger, who led 7th Infantry Brigade, 26 Assault Squadron Royal Engineers (26AS), knew the destination, but appreciated the visual help, 'I knew exactly where I was. The photographs we'd been working on were excellent'.[16] Deception and misinformation not only kept the

Germans guessing, but diverted their eyes from that stretch of the Normandy coastline between St. Martin de Varreville and Ouistreham, making them believe, as logic predisposed them to believe, that the Pas de Calais was the true target area. The disadvantages of the former were heavily outweighed by the greater chance of achieving surprise and the certain knowledge that however formidably the coastline might be defended, opposition there would not be quite as horrendous as further east.

D-DAY: THE TAKING OF JUNO BEACH

From west to east, the landings area was divided into five beaches, with the codenames Utah, Omaha, Gold, Juno and Sword. Put simplistically, the first two were for American troops, Sword and Gold were British, and Juno was Canadian. Each beach was subdivided into sectors and subsectors.

Juno Beach stretched from La Rivière eastwards to St. Aubin, bisected at Courseulles-sur-Mer by the River Seulles that wriggled its way north. At

BELOW: The broad expanse of Juno Beach that became a killing ground on D-Day. Looking back, John Hadley of Queen's Own Rifles of Canada commented: 'I was a boy when I went into France but I ended up, within a couple of days, a man. I'd seen things that I'd never seen in my life before and I hoped never to see again ....'

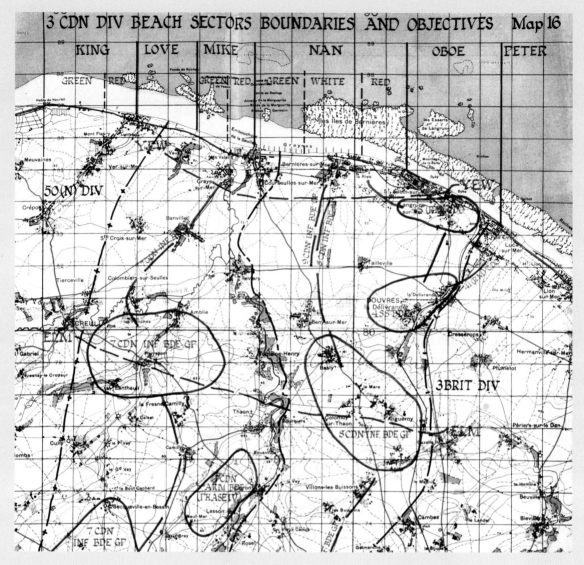

ABOVE: The sectors of Juno Beach and objectives of the Canadian divisions.

the coastal village of Graye-sur-Mer it showed reluctance to proceed directly to the sea, making a few broad curves and then turning right towards Courseulles, to run behind the sand dunes, parallel to the sea, for a quarter of a mile (400 metres) before it finally emptied into the dock at Courseulles. West of the river mouth, Juno was divided into two sectors, Love and Mike, with Mike subdivided into Mike Green and Mike Red; to the east, a single sector, Nan, was subdivided into Nan Green, Nan White and Nan Red.

Tasked with taking Mike and Love were four companies of the Royal Winnipeg Rifles, a Manitoba regiment fondly known as the 'Little Black Devils', augmented by 15 Platoon, 'C' Company of the 1st Canadian Scottish Regiment and sappers of the Royal Canadian Engineers. The 12th and 13th field regiments of the Royal Canadian Artillery (RCA) were to provide the artillery, while armoured support was in the hands of 'A' Squadron of the First Hussars and their Duplex Drive (DD) tanks, 'B' Squadron of the 22nd

Dragoons with their Crab flail tanks, and 26AS with their fascine and box girder tanks. These strange creations were designed to surmount many of the German defences that the Allies knew they would encounter.

NO LAUGHING MATTER: HOBART'S FUNNIES

Necessity is the mother of invention, especially in wartime. While the No. 74 (ST) hand grenade, known as the 'Sticky Bomb', was less than ideal because it preferred to stick to the khaki uniform of the soldier trying to throw it than to adhere to the target – the muddy sides of an enemy tank, Hobart's (or Hobo's) Funnies, as they became known from their unusual appearance, were in a different league. These ingeniously modified tanks overcame many of the problems faced by Allied troops from D-Day onwards, and although Sir Percy Hobart did not invent the modifications himself, he embraced them and brought them into his 79th Armoured Division. The most famous example was arguably the DD Sherman developed by the Hungarian engineer Nicholas Straussler, who arrived in Britain in the inter-war years.

A landing craft offloading its tanks onto a beach defended by a heavily armed and entrenched enemy is a sitting duck. A tank propelling itself ashore from 2 miles (3 kilometres) out, disguised as a small boat, is a smaller and rather less interesting target. Straussler devised a canvas skirt that incorporated flotation tubes and a lightweight frame, and he attached this around the hull of a Sherman tank, sealing the join with rubber. When raised vertically and inflated, the skirt created a canvas-sided dinghy, displacing a mass of water greater than that of the tank itself – thus allowing the tank to float with about 3 feet (0.9 metres) of freeboard and conveniently disguising the 'upper works' to fool observers. The underside of the tank was sealed to prevent flooding from below, a bilge pump was fitted to deal with any excess water, and the tank's own powerful engine was equipped with a Duplex Drive. At sea, the engine powered propellers; once on land, the skirt was quickly deflated and pulled down, and the engine once again drove the tank's wheels. It was this Duplex Drive, not D-Day, that gave the vehicle its DD Sherman designation.

The DD Shermans played a remarkable part in allowing the Allies to establish their bridgehead on D-Day. One sergeant recalled:

'I was the first tank coming ashore and the Germans started opening up with machine-gun bullets. But when we came to a halt on the beach, it was only then that they realized we were a tank when we pulled down our canvas skirt, the flotation gear. Then they saw that we were Shermans. It was quite amazing. I still remember very vividly some of the machine-gunners standing up in their posts looking at us with their mouths wide open. To see tanks coming out of the water shook them rigid.'[17]

Although the seas were rougher than envisaged, 29 of 30 tanks launched reached Utah Beach, the best result. Omaha, however, was a disaster: the DDs were launched too far out and in

THESE PAGES: A Duplex Drive Sherman tank with its flotation skirt raised and inflated. And the same tank with the skirt collapsed – now ready for action.

trying to steer for their precise landing spot they found themselves broadside to the waves. Only two out of 29 were able to land, and loss of life among the crews was appalling.

Other 'Funnies' were designated AVREs (Armoured Vehicle Royal Engineers), pronounced by the troops as 'Avrees', and these included the Churchill AVRE, Crab, Crocodile, Bobbin and Fascine. The Churchill AVRE was a Churchill tank on which the standard turret gun had been replaced by a spigot mortar that fired a 40-pound (18-kilogram) round known as the 'Flying Dustbin'. Like its unloved Home Guard predecessor, the mortar had to engage at 100 yards (90 metres) or less, and the gun loader was exposed while he reloaded, but it was specifically for use against fortifications

such as bunkers and pillboxes. The Crab was a Sherman tank with two arms that held a raised, rotating cylinder in front of it. Numerous chains, attached by one end across the width of the roller, acted as a flail, thrashing the ground with their weighted ends to explode mines or cut through barbed wire to make a safe path that others could follow. The Bobbin unrolled a canvas carpet to create a road over soft ground – such as the blue clay on Gold Beach – that could not support armour; it was nicknamed the Bog Roll. The Crocodile came equipped with a flame-thrower, the fuel for which was towed in a separate tank, and large gaps such as rivers were bridged by tanks modified to carry box girder bridges. Ditches and culverts were dealt with by the Fascine.

William Dunn joined the Royal Engineers in 1940 at the age of 17, becoming a driver mechanic in 'C' Company, 26AS. Before D-Day he trained on an AVRE that carried a fascine, which he described as:

'A big bundle of paling, I'd say about 15 to twenty feet across, lightly bound up into a big round bundle… It was on the front of your tank… Two hawsers came over the top of the tank and held it in place just above the turret. It was to drop into ditches… The commander would release it, it'd drop down into the ditch so you could just run over the top of it… And if you left it, the other tanks could follow on 'cause it was pretty strong and would carry the weight of a tank alright.'[18]

Only the DD tanks had swimming capability; the AVREs would be launched into shallow water and had to be made watertight below by being covered with a thick black compound that dried to a hard coating. Temporary extended exhausts and air louvres were also fitted to let gas out and air in. Once the tank was ashore these could be blown off by a small charge.

ON THE RIGHT TRACKS – PERCY HOBART

The celebrated military analyst Captain B.H. Liddell Hart regarded Major-General Percy Hobart as a genius. Both looked to the example of the Mongol armies who in a different age had swept across Europe on horseback, rather than plodding along at the pace of a supply

ABOVE: A Crab flail in action.

train. Fast tank units protected by their armour and self-supporting, even supplied by air drop – could have that same ability to smash and tear into the enemy. In 1927 Hobart was allowed to set up an experimental mechanized force, but even after it had demonstrated the effectiveness of this strategic mobility the hidebound military establishment embarked on a vindictive campaign to close ranks against him and anyone else espousing the idea.

More than a theorist, Hobart was also an inspirational leader who explained his tactics to those, at all levels, who would put them into practice, thereby gaining their confidence and loyalty. A brigadier by

1934, he founded and commanded the 1st Tank Brigade, and in military exercises not only reached the 'enemy's' rear but also proved that tanks could fight at night.

The military establishment still wilfully closed its eyes to the potential of the tank, much as many in the inter-war Royal Navy closed theirs to the aircraft carrier, and Hobart's one failing was that he lacked the diplomatic skills to reach their brains via their ears. He had, however, one ardent admirer in high places: Heinz Guderian, who in 1940 would put Hobart's ideas into practice – for Germany.

The War Office fought off the attempt by its own Secretary of State,

Leslie Hore-Belisha, to put Hobart in charge of a new armoured division, and in 1938 Hobart was shuffled off to Egypt to raise from scratch a second tank unit to counter the expected threat from Italy. Despite the hostility of General Sir Robert Gordon-Finlayson, C-in-C of British Troops in Egypt, Hobart trained the widely admired 7th Armoured Division – the 'Desert Rats' – that had been formed out of three Hussar regiments, two battalions of the Royal Tank Corps, the 3rd Regiment Royal Horse Artillery (RHA) and the 60th Rifles, but 1940 found him back home, dismissed by Wavell who had evidently yielded to the weight of prejudice against him. Hobart joined the Home Guard as a corporal, and might have lingered there, albeit at a higher rank, had not Liddell Hart gone to the Press with a scathing denunciation of the waste of military talent, Hobart's in particular. Churchill,

now Prime Minister, angrily swept aside all protestations and demanded he be brought back.

October 19, 1940
Prime Minister to Chief of Imperial General Staff:

    … I think very highly of this officer, and I am not at all impressed by the prejudices against him in certain quarters. Such prejudices attach frequently to persons of strong personality and original view. In this case, General Hobart's views have been only too tragically borne out. The neglect by the General Staff even to devise proper patterns of tanks before the war has robbed us of all the fruits of this invention. These fruits have been reaped by the enemy, with terrible consequences. We should, therefore, remember that this was an officer who had the root of the matter in him, and also vision….'[19]

BELOW: Sir Percy Hobart (right) during an invasion exercise on 1 May 1944. The vehicle behind him is an amphibious jeep.

Hobart raised the 11th Armoured Division, but as he was about to go out to North Africa with them, his enemies demanded he be retired on grounds of age. Once again, Churchill penned a venomous letter, dated 4 September 1942, to the Secretary of State for War, demolishing their argument and pointedly alluding to the reverses that the British had met with when faced with Rommel's Afrika Korps during the North Africa Campaign:

'I have been shocked at the persecution to which he has been subjected. I am quite sure that if, when I had him transferred from a corporal in the Home Guard to the command of one of the new armoured divisions, I had insisted instead on his controlling the whole of the tank developments, with a seat on the Army Council, many of the grievous errors from which we have suffered would not have been committed.'[20]

Hobart was persuaded by Liddell Hart and others to take on the task of devising the armour that would help to achieve victory when the time came for Operation Overlord. The result was not just his famous 'Funnies' but also the creation of the 79th Armoured Division, units of which were distributed among the various Allied armies, even those of the USA. After D-Day Eisenhower acknowledged that his 'Funnies' and their brilliantly trained crews had saved many infantry lives.

The 79th and Hobart went with the Allied armies across Europe until the end of the war. He then voluntarily retired and was honoured with a knighthood to add to the gallantry medals he had won in the First World War. A grateful USA awarded him the Legion of Merit, Degree of Commander. He died in 1957.

FINAL PREPARATIONS

On 1 June the Winnipegs were sealed in their camps near Southampton, and the following day – as Clark was leading his men towards Rome – the 'Little Black Devils' were issued with survival kits in case they found themselves stranded in Normandy: food pack, sterilization tablets, maps of France printed on fine silk for concealment, and compasses in the form of buttons. Now the officers were told the details of the operation.

That afternoon 'A' and 'C' companies of the Winnipegs boarded their LSI [Landing Ship Infantry], HMS *Llangibby Castle*,[21] well known to them from exercises and with a particularly fine catering department. The former passenger ship combined a magnetic attraction to trouble with a genius for survival. Bombed by the Luftwaffe in Liverpool in 1940, in 1942 she had her stern blown off by a U-boat and in 1942 took a hit from a Vichy French army shell. After damaging her bow in 1943 she was converted to an LSI for 1,590 troops and 15 landing craft and did sterling work in the Mediterranean.

'B' and 'D' companies of the Winnipegs and the Canadian Scottish were to carry out the first assault, and they were split between the former cross-Channel ferries *Canterbury* and *Lairds Isle* (ex-*Riviera*) – the latter having served during the First World

War as one of the world's first aircraft carriers.

'A' and 'B' squadrons First Hussars and their tanks arrived at Southampton. Some of the crews were allowed down to the NAAFI to enjoy a show; others remained aboard their Landing Craft Tanks (LCTs) with the DD Shermans. Major Younger saw 26AS's tanks loaded into eight landing craft. Two Crab flails from 22nd Dragoons were sent in each LCT; one half of 26AS would go to Nan, the other to Mike and Love.

The weather worsened during Sunday 4th; at noon General Eisenhower postponed Operation Neptune for 24 hours following meteorological reports that the seas would calm on the 6th. During Monday morning, the First Hussars went on a route march round the docks, which were now sealed off; the Winnipegs and the Canadian Scottish cleaned the mess decks. Weapons were inspected. The weather was still not ideal, but men were told to rest in expectation that the order to sail would come.

It did, and at 21:00 the LSIs began to pass through the boom gate into the choppy waters of the Solent and out into the rougher Channel. Now all ranks could be briefed. Hot food and seasickness tablets were served aboard the big LSIs; the troops on the LSTs had to make their own meals because of the lack of facilities. The transports rendezvoused with their escorts. By now the Royal Navy and the RAF had done as much as they could to deny the Kriegsmarine any opportunity to disrupt the crossing – mines had been dropped, and patrols continually looked out for submarines and torpedo boats. Major Tony Younger's LCT was

the front craft, following the escorting frigate. His second lieutenant was prostrate with seasickness, and he was not feeling too good. Having eaten his dinner he went to lie down.

Younger had told his crews to keep out of their vehicles and just walk around or try their hand at aircraft spotting. William Dunn, the fascine tank driver in 'C' Company, took the advice. There was no shortage of Allied aircraft in the dark skies: some packed with paratroopers, others towing gliders full of men and equipment, others carrying bombs; there were vital tasks to perform before the troops arrived.

THE AIRBORNE GO IN

The opposition faced by the Allied troops would come not just from the German units manning the Atlantic Wall immediately ahead of them, but from powerful defensive positions

ABOVE: Home cooking for troops of the Light Infantry of Canada aboard Landing Craft Infantry (Large) 306 of the 2nd Canadian (262nd RN) Flotilla during the D-Day crossing.

located further inland on the east and west flanks of the invasion zone. Out to the west, on the Cotentin Peninsula behind Utah Beach, Rommel had ordered his men to flood the land by opening the lock at the mouth of the River Douve at high tide and closing it at low tide, leaving just four heavily defended 'causeways' as the only means of exiting the beach. Positions to the east controlled vital roads and bridges that had to be captured to protect the bridgehead from any German counter-attack. Therefore these airborne operations were not small commando raids but large-scale attacks, involving more than 20,000 men.

Just after midnight, on D-Day, scouts from the British 6th Airborne Division parachuted into the area east of Caen. They were soon followed by the main drop of the rest of the force, some 7,000 together with their vehicles and heavy weapons. BBC journalist Guy Byam recorded his drop: 'One minute, thirty seconds. Red light – green and out, get on, out, out fast into the cool night air over France ... We're jumping into fields covered with poles … And the ground comes up to hit me. And I find myself in the middle of a cornfield … and, overhead, hundreds of containers are coming down.'

Nothing went smoothly. The paratroopers – British and Canadian, and even several journalists – were dispersed. Units were badly under strength, their personnel scattered or dead: killed in crashes, drowned in the marshes, or shot as they hung from their parachutes in the trees. Nevertheless, they succeeded in taking the vital bridges at Ranville and

Bénouville,[22] and despite having little equipment and only 150 of his 700 commandos with him, Lieutenant Colonel Terence Otway captured the battery at Merville that covered Sword Beach. Before Otway could fire the rocket announcing that the battery was out of action, 20 officers and men had been killed.

Meanwhile, on the Cotentin Peninsula, the Americans were experiencing similar problems following their drops. Personnel were dispersed over some 230 square miles (600 square kilometres); equipment was lost, men also shot and drowned. With their formations in disarray, the Americans, like the British, had to rely on initiative and determination to meet their objectives, and among their finest achievements, and still regarded as a textbook operation, was the capture of the German batteries at Brécourt, a farm north of Sainte-Marie-du-Mont, by Easy Company, 506th Parachute Infantry Regiment, 101st Airborne Division. The exploit was made internationally famous by the book, and subsequent television series, *Band of Brothers*.

SILENCING THE GUNS OF BRÉCOURT

Eighty-one aircraft took off before midnight on the eve of D-Day, formed up, and headed for Normandy with the men of Easy Company divided between aircraft numbers 66 to 73. Descending to a height of some 500 feet (150 metres) and at a speed of 150 miles (240 kilometres) per hour they entered the drop zones through a storm of German flak.

When Lieutenant Dick Winters was given the order to jump from aircraft No. 67 at 01:10 he did not know that aircraft No. 66 had crashed, killing all on board including, the company commander, Lieutenant Thomas Meehan, and that he was now the unit's senior officer. He landed in the vicinity of Sainte Mère-Eglise, minus all his equipment, even his rifle. Most paratroopers packed their kit, including weapons, into a canvas leg bag, and many of these were torn off by the blast from the aircraft props as the men jumped. In company with another paratrooper he began heading towards the beach some 5 miles (8 kilometres) away, meeting up en route with various members of his own unit, and gathering strays from others. A chance skirmish with some German soldiers and the discovery of a wrecked wagon gave Winters the comforting protection of an M1 Garand rifle and plenty of ammunition. At around 06:00, they joined up with the staff, giving a battalion strength of 200 under Colonel Strayer. As they carried on towards their objective, Winters was the commander of nine riflemen, one other officer, and a rather limited amount of firepower.

The flooding of the low-lying land behind Utah Beach left just four exits in the form of parallel causeways, standing 6 feet (1.8 metres) or so above the marshes and deep drainage ditches, that were easy to defend. Troops who got past the 50-millimetre guns in their casemates and the machine gun fire from the Tobrukstands might be able to wade across the marshes, though the drainage ditches, lurking in wait beneath the floodwater, would be deathtraps. However, the armoured support could

cross only on the causeways. Easy Company's task was to capture the exit to the second causeway, which led from the beach at La Madeine, between the hamlets of Haudienville and La Vienville, crossed the main road near the village of Le Grand Chemin and entered Sainte-Marie-du-Mont. The exit was covered by a four gun 105mm German battery established in a hedge running along a field at Brécourt Manor, and although the German gunners could not see their targets at such a distance they were directed from an observation point in the bell tower of the church at nearby Sainte-Marie-du-Mont.

ABOVE: The bell tower of the church at Sainte-Marie-du-Mont commands a perfect view of the flat countryside and causeways behind Utah Beach.

Easy Company possessed two machine guns. Winters ordered them to be set up in the inner and outer corner of a 'dogleg' in the hedge, trained on the muzzle of the first gun, to give covering fire if required. Then he split his men into two groups, one under his command, the other under Lieutenant Lynn 'Buck' Compton. While the latter group crept down the far side of the hedge at right angles to the trench-hedge, and sneaked up behind the first gun, Winters's group made a frontal approach in the open, crawling up to the emplacement.

They attacked simultaneously, with rifles and grenades. The noise of their assault must have been masked by the crumps of the other three guns, mingled with the sound of battle coming from the beach 5,000 yards (4,570 metres) away, where the landing had already begun. The German response when it came was completely uncoordinated. It appears that they may well have positioned their own defensive machine guns on an intruding corner on the opposite side of the field to the battery, to counter the expected attack from the direction of Sainte Mère-Eglise. To fire from that position on Easy Company was also to shoot their own troops in the back. Winters's men had taken out the first three guns and were thinly stretched and low on ammunition before their promised reinforcements finally arrived and took the fourth gun.

By this time machine gun fire from the Germans occupying Brécourt Manor had become fierce; Winters withdrew the men, and some of the Sherman tanks that had landed on the beach came up to lend a hand clearing out the German machine gun posts

As the US paratroopers reached the hamlet of Le Grand Chemin the battery opened up comparatively close at hand on their right. Evidently it had not been knocked out by the earlier bombing raids that had plastered the Normandy coast. Winters was ordered to 'take care of it'.

Reconnoitring the position by crawling along another hedge, he could see that the battery was firing down the causeway he had originally been charged with securing, and it had to be set in a ditch or trench running along a hedge. The only way of dealing with it was by stealth. He laid his plans for a flank attack, one gun at a time.

around the field. The capture of the battery took three hours and cost four American lives and six wounded; it saved many more on Utah Beach where the silencing of those guns was very apparent to the soldiers fighting their way off the beach. A highly significant bonus was Winters's discovery of a map giving the positions of all the machine guns and 105-millimetre guns in the Cotentin Peninsula.

Brécourt Manor was the home of the elderly Colonel de Vallavieille, his wife and two surviving sons – two other sons having already been killed in the war. When 24-year-old Michel came out of the house, he was shot in the back by a jumpy American soldier who apparently thought he was one of the Germans who had taken over the building. Critically wounded, he was quickly evacuated off the beach and taken to England for life-saving treatment – and never bore any grudge.

A SEARCH FOR GUNS UNEARTHS A FIELD HOSPITAL

Although the story of Dick Winters and his men has been retold many times, and many visitors to Normandy have stood by the gate to the field in which the action took place, no archaeological dig has ever been permitted on the land. Historian and battlefield guide Paul Woodage had studied the site for some years and corresponded with members of Easy Company, including Major Winters, to work out exactly what had happened that morning. His research raised doubt over one aspect of the assault: the precise position of one of the guns. The default position was that the guns were in a single row along the eastern edge of the field, but Major Winters had also drawn a sketch showing only three guns on that axis, and the fourth set into the northern boundary of the field to point north.

BELOW: The field at Brécourt; the guns were believed to be sited along the hedge bordering the right-hand side.

A Second World War reconnaissance photograph showed distinct pale patches in three positions along the eastern hedge, but no trace of a fourth, though there was a suggestion of something around the northeastern corner. An excavation of the site could probably settle the matter once and for all.

With the permission of Charles de Vallavieille, the colonel's grandson, Woodage joined forces with the *Dig WW2* team to conduct the work.

The whole area is so quiet and peaceful today that it is impossible to imagine the noise, bloodshed and sheer volume of men and materials that fought so hard in this rural, patchwork area of France during and after D-Day. The grazing field out of which the guns fired is almost flat, with the hedge along the ditch thinner than it had been. Visually, there is no evidence of anything violent having occurred.

The quietness at Brécourt created a problem for Eamonn McKenna, the soundman, who, like cameraman Mark McCauley, wanted the immediacy captured by a 'first take'. Because of the sensitivity of the book microphone, everyone on the site, even a hundred yards away from the 'action', had to keep quiet. 'Sometimes you've got something recorded on sound and it just needs lifting, and in the process of lifting the person saying "yes, I've got something here!" you lift all the background noise as well, and that's when you hear other people talking. If we're doing landscapes, we can hear people talking because the sound is being boosted so we can get bird sounds.'

The grey Normandy morning was spent in a non-invasive survey of the area by Dr Alastair Ruffell from the School of Geography, Archaeology and Palaeoecology, Queen's University Belfast, using ground penetrating radar to detect buried objects or changes in the subsoils that might indicate disturbance caused by, for example, backfilling a pit. The survey was done at high and low penetration: the deeper the penetration, the lower the resolution. At the same time, bomb disposal expert, Bill Shuttleworth of IDPL, on hand in case unexploded ordnance turned up, swept the area with a powerful £45,000 ferrous metal detector that had the ability to detect iron and steel at depths of up to 30 feet (9 metres).

By lunchtime, only two anomalies had been found, both by the metal detector: one was tiny and insignificant, but the other was, according to Shuttleworth, 'off the scale'. The site was located towards the end of the field and close to the hedge, and whatever was responsible lay at a depth of a little under 5 feet (1.5 metres). The bulldozer arrived to begin scraping the site, while the team tried to curb their excitement, remembering that an old coil of barbed wire would create a similar reading to the remains of a gun position. Not that a coil of German barbed wire would have been without interest. Starting in North Africa, the Germans evaluated Allied wire cutters taken from captured prisoners, and, wherever necessary, upped the specification of their barbed wire to try to keep ahead of the enemy.

The first object to be uncovered from the site was … a US Army toothbrush. This was somewhat surprising, given that Winters had told his men to leave their kit behind, but not as perplexing as the small brass bell that followed.

A badly corroded container was recovered, leaking a gooey substance that raised initial fears of something dangerously unpleasant such as Amytol, but it turned out to be thick grease.

Initially, the unearthing of some heavily rusted pieces of connected iron tubing raised hopes that a machine gun support had been found, but the find was positively identified as belonging to a heavy duty stretcher used for transporting casualties by jeep.

By now everyone was looking bemused as the spoil heap yielded numerous small glass phials, some still full, a British toothbrush bearing the War Office mark, a comb, an American lightbulb, a glass Horlicks container, and a couple of wine bottles. The most bizarre find was a saline drip, still half full. A rusty light – of a type that could have been rigged up to help doctors working in a field hospital, complete with wire – was carefully extracted, along with more bottles of medicinal appearance and US markings. Dan summed up:

'So this, according to Paul, was a huge field hospital. We're not that far now from Utah Beach and thousands of men wounded on D-Day, and in the days following it, would have needed somewhere to be looked after… And of course when the orderlies came to remove all the rubbish and medical supplies that had been used, they found these perfect pits, which of course had housed the German guns, and they must have just thrown it all into there. Today has really illustrated what's so

great about digging up battlefields, and that is: you can start out looking for one thing and you end up finding something completely different, but it's equally fascinating.'

The finds have been handed over to Charles de Vallavieille, and many will be exhibited in the nearby museum with which he is closely associated.

CLOSING THE BEACHES

The rough crossing was wretched for most of the thousands of troops, many of whom had been cooped up in their craft for days before they sailed. It was bad enough to feel, or to be, seasick; it was worse to vomit their last substantial meal and have no idea when they might get another. At 04:00 the Winnipegs were given a final cup of hot tea and a cold snack. Sub-Lieutenant Hugh Dinwiddy RNVR, a teacher and former county cricket player who had swapped his gown for a naval uniform and was commanding *LCT 441*, recalled: 'When dawn broke we became aware of the awesome shape of a British battleship on our starboard side. This silent monster, which had slid into position unnoticed, was very soon to open fire with its 16-inch guns in the direction of Caen.'[23]

John Hadley of Queen's Own Rifles of Canada remembered that, 'There were literally hundreds of aircraft that could be seen. The sky was black with aeroplanes and so forth, all heading inland. It didn't enter our heads that the Germans could stop the army, I don't think. It seemed to be such an overwhelming force that they were bound to get to their objective sooner or later.'

In the run-up to D-Day Allied fighters and bombers had attacked targets across France, from radar stations and railways to missile sites and fortifications, careful not to put any tell-tale emphasis on the chosen landing sites. As the landing ships sailed through the night, the RAF had bombed strategically; at dawn it was the turn of USAAF to attack the German positions, bombing and strafing the coast.

Unfortunately, the weather made the bomber pilots understandably wary of hitting the Allied fleet as it sailed beneath the cover of the low clouds, and they dropped too many of their bombs behind the powerful coastal fortifications.

At 05:15, still 10 miles (16 kilometres) from the coast, 'D' and 'B' companies of the Winnipegs and 'C' Company Canadian Scottish, climbed into their LCAs (Landing Craft Assault) and were lowered from their large LSIs onto the water. Tony Younger got up and shaved. By now the beach was in sight. The waves were around 5 feet (1.5 metres), higher than desirable. So far, there was no gunfire from the French coast. The assault was on its way in, the shallow-bottomed landing craft pitching, rolling and wallowing among the white-capped waves.

John Hadley was to land on Nan sector: 'We went in and finally we sighted land and it was very quiet; it was eerie. There was a long beach and a wall and there wasn't a sound or a sight and we couldn't see anything.'

The naval support began at 05:15, fired over the top of the advancing landing craft. Rear Admiral Vian's Eastern Task Force, which covered Sword, Juno and Gold beaches, began to bombard the German emplacements. The guns of the British and Canadian and French destroyers thundered out; rockets flashed out of the guns of the LCTs. Ninety-six 105-

ABOVE: A stream of small landing craft carry Canadian infantry from a large Landing Ship Infantry to Nan Sector, Juno Beach.

OPPOSITE ABOVE: A hospital jeep carrying stretcher cases, conspicuously flying the Red Cross.

OPPOSITE: A comforting taste of home: a Horlicks bottle found in the spoil heap at Brécourt.

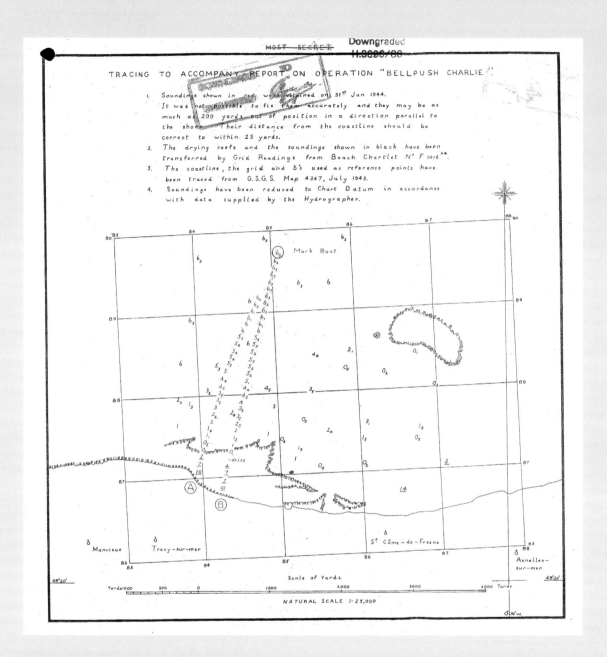

ABOVE: Existing charts of the beaches were decades out of date
and vital new data was obtained by highly dangerous covert surveying
operations codenamed 'Bellpush' and led by Lieutenant
Commander Frank Berncastle. Reconnaissance by midget submarine
and motor boat took place, notably those by Sergeant Bruce Ogden-
Smith and Major Logan Scott-Bowden who swam to shore from
a couple of miles out to collect beach samples. This one of Juno Beach
identifies the reefs that caused so much trouble for the landings.

millimetre self-propelled guns of the Royal Canadian Artillery aboard their landing craft augmented the barrage, with the 13th Field Regiment targeting the beach west of Courseulles. Rockets, too, were fired. Only when the landing craft drew closer to the shore did the tanks and infantry learn to their cost that the success of the bombardment and the aerial bombing had been totally disproportionate to its ferocity and spectacle. For the moment, their overriding concerns were their own sickness and the obstacles in their path.

If D-Day had been governed by the weather, H-hour was dependent on the tides. At low tide, all the beach obstacles were visible and could be avoided, but the infantry would have to disembark and cross hundreds of yards of exposed sand, at the mercy of the guns that swept the beaches. To land at high tide would shorten the distance on the beach, but make the landing craft vulnerable to Rommel's 'devil's garden'. The result was a compromise: land when the tide was halfway in. Juno Beach, however, presented a natural hazard not encountered elsewhere: an offshore reef, so H-Hour had to be 07:45, half an hour later than elsewhere, to allow craft to clear the shoal. Reconnaissance had told them exactly what to expect once they did:

'A system of anti-craft obstacles, running across all of MIKE sector and nearly all of NAN sector, incorporates hedgehogs, Element 'C's, pointed stakes and ramp-type obstacles. Hedgehogs are constructed of three 6˝ angle irons each 6ft 6˝ long, joined at their middles to form double tripods. The vertical height is approximately 5ft 7 in. the hedgehogs have been placed in staggered rows, with 12 to 15 ft between individual obstacles, and 25 to 30 yds between rows. Spacing between units of Element 'C' varies from 70 to 140ft. Pointed timber stakes are approx 10ft high and 6-ft apart. Ramp-style steel obstacles have been erected only on the WEST half of MIKE sector.

The latest available air phs show that mines, probably tellermines, have been placed on top of all types of offshore obstacles. Mines are secured in top of the hedgehogs, and on top of the timber stakes and Element 'C's. Except at extreme high tide the mines will be plainly visible.'[24]

STORMING THE STRONGPOINTS

John Hadley: 'And when that ramp went down and we went through the water onto the beach we just ran and ran. If you stopped on the beach you were dead. They would kill you. There wasn't much time to look around. The only time you had to look around was when you got up to the wall. We looked down and saw the dead bodies and the boats washing around.'

The task of the forces landing on Juno was very simple to describe: advance 10 miles (16 kilometres) inland and secure the Caen-Bayeux road by the end of the day. For Captain Gower and the 150 men of 'B' Company, which included a platoon from 'C' Company and sappers from the 6th

ABOVE: Beneath the casemates at Courseulles, wounded Canadian soldiers wait for transfer to a casualty clearing station.

OPPOSITE: Dan examines the results of allied firepower against this bunker, known now as Cosy's Bunker, guarding one of the beach exits. The effect of the concussion on any Germans manning it would have been severe; however, ultimately it was taken by Lieutenant Aitken's platoon.

Field Company Royal Canadian Engineers, trying to achieve it on Mike Red was a nightmare from the beginning, well before they had reached dry land. Four days after the landing, an 'informal report' as they described it, was penned for their colonel by a handful of Gower's men who described themselves as 'The only remaining D-Day personnel'.

'6 June 44 – D Day
Coy was engaged by heavy machine gun fire together with 75mm and mortar fire, starting when LCAs were 700 yards from the shore. This fire continued steadily as we touched down and on *doors down* crafts were being badly hit, but the men cleared the craft without hesitation. A large per cent were hit while still chest high in the water, the remainder pushed on into the heavy wall of fire with seemingly little regard for the terrific barrage.'

Gower's men struggled ashore on Mike Red through the floating bodies of their own dead and wounded to take on the formidable emplacements of *Widerstandsnest* 31 (see also page 177) overlooking the beach from the dune. This concrete warren of interconnecting bunkers and trenches, embraced on two sides by the Seulles and defended by barbed wire and machine guns set at stomach height, was fronted by a line of five thick casemates that housed 75-millimetre guns or 50-millimetre *KwK* (*Kampfwagenkanonem* – 'anti-tank') guns and a centrally located Renault tank turret. The armour had not arrived ahead of Gower's men; their numbers were already depleted, and many had rifles rendered useless by the seawater. But they had grenades and knives, and the Winnipegs found less conventional ways to knock out a gun. One was to work in pairs. A man would climb up on the shoulders of another, gain the roof of the emplacement and then pop a

"COSY'S BUNKER"

THIS BUNKER WAS STORMED AND TAKEN BY
LT W.F. (COSY) AITKEN AND 10 PLATOON OF
"B" COMPANY, THE ROYAL WINNIPEG RIFLES,
ON 6 JUNE 1944. "B" COMPANY SUFFERED 78%
CASUALTIES ASSAULTING "MIKE GREEN" BEACH

DEDICATED 6 JUNE 2004

"TALUS DE COSY"

CETTE BUNKER FUT PRISE D'ASSAUT PAR LE
LIEUTENANT W.F. (COSY) AITKEN ET LES
MEMBRES DE 10 PELATON DE LA COMPAGNIE "B"
DU ROYAL WINNIPEG RIFLES, LE 6 JUIN 1944 EN
PRENANT D'ASSAUT LA PLAGE "MIKE GREEN" IL
EUT 78% DE BLESSÉS ET DE MORTS

DEDICATED 6 JUIN 2004

ABOVE: A couple of days after the landings, men from the Highland Light Infantry of Canada examine the wreckage of the Landing Ship Infantry that had brought them ashore.

grenade in through the embrasure. Lieutenant Bill 'Cosy' Aitken, leading 12 Platoon of 'B' Company, was badly wounded in the head while taking one such bunker, and lost many of his men in the attack. Sometimes it came down to hand-to-hand fighting with knives. This battalion of the Winnipegs had not been in action before, and their opponents, while likewise inexperienced, were the fanatical young men of the Hitler Youth, products of a lifetime's Nazi indoctrination.

'The sand dunes were reached, and the pill boxes taken, by sheer guts and initiative of the individual. The following are reports made to CSM Belton and Sgt Walsh by word of mouth by personnel who are no longer with us. Men who are mentioned below could still possibly be alive.

'Rfn Kimmel, a signaller attached to the coy, showed outstanding courage in silencing one pill box. Cpl

Slatter E T, after being hit in the stomach, was seen on his hands and knees still trying to get up to the pill box, at the same time trying to direct his remaining section by shouting orders. It is reported that Cpl Klos W J was badly wounded in the stomach and legs while leaving the craft but made his way to the [missing word] and was found dead there, apparently having killed two of the Hun and was sitting on one, with his hands still gripped on his throat. This story was told by a man who had a minor injury and remained on the beach, later returning to the coy but is no longer with us, therefore no confirmation can be obtained. Capt Gower, without thought of safety for himself, encouraged his men and controlled the situation in full view of the enemy, bare headed as he had lost his helmet after an incident in the water. It is the opinion of the remaining few that his courage and amazing coolness, was one of the outstanding factors in our success in pushing through the first objective. When asked by CSM Belton if any of the company could be recommended for bravery he replied "no individual that he knew of could be recommended more than another as the whole company faced the hail of bullets unflinchingly, and there was not a man went to ground until he was hit. Almost every man who was wounded refused any aid offered and encouraged the other to get on with the job. ["]. Captain Gower mentioned that the show on the beach put on by B Company was almost unbelievable and most admirable.'

By 09:00 they had attacked three casemates and 12 machine gun emplacements, and 15 Platoon had crossed the river to drive the Germans out of four positions on ground almost encircled by the River Seulles. In so doing, the unit had suffered a staggering 80 percent casualties. Out of more than 150 who had embarked at Southampton, only 27, including Captain Gower – who was awarded the Military Cross – ended the day if not unscathed then at least fit to fight another day.

LOG-JAM

What had happened to the promised armour? The tanks that would swim ashore and bust the bunkers, the flails that could destroy the minefields and tear through the coils of barbed wire to open the beach exits?

Essentially, the sea was too rough for the DD tanks with their comparatively fragile canvas flotation skirts. At 05:30 the commanders of both 'A' and 'B' squadrons of the First Hussars had declared that it was impossible to launch. The LCTs then advanced to 7,000 yards (6,400 metres), hoping for calmer water, but the waves were still too high. The decision was taken to go for a conventional landing, and the craft approached the beaches until, with 3,300 yards (3,000 metres) to go, they were informed that they were arriving ahead of schedule. The order for a 360-degree turn went out, and the manoeuvre was completed by 07:15, by which time the naval bombardment had got underway. At this point, and to the dismay of the crews who had removed a great deal of equipment

ABOVE: Extended trials of the DD Tank were required to ensure its suitability for the D-Day landings. Here, Valentine III DD tanks prepare to test their flotation skirts by disembarking from a landing craft.

from inside the tanks, the signal for 'down doors' rang. Sub-Lieutenant Dinwiddy's reaction was terse:

'I signalled back, "Too rough, propose to beach". Immediately the signal was repeated and I had to let the first tank go. Almost at once it sank, with the crew inevitably drowned. Whereupon I signalled, "Tank sunk, going in to beach". On approach to the beach we hit a mine, which blew a large hole at the point on the port side forward where the first tank had been. Fortunately there were no casualties and I was able to land the remaining 3 tanks in the normal way.'[25]

Just ten of 'A' Squadron's tanks were launched, and of those only seven reached the shore to join the six that landed dry. Three were lost on the beaches, but the squadron was at last able to bring some relief to the hard-pressed Manitoban troops, claiming two 75-millimetre guns and six light machine guns definitely destroyed, one 50-millimetre anti-tank gun knocked out (after it had scored three hits on the second-in-command's tank) and several 'probables'.

Lieutenant Gerald Ashcroft RNVR, commanding *LCT 507*, had a grandstand view of what a tank could do at close range:

'As we were approaching the beach, our particular point of the beach was on a pillbox in a corner of the sea wall, and when we were close enough to examine it through binoculars we could see that the gun barrel of the big gun was pointing to the westward along the beach, and the embrasure to the north side was completely open. And as we approached to the level of the mines, we saw the gun barrel come back in, and knowing full well they had to unscrew the barrel to swivel the gun inside the emplacement, it was obvious that they were now training the gun to come out of the embrasure immediately in front of us. I got the major in charge of tanks to get his forward tank close up the watertight door, got our bow ramp lowered and the watertight door opened, and arranged for the major to train the gun on the pillbox [with] rounds of solid shell to get the pillbox before the pillbox got us. Fortunately, we hit

the beach at full speed … first shot was straight through the pillbox.'[26]

The regiment's own mortars landed more or less on time, but depleted – not by enemy action but by the conduct of the LCT commander who refused to beach his craft and, instead, ordered the platoon to disembark with their equipment in 12 feet (3.5 metres) of water. Three men drowned and two mortars were lost before the rest of the platoon made it impossible for the commander to refuse the order to take them ashore.

Yet another serious issue compounded the problems for the Winnipegs. To continue support for the 'Little Black Devils', the tanks needed to get off the beaches, but while the troops were prepared to throw themselves onto the wire, both exits from Mike were blocked by mines and there was still no sign of the AVREs and the Crab flails that were supposed to be clearing those exits and dealing with the ditches and traps that lay ahead. For more than an hour the First Hussars were held up, though they used the time to attack the casements from the beach.

The 26AS had experienced their own troubles during the crossing, including navigational errors and engine weaknesses. Indeed, one American LCT landed its tanks on Juno instead of Sword, so Crab driver

Arthur Whelan cleared mines for the Canadians: '... we didn't know what we were coming into. As we came ashore the scene was chaotic, with gun fire and it wasn't clear what was going on. We were scared to death, because we didn't know what was over the hill and it actually took a couple of days to get used to it.'[27] On 8 June Whelan and his tank were to find themselves on the wrong end of an 88-millimetre shell:

> 'It was armour piercing and we got it. The co-driver alongside me was killed and I couldn't get out because the hatch was buckled. I must have sat about half an hour there, thinking all sorts of things, and the Canadian officer in charge got hold of a chain & they ripped the hatch off to get me out. I had shrapnel in the shoulder & both legs and was taken to a Field Hospital. My legs were smashed and both legs were placed in plaster with a metal bar between them, like an A frame, before being transferred to a hospital just outside Swansea.'[28]

Off Mike Sector Bill Dunn and the rest of the crews aboard their LCT were ordered to mount their tanks (armoured units still retained cavalry terms):

> 'The landing craft stopped, dropped the ramps for us to come down and everybody straightaway shouted good luck to each other. The first tank off the LC was a flail. One of those Canadian tanks came off in front of us and I had to follow him off, and we came through the narrow gap that they'd done for us. Those people that had been lying overnight, they'd made these gaps in the defences for us to get through them. And then you had to drive up onto the beach.'[29]

There was added tension inside, with the hatches battened down against the heavy fire directed against them, because the driver, Dunn, was the only one who could see. Machine gun rounds were raking the area, hitting the troops, and the crew's worst fear was of running over and killing their own infantry. If men were lying down on the sand, were they dead or wounded or just taking shelter? There was something horrible, too, about crushing a dead man. Bodies were caught on the wire. He was told to keep going. Up ahead, the Crab's flail was thrashing the ground: mines were exploding. Then it missed one. The explosion went off underneath, blowing the tracks off, leaving the Crab blocking the gap. The only thing to do was to bulldoze it aside.

Beyond the dunes, the beach exit became the straight road leading to the village of Graye-sur-Mer, and 'C' Squadron's objective was to secure the crossroads with the main coast road. However, a small stream, wandering along the land between the dunes and the River Seulles, was known to cross the beach exit through a culvert, so Dunn's fascine tank was ordered into action to 'plug' it. What nobody knew was that the Germans had blocked the stream to create a morass in which they had dug a tank trap that at more than 8-feet (2.5-metres) deep and 60-feet (18-metres) wide was far too large for a single fascine to fill. Unable to discern the culvert, Dunn put his tank into first gear and proceeded very cautiously. Suddenly the tank began to tip forwards. He stopped the tracks, but inexorably the heavy vehicle slid into the water that had been masked by the light covering of sand blown across it. Water began to pour in, and shells exploded: the German gunners had the crippled tank in their sights.

The six-man crew struggled to escape as the vehicle filled; Dunn started to swallow water. Someone managed to drag him out onto the turret and he got to the seaward side of the tank and behind the dunes where his mate kicked him in the stomach to expel the liquid. Mortar bombs were detonating around them. Three of the crew were killed outright; the rest, including Dunn, were wounded. Despite a hole in his back, the co-driver insisted on crawling for help, but had not gone far before he died. Dunn, the youngest of the crew and with five compound fractures in one leg, rolled into a minefield. He knew it was such because the sign above him read *Achtung Minen*. From there he was rescued and evacuated.

Tragic as the accident was for the crew, it was also a disaster for both the DDs coming up behind and for the Winnipegs still desperate for the support that should have preceded them. The beach was getting rapidly narrower and more congested as the tide came in and more landing craft tried to unload men, tanks and materials, but at last the AVREs carrying box girder bridges got through the exit to bridge the tank trap. It was too wide for a single span of bridge, but after removing the fascine from Dunn's sunken AVRE, they were able to use the tank as a central pier and create a crossing. At around 10:00, the traffic jam on Mike began to ease.

MOVING SOUTH

All three assault companies of the Winnipegs had landed within seven minutes of one another. Major Lockhart Fulton's 'D' Company came ashore a good 100 yards (90 metres) or so to the west of 'B' Company and although they had to cross more than 200 yards (180 metres) of shallow water and open beach they raced, zig-zagging, to the dunes, sustaining few casualties. In almost every respect they were luckier than 'B' Company, because not only were they away from the *Widerstandsnest* but an LCT came up shortly afterwards, disgorging tanks of the First Hussars. Together the two units got off the beach, and began to move through the minefields, rooting out the machine guns, before heading towards Graye-sur-Mer. By 09:00, barely an hour after landing, they had 'gapped' the minefield by probing with bayonets and marking the edges of the safe route, and their forward units were passing through Graye and heading south. They had found no trace of the enemy at Graye – not surprising because the troops ordered to hold the village had been Soviet POWs to whom their German captors had made an offer they could not refuse. Faced with the possibility of dying for their enemy, they had had no hesitation in abandoning their positions. From Graye, 'D' Company made for Banville.

Fortune had also smiled on the Canadian Scottish on Love Sector. On coming ashore they were faced with a large concrete pillbox housing a 75-millimetre gun, but it proved to be one of just 14 percent put out of action by the Royal Navy.

The Winnipegs' follow-up companies, 'A' and 'C', along with the battalion HQ, had arrived shortly after the assault units, and all three found themselves caught in the vicious beach gunfire. The battalion's wireless set was a magnet for German fire, so leaving HQ pinned down on the beach for the next two hours, 'A' Company headed south towards St. Croix-sur-Mer until they, too, found themselves held up by fire from at least half a dozen machine guns. Responding to an appeal for help, tanks from the First Hussars rode to the rescue and 'with cool disregard for mines and A Tk guns beat down the mg posns and permitted A Coy to mop up and advance to the south'.[30] 'C' Company made for Banville, weeding out pockets of resistance en route, but were halted short of the village by German machine guns dug in on the higher ground. They joined with 'D' Company to deal with the problem and together the two units then fought their way to Cruelly. By around 17:00 battalion HQ had finally got off the beach, abandoned the radio and caught up with them. The regiment established itself for the night at Creully, 5 miles (8 kilometres) inland.

Canadian Press reporter Ross reflected the desperation of the fight in his D-Day dispatch:

'Bloody fighting raged all along the beaches. On the right, the Winnipegs had to battle their way past five major concrete casements and 15 machine gun positions set in the dunes commanding a long sweep of beach. From dune to dune, along the German trench systems, and through the tunnels, these Manitoba troops fought every yard of the way. They broke into the casements, ferreted out the gun crews with machine guns, grenades, bayonets and knives. The Canadians ran into cross-fire. They were shelled and mortared even in the German positions, but they kept slugging away at the enemy. After a struggle that was ... bitter and savage ... the Winnipeg's[sic] broke through into the open country behind the beach.'

MEDEVAC – BEAM ME UP, CAPTAIN. . .

Just before midnight on D-Day Lieutenant James Doohan, 13th Field Regiment, Royal Canadian Artillery, was returning from patrol to his unit, dug in near Banville, when a burst of machine gun fire from a nervous sentry spat in his direction. Four rounds hit his leg, a fifth caught the middle finger on his right hand necessitating amputation and a sixth would have penetrated his chest had it not been stopped by his cigarette case.

Doohan was evacuated from Juno, and after his return to fitness he retrained as an artillery-officer pilot (AOP) with the Royal Canadian Air Force (RCAF). Exploits that included flying low-level slaloms around pylons, executing manoeuvres above Stonehenge and getting almost too close to a U-boat off the Dutch coast, gained him a reputation as a reckless daredevil. From the 1960s he became internationally famous as 'Scotty', chief engineer of the Starship *Enterprise* in *Star Trek*.

LIBERATION

For René Lemars in Creully, the Allies arrived in the nick of time:

'We all stayed inside the house because my parents were shop-owners. In Creully there is the big square with all the different shops, and we were living right in the middle of it, and we didn't have a garden so we couldn't dig any shelters, so we stayed indoors. The neighbours had trenches etc. I saw all the Germans, including the officers and the 2 or 3 wagons, had all assembled on the square – and suddenly they all went at once. My dad was required by the Germans to go and be forced to work in Germany. He was supposed to leave on 6 June at 5.00pm, and McCormick with his 3 tanks [First Hussars] arrived at 3.00pm. They liberated Creully at 3.00pm so my dad, of course, didn't leave. So we were not very afraid because we were so happy that he was not leaving – but we could still hear the bombardment on the coast and could see the red lights. When they arrived there was not too much damage, two shell holes in the Church Tower and a little machine gun damage here and there, but we could sense that the Germans wanted to leave, so all in all it was all good for us.'

If, as Churchill had said, Operation Torch might be the end of the beginning, then D-Day was the beginning of the end. Every beach had been successfully taken, and the bridgehead was established. True, it had been a close run thing for the Americans

on Omaha where resistance had been savage. There they had been painfully short of armour after their DD tanks had sunk after having been launched too far out, and they had rejected the Crabs that would have destroyed mines and ripped paths through barbed wire. On Utah, however, the Americans had been luckier, and not just because Easy Company had silenced the Brécourt battery. The weather had caused the landings to take place further south than planned, and thus they had avoided a particularly unpleasant *Widerstandsnest* in the Dunes de Varreville. Sword and Gold had been taken to plan by the British, and, despite suffering casualties second only to the Americans on Omaha, the Canadians had made the furthest progress south. No army had reached the objective, but they were all in contact; reinforcements were pouring onto the beaches now behind them; and overall casualties had been much lower than anticipated – well below the 20,000 that Churchill feared.

Estimates of the actual number of Allied troops killed on that first day have varied widely, but a ten-year research programme in the USA by the

ABOVE: Saint-Aubin-sur-Mer was held by around one hundred German defenders. Tank obstacles held up the Canadian armour and snipers forced the infantry to take cover.

National D-Day Memorial Foundation has produced a total of 4,413 verified dead, well below even the lowest previous estimate and a tribute to the quality of the training, leadership and planning.

John Hadley: 'Well that's a day that I'll never forget and I lost a lot of friends that day and I landed with a bunch of very good men and I'm very proud to have served with them. And I'll never forget them.'

German losses were higher than those of the Allies, but well below the 19,000 French civilians thought to have been killed in the bombardments and bombing raids. Eleven months of hard fighting lay ahead for both sides.

THE BRIDGE TOO FAR

After D-Day, the Allied advance was not easy, but it moved ahead of schedule. During August the Germans were driven out of most of northern France, and Paris had been liberated. British and Canadian troops had reached the River Somme, and in the south the troops who had landed at Toulon were close to Lyon. During September the Canadians pushed up the Channel coast, meeting dogged resistance from the Germans who were determined either to deny the Allies the vital ports or to ensure that they would be in ruins if they did fall. On the Canadian right, the British were sweeping through, liberating Brussels

on the 3rd. Antwerp celebrated freedom the following day.

Given the success, General Montgomery proposed a swift strike north that should see the Allies in Germany by the end of the year. Eisenhower was unenthusiastic but agreed to a scaled-down version of the plan: a two-phase operation codenamed Market Garden. Operation Market required the taking of the five bridges along the road that ran north from Eindhoven to Arnhem, and had to be carried out by airborne assault. Once the bridges were in Allied hands, Operation Garden would see the XXX Corps come up that road and relieve the infantry. The two canal bridges between Eindhoven and Veghel were allotted to the US Army's 101st Airborne Division; and those over the Rivers Maas at Grave and the River Waal at Nijmegen were the objectives for the 82nd Airborne. The task of taking the final bridge, across the Lower Rhine at Arnhem, fell to the British 1st Airborne Division, which would be landing on the *north* side of the Lower Rhine, west of Arnhem.

'Off at last. After having been briefed for so many operations which have been postponed and eventually cancelled, the [Battalion] really got away this morning. Operation "Market" in which we are taking part is designed to seize the river crossing

at Grave, Nijmegen and Arnhem and to hold them until 30 Corps of the 2nd Army comes up to take them over and use them. 1 Airborne Div is to seize and hold the Arnhem bridge and form a bridge-head north of it around the town. There is a scene of suppressed excitement as we embark in our gliders….'[31]

Did Private Sam Cassidy, of the 7th Battalion, King's Own Scottish Borderers (7/KSOB), share that 'suppressed excitement', or did he sit quietly in the Horsa glider, perhaps reading or thinking about his wife and toddler back in Belfast? There must have been some trepidation as the glider armada streamed above the misty late summer farmland of eastern England and out over the North Sea, because although he had been in the army since 1942 this was going to be his, and the battalion's, first experience of action.

They crossed the coast just south of Antwerp. No dreaded flak met them, just a little small arms fire, and once inland they swung north. At around 13:30, and 2 miles (3 kilometres) from their destination, Cassidy's Horsa, like dozens of others, was released from the tow of the bombers to glide down onto the fields of the landing zone.

A few British gliders had aborted in England and one had force-landed near Antwerp, but more than 120 gliders came down in the soft fields east of Ede, causing damage to some of the undercarriages. A pair that went into the trees were badly smashed up and one man died, and it may well be that Cassidy was in one of those, because an incorrect rumour went round that he was injured or dead.

By 15:00 hours all the gliders had been unloaded and the men were ready to carry out the first objective: to hold the landing zone for the 4th Parachute

Brigade (4 Para), who were expected to land the following day. Opposition had been almost non-existent, but when the troops dug in for the night they soon came under heavy fire. The thick woodland of the area disrupted mobile communications between companies, and attempts to send reinforcements were never completely successful. However, the drop zone was held and 4 Para landed safely, albeit some four hours late.

From brigade HQ came the news that elements of 1 Para had seized the bridge at Arnhem and established themselves on the north side, though they were now cut off from the rest of their brigade. Some of 4 Para were sent off to reinforce them, but they would be unable to get through. The Borderers (7/KSOB) regrouped and enjoyed their first hot meal since leaving England before setting off on the north side of the railway from Ede to Wolfheze along a road congested with the transport and equipment of 4 Para. Just after Wolfheze the Borderers got past, and headed slightly northeast. Despite being strafed from the air the Borderers cleared the road of Germans as they advanced, and around 01:00 on the 19th they reached the farm of Johannahoeve, which 'B' Company captured more easily than anticipated. The machine gun fire intensified against the other companies, and with darkness making an attack impractical the battalion dug in around the farm in the early hours.

The rest of that day, 19 September, was chaotic; 7/KSOB came under sustained attack and at the same time they had to defend the landing by the 1st (Polish) Independent Parachute Brigade. The companies that could be gathered up moved under cover of darkness to the small town of Oosterbeek, just west of Arnhem, where what was left of the 1st Airborne Division would try to hold a bridgehead until the hoped-for relief arrived.

A ragged perimeter defence was hastily being organized; streets and houses were allocated to miscellaneous platoons, battalions and squadrons. Private Sam Cassidy and the remains of 7/KSOB were charged with holding a small wooded area on the northeastern corner that proved to be the gardens of two large houses. One of these was the Hotel Dreyeroord – or, as the troops were to call it, the 'White House' – and Private John Crosson would not easily forget the drama: 'It was a target for the Germans all the time. Once they could get through there they could get into the streets of Oosterbeg. There was a lot of bombardment. They were using bombs, obviously, mortars, and machine guns mostly – and snipers. It was not a good place to be. There was absolutely no security there. At any moment something would happen and you'd have to do your best to fight against it.' The severity of the first day's fighting comes through in the war diary:

'… effective mortar fire brought to bear on the enemy posns but shortly afterwards Lt Creighton was shot by a sniper and killed. The enemy now commenced to out-flank our [machine guns], which had to be withdrawn to prevent being over-run, and came back into D Coy's section of the perimeter. Our [anti tank] guns were active during the morning. The

first "kill" was an armoured car which was blown up and set on fire by the [anti tank] gun covering the north face. Later another [anti tank] gun under Lt Hannah, and escorted by a [platoon] of B Coy, went out to watch the [road] leading south from the [road] and [railway] crossing at 699791. Soon after it was in [position] a Tiger tk, towing a flame-throwing apparatus, appeared and a spirited action took place. As a result of the courageous behaviour of our [anti tank] gun crew, and of Cpl Watson and Pte McWhirter in particular, the Tiger tk was completely knocked out and the crew killed. As the enemy began to locate our position, shelling,

mortar fire and sniping began, and this continued with ever increasing violence throughout the day. …Progress to and from the White House became a case of running the gauntlet of very accurate sniper fire and in doing this the 2IC (Major Coke) was hit in the leg and put out of action.

1300 to 1900 — Early in the afternoon the enemy brought [forward a self-propelled] gun which, while remaining out of sight of our [anti tank] guns, shelled our [positions] at close range. In doing so it scored a series of direct hits on the White House, partially demolishing it and causing D Coy HQ and its other garrison to vacate it after having suffered casualties. The fire-fight continued all afternoon, our mortars, [anti tank] guns and MGs replying strongly whenever an opportunity or target offered.'[32]

The following morning was no less difficult, and late in the afternoon:

'This attack came in strongly, being made by fully a [Company] of SS troops. The enemy got as far as the White House and the slit-trenches which we had vacated in that vicinity, but every move he attempted to make beyond there was frustrated by a deluge of fire from the [Battalion]. Every weapon was got into action, the [medium machine guns], which simply belched forth unceasing fire, proving particularly effective. Once the enemy had been checked, the CO arranged a two-minutes "crescendo", - 3″ Mortars on the woods, [medium machine guns], on the trenches, and [anti tank] guns on the White House, – at the end of which he led the [Battalion] in a bayonet charge which swept any remaining enemy off the field. The White House and nearby trenches were filled with the bodies of the dead Germans, with many more lying all over the open. The German attackers, except for those who had fled, were killed to a man. "The battle of the White House", as this will be known, will live in the memories of all who took part in it.'

For two days the Borderers had fought to hold the White House against impossible odds. They had no company commanders and only one company sergeant major left in action. Losses among other ranks were high. During the night of the 21st they withdrew a mile south to the village-suburb of Hartenstein, closer to the river.

The whole 'Market' plan had completely unravelled. A mere 740 men under Lieutenant Colonel John Frost (later Major General Frost CB, DSO*, MC, DL) had managed to reach the bridge at Arnhem, and they fought for four days to hold it before, out of ammunition, they had to surrender. The 82nd Airborne had not taken the bridge at Nijmegen on schedule, and the tanks of XXX Corps had delayed before making the advance towards Arnhem that was so desperately needed. The Borderers and the rest of the ragged units of the 1st Airborne Division were left to hold on, incurring further heavy casualties, until the night of Monday the 25th when an evacuation across the Rhine, organized by British and Canadian units, rescued just under 2,400. More than 6,000 were taken prisoner.

Sammy Cassidy was not among the rescued: he was one of the 1,485 dead of Operation Market, killed on the second day's fighting in Oosterbeek.

BELOW: Desperate attempts to hold the Oosterbeek perimeter. An Allied soldier fires from what looks like the Hartenstein Hotel – now the Airborne Museum.

His daughter, Betty, grew up knowing little: 'Mother never talked about it and her family and sisters never talked about it either. … I just knew that he was in the war and he was a soldier and he died.'

Only after Betty's own daughter, Lynda Ross, had grown up did the family start to make inquiries into Sam's death. When Lynda's appeal for information appeared in the magazine of the Arnhem Veterans Club it was read by Private John Crosson. He had served alongside Sam at the White House, but he hesitated to respond. When, however, the request was repeated he did make contact to tell her what he had witnessed on Thursday 21 September 1944.

Crosson had been a sniper in one of the houses overlooking numbers 7–9 Cronjeweg, a street close to the White House. A tank was reported to be in the area, and some of the battalion were in position on the street, hoping for a chance to ambush it. German soldiers suddenly appeared. Cassidy called for a Bren gun, a type of light machine gun. Crosson watched as:

'Somebody gave him the Bren gun and he tried to fire it from the hip but it jammed as they sometimes do. Well there is a procedure for unjamming a Bren, but of course it takes time, but he banged the butt of the gun on the ground, tried it again and it still jammed. Getting a bit agitated now, he banged it again and this time it went off but the gun was facing upwards and shot him up through the head. He fell instantly dead with a great clatter. Everybody thought these Germans had shot him

but they got up and ran away. I realized what had happened because I was just behind him.'

The White House was repaired and still welcomes guests. Visiting Oosterbeek with *Dig WW2*, Lynda Ross found it 'strange to stay in the place that he died defending'. The legacy of the war remains in the gardens, where the Dutch metal detectorist Hans van der Velder has permission to work. He showed Dan how easy it is to find proof of the ferocious 24-hour combat. Grubbing among the shallow roots of a rhododendron on the north side he uncovered the cap of one of the 3-inch mortars mentioned in the war diary; handfuls of live ammunition emerged, together with pieces of an ammunition belt and a very well-preserved gun magazine. It all fitted with the disposition of the troops as recorded in the war diary:

'C Coy which was strongest held the western face and part of the northern and southern faces. D Coy held the remainder of the northern face and the whole of the eastern face (having a party of Glider Pilots under Comd). B Coy which was very weak held the remainder of the southern face. Mortars were centrally situated and [anti tank] guns covered every face and [road] approach. [Medium machine guns] were in D Coy area.'

German records state that Sam Cassidy was buried in a mass grave in the garden of the White House. After the war, the bodies of those killed in the fighting were exhumed and reburied in the military cemetery in Oosterbeek, but somehow Sam's body was never identified as such. There are eight graves of unnamed privates of the Borderers, and Betty and Lynda Ross believe that one of them is his. When they visit they lay a cross on each. There is some comfort for Betty: 'At least we know he's somewhere.'

LAST POST

Hopes of bypassing the fortifications of the Westwall ended in Arnhem and Oosterbeek, and the conflict ran its course, ending in May 1945. As the politicians reshaped Europe, surplus service personnel collected demob suits, families started to rebuild their lives and bulldozers began to clear the rubble. Organizations such as the Commonwealth War Graves Commission and the German War Graves Commission quietly got on with the work of bringing dignity to the dead soldiers of the Second World War: exhuming bodies from the anonymity of mass graves, identifying them where possible and reinterring them in dedicated cemeteries.

Even today, bodies are still being recovered and men identified. During work on the Gustav Line, Damiano Parravano discovered a 'dog tag' bearing the name 'Clinton W. Thomas'. 'From the moment I found it, it was clear to me that the piece of metal in my hands was really important, because it was connected to a man and consequently to a family.'[33] In the following days Parravano devoted himself to finding out information about Thomas. 'I discovered that he was reported Missing in Action: his body had never been found or

identified after the war, so I tried to make contact with the living members of his family. His relatives thought that he died defending a bridge, but we have discovered that Clinton died during an attack in the mountain sector of the Gustav Line.' Later, the family sent him photographs of Clinton 'taken at the time of his enlistment and earlier, as a child, with his parents and his brothers. It was a very moving moment for me, to see his face, just twenty years old, and like many other soldiers he died much too soon, fighting for an ideal or simply doing his duty.' Parravano sent the dog tag to the family, so 'at least something of him could be back at home'. As a direct result of the discovery, Thomas was reclassified as Killed in Action (KIA) and, even though his body has never been found, given a funeral.

In January 1945, well before the end of the war, the Dutch Ministry of Defence set up the Recovery and Identification Unit (RIU) to help deal with the many bodies – civilian and military, Allied and Axis – buried in makeshift graves or sometimes left in the

ABOVE: Lynda and Betty Ross at the Oosterbeek Military Cemetery.

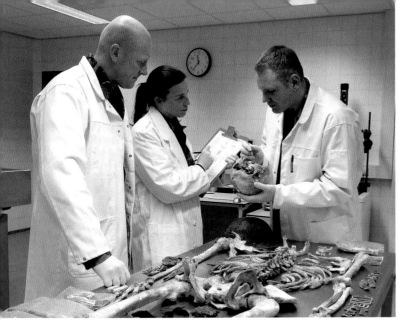

wreckage of tanks and aircraft. The Allied Graves Registration Units began their work after VE Day, and the RIU has dealt with their own civilian dead and something like 35,000 Germans. The RIU is still active and working on around 35 bodies a year. These have included an entire bomber crew. Clues from the location of the grave and the artefacts recovered with the body may determine the person's unit, and the team can use dental records and other anthropological and forensic techniques, including facial reconstruction, to try to establish their identity.

When Dan visited the laboratory, the head of the unit, Warrant Officer Class 2 (WO2) Geert Jonker, was working on three skeletons, all from the war. On the first table lay the remains of a German paratrooper, identified as such by the characteristic zip from a German airborne smock and blue buttons of a type worn by the Luftwaffe. His identity tag had survived, and the Germans had been able to identify him.

That was a typical case; the next, very different, and the skeleton was of a Dutchman. 'This individual,' explained Jonker, 'comes from a group of three men, three individuals, that were shot by the Resistance and were buried together. ... so most probably... they had to kneel and then they were shot in the head, execution style, and the skull has completely fractured. This is what we call *primary fractures*, so all the energy from the impact is released in the skull and it just explodes.'

Corroborating evidence was present in the form of the parachute line that had been used to tie the legs and arms together.

The sight made a deep impression on Dan. Afterwards he said: 'I was ready for death in battle. I was expecting to see the skeletons of young British, Polish and German soldiers who had paid the ultimate price. But when I was confronted with the body of a Dutchman, executed by his countrymen, his neighbours, as a collaborator I was stunned. This was not the war that we see on the newsreels, on the silver screen or read about in war memoirs, this was the sordid, vicious, hate-filled conflict that ruined so many millions of lives across the world.'

Jonker then showed Dan a set of personal photographs found with a body some time ago. All were in good condition, because the Germans often kept such precious possessions in their airtight gas mask containers, but all that could be established was that their owner must have served at some time in the Afrika Korp. Dan commented: 'Just extraordinary. He's even got pictures of what must be his home village there in the rolling countryside ...I've never really felt such a personal connection to a casualty in World War Two. I've never seen finds of this nature....'

Geert Jonker fully agrees with Damiano Parravano and Dan Snow on the importance of the individual: 'It just goes to show that there's really no difference between someone going missing in 1944 or someone going missing in 2004. For the next of kin the feeling of uncertainty stays the same. It doesn't wear off. And as long as the people are still alive that have known those who went missing during the war I am positive that the Dutch Government in the Netherlands will keep on doing this very important task.'

I've learned that battlefield archaeology allows you to fix a moment in time, a split second, the detonation of a shell or the crack of a bullet, in a way that reading sources and talking to veterans can't, and so it allows you to take a slice of time, which has been very exciting but also absolutely vital in trying to determine how the fortunes of war ebbed and flowed. For the first time I felt like I had a forensic understanding of the battle. I can imagine the assault on the Hitler Line or the landings on Juno beach unfolding minute by minute. Finds like the shattered Canadian helmet in front of the German machine gun post took the whole team to a split second on a battlefield 70 years ago. That is very rare.

Dan Snow

IN SEARCH OF WW2

There may be opportunities to 'dig' the Second World War for yourself, depending on skills and interests – whether through volunteering at a specialist museum or joining a group of battlefield/aviation/marine archaeologists. A number of academic institutions now offer studies in relevant subjects such as battlefield archaeology, from short courses lasting just a few days and designed for enthusiasts, to rigorous post-graduate research. Many sub-aqua clubs organize dives on Second World War wrecks for those with the appropriate certificates.

Remember that all military aviation wreckage in the United Kingdom is deemed to be the property of the Crown/the Ministry of Defence, a number of Second World War naval wrecks are classified as war graves, and most battlefields and fortifications are privately owned. Appropriate permissions must always be sought.

However, there is much to see while out and about in the local area or on holiday in western Europe. Numerous museums hold collections of objects from the Second World War, ranging from preserved warships to aircraft in flying condition, and almost all regimental museums will have artefacts from the period 1939 1945. Escorted tours of battlefields by knowledgeable and enthusiastic guides are very popular.

The following is just a small selection of museums; for details of online communities, please see the Further Reference. Please check the museum opening times before travelling.

AVIATION MUSEUMS

Aviation Archaeology Museum, Fort Perch Rock, New Brighton, Merseyside CH45 2JU

Battle of Britain Memorial Flight Centre, RAF Coningsby, Coningsby, Lincolnshire LN4 4SY

British Aviation Archaeological Council

Dumfries and Galloway Aviation Museum, Dumfries, DG1 3PH

Fleet Air Arm Museum, Yeovilton, Ilchester, Somerset, BA22 8HT

Imperial War Museum, Duxford, Cambridgeshire CB22 4QR

Lashenden Air Warfare Museum, Headcorn Aerodrome, Headcorn, Ashford, Kent, TN27 9HX

Luftwaffenmuseum der Bundeswehr, Berlin-Gatow, Germany

Montrose Air Station Heritage Centre, Broomfield, Montrose DD10 9BB

Norfolk and Suffolk Aviation Museum, Bungay, Suffolk, NR35 1NZ

RAF Museum Cosford, Shifnal, Shropshire TF11 8UP

RAF Museum, Hendon, London NW9 5LL

Spitfire and Hurricane Memorial Museum, Manston Airfield, Kent CT12 5DF

Thameside Aviation Museum, Coalhouse Fort, East Tilbury, Essex RM18 8PB

Yorkshire Air Museum, Elvington, York, YO1 4AU

NAVAL MUSEUMS AND PRESERVED SECOND WORLD WAR WARSHIPS

HMS *Alliance* and *X24*, RN Submarine Museum, Portsmouth PO12 2AS

HMS *Belfast* (Imperial War Museum), River Thames, London SE1 2JH

HMS *Cavalier*, the Historic Chatham Dockyard, Kent ME4 4TY

Merseyside Maritime Museum, Albert Dock, Liverpool, L3 4AQ

Motor Torpedo Boat 71, Imperial War Museum, Duxford, Cambridgeshire CB22 4QR

Royal Naval Museum, Portsmouth Historic Dockyard, Portsmouth PO1 3LA

Tamzine (smallest ship to rescue troops from Dunkirk), Imperial War Museum, Lambeth Road, London SE1 6HZ

U-534, U-Boat Story, Woodside Ferry Terminal, Birkenhead, Merseyside CH41 6DU

U-995, Laboe, Kiel, Germany

THE LAND WAR: MUSEUMS AND OTHER RESOURCES

The Defence of Britain project, carried out under the auspices of the Council for British Archaeology, has catalogued all known Second World War defences in Great Britain. The database can be accessed and downloaded via http://archaeologydataservice.ac.uk/archives/view/dob/ and users of Google Earth can download from this site a zipped KML file and see at a glance every defensive structure across the country or limited to a county of their choice. Beware: this can become an addictive pursuit.

Airborne Museum 'Hartenstein', 6862 AZ Oosterbeek, Netherlands

Bawdsey Radar Trust, Bawdsey, Suffolk

Domein Raversijde, Atlantic Wall Museum, 8400 Oostende/Ostend, Belgium

Historiale di Cassino, 03043 Cassino, Italy

Juno Beach Centre, 14470 Courseulles-sur-Mer, France

Le Grand Bunker, Musée Du Mur De L'Atlantique, 14150 Ouistreham Bella Riva, France

Musée du fort de Schoenenbourg (Maginot Line), 67250 Schoenenbourg, France

National Army Museum, Royal Hospital Road, Chelsea, London SW3 4HT

101st US Airborne Museum, 50480 Sainte Mère-Eglise, Normandy, France

Panzerwerk 'Katzenkopf' (Westwall), 54666 Irrel/Südeiffel, Germany

Stop Line Way (National Route 33) is being created for cyclists and when complete will run from Seaton, Devon, to Weston-Super-Mare, Somerset, following a Stop Line along which pillboxes, gun emplacements and tank traps can still be seen. The Seaton to Axminster stretch is already open.

Tank Museum, Bovington, Dorset BH20 6JG

Westwall Museum, 66955 Pirmasens, Germany

NOTES

PART 1

1 Dönitz became Führer der Unterseeboote (FdU) in January 1936. The title was changed to Befehlhaber der Unterseeboote (BdU) on 19 September 1939.

2 Most AMCs retained their names, but as the old Scott class destroyer HMS *Montrose* was in commission, Canadian Pacific's liner, *Montrose,* was commissioned into the Royal Navy as HMS *Forfar*.

3 National Archives reference ADM1/10889.

4 National Archives reference ADM1/10889.

5 KTB *U-56* eleventh patrol.

6 Private papers of D.J.C Hider RNVR, Imperial War Museum, Department of Documents, reference 97/24/1.

7 National Archives reference ADM1/10889.

8 AIR 28/473 RAF Station Limavady, ORB Appendices (Narrative).

9 AIR 28/473 RAF Station Limavady, ORB Appendices (Narrative).

10 The private papers of S. Blackstone, Imperial War Museum, Department of Documents, reference 219.

11 209 Squadron ORB ref AIR27/1294, and Report of Scouting and Search of PBY-5 No. AH545 Catalina for *Bismarck* 26 May, 1941. Issued by the Intelligence Division Office of Chief of Naval Operation, US Navy Department.

12 Reference AIR27/1833.

13 Per Ulster Aviation Museum.

14 Imperial War Museum Sound Archive Recording, reference 18097.

15 http://www.warsailors.com/singleships/brenas.html.

16 Message 1235, 8 December, from *Macharda* to the Admiralty, National Archives reference ADM223/552.

17 *Avenger* was one of several escort carriers built in the USA for the Royal Navy. US escort carriers in service with the US Navy were given CVE numbers, and wits among their crews – British and American – maintained that CVE stood for Combustible, Vulnerable, Expendable.

18 National Archives reference ADM1/17805.

19 National Archives reference ADM1/16168.

20 The first of these tactical responses became known as Raspberry because escort crews considered they were 'blowing a raspberry' at Hitler. Naturally, the rest were named after fruit and vegetables.

21 Time converted to GMT. U-boats worked on Central European Time; Britain was on double summertime.

22 Gibson, National Archives Reference ADM199/2147.

23 Webb to author, October 2011.

24 Gibson, National Archives reference ADM199/2147.

25 Armstrong, Whitworth & Co. brochure, Tyne and Wear Archives.

26 After the war, several navies turned to hydrogen peroxide in the concentrated form better known as HTP, particularly as a torpedo propellant, but an explosion on HMS *Sidon* in 1955 induced the Royal Navy to abandon its use on a precautionary basis. The Russian submarine *Kursk* was lost with all hands in 2000 following a cataclysmic explosion in her forward torpedo room – her torpedoes ran on a mix of HTP and kerosene.

27 Christopher Dobson, John Miller and Thomas Payne. *The Cruelest Night: Germany's Dunkirk and the Sinking of the Wilhelm Gustloff*. Boston: Little Brown, 1979, pages 83–84, 140–141. Other sources put the total as high as 9,400, so overloaded was the ship.

28 Spiegel TV documentary, 'An Incredible Rescue Against All Orders: *U-3505* and the Children of Hela', 2006.

29 Including HMS *Diadem*, HMS *Opportune* and the escort carriers HMS *Trumpeter* and HMS *Searcher*.

30 Ryan, Frank. *My Little Bit*. Imperial War Museum, Department of Documents, reference 98/568.

31 National Archives reference ADM1/19342.

32 Hamilton to author.

33 National Archives reference ADM116/5569.

34 The bomber's crew was rescued by a Sunderland III flying boat flown by Flight Lieutenant Bill Tilley DFC of 10 Squadron RAAF who managed to land and take off despite a heavy swell on the Atlantic. Source: Lake, Jon. *Sunderland Squadrons of World War 2*. Osprey Publishing: London, 2000, page 62.

35 Black, rather than white, because it would not merge with the boat's wake or the crests of waves.

36 'E for Edward', piloted by Flight Lieutenant G.W. Hill and crew.

PART 2

1 USAAF was formed in 1941; previously, it had been known as USAAC, in which the C stood for Corps. In 1947 it gained independence from the US Army and, renamed the United States Air Force, achieved the same relationship to the US Army and US Navy as the RAF to the Royal Navy and British Army.

2 National Archives reference AIR2/3715.

3 After his escape from the Curragh, Verity transferred to the dangerous world of the Special Operations Executive (SOE), flying Westland Lysanders in and out of Occupied France. He retired as a Group Captain.

4 Keefer, Ralph. *Grounded in Eire*. McGill-Queen's University Press: Montreal, Quebec, and Kingston, Ontario, 2001, page 93.

5 The private papers of Major D.S. Gentile, Imperial War

Museum, Department of Documents, reference 91/1/1.

6 Popularly thought of as a pure fighter, the Messerschmitt Bf 109 could and did carry bombs. Spitfires and Hurricanes had a similar capability.

7 The Vic was the standard V formation, devised during the First World War by Major Sholto Douglas of the Royal Flying Corps. The flight leader flew at the front with two wingmen just behind him, one on either side in echelon. Additional aircraft could be added in pairs to increase the size of the V. The Vic can still be seen in flying displays, but was discarded during the Second World War.

8 National Archives reference AIR50/169.

9 The *London Gazette* 26 November 1940.

10 Thomas to author, August 2011.

11 National Archives reference AIR27/2076.

12 http://www.spitfires.ukf.net/home.htm

13 Pronounced Fin-oo-kan.

14 Interestingly, there is no record in ADM199/2044, or via U-boat.net, of any escort destroyer being attacked in the North Sea or the North Atlantic at around this time.

15 RAF slang for lagging behind and/or not paying attention.

16 Operation Bowery file: National Archives reference ADM 223/552.

17 An RAF Spitfire allegedly made an emergency landing on USS *Wasp*, despite having no landing hook to catch the wires. Asked by the astonished crew how long he had been flying Spitfires he told them it was his first flight.

18 Operations Record Book, 601 Squadron.

19 *Hamilton Spectator* of 21 April 1943.

20 ORB 19 Squadron, National Archives reference AIR27/254.

21 Canadian Personnel Records, courtesy of Rick Schofield.

22 National Archives reference WO 208/3321.

23 The aircraft, piloted by Lieutenant John Leahy, appeared to have exploded in mid-air on 5 September an hour out of Gander, with the loss of all the crew. Strong, Russell A. *First Over Germany: A History of the 306th Bombardment Group.* Hunter Publishing Co.: Winston-Salem, North Carolina, 1982, page 25.

24 It had been developed originally for the Fleet Air Arm in response to its need for a low-altitude fighter/anti-submarine warfare aircraft and entered FAA service only in 1944, powering the Fairey Firefly.

25 Fifteen were powered by the Rolls Royce Griffon IV.

26 National Archives reference AIR27/742.

27 National Archives reference AIR 27/425.

28 91 Squadron ORB, National Archives reference AIR 27/740.

29 National Archives reference AIR27/742.

30 Jones, R.V. *Most Secret War: British Scientific Intelligence 1939–1945.* Wordsworth Military Classics: Ware, Hertfordshire, 1998, page 423.

31 National Archives reference AIR27/742.

PART 3

1 Jimmy Kennedy and Michael Carr, Peter Maurice Music Co. Ltd, 1939.

2 Information taken from *The GEC Journal of Research*, Vol.3, No.2, 1985, pages 73–83.

3 By kind permission of Bawdsey Radar.

4 Imperial War Museum, Private Papers of Mrs E.M. Lynch, catalogue Documents 11133.

5 Imperial War Museum, Private Papers of Mrs Irene Burchell (née Foxwell), catalogue Documents 946.

6 'Z' AA sites fired unguided rockets.

7 National Archives Ref HO186/391 Ministry of Home Security: Air Raid Precautions (ARP GEN).

8 National Archives Ref HO186/391 Ministry of Home Security: Air Raid Precautions (ARP GEN).

9 The memo records the name incorrectly; this is from the papers of Colonel Eric Herbert Larkcom, 1895–1982 (catalogued under Jacobs-Larkcom at the Liddell Hart Centre for Military Archives, King's College, London).

10 ibid

11 ibid

12 Imperial War Museum, Private Papers of R. Howlett, catalogue Documents 4808.

13 Imperial War Museum, Private Papers of R. Howlett, catalogue Documents 4808.

14 Imperial War Museum, Private Papers of R. Howlett, catalogue Documents 4808.

15 Imperial War Museum, Private Papers of R. Howlett, catalogue Documents 4808.

16 National Archives reference WO 199/1800.

17 National Archives WO 199/191–193. Acknowledgements, also, to Philip Clifford's article 'Love Hate and the Spigot Mortar' in *Loopholes: Journal for the Pillbox Study Group and the United Kingdom Fortifications Club*, No. 14, and to Graham G. Matthews of the Pillbox Study Group.

18 Imperial War Museum Sound Archive Recording, reference 23813.

19 Maunsell, 6 October 1940.

20 A list is available at www.islandfarm.fsnet.co.uk

21 *Küsten Verteidigung Abschnitt.*

22 Emplacements with a revolving machine gun turret on the ground-level roof, first seen in the North Africa campaign.

23 Lemars to author, July 2011.

PART 4

1 From the battle report held at the regimental archives.

2 From the battle report held at the regimental archives.

3 National Archives reference WO170/865.

4 National Archives reference WO 179/2956.

5 National Archives reference WO 179/2956.

6 National Archives reference WO 179/2956.

7 National Archives reference WO 179/2930.

8 National Archives reference WO 179/2956.

9 National Archives reference WO170/865.

10 National Archives reference WO 204/8209.

11 National Archives reference WO 204/8209.

12 National Archives reference WO170/865.

13 Wilmot, Laurence F. *Through the Hitler Line: memoirs of an infantry chaplain*. Wilfred Laurier University Press: Waterloo, Ontario, 2003.

14 National Archives reference WO 179/2956.

15 National Archives reference WO170/865.

16 Imperial War Museum Sound Archive Recording reference 8634.

17 Warren Tute, John Costello and Terry Hughes. *D-Day*. (rev. ed.) London: Pan Books Ltd, 1975, page 209.

18 Imperial War Museum Sound Archive Recording reference 12938.

19 From Churchill, Winston S. *The Second World War, Vol. II, 'Their Finest Hour'* (1st ed.) Cassell: London, 1949, pages 602 603. Quoted in Macksey, Kenneth. *Armoured Crusader: The Biography of Major-General Sir Percy 'Hobo' Hobart*. Grub Street: London, 2004, page 186.

20 From Churchill, Winston S. *The Second World War, Vol. IV, 'The Hinge of Fate'* (1st ed.) Cassell: London, 1950, page 791. Quoted in Macksey, Kenneth. *Armoured Crusader: The Biography of Major-General Sir Percy 'Hobo' Hobart*. Grub Street: London, 2004, page 231.

21 The ship is frequently referred to as *Llangby Castle*, an error probably originating from the misspelling in the Winnipegs' war diary.

22 This bridge was renamed in honour of the British 6th Airborne, taking its new name, Pegasus Bridge, from the division's badge.

23 The private papers of Hugh Dinwiddy, Imperial War Museum, Department of Documents, reference 04/31/1.

24 National Archives reference WO178/2839.

25 The private papers of Hugh Dinwiddy, Imperial War Museum, Department of Documents, reference 04/31/1.

26 Imperial War Museum Sound Archive Recording reference 10086.

27 Courtesy Mrs V. Whelan and Stockport and District Normandy Veterans, see http://stockportveterans.wordpress.com

28 Courtesy Mrs V. Whelan and Stockport and District Normandy Veterans, see http://stockportveterans.wordpress.com

29 Imperial War Museum Sound Archive Recording reference 12938.

30 National Archives reference WO179/2965.

31 War diary of the 7th Battalion King's Own Scottish Borderers, 1st Airborne Division, 17 September 1944.

32 War diary of the 7th Battalion King's Own Scottish Borderers, 1st Airborne Division, 17 September 1944.

33 Parravano to author November 2011.

SELECT BIBLIOGRAPHY

Books

Bagnasco, Erminio. *Submarines of World War Two*. Arms and Armour Press: London, 1977.

Bennett, David. *A Magnificent Disaster: The Failure of Market Garden, the Arnhem Operation September 1944*. Casemate Books: Newbury, 2008.

Caine, Philip D. *The RAF Eagle Squadrons: American Pilots Who Flew for the Royal Air Force*. Fulcrum Publishing: Golden, Colorado, 2009.

Copp, Terry. *Fields of Fire: The Canadians in Normandy*. University of Toronto Press: Toronto, Ontario, 2004.

Dobinson, Colin. *Fields of Deception: Britain's Bombing Decoys of World War II*. Methuen Publishing: London, 2000.

Doherty, Richard. *The North Irish Horse: A Hundred Years of Service*. Spellmount Publishers Ltd: Stroud, Gloucestershire, 2002.

Fisher Jr., Ernest F. *United States Army in World War II: The Mediterranean Theater of Operations Cassino to the Alps*. Center of Military History, United States Army: Washington, D.C., 1977.

Ford, Ken. *D-Day 1944 (4): Gold and Juno Beaches*. Osprey Publishing: Oxford, 2002.

François, Dominique. *Normandy: Breaching the Atlantic Wall. From D-Day to the Breakout and Liberation*. Zenith Press: Minneapolis, Minnesota, 2008.

Garlinski, Jozef. *Hitler's Last Weapons: The underground war against the V1 and V2*. Littlehampton Book Services Ltd: Littlehampton, 1979.

Goddard, Lance. *D-Day: Juno Beach Canada's 24 hours of destiny*. Dundurn: Toronto, 2004.

Hood, Jean. *Submarine: An anthology of first-hand accounts of the war under the sea, 1939 1945*. Conway: London, 2007.

Jones, R.V. *Most Secret War: British Scientific Intelligence 1939 1945*. Wordsworth Military Classics: Ware, Hertfordshire, 1998.

Jullian, Marcel. *Jean Maridor, chasseur de V1*. Amiot-Dumont: Paris, 1954.

Keefer, Ralph. *Grounded in Eire: The Story of Two RAF Fliers Interned in Ireland During World War II.* McGill-Queen's University Press: Montreal and London, 2001.

Lake, Jon. *Sunderland Squadrons of World War 2.* Osprey Publishing: Oxford, 2000.

Lavery, Brian. *River-class Frigates and the Battle of the Atlantic: A Technical and Social History.* National Maritime Museum: London, 2006.

Macksey, Kenneth. *Armoured Crusader: The Biography of Major-General Sir Percy 'Hobo' Hobart, One of the Most Influential Military Commanders of the Second World War.* Grub Street: London, 2004.

Malarkey, Don. (With Bob Welch.) *Easy Company Soldier: The Legendary Battles of a Sergeant from World War II's 'Band of Brothers'.* St. Martin's Press: New York, 2008.

Merseytravel. *The Story of U-534.* Merseytravel: Liverpool, undated.

Nesbit, Roy Conyers. *An Illustrated History of the RAF.* Salamander Books Ltd: London, 2002.

Nicholson, Lieutenant Colonel G.W.L. *The Canadians in Italy: 1943–1945.* Edmund Cloutier: Ottowa, 1956.

Parker, Matthew. *Monte Cassino: The Story of the Hardest-fought Battle of World War Two.* Headline Publishing Group: London, 2003.

Peterson, John. *Darkest before Dawn: U-482 and the sinking of Empire Heritage 1944.* The History Press: Stroud, Gloucestershire, 2011.

Pitt, Barrie and Frances. *The Chronological Atlas of World War II.* Macmillan: London, 1989.

Reid, Brian A. *Named by the Enemy: A History of the Royal Winnipeg Rifles.* Robin Brass Studio: Kingston, Ontario, 2010.

Robson, Martin (ed.). *The Spitfire Pocket Manual: 1939–1945.* Conway: London, 2010.

Routledge OBE TD, Brigadier N.W. *Anti-Aircraft Artillery 1914–1955.* Brassey's: London, 1994.

Saunders, Tim. *Juno Beach.* Pen and Sword Books: Barnsley, 2003.

Scoltock, Jack. *The Meltin' Pot: From Wreck to Rescue and Recovery.* The History Press: Stroud, 2008.

Short, Neil. *Tank Turret Fortifications.* Crowood Press: Marlborough, 2006.

Spooner, Tony. *Coastal Ace: The Biography of Squadron Leader Terence Malcolm Bulloch, DSO and Bar, DFC and Bar.* William Kimber: London, 1986

Stacey, Colonel C.P. *Official History of the Canadian Army in the Second World War.* Queen's Printers: Ottowa, 1955.

Strong, Russell A. *First Over Germany: A History of the 306th Bombardment Group.* Hunter Publishing Co.: Winston-Salem, North Carolina, 1982.

Suhren, Teddy and Brustat-Naval, Fritz. *Teddy Suhren Ace of Aces: Memoirs of a U-Boat Rebel.* Chatham Publishing: London, 2006.

Terraine, John. *The Right Of The Line: The Role of the RAF in World War Two.* Pen and Sword Books: Barnsley, 2010.

Turner, Frank R. *The Maunsell Sea Forts: The World War Two Naval Sea Forts of the Thames Estuary.* Privately Published: Gravesend, 1994.

Wilmot MC, Laurence F. *Through the Hitler Line: Memoirs of an Infantry Chaplain.* Wilfred Laurier University Press: Waterloo, Ontario, 2003.

Winters, Major Dick. *Beyond Band of Brothers: The War Memoirs of Major Dick Winters.* Ebury Press: London, 2011.

Zaloga, Steven J. *D-Day Fortifications in Normandy.* Osprey Publishing: Oxford, 2005.

Zaloga, Steven J. *The Atlantic Wall (1) – France.* Osprey Publishing: Oxford, 2007.

Zaloga, Steven J. *The Atlantic Wall (2) – Belgium, The Netherlands, Denmark and Norway.* Osprey Publishing: Oxford, 2009.

Articles

'CH – The first operational Radar' in *GEC Journal of Research*, Vol. 3, No.2, 1985, pages 73–83.

Clifford, Philip. 'Love Hate and the Spigot Mortar' in *Loopholes: Journal for the Pillbox Study Group and the United Kingdom Fortifications Club*, No. 14.

Constable, Trevor J. 'The Little-Known Story of Percy Hobart' in *The Journal of Historical Review*: Volume 18 Number 1, January/February 1999: Newport Beach, California.

Copp, Terry. 'Breaching The Hitler Line: Army, Part 75' in *Legion Magazine*, 7 March 2008: Kanata, Ontario.

Copp, Terry. 'Bridgehead On the Melfa: Army, Part 76' in *Legion Magazine*, 1 June 2008: Kanata, Ontario.

Daniels, Major Michael J. 'Innovation in the face of adversity: Major-General Sir Percy Hobart and the 79th Armoured Division (British)', a thesis presented to the Faculty of the U.S. Army Command and General Staff College in partial fulfillment of the requirements for the degree Master of Military Art And Science. Fort Leavenworth: Kansas, 2003.

Griffiths MBE, MC*, Lieutenant Colonel R.J. Speech given by him at the dinner commemorating the 50th anniversary of the Hitler Line battle. Imperial War Museum catalogue reference K93/1454.

'Rolls-Royce Griffon (65)' in *Flight Magazine*, 20 September 1945.

Online and film

Chadderton, H. Clifford. 'D-DAY: The Story of the Canadian Assault Troops.' DVD in the *War Amps Military Heritage Series*, Canada, 1998.

http://ahoy.tk-jk.net/
A wide-ranging website on Second World War naval and maritime history by Commander Mackenzie Gregory RAN Rtd.

http://archaeologydataservice.ac.uk/archives/view/dob/
The Council for British Archaeology's Defence of Britain Project.
Users of Google Earth can download a kmz file which provides
an overlay showing the sites: Extended Defence of Britain 09.kmz

www.airfieldinformationexchange.org
Online community for researching disused airfields.

www.anti-aircraft.co.uk/index.html
Covers all aspects of British and Commonwealth Anti-Aircraft
during
and just after the Second World War

www.associations.rafinfo.org.uk
Royal Air Force Register of Associations; includes comprehensive
guide to jargon.

http://atlanticwallbelgiumboulogne.110mb.com
Covers the Atlantic Wall from Belgium to Boulogne and the V1
and V2 sites in France and Belgium.

www.castlearchdale.net/id2.html
The history of the flying boat base.

http://coalhousefort-gallery.com/V1-flying-bomb-Vengance-
weapon-site-Hazebrouck. Very good images and descriptions of a
V1 site.

http://www.coalhousefort.co.uk/
Official site of Coalhouse Fort, a Napoleonic fort with Second
World War anti-aircraft additions, and home to Thameside
Aviation Museum.

www.controltowers.co.uk

www.dday.org
Website of The National D-day Memorial, Bedford, Virginia.

www.derelictplaces.co.uk
Online community dedicated to documenting the derelict and
abandoned buildings that are part of British military, industrial
and historical heritage.

www.english-heritage.org.uk/publications/ military-aircraft-
crash-sites/
English Heritage: 'Military Aircraft Crash Sites – Archaeological
guidance on their significance and future management', with a
website, comment and a useful downloadable 2002 document,
which includes many addresses to assist research.
www.jean.maridor.org
Website in memory of Free French Pilot Captain Jean Maridor.

www.kg6gb.org/pow_camps_in_uk.htm
A simple catalogue of Second World War POW camps in Britain.

www.nimc.co.uk (Northern Ireland Museums Council, Second
World War Online Learning Resource for Northern Ireland:
http://www.secondworldwarni.org/

http://northirishhorse.net/
Comprehensive history of the regiment by *Dig WW2* contributor
Gerry Chester.

www.pillboxesuk.co.uk/
Pillboxes in Britain.

www.pillbox-study-group.org.uk
A site committed to the study and preservation of 20th-century
United Kingdom and international pillboxes and anti-invasion
defences. Online magazine: *Loopholes*.

www.radarpages.co.uk
Dick Barrett's comprehensive site on Chain Home Radar.

www.rafbombercommand.com/
About the Royal Air Force's bomber aircrews, airmen and
airwomen 1939 1945.

www.royaltankregiment.com/
Goes beyond the history of the regiment.

www.spitfires.ukf.net
Identifies every Spitfire built, from contract through production
to final fate.

ww2ni.webs.com/
Andrew Glenfield's comprehensive website on the Second World
War in Northern Ireland.

www.uboat.net
Probably the definitive website on U-boats.

www.uboatarchive.net
The best site for U-Boat patrol reports and other records.

www.ulsteraviationsociety.org

www.warsailors.com
Excellent starting point for convoy research.

PICTURE CREDITS

ACKNOWLEDGEMENTS

First of all, let me thank Dan Snow and everyone at 360 Production without whom there would have been no book to write. I thoroughly enjoyed being on some of the digs with you. Next comes the Conway Publishing team, both in-house and freelance: Editors John Lee and Alison Moss for giving me the project, Jennifer Veall for sourcing so many of the images, Anna Matos Melgaco for the design, and, above all, my simply outstanding and understanding copy editor, Christopher Westhorp. Several of the experts featured in the film were extremely helpful: Gareth Baillie, Gerry Chester, Richard Doherty, W.O. Geert Jonker, Donal Neill, Damiano Parravano, Lynda Ross, Bill Shuttleworth, Rich Stevenson, Ian Wilson, and Paul and Myriam Woodage. A very big thank you to the National Archives, British Library, Imperial War Museum, Lloyd's Register of Shipping and Lashenden Air Warfare Museum for your help and for the preservation of items and records of inestimable value. I offer my gratitude to the following

individuals and organizations for generously sharing their knowledge or providing other assistance: Jean-Claude Augst; Bawdsey Radar; Irene Burchell; Jonathan Catton; Coalhouse Fort; Paul Diamond; Andy Glenfield; Mackenzie Gregory; René Lemars; Captain Jerry Mason USN Rtd; Andrew Pentland; John Peterson; Lieutenant Colonel Brian Reid Rtd; RAF Langham; the Royal Winnipeg Rifles Museum – not forgetting Commander David Hamilton; Rick Schofield; Alison Sieff; George Smith; Charles de Vallavieille; Linda Varley of Stockport Veterans Association; Rush Webb; Mrs V. Whelan; Natalie Worthington and Marie-Eve Vaillancourt-Deleris of the Centre Juno Beach; Elin Lindqvist; and my London friends Judy, Peter and Sarah Greenwood, with their convenient spare room. Finally, special thanks to my very tolerant husband, George – being married to an author is not easy.

INDEX

Figures in *italics* indicate captions.

CON LAW

CON LAW

Mark Gimenez

sphere

SPHERE

First published in Great Britain in 2013 by Sphere

A CIP catalogue record for this book is available from the British Library.

ISBN HB 978-1-84744-379-3
ISBN CF 978-1-84744-380-9

Typeset in Bembo by Hewer Text UK Ltd, Edinburgh
Printed and bound in Great Britain by Clays Ltd, St Ives plc

Papers used by Sphere are from well-managed forests
and other responsible sources.

MIX
Paper from
responsible sources
FSC® C104740

Sphere
An imprint of
Little, Brown Book Group
100 Victoria Embankment
London EC4Y 0DY

An Hachette UK Company
www.hachette.co.uk

www.littlebrown.co.uk

To Laurence J. ("Larry") Rice Jr. (1954–2009), devoted husband, father, son, brother, friend, and lawyer.

Acknowledgments

My sincere thanks and appreciation to David Shelley, Jade Chandler, Iain Hunt, and everyone else at Sphere/Little, Brown Book Group in London; Professor Emeritus of Law Charles E. Rice at the Notre Dame Law School, a scholar and a gentleman, for teaching me constitutional law (again); Barbara Hautanen for the Spanish translations; Joel Tarver at T Squared Design in Houston for my website and email blasts to my readers; and all of you who have emailed me. I hope to hear from you again.

The layman's constitutional view is that what he likes is constitutional and that which he doesn't like is unconstitutional.

—Supreme Court Justice Hugo L. Black, 1971

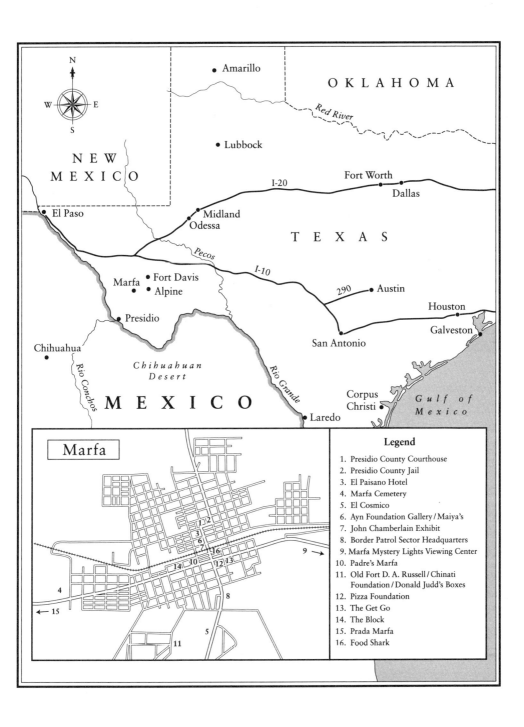

Prologue

'Professor—he's got a gun!'

'Get down, Renée.'

His young intern ducked down behind Book.

'Goddamn outsider,' the man holding the gun said, 'coming to our town and stirring up trouble.'

The three young men reeked of beer and sweat and testosterone. They sat on the tailgate of an old pickup truck; crushed beer cans littered the bed behind them. The gunman sat in the middle; he was unshaven and wore a cap on backwards and overalls over a bare chest that revealed a KKK tattoo on his right biceps. He held the gun with his right hand; that would be his strong side. The second man held a three-foot length of pipe with his left hand, slapping it into his right palm like a principal about to render corporal punishment to the class bully; he was a southpaw. He sat to the gunman's right and wore a camo cap and a wife-beater muscle shirt. The third man was empty-handed; he sat to the gunman's left. He wore a straw cowboy hat and a *Don't Mess with Texas* T-shirt. He shuffled his boots in the dirt of the parking lot.

Book took a small step to his left.

He and Renée had just eaten lunch with Ronald and his sister at a café situated hard against the railroad tracks on the black side of town. It was all laughs and good times as they walked out back to say their goodbyes and to ride home on the Harley. But they found these three hillbillies waiting for them; their truck blocked access to the motorcycle. A Confederate flag adorned the back window. Some folks simply refused to evolve. The Klan lived on in East Texas; these young men were the progeny of the three Klansmen who had made East Texas infamous by dragging a black man to his death behind their pickup in 1998. Book could imagine the same fate for Ronald. The man waved the gun at Book.

'You and your gal there, get on that motorbike and get the hell out of our town. Me and the boys, we're gonna take Ronnie for a ride out to the piney woods, remind him about the facts of life: black boys don't mess with white women.'

'I take it you boys aren't NBA fans.'

'You a funny goddamned Injun, ain't you?'

Book's coloring and coarse black hair often made people think he was at least part Native American; perhaps he was. As a boy, he would paint his face and pretend to be a great Comanche war chief. The moment did have a cowboys-and-Indians feel to it. But Book did not wear war paint that day; he did wear his hair too long for someone in his profession, jeans, boots, and a black Tommy Bahama T-shirt. These boys' fuses were already lit and fueled by alcohol and inbred racism, but he still tried to defuse the situation.

'Well, it's possible I have some Comanche blood in me, but—'

'You fixin' to have blood on you, you don't get on that bike, you goddamned skinny-ass Injun.'

Book stood six-one but weighed only one-seventy-five, so he was a bit on the lean side, especially compared to these three sides of beef. They were big and muscular twenty-somethings, and they had too much alcohol on board to succumb to reason or mild physical persuasion. He was thirty-five and skinny. But he did have skills.

'Ronald,' Book said without breaking eye contact with the gunman, 'you and Darlene take off.'

Ronald stepped in front of his sister.

'No way, Professor.'

'You just got out of prison. You don't need this.'

'I survived seventeen years in that prison. I know how to fight. You're a law professor.'

Ronald Westbrook had been incarcerated for the last seventeen years for a crime he did not commit: aggravated rape. Of a white woman. In East Texas. No DNA or other physical evidence of any kind had been collected or introduced at trial. But he was convicted nonetheless, guilty only of being a black man in his late twenties with tattoos covering his upper body, the same as the perpetrator. In his youth, Ronald had been a high school football star whose dream of a pro career ended with a knee injury; he had always lived on the right side of the law, but the law said he would live the rest of his life as an inmate in the state penitentiary.

He was not alone.

In the last decade, fifty innocent black men had been released from prison in Texas after being exonerated by DNA evidence. Ronald was not one of them. DNA testing was not standard police procedure seventeen years before in that small East Texas county. Ronald was convicted solely on the victim's testimony; she pointed him out in the courtroom before the jury, as certain as a witness could be. Studies have shown that eyewitness testimony is almost always unreliable; a terrified person with a gun stuck in her face remembers almost nothing with evidentiary clarity. Fear blinds a human being. But the local district attorney sent another black man to prison and earned another term in office. Ronald Westbrook resigned himself to dying in prison.

Until his sister wrote a letter to Professor John Bookman.

Book and Renée rode the Harley to East Texas. They

discovered that Ronald had in fact had sex with a white woman that night, but not with the victim; at the time of the alleged rape, he was in bed with Louise Parker, a respected widow in town who had met Ronald at the church where she worked. She was lonely; he was the janitor. They shared a love of the Bible and each other. But Louise could not face the social stigma she would have to endure in her small hometown if she testified to having sex with a black man. So she watched in silence as Ronald was convicted and sentenced to life.

Now it was her life that was ending.

She had terminal breast cancer. For seventeen years, she had kept her secret; and Ronald had never betrayed her. 'Professor, I grew up in this town. I know how it is. I would've been sentencing her to a place worse than prison,' he said when Book had asked, 'Why?' His sister knew there had been a woman, but not her color or her name; so Book and Renée played detective. They tracked Ronald's life from the football field to the church; they learned of Louise. They went to her home, but her son, now a respected lawyer in town, refused to talk to them or allow them to talk to his mother.

They found her in the hospital.

She too refused to talk. The nurse called her son, and he called the sheriff. Book's mind raced, trying to think of something that would get Louise to tell the truth. But the sheriff arrived and handcuffed them. Just as he pulled them to the door, Renée broke into tears and cried out to Louise.

'My mother died without saying she was sorry!'

Louise turned her eyes to Renée and held up a weak hand to the sheriff.

'What did she do?'

'She cheated on my father! She cheated on us!'

Tears came to Louise. She gestured the sheriff away and Renée close.

'I'm sorry,' she said. 'For what I did to Ronald.'

4

Louise Parker made amends before meeting her Maker. She revealed her secret on videotape. Two weeks later, Ronald Westbrook came home. His hair had turned gray, and his body had aged, but his handshake remained firm. He thanked Book, payment in full. His sister hugged Book and cried until his shirt was wet. Ronald forgave Louise before she died. They were the only witnesses to her burial; her son did not attend. There was no celebration in town upon Ronald's return. Book had learned that most people, even good people and especially people in small towns, preferred that their past acts of injustice remain in the past. And others were just one generation removed from white hoods. Like these three men. Book addressed the gunman.

'Ronald and Darlene are going home now.'

The gunman spat tobacco juice then stood; he was at least six-four.

'The hell you say. See, I don't figure you making any decisions, Injun. I believe this three-fifty-seven Magnum's making the decisions today.'

A .357 Magnum is one of the most powerful handguns manufactured in America, which is to say, in the world. One possible future played out in Book's mind: the gunman firing point-blank into Book's chest, the massive piece of lead piercing his sternum, exploding through his heart, blowing a fist-sized hole in his back, then striking and killing Renée; the man then turning the gun on Ronald and Darlene ducked behind her brother. Two shots and the four of them would be dead. One shot from a .357 Magnum twenty-one years before, and Book's father was dead.

'Ronnie, he's coming with us,' the gunman said. 'We got some unfinished business with him. And his pretty little sister.'

Darlene emerged from behind Ronald and gazed up at the gunman with a look of recognition.

'Wait. I know you. You're Dewey Randle. We went to school together. You were always looking at me. You didn't do that Klan stuff back then.'

Dewey glared down at her.

'Nig—'

He dropped his eyes. His expression softened slightly, almost as if embarrassed. His voice came out soft.

'Black man rapes your mama, you change.'

'It was your mama who pointed Ronald out in court, said he raped her.'

Dewey's face and voice turned hard again. His anger spilled out.

'It was my mama he raped. Now folks are sayin' she's a liar. I figure Ronnie and that dead woman, they're the liars. Maybe we take Ronnie out to the woods, he'll confess—or he'll watch us do to you what he did to my mama.'

Ronald took a step toward Dewey, but Book blocked him with an outstretched arm. He locked eyes with Dewey Randle, and in his eyes Book saw the same emptiness he had seen only once before, in the eyes of a convicted killer about to be executed.

'That's not going to happen.'

'I got nothin' to lose, Injun. I'm ready to die. Are you?'

'I am.'

Dewey gave Book a bemused look. 'You ain't afraid of dying?'

'I'm afraid of not living.'

'What's the difference?'

'Not living is worse than dying.'

'Good. 'Cause you fixin' to die, Crazy Horse.'

'Son . . . you don't know crazy.'

Dewey raised the gun to Book's head, all the opening he needed. His mind had already played out the three moves he would execute to disable Dewey; it all happened in less than two seconds, but the world seemed to move in slow motion as he swung his open right hand up and against Dewey's wrist, moving the gun away from his face . . . the gun discharged . . . Renée screamed . . . Book swung his left arm up from the inside and grasped Dewey's wrist . . . the tenets of martial

6

arts dictated that Book's next move would be to pull the gun hand down to the outside of his left hip, bringing Dewey's head down and close enough to strike, but that move would also bring the gun closer to Renée . . . so instead, Book jerked the gun hand hard and up past his own head . . . which brought Dewey's head close enough for a temple strike . . . Book tucked his right fist and launched himself into the taller man, slamming his right elbow into Dewey's left temple, knocking him unconscious. The gun fell to the ground, followed by Dewey Randle. Book kicked the gun away then spun to a knife-hand-guard position to face the man with the pipe; but he addressed his intern behind him.

'You okay, Renée?'

A timid voice from below: 'Unh-huh.'

'Ronald? Darlene?'

'We're good, Professor. But how did you . . .?'

The other two men's faces told him that either the alcohol or their egos would not allow a retreat. Book blamed it on the Alamo. No self-respecting Texan—or should he say, no self-respecting drunk Texan—would surrender without a fight. The wife-beater came at Book with the length of pipe; he stepped forward with his left foot and swung as if trying to hit a home run off a high fastball . . . Book ducked under the pipe swinging past his head and executed a spinning sweep, whipping his left leg against the back of the man's leg and knocking his feet out from under him, then a ridge hand strike to the bridge of his nose as the man fell over back-wards. He collapsed to the ground, writhing in pain and cupping his broken nose as blood gushed forth. Book spun to face the third man. 'Don't Mess with Texas' stood frozen over his buddies. He considered his options.

'Don't,' Book said.

He didn't.

The gunfire had brought a crowd out of the café and the sound of a distant siren. Ronald and Darlene would be safe, for now. Book turned to his intern; she was crouched on the ground as if saying a final prayer. He bent down and took her shoulders and lifted her up. She seemed to be in a state of shock.

'Renée, it's okay. You're safe now. I told you I would always protect you.'

He helped her onto the back seat of the big Harley. He swung a leg over and stood the bike upright. Renée leaned into him from behind and wrapped her arms tightly around his torso; he felt her body trembling.

'Thought you're a law professor?' Ronald said.

'I am.'

'Never seen no professor fight like that.'

'It's the Comanche blood.'

Book shook hands with Ronald then fired up the engine, shifted into gear, and gunned the motorcycle west on the highway to Austin. He let out a war cry that would have made Crazy Horse proud.

ONE MONTH LATER

Chapter 1

'Professor Bookman—'

'Answer the question.'

'But, Professor—'

'Ms. Edwards, do you or do you not have a constitutional right to take the pill?'

'I don't care.'

'You don't care if you have a right to use contraceptives?'

'No.' She shrugged. 'I'm a lesbian.'

Book sighed. His mind offered up a list of biting retorts—not to her lesbianism, but to her lack of interest—but he decided against uttering a word. Even a tenured law professor had to be careful with class lectures these days, when every cell phone and laptop doubled as a video camera; this morning's lecture might be that night's viral YouTube video. So he turned from Ms. Edwards and searched the sea of faces for another female student who might care or at least be willing to answer his question in front of the other hundred students. Most had their heads ducked behind their laptops, assured that Professor Bookman would not use his classroom authority to humiliate them in front of their peers. The days of law professors wearing bowties and suits—Book wore boots, jeans, and another Tommy Bahama T-shirt (*Nothing but Net* stenciled under a hammock strung between two palm trees)—and employing the Socratic method to browbeat their students were over. Students paying $30,000 a year (twice that at private schools) demanded a kinder, gentler law school experience. Consequently, Book prodded them to participate in the class debates, but he did not force it upon them. Although it seemed counter-intuitive for prospective lawyers, he knew it was not everyone's nature to seek attention.

It was, however, Ms. Garza's nature.

She sought attention. She demanded attention. She sat directly in front of Book on the front row to ensure his attention. She stuck her hand in the air and puffed her chest out proudly, not to show off her feminine attributes to her handsome professor but to display the message-of-the-day printed in big black letters on her white T-shirt: IF I WANTED THE GOVERNMENT IN MY WOMB, I'D FUCK A SENATOR. No doubt she had chosen her attire in honor of that day's constitutional law topic as stated on the class syllabus: 'The Right of Privacy and Women's Reproductive Rights.' Book admired Ms. Garza's commitment to social justice, but after facing her (and her T-shirts) on the front row for fifty minutes four mornings each week for eight months, her hand always waving frantically, desperate for another opportunity to espouse her political views to the class, the new had worn off. But she remained his go-to student to ignite a class debate.

'Ms. Garza, do you have a constitutional right to take the pill?'

'You're damn right I do.'

'Why?'

'Because in *Griswold v. Connecticut*, the Supreme Court found a right of privacy in the Bill of Rights—'

Book held up an open hand. 'Does the Bill of Rights—the first ten amendments to the Constitution—expressly mention a right of privacy?'

'No. But the Court found a right of privacy in the penumbras of the Bill of Rights—'

'*Penumbras?* What, Ms. Garza, is a penumbra?'

'Uh . . . I'm not really sure.'

'Look it up.'

While she typed on her laptop, Book sat on the front edge of his desk and surveyed the one hundred freshman students—'1Ls' in the vernacular, the first year of their transition from human being to lawyer almost complete—rising before him in the fan-shaped, theater-style seating in Classroom 2.138 at the University of Texas School of Law. They attended his constitutional law class, 'Con Law' as it was known in the curriculum catalog, only because it was a required course; they needed the class credit to earn a law degree. These students much preferred studying the nine million words of the tax code and regulations, for their lives would be lived among those words. Those legal dos and don'ts, rules and regulations borne of generous lobbying and conveniently painted in gray rather than black and white, allowed for a lawyer's creativity.

Many a legal career had been forged in the gray margins of the law.

But not his career. He had never been attracted to the words defining capital gains. After one reading of the Constitution—4,543 words; 7,591 including the twenty-seven amendments—back when he was a 1L, he knew his legal life would be lived among the words of James Madison. He had fallen in love with the Constitution at age twenty-two and the affair continued to this day. 'We the People of the United States, in Order to form a more perfect Union, establish Justice, insure domestic Tranquility, provide for the common defence, promote the general Welfare, and secure the Blessings of

Liberty to ourselves and our Posterity, do ordain and establish this Constitution for the United States of America.'

How could you not love those words?

But try though he did—and he did try Monday through Thursday from 9:10 A.M. until 10:00 A.M.—he could not instill the same love for the Constitution in these profit-minded students. If the Constitution had a Facebook page, few of these students would 'like' it. Few would follow it on Twitter. Few seemed to even entertain such lofty legal ideals as liberty and justice these days. Those were concepts you read about in the casebooks, not rights you fought for in the real world. They were not the children of the civil rights era; they were the grandchildren. Twenty-two, twenty-three, twenty-four years old, they had grown up in an era of affluence and entitlement, beneficiaries of the fights fought before they were born. Consequently, they cared more about their job prospects upon graduation, most hoping to become well-paid corporate servants.

Who else could pay $1,000 an hour?

And that was the role law schools now played: farm teams for the major league law firms. 'A' students were valuable commodities in the law business. They were currency. The schools funneled the best and the brightest to the plush offices on the fiftieth floors of skyscrapers across the nation. In return, the law firms endowed chairs at the law schools, ensuring the curriculum would be shaped to further corporate interests, offering such classes as: Corporations; Corporate Finance; Corporate Governance; Taxation of Corporations and Share-holders; Federal Income Taxation of Corporations; Corporate and Securities Law and Transactions; Corporation Law, Finance, Securities, and Regulation; Mergers and Acquisitions; and, of course, White Collar Crime.

Even for this millennial generation, a law degree was viewed as their ticket in life. Most, those sons and daughters of the working class, chose law school because their parents had not.

They borrowed a hundred thousand dollars to finance a legal education at UT law school (twice that at Harvard law school) because a law degree still constituted a viable vehicle for social mobility in America, a way to get ahead. To be successful. To have a better life. Perhaps even to get rich.

Others, those sons and daughters of the one percent, simply needed a station in life, a place to be when they weren't at the country club.

Only a few still came to law school with a desire to change the world. Like Ms. Garza here. She burned hot with political desire. She read off her laptop.

'*Webster's* defines penumbra as "the partial or imperfect shadow outside the complete shadow of an opaque body, such as a planet, where the light from the source of illumination is only partly cut off."'

'A shadow?' Book said. 'Let me get this straight: the Supreme Court found a right of privacy in the shadows of the Bill of Rights, where it had been lurking for almost a hundred and eighty years?'

'That's what they said.'

'But I thought the Bill of Rights lists all the rights of the people guaranteed by the Constitution?'

'That's not correct.'

'Please explain.'

'The Framers figured right-wing Republicans—'

'In seventeen eighty-nine?'

'—would read the Bill of Rights as an exclusive list of the people's rights, so James Madison added the Ninth Amendment specifically to negate that interpretation.'

'And the Ninth Amendment states what?'

She read: '"The enumeration in the Constitution, of certain rights, shall not be construed to deny or disparage others retained by the people."'

'To translate, the Framers wanted to make clear that there were other rights retained by the people, even if not specifically mentioned in the Bill of Rights?'

15

'Yes.'

'And in *Griswold*, the Court determined that one such unmentioned right was the right of privacy. The Court struck down a state law that banned the use of contraceptives, holding that that decision—whether or not to get pregnant—is within a woman's zone of privacy. That the government has no say in such a personal decision.'

Mr. Brennan, also seated on the first row, raised his hand. He tried to transcribe every word Book uttered in each class on his laptop, more court reporter than law student. Book nodded at him.

'Professor, after "whether or not to get pregnant," did you say—'

'Mr. Brennan, you don't need to record my lectures *verbatim*. Just listen. Or better yet, participate.'

Mr. Brennan's hands hovered over his keyboard. Book surrendered, as he had each class.

'I said, "that decision—whether or not to get pregnant—is within a woman's zone of privacy. That the government has no say in such a personal decision."'

Mr. Brennan typed furiously.

'Got it. So the rule of *Griswold* is—'

'Mr. Brennan, this is Con Law not Civ Proc. You're not trying to learn discrete rules of the Court. You're trying to learn to think for yourself, which, unfortunately, few of you will ever do in the private practice of law.'

Mr. Brennan held his gaze. Book again surrendered.

'The rule of *Griswold* is that there is an unwritten but fundamental right of privacy in the Bill of Rights, and a state ban on the use of contraceptives by a married couple violates that right. Which the Court extended to unmarried couples in *Eisenstadt v. Baird* in nineteen seventy-two.'

Mr. Brennan typed. He wore a Boston Red Sox jersey and cap on backwards. He was one of those working-class sons, intent on graduating in the top ten percent of his class, hiring on with a large Boston law firm, paying off his student loans, and living a better life than his father, a Boston cop. Mr. Brennan couldn't get into Harvard, so he had come south for law school. He kept his head down, his fingers moving across the keyboard, and his mind focused on final exams. Book addressed the class.

'*Griswold* was decided in nineteen sixty-five. Eight years later, the justices handed down perhaps the most controversial decision in the history of the Court: *Roe v. Wade*. In *Griswold*, the Court said a woman has a fundamental right not to get pregnant. In *Roe*, the Court said a woman has a fundamental right to end a pregnancy. Mr. Stanton, who was the appellee in *Roe*?'

Mr. Stanton occupied the top row, leaned back in his chair against the wall and dressed like the frat boy he was, his hands buried in his lap and his fingers tapping against his cell phone. Texting in Con Law class. Again, Book held his tongue. Mr. Stanton was smart and rich, and he acted the part. His father was a senior partner in a large Houston firm that had endowed two chairs at the law school. Consequently, Mr. Stanton acted more like a shareholder of the school than a student. The transition from the UT law school to the River Oaks Country Club would be smooth and seamless for E. Roger Stanton Jr.

'Mr. Stanton, if you have a moment, would you please answer the question?'

Mr. Stanton still did not look up from his phone.

'Sorry, Professor, I'm dumping my Facebook stock I got in the IPO. Henry Wade, the Dallas County district attorney, he was the appellee.'

'Who was the appellant?'

Still texting.

'Norma McCorvey, aka "Jane Roe, a pregnant single woman."'

'Who was her lawyer?'

'Uh . . . I don't know.'

'Read the opinion.'

Mr. Stanton's eyes lifted to his laptop.

'Sarah Weddington.'

'From what law school did she graduate?'

'Doesn't say.'

'Anyone?'

No one.

'Not even you, Ms. Garza?'

She turned her palms up. 'I wasn't born until nineteen ninety.'

Mr. Stanton, texting again: 'Didn't your mother know that abortion was legal in nineteen ninety, even in Del Rio?'

'Not funny, Mr. Stanton.'

But the class thought he was; they too had grown weary of Ms. Garza. She had been born poor on the border, at the opposite end of the socioeconomic spectrum from Mr. Stanton. She had entered UT an underprivileged female; she had graduated an in-your-face feminist. Book often saw her manning the pro-abortion booth on the West Mall, the free-speech zone on campus. He finally answered his own question, something law professors often had to do.

'Sarah attended this very law school. She graduated in nineteen sixty-seven. Only four years later, she argued *Roe v. Wade* and became the youngest lawyer ever to win a Supreme Court case.'

The students smiled, as if they could put her victory on their own resumés. Ms. Garza seemed especially proud. Perhaps Sarah the law student had burned hot with the same desire to change the world. She had certainly changed the world; some would argue for the better, some would argue for the worse, but no one could argue that she didn't change the world. Book had won two search-and-seizure cases at the Supreme Court. Both were groundbreaking—every Supreme Court case is groundbreaking—but neither had changed the world.

'Mr. Stanton, what law did the appellant challenge?'

Still texting. He did not look up.

'The Texas law that made all abortions criminal acts unless necessary to save the mother's life.'

'And what did the Court decide?'

'That the law violated Roe's right of privacy and was thus unconstitutional.'

'Mr. Stanton, in which article of the Bill of Rights is abortion mentioned?'

'It's not.'

'Why is that?'

Ms. Garza couldn't restrain herself.

'Because racist, misogynistic white men who owned slaves and didn't allow women to vote wrote the Constitution!'

Mr. Stanton coughed words that sounded like 'affirmative action.' His posse of fellow frat boys on the back row laughed. Book did not defend Ms. Garza. She needed no help. She turned in her chair and aimed a finger (not her middle one this time) at Mr. Stanton.

'Your days are numbered, Stanton. Apartheid in America is coming to an end. Enjoy it while you can.'

'I will. In a month, I'll be lying by the pool at the country club surrounded by white girls.'

'And if you get one of those girls pregnant, your rich daddy will pay for her abortion. A poor black or Latino girl gets pregnant, your daddy wants to force her to have the baby. Fifty million abortions since Roe—does your daddy want to pay more taxes to support all those babies?'

The senior Stanton was a prominent and very rich Republican in Texas.

'No, but I'll get him to endow a lifetime abortion pass for you. God knows we don't need any more Irma Garzas in this world.'

The junior Stanton shared a high-five with his posse. Book kicked the front panel of the desk as if the heel of his boot was a gavel, and order was soon restored. Book had warned the students that his classroom was an intellectual free-fire zone, like the Supreme Court but more civil.

'Mr. Stanton, if the Constitution says nothing about abortion, how did the Supreme Court determine that a woman has a constitutional right to have an abortion?'

'They discovered it.'

'Where?'

'In the right of privacy.'

'The same right of privacy they discovered in *Griswold*?'

'Yep.'

'Another unmentioned right lurking in the shadows?'

'Who knew?'

'But, as Ms. Garza correctly stated, the intent of the Ninth Amendment was to make clear that there are other rights not mentioned in the Bill of Rights that are nonetheless protected by the Constitution. The Court ruled in *Griswold* that one such unmentioned right is the right of privacy. Mr. Stanton, isn't abortion another such right?'

'No. Abortion was not an unmentioned right of the people at the time the Bill of Rights was ratified. In fact, it was a crime at common law in every state of the Union.'

Ms. Garza stood and faced Mr. Stanton. The debate was on.

'That's bullshit, Stanton. The Court said abortion was *not* a crime at common law.'

'They lied. The only authority the Court cited were two law review articles written by the general counsel of a pro-abortion group, which articles have been roundly discredited as distortions of the common law. In order to justify their hijacking of the Constitution to push their political agenda, the liberal justices misstated history by adopting one biased author's point of view.'

'History is just a point of view,' Ms. Garza said. 'Usually written by white men biased against women and minorities. The right to have an abortion was another right not mentioned in the Constitution because women did not serve on the Constitutional Convention. Women's voices were not heard at the time, Mr. Stanton.'

'Thank God.'

Which elicited a round of boos from the women in the classroom. Book kicked his desk again and gestured Ms. Garza into her chair.

'Mr. Stanton, what was the key ruling of *Roe*?'

'That the right of privacy includes the right to have an abortion.'

'No.'

Mr. Stanton frowned.

'Ms. Garza?'

'That before viability of the unborn child, the state has no legitimate interest in the unborn.'

'The Court so held, but was that really the key ruling of the case?'

No takers.

'Come on, people, you've read the case. Think.'

Heads ducked behind the façade of laptops.

'I know you're back there. You can hide but you can't run, at least not for'—he checked the clock on the back wall—'fifteen more minutes. Was viability the key ruling of *Roe*?'

'No.'

A small anonymous voice.

'Who said that?'

Book searched the laptops for a face.

'Come on, fess up.'

A hand slowly rose above a laptop.

'*Ms. Roberts*? Was that you?'

'Unh-huh.'

Ms. Roberts peeked over her laptop on the sixth row. She had never before spoken in class.

'Ms. Roberts, welcome to the debate. So what was the key ruling in *Roe*?'

21

She looked like the shy girl in high school who had never been on a date being asked to the prom by the football star. She took a handful of her hair hanging in her face and wrapped it around her left ear. With her index finger she pushed her black-framed glasses up on her nose. She took a deep breath then spoke in the softest of voices to the hushed classroom.

'That under the Constitution, an unborn child is not a living human being at any time prior to birth. As Justice Stevens said, it is only a, quote, "developing organism." Thus, the Constitution offers no protection whatsoever to an unborn child.'

'Correct. Please elaborate.'

'The Fourteenth Amendment states that, quote, "nor shall any state deprive any *person* of life, liberty, or property, without due process of law; nor deny to any *person* within its jurisdiction the equal protection of the laws." Thus, if an unborn child were a "person," Roe's case would fail because the Fourteenth Amendment would expressly protect the unborn child's right to life. So, in order to find a right to an abortion, the Court had to first rule that an unborn child is not a "person" under the Constitution. Which is exactly how they ruled: an unborn child is not a living human being and thus abortion is not the termination of a human life.'

Ms. Roberts had found her voice after eight months of Con Law classes. Another small victory for Professor John Bookman.

'So?'

'So, if the unborn child is not a living human being, what's growing inside the mother—a vegetable? Dogs and cats aren't persons under the Constitution either, but we have laws that prevent us from killing them for sport. And this ruling seems especially cruel given that the Court had previously ruled that corporations do qualify as persons under the Fourteenth Amendment and are thus entitled to the full protection of the Constitution.'

Mr. Stanton, from the back row: 'As my man Mitt said, "Corporations are people, too."'

Which evoked a round of laughter. Book kicked his desk again.

'People, this is important. Ms. Roberts is on to something. Listen up.' Back to Ms. Roberts. 'So corporations have more rights under the Constitution than an unborn child?'

'Yes. In fact, a rock has the same constitutional rights as an unborn child.'

'You're almost to the finish line, Ms. Roberts. Now tell us why that particular ruling matters.'

'Because it makes us question whether we matter. It makes us question our place in the grand scheme of things. Do human beings occupy a special place in the universe or are we just a species that has evolved to a higher state of cognitive ability than, say, chimpanzees? When our highest court of law says human beings have absolutely no rights until we're born, that delegates an unborn child to the same constitutional status as an earthworm or a tomato or a—'

'Rock?'

'Yes.'

'And you think you're more important in the universe than a rock?'

'I hope so.'

'So what are the possible legal consequences of this ruling?'

'What if the unborn child has a genetic defect? Can the government force the woman to abort in order to avoid costly future treatment for that child? What if the government decides to solve poverty by instituting mandatory abortions, like in China? New York City public schools are giving the abortion pill to eighth-grade girls without their parents' permission. When our highest court says that unborn humans are not "persons" under the Constitution and may be killed without constraint but corporations that manufacture weapons of war that kill millions of born humans are "persons" with constitutional rights, I say, Who are those guys? Why do they get to decide what is or isn't human? Who elected them God? How do we know they're right? If they're right, who are we and what are we and what is our place in the universe? Is human life nothing more than a biological coincidence? Are our lives no more important in the universe than road kill on I-Thirty-five? Do we matter? Or are we just matter?'

'And if they're wrong?'

'We're all in deep shit, so to speak.'

The students stared at her with stunned expressions. Except Ms. Garza. She glared at Ms. Roberts.

'What, now you're Sarah Palin? You want women to go back to coat hangers and poison?'

Ms. Roberts did not wither under Ms. Garza's hot glare.

'I had an abortion, Ms. Garza. I was ra—'

She ducked her head, and an awkward silence fell upon the room, until Mr. Stanton said from the back row, 'Ms. Garza, you are the poster child for abortion on demand.' Which evoked a round of supportive hoots.

'Unacceptable, Mr. Stanton,' Book said. 'In this classroom we are civil lawyers, able to disagree without being disagreeable. What is my absolute rule of conduct?'

'We shall remain civil at all times.'

'You have violated that rule. An apology, please.'

Mr. Stanton seemed contrite.

'My sincere apology for my incivility, Ms. Garza.'

She faced him.

'Fuck off, Stanton.'

He threw up his hands.

The first time a student had blurted out the F-word in his class, Book had sent him packing. Eight years later, he didn't blink an eye. He was beyond being shocked by profanity—in class, in the corridors, anywhere in public for that matter. Profanity was as much a part of speech for this generation as 'howdy' was for Book's. The F-word had made its way from the locker room to the law school. Athletes, actors, CEOs, and even vice presidents employed the F-word. It's a noun, verb, adverb, adjective, and interjection. It's mainstream speech. It's freedom of speech. The Supreme Court had in fact ruled that the government could not fine a broadcast company for the singer Bono blurting out the F-word during an award show. Book often wondered if the Framers had anticipated that the First Amendment would one day give constitutional protection to 'fuck off.'

'Not gracious, Ms. Garza,' Book said. 'People, I know this is an emotional issue. But as lawyers we must keep our heads while others around us are losing theirs. In this classroom, we are lawyers, not protestors.'

'But we're one Supreme Court justice away from abortion being banned in America!' Ms. Garza said.

'Who told you that?'

'Biden. He said so on TV.'

'He's wrong.'

'He's the vice president.'

'He's still wrong.'

'But Justice Scalia wants to ban abortions!'

'No, he doesn't. Scalia said that as far as he's concerned, the states may permit abortion on demand. The conservative justices don't think there's a constitutional right to have an abortion, but they've never said that the Constitution bans abortion or that an unborn child is a "person" under the Constitution. They've never disagreed with the key ruling of *Roe*, that abortion is not the taking of human life under the Constitution.'

'You sure about that?'

'I'm teaching Con Law, Ms. Garza.'

'Professor,' Mr. Brennan said, taking a respite from his furious typing, 'do you think the Court correctly decided *Roe*?'

'Mr. Brennan, in this classroom what I think is irrelevant. What you think is relevant. And that you think. I don't care whether you agree or disagree with the *Roe* case, only that you

25

think about the case. As students of the Constitution, we are more concerned with the Supreme Court's reasoning than with its decisions, its thought process rather than who wins or loses the case.'

'Bullshit.'

'Ah, a dissenting opinion from Ms. Garza. In any event, we may disagree with the Court's decisions, but so long as the justices *interpret* the Constitution, they are acting within their authority. If, however, they *amend* the Constitution, they are usurping we the people's authority.'

Mr. Stanton: 'And that's exactly what they did in *Roe*. The Court can't *interpret* words that don't even exist.'

'Ms. Garza, doesn't Mr. Stanton make a good point? If the Framers of the Constitution—'

'White men.'

'Yes, we know that, Ms. Garza. If the Framers wanted to give a woman the right to have an abortion, wouldn't they have just written it into the Bill of Rights?'

'Their misogynistic belief system prevented them from considering the plight of women, just as their racist attitudes prevented them from freeing the slaves.'

'All right. Let's assume that to be true, that our Founding Fathers were unable, due to their upbringing, their religious beliefs, their views about women's place in society . . . for whatever reason, they were incapable of including a right to an abortion in the Constitution. Now, fast forward to nineteen seventy-three. Women may vote, use contraceptives, attend law school. States are liberalizing abortion laws. Why didn't the Court just say to Roe, "We're sorry, but the Constitution does not address abortion. Therefore, you must take your complaint to your state legislature to change the law." Isn't that the correct action for the Court to take, to defer to the demo-cratic process?'

'Changing the law through fifty state legislatures would have taken decades, and without a national abortion right poor women like Roe might have to travel to another state to obtain an abortion. A Supreme Court opinion is the law of the land. It changes the law in all fifty states in a single moment. Like that.'

She snapped her fingers.

'But, Ms. Garza, isn't the appropriate avenue to a national abortion right a constitutional amendment? The Constitution has been amended twenty-seven times to add the Bill of Rights, end slavery, guarantee the right to vote to women and persons of all races, create an income tax, begin and end prohibition . . . Why not abortion?'

'Because the justices knew right-wing religious nuts would block a constitutional amendment granting women the right to an abortion.'

'But isn't that the nature of democracy? We the people determining our own rights?'

'Not when they the Republicans deny me my rights.'

'But what do you do in a democracy when you can't convince a majority that you should in fact possess a particular right?'

'I do what Roe did—I get the Supreme Court to give me the right I want.'

'So, in a nation of three hundred twenty million people, nine unelected lawyers sitting as the Supreme Court should circumvent democracy by removing certain issues from the democratic process and declaring those issues constitutional in nature?'

'Yes. And it only takes five justices to win.'

'But by removing abortion from the democratic process, didn't the Court poison political discourse in America? Abortion wasn't even part of the political conversation before *Roe*. Now it's a litmus test for judges and politicians, and it has polarized the nation. *Roe* didn't settle a political fight; it started one.'

'It gave women control over their reproductive decisions. Just like men enjoy.'

'Oh, yeah,' Mr. Stanton said from the back row. 'We've got it real good. A girl lies about being on the pill, and we're paying child support for the next eighteen years. Try telling that to your dad.'

Another awkward silence captured the classroom.

'Uh, okay, let's move on. In nineteen ninety-two, after two decades of protests, political fights, and contentious judicial nominations, the Court again took up a major abortion case, *Planned Parenthood v. Casey*. The Court's stated intent was to put an end to the abortion wars in the country. In a five-to-four decision, the Court reaffirmed *Roe* but allowed the states more leeway in regulating abortions. Justice Kennedy's lead opinion appealed to the American people to respect their decision and accept a woman's right to an abortion as the law of the land, a lawyer's way of saying, "Trust us. We know what we're doing."'

Ms. Roberts jumped back into the fray.

'How are we supposed to trust those guys when Kennedy can write that nonsense in *Casey*?' She read off her laptop: 'Quote, "At the heart of liberty is the right to define one's own concept of existence, of meaning, of the universe, and of the mystery of human life." Really? Maybe it's just me, but it's hard to imagine Jefferson or Madison saying goofy stuff like that.'

Mr. Stanton, from the back row: 'I said goofy stuff like that back in college, but I was stoned at the time. I made a video and posted it on YouTube, got a hundred thousand hits.'

'And you still got into this law school?'

'Rich daddy,' Ms. Garza said.

Mr. Stanton shared a fist-bump with his buddies.

'Was Kennedy like that when you clerked for him?' Mr. Brennan asked.

Book's clerkship for Justice Kennedy had made him a hot commodity among constitutional lawyers because Kennedy was often the swing vote in crucial five–four decisions.

'I came on board ten years after *Casey*. Kennedy was just trying to broker a peace in the abortion war. He respects the Court, and he wants the people to respect it as well.'

'Too late for that,' Ms. Garza said. 'We're not stupid. We know the Court's just another political branch.'

'The Constitution is just politics?'

'Professor, everything is just politics.'

Book felt as if he had just been told that the love of his life had cheated on him. The Constitution is just politics? The Court no less partisan than the Congress? Ms. Garza read his mind.

'The only difference between Congress and the Court is that we can vote those Republican bastards out of Congress.'

'Mr. Stanton—'

He looked up from his texting.

'Ms. Garza is mistaken, isn't she?'

'In so many ways, Professor.'

'Make your case.'

'First, her T-shirts are getting old. Second, she—'

'About the Court being a political branch.'

'Oh. The Court is perceived as being political because the justices subverted democracy in *Roe*. In America, we don't stage violent protests and burn down cities when our side loses an election. We organize for the next election. But we want to vote. The people didn't get to vote on abortion.'

Ms. Roberts again: 'As Scalia said in his *Casey* dissent, quote, "value judgments should be voted on, not dictated." And quote, "the people know that their value judgments are quite as good as those taught in any law school—maybe better." I like that.'

Ms. Garza again glared at her classmate.

'Now you're quoting Scalia? Jesus, Liz, you wouldn't talk for eight months, now you won't shut up. Quote this.'

Ms. Garza jabbed her middle finger at Ms. Roberts.

'Unacceptable, Ms. Garza. An apology, please.'

'Oh, I'm really fucking sorry, Ms. Roberts.'

That constituted sincere for Ms. Garza.

'Civility, people. This is a classroom, not the Supreme Court conference room on decision day. Ms. Garza, your rebuttal to Mr. Stanton's case—the rebuttal that does not include your middle finger.'

'Two generations of women have grown up with total control over their reproductive decisions, both contraceptives and abortion. If men get to vote on our right to abortion, they'll take that right away from us. Then they'll take the right to use contraceptives. Because men want desperately to control women—our lives, our liberties, our work, our pay, our sexual activity, our bodies, and most of all, our wombs.'

Mr. Stanton: 'Trust me, I don't want anywhere near your womb.'

The class laughed. Ms. Garza did not.

'Stanton, you're just mad because women won a right to an abortion.'

'I'm mad because the liberal justices hijacked the Constitution—they made it up!'

'You don't know that.'

Mr. Stanton pointed down at Book. 'He said so in his last book.'

Another round of laughter.

'How do you know I'm right?' Book said.

'Because you're down there lecturing, and we're up here taking notes.'

More laughter.

'How do you know I'm not just another tenured professor pushing my personal political beliefs on his captive audience of impressionable students?'

'Because you're not teaching over in the English department.'

The entire class laughed and let out a collective sigh of relief when the bell rang. They rose as one and gathered their belongings. Book yelled over the noise.

'Read *National Federation of Independent Business v. Sebelius,* aka Obamacare, for the next class.'

The mass of students parted like the Red Sea before Moses. Half rushed for the doors. The other half surged down to the front and around Book, peppering him with questions and pushing copies of his latest book, *Con Law: Why Constitutional Law is the Greatest Hoax Ever Perpetrated on the American People,* for him to sign. It was currently number one on the *New York Times* nonfiction print and digital bestseller lists.

'Professor, would you sign your book for my mom? Her name's Sherry.'

He signed the book with a Sharpie. Another came forward.

'Sign my book, for my dad. Ken.'

He signed. Another hand came forward.

'Sign my Kindle.'

'Your Kindle?'

'I have your e-book on it.'

He signed her Kindle. She then stepped close and held out her cell phone in front of them.

'Can I take a picture of us? For my dad? He said when you're on the Supreme Court—'

Book had made many shortlists of potential candidates.

'—you'll straighten those crazy bastards out.'

She snapped a photo.

'My dad never misses you on those Sunday morning talk shows. He loved that line yesterday on *Face the Nation*—'

Book had participated via a satellite feed from the local Austin studio.

'—when you told that senator that you were neither liberal nor conservative, Republican nor Democrat, but that instead you were the last known practicing Jeffersonian in America.'

'It wasn't a line.'

The students drifted off. Book gathered his casebook and notes and walked out the door and down the narrow corridor crowded and noisy with aspiring lawyers chatting about their

31

lucrative job offers from large law firms. Thirteen years before, he had walked the corridors of Harvard law school, aiming to do something important with his life, perhaps even to change the world. But not to get rich. Money had never motivated him. He had found that he needed few material things in life. He lived in a small house near campus. He had acquired the Harley secondhand and made it his own. He had never owned a car, and he no longer owned a suit. Having things meant nothing to him. Doing things meant everything. And he did everything at a fast pace.

Because he knew he didn't have much time.

Chapter 2

'Get a haircut, Bookman.'

Book took the stairs two steps at a time, so he was quickly past the white-haired man dressed immaculately in a suit and tie walking down the stairs. He was the dean of the law school.

'Right away, Roscoe.'

Tenure had earned Book a fifteen-foot-by-twenty-foot office, a lifetime salary, a secretary, and the right to wear his hair long. He arrived at the fifth floor, turned a corner, ducked between students, and entered the front room of the two-room office suite where a middle-aged woman wearing reading glasses secured to her neck by a glittery strand of beads sat at a desk and held a phone to her ear.

'Here he is,' Myrna said into the phone. She covered the mouthpiece and whispered, 'The police. Again.'

Book put the phone to his ear. 'John Bookman.'

'Yeah, uh, Professor, this is Sergeant Taylor, Austin PD. We found your mother.'

'She wandered off again?'

'Yes, sir. She was at the mall. Victoria's Secret. Walked out with an armful of lingerie, said she had a date tonight. They called us, we took her home. I called your sister. She's on the way. I'll stay till she gets here.'

'Thanks, Sergeant.'

'Don't mention it. I worked with your dad.' He paused. 'Uh, Professor, I don't mean to mind your business, but you should really consider putting your mom in a home. Folks in her condition, they wander off, get lost, end up outside all night. One day we might not find her in time. Your dad wouldn't have wanted that.'

Book thanked the officer and hung up the phone. He could not abide the thought of his mother in a nursing home. Myrna regarded him over her reading glasses.

'You okay?'

He wasn't, but he nodded yes.

'Messages?'

Myrna held up pink call slips. 'Fox wants you on the Sunday morning show, by satellite. To debate the Supreme Court's decision on Obamacare.'

'With whom?'

'McConnell.'

'Again? After our last debate?'

'He's a politician, doesn't know you made him look like a fool.'

'Wasn't exactly hard work.'

'And *Meet the Press* wants you to debate Schumer.'

'Him, too?'

She shrugged. 'They're gluttons for punishment.'

'What else?'

'They're stupid, they're egomaniacs, they're—'

'The messages.'

'The *Wall Street Journal* and the *New York Times* want your comments on the case.'

'When?'

'Today. Front-page articles in tomorrow's editions. And you're late for the faculty meeting.'

Myrna reached down to her oversized purse and came up again with a sealed plastic container. Several years back, she started bringing him leftovers from dinner the night before because he ate protein bars for breakfast, bachelor and all; it was now a daily ritual.

'Chicken quesadillas,' she said.

'With your guacamole?'

'Of course.'

'Thanks.'

'Stu said I should charge you, even if they are just leftovers.'

'Remind Stu that I didn't charge him for his murder case.'

A year before, Myrna's husband had accidentally run over an armadillo in his four-wheel-drive pickup truck. An animal-rights activist, which is to say, a resident of Austin, had witnessed the 'murder' and called the police. The district attorney, up for reelection, charged Stu with animal cruelty. Book defended him and won an acquittal.

'Mail?'

Myrna pointed a thumb at his office door behind her. He walked through the open door and into his office crowded with a leather couch, a bookshelf filled with casebooks and a crash helmet, law review articles stacked along the walls, Southwestern art and framed photographs of himself with Willie Nelson and ZZ Top and other Texas musicians, a cluttered desk with an open laptop, and a work table where a young woman sat reading his mail.

'Who are you?'

'Nadine Honeywell. I'm a two-L. The dean of students sent me over. I'm your new intern.'

Tenure had also earned Book a paid student assistant to help with his research, his law review articles, and his correspondence.

'Where's Renée?'

'She quit.'

'*Why?*'

Nadine shrugged. 'All she said was, "I didn't go to law school to get shot at." She was just joking, right, Professor?'

Book dropped the armload of books and notes and Myrna's plastic container onto the couch then stepped to the solitary window and stared out at the treed campus. He had grown to like Renée. Just as he had grown to like all of his interns. But sooner or later, they all quit.

'Right, Professor?'

He sighed. 'Yes, Ms. Honeywell. She was just joking.'

'I thought so.'

He turned from the window. Nadine squirted hand sanitizer from a small plastic bottle into one palm then rubbed her hands together. The room now reeked of alcohol. She wore a T-shirt, shorts, sandals, and black-framed glasses riding low on her nose. Her black hair was pulled back in a ponytail, and Book could discern no sign of makeup or scent of perfume. She was skinny and looked thirteen. She picked up an envelope and used a pocketknife to slice open the flap.

'Is that my pearl-handled pocketknife?' Book asked.

'Must be. I found it on your desk.'

She gestured with his knife at the pile of mail on the table in front of her.

'Myrna said you get hundreds of these letters every week.'

'Every week.'

'So people all over the country write to you and ask for help? Like you're some kind of superhero or something?'

'Or something.'

'And do you?'

'Do I what?'

'Help them.'

'A few.'

'Why the snail mail? Haven't they heard of email?'

'I don't publish my email address. I figure if they want my help, they should at least be willing to write a real letter. And you can tell a lot more about a person from a letter.'

'I can tell there are a lot of sad people out there. Single mothers not getting their child support—'

'Send those over to the Attorney General's Child Support Office.'

'—inmates claiming innocence and wanting DNA tests—'

'Send those to the Innocence Project.'

'—people wanting to sue somebody—'

'No civil cases.' Book took a step toward his desk. 'Tell me if you find something interesting.'

'I did.'

Nadine held up an envelope.

'You should read this one.'

Book took the envelope, walked over to his desk, and was about to drop down into his chair when he heard Myrna's voice from outside.

'Faculty meeting!'

He pushed the envelope into the back pocket of his jeans, grabbed the plastic container with Myrna's quesadillas, and walked out of his office and down the corridor.

Chapter 3

The University of Texas School of Law opened its doors in 1883 with two professors teaching fifty-two students. White students. State law forbade admission of black students. In 1946, a black man named Heman Sweatt applied for admission to the UT law school; his admission was denied solely because of his race. The infamous 1896 Supreme Court ruling in *Plessy v. Ferguson* had deemed the Equal Protection Clause of the Fourteenth Amendment satisfied if a state provided 'separate but equal' accommodations for the races. So, rather than admit Mr. Sweatt, UT opened a separate law school for blacks only. But while the UT law school then had sixteen professors, eight hundred fifty students, a 65,000-volume library, and alumni in positions of legal power throughout the state, the blacks-only law school had three professors, twenty-three students, a 16,500-volume library, and exactly one graduate who was a member of the Texas bar. Mr. Sweatt sued but lost in the state trial court, state appeals court, and state supreme court. So he took his case to the U.S. Supreme Court. In *Sweatt v. Painter*, the Court ruled in 1950 that the blacks-only law school did not offer a legal education equal to that offered whites and ordered Mr. Sweatt admitted to the UT law school. Sixty-two years later, the University of Texas School of Law had seventy-two full-time professors, 1,178 students, a million-volume library, and sixty-two black students.

Book opened the door and stepped inside the faculty conference room where most of the full-time faculty were already engaged in vigorous debate. He tried to walk unnoticed around the perimeter of the large room, but the discussion abruptly stopped, and all heads turned his way, as if a student had invaded their private sanctum.

'Ah, our very own Indiana Jones is honoring us with his presence this morning. How wonderful. My, the press does love our dashing young professor, don't they?'

Addressing Book from the head of the long conference table was Professor Jonah Goldman (Harvard, 1973, Environmental Law), the faculty president. Book's exploits in East Texas had made the national press.

'And your book is still number one on the *New York Times*, I see. I would think you could afford a suit with all those royalties.'

Professor Goldman had lived the last thirty-five years of his life in this law school, seldom venturing far from campus, preferring instead to live like a nun cloistered inside a convent. Like many of his contemporaries, he had entered law school to avoid the draft during the Vietnam War and had stayed on to enjoy the benefits of lifetime tenure. He was short and portly and sported fluffy white hair and a trimmed white beard; he wore a brown plaid three-piece suit and a brown bowtie; there was still one law professor in America wearing bowties. Book ignored him (and his bowtie) and found a seat in the back corner next to his best friend among the faculty, which is to say, his only friend among the faculty.

'Henry.'

'Book.'

Henry Lawson (UT, 1997, Oil and Gas Law) was an associate professor of law. His face held the expression of a middle-aged man with no job security. Which was what he was. He occupied a rung on the academic career ladder one below that of a tenured professor of law. And his tenure was on the agenda that day.

His chances were not good. First, forty-three of the seventy-two professors in the room held law degrees from Harvard and Yale while Henry held a law degree from this very law school. Only four other professors on the full-time faculty were UT law graduates; no other Texas law school, or Southern law school for that matter, was represented on the faculty. When Harvard- and Yale-educated professors did the hiring, they hired Harvard and Yale graduates, not Texas and Alabama graduates. They demanded diversity in all things academic, except professors' law schools and political ideology.

Second, Henry had spent five years working in the legal department of an international oil company. That experience served him well as a professor teaching oil and gas law, but as far as the Harvard and Yale professors were concerned, he might as well have been in-house counsel to the Grand Order of the Ku Klux Klan. Which at one time would not have disqualified one from teaching at UT. William Stewart Simkins, a Klansman turned law professor, taught at the UT law school from 1899 to 1929; the university even named a dormitory in his honor in 1954, coincidentally the same year the Supreme Court handed down its landmark ruling in *Brown v. Board of Education* overturning *Plessy* and declaring that 'separate but equal' violated the Constitution. The Board of Regents had renamed the dorm just the past year.

And third, the slim chance Henry did have would become no chance at all if the Harvard–Yale cartel discovered that he had voted for George W. Bush. Twice. Henry's expression revealed his despair.

'I'm forty-one, Book,' he said in a low voice. 'There's no other law school out there for me. With this economy and law jobs plummeting, schools are freezing new hires. I've been denied tenure twice. Three strikes, and I'm out.'

He put his elbows on his knees and his face in his hands. After a long moment, he turned to Book.

'Ann's pregnant again.'

Book chucked him on the shoulder.

'Congratulations.'

Henry did not seem thrilled at the prospect of becoming a father for the third time. So Book did the only thing he knew to perk up his friend's spirits: he popped the top on the plastic container and offered Henry a quesadilla.

'Chicken.'

'With Myrna's guacamole?'

'Of course.'

They ate the quesadillas while the other professors renewed their debate in earnest.

'What are they fighting about today?' Book asked.

'What else? Money and tenure. And the vacant assistant deanship.'

The assistant dean had been fired when it came to light that the UT Law School Foundation, a nonprofit run by alumni, had handed out—on the dean's sole recommendation—$4.65 million in 'forgivable loans' to twenty-two professors in amounts ranging from $75,000 to $500,000. Purportedly to attract and retain key faculty by allowing them to purchase homes in the high-dollar Austin residential market, the loans were forgiven if the professor remained on the faculty for a negotiated term of three to ten years. The assistant dean himself had received a $500,000 loan, apparently to ensure his loyalty to UT. The secret faculty compensation numbers had become public when several professors made an open records request; the information ignited a firestorm among the faculty, not because the other professors thought the loans too 'Wall Street' during this Great Recession when the law school was increasing tuition on its middle-class students by double digits, but because they wanted in on the action. The controversy reached the university president, and worse, the Austin newspaper and the legal blogosphere, which proved an embarrassment to the administration; the president then fired the assistant dean. He couldn't fire the dean who doled out the money because the Longhorn football coach and the law school dean—a legendary law professor at UT who had taught most of the senior partners at the major Texas law firms and who was now a legendary accumulator of donations and endowments from those law firms—ran the only two profit centers on the UT campus. But someone had to be fired.

'I want more money!'

Professor Sheila Manfried (Yale, 1990, Feminist Legal Theory and Gender Crimes) was addressing the faculty. She waved a thick document in the air.

'I have the faculty compensation numbers. I knew I was getting screwed, and this proves it. I can't believe how many male professors are making more money than me. I want a salary increase, and I want one of those forgivable loans. I've been on this faculty for eighteen years. I've been tenured for twelve. I publish more articles than the rest of you combined. My law review articles have been published in the *Yale Law Review*, the *Harvard Law Review*, the *Michigan Law Review* . . .'

She pointed at male professors (who referred to her as 'Professor Mankiller' behind her back) in succession as if identifying guilty defendants in court.

'. . . But you're making more than me? And you? And you? You guys haven't published anything in years.'

Professor Herbert Johnson (UT, 1974, Contracts), one of those guys, offered the male rebuttal.

'Well, Sheila, when I did publish something, it was useful, not your feminist crap. What's your latest article? "The Tort of Wrongful Seduction." You want men to be liable for damages if they really didn't mean it when they said, "I love you." How stupid is that?'

Professor Manfried glared at him then jabbed a long finger in the air as if to stab him.

'That's it, Herb. I'm putting you on my witness list.'

Professor Manfried had sued the university for gender discrimination over her compensation. She made $275,000.

'Liberals fighting over money like Republicans,' Henry said.

'The desire for money transcends politics.'

'But tenure doesn't.' Henry shook his head. 'I was ROTC at A&M, served in the army for four years, graduated top of my class at this law school, worked to pay off my student loans . . . but I'm an outcast here because I worked for an oil company.'

'And voted Republican,' Book whispered.

'Shh! They don't know.'

Book could count the number of professors who might have voted Republican on his fingers and toes, and he didn't need to take his boots off. Of course, it was mere speculation; one did not speak publicly about such things inside an American law school, not if one wanted tenure or a salary hike. Law school faculties leaned hard to the left, which was to be expected at Harvard and Yale, but at Texas? That fact—that Ivy League-educated liberals who disdained all things Texan (except their University of Texas paychecks) and whose fondest dream was to be called home to Harvard and Yale were teaching the sons and daughters of conservative UT alumni— had always amused him. If only those conservatives knew that their beloved university had a faculty only slightly to the left of the ruling party in Havana.

'I propose a faculty resolution demanding that the new

assistant dean be a woman,' Professor Manfried said. 'Better yet, a lesbian.'

'They're bringing in an outsider,' Professor Goldman said. 'A heterosexual male.'

'How do you know?'

'He's married with two children.'

'That they hired a man?'

'I have my sources in Admin. I hear that Roscoe will finalize the deal before the semester is out.'

'Then I propose a resolution that Roscoe be fired and replaced with a lesbian.'

Roscoe Chambers was the law school dean. He was seventy-seven years old and a crusty old fart who ran the law school with an iron fist.

'He's untouchable, Sheila,' Professor Goldman said.

'He's a Republican dinosaur. It's embarrassing to go to law school conferences and have professors from other schools laugh at us because we have a Republican dean.'

'He controls too much alumni money to be fired. He can pick up the phone and pull in five million today. He'll hire whomever the alumni want for the next assistant dean.'

'Well, he might control who runs this school, but we control who teaches here.'

Professor Manfried sat, and the collective blood pressure of the faculty receded to normal levels. Which gave Professor Robert Stone (Chicago, 2006, Law and Economics) an opening. He stood to groans. He had a law degree and a Ph.D. in economics and looked like Book's accountant. He was one of the new breed of law professors, a multi-disciplinarian who thought outside the box, normally not considered a positive character trait in a non-tenured professor. Book didn't know him well, but he liked what he did know.

'My fellow colleagues, in one month, accredited law schools across the country will graduate forty-eight thousand new lawyers, the most in history. But only twenty thousand

44

legal jobs await them. The big corporate law firms are hiring fewer graduates, they're firing attorneys, and they're outsourcing their low-level legal work overseas to lawyers in India and the Philippines just like the tech companies do their call centers.'

Professor Goldman: 'Where'd you read that?'

'The *Wall Street Journal*.'

'You read the *Wall Street Journal*?'

'Of course. Don't you?'

'No. I read the *New York Times*. If it's not in the *Times*, I don't need to know it.'

'Jonah, you need to know that our graduates are facing the worst legal job market in two decades. We're dramatically oversupplying the market. But we're immune from market forces because the federal government is now the sole provider of student loans and lends the full sticker price for law school, including cost of living, whatever the cost. Last year's graduating law class nationwide owed a collective three-point-six billion in student loans. The students don't have a prayer of repaying that debt.'

'What's your point, Bob?'

'My point is, Jonah, we can't keep bringing four hundred new students into the law school each year, charge them thirty thousand dollars a year, and put them into a market where there aren't enough jobs to go around. Nationally, one hundred fifty thousand students at two hundred law schools pay five billion a year in tuition. Law schools are cash cows on university campuses, Jonah, but in this job market, a law degree will be worthless for three-fourths of the students. Actually, less than worthless since they'll owe a hundred thousand or more in debt.'

'Why's that our fault?'

'Because we continue to raise the cost of a legal education. Over the last decade, we tripled tuition and doubled our salaries.'

'But they keep paying it.'

'With federal loans, debt that pays our salaries. We're like peanut farmers, Jonah, subsidized by the federal government.'

'How many peanut farmers have advanced degrees from Harvard?'

Professor Goldman let out an exasperated sigh.

'Okay, Bob, so what's your brilliant proposal this time?'

'We need to teach more and be paid less. We need to be honest with our students about their job prospects. We need to reduce the supply of lawyers to the demand for lawyers. I propose a faculty resolution that we reduce next year's incoming class by twenty-five percent.'

Professor Stone's proposal evoked a collective gasp from the faculty. Professor Goldman stared at his younger and untenured colleague as if he were a homeless person urinating at the corner of Eleventh and Congress downtown.

'Have you lost your mind? Twenty-five percent, that's a hundred tuition-payers—'

'*Tuition-payers?* You mean, students?'

'Yes. Them. And that's over three million dollars in lost tuition revenue. You know what that would mean? Pay cuts. No summer stipends. No research funds. Maybe no secretaries or interns. You want that? Besides, these tuition-payers— excuse me, these students—aren't here to save mankind. They're here to get a law degree and hire on with those corporate law firms and get rich. Just this morning, I posed a hypothetical fact situation to my class and asked a student which side he wanted to represent. He said, "Whichever side can pay more." We didn't teach them that. The world did. These kids are capitalists through and through.'

'And we're not? Fifty-one of us in this room make more than two hundred thousand and nineteen more than three hundred thousand, for teaching, what, six hours a week for twenty-eight weeks? We're paid summer stipends of sixty, seventy, even eighty thousand dollars to write on a beach. This public law school paid the seventy-two full-time professors in this room a total of eighteen million dollars in compensation last year—not including those forgivable loans some of you got—for part-time work.'

'*Part-time?* My God, man, we're in class six hours each week. At Harvard, they're in class only three hours. Besides, we're a top-tier law school—we shouldn't have to teach.'

'Someone's got to, Jonah. It's a school, which implies teachers. So the school has to hire twenty lecturers and one hundred thirty-five adjuncts to teach for us. And it's all paid for by increasing tuition on middle-class students who borrow to pay it. Total student debt now exceeds one trillion dollars, more than credit card debt, and it can't be discharged in bankruptcy. It's a huge drag on the economy. Even the employed grads can't qualify for home mortgages.'

'They need forgivable loans,' Professor Manfried said.

'They've got them,' Professor Goldman said. 'I hear Obama's going to forgive all that student debt—it's all owed to the federal government anyway, so we're just passing the cost on to the taxpayers, like the General Motors bailout.'

Henry whispered to Book, 'And the public thinks we spend our time teaching contracts and torts.'

Professor Goldman turned back to Professor Stone. 'Why shouldn't we be well paid? My Harvard classmates sitting atop those corporate law firms in New York are making millions.'

'They're real lawyers, Jonah, working for real clients paying real money. That has value in the marketplace. Most of us don't have a clue what real lawyers do.'

'I don't want a clue. We're not practitioners, Bob. We're not a trade school. It's not our job to teach students how to practice law. We're here to teach the theory of law. And we do have value—we're the only path to the legal profession. If you want to be a real lawyer, you've got to go to law school. That gives us value.'

'A hundred-thousand-dollar value?'

Professor Goldman addressed Professor Stone as if he were a 1L who hadn't answered a question correctly.

'Tell you what, Bob, let's take a quick vote. A show of hands from those in favor of Professor Stone's proposal to reduce enrollment, tuition, and our salaries.'

Book raised his hand. Henry couldn't; without tenure, he had no academic freedom. No other professor raised a hand.

'Yes, we know you would be in favor of something like that, Professor Bookman.'

Professor Stone sat and slumped in his chair. His regular economic analyses of law school finances over the last few years of the Great Recession had always proven unpopular with the faculty. Denial was far more popular; in fact, denial defined the Academy, aristocrats blissfully ignorant of the plight of the masses living off-campus. They fought over forgivable loans and summer stipends, they wrote law review articles with four thousand footnotes, they dreamed of being appointed to a federal appeals court; they taught the theory of law and lived theoretical lives, 'what-if' lives as if life were a hypothetical fact situation. They railed against Republicans and Wall Street and the one-ercenters, but they sat happily ensconced in chairs endowed by corporate law firms in Houston and Dallas, by Joe Jamail, the billionaire plaintiff's lawyer famous for winning a $3 billion verdict in *Pennzoil v. Texaco*, and even by Frederick Baron, the now-deceased millionaire asbestos lawyer infamous for funding John Edwards' mistress during his failed presidential campaign.

Such was the Academy.

Book did not live an Academy life. He lived out there, among the people. In the real world. On the road. Less traveled or more traveled, but at least traveled. He didn't want to teach theory; he wanted to live reality. With each passing day, he became more disillusioned with the Academy. It seemed less relevant, less in touch with the real world, less concerned with the problems of real people. More disconnected from life. More unconcerned with life off-campus.

'All right,' Professor Goldman said. 'Let's move on to tenure. Would those professors up for tenure please exit the meeting?'

Henry stood. He looked like a man about to face a firing squad.

'I love teaching the law.'

'You'll still be teaching the law next year, Henry.'

After Henry and Professor Stone and the other tenure candidates had departed, Professor Goldman, as chair of the Tenure Committee, opened the meeting for discussion.

Book stood. 'I propose Henry Lawson for tenure. For the third time. Henry is a gentleman and a scholar. He has published five law review articles—'

Professor Goldman interrupted: 'In what reviews?'

'Texas Tech, Tulsa . . .'

'Texas Tech and Tulsa. Not exactly the "A" list, is it? Any in the Harvard or Yale reviews?'

'Those reviews aren't interested in articles about oil and gas law, Jonah.'

'Then how important can his articles be? How much value can we attach to publications in the *Texas Tech Law Review*?'

'You write about the rights of trees, Jonah—how valuable are your articles, except perhaps to an evergreen? How many people read your articles? How many times have your articles been cited, anywhere? Truth is, no one reads our law review articles, you know that. We write them to get tenure. Most legal scholarship is worthless drivel. But Henry is a nationally recognized expert in oil and gas law—'

'Yippee.'

'—He's served on the White House's Energy Task Force—'

'Promoting oil and gas drilling—including fracking, for God's sake!'

'—He's in demand as a speaker to industry groups—'

'Oil company executives.'

'—We all know that Henry is smart enough, dedicated enough, a hell of a teacher, his students love him—'

'Tenure is not a popularity contest.'

'—Henry worked in the real world—'

'For an oil company.'

'—Which means he can teach the students about being real lawyers.'

'So?'

'So he can relate to the very alumni who support this university and this law school. For all of you Harvard and Yale grads who don't know, this university was built on oil money. And I remind you that Henry—'

'Voted for Bush! Twice!'

Another even louder collective gasp went up from the professors.

'How do you know?'

'I have my sources. He can't have voted for Bush and be our next tenured professor.'

'You're right, Jonah. Henry shouldn't be the next tenured professor. He should be the next assistant dean, and then the next dean when Roscoe retires. He could run this school better than any of us.'

'Having a Republican dean like Roscoe is why we dropped in the rankings. If word gets out that one of our tenured faculty members voted for Bush, we'll be a joke in the Academy. Our reputation among our peers—which accounts for twenty-five percent of our *U.S. News* ranking, I remind you—will take a dive. Do you want that?'

UT law school had dropped from fourteenth to sixteenth in the latest *U.S. News and World Report* law school rankings; panic had ensued. Twenty years before, *U.S. News* began the rankings. At first, the rankings were viewed by the Academy as amusing anecdotes; today, the rankings are viewed as critical to a law school's success. Move up in the rankings, and celebrations begin in the faculty lounge; move down, and heads roll. Prospective law students decide which schools to apply to based upon the rankings; thus, rankings drive applications; and applications put butts in seats worth $30,000 to $50,000 each. With so much money riding on the rankings, some schools had gamed their reports to achieve higher rankings, inflating their Law School Admission Test numbers, including among 'graduates known to be employed nine months after graduation' those grads working at Starbucks because they couldn't find legal jobs, and even hiring their own unemployed grads for short-term stints spanning February 15—the effective date for the schools' reports—so those students could be counted as employed. Rankings now drive every decision made in law schools across America.

'If we hope to move up in the rankings, we must hire and grant tenure to star professors,' Professor Goldman said.

'And all the stars come from Harvard and Yale?'

'They're sure as hell not Republicans from UT.'

'But we're top ten in football,' Professor Al Harvey (UT, 1985, Property Law) said. 'Can't be tops in football and law.'

'Tell the alumni that,' Professor Goldman said.

'Did you see the spring game? The team's looking good.'

'Shut up, Al.'

'I'm just saying.'

'Jonah,' Book said, 'this isn't about rankings.'

'Everything's about rankings. If we grant tenure to Henry, we'll be lucky to stay in the top tier. Are we going to be the Harvard of the Southwest or not?'

'Not. Jonah, we're chasing Harvard and Yale in the rankings even though we all know the methodology employed by *U.S. News* is flawed and their results laughable. I've got a better idea: let's drop out of the rankings.'

'You've gone mad! If we take ourselves out of the rankings game, we'll never hire another Harvard or Yale graduate.'

'Good.'

Jonah Goldman's pale face turned bright red, which clashed with his brown suit. Book figured, what the hell, might as well go all the way.

'Jonah, you're living in the past. But our students will live in the future, so this school must look to the future. And that future will not be made following in the footsteps of Harvard and Yale. It will be made by cutting our own path right here in Texas. Therefore, I propose that we refuse to participate in the rankings. I propose that we teach our students to be real lawyers. And I propose the best person I know to lead this school into that future: Henry Lawson. I propose Henry for tenure and to be our next assistant dean.'

'Fine,' Professor Goldman said. 'All in favor of Professor Bookman's proposals, raise your hands.'

Book stuck his hand defiantly in the air and waited for reinforcements . . . and waited. Four other hands finally went up, all from the UT professors. But no Harvard or Yale hand. Or Columbia. Or Stanford. Or the others. Professor Goldman turned to Book with the smug look of the rich boy in grade school who always got the best toys money could buy.

'Your propositions fail, Professor Bookman.'

Book dropped down in his chair. Institutional inertia prevailed. Fear of the future. Professors hanging on to the past. Hoping the past lasts until they retire with full benefits. The school would continue to chase Harvard and Yale in the rankings, and the students would lose. Henry Lawson would not be the new assistant dean. He would not be granted tenure. Not that year. Not any year. He was the best teacher on the faculty, but he would soon be teaching at another law school. Or perhaps at a high school.

Other professors stood and championed their protégés. Book slumped down in his chair and felt something in his back pocket. He pulled out the envelope Nadine had given him. It

52

was postmarked 'Marfa, Texas,' on April 5, four days before. He removed the letter, unfolded the single sheet, and read the handwritten note.

Dear Professor Bookman,

Remember me? Nathan Jones? I was your intern for one month four years ago. I'm sorry I quit so abruptly back then, but I didn't want to die before getting my law degree. (Just kidding.) Anyway, I'm married now, my wife's pregnant, and I'm a third-year associate at the Dunn firm in West Texas. I work in our Marfa office which we established to represent our largest client, an oil and gas company. Mostly gas. They're fracking in the Woodford shale field north of town. Professor, our client is contaminating the aquifer with the frack fluids. I have proof. That aquifer is the sole source of drinking water for this part of West Texas. I took the matter to my senior partner in Midland. He told me to keep my mouth shut, that any information I have is confidential under our ethics rules. Which means if I go public, I'll get disbarred. So I'm required to keep this secret while our client contaminates the aquifer with toxic chemicals. That doesn't seem right. But I don't know what to do. Can you help me? Funny. Now I'm writing one of those letters to you.

Regards,
Nathan

PS: I think someone followed me home last night. My wife is scared.

Book walked down the corridor at a fast pace then stopped and stuck his head into Henry's office. Henry looked up.

'I'm sorry, Henry.'

'They know I voted for Bush?'

Book nodded.

'Damn.'

Book continued down the hall. He had secured tenure four years before, at age thirty-one. Clerking for Justice Kennedy, winning two Supreme Court cases, and making the shortlist of potential candidates for the Court does that sort of thing for a law professor. The law school would be embarrassed to have a faculty member nominated for the Supreme Court but denied tenure. Henry Lawson was not a Supreme Court candidate.

Nor was he a celebrity law professor.

Book was. After his Supreme Court clerkship, he could have taught at any law school in America. But he came home to be near his mother after she had been diagnosed with early-onset Alzheimer's. Eight years later, she still lived in the same house where she had raised her children, but she did not know her children and could not find her way home. Book entered the outer office of his suite. Myrna held pink message slips in the air.

'Your sister called. She wants to put your mother in a home.'

'Did you tell her, "Hell no"?'

Myrna knew not to answer. 'And James Welch called.'

'Who's he?'

'Our boss. Chairman of the Board of Regents. Appointed by the governor himself.'

'Another billionaire alumnus wanting to fire me because he didn't like what I said on *Face the Nation*.'

'He doesn't want to fire you. He wants to hire you.'

'For what?'

'Didn't say. Might have something to do with his son.'

'Who's his son?'

'Sophomore. Arrested for drug possession. On Sixth Street. It made the paper.'

Book took the pink slip. 'I'll call him from Marfa.'

'*Marfa?*' She groaned. 'Oh, no, not another letter.'

Book waved Nathan Jones's letter in the air as he walked

into his office where Nadine Honeywell still sat reading his mail. He grabbed the crash helmet off the bookshelf and held it out to her. She frowned at the helmet as if it were a bloody murder weapon.

'What's that for?'

Chapter 4

'I'm hungry, my butt's numb, and I think I swallowed a bug!'

It was just after eleven the next morning. Nadine Honeywell required twenty-four hours' advance notice prior to leaving town. She wore the crash helmet, goggles over her black glasses, and number 100 sunblock on all skin exposed by her short-sleeve shirt and shorts. She sat higher in the second seat. Book wore jeans, boots, a black T-shirt, black doo-rag, and sunglasses. He glanced back at his intern; she was holding her cell phone out. He yelled over the engine noise.

'What are you doing?'

'Trying to text!'

'Why?'

'I always text when I drive!'

'You're not driving. You're riding.'

'Close enough!'

Book had installed the windshield so they didn't eat (all the) bugs for four hundred miles, the leather saddlebags to hold their gear, and the second seat for Nadine. He had picked her up at seven. Four hours and three hundred miles on the back of the big Harley hadn't improved her mood.

'There's a rest stop up ahead. I'll pull over. We can stretch.'

'I've got a better idea. Let's turn back!'

They had ridden west out of Austin on Highway 290 through the Hill Country then picked up Interstate 10, the 'Cowboy Autobahn' where the posted speed limit was eighty but the actual limit pushed one hundred. They were now deep in the parched high plains of West Texas. Other than the four-lane interstate and the wind farms—thousands of three-hundred-foot-tall turbine windmills dotted the land-scape on both sides, their blades rotating as if propellers trying to push Texas eastward—the landscape remained as desolate and untouched as it had been at the beginning of time. Book steered off the highway and into the rest stop. He slowed to a stop, cut the engine, and kicked the stand down. Nadine hopped off as if she had been adrift at sea and now touched land for the first time in a year.

'My God, you never heard of cars? With climate control and CD players?'

She yanked off the helmet and goggles, shook out her shoulder-length hair, and wiped sweat from her face. Book removed his sunglasses and the doo-rag then pulled two bottles of water from a saddlebag. He handed one bottle to his intern; she drank half.

'I could really use a caramel frappuccino right about now, but I haven't seen a Starbucks since we left Austin.'

'I don't think you're going to find one out here, Ms. Honeywell.'

'It's like a desert.'

'It is a desert. The upper reaches of the Chihuahuan Desert.'

'What are those?'

She pointed to the horizon where a low ridgeline with craggy peaks stood silhouetted against the blue sky.

'Mountains.'

'In Texas?'

Mountains in Texas. Book had ridden the Harley through much of Texas, but not this part of Texas. Of course, it took some amount of riding to cover all of Texas; the state encompassed 268,000 square miles.

'How much longer?' Nadine asked.

'Couple of hours.'

'I'm hungry.'

Book reached into a pocket of his jeans and pulled out a package of beef jerky. He handed a strip to Nadine. She took the jerky with her fingertips and held it out as if examining a dead rat.

'You're joking?'

'High in protein.'

She made a face and extended the jerky his way. He took the jerky and clamped the strip between his teeth then reached into another pocket and removed a granola bar. He offered it to her.

'Good carbs.'

She regarded the granola bar a moment then gestured at his clothing.

'You got another pocket with hot dogs?'

'Sorry.'

Her shoulders slumped in surrender. She set the water bottle on the bike and pulled out a bottle of Purell hand sanitizer; she squirted the gel and rubbed her hands together then took the granola bar and bit off a piece. He chewed the jerky.

'I'm missing my Civ Proc class,' she said.

'You can learn rules anytime.' Book spread his arms. 'This is where a real lawyer works, Ms. Honeywell—in the real world. Not in an air-conditioned office on the fiftieth floor.'

'I'm going to write wills.'

'Why? That's boring.'

She shrugged. 'Not a lot of danger in estate planning.'

'You ever meet an heir cut out of his daddy's will?'

They came to law school without a clue what it meant to be

a lawyer. It wasn't sitting in a fancy office poring over discovery for eight hours and billing ten. Being a lawyer was about helping people in need. Real people, not rich people. Book was determined to teach his interns that the law wasn't found in the casebooks but out here in the world beyond the classroom. They came to him as law students; they would leave as lawyers.

'Professor, can I ask you a question?'

He chewed the jerky and nodded.

'Why are you doing this? You read that letter then jump onto this motorcycle and ride to the middle of a desert? And drag me along? Why? Why do you care so much about Nathan Jones?'

'He was my student four years ago.'

'How many students have you taught? A few thousand? What makes him so special?'

'He was also my intern.'

'For how long?'

'One month.'

'You knew him for one month four years ago, and now you're dropping everything to help him?'

Book stared at the distant ridgeline and thought of Nathan Jones.

'He saved my life.'

She frowned. '*How?*'

'Long story. And we've still got a long ride.'

She regarded him for a long moment while she finished off the granola bar. Then she said, 'Next time, get the kind with the chocolate coating.'

Book donned the doo-rag and sunglasses then swung a leg over the Harley.

'You ready?'

'No.'

But she bucked herself up then strapped on the goggles, pulled on the helmet, and climbed on behind him. He started the engine, shifted into gear, and accelerated past roadside signs that read 'Burn Ban in Effect' and 'Water 4 Sale' and onto the long black ribbon of asphalt disappearing into the distant horizon.

One hundred thirty years before, Hanna Maria Strobridge saw the same distant horizon from her seat inside her husband's private railroad car. His name was James Harvey Strobridge, and he built railroad lines for the Galveston, Harrisburg, and San Antonio Railroad. He had built the very line they rode on that day. Hanna had ridden in that private car from California to Texas; she had even been at Promontory Point in the Utah Territory for the driving of the golden spike in 1869 when the first transcontinental railroad was completed. At the time, James was the foreman for Central Pacific Railroad, which built the track eastward from California. After a moment, Hanna dropped her eyes from the horizon to her book, Feodora Dostoyevsky's latest, *The Brothers Karamazov*. She fancied Russian novels and striped skirts.

Two hours later, the train stopped at a water depot bordered by three mountain ranges. Hanna had no idea where they were because the depot had no name. Her husband, as superintendent of railroad construction, possessed the sole and absolute authority to name every water depot and other unnamed locale within the railroad's right-of-way. But he had no imagination for naming persons or places, so he had delegated his authority to his wife.

'Well, Hanna, what are you gonna name this little no-count place?'

She pondered a moment and thought of the servant in her book named Martha Ignatyevna. Of course, 'Martha' was the English translation; in Russian, her name was—

'Marfa.'

And so it was.

'And that's how Marfa got its name,' Book said.

From the back seat: 'Fascinating.'

Sitting four hundred miles due west of Austin, two hundred miles southeast of El Paso, sixty miles north of the Rio Grande, and a mile above sea level, the high desert land colloquially known as *el despoblado*—'the unpopulated'—and geologically as the Marfa Plateau is generally unfit for human occupancy. It's not bad for cattle, if it rains. If it doesn't, it's not so hospitable to them either. But man's nature drives him to settle the unsettled frontier; and so men have tried in Marfa, Texas.

From a distance, as you come down off the Chisos Mountains from the east and onto the plateau, you see the Davis Mountains to the north and the Chinati Mountains to the south; between the ranges lies a vast expanse of yellow grassland. And smack in the middle you see a small stand of trees, hunched together as if seeking safety in numbers against the relentless wind whipping across the land. The trees, planted by the first settlers, offer the only shade for a hundred miles in any direction and define the boundaries of the town of Marfa. As you come closer, you see the peach-colored cupola atop the Presidio County Courthouse peeking above the treetops as if on lookout for rampaging Indian war parties. But no savage Comanche galloping across the land on horseback threatened the peace in Marfa that day; only a Con Law professor riding a Harley with his reluctant intern perched behind him.

Book downshifted the Harley as they entered town on San Antonio Street and rode past a Dollar General store on the north side and dilapidated adobe homes on the south; Presidio County ranked as the poorest in Texas and looked it, except for a few renovated buildings housing art galleries. He braked at the only red light in town then pointed to the blue sky where a yellow glider soared overhead in silence. Nadine pointed south at an old gas station on the corner that had been converted into a restaurant called the Pizza Foundation; her face was that of a child who had spotted Santa Claus at the mall.

61

'Pizza!'

'Let's talk to Nathan Jones first. Maybe he'll have lunch with us, tell us his story.'

'What time's your appointment?'

'Didn't make one.'

'Why not?'

'Better to arrive unannounced. Nathan was always given to drama, probably read too many Grisham novels.'

'Just so you know, if he made me ride six hours on this motorcycle for nothing, I'm going to beat him like a redheaded stepchild.'

In the rearview mirror, Book saw a green-and-white Border Patrol SUV pull up behind the Harley and hit its lights. He cut the engine and kicked the stand down; he noticed Hispanics on nearby sidewalks scurrying away. Two agents wearing green uniforms and packing holstered weapons got out of the SUV and sauntered over. Both were young men; one was Anglo and looked like a thug, the other Hispanic and an altar boy. The thug eyed the Harley.

'What's that, an eighty-nine softtail classic?'

'Eighty-eight.'

'You restore it yourself?'

'I did.'

'Turquoise and black, I like that. And the black leather saddlebags with the silver studs. Cool. What engine is that?'

'Evo V-2.'

'Damn, that's a fine ride.'

The thug admired the bike then Nadine perched high in the back seat and finally turned his attention to Book.

'You Mexican?'

Book glared at the agent.

'Do I look Mexican?'

'You look like an Injun, but we don't get Injuns around here no more, just Mexicans.'

The Hispanic agent's expression seemed pained. He took a

step slightly in front of the thug. He was either the good cop in a good cop/bad cop routine or genuinely embarrassed by his partner.

'You look familiar. Where have I seen you?'

'On national TV, you dopes,' Nadine said from behind. 'He's famous.'

'Who you calling dopes?' the thug said. Then he turned to Book and said, 'Were you the bachelor?'

A look of recognition came across the Hispanic agent's face; he smiled broadly.

'No, he's the professor. Bookman. I watch you every Sunday morning. It's an honor to meet you, sir. I'm Agent Angel'— *AHN-hell*—'Acosta.'

'John Bookman.' They shook hands then Book aimed a thumb at the back seat. 'My intern, Nadine Honeywell.'

'And this is my partner, Wesley Crum. Please excuse his bad manners, Professor, he was raised by the scorpions in the desert.'

'Funny,' the thug named Wesley said.

'Did you come to Marfa to see the art?' Agent Acosta said. 'Judd's boxes? Chamberlain's crushed cars? Flavin's fluorescent lights?'

'Uh, yes,' Book said. 'That's why we're here.'

Agent Crum's eyes loitered on Book's back-seat passenger. 'I got fluorescent lights in my trailer,' he said with a grin, 'if you want to see them.'

Nadine sighed. 'Dope.'

Agent Crum's grin turned into a frown.

'Enjoy your stay, Professor,' Agent Acosta said. '*Bienvenidos.*'

Book fired up the engine and gunned the Harley through the light and turned north on Highland Avenue. He saw in the rearview the two agents engaged in an animated conversation.

'Dopes, Ms. Honeywell?'

'I call them as I see them, Professor.'

They cruised slowly up Highland, apparently the main street in town. It dead-ended at the courthouse that loomed large above the low-slung buildings. They rode past the Marfa City Hall on the right and then a row of refurbished storefronts occupied by the Marfa Public Radio station, the Marfa Book Company, and a shop called Tiend M that sold handmade jewelry. On the very visible side exterior wall of one building graffiti had been painted in large strokes like a billboard: *The Real Axis of Evil is the US, UK, and Israel.* A city crew with brushes prepared to paint over the message, no doubt unappreciated in West Texas. They crossed El Paso Street, and Nadine pointed again.

'Food Shark!'

Parked under a large shed with picnic tables was a silver food truck with 'Food Shark' stenciled across the side and a few customers at the service window. A sign read *Marfa Lights Up My Judd.* Bicycles were parked under the shed and foreign-made hybrids at the curb; one had a bumper sticker that read *WWDJD?* On the north side of the shed ran railroad tracks; Book hit the brakes hard as the crossing arms came down. The red lights flashed, and a train whistle sounded; a cargo train soon roared through downtown Marfa on its way west to El Paso. Hanna's train still came through town, but it was now the Union Pacific.

When the arms rose, Book accelerated over the tracks and across Oak Street and past Quintana's Barber Shop, the state Child Protective Services office, and the Iron Heart Gym. Other than the activity under the shed, downtown Marfa sat silent—no car horns, no sirens, no squealing tires, no sounds of the city. There was no traffic and few pedestrians. No joggers, cabs, pedicabs, or panhandling homeless people that one encountered in downtown Austin. It was as if the town were taking a siesta. Across Texas Street was a building with a replica of an oil rig on the roof; on the far side of Highland sat the two-story, white stucco El Paisano Hotel.

'Back in the fifties, they filmed *Giant* here,' Book said. 'All the stars stayed there.'

'That was a movie?'

'You've never heard of *Giant*?'

'Nope.'

'It's an epic about Texas' transformation from a cattle economy to an oil economy.'

'Sounds exciting.'

'It's a classic. Rock Hudson played a cattle baron.'

'Never heard of him.'

'He's dead. James Dean played a ranch hand turned oil tycoon.'

'Never heard of him either.'

'You've never heard of James Dean?'

'Is he on Twitter?'

'He's dead.'

'Well, there you go.'

'What about Elizabeth Taylor? She played the cattle baron's wife.'

'Is she that blonde movie star who used to date Clinton then committed suicide a long time ago?'

'That'd be Marilyn Monroe. She dated Kennedy. Overdosed on pills.'

'Never heard of her.'

'She's dead, too.'

'How am I supposed to know about dead people?'

'How about Donald Judd?'

'You're making these names up, right?'

'No.'

'Who did he play in *Giant*?'

'No one. He was an artist here in Marfa.'

'Let me guess: he's dead, too?'

'He is.'

'Is there anyone in this town who's not dead?'

Book turned right at the shuttered Palace Theater onto Lincoln Street and parked in front of a one-story building facing the courthouse. A small sign on the stucco façade read:

THE DUNN LAW FIRM with MIDLAND–LUBBOCK–AMARILLO–MARFA in smaller letters below. They got off the Harley. Book removed his sunglasses and doo-rag and knocked the dust off his T-shirt and jeans. Nadine removed the crash helmet and goggles and smoothed back her hair. They entered the law firm offices and stepped into a well-appointed reception area. Hallways extended off both sides. In the center along the back wall sat a receptionist behind a desk. Her head was down. They walked over to her. She wore a black dress. She wiped tears from her red face with a white tissue then blew her nose. She finally looked up at Book.

'You okay?' he asked.

'Funeral.' She wiped tears again. 'This afternoon.'

'I'm sorry for your loss.'

She nodded then forced a professional expression.

'Can I help you?'

'I'm John Bookman, to see Nathan Jones.'

Her professional expression evaporated; she frowned and appeared confused.

'*Nathan?* But . . . it's his funeral.'

Chapter 5

'Rock Hudson, James Dean, Elizabeth Taylor, Donald Judd, Nathan Jones . . . does everyone in Marfa die?' Nadine Honeywell asked.

'Eventually.'

On the western edge of town, out on San Antonio Street past the Thunderbird Motel and the Pueblo Market, across the street from a junkyard and adjacent to a mobile home park, was the Marfa Cemetery. A chain link fence ran down the center of the cemetery. West of the fence were the graves of the deceased of Mexican descent; some of the gravesites would qualify as religious shrines. East of the fence were the graves of Anglos; small American flags fluttering in the wind marked many of the gravesites. A dirt road crisscrossed the cemetery. They had ridden the Harley in and now leaned against the bike a respectful distance from the burial of Nathan Jones.

'A car accident,' Book said. 'Same day he mailed the letter.'

Through tears, the receptionist had provided the basics of Nathan's death.

'Coincidence.' Nadine turned to him. 'Can we go home now?'

'No.'

'Why not?'

'Because I don't believe in coincidences.'

'I was afraid you were going to say that.'

Book hadn't been to a funeral in twenty-one years. Five hundred police officers from around the state of Texas had turned out in full uniform for Ben Bookman's funeral; they do that for a fellow officer killed in the line of duty. Not so much for lawyers. Only a few dozen people were gathered at the gravesite. Some were dressed like lawyers, most like cowboys in jeans and boots and plaid shirts. A young woman wearing jeans and a black T-shirt stood alone off to one side; she looked their way for a moment then looked away. Book spotted the receptionist in her black dress; she dabbed her eyes with a handkerchief. An older couple seemed distraught; probably Nathan's parents. A young, very pregnant woman stood next to them; she stepped forward and placed a red rose on the casket. No doubt Nathan's wife. Next to her stood one of those locals, a large young man with blond curly hair; he put an arm around her shoulders. Family or family friend. A white-haired man snapped photographs from the perimeter. After the service ended and the crowd began to disperse, Book approached the pregnant woman.

'Ms. Jones?'

'Yes.'

'I'm Professor Bookman. From UT. Nathan wrote to me.'

Her eyes darted around then she stepped close and lowered her voice.

'Not here. They're watching. Come to my house. Tonight. I'm in the book.'

'I'm not sleeping in a teepee.'

El Cosmico occupied eighteen acres just south of town and adjacent to the Border Patrol station. Its website touted a 'unique communal outpost in West Texas,' but Nadine wasn't convinced. Accommodations ranged from refurbished Airstream trailers to safari tents and authentic Sioux teepees. A community bathhouse with a tub and toilet came with the price. Dubbed a 'hippie campground' by the locals, El Cosmico was the latest venture of the woman behind the Hotel San José and Jo's Coffee in Austin. Book was a regular at Jo's, so he had decided to give it a try. But his intern was having none of it.

'And I don't share toilets with strangers.'

She sighed and shook her head as if faced with an impossible task.

'I can't even imagine how many sanitizing wipes I'd go through.'

'Ms. Honeywell, you're a mighty picky traveling companion, you do know that?'

'So sue me.'

'Spoken like a true lawyer.'

Ten minutes later, they stood at the front desk of the El Paisano Hotel. The lobby of the Spanish baroque, pueblo-deco style hotel featured leather chairs and ottomans, colorful Mexican tiled floors, exposed wood beams, and—

'OMG,' Nadine said. 'Is that a buffalo head on the wall?'

'And a longhorn.' Book turned to the desk clerk. 'Just one night.'

Nadine dug her cell phone out of her canvas bag and took a photo of the stuffed heads.

'No one back home will believe this.'

'Your name?' the clerk said.

'John Bookman.'

The clerk broke into a big smile. 'Professor Bookman, welcome to the Paisano. We were expecting you.'

'You were?'

'Your secretary—Myrna?—she called ahead and made reservations for you and Miss Honeywell. I have some messages for you.'

69

The clerk disappeared behind the counter.

'Where's the nearest Starbucks?' Nadine asked. 'I'm dying for caffeine.'

The clerk reappeared and said, 'No Starbucks in Marfa.'

Nadine stared as if the clerk had said, 'No oxygen in Marfa.' 'You're joking?'

The clerk shrugged at her then handed three message slips to Book: Myrna, his sister, and James Welch. Nadine shook off her Starbucks shock and held her phone up as if trying to gauge the wind in the lobby.

'Why can't I get through?'

'Cell phone service,' the clerk said, 'it's a bit sketchy out here.'

Nadine responded with the same look of utter disbelief.

'No Starbucks or texting—are we still in America?'

'You're still in Texas.'

The clerk handed room keys to Book.

'Professor, you're in the Rock Hudson suite, and Miss Honeywell is in the Elizabeth Taylor suite. Rooms two-eleven and two-twelve.'

'Great, now we're sleeping in dead people's beds,' she said.

'They were alive when they slept here. Let's wash up and get some lunch, figure out where we go from here.'

'Home.'

'Enjoy the art,' the desk clerk said.

Book carried their gear up the flight of stairs—there was no elevator—and down the corridor to their rooms.

James Dean practiced rope tricks in the courtyard of the El Paisano Hotel. Rock Hudson and Elizabeth Taylor partied with the cast and crew in the dining room. Director George Stevens reviewed the 'dailies' in the ballroom each evening; locals were welcome. And they came. For six weeks in the summer of 1955, Hollywood lived in the Paisano, and Marfa was Cinderella at the ball.

But the ball ended, Hollywood went home, and Marfa was left to its old life. The town and the hotel began a steady slide. By 2001, Marfa was the county seat of the poorest county in Texas, and the Paisano was sold at a tax foreclosure auction on the steps of the Presidio County Courthouse. No one imagined that day that there would be a Hollywood ending for both the town and the hotel. But there was—but not because of Hollywood.

Because of art.

Book deposited Nadine in Elizabeth Taylor's room then went next door to his room. Rock Hudson had been comfortable: living room, full kitchen, bedroom, and private rooftop balcony. Book dropped his bag then looked for the room phone. There wasn't one. So he dialed Myrna on his cell then stepped out onto the balcony. Myrna's voice soon came over, a bit scratchy but audible.

'You made it to Marfa safely?'

The mother in Myrna.

'We did.'

'How's Nadine?'

'Homesick. How'd you know we'd stay at the Paisano?'

'Nadine didn't seem like the camping-out type, not with all that hand sanitizer. When are you coming back?'

'Tomorrow, probably. You remember Nathan Jones? He interned for me four years back?'

'Of course I remember Nathan. He saved my job.' She thought that was funny. 'Why?'

'He wrote me that letter, asking for help.'

'Are you going to help him?'

'No.'

'Why not?'

'He's dead.'

Book called his sister next. Joanie was thirty-one and a new mother. He had given her away at her wedding three years before to a doctor named Dennis. Book's new brother-in-law

71

had advised them to put their mother in a home. But what the hell did he know about Alzheimer's? He was a proctologist.

'Book, we've got to talk about putting Mom in a home.'

'No.'

'I know you don't want to, but—'

'She didn't put us in a home. She went back to work after Dad died.'

Clare Bookman had kept the books and paid the bills for a dozen small businesses in Austin; now she couldn't balance her own checkbook.

'And Dad sure as hell wouldn't have put her in a home.'

Alzheimer's had made his mother a stranger in her own body. In her own house. To her own children. She would not have wanted to live like that. But it was too late for her to make that choice. The disease had made the choice for her. When the time came for Book, he would make the choice before the disease made it for him.

'Book, she doesn't even know who we are anymore.'

'We know who she is.'

'Book—'

'Joanie—that's not going to happen. She can live with me.'

'And all your sleep-over girlfriends?'

'They won't sleep over anymore.'

'And how will you take her anywhere? On the back of that Harley?'

'I'll buy a car.'

'What would you buy that's fast enough and dangerous enough?'

'A minivan.'

She laughed. He liked Joanie's laugh.

'Indiana Jones in a minivan? I don't think so. Besides, Book, you're always gone. Like now.'

'I'll hire around-the-clock caregivers.'

'That's expensive.'

'Can you say "book royalties"?'

'I thought that was going to be your retirement fund?'

From the rooftop balcony two stories up, Book could see all of Marfa and the desert beyond. The prairie grass gleamed yellow in the sun.

'I don't figure on living to retirement age.'

'Oh, Book, don't talk like that. Just because Mom . . . that doesn't mean . . .' She sighed into the phone. 'What are you doing in Marfa?'

'Working.'

'Another adventure?'

'A dead lawyer.'

His last call was to James Welch, chairman of the Board of Regents for the University of Texas System, a nonprofit organization possessing a $21 billion endowment, numerous real-estate developments, two million acres of prime oil land, stakes in a world-class golf club, a radio station and a cable TV sports channel, the most expensive and profitable football team in America, and fifteen universities and medical schools throughout Texas educating over two hundred thousand students. The University of Texas at Austin is the flagship campus. James Welch had earned an MBA from UT thirty-three years before; today, he boasted a $3 billion net worth. He was the most powerful man in higher education in Texas.

'Professor Bookman, thanks for calling me back.'

'Sorry for the delay, Mr. Welch. I had to leave town unexpectedly.'

'Your secretary said you were in Marfa. The wife and I went out there a few years back. She wanted to see the art. Boxes and crushed cars and fluorescent lights—I didn't get it.'

He exhaled.

'Well, as you may have heard, Professor, my son, Robert, was arrested for drug possession with intent to distribute. They took his blood without his consent.'

'What was he doing when the police arrested him?'

'Leaning against his car parked on Sixth Street. Cop came along and arrested him.'

'He didn't say or do anything to the police officer?'

'Knowing Bobby, he probably smarted off. Never been one to keep his mouth shut. Like his mother. But how can they do that, take his blood without his consent? Is that constitutional?'

The definition of a liberal: a conservative who had been arrested.

'Good question. No answer as yet. So they arrested your son, searched his car, and found drugs?'

'Cocaine.'

'How much?'

'The police report says a pound.'

'That's more than recreational.'

'Bobby's not a drug dealer, Professor. He's a user. And he's going into rehab at the Betty Ford Clinic, if he gets out of jail. And the case is dismissed. And his record expunged.'

'Mr. Welch, you should hire an experienced criminal defense lawyer.'

'I did. Scotty Raines. He said the search and seizure was illegal, no probable cause to search his Beemer or take a blood sample. He suggested I hire you.'

'Why?'

'Because if Scotty says the search and seizure was illegal, the judge will still hold a trial. But you're a famous constitutional law expert. If you say the search and seizure was illegal, the judge will dismiss the case.'

'You want me to write a brief?'

'And argue the issue in court, if necessary. I'm prepared to pay you handsomely.'

'You don't think your status is enough to'—Book wanted to say, 'Get him off,' but didn't—'remedy this situation?'

'In Dallas, sure. But this is Austin, not exactly a hotbed of Republicans. The D.A. is a Democrat. I'm a big Republican donor in Texas, and I supported the D.A.'s opponent in the last election.'

'Whoops.'

'Whoops is right, Professor.'

Book pondered a moment. Sitting in the Travis County Jail for six months to a year with hardened criminals wouldn't do the young Welch any good. He needed to be in rehab.

'Professor?'

'I'll do it. I'll talk to your lawyer and write your brief.'

'Thank you. What do I owe you?'

'Nothing.'

'You're going to work for free?'

As if Book had said a recount had made Romney the winner.

'No. In return, I want two promises from you. And these are non-negotiable, Mr. Welch.'

'Shoot.'

'First, your son goes into residential rehab, not some one-hour-a-week outpatient therapy. Six months minimum.'

'Six months? He'll fall behind in school.'

'Better than falling behind in life.'

'All right. Six months. I'm taking him out there myself. Professor, I love my son. I will take care of him.' He hesitated a moment then said, 'When I was at UT, we got drunk on Lone Star beer. Now it's cocaine. Why do kids use drugs?'

'I don't know, Mr. Welch.'

The line was silent for a long moment then Welch's voice came across.

'What's the second promise?'

Chapter 6

His intern didn't answer her door when Book rang the bell—
the Rock Hudson and Elizabeth Taylor suites had doorbells—so
he went downstairs. He checked the phone book at the front
desk for Nathan Jones's home address and jotted it down in the
small notebook he always carried in his back pocket. He asked
the desk clerk for the local paper, but it was a weekly and the last
edition had come out the day before Nathan died; the new
edition would come out the next day. He asked the clerk for the
location of the newspaper office. He then searched for his intern.

He found her in the *Giant* museum.

In a small space off the lobby, *Giant* memorabilia, movie
posters, photographs, coffee mugs, T-shirts, caps, and shot
glasses were offered for sale, and on a small television the film
ran in a loop. Nadine Honeywell sat in a leather chair in front
of the screen with her feet kicked up on an ottoman and her
eyes focused through her black glasses on the movie. Book had
watched *Giant* several times, as had every Texan of age; it was
the national movie of Texas. On the screen, Jett Rink, the
ranch hand turned oil tycoon played by James Dean, had just
struck oil on the small tract of land he had inherited from Luz

Benedict. He drove straight to the Reata ranch house and sucker-punched his former employer, Bick Benedict, the cattle baron played by Rock Hudson.

'He's gorgeous,' Nadine said. 'And gay.'

'Jett Rink?'

'James Dean.'

'He died a few weeks after they finished shooting the movie here. He was driving fast, heading to a road race in southern California in his Porsche, truck pulled out in front of him, he couldn't stop in time. He was only twenty-four. Lived fast and died young. Never saw the movie, but he was nominated for an Oscar. He made only three films: *Giant*, *East of Eden*, and *Rebel Without a Cause*.'

Nadine's eyes turned up from the screen to Book. 'So, what, you're trying to be another James Dean?'

'I'm not gay.'

'A rebel without a cause . . . except you're a rebel with too many causes.'

Jett's Grill fronts the courtyard just off the hotel lobby. It's a civilized place with cloth tablecloths, a pink-and-green tile floor, and a wait staff dressed in black. Book ordered tilapia tacos and iced tea. Nadine ordered the *Giant* cheeseburger— one-half pound of Black Angus beef—Parmesan fries, a root beer, and coffee and a chocolate brownie for dessert.

'Ms. Honeywell, would you like a stick of butter with that?'

'No.'

She looked up at the waitress, a young woman with a rose tattoo on her ample bosom. She was an artist; waiting tables was her day job.

'I want ice cream. Vanilla.'

'You know what you're putting inside yourself?'

'Better than a man.'

'Amen,' the waitress said. She winked at Nadine then left with their orders.

His intern had cleaned up and pulled her hair back in a ponytail. Her face was innocent and unadorned. She dug in her canvas bag and pulled out a sanitary wipe packet; she tore open the packet, removed the wipe, and proceeded to rub down the salt and pepper shakers, the silverware—she reached for his, but he moved them away—and her water glass.

'You can't be too careful,' she said.

'I don't know. Maybe you can.'

She again reached into her bag and came out with the Purell hand sanitizer. She squirted the gel into her palm and rubbed her hands as if she were a doctor prepping for surgery. Their table now smelled like a hospital.

'You like that stuff?' Book said.

'Purell is pretty good. Sixty-two percent ethyl alcohol content. Germ-X has sixty-five percent. My favorite is Outlast. It has seventy percent ethyl alcohol, it kills ninety-nine-point-ninety-nine percent of germs, and it lasts six hours. But it's kind of hard on my skin.'

'You don't get out much, do you?'

'The world is full of dangerous germs.'

'Life is dangerous.'

'It was for Nathan.'

Nathan Jones was dead at twenty-nine. He had been Book's intern at twenty-five. For one month. Until that first letter had arrived in the mail. And they had gone to South Texas.

'Was it dangerous for Renée?'

'I guess she thought it was. But I always protected her.'

She sat silent for a moment then said, 'You're right.'

'About what?'

'I don't get out much.'

'You will as my intern.'

Nadine contemplated her sanitized hands.

'Professor . . .'

She turned to him; she was that thirteen-year-old kid again.

'. . . can you protect me?'

'Yes, Ms. Honeywell, I can. And I will.'

'Nothing personal, but you're a law professor. And it's a harsh world.'

'I have skills.'

She regarded him a moment then finished rubbing her hands. She offered the sanitizer to Book.

'I washed upstairs.'

The waitress returned. She placed their drinks on the table then handed a card to Nadine.

'Text me.'

She winked again then walked away.

'I attract lesbians,' Nadine said. 'And no, I'm not.'

Book emptied a sweetener into his iced tea, stirred, and took a long drink. Nadine sucked her root beer through a long straw.

'You ever write a brief?' Book asked.

'In law school?'

'Time you learned.'

'What's the issue?'

'Search and seizure. Fourth Amendment.'

'Who's the client?'

'Bobby Welch.'

'That regent's son.'

'You don't know who Elizabeth Taylor was, but you know who Bobby Welch is?'

'Someone tweeted me that he got arrested for drug possession.'

'That's how you get your news? On Twitter?'

'That's how everyone my age gets the news.' She shrugged. 'No commercials.'

'If I owned CBS stock, I'd sell.'

'What's CBS?'

Book sat back and reread Nathan Jones's letter.

'He said his client was contaminating the groundwater, but didn't say who his client was. Said someone followed him home. Said his wife was scared. Said he had proof. Said he needed my help.'

Book blew out a breath.

'How do I help a dead person?'

'So what are we going to do?'

'If you die from unnatural causes in a small town, there'll usually be an article in the local paper. And an obituary. So, Ms. Honeywell, we're going to find the newspaper office, see what we can learn there. Then we'll ask around town, try to learn the identity of Nathan's mystery client. And we'll visit his wife tonight, see if she has his proof.'

'And go home tomorrow?'

'Probably.'

'*Probably?*'

Book folded and replaced the letter inside the envelope then checked the postmark again.

'He mailed this letter on the fifth, died that night.'

'Coincidence.'

Chapter 7

His intern brushed and flossed her teeth after every meal to prevent cavities and gum disease, or so she had advised him. When she returned downstairs, they proceeded through the hotel courtyard, across Texas Street, and south on Highland Avenue past a row of renovated storefronts. The first display window featured a sleek wood desk; stenciled on the window was *Evan Hughes, Furniture Design and Fabrication*, and below that *Marfa, TX – Brooklyn, NY*. The next storefront sat vacant, but after that was a shop called Stuff that sold stuff. Parked at the curb was an old hearse painted in a Wild West motif with horses and cattle and gunslingers; longhorns had been mounted on the grill.

'Odd,' Nadine said.

She abruptly stopped and examined her arm then stuck her hand inside the canvas bag looped over her shoulder and came out with an aerosol can. She sprayed her arms and legs and neck.

'Germs?' Book asked.

She turned the can so he could read the label: OFF!

'Mosquitoes. They carry the West Nile virus. It's an epidemic.'

'In April?'

'You can't be too careful.'

She offered the can to him, but he declined. She was now cleared to continue down the sidewalk. A white two-story adobe-style building with inlaid tile, elaborate wrought iron, and *Brite Building 1931* in black print across the front façade occupied the next block. It housed a restaurant called Maiya's behind a red door, the old Marfa National Bank, and the Ayn Foundation gallery. The featured exhibits were by Maria Zerres and Andy Warhol.

'Let's check it out,' Book said.

They entered the gallery. Displayed inside the bare space were three of Andy Warhol's works based on Da Vinci's *The Last Supper*. A large black-and-white sketch on one wall depicted Jesus at the Last Supper. On another wall was a color version of Jesus. Another had Jesus next to a bodybuilder with the caption, 'Be a Somebody with a Body.'

'Also odd,' Nadine said.

'What's odd is an Andy Warhol exhibit in Marfa, Texas,' Book said.

'You're doing it again.'

'What?'

'Making up names.'

'I'm not making it up. Andy Warhol's a famous artist.'

'Is he dead?'

'He is.'

They walked outside just as two young men bounced in as if entering a trendy coffee shop in SoHo; they carried iPhones and wore Keds, skinny jeans, white T-shirts—one had *WWDJD?* stenciled across the front—and porkpie hats like the cop in *The French Connection*.

'They're gay,' Nadine said when they stepped onto the sidewalk.

They continued south and encountered similar young men engaged in their electronic devices and animated conversations. Book said 'howdy' to the next group and got a look in response. He tried 'hidee' on the next ones and got nothing. They wore black-framed glasses, mismatched clothing, fedoras and bowler hats, colorful hair that stuck out like porcupine quills, tattoos, and piercings. Boys walked hand in hand, about as common a sight in West Texas as cattle being herded down Fifth Avenue in New York City. The young men acted with the same aloofness the hipster creative types in the SoCo part of Austin displayed, as if trying too hard to appear endowed by God with genius; which is to say, they acted much the same as law students at UT.

'Also gay,' Nadine said.

'Stop.'

'Just saying.'

'Don't.'

She made a face.

Situated on the north side of the railroad tracks was the old Marfa Wool and Mohair Building. The sandstone-colored building had been converted into an art gallery featuring the works of John Chamberlain. They went inside and were greeted by a young docent wearing a pink T-shirt with *Chinati* printed across the front. He explained the layout of the exhibit then left them to tour on their own.

'Gay,' Nadine whispered.

Book sighed then turned to his intern.

'Why do you do that?'

A perfectly innocent face.

'What?'

'Your gay or straight game.'

She shrugged. 'It's not a game. It's a basic survival skill in San Francisco. For girls. You know, you get all gooey-eyed over this great-looking guy, turns out he likes boys. It can be pretty embarrassing, especially if you've already taken your clothes off.'

'I would think so.'

'You wouldn't believe how many times that's happened to me.'

'Taking your clothes off?'

'Romancing a gay guy. That ever happened to you?'

'Romancing a gay guy? No.'

'Romancing a lesbian and not knowing it?'

'If I didn't know it, how would I know if it happened?'

'Sounds like a law professor's answer. Of course, the odds of finding a straight guy in San Francisco are about the same as finding a gay guy in West Texas.'

She regarded the gay docent.

'Or not.'

John Chamberlain was not gay. He had four wives and three sons and was a renowned sculptor of automotive steel. Bumpers, door panels, fenders—he crushed and twisted the pieces into massive modern art. One of his sculptures had sold for $4.7 million just prior to his demise. Twenty-two of his works were displayed in the building in which Book and Nadine now stood. She stared at a mangled steel sculpture titled *Chili Terlingua*.

'That's art?'

'Well . . .'

'Exactly. Does this Chamberlain guy live here?'

'He's dead.'

'Figures.'

'Marfa sits at the same altitude as Denver,' Book said. 'Hence, the cooler air.'

'But Denver has a Starbucks,' his intern said. 'Hence, I'd rather be in Denver.'

They proceeded along Highland Avenue until they arrived at a storefront with *The Times of Marfa* stenciled across the front plate glass window. Taped to the window was a 'Burn Ban in Effect' notice.

'Small-town publishers, they know everything about

everyone—and they trade in information. You give them a little, they'll give you a lot.'

'Like my aunt.'

'Is she in the newspaper business?'

'The gossip business. If I want my mother to know something, I tell my aunt. Faster that way.'

'Well, if you want to know what's going on in a small town, you read the local paper. And if you want to stir the pot in a small town, you put a story in the paper.'

'And do we?'

'Do we what?'

'Want to stir the pot?'

'Yes, Ms. Honeywell, we do.'

'That sounds dangerous.'

'It can be.'

They opened the screen door—the inside door was propped open with a large rock—and stepped into a small office. An older man sat at a desk behind a waist-high counter with his head cocked back slightly, apparently so he could focus on the computer screen in front of him through his reading glasses. He glanced at them over his glasses then went back to his typing. After a moment, he stood and walked over. He looked like one of the Beach Boys on their fiftieth reunion tour; his hair was white, his eyes blue, and his shirt Hawaiian. He wore a red 'MARFA' cap. A toothpick dangled from his lips like a cigarette. He was the photographer at Nathan Jones's funeral. He stuck a weathered hand across the counter.

'Professor Bookman, I presume.'

They shook hands.

'Sam Walker . . . owner, publisher, reporter, typesetter, printer, and delivery boy. I write the paper up front and print it out back. That's what you're smelling, the ink.'

'John Bookman. And Nadine Honeywell, my intern.'

'Welcome to Marfa.' Sam Walker chuckled. 'Boy, you really

lit into McConnell and Schumer last Sunday. I like that—you don't play favorites.'

'I don't have favorites.'

'I expect not.'

'How'd you know I was in town?'

'Word travels fast from the Paisano. We know who's in town before they get up to their rooms. We get all kinds of celebrities these days. Robert Redford was in town last week, flew in to see the art. And that Quaid boy—not the one that was in *G.I. Joe*—'

'*G.I. Joe?*'

'No, the other one. He and his wife moved here, bought a storefront on Highland next to Evan Hughes's furniture shop, figured on fixin' it up for their home, but then Hollywood hit men came gunning for them so they hightailed it up to Canada.'

'Hollywood hit men?'

'That's what they said. Course, I'm not sure all the lights are on. Anyway, he defaulted on the purchase note, the owner foreclosed, and they had a sheriff's auction on the sidewalk, sold all his stuff.'

'Sounds like you know everything going on in your town.'

'I've lived seventy-two years now, Professor, all but my four college years right here in Marfa and the last fifty right in this spot, observing and reporting. So I keep up with things. Course, it ain't that hard, not when there's only two folks per square mile in all of Presidio County. Only so much news those few folks can create.'

'Is Marfa a better place now than when you started the paper?'

'It's different. Better is a point of view, not a fact.'

'You sound like an old-style newsman.'

'Well, I am old.'

'This the only newspaper in town?'

'In the county. Weekly. Next edition comes out tomorrow.'

86

Sam held up two mock front pages.

'Slow news week, so I'm trying to decide on the lead story. I got one story about the roller derby returning to Marfa and another about a ton of marijuana found by the Border Patrol in a bulldozer blade. What do you think, Professor?'

'Roller derby.'

'That's what I figured.'

'Mr. Walker—'

'Sam. So you folks come out to see Judd's boxes and Flavin's fluorescent lights?'

'And a former student. Nathan Jones.'

Sam grimaced. 'Boy, that was a damn shame. Married, about to be a daddy.'

'Did you know him?'

'Never heard of him till he died last week. Must've been low profile, for me not to know him. Bad accident out on Sixty-seven. Folks out here drive too damn fast. Course, when you drive a hundred miles for lunch, hard to drive the speed limit, even if it is eighty.'

'Did you write an article about the accident or an obituary?'

'Both. They'll be in tomorrow's paper.'

'Mind if I read them today?'

Sam shrugged. 'Sure. Why not?'

He walked over to his desk and returned with two short articles. He placed them on the counter. Book read the first article.

LOCAL LAWYER DIES IN ONE-CAR ACCIDENT

Nathan Jones, 29, a lawyer with The Dunn Law Firm in Marfa, was killed in a one-car accident on the north side of Highway 67 nine miles east of town Thursday night about 11 P.M. Sheriff Brady Munn investigated the accident and reported that Jones apparently fell asleep, ran off the road, lost control of his vehicle, and crashed into a pump jack.

The pickup truck's gas tank ruptured and exploded. Jones died at the scene. 'Speed was a contributing factor in the accident,' Sheriff Munn said. Jones was returning to Marfa from Midland where he had business at his law firm's offices. Thomas A. Dunn, senior partner at the firm in Midland, expressed shock at Jones's death. 'He was a fine young lawyer and a fine young man. We will miss Nathan.'

'Good-looking boy,' Sam said.
A photograph of Nathan accompanied the obituary.

JONES, NATHANIEL WILLIAM, 29, went to be with his Lord and Savior on April 5th. Nathan was born on February 12, 1983. He grew up on his family's cattle ranch west of Marfa. He graduated from Marfa High School then Texas Tech University with a degree in English. He attended law school at the University of Texas in Austin and received his law degree in 2009. He was a member of the Texas Bar Association and was employed with The Dunn Law Firm in Marfa. Nathan is survived by his wife, Brenda, who is expecting their first child, and his parents, William and Edna. Funeral services were at the First Baptist Church with burial at the Marfa Cemetery.

'Only problem with a weekly,' Sam said. 'Sometimes the deceased is already in the ground before the obituary comes out. Least he had a nice funeral.'

'We saw you there. You went even though you didn't know him?'

'When there's not but two thousand folks in town, one dies, it means something. Out here, Professor, folks aren't fungible.'

As law students often seemed to be.

Book had lost contact with Nathan after he had graduated from the law school. He viewed his role as similar to a parent's: to teach the students skills for life in the legal world so they could survive on their own. Consequently, the students leave law school and their professors behind; they get on with their lives and legal careers. They seldom have contact with their professors except to shake hands at continuing legal education seminars. They return to campus for football games, and if they're successful, to make a donation to the school. If they're very successful, their firms might endow a chair. If they become fabulously rich, they might buy the naming rights for a building or space on campus. Hence, the law school had the Susman Godfrey Atrium, the Joseph D. Jamail Pavilion, the Jamail Center for Legal Research, the Kraft Eidman Courtroom, and the Robin C. Gibbs Atrium. His former intern had not become a rich and famous lawyer. He had not made a donation, endowed a chair, or bought a naming right. He had simply returned home to Marfa and gotten on with his life. And now his life was over. Book could not help but feel that he owed an unpaid debt to Nathan Jones.

'And I took some photos of the funeral service,' Sam said.

'Why?'

'A life ended. Deserves to be documented. So folks won't forget.'

'Do you have a photo of the guests at Nathan's funeral?'

Sam again went to his desk and returned with a computer-generated photograph. He placed it on the counter in front of Book.

'Who are these people?' Book asked.

Sam pointed at faces in the photo. 'She's the wife . . . his parents . . . lawyers, I figure, who else would wear suits? . . . the sheriff . . . Sadie, the court clerk . . . other locals.'

'May I have this photo?'

'Sure.' Sam's eyes turned up to Book. 'You looking into his death, figure maybe it wasn't an accident?'

'What makes you say that?'

'Just hoping for a lead story better than the roller derby.'

'Sorry to disappoint you.'

'Then what brings you to Marfa?'

'We came for the art, stopped in to say hello to Nathan, learned he had died.'

'Same day the boy was buried?'

'Coincidence.'

'Myself, I don't believe in coincidences.'

Nadine threw her hands up. 'What does everyone have against coincidences?'

Sam picked up a digital camera from his desk.

'Mind if I take your picture? For my wall.'

He gestured to the side wall on which photos of celebrities were hung. Book shrugged an okay. He figured Sam Walker might be a friend in Marfa—and he might need a friend. Sam snapped a few photos then held the camera out to Nadine.

'Would you take one of me and the professor?'

Sam came around the counter and stood next to Book. Nadine took their photo and handed the camera back to Sam. He went over to his desk, put the camera down, and picked up a book.

'Would you sign my book? I mean, your book?'

Book autographed the title page.

'I read that article about you in the *New York Times*,' Sam said. 'How people write you letters asking for help and you go off on these adventures, crusades they called them . . . photo didn't do you justice.'

Book decided to take Sam Walker into his confidence.

'Sam, can I trust you?'

Sam leaned in a bit.

'Sure, Professor.'

'Nathan Jones wrote me one of those letters.'

Book pulled out Nathan's letter and handed it to Sam. He looked at both sides of the envelope then removed the letter and read it. His expression turned somber. He slowly folded the letter, put it back inside the envelope, and handed it back to Book, almost as if he didn't want it in his possession.

'Noticed the postmark,' Sam said. 'Same day he died. Another coincidence.'

Book nodded.

'So you came to Marfa because he wrote this letter, only to find him dead. Said someone followed him home, said his wife was scared. Might make a man suspicious.'

'It might.'

'You seen his proof?'

'Not yet.'

'That'd be a big story, fracking contaminating the water. Hope it's not true.'

'Because of the water?'

'Because something like that could blow this town apart.'

'Or get someone killed.'

'Might could.'

Sam studied Book a long moment.

'Professor, mind if I ask you something?'

'Shoot.'

'Why do you care so much about Nathan Jones?'

'I owe him.'

Sam nodded slowly. 'Sheriff said his death was an accident.'

'You trust him?'

'Brady Munn? He's as honest as the desert.'

'Know who Nathan's client might be?'

Sam tapped the image of a big bald man in the funeral photo.

'Gotta be Billy Bob Barnett. Why else would he be at a lawyer's funeral? Biggest fracking guy in the Big Bend. Rolled into town five years back from Odessa. Office is just down the street, oil rig on the roof, can't miss it.'

'I didn't. So Mr. Barnett is an important person in town?'

'You could say that. Twice.'

'Why?'

'Because he's got what Marfa's never had and everyone wants: jobs. Before he came to town, we had damn near twenty-five percent unemployment. Now it's damn near zero. We're still a poor county, just not as poor. Which makes you feel rich, after you've been so poor for so long.'

'So tell me about Marfa.'

Book had shared information with Sam Walker, and now Sam wanted to share with Book. Most lawyers view every conversation as an opportunity to practice their interrogation of a hostile witness; but Book had learned a skill most lawyers never learn: to listen to other people. Sam stepped to the wall and pointed at an old black-and-white photo. The courthouse towered over the town.

'That was Marfa back in the late eighteen-hundreds, only about eight hundred residents. Then they built the courthouse, and we became the county seat. Town started to grow. Government stationed the cavalry here during the Mexican Revolution—they called it Camp Marfa until they changed the name to Fort D. A. Russell. By nineteen thirty, we had almost four thousand residents.'

Sam tapped a framed photograph that showed cavalry soldiers in formation on horseback.

'That's the way the fort looked back then. During World War Two, the government built a POW camp out there, brought in a few hundred German prisoners from Rommel's Afrika Korps. Geneva Convention says prisoners are supposed to be detained in the same climate they were captured in, so it was desert to desert for them. Not sure those Germans might not have opted for California or Colorado if given the choice, but they got Marfa. Apparently they were well behaved, didn't try to escape. Grew vegetables in a garden and painted murals on their barracks, old Building Ninety-Eight. You can go look at it. And we had the Marfa Army Air Field east of town, brought pilots in for flight training. Can't see much from the highway, but go on that Google Earth, you can still see the runways. That was our peak time, over five thousand folks lived here.'

'What happened?'

'We won the war. The army closed up shop, and the Germans went home. Shut down the fort, except for the part used by the Border Patrol to stop bootleg coming across the border. Beer and whiskey, seems kind of quaint now, doesn't it, compared to cocaine and heroin?'

He worked the toothpick.

'And then the rain stopped. Seven years it didn't rain, in the fifties. The great drought. Destroyed cattle ranching and the local economy, such as it was. Old-timers had to sell the herds then the land. Only break from the suffering was when *Giant* came to town. I was fifteen back then. Exciting time. They hired locals for extras, money people damn sure needed. My folks were in the barbecue scene, when Rock brought Liz home to Texas. Cast mingled with the locals between shots, nights at the Paisano—I watched the dailies in the ballroom every night, me and the rest of Marfa. I thought Jimmy Dean was about the coolest guy I'd ever seen, started combing my hair like him. Never knew he was gay. Or Rock Hudson till he died of AIDS.'

Nadine gasped. 'OMG—Bick Benedict was gay?'

Sam eyed her, apparently unsure if she was serious.

'She's been watching the movie at the Paisano,' Book said.

'Oh. Well, I'm afraid he was, little lady.'

'Wow. I didn't see that one coming.'

'Anyway, *Giant* allowed us to forget our troubles for a few months. When they packed up and that train pulled out of town, it was like Marfa's funeral procession. Population's been dropping ever since. Kids get out of high school then out of town—last census, we were down to nineteen hundred and eighty-one souls living here full time. This place was damn near a ghost town. Last one to leave, turn out the lights.'

Sam removed the cap and scratched his head.

'That was before Judd.'

Sam pointed at a photo of an older bearded man.

'Donald Judd. Big-time artist up in New York City, decided to move his operation to Marfa in nineteen seventy-three. Wanted his art to be set in place permanently. "Installation art," they call it. Judd bought vacant buildings on Highland—there were many to choose from—the Marfa National Bank Building, the Crews Hotel, the Safeway grocery store, the Wool and Mohair Building . . . renovated them into studios and galleries.'

'We checked out the Chamberlain exhibit in the Wool and Mohair Building.'

Sam gestured with the toothpick. 'I'm an open-minded sort of man. I've actually grown fond of Judd's boxes, and I'm warming up to Flavin's lights. But crushed car parts? That's art?'

'See?' Nadine said to Book. 'I'm not the only non-believer.'

'Then Judd bought the fort. Three hundred forty acres. Turned the artillery sheds and barracks into galleries, put up outside art—sixty big concrete boxes, damnedest thing you've ever seen, right on the field where Patton played polo. He was an interesting man, Judd. Loved bagpipes. I don't know why.'

'You knew him? Personally?'

'I did. Talked to him many times. Said he moved to Marfa because he hated the show business and commerce art had become in New York. Wanted to get away from that world. And if you want to get away from the world, by God, this is your place. From here to Hell Paso—thirty thousand square miles—there's not but thirty thousand people. Judd kept to himself, and locals didn't bother him—hell, no one knew who he was, or cared. He fell in love with this land, bought forty thousand acres south of town, called it Las Casas. He's buried out there, died in ninety-four. Lymphoma. Place was still a ghost town when he died. No jobs, no celebrities, no businesses, the Paisano was shuttered, tourists came for the Marfa Lights not the art, and Highland Avenue was nothing but vacant storefronts except for Judd's galleries.'

'People weren't coming to see his art?'

'Judd shunned publicity like the Amish shun the modern world. He lived like a monk out there on his ranch, no electricity, no hot water, no people. Like I said, he came here to escape the world, not invite it in.'

'What happened? The buildings on Highland aren't vacant now.'

'After Judd died, the mayor and other movers and shakers in town, people in the game—'

'What game?'

'The money game.'

'And you don't play that game?'

Sam Walker spread his arms to the small office.

'My media empire. Professor, I publish this paper because the history of Marfa and the Big Bend needs to be recorded. I think that's important. This isn't a business to me—hell, I barely break even most months. I expect constitutional law means more to you than your paycheck.'

'It does.'

'The mayor asked me to join in, but I declined. I don't make news, I just report it.'

'Maybe I should meet the mayor.'

'Just walk around town, he'll find you. He can sniff out a celebrity like a bird dog on a hunt. Man was born kissing ass.'

'You and the mayor enemies?'

'Enemies? Nah. You want enemies, go to Houston or Dallas. Me and the mayor, we just look at the world from different angles. Anyway, him and those ol' boys got together, decided to market the "Marfa concept," they call it, the art, a way to put Marfa on the map. "Marfa myth" is what it is. But the national media bought it, descended on our little town, told the art world that this is the place to be. We don't have a doctor, a dentist, a drug store, a movie theater, a McDonald's, a Walmart—'

'A Starbucks,' Nadine said.

'—but Marfa's the place to be? I don't get it. But everyone drank the Kool-Aid. Then the Triple As descended on us.'

'The Triple As?'

'Attorneys, artists, and assholes. That's what the locals call them, the Triple As, outsiders who came to town to make Marfa their own. Attorneys came first, double-barreled rich, flying out here from Dallas and Houston in their private jets, acting like they had discovered Judd's art, buying up old adobes and downtown buildings like they were buying lunch. Then the artists came, from New York, gays mostly, bit of a culture shock to cowboys.'

'I told you,' Nadine said.

'We're like L.A. now, except with artists instead of actors. Everyone making coffee, scooping ice cream, or waiting tables is an artist hoping to be discovered.'

'In Marfa?'

'Like an artist version of *American Idol*. They're all young and hip and hate Bush, but bottom line, they're all desperate to be as rich as Republicans and as famous as that Kardashian gal.'

'Khloe?' Nadine said.

'No. The other one.'

'Oh. Kim.'

'They're just passing through, like the trains. But they brought a little variety to town, opened these fancy restaurants serving French food and Italian cuisine, little place called Maiya's—'

'We walked past it. Red door, in the Brite Building.'

'Gal from Rhode Island, she owns it. New Yorker came to town to design costumes for that movie *There Will Be Blood*, decided to stay, started a dry goods store. Others came and opened up more restaurants, galleries, jewelry shops, a bookstore, organic grocery store, coffee houses, live music bars, and that Ballroom Marfa, what they call a multimedia art space. Now, with Judd's and Flavin's and Chamberlain's masterpieces installed here, they say Marfa's the new art Mecca, so New York artsy types trek out here like they're making some kind of religious pilgrimage.'

Sam seemed to reflect on his own words a moment.

'Funny how things worked out. We were a ghost town of old ranchers, old-timers, old Mexicans, and old buildings, only two places to eat, but hell, you can't eat but one place at a time. We were here because we belonged here. On this harsh, unforgiving land. Then Judd moved here because he didn't belong in New York anymore. Twenty years, he made his art and his home here, became a bona fide Texan—I told him so the day he bought that ranch, that's every Texan's dream, to own a part of Texas. Now, twenty years after he died, the mayor and the Triple As have taken something real and made it something phony, turned this town into Santa Fe South or Marfa's Vineyard, take your pick, and Judd's art into the commerce and show business he hated. Marfa's a goddamned art theme park, and we're just running the rides for the tourists.'

Sam returned to Donald Judd's photo.

'Don wouldn't want to live here now. All the New Yorkers followed him here—hell, we got more Yankees than cattle. Folks fly in for the weekend, pay two hundred thousand for adobes worth twenty 'cause they think they're cute, then they triple the size and turn the places into walled compounds like they're living in Guadalajara in fear of the cartels. Drove real-estate prices and taxes up and the locals out. What you call ironic, New York liberals who profess to care so much about the poor and Mexicans, but they're buying third and fourth homes as trinkets and driving the poor and Mexicans out of Marfa. I tell them that, and they just smile and shrug their shoulders, as if it's out of their control. Like the weather.'

Sam dug at his teeth with the toothpick.

'Before the Triple As, this town was peaceful, hardly any conflict, just the normal stuff between the Anglos and the Mexicans—this *is* Texas—but basically everyone minded their own business and got along.'

'Not now?'

'Not hardly. Now we've got conflict. Hell, it's a goddamned civil war. "New Marfa" versus "old Marfa." Haves versus have-nots. Anglos versus Mexicans. Mexicans versus the Border Patrol. Artists versus cowboys. Homosexuals versus heterosexuals. And we're all at odds with Mother Nature, trying to make a life in this desert. Now we've got the fights over fracking.'

Sam waved at a passer-by outside.

'Is Mr. Barnett the only fracker in town?'

'Far as I know. He's the man in Marfa. Employs damn near everyone in town who ain't a Border Patrol agent or an artist. Bought up leases, hired locals to work the rigs, and started punching holes. Pays good wages—some of those boys had been unemployed for years, all of a sudden they're able to buy new pickups. Art made Marfa fashionable. Fracking made us profitable.'

'So where's the fight?'

'Fights. Plural. We got the environmentalists and artists trying to stop the fracking 'cause they think it's the end of the world, and we got the cattle ranchers fighting the pipeline easements. Can't truck gas out like you can oil, so Billy Bob's laying pipelines. If folks won't sell—and they won't—he's condemning their land, which is apparently legal in Texas.'

'It is.'

'Hell of a law.'

'Has Billy Bob filed condemnation suits?'

'Yep.'

'I assumed that didn't make him any friends?'

'Nope.'

'So what's your opinion of Mr. Barnett?'

'My opinion? Fact is, he's one of the assholes.' Sam glanced at Nadine. 'Pardon my French.' Back to Book: 'Out here, you don't mess with a man's land. It can be dangerous.'

Chapter 8

They had seen Marfa from the outside looking in; now they saw Marfa from the inside looking out. Standing in the cupola atop the three-story, Renaissance-revival-style Presidio County Courthouse that offered a 360-degree panorama of the Marfa Plateau, they could see the entirety of the town, all the way to the edges where civilization petered out into desert. The land beyond lay stark and yellow and bare of trees all the way to the brown mountain ridges that framed the plateau.

'I'm scared of heights.'

'Ms. Honeywell, you're only four stories up.'

'I think I'm going to throw up.'

They walked back down the stairs to the district courtroom on the second floor. The courthouse had been built in 1886 for only $60,000, but the solitary courtroom was the grandest Book had ever seen, and he had seen a few. It had a ceiling twenty feet high, elaborate crown molding, and old-style seating with individual chairs secured to the wood floor. They sat and took in the space.

'You let Mr. Walker go on and on about Marfa. Why didn't you question him about fracking?'

'Most folks get defensive when a lawyer interrogates them like a guilty defendant, Ms. Honeywell. They don't open up. They shut down. So I've learned to listen. Everyone has a story to tell, and they want to tell it. We learned a lot from Sam Walker.'

'We did?'

'We did.'

'I thought you wanted him to put a story in the paper?'

'I do. And he will.'

Her eyebrows crunched down. 'You say that as if you've done this before.'

'I have.'

'Why does that make me nervous?'

Book gestured at the grand courtroom that bespoke the history of West Texas.

'So, Ms. Honeywell, what's your career plan? To be a small-town lawyer and probate wills in a courtroom like this? Or a big-city lawyer?'

'I don't want to be a lawyer.'

Book turned to his intern. 'Then why are you in law school?'

'My dad didn't have a son to take into his practice, so he's making do with me.'

'What do you want to be?'

'A chef.'

'A law student who wants to be a chef? That's different.'

'A law professor who rides a Harley? That's different.'

If you want to sue over a contract, a car accident, or condemnation of land for a gas pipeline in Presidio County, you file a lawsuit in that courthouse. With the district clerk. Who smiled at Book.

'Professor Bookman,' she said. 'Sam Walker called, said you were heading my way. I'm Sadie Thomas. I think you should be on the Supreme Court.'

'You should take my Con Law class first.'

She was a middle-aged woman with a sweet face. Which face appeared in the funeral photo.

'So what brings you to our courthouse?'

'I need some information.'

'About what?'

'Whom. Billy Bob Barnett.'

Her smile disappeared.

'I understand he filed lawsuits against landowners?'

'Pipeline condemnation cases, about two dozen so far.'

'Who represents him?'

'The Dunn Law Firm.'

'What lawyer?'

'Nathan Jones. But he died in a car accident last week.'

'He was my intern four years ago. Did he file lawsuits for any other clients?'

'As far as I know, Billy Bob was his only client. He always joked about being a one-client lawyer. Too bad his only client was an asshole.'

'So I've heard.'

'You'll hear it more. Condemning folks' land for a pipeline, it's legal, but it's not right. Landowners got together, hired the same lawyer out of Santa Fe, but they always lose. Billy Bob's got the law on his side. Folks are fighting mad.'

'Mad enough to kill?'

'Him, but not his lawyer.' Sadie exhaled heavily. 'He was a sweet boy, Nathan. Brought me a red rose on my birthday. Every year. He was really excited about becoming a daddy.'

Book thanked her and turned to leave.

'Professor—'

He turned back.

'I wouldn't get in the middle of this fight. Might not be healthy.'

★   ★   ★

'They killed Nathan, Professor.'

At half past seven, Book and Nadine rode over to Nathan Jones's house on Austin Street north of the railroad tracks. It was a neat frame house with a black 4x4 Ford pickup truck parked out front. The large young man with curly blond hair who had stood next to the wife at the funeral met them at the door. His name was Jimmy John Dale. He and Nathan had been best friends since childhood. He smelled like a brewery.

'Why do you say that, Ms. Jones?'

'Brenda. Because they said he was speeding, but Nathan never drives fast.'

Only five days after her husband's death, she still spoke of him in the present tense.

'He was a boy scout?'

'Eagle.'

She was due in three weeks; it was a boy. She sat uncomfortably in an armchair. Book and Nadine sat on the couch; Jimmy John paced the wood floor with a beer in his hand and a frown on his face, as if he had something on his mind and that something had irritated him. A wedding portrait of Nathan and Brenda hung on one wall of the small living room. She wore a white wedding dress, he a black tuxedo.

'Wow,' Nadine said. 'He's James Dean's identical twin.'

'That's what everyone says,' Brenda said.

Several other photos of Brenda and Nathan showed them walking a beach, lying on a picnic blanket, and dancing at a party. They were an odd couple, physically. Brenda was a cute girl with a round face who would struggle with the baby weight after giving birth, the same as Book's sister was now struggling. Nathan Jones looked like a male model in one of those glossy fashion magazines; his features were sharp, his eyes dark, and his body lean. He seemed almost too perfect to be a real man, just as he had seemed too introverted to be a lawyer; next to him, Ms. Roberts seemed like a talk show host. He made an A in Con Law; he often drew in a small sketchbook he carried.

'Check out his crazy photos,' Jimmy John said.

On another wall were framed black-and-white photos, all of the stark West Texas landscape. One showed cowboys on horseback herding cattle across the dusty plains, but in the foreground as if observing the scene was a perfectly clothed Barbie doll, its vivid color a sharp contrast to the black-and-white scene. Another was of the open land and a low mountain range in the distance with a tall red rose stuck in the dirt in the foreground. A third showed a drilling rig standing tall above the land, roughnecks working on the deck, and in the foreground pink lacy lingerie. Nadine stood and examined each photo as if she were an art critic.

'I know,' Brenda said. 'They're weird. I didn't get them either. But Nathan loves to take those photos. It's his passion.'

'He had an eye for the landscape,' Book said. 'Did he ever try to sell his photos?'

'No. It's just a hobby. He's happy being a lawyer. Was. Which was good, because he works . . . worked a lot of late nights.'

'What else did he do? When he wasn't working?'

'Nothing. He works at the firm and spends the rest of his time with me. And Jimmy John.'

'What did you and he do?'

She shrugged. 'Normal stuff. Sundays after church, we'll pack a lunch and drive the desert looking for landscape for him to shoot. We'll put out a blanket, and he'll take hundreds of pictures from different angles. He's got some great photos from up in the Davis Mountains.'

'Did he hang out with anyone else?'

'He doesn't have a lot of friends in Marfa.'

'But he grew up here.'

'He wasn't a cowboy,' Jimmy John said.

'Any siblings?'

'He's an only child,' Brenda said.

'So how'd you two meet?'

'We all grew up together, here in Marfa. Nathan and I, we've been sweethearts since grade school. After high school, we went to Tech together. I got a degree in education, he majored in English. I came home, been teaching kindergarten in the public school seven years now. Nathan went to UT for law school. You were his hero, Professor. He talked about you a lot. We always watched you on TV.'

'You really got a black belt in kung fu?' Jimmy John said.

'Taekwondo.'

'When he got his law degree,' Brenda said, 'he came home, we got married, and he hired on with the Dunn firm. That was right when they opened the office here.'

Book addressed Jimmy John. He had a red face and a thick body. His jeans dragged the ground in the fashion of cowboys. Given his obvious state of inebriation and irritation, Book decided not to pepper him with questions but to just let him talk—and he seemed anxious to talk.

'So, Jimmy John, what's your story?'

Jimmy John took a swig of his beer then swiped a sleeve across his mouth.

'My *story*?' He snorted as if amused by the question. 'My story is, Brenda and Nathan went off to college, I stayed here. I only got a high school education, so I was low man on the totem pole for jobs around here, right below the Mexicans 'cause they'll live twenty to a trailer so they can send money back home to Mexico. You know they send thirty billion dollars back home every year? But they ain't taking money from American workers. Yeah, right. So I worked the cattle, dug holes and laid asphalt for the city, whatever work there was. Then this place becomes some kind of hot spot for art and all of a sudden every goddamn homosexual in New York City is moving to Marfa, artists with more money than sense, paying too much for homes, driving up the prices, now locals like me, we can't afford nothing but trailers on the Mexican side of town. Biggest employers in town were the tomato farm and Border Patrol. I applied, but they want agents who can speak Spanish.'

'You could learn.'

'We shouldn't have to speak Spanish to work in America, Professor, especially not for our own government. But we speak English on the rigs.'

'Who do you work for?'

'Billy Bob Barnett. He don't hire wets.'

'You like the work?'

'I like to work. Never had a regular job till fracking came to town. Give people like me a chance.'

'For what?'

'A life.'

The economy had left the Jimmy Johns of America behind. Manufacturing jobs had gone offshore to Mexico and Asia, and the oil and gas business had gone to the Middle East. Twenty-three million Americans were unemployed; most felt betrayed by their country. Bitter. Angry. Most had no hope for a steady job. Ever. Until fracking came along. But it came with a price. Jimmy John pulled out a white handkerchief from his back pocket and blew his nose. Blood stained the white cloth.

'He gets nosebleeds,' Brenda said. 'And headaches. From working the rigs.'

Jimmy John shrugged. 'Lot of chemicals and gases coming up the well hole.'

'You have a doctor check you out?'

'No doctor in Marfa.'

He dug in his shirt pocket and pulled out a small container and swallowed two pills then chased them with the beer.

'He takes Advil like he's eating candy,' Brenda said. 'Nathan begged him to go to Alpine, see a doctor there.'

Jimmy John waved off her concerns with his beer can. 'Ain't like I'm gonna quit my job.'

'You married?' Book asked.

That question amused Jimmy John even more.

'*Me?* Hell, ain't no white girls in town.'

Book turned back to Brenda Jones. 'Did you know that Nathan had written a letter to me?'

'He said he was going to.'

'Did you know why?'

'He said something wasn't right. With the water. Said Billy Bob was cutting corners. Nathan was scared to death of him.'

'His own client?'

'Billy Bob bullied him. He bullied everyone.'

'Aw,' Jimmy John said, 'he's all bark and no bite. Oil men are rough around the edges, is all.'

Book pulled out Nathan's letter and handed it to Brenda. She read it then gave it to Jimmy John.

'He asked for your help, Professor,' Brenda said.

'How do I help him now?'

'Find the truth.'

Jimmy John handed the letter back to Book and said, 'Well, Billy Bob's the only fracker in Marfa.'

'And Nathan's only client,' Brenda said. 'If you work for the Dunn firm in Marfa, you work for Billy Bob Barnett. Nathan worried about it, having only one client. If Billy Bob got mad at him, he'd be out of a job.'

'But he still wrote this letter to me.'

'Professor,' Jimmy John said, 'them environmentalists been claiming that bullshit about groundwater contamination since we fracked the first well out here. Now they got the artists joining in, gives 'em something to do, I guess. They're liberals who hate the oil and gas industry. They want us all to ride bicycles like they do. I've worked those rigs for five years, and I can tell you, there's no contamination. I see the pressure readings on the casing. We've never had a leak.'

'Then why did Nathan say in his letter he had proof of contamination?'

'I don't know. He asked me, I told him we go by the book. He never told me he had any proof.'

Book turned back to Brenda. 'Did he show you any proof?'

'No. Nothing.'

'Did he tell you that he had shown the proof to his senior partner?'

She shook her head.

'Do you know him?'

She nodded. 'Tom Dunn. I met him once before the funeral. He gave me the creeps. He's the type who talks to a woman's breasts instead of her face.'

'If Nathan had proof and went public with it, the government would've shut down the frack wells.'

'Maybe,' Jimmy John said. 'Maybe not. This is Texas, Professor.'

'I told him to keep quiet about it,' Brenda said.

'Why?'

'Because if he went public, he'd either be out of a job or dead. He sent you that letter, and now he's dead. That seem like a coincidence to you, Professor?' She fought back tears. 'They killed him. Billy Bob's men.'

'Why?'

'Money.' She pointed at the floor. 'That gas down there is worth billions.'

Jimmy John put his free hand on Brenda's shoulder.

'It was an accident. Billy Bob, he's already rich.'

'People like him, they never have enough money.'

She could no longer fight the tears.

'They followed me home.'

Jimmy John shook his head. 'Nathan had her so scared she was seeing ghosts. Look, Professor, I loved Nathan like a brother. I miss him every minute. But it was just an accident. He was driving back from Midland late, and he fell asleep at the wheel.'

'That's what he said,' Brenda said.

'Who?' Book said.

'The sheriff.'

When they said their goodbyes, Brenda Jones gave Book a hug and whispered, 'Professor, you were his hero. Be his hero now. Give him justice. Find his truth. It wasn't an accident.'

He and Nadine walked outside and climbed on the Harley, but Book did not start the engine. Instead, he stared at the stars above them. He had pursued truth and justice—or as close thereto as the law allows—on enough occasions now to know that justice was more crushed car art than an act certain—in the eye of the beholder rather than an eye for an eye—and truth was found in one's heart rather than one's head. Maybe Justice Kennedy was correct: perhaps we are each entitled to define our own existence, our own meaning, our own truth. So he would not search for the truth, but for Nathan's truth. He owed him that much.

'What did we learn today, Ms. Honeywell?'

'I don't like riding six hours on a Harley.'

'About Nathan Jones's death.'

'A, official cause of death was accidental.'

'And?'

'B, Billy Bob Barnett is the client in his letter who is allegedly contaminating the groundwater.'

'And?'

'C, he didn't show his proof to either his wife or his best friend.'

'Very good.'

'And D, he was gay.'

'*Who?* Jimmy John?'

'Nathan Jones.'

Chapter 9

Border Patrol Agent Wesley Crum yelled back to his partner: 'Angel, you run like a goddamn queer! Hurry, they're getting away!'

It was after midnight, and Wesley and Angel were chasing wets through the desert again. Wesley wore night-vision goggles which allowed him to spot the wets running through the brush—not as good as the Predator's 'eyes in the sky,' but the goggles gave him an on-the-ground advantage over the wets. He was after two males and two females, no doubt a mom-and-pop operation who brought the kids with them for a lifetime in America. A chance at the American Dream: free education, free healthcare, free welfare, free this, free that, free everything, living at the expense of hard-working, tax-paying Americans. What a deal. First thing they do is get pregnant and punch out a baby in America—an American citizen with exactly the same rights as Wesley Crum—which guarantees them an extended stay in the U.S. of A. Consequently, Wesley viewed his job as deficit reduction: every Mexican he caught and deported back across the river equaled four or five Mexican babies the federal government wouldn't have to support.

Hell, if he caught enough wets, he could single-handedly balance the fucking budget.

Wesley Crum was thirty years old and had been on the job twelve years. He had grown up in Marfa and wanted to stay in Marfa, but there were no jobs in Marfa. Most of his high school buddies had moved away to Odessa to work the oil fields. Wesley hired on with the U.S. Customs and Border Protection Agency, now part of the Department of Homeland Security. That was back when agents didn't have to speak Spanish to get hired. Now Border Patrol hired Hispanics like Angel.

His partner was an odd duck. Read books. Listened to Marfa Public Radio. Knew stuff. Liked art and the artists. Three years younger than Wesley, Angel had grown up in Presidio and went to college at Texas A&M. Graduated, but he came back to work the border. They were as different as night and day—or Anglo and Hispanic—but they had forged a partnership that had lasted Angel's entire five years on the job, which was five years longer than any other relationship in Wesley's adult life. Of course, everyone liked Angel Acosta. He was that kind of guy. They worked the Big Bend Sector, which covered 165,000 square miles including seventy-seven counties in Texas and all of Oklahoma and 510 miles of the Rio Grande. Which pretty much guaranteed that they would chase wets every night. But Wesley liked the desert at night. He stopped and waited for his partner to catch up. Angel arrived; he was breathing hard. They addressed each other through the night-vision goggles.

'Let them go, Wesley. They just want to work.'

'Are you having one of them eccentric crises I heard about on TV?'

'Existential. You watching Dr. Phil again?'

'Are you?'

'You've got to do something else during the day when we work the night shift.'

'Like what?'

'Well, you could try reading.'

'*Reading?*'

As if Angel had said 'yoga.'

'I just don't see why we chase these people when they just want to work.'

'So we can keep working. So we keep our jobs, that's why we chase wets. Angel, there ain't no other jobs in Presidio County for guys like us, especially me. We either chase wets or collect unemployment.'

'We could work the frack rigs.'

'Man, chasing wets is a hell of a lot easier than that. And the federal government's benefit plan is much better than anything in the private sector.'

Angel shrugged. 'That's true.'

'Okay. You got your head on straight?'

'Yeah, I guess.'

'Good. They're hunkered down about a hundred yards due north. You circle around east, I'll go west. We'll trap these wets and deport their Mexican butts back to Chihuahua.'

They ran into the dark desert.

Chapter 10

'Saw you out running this morning,' Presidio County Sheriff Brady Munn said from the other side of his man-sized desk. 'Dawn in the desert's nice, ain't it?'

Nadine eyed Book through her black glasses. 'You ran at dawn? What is that, like, eight A.M.?'

'Six. I always run at dawn.'

'I sleep at dawn.'

'You folks want a cup of coffee?'

'No, thanks,' Book said.

'Sure,' his intern said. 'With cream. The real stuff, not the powdered.'

The sheriff cracked a little smile. 'I'll get the jail chef right on it.' Instead, he called out through the open door: 'Rosa, two coffees. With real cream.'

A hearty laugh came back. Then a voice with a Spanish accent.

'Real cream? Are you serious?'

'Run across the street to SqueezeMarfa, they'll have some.'

Now Spanish words came back, which turned the sheriff's smile into a chuckle.

'You folks speak Spanish?'

'No,' Book said.

'Nunh-huh,' Nadine said.

'Good.'

It was nine the next morning, and they sat in the sheriff's office in the county jail across the street from the Presidio County Courthouse. They had arrived without an appointment, but the sheriff had agreed to see them. He greeted them in the lobby then escorted them to his office. When he turned his back, Nadine had whispered to Book, 'Not gay.' Her San Francisco skills were not required to render that verdict in Presidio County. Sheriff Munn stood well over six feet tall and outweighed Book by at least fifty pounds; his body appeared as solid as an oak tree, even in middle age. He had thick hair with gray streaks and wore a Western-style uniform, tan cowboy boots, a massive handgun on his hip, and a droopy mustache. He smelled like leather and looked like Wyatt Earp; he called everyone 'podna.'

'So, podna, you figure you can do my job better than me?' the sheriff said.

'Pardon me?'

The sheriff tossed a newspaper onto the desk in front of Book. It was the latest edition of *The Times of Marfa*, just out that morning. On the front page was the photo of Book that Sam Walker had taken the day before. The sheriff pointed a gnarly finger at the newspaper.

'Says you're a famous law professor, come to Marfa to figure out what happened to the lawyer. Says his death might have something to do with fracking.'

Book had already read the article. The desk clerk at the Paisano had handed the newspaper to Book on his way back up to his room after his morning run, when Book had advised him that they would be staying another night. (He hadn't yet broken the news to his intern.) His hunch had played out; Sam Walker couldn't resist a better front-page story than the roller

114

derby. But he picked up the paper anyway and read the article as if for the first time. He then folded the paper and set it on the desk. He looked at the sheriff.

'Nathan was my student intern four years ago. He wrote me a letter six days ago.'

Book handed Nathan's letter across the desk to the sheriff just as a Hispanic woman entered with two cups of coffee on a little tray with sugars and real cream. She placed the tray on the desk but eyed Book with suspicion. He held his hands up in mock surrender then pointed at Nadine, who practically dove for the coffee.

The sheriff said, '*Gracias*, Rosa,' without diverting his eyes from the envelope. He checked the postmark then removed the letter and stroked his mustache and randomly grunted as he read. The sheriff's office was spacious and manly and filled with weapons. Modern military-style rifles stood in a glass case; vintage Western-style rifles were mounted on the walls next to photos of the sheriff on horseback in calf-roping competitions. A police radio sat on a table behind the sheriff; voices of law enforcement personnel came over sporadically. The sheriff finally looked up from the letter.

'Pretty serious accusation.'

Book nodded.

'I reckon he meant Billy Bob Barnett.'

'Nathan's only client.'

'You talk to him? Billy Bob?'

'I will.'

'You figure what the lawyer says in this letter might be a motive for murder? Someone who didn't want that proof made public?'

'It's a developing theory.'

'You got any facts to back it up?'

'Not yet.'

The sheriff grunted again then eyed the envelope again. 'Postmarked same day he died.'

'How do you feel about coincidences?' Nadine asked.

'Reckon they happen.'

'Good.' She turned to Book. 'Can we go home now?'

She had been packed and ready to roll when he returned from his run.

'Tomorrow.'

'*Tomorrow?* I've got to study for my Crim Law final.'

'You're learning criminal law in the real world, Ms. Honeywell.'

'I feel safer in a classroom.'

The sheriff took his coffee, poured sugar and cream, and sipped. He addressed Nadine.

'Good call on the cream.'

Static then a loud voice came across the radio; the sheriff cocked his head that way.

'Rosa, tell the sheriff we got us a dead Mexican out Ninety past the Aerostat. Looks like he was walking north barefooted, got bit by a rattler. Leg's swollen up like a damn balloon.'

'Rosa doubles as the dispatcher,' the sheriff said.

He reached back and grabbed the mike. He clicked a button.

'Rusty, I'm in an important meeting with a couple of folks from Austin. I can't come running out there for a dead Mexi-can. Rosa's gonna call Border Patrol, get them to handle it. Their jurisdiction—"Securing America's Borders," like their motto says.'

The sheriff smiled, as if at an inside joke.

'Reporters?' Rusty said over the radio.

'What?' the sheriff said.

'That *Vanity Fair* reporter back in town? She's a cutie.'

'*Vanity Fair* reporter? Rusty, get your head out your butt and get to work. After the Border Patrol takes over there, get over to the Randolph spread, see about their rustling complaint. Probably just lost count and not cows.'

The sheriff clicked the button on the mike and exhaled.

'County pay don't attract Ph.D.s for deputies.'

He replaced the mike on the table and turned back to Book.

'I agree the timing's a mite suspicious, Professor, but we don't do murder in Marfa. We get calls on dead Mexicans, stranded motorists, stoned artists riding bicycles naked, that sort of thing. Our big crimes are drug busts, shipments coming north across the border—Presidio County stretches all the way south to the Rio Grande. But we don't get violent crimes like in the cities.'

'Did you know Nathan Jones?' Book asked.

'Nope.'

'You were at his funeral.'

'He was a Marfan. One of us. That's why I was there. That's why I cared.'

He sipped his coffee.

'What about you, Professor? Why do you care so much about Nathan Jones?'

'I owe him.'

The sheriff grunted. 'Well, I never crossed paths with him. Must not have done criminal defense work.'

'Oil and gas. Mostly gas.'

'Lot of that going around these days.'

He drank his coffee.

'I worked up the accident scene myself, Professor. No signs of foul play. Everything I saw said it was just an accident. So that was my official cause of death: accidental. We get half a dozen of these car crashes every year, main cause of death in Presidio County, right after old age and boredom.'

'Sheriff, have you ever heard anything about fracking contaminating the groundwater?'

'Nope. No brown water, no one's been lighting their tap water on fire like I seen on TV. We still drink the water, don't need to pay extra to have it served in a bottle.'

He held up his cup of coffee.

'Tap water.'

Nadine frowned at her coffee cup. The sheriff noticed and half smiled.

'But environmentalists been crawling all over West Texas, trying to prove up contamination, which would be a pretty serious matter around here.'

'Because of the water?'

'Because of the jobs. Fracking brought jobs to Marfa, Professor, good jobs for good ol' boys. When you got a family to feed, you don't worry about a little arsenic in your drinking water.'

Nadine's eyes got wide; the sheriff chuckled.

'Look, Professor, I don't want to drink frack fluids either, but I've never heard anyone complaining about contamination. And trust me, folks would call us—hell, we're the only thing resembling authority in Presidio County. Damn near four thousand square miles we cover.'

'Nathan said he had proof.'

'Find it.'

He replaced the letter inside the envelope and flipped it across the desk to Book.

'In the meantime, I wouldn't go waving that letter around town, Professor. You're threatening a lot of people's jobs. Folks around here don't abide outsiders stirring up trouble.'

'Not the first time I've heard that.'

'I don't want it to be the last time.'

The two men regarded each other for a long moment.

'May I see the autopsy report?' Book asked.

The sheriff grunted again, which apparently was a basic form of communication for him.

'Well, you see, Professor, there wasn't enough left to autopsy.'

'Fire got real hot, I expect.'

Book, Nadine, and the sheriff stood in the impound lot on the northern edge of town. The prairie stretched in front of

118

them all the way to the Davis Mountains. Nathan Jones's pickup truck—or what was left of it—sat before them on the dirt ground. The vehicle had been cut nearly in half and burned down to the steel frame. With Nathan Jones strapped in his seat. Book could hear his screams.

'Figure he fell asleep.'

'The rumble strip didn't wake him?'

Rumble strips ran along the shoulders of most Texas highways, grooves cut into the asphalt that cause a vehicle to vibrate if the driver veers out of his lane. Intended as a safety feature to alert inattentive drivers, they were dangerous to motorcyclists. Book always took care to avoid rumble strips while on the Harley.

'Apparently not. He must've been running ninety, ninety-five. Got sleepy, lost control, ran off the road, slammed into a pump jack on the passenger's side. Impact split the vehicle, ruptured the gas tank, knocked the pump jack loose. Between the oil and the gas, must've been one hell of a fire. Damn lucky the wind was down, or it might've burned half the county to dirt.'

The sheriff grunted.

'Bad way to go,' he said. 'Course, there ain't no good way. I got photos from that night, if you want to see them.'

'No, thanks.'

Book wanted to remember Nathan Jones as the law student he knew, not as a charred corpse.

'Where'd this happen?'

'East of town, north side of Highway Sixty-seven, just past the Marfa Mystery Lights Viewing Center.'

Every evening the hopeful gather at a man-made rock structure nine miles east of Marfa on the south side of Highway 67. When night falls, they stand at the low rock wall and face south. They stare out beyond the runways of the old Marfa Army Air Field and into the dark desert toward the Chinati

Mountains, focused on an area known as Mitchell Flat situated between the Marfa and Paisano passes.

They are hoping to see the lights.

Since 1883 when a young cowboy reported seeing mysterious lights between the passes, the 'Marfa Mystery Lights' have drawn tourists from around the country to that very spot. A few see the lights—red, green, orange, or yellow balls—hovering above the land, darting back and forth, even giving chase—but most do not. But that does not dissuade more tourists from coming. For ninety years, the mystery lights defined Marfa—until Donald Judd moved to town.

The Viewing Center sits on the south side of Highway 67. Nathan Jones died on the north side. Book slowed the Harley and made a U-turn. They rode slowly along the shoulder until they came to a spot where a wide swath of the tall prairie grass had been scorched bare, as if a wildfire had swept across the land. He stopped and cut the engine.

'He ran off the road here.'

They got off the Harley and followed the tire tracks across the burnt earth. Small pieces of debris from the vehicle littered the ground. The wind blew strong from Mexico.

'Veered off at an angle, then the truck slid sideways, hit the pump jack.'

They stood at the pump jack. It had not yet been repaired. Book could play out the scene in his head like a movie, Nathan Jones driving this dark road late at night, getting drowsy, falling asleep then jerking awake when the truck left the smooth asphalt and hit the rough ground, panicking, yanking hard on the wheel, the truck sliding sideways, slamming into the pump jack, exploding into flames . . . screaming.

'Nathan Jones died right here.'

The young man who had saved Book's life had lost his own life at the very spot where Book now stood. They remained quiet for a time. Then Book turned back to the highway. Nathan had come off the road a long way.

'He must've been going really fast.'

'Like James Dean,' Nadine said.

Chapter 11

They rode a hundred miles in silence. Nadine didn't ask to go home or complain that she was hungry. They rode east through Alpine then turned north and descended from the high desert plateau and onto the plains. The mountains disappeared behind them and were soon replaced by pump jacks as they rode above the great Permian Basin oil field where vast Texas fortunes had been made during the boom and lost during the bust. The land lay flat and bare and depressing, inhabited only by cell phone towers and power lines and thousands of black-and-yellow pump jacks, their horse heads bobbing up and down rhythmically, as relentless as the wind but more profitable, ten strokes pumping one barrel of black gold—and at $100 a barrel, it was black gold—up from the depths of the earth. The foul smell of the oil industry clung to the landscape like wet toilet paper. Nadine yelled over the engine noise and the wind.

'What's that smell?'

'Money.'

They came upon Odessa from the south; the view was no better from the north, east, or west. The town was nothing more than a glorified oil camp inhabited by one hundred thousand people. Oil fed them, clothed them, transported them, and sheltered them. Oil was their past, their present, and their future. Oil was their hope and their fear. Oil was their life.

'Yuk.'

'Don't say yuk, Ms. Honeywell. That oil subsidizes your education. A lot of those pump jacks belong to UT. The school has made about five billion dollars so far from this field.'

'Then why do they keep raising my tuition?'

Refineries, low-rent motels, and strip joints occupied both sides of the highway; one sign touted 'Joe's Steakhouse and Fabric Free Entertainment.' Only a few pickup trucks sat in Joe's parking lot. Either Joe's steaks were lousy or his sign too subtle for Odessa; the strip joint next door offered 'Totally Naked Gals,' and its parking lot was packed. Drilling rigs and casing pipes were stacked high on frontage lots, awaiting the next well hole to be punched into the earth. Eighteen-wheelers and pickup trucks crowded the lanes adjacent to the Harley; tattooed arms hung out the windows and hard-looking men gazed down at them. Book had visited inmates at the state penitentiary on several occasions; these men's eyes told the same story: they were doing hard time.

'Why's the land so bare?' Nadine asked after they had cleared the city limits.

Much of the land looked like a moonscape. No trees, no brush, no grass. Just gray dirt.

'Salt water, from the oil wells. Back in the old days, they pumped the salt water into unlined evaporation pits. The salt water seeped into the ground, killed the vegetation. That was thirty or forty years ago. Nothing's ever grown back, probably never will.'

'Place makes me want to throw up,' Nadine said. 'Why do people live here?'

'Jobs. When you don't have a job, you'll live anywhere for a job. Do anything for a job. You hear politicians on TV talking about the working class? This is it, Ms. Honeywell. High school educated workers. Most of their jobs were outsourced overseas for cheap labor, but the oil is here so these jobs are still here.'

'I don't want to live here.'

'You won't have to. You're educated. But never forget what these people's lives are like. Never forget that these people need jobs, too.'

Book accelerated the Harley east on Interstate 20 toward Midland as if trying to keep pace with the train running on the tracks that paralleled the interstate. A vulture circled overhead.

'Most people make an appointment.'

'We were in the neighborhood.'

'You were in Marfa. I get the paper.'

From a distance, the buildings of downtown Midland seemed to pop up out of the prairie like yucca plants. Midland was known for oil and gas and George W. Bush. He had grown up here. When he left the White House for the final time, his first stop back in Texas was Midland; twenty thousand locals turned out to welcome him home. Then George W. retired to Dallas.

Thomas A. Dunn had also grown up in Midland. He left for college and law school at UT then returned home for good. He was now sixty-three years old and the senior partner at The Dunn Law Firm, which employed one hundred thirty lawyers and maintained offices in Midland, Lubbock, Amarillo, and Marfa. From a corner office on the twentieth floor, Tom Dunn oversaw a legal empire that spanned West Texas. He was an oil and gas lawyer, and West Texas was oil and gas country. The Permian Basin covered seventeen counties and seventy-five thousand square miles; an estimated thirty billion barrels remained to be extracted. It was a very good time to be in the oil and gas business. Or a lawyer to the oil and gas business. And Tom Dunn was all business, the kind of lawyer who probably had sex by the billable hour. Book didn't know Mrs. Dunn, but he felt a twinge of sympathy for her nonetheless.

'Saw you at Nathan's funeral,' he said.

'He worked for me. Nathan was a good young lawyer, billed his quota every month without complaint.'

'What's the quota for young lawyers these days, Mr. Dunn, so I can tell my students?'

'Three thousand hours a year.'

Nadine gasped. 'OMG.'

Dunn chuckled. 'A common reaction among our new associates.'

'That's what, two hundred fifty billable hours a month?' Book said. 'Doesn't seem realistic.'

'Reality is, Professor, I start billing when I wake up in the morning and stop when I fall asleep that night. I'm always thinking about my clients. And that's what I'm paid to do: think.'

'It's easier once you can rationalize it, isn't it?'

'Much.'

Book had met many senior partners at many large law firms; when they visited the school, the famous Professor Bookman was always part of the dog-and-pony show, a circus act to attract endowments. Senior partners were more Wall Street than Main Street, more businessmen—every senior partner he had met had been male—than lawyers. Perhaps the law was just a business these days, and lawyers were in the business of buying and selling the law. Some firms boasted thousands of lawyers and billions in revenues. Billable hours were inventory, and young lawyers fungible commodities. Book had never regretted his decision to forgo the private practice of law. He hadn't gone to law school to be a businessman. He had gone to be a hero like his dad, but wielding the law instead of a gun.

'So you rode four hundred miles on that Harley to investigate Nathan's death?'

'With me on the back,' Nadine said.

'That's not why I came.'

'Newspaper said that's why you came.'

'Nathan wrote a letter to me.'

Book handed Nathan's letter to Dunn. He sat down behind his desk, put on reading glasses, removed the letter from the envelope, and read. Book pulled out the funeral photo and circled Dunn's face, as he had circled the faces of all the other locals they had met. He then surveyed Dunn's office. The same interior decorator must design every law office in America, or at least every one he had been in. The furniture, the rugs on the floor and the art on the wall, even the photos scattered about seemed to be from a stock lawyer template. Perhaps lawyers were comforted by conformity, soothed by sameness, as they fought boredom and billed hours. Book could not imagine himself in Tom Dunn's chair. Dunn removed his glasses and exhaled heavily, as if he had just learned that his wife was cheating on him; or worse, that she had embezzled funds from their joint bank account.

'Nathan wrote this?'

'He did. I've learned that Billy Bob Barnett was the client he referenced.'

'Professor, I don't know what Nathan thought he found, but it wasn't evidence of groundwater contamination. Frack well holes are encased in redundant layers of steel and cement. Billy Bob doesn't cut corners with his drilling.' He chuckled. 'Hell, Billy Bob's a walking Aggie joke—he's too dumb to be a crook.'

'But he's rich enough to hire your firm. How much does he pay you each year?'

'That's confidential, Professor.'

But he couldn't restrain a thin smile.

'Eighteen million last fiscal year.'

'That buys a lot of loyalty from a lawyer.'

'Part of the job description.'

'Nathan said in his letter that he brought your client's contamination to your attention.'

126

'He didn't.'

'Wonder why he said he did?'

'I don't know.'

'May I look in his office?'

'You know better than that, Professor. Client confidentiality.'

Tom Dunn stood and walked to the window. He was a tall, gray-haired man who seemed as hard as the land. He gestured at West Texas beyond the plate glass.

'See all those pump jacks pumping oil out of the ground twenty-four/seven? You know what that means around here, Professor? Jobs. Midland–Odessa, we're booming again. One hundred and fifty thousand producing wells in the Permian Basin. Thirty-six billion a year in revenues. That pays a lot of wages to a lot of workers. But not that long ago those pump jacks were still, the wells shut in, workers sitting idle, oil field equipment rusting on the side of the interstate. Old wells and low prices, couldn't produce enough oil to make economic sense. Billy Bob changed all that.'

'How?'

'Fracking.'

'On oil wells?'

'You bet. See, he grew up in Odessa, his dad was a roughneck. Billy Bob decided he wanted to own the oil not just work the oil. So he went to A&M, got a degree in petroleum engineering. Learned about hydraulic fracturing. Fracking's been around sixty years, but no one thought about reworking these old oil wells with fracking, going deeper, going horizontal, to open up the reservoir to let more oil out faster. Billy Bob did. Now everyone is. Then he started fracking for natural gas before anyone else. He knows more about fracking than anyone in Texas, which means anyone in the world. Fracking started right out there.'

He turned from the window.

'Point is, Professor, folks around here are real happy to have work again. They need the jobs. They're not going to take kindly to some liberal law professor messing with their livelihoods.'

'Is that a threat?'

'An observation.'

'I'm not liberal.'

'You're sure as hell not conservative.'

'What's Billy Bob?'

'Rich.'

'He's taking people's land for his pipelines.'

'Which is perfectly legal in Texas, as you well know.'

'Legal doesn't mean right.'

'Please, Professor, this isn't first-year law school.'

'I heard the landowners aren't too happy.'

Tom Dunn shrugged. 'Hell, I wouldn't be either.'

'Nathan was handling those lawsuits. Think one of the land-owners might've run him off the road because of that?'

Dunn shook his head. 'Too much trouble. If they wanted to kill Nathan, they would've just shot him. This is West Texas, Professor. Everyone's got a gun. Or ten.'

'Mind if I meet with your client?'

'Yes, I do mind.'

'Well, since we're not opposing lawyers in litigation or a transaction, I guess I can meet with him whether you mind or not.'

'I'll let him know to expect you.'

Book stood. 'Thanks for your time, Mr. Dunn.'

'Professor, why do you care so much about Nathan Jones?'

'I owe him.'

'Must be a big debt, to come way out here. That's why I avoid owing anyone.'

'Even your biggest client?'

Book walked to the door; Nadine followed. But Book stopped and turned back.

'You know, Mr. Dunn, if a lawyer aids and abets a criminal violation of the federal environmental laws, he gets to share a prison cell with his client. Most lawyers aren't willing to go to jail for their clients. I wonder how much money a client would have to pay a lawyer to get him to risk prison time. What do you think, maybe eighteen million a year?'

Dunn fixed Book with a searing glare, as if he were a young associate who had failed to bill his monthly quota—for the second consecutive month.

'First, I'm not in your Con Law class, Professor, so don't lecture me. And second, I hope that's a law professor's hypothetical fact situation and not an accusation because if you're accusing me of a crime, I'd have to pick up that phone and call the UT law school dean and express my displeasure, which might have repercussions for the professor making those false and defamatory accusations.'

'I'm tenured, Mr. Dunn.'

'I'm pissed, Professor.'

'And Nathan's dead.'

'I didn't kill him, and neither did Billy Bob. The sheriff said it was an accident.'

'Then neither you nor your client has anything to fear.'

'From what?'

'Not what. Whom.'

'From whom?'

'Me.'

'I thought that went well,' Nadine said. 'Is that what you call stirring the pot?'

'It is.'

'Do you do that often?'

'I do.'

'Has anyone ever taken offense?'

'Define "taken offense."'

'Attempted injury upon your body.'

'They have.'

'Was there gunfire?'

129

'On occasion.'

'How many occasions?'

'A few.'

'Define "a few."'

'Seven.'

'People shot at you seven times?'

'Maybe eight.'

His intern sighed heavily. 'So in the newspaper reports, I'll be the "innocent bystander caught in the crossfire."'

'I promised to protect you, Ms. Honeywell.'

Sit on a bench in downtown Austin for five minutes and five panhandlers would've already hit on you. Not so in downtown Midland. Law and order—mostly order—prevailed. They sat on a bench outside the Dunn Building, taking a breather before riding back to Marfa. The West Texas wind funneled between the buildings and threatened to blow them over. Pedestrians leaned into the wind, making it seem as if the earth had tilted on its axis. Young men in suits and women in dresses walked past and into the building, apparently lawyers returning from lunch.

'Thomas A. Dunn,' Nadine said. 'The "A" must be for asshole.'

'Fortunately, it's not a crime in Texas, or we'd have a lot more lawyers in prison.'

'Professor, why didn't you ever practice law? You could've been another Tom Dunn.'

'That's why.'

Book pointed up, as if to the corner office on the twentieth floor.

'I knew that life wasn't for me. Working inside. Wearing suits. Counting my life away by the billable hour.'

'He looks rich.'

'I'm sure he is. Each lawyer chooses the life he or she wants, Ms. Honeywell, just as you will have to choose. I chose a life on a Harley instead of in a Mercedes-Benz.'

130

'You ever regret that choice?'

'Only when it rains.'

She smiled.

'You could've worked at a nonprofit.'

'It's called teaching law school.'

'Hey, I read about those forgivable loans.'

'They made Twitter?'

'Oh, yeah.'

'Well, I didn't get one.'

'You could've done legal aid for the needy.'

'That's why we're here—to use our legal skills to aid someone in need.'

'But the person in need is dead.'

'So he is.'

'Professor, Tom Dunn is an asshole, but he's right: Nathan's death was an accident.'

'Are you just saying that so I'll take you home?'

'I want to go home, but I believe it was an accident.'

'Why?'

'The sheriff doesn't seem like a fool. He's investigated a lot of car accidents. If Nathan was murdered, he'd know it. And why would Billy Bob murder his own lawyer? For money? He's rich enough to pay eighteen million in legal fees to Dunn. To stay out of prison? How many rich guys go to prison? He'd blame any contamination on his employees, the company would pay a fine, and he'd stay in business. And if Nathan had proof, he would've shown it to his wife or his best friend. Professor, you're emotionally invested in this case. You're not looking at it objectively. Because Nathan saved your life.'

'He saved my life, but I wasn't there to save his. I owe it to him to find out how he died.'

'You did. Nathan Jones died in an accident.'

'He shouldn't have died that way.'

'And my sister shouldn't have died of cancer when she was eight.'

'*Eight?*'

His intern's voice cracked. 'It destroyed my parents. Their marriage. Our family.'

She paused.

'After she died, we never had a real Christmas tree. My mother bought an artificial one.'

Book's instinct was to embrace his intern, but he resisted.

'I'm sorry, Ms. Honeywell. That's just not . . .'

'Fair? One thing I've learned, Professor, life is unfair. I couldn't make it fair for my sister, and you can't make it fair for Nathan.'

Or his own mother.

'Professor Bookman?'

Book looked up to a young man smiling down at him. He stood.

'I'm Tim Egan. I took your class five years ago. What brings you to Midland?'

'Nathan Jones.'

The smile left his face. 'Bad deal. He was a good guy.'

'You work at the Dunn firm?'

'We all do.'

'Oil and gas?'

'Yep.'

'Fracking?'

'Fracking *is* the oil and gas business today.'

'You know anything about groundwater contamination caused by fracking?'

'Nope. And I don't want to know. I do what I'm told and keep my mouth shut.'

Book's thoughts of disapproval must have registered on his face.

'Look, Professor, we're not cops. Our clients hire us to do their bidding, not to turn them in to the Feds.'

'I take it you didn't go to law school to make the world a better place?'

'I went to law school to make money.'

Disapproval turned to—

'Don't look so disgusted, Professor. I graduated with a hundred thousand dollars in student loan debt, money I borrowed so UT law professors can make three hundred thousand a year teaching two classes a semester. I couldn't pay my loans off working at a nonprofit. So you guys are as much to blame for the state of the legal profession as we are.'

'What grade did I give you?'

'B.'

'I should've given you a C.'

Nadine had scooted down the bench when the lawyer had engaged the professor. She now smiled. The professor was growing on her.

'*Nadine?*'

She turned to the familiar voice and saw a familiar face.

'*Sylvia?*'

She stood, and they hugged. Sylvia Unger had graduated law school the year before. She was holding a venti Starbucks cup.

'There's a Starbucks here?'

'Right around the corner.'

'Oh, thank God.'

Nadine fought the urge to snatch Sylvia's cup and suck the coffee into her caffeine-depleted body.

'I thought you wanted to work in Dallas?'

Sylvia shrugged. 'No jobs in Dallas, so I came to Midland.'

'You still dating that lawyer in Dallas?'

'He dumped me for an SMU cheerleader.'

Nadine shook her head. 'Guys say they want brains and personality, but what they really want are big tits and a tight ass.'

'He left me for a male cheerleader.'

Nadine groaned. 'I hate it when they do that. Leaving you for another girl is bad enough, but for another boy?'

'Tell me.'

Sylvia was not from San Francisco, so it was probably her first experience with romancing a gay guy. Her expression said she had not gotten over him. Nadine thought it best to change the subject.

'You like it out here?'

'Beggars can't be choosers.'

The wind tried to blow Sylvia's dress over her head. She clamped her arms down both sides of her body like a vise.

'Does the wind ever stop blowing?' Nadine asked.

'No. It doesn't. And the oil smell never goes away.'

'Is the practice of law fun?'

'*Fun?*' Sylvia almost laughed. 'Nadine, "fun" and "the practice of law" do not belong in the same sentence.'

'What kind of work are you doing?'

'Estate planning.'

'Do you like it?'

'It's a living. So what are you doing here?'

Nadine aimed a thumb at the professor. 'Working for Bookman.'

'Wait—you're not his intern?'

'Uh . . . yes, I am.'

'Be careful.'

'He's a nice guy.'

'He's crazy. He's got a death wish or something.'

'We rode out here on his Harley.'

'See?'

'Sylvia, did you know Nathan Jones?'

'We met. I'm up here, he's in Marfa. Was. He seemed like a nice guy. I didn't work with him, but he must've been a good lawyer, working for the firm's biggest client.'

'Billy Bob Barnett?'

'Yeah. What are you and Bookman doing in Midland?'

'We came to see Tom Dunn.'

Sylvia frowned. 'The dark lord. He's so creepy. When he talks to me, he talks to my breasts.'

'I noticed. And I barely have breasts.'

'It's just the thought of it, for guys like Dunn.'

They shared a giggle.

'I didn't see you at Nathan's funeral yesterday,' Nadine said. 'Did you go?'

Sylvia shook her head. 'Dunn said he was going for the firm, told us to stay here and bill hours. He's sentimental like that.'

'Nathan wrote a letter to the professor, said there was some funny business going on with fracking. Is there?'

Sylvia shrugged. 'I don't know. Those guys in the oil and gas department, they're like a fraternity. They don't talk to us girls in estate planning. And the first thing you learn in the practice is to not ask questions and to keep your mouth shut.'

'Nathan must have missed that class. Anyone else who might know if anything odd was going on?'

'Becky.'

'Who's she?'

'Nathan's secretary.'

'Nathan treated all the girls like sisters instead of secretaries,' Becky Oakes said. 'Most lawyers treat us like slaves.'

Becky had been Nathan's secretary for the entirety of his legal career.

'Becky, did you know about the letter Nathan sent to me?'

Nadine had passed on a tour of the Petroleum Museum in Midland, so after a quick stop at the Starbucks—Nadine had drunk a venti frappuccino on the ride back—

'Don't spill that down my saddlebags,' Book had cautioned her.

'Nobody likes a tidy freak,' she had responded.

—they had returned to Marfa and caught Becky as she was leaving for the day. She glanced up and down the sidewalk then lowered her voice.

'He told me about it. What he thought was happening, with the groundwater.'

'Did you tell anyone?'

'No. I swear. No one.' She hesitated. 'Except my husband.'

'What does he do? Your husband.'

'He's a roughneck. For Billy Bob.'

Chapter 12

Padre's Marfa on West El Paso Street across from the Godbold Feed Store had once been the place to die for in Marfa. It used to be a funeral home. It was now a restaurant/bar/live music venue. Outside, the white adobe gave it the appearance of an old Spanish mission; inside, the wood bar and neon signs gave it the appearance of an old Texas honkytonk. Book fully expected his intern to break out latex gloves, but she apparently satisfied her sanitary concerns by wiping down the entire table and then her glass, utensils, and chair. They sat at a table along the wall opposite the bar; Sean Lennon sang onstage.

'He's John Lennon's son.'

'Who's that?'

'Ms. Honeywell, please tell me you're not serious.'

Her innocent expression.

'What?'

'John Lennon? The Beatles?'

'Wait, don't tell me. He's dead.'

'He is, shot by an insane fan in nineteen eighty.'

'I wasn't born until nineteen eighty-nine.'

'Still, you haven't heard of Rock Hudson, James Dean, Elizabeth Taylor, Donald Judd, Andy Warhol, or John Lennon?'

'If it's not on Twitter, I don't need to know it. And, Professor, I can name a dozen people everyone my age knows but you've never heard of.'

'True enough, Ms. Honeywell. But what about the events of the day? What's happening in China, North Korea, the Middle East . . . or the east and west coasts of America?'

'I especially don't want to know that stuff.'

'Why not?'

'Because it's all bad stuff. Last time I watched the news on TV, I had to get a prescription for an antidepressant. A mass murder at an elementary school . . . politicians pushing the country over a fiscal cliff . . . suburban stay-at-home moms reading porn, which really creeped me out, by the way. Who wants to know that stuff? My generation turned off the TV, Professor.'

'Willful ignorance.'

''Willful ignorance' is a legal term, also known as 'conscious indifference,' for intentionally not knowing some fact, typically CEOs intentionally avoiding knowledge that their companies' subcontractors produce their apparel in Asian sweatshops or that nicotine is addictive, thus allowing the CEOs to testify under oath, 'I didn't know,' when in fact the correct response was, 'I didn't want to know.'

'Exactly,' his intern said. 'We live our lives that way. It's safer.'

Book gestured at her hand sanitizer. 'You sanitize your hands and yourself from all the bad things in life.'

'What's wrong with that?'

'You're not experiencing the world you live in.'

'It's your world. Not ours. Your generation screwed it up. Not us.'

'You could change the world. Make it a better place.'

She appeared bemused. 'Please, Professor.'

'You're a law student.'

'I'm in law school because I possess the two attributes required to gain admission to the finest law schools in the country: A, I'm book smart, which allowed me to score high on the LSAT'—the Law School Admissions Test—'and B, my daddy can pay the tuition. Anyone with those two attributes can get into any law school today. You don't have to know what's happening in the world . . . or care.'

She was right. And a typical law student. A few students like Ms. Garza and perhaps Mr. Stanton seemed engaged in the world outside the law school, but only a few. Most were singularly focused on grades: those in the top ten percent of their class would have jobs upon graduation; those who were not would not. So they had no desire or time to keep up with current events. They did not watch the news or read newspapers. They read casebooks. Torts. Contracts. Property. Civil Procedure. Criminal Procedure. Con Law. For three years, the study of law constituted life.

'Well, John Lennon was a musician, singer, and songwriter, one of the best ever.'

'If you say so.'

They had first tried the outdoor patio with Christmas lights strung overhead and gravel underfoot and Willie Nelson on the jukebox, but the tables were taken by artists on iPads and hippies past their prime and a young woman who looked out of place in a glittery red cocktail dress; her black cowboy boots said she was making a fashion statement. A pit bull wearing a red bandanna lounged beneath her long crossed legs; a metal sculpture of a sombrero-clad mariachi stood behind her. The dance floor and adjacent game room with pool tables, shuffleboard, and foosball were crowded with young women in short-shorts and young men in jeans and boots and T-shirts. Of course, Book also wore jeans, boots, and a T-shirt. But he was a skinny law professor; they were thick-bodied roughnecks who worked the fracking rigs. Some wore red jumpsuits with *Barnett Oil and Gas* stenciled across the back. Their waitress was an artist; waiting tables was her night job. Book had ordered the tuna melt on sourdough, a cold pickle, and iced tea. Nadine went for chips and queso, frito pie with cheese and onions, chili cheese fries, a chocolate soda, and a moon pie. Book circled Becky Oakes's face in the funeral photo then consulted his pocket notebook.

'What did we learn today, Ms. Honeywell?'

'Are we going to have a pop quiz every night, Professor?'

'We are indeed.'

She exhaled dramatically.

'A, Tom Dunn is a creep.'

'Agreed. What else?'

'B, either he's a liar or Nathan Jones was a liar.'

'Nathan said he showed his proof to Dunn, but Dunn denied it.'

'My money's on Dunn. He's the liar.'

'Agreed.'

'We talked to the sheriff, Nathan's senior partner, and his secretary, but we uncovered no proof of contamination or evidence of murder. All we have is coincidence.'

'Nathan's wife seemed convinced that he was murdered.'

'She's emotional about his death. Which is to be expected. But we can't be. What did you always say in class? "We're lawyers. We must keep our heads while everyone around us is losing theirs."'

'You took my class?'

'Last year.'

'At least you listened.'

'Can I eat my moon pie now?'

From across the room, Jimmy John Dale watched the professor and the girl named Nadine eating dinner. You don't generally see white girls eating moon pies like that. He sat at a table with five other roughnecks who also worked for Billy Bob Barnett; they had just gotten off their shift and still wore their red

140

jumpsuits. While he was watching Nadine, they were watching another woman across the room.

'I'd love to jump her bones,' Mitch said.

'I'd love to beat the shit out of her,' Sonny said. 'She's trying to shut down fracking, take our jobs.'

'Still, Carla's got a great body.'

Mitch was always practical like that. Jimmy John rubbed his temples. The headache was coming back.

'Can we go home now?'

'No.'

The band took a break. Book was watching his intern devour the moon pie when a young woman walked up and sat down at their table across from Book and next to Nadine and scooted in close. Nadine frowned at her then moved her chair over a bit. Book read her shirt: *Fracking is for Gas Holes*—

'Funny,' he said.

—and she read his Tommy Bahama shirt: *I Plead the Fifth* with a bottle of rum.

'Yours, too.'

She seemed familiar. He had seen her before. He looked at the funeral photo in front of him. She was the young woman standing off to the side during the burial of Nathan Jones.

'Professor Bookman, I'm Carla Kent. I need to talk to you.'

'I'm listening.'

'Nathan came to me.'

'Where?'

'My teepee at El Cosmico.'

'You have your own teepee?'

'Long-term stay.'

'What did he come to you about?'

'Fracking.'

'Why you?'

'Everyone in town knows me. I'm trying to shut down fracking.'

'You're an environmentalist?'

'From Santa Fe. Professor, Nathan was scared. Now he's dead. Because he knew something he wasn't supposed to know.'

'What?'

'Billy Bob's fracking is contaminating the Igneous Aquifer, the sole water source for this whole area—Marfa, Fort Davis, Alpine. Nathan said he had proof. They killed him to prevent that proof from becoming public.'

'It was an accident,' Nadine said.

'It was murder.'

'Billy Bob Barnett is a murderer?' Book asked.

'He is.' She seemed deadly serious. 'Professor, help me put that bastard in prison where he belongs.'

'Do you have any evidence of murder?'

'No.'

'Did you see Nathan's proof of contamination?'

'No.'

'Ms. Kent, I'm not here to shut down fracking. I'm just trying to find out how my student died.'

'And I'm trying to tell you how he died—he was murdered!'

Her emotions resided close to the surface. She took a deep breath to gather herself.

'Professor, I cared about Nathan.'

'You were at his funeral.'

'And Nathan cared about this land. And the people who live on it. The water they drink. He didn't know what to do, but he said he knew someone who would help us—he said *us*—a professor at UT. I thought he meant a petroleum engineering professor. Not a law professor.'

'I have other skills.'

'The paper said you came here for Nathan.'

'I might've come for the art.'

'Can I see it?'

'The art?'

'The letter.'

'Ms. Kent . . .'

'You showed it to everyone else in town.'

'That's true,' Nadine said.

Book gave his intern a sharp look then handed the letter to Carla. She read it.

'See, he said his client is contaminating the aquifer. He meant Billy Bob. And now he's dead.' She checked the post-mark on the envelope. 'Died the same day he mailed the letter. That seem odd to you?'

'Oh, God,' Nadine said. 'Don't tell me you don't believe in coincidences?'

'Not that much of a coincidence. Professor, Nathan said he hadn't put all the pieces together yet, said he'd come back to me when he did. Maybe he did. Maybe he put the pieces together. Maybe Billy Bob killed him. Professor, work with me. Please.'

'I'm sorry, Ms. Kent. I work alone.'

'Then why'd you bring me?' Nadine said.

'I mean, alone with an intern. This is Nadine Honeywell.'

'If you didn't come to Marfa to find the truth,' Carla said, 'then why'd you come?'

'To fish.'

'*Fish? Where?* There's no water between here and the Rio Grande, and if you eat fish from that cesspool you'll die.'

Carla now gave him a sharp look; she stood.

'Don't toy with me, Professor.'

She marched over to the bar. Book watched after her. She was an attractive woman, lean with a low body mass index, no older than thirty, with dark hair and eyes. She wore tight jeans, boots, and the T-shirt. She looked tough.

'Don't worry,' Nadine said. 'You won't be romancing a lesbian.'

'I don't plan on romancing her, but how do you know she's not a lesbian?'

143

'Because I attract lesbians. I don't know why. But she wasn't attracted to me. She was to you. She'll be back.'

Nadine sipped her soda.

'Why'd you play coy with her?'

'Because I don't know her.'

Nadine nodded at the bar.

'Everyone else does.'

The locals at the bar regarded Carla as if she had a communicable disease; she was apparently well known but not welcome. She stood alone.

'Come on,' Sonny said. 'Let's have some fun with Carla.'

'I wouldn't do that if I was you,' Jimmy John said.

'Why not?'

'Looks like she's friends with the professor.'

'What professor?'

'Don't you read the newspaper?'

'Hell, no.'

Jimmy John pointed with his forehead in the professor's direction.

'Him?' Sonny said. 'That skinny-ass guy she was talking to, he's a professor?'

'Yep.'

'That long hair, he looks like one of them queer artists. We're supposed to be scared of him?'

Sonny grabbed his Lone Star longneck and headed over to Carla at the bar. Mitch and the others followed. Jimmy John popped two Advil and chased them with a beer.

'We'll get started on the Welch brief tonight,' Book said to his intern. But his eyes were on the bar where several roughnecks wearing red *Barnett Oil and Gas* jumpsuits and holding longnecks walked up and bookended Carla. They said something to her, and she said something to them. It was obviously not polite conversation. She got in one man's face and said what

144

appeared to be the F-word and not 'fracking.' She turned to leave, but the roughnecks grabbed her arms. She struggled against their holds. Her eyes went to Book. She no longer looked tough.

He groaned then pushed himself up and walked over to Carla and the roughnecks. They were bigger, stronger, younger, and drunker.

'How about a dance, Ms. Kent?'

'I'd love to.'

She again tried to pull away, but the roughnecks maintained their hold.

'The lady wants to dance,' Book said.

The biggest roughneck held up one finger and said, 'A, she ain't no lady.'

A second finger.

'Two, there ain't no music playing.'

A third finger.

'And D, this ain't—'

'No, no, no,' Book said. 'You either say "three" or "C," not "D." D would be four fingers.'

'Oh.'

The roughneck held up four fingers.

'And C, this ain't none of your goddamned business, Pocahontas.'

Book sighed. The Indian thing again. A few more rough-necks holding longnecks joined the party. They had Book pinned to the bar.

'Oh, shit.'

Those big brutes would beat up the professor for sure. He really was crazy. Nadine searched the crowded room and spotted a familiar face. She stuffed the rest of the moon pie into her mouth then jumped up and hurried over to the young man sitting alone at a table. His eyes turned up to her; she pointed at the professor.

145

'He needs help! Do something!'

Her words sounded garbled through the moon pie. She swallowed and tried again.

'He needs help! Do something!'

The Border Patrol agent named Wesley Crum offered only a lame shrug.

'No jurisdiction. He's an Injun, not a Mexican. Call someone at the Bureau of Indian Affairs.'

He thought that was funny.

Book pointed a finger as he counted the men in the red jumpsuits.

'One, two, three, four . . . Are you with them? . . . Five. You know, this really isn't a fair fight.'

'So?'

'So there are only five of you.'

'He's a funny Injun,' the big roughneck to his right said.

Five men, five moves, five seconds max. Right to left down the line. They would go down like dominoes. Book needed the big roughneck to his right to start the action, so he said, 'And you're an asshole.'

The roughneck reached for Book with his non-beer-holding hand and took a step closer. That was a mistake. Book drove his left knee into the man's groin . . . he went down to his knees . . . then a right-hand throat strike to the second man . . . he gagged and fell backwards . . . now a left-hand back fist to the third man's temple . . . he stumbled back and grabbed his head . . . then a reverse punch to the fourth man's face . . . he collapsed to the floor . . . and finally a—but the fifth man stepped back out of range.

Book gestured with his fingers for him to come closer. He shook his head. Book gestured again. The man's eyes turned from Book to behind Book. He spun around just in time to see Nadine slam a beer bottle over the bald head of another roughneck holding a pool cue as if he were about to clock Book in the head. The roughneck's eyes rolled back, and he crumpled to the floor. Nadine held the broken beer bottle in one hand and the chocolate soda in the other. She sucked from the straw.

'Can we go home now?'

Carla's eyes went from Book to the roughnecks groaning and holding various parts of their bodies and then back to Book.

'I thought you're a law professor?'

'I said I had other skills.'

Her eyes twinkled. 'Are those all your physical skills?'

They shared a long gaze, which was not interrupted when a meaty hand clamped down on Book's right arm and a gruff voice said, 'Time for you to leave, buddy.'

Book maintained his gaze with Carla but grabbed the man's hand and turned his wrist counterclockwise and dug his fingers into the man's palm pressure point until his knees buckled and he went down to the floor.

'I'll leave when I damn well please.'

He broke eye contact with Carla, released the man, and then turned to Nadine.

'Let's leave, Ms. Honeywell.'

'Town?'

'This bar.'

They headed to the door, but he heard Carla's voice from behind.

'I'll take a rain check on that dance, Professor.'

From across the bar, Jimmy John shook his head. He hated to be an 'I told you so,' but Sonny and Mitch never listened. The girl named Nadine was kind of cute and good with a beer bottle to boot.

'Is it unconstitutional under the Fourth Amendment's prohibition against unreasonable searches and seizures for the police to draw a suspect's blood without consent?'

Nadine Honeywell typed on the laptop, but she couldn't focus on the Welch brief because her body still tingled with fear and excitement and adrenaline—she had actually smashed a beer bottle over that big brute's bald head! OMG! She had never done anything like that in her entire life! Normally, when faced with such a physical conflict, she would have grabbed the moon pie and chocolate soda and dove under the table and hidden from the danger. But the professor's kung fu butt-kicking had shifted her adrenal glands into high gear, and she had just acted out all her fantasies—well, not the one with that tall guy at the fish shop in San Francisco, where she's at home cooking in her apron and nothing else and he delivers a big salmon and one thing leads to another and soon their bodies are covered in extra virgin olive oil and . . . she blew out a breath . . . God, that's a great fantasy . . . but the one where she wasn't a timid law student afraid of life who cowered before conflict and ran from . . . okay, okay, we've been through that too many times, just let it go . . . Where was she? Oh, yeah, she hadn't even made a conscious decision to do it; she had just done it. She saw him advance on the professor from behind with the pool cue and knew he was going to hit the professor. He could have been killed. Her future flashed before her eyes: the professor is dead; she's stuck in Marfa; no one to call but her father; he flies in from San Francisco; he is not happy with his daughter. That dire prospect gave her the incentive to grab the bottle and swing it as hard as she could at the guy's head. She still couldn't believe she had knocked him unconscious. But she was always strong for her size.

It felt really good. Not to be afraid.

She sat propped up in Elizabeth Taylor's bed. The professor had put her to work on the Welch brief then gone next door to Rock Hudson's room to return phone calls. Cell phone reception was better on the outdoor patio.

★   ★   ★

148

Joanie had left three messages for Book at the Paisano. He called his sister back from the rooftop patio. The sky was dark and the stars bright. And a young lawyer was dead. Did he fall asleep at the wheel or was he run off the road? Was his death an accident or a murder? Was it just a coincidence that he died the same day he mailed the letter? And the most perplexing question of all: how do you find a dead man's truth?

Chapter 13

At dawn, Book exited the courtyard at the Paisano and ran south on Highland Avenue past the Andy Warhol and John Chamberlain exhibits and the railroad tracks just before the crossing arms came down and a train roared through town and the yellow corrugated buildings at the Border Patrol sector headquarters and the sign that read 'Chinati Foundation' and the teepees at El Cosmico—

Carla Kent stood under the shower and let the water wash over her body. The air was cold, but the water was hot. The open-air community bathhouse had a roof and partial wood sides that provided some modesty if one were modest, but it offered a majestic view of the mountain ranges that surrounded the Marfa Plateau and Cathedral Rock to the east, a mountain peak shaped like the Great Sphinx. She loved dawn in the desert. An unspoiled land she would fight to protect from fracking. It was her mission in life. That and to see Billy Bob Barnett in prison or dead. Preferably dead. She rinsed the shampoo from her hair; when she opened her eyes, she saw a lone runner heading south on Highway 67 that fronted El Cosmico.

The professor.

—and a strange configuration of large concrete boxes aligned in an open field parallel to the road; his breath fogged in the morning air. He cleared civilization and ran on the strip of asphalt cutting through the desert; not a single car passed him. He thought of the Comanche when they had roamed this same desert; they accepted it on its own terms with no need to make it something more. Then Hanna's train had come and changed the desert and their lives. He felt the desert changing him—and he knew it would change him more before he rode the Harley home. He ran several more miles then turned back and headed north. But he stopped to observe the shadows cast onto the yellow prairie grass by the rising sun off the concrete boxes.

It was oddly mesmerizing.

When he arrived back at the hotel, he did not enter the lobby. The Paisano did not serve breakfast, so he continued up the sidewalk past the small Chamber of Commerce office and Consuelo's Bookkeeping and Tax Service and then turned west on Lincoln Street. Half a block down, he ducked into the small courtyard of SqueezeMarfa, the sheriff's favorite breakfast spot. He went inside and ordered a Strawberry Banana Cabana smoothie with nonfat vanilla yogurt then sat outside and pondered the life and death of Nathan Jones.

His life was short.

His death was fast.

Was it murder?

Or just an accident?

Book wanted Nathan's death to be something more than an accident—just as he had wanted his father's death to be something more than a drug-addicted homeless man grabbing his

151

service gun and shooting him. Perhaps that was the human ego at work: his father had been important in his life; *ergo*, his life should warrant an important ending. Nathan had saved his life; therefore, his life should warrant a more important ending than a car accident.

But that was not life.

Life seemed to be one continuous accident. Birth—where, when, and to whom—is just an accident of fate, a genetic lottery. Win that lottery, and you're born in a first-world country with opportunities in life and a life expectancy of seventy-eight years or more. Lose, and you're born in a third-world country with no opportunities and a life expectancy of forty-eight years or less. Death—early, late, natural, violent—no matter your station in life, death would come to you. Would it come at age five, thirty-five, or seventy-five? Would it come by crime or disease or old age? Was that destiny or luck? God's will or man's mistake? In the end, it didn't really matter. It is what happens between birth and death that matters. That makes us matter. As Ms. Roberts had said in class, 'Do we matter? Or are we just matter?' And so Book was left to wonder:

Had Nathan Jones's life mattered?

Had Ben Bookman's life mattered?

Would his own life matter?

Book entered the hotel and stopped at the front desk.

'Another night, please.'

'Yes, sir, Professor,' the desk clerk said. 'But Miss Honeywell won't be happy.'

He took breakfast back to Nadine—a large coffee, sandwich baguette (scrambled eggs, Swiss cheese, and ham on a toasted demi-baguette), and a waffle with chocolate syrup and whipped cream. He figured that would hold her until lunch. He had granola and more yogurt.

But she wasn't in her room.

152

Fear shot through him like a bullet. Perhaps the bald guy she had clocked at Padre's had come looking for her. Book had promised to protect her. He ran back downstairs and checked the *Giant* museum; she wasn't there. Or in Jett's Grill. Or in the small library. Or in the ballroom. Or in the—

She was in the pool.

It had been built just off the ballroom where an outdoor patio had once stood, surrounded by thick adobe walls but open to the sky. The sun was now shut out by a plastic corrugated cover, which created a sauna-like atmosphere at pool level. Steam rose off the water; it was a heated pool. The space smelled of chlorine. Nadine Honeywell was alone in the pool, swimming laps. He breathed a sigh of relief. When she swam back his way, she saw him and stood. Her skin looked like a sheet of white paper against the blue water.

'Ms. Honeywell, has your skin ever seen the sun?'

'I don't think so. I use sunblock with a two hundred SPF rating.'

'They go that high?'

'No. I put on two coats of a hundred.'

'Why?'

She gave him a puzzled look. '*Hel-lo?* Melanoma?'

Book pointed up. 'The pool is covered. And it's still morning. The sun's not overhead yet.'

'Can't be too careful.'

She climbed out of the pool.

'I found this suit in the gift shop.'

The snug one-piece suit revealed a lean body he hadn't noticed before with her baggy clothes. She caught him appraising her.

'I have a swimmer's body. Might be why lesbians are attracted to me.'

She wrapped a green-and-white striped towel around herself. They sat in patio chairs around a small table. She dug her sanitizing materials out of her canvas bag and went through her standard routine. Then they ate breakfast.

'You're a good swimmer.'

'I trained when I was a teenager.'

'Is that why you eat so much, your swim training?'

'You should've seen what I used to eat. Four hours a day in the pool burns some calories. And I have a high metabolism.'

'Did you compete?'

'No.'

'Why not?'

'Afraid.'

'Of drowning?'

'Losing.'

'So you never won?'

'Story of my life.'

She finished the last of the waffle and drank the coffee.

'Thanks for last night,' Book said. 'That pool cue wouldn't have done my head much good.'

'I guess that means if I ever get into trouble, you'll have to help me.'

'Ms. Honeywell, you've earned a lifetime pass.'

She pondered that prospect a moment then smiled.

'Okay,' Book said, 'what have we learned since the last quiz?'

'A, I know you can protect me now, that kung fu fighting.'

'Taekwondo.'

'B, I like to hit bad guys with beer bottles.'

'Do you now?'

'I do. And C, Nathan didn't show his proof to that Carla girl either. Which makes me question if there ever was any actual proof. Maybe Nathan just wanted there to be proof.'

'Very good, Ms. Honeywell. You're questioning every assumption and every supposed fact. You'll make a good lawyer.'

'Chef.'

She sipped her coffee.

'Professor, can I ask you something?'

'Of course.'

'So far you've shown Nathan's letter to everyone we've met in town except the desk clerk. Why?'

'Bait.'

'Bait?'

'See if anyone bites.'

'Fish. You told Carla you were here to fish. Funny. So who do you want to catch?'

'Whoever killed Nathan.'

'What if no one bites?'

'Then it was just an accident.'

She considered that through several sips of coffee. Then she said, 'You're kind of sneaky, aren't you?'

'Comanche.'

Chapter 14

'Professor, I've heard "fracking this" and "fracking that" ever since we rode into town, but I don't even know what fracking is.'

'You're about to find out.'

'From whom?'

Book unfolded the funeral photo and pointed at the big man with the bald head.

'The big fish.'

A four-wheel-drive maroon Cadillac pickup truck with a *Gig 'em, Aggies* decal on the back window sat parked at the curb outside the Barnett Oil and Gas Company Building on Highland Avenue just down from the hotel. They walked inside. On the floor was maroon carpet; on the walls were photos of the Texas A&M University football field, the football team, and the male cheerleaders. The school's colors were maroon and white. Book stepped over to the receptionist—a broad-shouldered young woman who looked a bit manly—and asked to see Billy Bob Barnett.

'And you are?'

'Professor John Bookman, from UT.'

'A professor?'

'Is that a problem?'

'The UT might be. Billy Bob hates the Longhorns.'

'The cattle or the people?'

'Funny. What do you teach?'

'Constitutional law,' a deep male voice behind them said.

Book turned to the same big man in the funeral photo. He had a bald head—not bald with fuzz on the sides but shaved-to-the-bare-skin bald, as if a white bowling ball sat atop his shoulders—and a black goatee streaked with gray. He wore jeans, a maroon cowboy belt with a fancy silver buckle, maroon boots, and a maroon A&M golf shirt. He looked to be in his late forties, stood six-two, and weighed two-fifty or more.

'He's the famous law professor, Earlene. He's on TV damn near every Sunday morning, making those senators look stupid. Course, that ain't exactly man's work.'

He sniffled and swiped the back of his hand across his nose then walked over, stuck out the same hand to Book, and flashed a big smile.

'Billy Bob Barnett.'

Book hesitated then shook hands.

'John Bookman.'

'Professor, it's an honor. Course, you didn't have to dress up for me.'

He hadn't. Book wore jeans, boots, a blue Tommy Bahama T-shirt, sunglasses on a braided cord around his neck, and his black running watch. No rings.

'And my intern, Nadine Honeywell.'

She wore shorts that revealed her swimmer's legs. Billy Bob's eyes roamed her body with lascivious intent.

'Well, honey.'

He had amused himself with his play on her name. Book gestured at the photos on the wall to divert Billy Bob's leer from his intern.

'Did you play football at A&M?'

157

'Yell leader.'

Unlike the University of Texas, which offers gorgeous coeds in leather chaps, biker shorts, and torso-revealing fringed cowgirl shirts as cheerleaders at football games, Texas A&M offers five male students in white shirts and trousers as 'yell leaders.' The former Aggie yell leader standing before Book abruptly threw his arms out and broke into a yell.

Squads left! Squads right!
Farmers, farmers, we're all right!
Load, ready, aim, fire, BOOM!
Reload!

Nadine had recoiled in fright when Billy Bob began his yell.
'Wow,' she now said. 'That's really scary.'
'It is for Longhorns,' Billy Bob said with a big grin.

A&M boasted a proud agricultural and military tradition, although the A and the M originally stood for 'Agricultural' and 'Mechanical,' and the students were initially called 'Farmers,' but later became 'Aggies,' a common nickname for students at Ag schools. The downside is that the nickname encouraged UT Longhorn students to make up jokes mocking Aggies as dumb farmers, such as:

How do Aggies practice safe sex?
They get rid of all the animals that kick.

'Anyway,' Billy Bob said, 'I got a degree in petroleum engineering, minor in international politics, which is damn near required knowledge to play the oil and gas game today. Not like back in the day, when the Texas Railroad Commission controlled the price of oil in the world, before OPEC came on the scene. Before my time, but old-timers tell me the oil and gas business was really fun back then. How 'bout some coffee and donuts?'

'No, thank—'

'What kind of donuts?' Nadine asked.

'Honeywell, we got chocolate donuts and glazed donuts and sprinkled donuts and crème-filled donuts and just about every kind of donut they make. You like donuts?'

'I love donuts.'

'Me, too. Come on back, we'll get you sugared up . . . sugar.'

Billy Bob abruptly turned away and sneezed—Nadine used the opportunity to make a gagging gesture with her finger at her mouth—then he blew his nose into a white handkerchief.

'Damn head cold.'

They followed him down a hallway; he jabbed a thumb behind them.

'Receptionist, she's more an Earl than an Earlene, but she can double as my bodyguard in a pinch.'

'You need a bodyguard in Marfa?' Book asked.

'Never know, all these artists and environmentalists.'

Nadine pulled out her hand sanitizer and offered Book a squirt; he was about to decline when Billy Bob sniffled and then wiped his hand across his nose again. Book stuck an open palm out to her; she gave him a good squirt. He rubbed the gel into his hands as they followed Billy Bob into a lunchroom. On a table sat a platter of donut paradise. Nadine's eyes sparkled.

'Oh, boy.'

She squirted sanitizer into her hand and rubbed quickly while she studied the donuts. Billy Bob grabbed a massive donut with colorful sprinkles on top; his belly testified to a serious donut habit. He waved a hand at the platter of sugar.

'Take what you want, Honeywell.'

She did. A big chocolate-covered donut.

'Can I have coffee, too?'

'Help yourself.'

She did. A tall Styrofoam cup of caffeine.

'Read in the paper you were in town, Professor,' Billy Bob said. He stuffed half the donut in his mouth. Blue and red and pink sprinkles now dotted his goatee. 'And I heard you roughed up a couple of my boys last night at Padre's. With that kung fu crap.'

'Taekwondo. Only after your boys accosted a lady.'

'Carla's no lady. Cusses like a roughneck and votes like a Commie. She's an environmentalist.' He had amused himself again. 'Course, she fits right in now, all those New York homosexuals moving down here, voting Democrat . . . Hell, Presidio County went for Obama, only county in all of West Texas. That's pretty goddamn embarrassing, if you ask me.'

'I didn't.'

'If you did.' He finished off the donut. 'You know, Carla, her—'

Billy Bob stopped short his sentence as if he had thought better of it. He abruptly pivoted and lumbered out. Nadine crammed the last of her donut into her mouth as if she were in a donut-eating contest then quickly grabbed another chocolate one; they followed Billy Bob farther down the hallway. Book whispered to Nadine.

'You know how much sugar you're putting in your body?'

'Better than a man,' she said through a mouthful of donut.

They entered an expansive office with the courthouse cupola framed in a wall of glass. Billy Bob gestured at two chairs in front of a massive wood desk that looked as if it had been carved out of a redwood tree.

'Take a load off.'

He circled the desk and dropped into a leather chair that resembled a throne. They sat in the visitors' chairs. The office featured wood and leather and the aroma of cigars. A tall bookshelf behind Billy Bob held more Aggie memorabilia, signed footballs and framed photographs of Billy Bob with coaches and the governor of Texas, a former yell leader himself. On the wall opposite the desk hung a huge flat screen television; on the side wall were large maps of Texas, the U.S., and the world. The desktop was clean except for a copy of *The Times of Marfa* with Book's photo on the front page, a remote control, and a Western-style handgun sitting atop a thick stack of papers. Billy Bob swiveled in his chair, reached into a cigar box on the shelf, and removed a long cigar. He held it out to Book, but Book shook his head. Billy Bob clamped his teeth around the cigar.

'I hate Commies, but the Cubans do make good cigars.'

He picked up the handgun, pointed the barrel at Book, and pulled the trigger. A flame shot out the barrel.

'Lighter.'

He moved the flame to the end of the cigar, but Book's intern stopped him cold.

'No!'

Billy Bob looked at her. 'What?'

'I have allergies.'

Billy Bob studied her a moment then released the trigger of the handgun-lighter. The flame disappeared. He replaced the lighter on the stack of papers. His gaze returned to Nadine, as if expecting a show of appreciation for his chivalry. But all he got was, 'Thanks.' Book decided to use the moment to begin his cross-examination of Billy Bob Barnett.

'Mr. Barnett, are your fracking operations contaminating the groundwater?'

Some lawyers believe that aggressive rapid-fire questioning is the most effective form of cross. Perhaps it is in a courtroom where the witness knows he is the target. But outside a court-room, when you're still stalking the target, when the witness does not yet know he is the target—when you're not even sure he is the target—such questioning is not effective. The witness simply refuses to answer your questions; and there is no judge to force an answer.

Book wanted answers from Billy Bob Barnett.

So he opted for a different technique. One that encour-aged the witness to talk—about himself, his work, and his life. That technique required a provocative opening inquiry

161

and a certain amount of patience. Most people want to convince you that they're good, that their work is important, that their lives are relevant. If given the opportunity, they will talk. And if their favorite topic of conversation happens to be the person they see in the mirror—and Billy Bob Barnett seemed that type of man—they will talk a lot. Reveal a lot. Perhaps even incriminate themselves. Book felt certain that the man sitting across the desk had much to offer in the way of self-incrimination.

Billy Bob's eyes slowly came off Nadine and onto Book; he held his expression a moment then broke into a hearty laugh.

'Well, good morning to you, too, Professor. Damn, you sure don't waste any time with small talk, do you? Hell, and I was gonna try and recruit you away from UT for our new A&M law school. Professor of your stature, just what we need to get it off the ground. Five years from now, our law school will be better than yours.'

Only a hundred miles separates the University of Texas at Austin and Texas A&M University at College Station, but the two schools have been bitter archrivals for over a hundred years. Both enroll fifty thousand students, but the student bodies resemble the national political parties: UT is liberal, green, anti-war, and Democrat; A&M is conservative, oil and gas, the corps, and Republican. The Lyndon Baines Johnson Library and Museum stands on the UT campus; the George H. W. Bush Presidential Library stands on the A&M campus. The schools have competed in putting prominent politicians, business leaders, scientists, military officers, academics, artists, actors, and athletes into the world—but never lawyers. Because A&M had no law school. Until now. The A&M alumni had finally gotten their law school, and they were determined to fund it to whatever extent necessary to top UT. Billy Bob jabbed the unlit cigar in the air.

'And we're sure as hell not gonna hire a bunch of goddamn left-wing professors from Harvard and Yale, I guarandamntee you.'

'Not enough jobs for law grads as it is, might not be the best time to start a new law school.'

'Not to worry, Professor. Aggies take care of each other. We're akin to a cult, like Mormons without the extra wives. We'll make damn sure every graduate gets a job. And Mr. Barnett was my daddy. I'm just Billy Bob.'

'Billy Bob. Same question. Are your fracking—'

'Hydraulic fracturing,' he said, carefully pronouncing each syllable as if he were a kindergartner sounding out the words. 'We don't say "fracking." Myself, I prefer "hydraulic stimulation."'

'Why not fracking?'

'Stimulation sounds fun; not so much fracking. And some sci-fi movie used it like the F-word, to mean sex. Environmentalists picked up on it, plastered it on T-shirts, billboards, bumper stickers. "Frack Me" . . . "Frack You" . . . "Frack Off" . . . "Frack This" . . . "Frack That" . . .'

Nadine giggled.

'It ain't funny,' Billy Bob said.

'It's pretty funny.'

Billy Bob bit down on the cigar, leaned back in his throne, crossed his thick arms, and studied Nadine Honeywell a long uncomfortable moment. He removed the cigar.

'You want a job, Honeywell?'

'I want to be a chef.'

'The hell you doing in law school?'

'My dad wants me to be a lawyer.'

Billy Bob nodded. 'My dad wanted me to be a lawyer, too. Respectable. Instead, I'm rich. Course, I wouldn't have been a good lawyer, never was much for book work. So I went to A&M.'

'Was he mad when you didn't go to law school?'

Billy Bob grinned. 'Fit to be tied.'

'Did he ever forgive you?'

'He died.'

That thought lingered like cigar smoke until Book broke the silence.

'Billy Bob, is your hydraulic stimulation contaminating the groundwater?'

Billy Bob snapped back to the moment. 'Hell, no. The Energy Institute at your own UT confirmed that, said there's no direct connection between hydraulic stimulation and groundwater contamination.'

'Well, that might be so, but your own lawyer said otherwise.'

'The hell you talking about?'

Book pulled out Nathan's letter and slid it across the desk. Billy Bob examined the envelope then removed and read the letter. He sniffled and breathed through his mouth. He finally looked up with a frown.

'Aren't lawyers supposed to be loyal to their clients?'

'Some lawyers have consciences.'

'Not the ones I hire.'

The frown left, and he sighed.

'Nathan was a good boy and a good lawyer. Smart and dependable. Cute gal for a wife. What's her name?'

'Brenda.'

'Yeah, Brenda.' He shook his head. 'His kid's gonna grow up without a dad.'

'Was Nathan your primary lawyer?'

'Here in Marfa. Tom Dunn—you met him, I heard—he's my main lawyer. Nathan handled my day-to-day matters down here—lawsuits, leases, permits, contracts, that sort of thing. He was a hard-working lawyer. I liked him. Real sorry he died. Terrible accident. I told him to slow down—'

'He drove fast?'

'This is West Texas. Everyone drives fast. But I don't have a clue what he's talking about in this letter, Professor. I'm a fracker'—he grimaced—'a stimulator and damn proud of it. I'm saving America from the Muslims and Europe from the Russians.'

'What do you do on weekends?'

'And contrary to what you hear and read in the left-wing media, fracking'—another grimace—'stimulation is completely safe to humans and the environment.'

He picked up the remote control and pointed it at the TV. The screen flashed on to a YouTube video showing a drilling rig.

'Watch and learn, Professor—the ABCs of hydraulic stimulation.'

The video played on the screen narrated by a friendly male voice, as if Mister Rogers were explaining fracking to the neighborhood kids.

The narrator: '*Geologists have known for years that substantial deposits of oil and natural gas are trapped in deep shale formations. These shale reservoirs were created tens of millions of years ago. Around the world today, with modern horizontal drilling techniques and hydraulic fracturing, the trapped oil and natural gas in these shale reservoirs is being safely and efficiently produced, gathered, and distributed to customers. Let's look at the drilling and completion process of a typical oil and natural gas well.*'

A color animation depicted the drilling of a well through a cross-section of the earth.

'*Shale reservoirs are usually one mile or more below the surface, well below any underground source of drinking water, which is typically no more than three hundred to one thousand feet below the surface.*'

The video showed a drill bit cutting through a blue aquifer at '300–1,000 feet' and then descending down to a gas reservoir at '5,000–13,000 feet.'

'*Additionally, steel pipes, called casing, cemented in place, provide a multi-layered barrier to protect fresh-water aquifers.*'

Book raised his hand, as if he were back in third grade. Billy Bob paused the video and raised his eyebrows.

'Yes, Professor?'

'Steel and cement casing,' Book said. 'Isn't that what they had on that offshore rig that blew out, spilled millions of gallons of crude oil in the Gulf of Mexico?'

'What they had were idiots making decisions.'

Billy Bob clicked the remote and resumed the video.

'*During the past sixty years, the oil and gas industry has conducted fracture stimulations in over one million wells worldwide. The initial steps are the same as for any conventional well. A hole is drilled straight down using fresh-water-based fluid, which cools the drill bit, carries the rock cuttings back to the surface, and stabilizes the wall of the well bore. Once the hole extends below the deepest fresh-water aquifer, the drill pipe is removed and replaced with steel pipe, called surface casing. Next, cement is pumped down the casing. When it reaches the bottom, it is pumped down and then back up between the casing and the bore hole wall, creating an impermeable additional protective barrier between the well bore and any fresh-water sources.*'

Book raised his hand again. Billy Bob paused the video again.

'Impermeable?' Book said. 'Cement sidewalks crack over time, why not cement casings? Can you guarantee no leakage?'

'Industry guidelines only require no *significant* leakage.'

'Significant? What does that mean?'

'More than insignificant.'

Billy Bob restarted the video.

'*What makes drilling for hydrocarbons in a shale formation unique is the necessity to drill horizontally. Vertical drilling continues to a depth called the "kickoff point." This is where the well bore begins curving to become horizontal.*'

The animation showed the drill bit slowly turning to a ninety-degree course through the earth.

'*When the targeted distance is reached, the drill pipe is removed and additional steel casing is inserted through the full length of the well bore. Once again, the casing is cemented in place. Once the drilling is finished and the final casing has been installed, the drilling rig is removed and preparations are made for the next steps: well completion. The first step in completing a well is the creation of a connection between the final casing and the reservoir rock. This consists of lowering a specialized tool called a perforating gun, which is equipped with shaped explosive charges, down to the rock layer containing oil or natural gas. This perforating gun is then fired, which creates holes through the casing, cement, and into the target rock. These perforating holes connect the reservoir and the well bore. Since these perforations are only a few inches long and are performed more than a mile underground, the entire process is imperceptible on the surface.'*

Book held up a hand. Billy Bob exhaled then stopped the video.

'You're setting off explosive charges inside the earth?'

'Same thing they do in mining.'

'I read something about fracking causing earthquakes.'

Billy Bob snorted. '*Minor* earthquakes.'

He resumed the video.

'*The perforation gun is then removed in preparation for the next step: hydraulic fracturing. The process consists of pumping a mixture of mostly water . . .*'

Book raised a finger; he felt almost apologetic. Billy Bob paused the video.

'How much water?'

'Five million gallons.'

'Per well?'

'Yep.'

'What's your source?'

'Aquifer.'

'That's drinking water.'

'Not after I use it to fracture a well.'

'Lot of water.'

'Lot of gas. But actually, Professor, it's not that much water because it's a one-time usage with fracturing. A regulation golf course uses five million gallons of water every month. And we only use two gallons of water per million BTUs. Ethanol production uses twenty-five hundred gallons to produce the same amount of energy.' Another snort of disgust. 'What a joke that is. And Bush gave 'em the ethanol tax break. Now every farmer in America is growing corn for the ethanol plants.'

He restarted the video.

'. . . and sand plus a few chemicals . . .'

Nadine shot her hand into the air and waved it like Ms. Garza wanting attention. Billy Bob paused the video and regarded her.

'You too, Honeywell?'

'What chemicals?'

'Same stuff you find under your kitchen sink.'

'Like Drano?'

'You want your kids drinking frack fluids?' Book said.

'Maybe, but the little bastards live in Houston with their mother. My first ex. Second ex, she lives in Dallas. Third, she got my house in Aspen. Goddamn community property laws. You'd think I'd learn about women.'

'Or they'd learn about you.'

'Hey, they did just fine by me.'

Almost as if he were bragging about how much he had lost in his divorces.

'But not to worry, Professor, we're not contaminating the groundwater. The chemicals we use, they're harmless. Watch.'

He restarted the video. On the screen a list of chemicals came up. Book read the list aloud.

'Chloride.'

'Table salt,' Billy Bob said.

'Polyacrylamide.'

'In contact lenses.'

'Ethylene glycol.'

'Household cleaners.'

'Sodium and potassium carbonate.'

'Laundry detergent.'

'Glutaraldehyde.'

'Disinfectant.'

'Guar gum.'

'Ice cream.'

'Citric acid.'

'Sodas, ice cream, cosmetics.'

'Isopropanol.'

'Deodorant.'

Billy Bob turned his hands up as if innocent of all charges.

'See, Professor, that's just regular stuff. We ain't putting diesel fuel down the hole anymore.'

'You used to?'

'Back in the day. But the Environmental Protection Agency banned diesel in slick water back in oh-five.'

'Slick water? Is that the same as frack fluid?'

'We don't say frack, so we call it slick water.'

'I guess that does sound better than "toxic brew" or "chemical cocktail."'

'Much.'

'. . . under controlled conditions into deep underground reservoir formations. The chemicals are generally for lubrication, to keep bacteria from forming, and help carry the sand. These chemicals typically range in concentration from zero-point-one to zero-point-five percent by volume . . .'

Book raised his hand; Billy Bob sighed and stopped the video.

'Damn, Professor, I wouldn't want to go to a movie show with you.'

'One-half percent of five million gallons is still, what—'

'Twenty-five thousand gallons,' Nadine said

Book and Billy Bob both cut their eyes to her. She shrugged.

'I'm good with numbers.'

169

Book turned back to Billy Bob. 'Twenty-five thousand gallons of toxic chemicals pumped down into the earth? In each well?'

'Can we watch the video? This is the good part.'

Billy Bob pointed the remote, and the animation went into action.

'. . . and help to improve the performance of the stimulation. This stimulation fluid is sent to trucks that pump the fluid into the well bore and out through the perforations that were noted earlier. This process creates fractures in the oil and gas reservoir rock. The sand in the frack fluid—'

Nadine gave a fake gasp. 'OMG—he said frack.'

Billy Bob shook his head as if exasperated with a child.

'—remains in these fractures in the rock and keeps them open when the pump pressure is relieved. This allows the previously trapped oil or natural gas to flow to the well bore more easily. This initial stimulation segment is then isolated with a specially designed plug and the perforating guns are used to perforate the next stage. This stage is then hydraulically fractured in the same manner. This process is repeated along the entire horizontal section of the well, which can extend several miles. Once the stimulation is complete, the isolation plugs are drilled out and production begins. Initially water, and then natural gas or oil, flows into the horizontal casing and up the well bore. In the course of initial production of the well, approximately fifteen to fifty percent of the fracturing fluid is recovered.'

Book raised his hand. Billy Bob stopped the video.

'So only fifteen to fifty percent of five million gallons—'

He glanced at Nadine.

'Seven hundred fifty thousand to two-and-a-half million gallons.'

'—is recovered. Which means at least fifty percent of those chemicals—'

'Twelve thousand five hundred gallons.'

'—and maybe as much as eighty-five percent—'

'Twenty-one thousand two hundred fifty gallons.'

'—isn't recovered. What happens to all those chemicals?'

Billy Bob shrugged. 'They stay in the reservoir. There's five to ten thousand feet of rock between the gas formation and the aquifer, Professor. Fluids can't migrate through a mile or two of rock. That's why they call it rock. Those chemicals ain't going anywhere.'

'You sure?'

'Pretty sure.'

Billy Bob restarted the video.

'This fluid is either recycled to be used on other fracturing operations or safely disposed of according to government regulations.'

Billy Bob paused the video before Book could raise his hand.

'Do you recycle your frack fluid?' Book asked.

'Slick water. And no. Too damn expensive.'

'What do you do with it?'

'Pump it down disposal wells.'

'What's a disposal well?'

'Deep salt-water wells. We dump everything from sewage to radioactive substances down those holes—'

'Like frack fluids?'

'—stuff the law won't allow to be disposed in rivers and streams. We got fifty-two thousand disposal wells in Texas, more than any other state.'

'Is that something to brag about? That we're putting more toxic chemicals into the earth than any other state?'

'Don't worry, Professor. The Railroad Commission regulates what goes down the hole.'

'Why doesn't that make me feel better?'

Billy Bob resumed the video.

'The whole process of developing a well typically takes from three to five months. A few weeks to prepare the site, four to six weeks to drill the well, and then one to three months of completion activities, which includes one to seven days of stimulation. But this three- to five-month investment can result in a well that will produce oil or natural gas for twenty to forty years or more.'

Billy Bob ended the video. He sighed wistfully. 'I love that movie.'

As if he had just watched *Casablanca*.

'I take it that video wasn't put out by the Sierra Club?' Book said.

'Marathon Oil. Put it on YouTube.'

Billy Bob Barnett seemed satisfied with his defense of fracking. But Book wanted him to continue, in the hope that he would over-talk, as guilty witnesses often felt compelled to do. Thus, another provocative question was called for, an inquiry that called into question the validity of his life's work, which is to say, his manhood.

'Billy Bob, is it really worth it?'

'Is what worth what?'

'Fracking. I mean, it's a huge environmental controversy, here and around the world. Is it really worth fighting over?'

Billy Bob's face registered an expression of absolute disbelief. He pointed at the screen on the wall.

'Did you hear what he just said? Twenty to forty years, Professor. Twenty to forty years of turning the lights on, cooking on the stove, heating and cooling your home, watching reality shows on TV . . . twenty to forty years of electricity. Unless you want to live in the dark, it's damn sure worth fighting for.'

His face glowed red.

'Why not solar and wind power?'

Billy Bob rolled his eyes. 'You liberals think the sun and the wind can do it all. They can't. Not yet. I want us to be energy independent, too, Professor, so I'm all for solar, wind, geothermal, hydro, you name it. Anything that'll get us off Muslim oil. And maybe in twenty or thirty years those technologies will be able to power the planet or at least America. But not today. Oil, gas, and coal supply eighty-five percent of our energy today. And we need energy today. Easy to sit in your ivy tower—'

'Ivory. Like the elephant tusk, not ivy like the plant.'

'Oh.' He rebooted his thought. 'Easy to sit in your ivory tower and preach your liberal politics, but what'll happen to America when the Muslims decide to sell their oil to the Chinese instead of us 'cause they'll pay more? When we don't have the energy to power our factories and light our homes? Our cars, trains, and planes? What happens to America then, Professor?'

Billy Bob stood and walked over to the U.S. map on the side wall. They followed.

'Current estimate is that we've got a hundred years' supply of natural gas in North America.' He pointed the cigar at shaded areas on the map. 'The big shale plays are the Horn River and Montney up in Canada, the Barnett—no relation—Eagle Ford, and the Woodford in Texas, Haynesville in Louisiana, Fayetteville in Arkansas, and the big daddy of them all, the Marcellus Shale. That one field covers ninety-five thousand square miles of New York, Pennsylvania, Ohio, and West Virginia, contains two-thirds of U.S. reserves.'

'I thought they put a moratorium on fracking in New York?'

Billy Bob nodded. 'Vermont, too, even though no one's found shale gas in the state. Said it was a show of solidarity. Goofy liberals.'

He now stepped to the world map and again used the cigar as a pointer.

'Shale gas has been found in northern UK and Europe—Poland, Austria, Sweden, Romania, Germany, France . . .'

'Didn't the French ban fracking?'

He shrugged. 'They're French.'

Billy Bob pointed the cigar at other nations.

'China, they've got more recoverable shale gas than us, about thirteen hundred trillion cubic feet. Argentina, they've got almost eight hundred. Mexico, seven hundred. South Africa, five hundred. Australia, four hundred. And all that shale gas requires hydraulic stimulation. That's our technology. We're not outsourcing American jobs, Professor, we're creating American jobs by outsourcing our technology. Our hydraulic stimulation is taking over the world.'

'Like our fast food?'

'Except it's better for you. Gas is good, Professor.'

Billy Bob held up one finger.

'It's cleaner than coal and safer than nuclear. Right now we're using mostly coal-fired plants to generate electricity. We switch over to natural gas, greenhouse gases are cut in half. And we don't risk a Chernobyl or Fukushima.'

A second finger.

'It's cheap and abundant. The same amount of energy from gas costs one-fourth what it takes in oil to produce. And we've identified twenty-five thousand trillion cubic feet of extractable gas in the world—outside the Middle East. That's enough to power the world on natural gas alone for fifty years.'

A third finger.

'It's ours, not the Arabs'. Right now we're sending a trillion dollars a year to Muslims who want to kill us. We get off Muslim oil, we keep one trillion dollars a year, every year, here at home. It's simple: drill at home or get killed at home.'

A fourth finger.

'Jobs. The world is starving for jobs, Professor, and hydraulic stimulation provides jobs. Lots of jobs. But Ivory League-educated environmentalists—'

'No, that one is Ivy.'

'But you just said . . . never mind. Liberal environmentalists drive around in their Priuses and don't give a damn about the unemployed working class. People are desperate for jobs. We got workers living in man camps in shale plays all over the country.'

'Man camps?'

'Trailers, cheap motels and rent houses, ten to twenty men living in each, because there's not enough housing in these boom towns. Men leave their families so they can work in South Texas or out here, send money home to Houston or Chicago, to mama and the kids like Mexicans send money home to Chihuahua. I guess we're all migrants when it comes to jobs.'

He added his thumb.

'And most important of all, Professor, shale gas is single-handedly causing a shift in the world's geopolitical balance of power.'

'How?'

'I'm fixin' to tell you how.' Back to the world map. 'Seventy percent of the world's conventional natural gas—that's everything except shale gas—is located in exactly two countries: Russia and Iran. What's that tell you?'

'God has an odd sense of humor?'

Billy Bob chuckled. 'That He does. What it tells us is that we can't let the bad guys control the world's natural gas supply like they do the oil supply. See, most of Europe is tied to Russian natural gas, the rest to Iran. So Putin carteled up with that loony bastard Ahmadinejad, put European countries in a political and economic vise. Remember back in oh-eight when Russia invaded Georgia—'

'The Russians invaded Georgia?' Nadine said. 'OMG, my aunt lives in Atlanta. Will she be okay?'

Billy Bob regarded Book's intern as one might Paris Hilton giving financial advice.

'She gets her news on Twitter,' Book said.

Billy Bob grunted. 'Anyway, the Euros, they opposed UN sanctions because they couldn't risk Putin cutting off their gas supply. Which is how Putin operates—he ain't selling gas, he's wielding a political sledgehammer. And he vetoes every UN sanction on Iran because they're partnered up, so Iran just goes merrily down the path to a nuclear weapon. And where does that path end? With Israel bombing Tehran back to the fifties. Which ignites the Middle East and puts U.S. troops on the ground again.'

'And shale gas can prevent all that?'

'Damn straight it can. Shale gas makes the U.S. energy independent and gives Europe the chance to tell Putin and Ahmadinejad to pump their gas up their—'

He glanced at Nadine.

'—where the sun don't shine. If they'll just go get it. Poland's got almost two hundred trillion cubic feet of shale gas—that's a two-hundred-year supply—and they're damn sure going after that gas. But France, they're not, even though they've got a hundred-year supply. They'd rather depend on nuclear power. How stupid is that? Waiting for another Fukushima? But that's what happens when environmental socialists are making the decisions. They'd rather hand the world over to Putin and Ahmadinejad. They don't get it. This ain't about a frackin' well dirtying a little water—it's about the future of the goddamn free world!'

He caught himself.

'Hydraulic stimulation,' he said carefully. 'What happens then, Professor? What happens when no one in the world needs Russian or Iranian gas? When Putin can't tell the Euros how to vote at the UN? Putin's power drops with the price of gas. The UN pushes Ahmadinejad back under his rock. Which makes the world a safer place. A better place. The good guys win, and the bad guys lose. That's got to sound good even to a liberal.'

'I like it!' Nadine said. 'And I don't even know who Putin and Ack . . . Achjim . . . that guy are. His name probably has too many characters for Twitter.'

Billy Bob smiled at her, as if she were a precocious child.

'You're a pistol, Honeywell. You sure you don't want a job?'

'I'm sure.'

'All the donuts you can eat.'

'On the other hand . . .'

Billy Bob turned back to Book and put the cigar in the air.

'And never forget, Professor—we are the good guys.'

'But we need clean water. And fracking is dangerous.'

Billy Bob shook his head with a bemused expression on his face. 'Liberals. God bless the children. Professor, people texting while driving is dangerous. Riding that Harley is dangerous . . .'

'Amen,' Nadine said.

'. . . Life is dangerous. Hell, yes, drilling is dangerous. Accidents happen. Get over it. Or start riding a bike, and not that Harley. The kind you pedal.'

Billy Bob stepped over to another map that depicted a satellite view of the world at night. Most of North America was brightly lit. As were the UK, Europe, India, Japan, and the perimeter of South America. But much of Russia and China was dark, as was all of Africa except the northern nations and South Africa. It was a telling view of the world.

'You want to live with light or in the dark? You don't get light without electricity. You generate electricity with oil, coal, nuclear, or natural gas. Pick your poison, Professor.'

He turned his hands up.

'Gas is the best choice, and shale gas gives us that choice. The world needs to cut carbon emissions, the world needs a bridge from oil to alternative energy sources, the world needs to get off Middle Eastern oil and Russian and Iranian gas . . . Shale gas does all that and more. Is it perfect? No. But what is? But shale gas makes for a more perfect world. It's a no-brainer, Professor, even for a liberal like yourself.'

He stepped over to the desk, grabbed the thick document under the handgun-lighter, and returned. He handed the document to Book then gestured with the cigar.

'Don't take my word for it, Professor. Take MIT's word. And Harvard's. And the Baker Institute at Rice. Read their reports on shale gas and geopolitics. I'm not making this stuff up.'

Nadine raised her hand.

'You got a question, Honeywell?'

'Where's the girls' restroom? Coffee goes right through me. Sorry, that's an over-share.'

'Down the hall, past the donuts.'

Nadine pivoted and walked to the door; Billy Bob's eyes followed her out.

'Boy, I'd sure like to have her on my payroll.'

'She's my intern.'

'Keep your prick out of the payroll—I learned that lesson the hard way. Several times. You know, it's outrageous what a gal can get for sexual harassment these days.'

He chuckled then walked around his desk and sat in his leather throne. Book took his seat again. Billy Bob chewed on the cigar and regarded him.

'Professor, why do you care so much about Nathan Jones?'

'I owe him.'

'You rode that Harley four hundred miles just because you owed Nathan a favor?'

'Because he wrote me that letter.'

'Well, Professor, I don't know what Nathan thought he knew or what you've heard around town, but I'm a good guy.'

Book had spent the last hour trying to get Billy Bob Barnett to incriminate himself in the death of Nathan Jones; Billy Bob Barnett had spent the last hour trying to convince Book that fracking was good for the world. Neither had succeeded. Nadine returned with another donut.

'I couldn't resist.'

Billy Bob winked at her. 'I like women who don't resist.'

She sat and ate the donut then licked chocolate from her fingers. Billy Bob watched her like a teenage boy with a serious case of puppy love. He finally broke away and tapped the newspaper on the desktop.

'There's no murder mystery in Marfa, Professor. Nathan drove too damn fast, like everyone else in West Texas. He fell asleep at the wheel. He ran off the road and hit a pump jack. He died. It's a damn shame. But it wasn't a crime.'

He tossed Nathan's letter across the desk to Book.

'My operations are run by the book. Hell, I'm an Aggie. We don't cheat. If we did, we'd have a better football team.'

He grinned. Billy Bob Barnett had not taken the bait. Perhaps he was guilty of nothing more criminal than being a boor. Or perhaps he was smarter than he put on; perhaps his good ol' boy routine was just that. Book decided to take one last shot at baiting Billy Bob, to lure him with a big piece of in-your-face red meat. He held up Nathan's letter.

'You know, Billy Bob, what Nathan wrote, some people might consider that a motive for murder. Your own lawyer accuses you of environmental crimes that could destroy your company and put you in prison for the rest of your life and says he has the evidence to prove it, that might make a person take action. Maybe even murder.'

Billy Bob's grin was gone. His jaw muscles clenched so tightly he bit the cigar in two; the end dangled from his mouth. The clenching spread upward until his entire bald head seemed to clench; his skin turned red and his dark eyes stared Book down, like two kids seeing who'd blink first. Book thought, Wait for it . . . like when he went fishing as a kid, watching a big catfish circling the bait, trying to decide . . . but the big fish didn't bite. Instead he took the cigar and tossed it into a trash basket.

'And some people, Professor, might consider it rude to walk into my office uninvited, eat my goddamn donuts, and then accuse me of murdering my own lawyer.'

His expression softened. He blew out a breath.

'Professor, I punch holes in the ground. I don't break laws and I don't kill lawyers, although we'd be a hell of a lot better off if we followed Shakespeare's advice. So why don't you and Honeywell play tourist today, go look at Judd's boxes, eat at Maiya's, maybe take in the Marfa Lights tonight, then get up tomorrow morning and ride that Harley back to Austin and wait with all those other liberals for the sun and the wind to power your world.'

'Are you trying to run me out of town?'

'Is it working?'

'No.'

'Then I'm not.'

'Good. And I'm not a liberal.'

'Professor, if it waddles like a duck and quacks like a duck, it's a duck.'

Billy Bob Barnett, fracking zoologist, escorted them out of his office and down the hallway—Nadine ducked into the lunchroom and grabbed another chocolate donut—past Earlene the receptionist, and out the building. They stood on the sidewalk; Nadine finished the donut and licked her fingers.

'So, Ms. Honeywell, what did we learn in there?' Book said.

'Billy Bob's a creep who breathes through his mouth. I generally don't trust mouth-breathers, but he's got good donuts.'

'What else did we learn in there?'

'Earlene is a lesbian.'

'No. We learned that Billy Bob Barnett didn't take the bait.'

'And Earlene's a lesbian.'

Book exhaled. He was trying to be patient with his intern.

'Okay, so this gay-and-lesbian identification skill you've mastered allows you to assess a person's sexuality simply by looking at them, is that correct, Ms. Honeywell?'

She shrugged a yes. He decided to demonstrate for his intern's benefit how skillful cross-examination can make such assertions seem utterly foolish and the person making such assertions even more foolish. He employed his courtroom voice and questioned her as if she were sitting in the witness chair.

'So what gave Earlene away as a lesbian? Her clothes? Her hair? Her lack of makeup? The way she looked at you and not

180

me? The fact that she's got shoulders like Michael Phelps? Ms. Honeywell, please tell the jury how you can know conclusively that Earlene the receptionist is in fact a lesbian?'

Nadine shrugged again.

'She grabbed my butt in the bathroom.'

Chapter 15

'They're boxes.'

'Works of art, Ms. Honeywell.'

Nadine Honeywell stared.

'Boxes.'

They stood in a renovated artillery shed on an abandoned cavalry outpost just south of town; it was more monastery than museum. Arrayed before them were fifty-two of Donald Judd's *100 Untitled Works in Milled Aluminum*. The other forty-eight were installed in an adjacent shed. The works were rectangular boxes, each with identical exterior dimensions—41 × 51 × 72 inches—but unique interior configurations—a box within a box, a floating box, partitions like cards in a deck or slanted shelves on the wall—that created optical illusions; each was open to the inside, each weighed one ton, each had been factory fabricated to exacting specifications, each cost $5,000. The boxes were perfectly aligned in three north–south rows under a high ceiling topped by a Quonset hut roof; massive east- and west-facing windows allowed the sun to bathe the boxes in light and set the shiny surfaces aglow. A young man sat cross-legged on the floor before one box, his elbows on his knees and his hands cupping his chin, and stared as if in a trance, like a disciple before a religious shrine. Donald Judd was a crusty gray-haired and bearded Midwesterner; he lived on a ranch overlooking Mexico; he was a towering figure in contemporary art in New York; and he created his life's masterpiece in Marfa, Texas.

Which masterpiece was funded by oil money.

Donald Judd began his artistic career as a painter but became renowned as a sculptor of boxes. He was a leader of the Minimalist art movement in New York in the sixties, but he became disenchanted with the New York art scene. He hated museums. 'Art is not commerce or show business,' he said. He believed that art cannot be separated from the space around it and said he put as much thought into 'the placement of the piece as into the piece itself.' He wanted to permanently install his art in big open spaces, inside and outside, where it would exist forever. In 1973, he moved to Marfa to realize his vision.

Which required money. A lot of money.

Philippa de Menil had a lot of money and a love of contemporary art. Her money came from oil; she was the granddaughter of Conrad Schlumberger, the French physicist who founded Schlumberger Ltd., an international oilfield service company. Her love of art came from her mother, Dominique de Menil, who founded the Menil Collection, a contemporary art museum in Houston. In 1974, Philippa founded the Dia Art Foundation in New York with her husband, Heiner Friedrich, and her inheritance, Schlumberger stock. Their vision was 'one artist, one place, forever,' to be achieved by funding permanent installations of major art projects; that is, one-man museums.

Heiner had long been a dealer of Donald Judd's work, both in his native Germany and in New York. Dia's vision matched up perfectly with Judd's. In 1978, Philippa and Heiner agreed to fund Judd's Marfa project, including the one hundred aluminum boxes as well as sixty large concrete boxes to be installed in an adjacent field just to the east of the artillery sheds. Dia purchased the decommissioned Fort D. A. Russell, paid Judd a monthly stipend of $17,500, and poured $5 million into the project. Dia funded other artists as well, including John Chamberlain and Dan Flavin; it acquired hundreds of artworks, many by Andy Warhol. It was a heady time indeed for the Dia Foundation and Philippa's Schlumberger stock, which traded in the $90 range.

But the oil crash of 1982 hit oil stocks hard; Schlumberger's stock price plunged to under $30. Despite putting $35 million of her inheritance into Dia, the foundation faced financial ruin. Philippa and Heiner told Judd that Dia could no longer fund his Marfa project.

Judd was not pleased.

After he threatened a lawsuit, Dominique de Menil stepped in to save Dia and her daughter's fortune. Heiner was removed from the board; Philippa's inheritance was placed in a trust overseen by her brothers. Dia conveyed the entire Marfa project—the buildings, the fort, and the art—and $2 million to Judd's new Chinati Foundation. They parted ways. Judd completed his masterpiece in 1986.

Judd's boxes are now something of a shrine. Art lovers from around the world make the pilgrimage to the old fort. With permanent installations of masterpieces by three giants of contemporary art—Judd's one hundred boxes, Chamberlain's twenty-two crushed cars, and Flavin's 336, eight-foot-long fluorescent lights in four colors (green, pink, blue, and yellow) installed in six U-shaped barracks at the fort, which the *New York Times* dubbed 'the last great work of 20th-century American art'—Marfa itself has been deemed 'Minimalism's masterpiece'; but Marfa will always be about Donald Judd. Marfa is a one-man museum; one artist, one place, forever. The vision of Judd, Heiner, Philippa, and Dia was realized and validated. The vision lives on without them.

Donald Judd fell ill on a trip to Germany in early 1994 and died in a New York hospital at the age of sixty-five. He is buried on his beloved ranch south of Marfa. The Dia Foundation survived but without Heiner or Philippa. Heiner Friedrich, now seventy-four, recently opened a museum in Germany and bought a $2 million home in the Hamptons. Philippa de Menil, now sixty-five, converted to Sufi Islam and is known as Shaykha Fariha Fatima al-Jerrahi; she is on Facebook. And the source of it all—Schlumberger stock—now trades near $80, giving it a market cap of $103 billion. The company is a leading international player in shale gas fracking.

'You reading a book at lunch?'

Border Patrol Agent Wesley Crum stuffed the last of the large pepperoni pizza into his mouth. He and Angel Acosta sat on stools at the counter.

'What are you reading?'

His words came out garbled through the pizza he was chewing. Angel looked up from the book.

'What?'

'What are you reading? That *Shades of Grey* book they was talking about on *The View*?'

'No, I'm reading his book.'

'Whose?'

Angel nodded past Wesley; he turned and saw the professor and his gal walk into the place. Angel waved like a kid to a sports star. Wesley shook his head. This was goddamn embarrassing.

'Professor,' Angel said. He held up the book. 'Would you sign my book?'

The professor stepped over, greeted them, and autographed the title page.

'It's very enlightening,' Angel said.

'Thanks, Agent Acosta,' the professor said.

He and the girl found a table across the room. Angel stared at the professor's signature on his book. Wesley sighed.

'Jesus, Angel—he ain't one of the Kardashian sisters.'

'It smells great in here,' Book's intern said. She inhaled the place. 'Olive oil. I love extra virgin olive oil.'

Her eyes glazed over and her mind seemed to drift off into another world.

'Ms. Honeywell?'

Nothing. He spoke louder.

'Ms. Honeywell.'

She snapped.

'What?'

She had a wistful expression on her young face.

'Oh, sorry, Professor, I was, uh . . . thinking about olive oil.'

'Cooking with it?'

'Something like that.'

She shook it off with a full-body shiver.

'So why'd we go look at the art?'

'You're a student. I'm a professor. I'm trying to educate you.'

'In art?'

'In life.'

She eyed him with suspicion. 'You're not telling me the whole truth.'

'See? You've already learned an important life lesson.'

'Don't trust law professors?'

Book smiled.

'Can we go home now?'

'No.'

'When?'

'Tomorrow.'

She groaned then pulled out her cell phone and began tapping with her thumbs on the little keyboard.

'What are you doing?'

'Tweeting.'

'What?'

She read off her phone: '"Help! I'm being held hostage in West Texas by a deranged law professor."'

'How many followers do you have?'

'Two. Including my mom.'

She replaced the phone and folded her hands on the table.

'Most law professors love to hear their own voices so they lecture the entire class. You didn't.'

'I don't lecture. I'm just a tour guide through Con Law.'

'Problem is, we never knew what you were thinking.'

'Good.'

'But we're not in your classroom, Professor. We're in Marfa. So tell me what you're thinking.'

It was past noon, and Nadine was homesick and hungry. He had not yet found Nathan's truth, so he couldn't take her home, but he could feed her. They had ridden back into town for lunch at the Pizza Foundation, just a few blocks up Highland Avenue from the Border Patrol headquarters. The building had been a gas station in a prior life. A purple Vespa was parked outside.

'I'm thinking there's a connection. Between Nathan, the art, fracking, his death . . . my gut tells me it's all tied together.'

'Maybe your gut's just telling you it's hungry.'

'Could be.'

'Connected by what?'

'Not what. Whom.'

'Hi, I'm Kenni with an "i." I'll be your waiter.'

A skinny young man wearing skinny jeans and a T-shirt that read *Frack Off* stood at their table. He seemed too somber to be a waiter in Marfa. He wore purple with a passion—in his hair, on his back, and on his feet. He was young, pierced, and tattooed. On the fingers of his left hand letters had been inked into his skin, one letter per finger: WWDJD.

'I've seen that WWDJD all over town,' Nadine said. 'What's it stand for?'

187

' "What would Donald Judd do?" '

Nadine frowned. 'Isn't it supposed to be WWJD? "What would Jesus do?" '

'Not in Marfa.'

Kenni's face was puffy, and his eyes were red, as if he had been crying. Or as if he were stoned. Or both.

'You okay?' Book asked.

Kenni gave a weak nod. 'Just sad.'

He offered no more, so Book ordered the chicken, tomatoes, spinach, and olive oil on thin crust. Nadine went for pepperoni, sausage, Canadian bacon, and extra cheese and her hand sanitizer. When Kenni left, Nadine said, 'He's gay.'

'You're not going to stop, are you?'

She shrugged. 'Just stating the obvious. He walks with his palms to the ground.'

Book turned and observed Kenni. He walked with his arms tight to his body and his wrists angled up so his palms faced the floor.

'Telltale sign,' his intern said.

'All right, Ms. Honeywell, since you're apparently an expert on this sort of thing, why do you think Nathan was gay?'

'His photos.'

'Explain.'

'What did you see?'

Book shrugged. 'Black-and-white photos.'

'You're not gay.'

'I know. But why do you think Nathan was?'

'The brilliant law professor is clueless. I love it.' She smiled and wiped the table down then rubbed sanitizer on her hands. 'All the photos were black and white, manly scenes, cattle and cowboys, the rugged landscape, a drilling rig, but in each photo there was one object in color, one thing that didn't belong in the scene—a Barbie doll, a red rose, pink underwear.'

'Okay.'

188

'Like Nathan. He was saying he didn't belong here. He was a gay guy in manly West Texas, living a black-and-white life, forced to hide his true colors.'

Book pondered her words a moment.

'Ms. Honeywell, either you're really smart or all that ethyl alcohol is poisoning your brain.'

A gray-haired man wearing a plaid shirt, creased khakis, and cowboy boots walked up and stuck his hand out to Book.

'Ward Weaver, mayor of Marfa.'

They shook.

'John Bookman. And Nadine Honeywell.'

'Read in the paper you were in town, Professor. Mind signing my Nook? Got your e-book on it. Been carrying it everywhere with me the last couple days, hoping to run into you.'

Book used a Sharpie to sign the mayor's Nook.

'Mind if I sit?'

'Pull up a chair.'

The mayor sat then sniffed the air. 'Smells like a hospital.'

He waved at Kenni across the room.

'So how do you folks like our little town? Number eight on the Smithsonian's "twenty best small towns in America" list.'

'The museum?' Nadine said.

'The magazine.'

He reached into his shirt pocket and pulled out a newspaper clipping.

'Got the article right here.'

He unfolded it on the table like a teenage boy with a *Playboy* centerfold. He read.

'"It's just a flyspeck in the flat, hot, dusty cattle country of southwest Texas—closer to Chihuahua than Manhattan. But it's cooking, thanks to an influx of creative types from way downtown."'

The mayor looked up with a grin.

'We beat out Key West.'

He carefully folded the article and replaced it in his pocket. He then reached into his other shirt pocket and removed another clipping. He spread it on the table and read.

'"The Art Land. In Marfa, the worlds of beef and art collide, giving the town a unique kick." *New York Times*. Course, you know what that's like, being in the *Times*, don't you, Professor? I read that story, "Indiana Jones Goes to Law School." Was all that true?'

'It was.'

The mayor grunted then folded and replaced that article. He patted his shirt and then the pockets of his khakis. He returned with several more clippings.

'"Marfa makes an art out of quirky." *Chicago Tribune*. "Minimal, marvelous Marfa: avant-garde art, deep in Texas." *Pittsburgh Post-Gazette*. "Marfa, oasis d'artistes." *Le Monde*. You read French?'

Book shook his head.

'Don't know what it says, been hoping someone could translate it.'

Nadine reached over, took the article, and read: '"This is a charming and strange village, a world apart. In the late afternoon, you can enjoy a Spritz (Champagne, Campari, seltzer water) on the terrace of the only restaurant on the main street . . ."'

The mayor smiled and nodded in approval. 'That's nice.'

Nadine scanned down the article. 'It goes on to tell the history of the town, how Marfa got its name, blah, blah, blah, Judd's story, the boxes, blah, blah, blah . . . Oh, this is interesting.'

'Read it to me,' the mayor said like a kid wanting his mother to read the ending to a Harry Potter book.

Nadine translated. '"The widening gap between the arts and the Marfa 'from below' also casts a shadow on the picture. At the last census, the population was seventy percent Hispanic, and the median income less than half of

Texas. But there are few artists who are interested in Marfa's poor and Mexicans. Chicanos, for their part, do not mix with the 'chinatis,' as they call the newcomers . . . The next contention could focus on education. Founded by two personalities from the art world, an international private school will open in September for twenty students. Do we want to educate the entire community or a few? Donald Judd enrolled his children in the public schools. This is one of the poorest counties in Texas or in the United States. Our schools are starving for money."'

The mayor's excited child's face had turned into a deeper frown with each word of Nadine's translation. He gestured at the article.

'That's what those French words say? You sure about that?'

'Unh-huh.'

'Well, hell's bells, that ain't a good story at all. And I've been carrying it around all this time. Goddamn French people.'

He snatched the article and wadded it into a ball and threw it at a distant trash basket. Nadine turned to Book; she was trying not to laugh.

'French, Ms. Honeywell?'

'The finest private school education available in San Francisco.'

The mayor spit out the bad taste of French and put his other prized articles away.

'Anyway, we've been written up in *GQ*, *Vogue*, *Vanity Fair*, *Wall Street Journal*, *Texas Monthly*, papers and magazines from California clear to New York City. Before Judd, all we had was the Marfa Mystery Lights. After Judd, we got art. And that's a marketable concept.'

'A concept?'

'You know, a promotional gimmick.'

'Judd's art is a gimmick?'

The mayor shrugged. 'Disneyland has Mickey Mouse.'

Kenni brought a glass of iced tea for the mayor. He grabbed

the sugar dispenser and turned it up. And left it there, dispensing a load of sugar into the tea.

'You like a little tea with your sugar?' Book said.

'What? Oh, I've got a bit of a sweet tooth.'

'Lucky you still have teeth.'

'Don't pay him any mind, Mayor,' Nadine said. 'He doesn't know anything about the sweeter things in life. Like sweet tea and chocolate-covered donuts and . . . pizza!'

Kenni had returned with their pizzas, which kept Nadine quiet.

'See,' the mayor said, 'when you think of Dallas, you think of J. R. Ewing and the Cowboys. Austin, you think of music and hippies. Houston, you think of . . . mosquitoes. We want you to think of art when you think of Marfa. And let me tell you, Professor, art is a promotional gimmick that works.'

He drank his sugar with tea then continued.

'I mean, we're an airplane flight and a four-hour drive from anywhere, but ten thousand art tourists make the pilgrimage every year. And that's what it is for those folks, a religious experience, like Judd was a god and Marfa's a shrine. I don't get it myself—hell, they're just boxes—but they come and they see and they spend. We got a bookstore, fourteen art galleries'—the mayor pointed out the window—'right over there, that's the inde/jacobs gallery, two homosexuals from Minnesota moved down here and opened it—and nine restaurants. Got a French place called Cochineal, gay couple owns it, they had a place in New York called États-Unis, cost you a hundred bucks to eat there, place is packed—homosexuals, they can cook. We got Italian, Mediterranean—that's the Food Shark. Serves falafel, hummus, fatoush salad . . . folks like the stuff, but it gives me gas.'

'Good to know.'

'But it gives the town a bit of flavor. And they buy real estate. Home values, they've skyrocketed.'

'Taxes, too, which I've heard is forcing locals to sell and move out of town.'

The mayor shrugged away any such concern. 'Price of progress. I've got a house listed for half a million dollars. Ten years ago, you could buy all the houses in town for less than that. That's progress.'

'You're a real-estate broker?'

The mayor nodded. 'I was an accountant, but never much money in Marfa to count, so I got my real-estate license. And business is booming, all the newcomers buying up homes and land. The Ryan Ranch, where they filmed *Giant*, it's up for sale—for twenty-seven million.'

'Is it a big ranch?'

'Nah. Only about thirty-four thousand acres. But I read it's half as big again as Manhattan Island, and only the son lives on it now. Maybe he'll get his price. New Yorkers, they think our prices are cheap. Homosexuals, they've got beaucoup bucks, I guess because they don't got children. Kids are expensive.'

He shook his head as if in wonderment at the world around him.

'Art and homosexuals on the plains of West Texas. Is life funny or what?'

'Or what.'

The mayor looked around, leaned in, and lowered his voice.

'These homosexuals, they're the best thing to ever happen to Marfa, even if they are abominations in the Lord's eyes.'

'Good of you to look past their human faults.'

'I'm a Christian man.'

'And a real-estate broker.'

'That, too.' He leaned back. 'Before the artists, don't believe we had a homosexual in town . . . well, there was the Johnson boy, everyone wondered about him. But he moved over to Alpine. They got a university there.'

As if that explained the Johnson boy's change of venue.

'During the Chinati Open House in October, we'll have more homosexuals per square foot in Marfa than in San Francisco'—Nadine gave Book an 'I told you so' look—'and most of them are Jewish to boot. Got me to thinking about a motto for Marfa, you know, like "Muslims to Mecca."'

'That's Mecca's motto?'

The mayor had the look of a man about to make a big announcement.

'"Jews to Judd." What do you think? Kinda catchy, ain't it?'

The mayor smiled proudly, as if he had just coined another 'What happens in Vegas stays in Vegas.' Nadine eyed the mayor as she had the Border Patrol agents that first day; Book hoped she would not express the same evaluation of the mayor.

'*Jews to Judd?* Are you a dope?'

'I'm the mayor.' He turned his hands up as if innocent. 'I figured we could run an ad in the *New York Times*.'

Book shook his head. 'I wouldn't go there, Mayor.'

The mayor seemed perplexed. But he quickly shook it off and continued with his sales pitch.

'Anyway, we got the largest hydroponic tomato farm in the world, they produce twenty million pounds of tomatoes every year.'

'Lot of tomatoes.'

'Damn straight it is. We got that El Cosmico hippie camp-ground. I heard tell folks smoke dope out there.'

'You're kidding?'

'Nope. And we're fixin' to have an art-house drive-in movie theater, designed by the same architects that designed the Museum of Modern Art in New York.'

'You need a Starbucks,' Nadine said.

'We got a Frama's.'

'Coffee shop?'

'Yep.'

'Fresh ground beans?'

'Yep.'

'Real cream?'

'Yep.'

'Where?'

'Block west of the Paisano.'

'I'm there.'

'How much coffee do you drink?' Book asked his intern.

'As much as I can.'

The mayor pressed on. 'Press calls us "Santa Fe South" and "Marfa's Vineyard."'

'Is that a compliment?'

'Yankees like the sound of it. And it brings the celebrities to town. Robert Redford was just here—'

'We heard.'

'—and Michael Nesmith performed here last year.'

'Who's he?' Nadine asked.

'The Monkees.'

'He's a monkey?'

'*The* Monkees. TV show about a band back in the late sixties.'

'I wasn't born until the late eighties. Is he dead, too?'

'He wasn't when he sang here.'

'We heard there's some conflict between the newcomers and the old-timers?' Book said.

'Sounds like you've been talking to Sam Walker?'

'We have.'

'He tell you about the Triple As?'

'He did.'

'Well, those attorneys, artists, and assholes brought a lot of money to Marfa. See, I want this town to grow. Sam wants to write about the dying West. Sometimes I think he'll only be happy when he's the last person left in town to read his paper.' He shook his head. 'Sam, he's . . . he's just not a big thinker.'

'Like you?'

The mayor turned his palms up and offered a 'What can I say?' expression. 'Marketing the art, that was my idea.'

'And "Jews to Judd,"' Nadine said.

'I'm trying to get folks interested in making a sequel to *Giant*, like they did with *Dallas*.'

'But all the stars are dead,' Nadine said.

'That is an obstacle. I was thinking, maybe we could pick up the story after Bick and Jett are dead. Remember at the end they showed Bick's two grandsons, one was Anglo, the other Mexican? Hollywood loves that multicultural angle. We could even make one of them a homosexual. I was hoping the Quaid boy could star in it, but he had to leave town pretty fast, to escape those assassins.'

'We heard.'

'Hell of a deal, Hollywood assassins running around Marfa.'

'So Sam says there's conflict in town . . . other than assassins after old movie stars.'

'Oh, there's a little friction, is all.'

'Friction?'

The mayor nodded. 'Friction. When you've lived your life a certain way among similar people for fifty, sixty years, then new folks come to town who live a different way, they rub each other the wrong way, creates a little friction. Nothing to fret about . . . long as it don't slow down the real-estate market.'

'We wouldn't want that.'

'Nope.'

'Well, glad things are going well in Marfa, Mayor.'

The mayor regarded Book a moment. His civic booster expression turned serious.

'We got a good thing going, Professor. Don't screw it up for us.'

'And how would I do that?'

'Acting like we got a murder mystery in Marfa.'

Book unfolded the funeral photo on the table. He could not find the mayor's face among the funeral guests.

'You didn't go to Nathan Jones's funeral?'

'I didn't know him. When they said Billy Bob's lawyer was killed in a car wreck, I said, "Who?" Which is odd since I make it a point to know every voter in town. Can I see it?'

'What?'

'The letter.'

'You know about the letter?'

'Hell, Professor, everyone in town knows about the letter. You been showing it off like it's a war medal.'

Nadine nodded in agreement. Book handed Nathan's letter to the mayor. He read it and then exhaled.

'You see his proof?'

'Not yet.'

'You've been in town, what, three days, and you haven't seen his proof?'

'No.'

'Maybe there is no proof. You think about that?'

'I have.'

'Heard you met Billy Bob this morning.'

'We did.'

'He do a yell for you?'

'He did.'

'I wish he hadn't,' Nadine said.

'Didn't he tell you fracking was safe?'

'He did.'

'He show you that fracking video?'

'He did.'

'Then what's the problem?'

'In my experience, Mayor, when there's money at stake, people tend to slant their testimony.'

'You saying Billy Bob's a liar?'

'I'm saying there are two sides to every story.'

'And you're getting the other side from Carla?'

'You know Carla?'

'Everyone knows Carla. Heard you had a meeting with her at Padre's last night.'

'We met. We didn't have a meeting.'

'You sure beat up those roughnecks for her.'

'They were rude.'

'They're roughnecks. So what'd you think of their boss?'

'He's a mouth-breathing creep,' Nadine said through her pizza.

'Says he's got sinus problems. And gals tend to think he's a little creepy, but, hell, he's an Aggie.' The mayor chuckled. 'Look, I've known Billy Bob since he moved to town. I've seen him sober and I've seen him drunk—don't invite him to your Christmas party, by the way. He's a skirt-chasing fool, but he ain't a killer.'

He held up the letter.

'This is pretty serious stuff.'

'Enough to get Nathan Jones killed?'

'Sheriff ruled it an accident, boy driving too fast. You met him, Brady. He seem like he knows what he's doing?'

'He did.'

'He does. If Brady Munn says it was an accident, it was an accident. Case closed. Folks don't murder each other in Marfa.'

The mayor downed his iced tea like a drunk downing his last shot of whiskey and stood as if to leave. But he hesitated; he had one more question for Book.

'Why do you care so much about Nathan Jones?'

'He was my student. I owe it to him to learn the truth.'

'The truth?' The mayor seemed amused. 'I've lived sixty years now, Professor, and I've learned there's no such thing as truth. There's just points of view.' He paused a moment, as if contemplating his own words, then said, 'Speaking of students, don't you still have classes to teach in Austin?'

The mayor walked away. They watched him glad-hand a few folks on their lunch break, then exit the establishment. Book turned to his intern.

'You get the feeling people want us to leave town?'

'I know I do.'

Chapter 16

'Henry, thanks for calling me back.'

'Just updating my resumé. How's Marfa?'

'Different.'

Book sat on Rock Hudson's rooftop patio. The sky was blue, and the afternoon warm. He had called Henry Lawson at the law school for legal advice. He often consulted Henry because he had worked in the real world. He had dealt with the reality of the law and not just the theory. He provided an objective view of the world. And he was smart.

'What are you doing in Marfa? You left kind of fast.'

'A former intern named Nathan Jones wrote me a letter—'

'Uh-oh, another letter.'

'—said he was now a lawyer here in Marfa representing an oil and gas client involved in fracking. Said his client was contaminating the groundwater. Said he had proof.'

'So what'd he have to say?'

'Nothing. He's dead. Died in a car accident, same day he mailed the letter to me.'

'Odd timing.'

'I thought so.'

'You suspect foul play?'

'I do.'

'Another quest for justice?'

'I'm afraid so.'

'Why do you care so much about Nathan Jones?'

'He saved my life.'

'He was the one? Down in South Texas?'

'He was. His wife's pregnant, due in a few weeks.'

'Damn. So you're playing detective again?'

'I talked to the sheriff—'

'What did he have to say?'

'Accident.'

'He got a stake in the game?'

'No.'

'Go on.'

'Then we visited the accident scene, talked to Nathan's senior partner in Midland—'

'Who's that?'

'Tom Dunn.'

'He's an important lawyer in West Texas.'

'Nathan said he took his proof to Dunn, but Dunn denied it.'

'That's what lawyers do.'

'Then we met with his client.'

'Who?'

'A fracker named Billy Bob Barnett.'

Henry laughed. 'You met Billy Bob?'

'You know him?'

'Everyone in the business knows Billy Bob. He's like a character out of a movie, a modern-day Jett Rink. Last I heard, he was sitting on a gold mine out there, held oil and gas leases on all the land in the Big Bend. So this dead lawyer had proof that Billy Bob is contaminating the groundwater?'

'Said he did. But I can't find it.'

'That kind of proof wouldn't be good for Billy Bob. You think he killed the lawyer, to shut him up?'

'It's a theory.'

'Book, I trust Billy Bob as far as I can throw the fat bastard, but a murderer? People murder for money, and he's already got lots of money.'

'He doesn't have a good reputation in the industry?'

'When he dies, they're going to have to screw him in the ground. He's like a lawyer—you figure he's lying anytime his lips are moving.'

'Not a straight shooter?'

'Only when he's shooting you in the back.'

'So the lesson is . . .?'

'Don't turn your back on Billy Bob Barnett.'

'I'll try to remember that.'

'So how can I help?'

'What do you know about fracking?'

'Everything. Fracking *is* the oil and gas business today. Virtually every gas well in the U.S. is fracked, and sixty percent of oil wells. Fracking accounts for fifty percent of all natural gas production, twenty-five percent of oil.'

'Billy Bob took me through the process. I thought I'd fact-check with you.'

'Shoot.'

'Water usage. Billy Bob said he uses five million gallons of water to frack a well, but says that's really not much water compared to ethanol.'

'He's right. Relative to other energy production, fracking uses very little water. But he didn't tell you the whole story.'

'Which is?'

'Which is, shale gas wells are short-life wells because the gas flows very fast out of the reservoir. The decline curves are steep, production levels drop off fast. So they have to constantly frack more wells to keep their production revenues up to cover expenses—fracking is expensive, about seven million dollars per well—and turn a profit. So even though on a per-well basis water usage is relatively low, the fracking industry uses a massive amount of water in total, something like three to four trillion gallons annually, mostly from lakes and aquifers, the sources for our drinking water.'

'He didn't mention that.'

'They never do.'

'Groundwater contamination.'

'Environmentalists have been trying to connect the dots from a frack well to a contaminated aquifer for the last decade. If they ever do, the Feds might shut down fracking. Which is what they want.'

'Why? Billy Bob said switching from coal to gas cuts carbon emissions in half.'

'And switching to green energy cuts it to zero. That's what the environmentalists want, to shut down the oil and gas industry and go straight to renewables—without a bridge. Just a big leap from eighty-five percent carbon energy to one hundred percent renewable. We're three, maybe four decades from that.'

'Billy Bob said the Energy Institute at UT found no direct connection between groundwater contamination and fracking.'

Henry laughed again.

'He didn't read the entire report. They also said that contamination is not unique to fracking, that casing failures and improper cement jobs occur in conventional drilling as well. But so far, no one's found direct evidence of contamination, not even the EPA. There's some anecdotal evidence—tap water turning brown and smelling foul, folks in Pennsylvania lighting their water on fire because of methane, the so-called "flammable faucets"—but hard to know if it's caused by fracking. So that's the first potential for contamination, failure of the well hole casing, which would allow frack fluids to flow directly into the aquifer. And we don't want those chemicals in our drinking water.'

'He said it's all under-the-kitchen-sink-type stuff.'

'But you don't want to drink any of that stuff. And some

frackers have used known carcinogens like benzene and formaldehyde in their frack fluids. We don't know who or when or where because they're not required to disclose their chemicals.'

'Federal water and pollution laws don't regulate this stuff?'

'If you want to inject any chemical into the earth for any reason, you're subject to the EPA rules and regulations under the Safe Drinking Water Act . . . unless you're fracking. Then you're free to pump any chemical you want down that hole.'

'Why?'

'Back in oh-five, Congress exempted fracking from the Water Act at the behest of Halliburton's ex-CEO, Vice President Cheney. Since Halliburton invented fracking, the exemption became known as the "Halliburton Loophole." So they can put anything except diesel fuel down the well hole without a permit or disclosure.'

'Doesn't sound smart.'

'What about politics is?'

'You said first potential for contamination. What's the second?'

'Migration. Even if the frack fluid goes down the hole without leakage, most of it stays in the reservoir. Over time it might migrate up through the rock and contaminate the aquifers from below.'

'What's the likelihood?'

'Shale gas formations are two or three miles below the aquifers, so migration through the rock is highly unlikely, at least that's what the geologists say. But they've been wrong before. And now they're "super fracking," using more powerful explosives to make even deeper cracks in the shale rock, which offers more migration paths. Problem is, migration contamination would be worse because the fracking process releases arsenic, underground shale gases like radon, radium two-two-six, methane, benzene, and what they call "NORM," naturally occurring radioactive material—'

'I see why they use an acronym.'

'—all of which is picked up by the fluid and transported up. That stuff gets into the drinking water, we're in a world of hurt.'

'Is there a third potential?'

'Flow-back. That portion of the frack fluid that's pushed up the hole by the gas. It's highly toxic after the fracking process, so you can't just dump the stuff into surface waters, rivers and lakes. You can recycle and reuse the flow-back, which is the best solution because we'd also cut down on the total water usage in fracking. But recycling is expensive. A few of the majors are recycling some of their frack fluid, but the independents like Billy Bob, they can't afford to. So they inject it down Class Two disposal wells. Should be Class One wells for hazardous wastes, but the industry got oil and gas waste exempted under the Resource Conservation and Recovery Act, so flow-back is deemed nonhazardous no matter what's in it.'

'Why'd they want flow-back exempted?'

'Cheaper to dispose in Class Two wells. We've got a hundred forty thousand of those wells, only five hundred Class Ones. We're putting every waste imaginable down those wells.'

'Why?'

'We've got to put it somewhere. Problem is, the industry disposes of a trillion gallons of flow-back every year, so Class Two disposal is getting more expensive. Supply and demand. Some operators push too much down the hole under too much pressure, and that's caused the reservoir walls to crack and the flow-back to migrate and contaminate nearby water wells. The Railroad Commission is supposed to regulate that sort of thing, but they've always been puppets of the industry. When you're in the industry, you like that. When you're out, you wish to hell they'd do their job.'

'Jobs.'

'Lots of jobs. Fracking employs fifty thousand workers in the Eagle Ford in South Texas, a hundred thousand in the Barnett, maybe three hundred thousand if the Marcellus is developed. And those jobs pay well—roughnecks can make a hundred thousand—and that's money to buy homes and cars, food and clothes, pay taxes. And gas powers factories, so cheaper gas makes the U.S. more competitive in the global economy. Which means more manufacturing jobs, more income, more prosperity. Which in turn creates more jobs in the service and retail industries. The economy grows. Cheap energy is good for America. Good for the world. And shale gas is cheap energy. For a long time.'

'Last thing: tell me about the geopolitics of shale gas.'

'It's a game-changer. If shale wins, the West wins and Russia and Iran lose big-time. If shale loses, they win and we lose. Energy equals political and economic power. It's that simple.'

'That's what Billy Bob said.'

'He's right about that.'

'So Billy Bob Barnett's not just a dumb-ass Aggie?'

'That "I'm just a dumb ol' Aggie" routine is a role he plays. Figures it's better to have people underestimate him. But don't you make that mistake. He's not stupid. He knows the business. He knows how to find oil and gas and how to make money. He's rich, and he's made a lot of important Aggies in Texas rich. Not me, but other Aggies.'

Henry paused.

'I'm applying to the new Aggie law school. Next time you see Billy Bob, ask him to put a good word in for me.' He laughed. 'Just kidding. Look, Billy Bob Barnett's a driller. He knows how to punch holes in the earth. He's fracked maybe a thousand wells over the last decade—he was fracking before fracking was fashionable. He knows the environmentalists are gunning for fracking, praying a fracker contaminates an aquifer so they can shut it all down. He's not dumb enough to kill his golden goose. Fracking is a money machine for him. He's not going to blow it all by intentionally contaminating ground-water. You don't get rich in the oil business by being a dumb-ass.'

'So what's your advice, counselor?'

'Get the lawyer's proof.'

'I've shown his letter all over town, trying to get a bite. No takers. I've talked to everyone who might know anything about that proof, but no one does. Nathan didn't show his proof to his wife, his best friend, or the environmentalist he was working with.'

'Okay, Book, let's take an objective look at the facts: first, the lawyer said he had proof, but no one's seen it and you can't find it. Second, the sheriff said there was no evidence of foul play. All facts point to an accidental death. Third, Billy Bob's too rich and too smart to shoot himself in the foot. He doesn't need to cheat to make money. And fourth, you're suffering a serious sense of guilt about this intern, so you're searching for something that's not there. All of which leads me to conclude that there is no proof. And no murder. It was just an accident.'

Henry paused.

'Sometimes, Book, there is no mystery. Sometimes things are exactly what they seem to be.'

Chapter 17

'Nothing in this movie is what it seems to be.'

Book had again found his intern in the *Giant* museum watching the movie. She held a large coffee cup with one hand—'I found that Frama's'—and pointed at the screen with the other.

'The big Reata ranch house, it was just a façade. There was no inside or back to it. They only built the front, made it look like a mansion.'

'The magic of movies.'

'Bick Benedict's this macho cattleman and Jett Rink's a surly ranch hand turned ruthless oil tycoon, but in real life Rock Hudson and James Dean were both gay.'

'Back then, if the world knew they were gay, their acting careers would've been over. So the studios kept up their heterosexual images, had them appear with starlets around Hollywood. They had to keep their true lives secret. They lived façade lives, like the ranch house.'

'Like Nathan Jones.'

Book watched the movie, Rock Hudson and James Dean in the big fight scene on the front porch of the ranch house, all pretending to be something they weren't. All just acting out roles in Marfa, Texas. Had Nathan Jones pretended to be someone he wasn't? Had he just acted a role in Marfa, Texas? If Nadine were right, Nathan had lived a hard life out here, hiding himself from his wife and his friends. That thought made Book sad for his intern. But it didn't make Nathan's death anything more than just a tragic accident.

He had found Nathan Jones's truth.

His truth—the truth—was that he had died in a horrible accident. The sheriff was right: there was no evidence of foul play. No evidence of murder. No proof of contamination. Nadine was right: Book was emotionally invested in Nathan's death. He had not remained objective. He had searched for a murder instead of the truth. For something that wasn't there. There was no murder. It was time to close this case and return to the law school. Henry was right: sometimes things are exactly what they seem to be.

'I'm just like Rock and James and Nathan,' Nadine said.

'Gay?'

'A pretender. They were gays pretending to be straight. I'm a chef pretending to be a law student.'

'Perhaps you are, Ms. Honeywell. So I suggest we see what chefs do here in Marfa, try out one of those fancy restaurants tonight. Before we leave town tomorrow morning.'

Nadine's mouth gaped, and her eyes got big.

'Well, shut the front door.'

The red front door of Maiya's contrasted with the white adobe of the Brite Building where the restaurant occupied a ground-floor space. Marfa gathered at Maiya's for drinks and dinner each night Wednesday through Saturday. They walked in and saw the mayor at a table, apparently selling the Marfa concept to his dining companions. He waved at Book, and Book waved back. At one end of the bar was Border Patrol Agent Angel Acosta with a young woman; he was not dressed in a green uniform but in all black. He waved, and Book waved back. At the other end of the bar was a group of young males in hipster attire, no doubt artists. Talking to them as if lecturing a class were Carla Kent and a young man dressed in a suit without a tie. She saw Book and came over with the man in the suit.

'Professor,' Carla said, 'this is Fred Phillips. He's an environmental lawyer from Santa Fe.'

Book shook hands with Fred and introduced him to Nadine.

'Professor, it's an honor. I've read all your books and watched you on TV. I really appreciate your point of view.'

'So what brings you to Marfa?'

'Carla got me down here, to represent landowners in condemnation suits brought by Barnett Oil and Gas.'

'Tough cases given the law in Texas.'

'We can't win, but we can drag it out, slow him down, make it very expensive.'

'Well, good luck.'

'Thank you, Professor.'

Fred returned to the bar. Carla took a step closer to Book.

'Saw you out running this morning,' she said. 'While I was showering. At the El Cosmico.'

'Must've been cold.'

'Water was hot.'

'Ms. Kent, we're leaving in the morning.'

She took a step back.

'Nathan Jones was murdered,' she said.

Book showed her the funeral photo with the circled faces.

'Ms. Kent, I've interviewed everyone in Marfa who had a connection with Nathan—his wife and best friend, his senior partner, his secretary, his co-workers, his client, the sheriff, the mayor . . . no one took the bait.'

'What bait?'

'His letter. I found no evidence of murder and no proof of contamination. His death was an accident.'

'Same day he mailed the letter to you?'

'Just a coincidence.'

She pointed a finger in his face. 'You're wrong, Professor.'

She returned to her place at the bar but gave him a long stern look. She seemed a very intense woman. His prior experience with such women proved to be too intense to last; the relationships burned hot, then quickly burned out. But he had to confess, such relationships were exciting while they lasted—which could explain his attraction to such women. That or the fact that he would never marry, and such women never entertained marriage.

'Told you,' his intern said.

'What?'

'There would be romance.'

'No time for romance. We're leaving in the morning.'

'What about Nathan's wife?'

'We'll talk to Brenda on our way out of town.'

They were led to a table by their waiter; he was an artist. Maiya's was elegant and expensive with white tablecloths and a $150 price tag for two, but that did not dissuade Nadine from wiping down the silverware and table accessories and then her hands.

'What did Professor Lawson say about fracking?'

'That Billy Bob didn't tell the whole truth—'

'Like law professors.'

'—but that what he said was basically true.'

'So what's the truth about fracking?'

'The truth? That's a hard thing to know, Ms. Honeywell. What do the words of the Constitution mean? Which politician is correct about fixing the economy? Is global warming real? Was Oswald the lone gunman? Should Roger Clemens be in the Hall of Fame? Is fracking good or bad? I don't have any answers. Maybe there's no such thing as the truth. Maybe it's all just a point of view, like the mayor and Ms. Garza said.'

'Irma?'

Book nodded.

'She scares me sometimes, she's so committed. Like that Carla girl.'

Maiya's smelled of food and sounded of life. Patrons talked and laughed. Judd's boxes and Maiya's food; Marfa was growing on Book. He had the spinach lasagna; Nadine had the grilled rib eye steak with Gorgonzola butter, red-skinned mashed potatoes, and pistachio ice cream with dark Belgian chocolate. She finished off the last bite then sat back and sighed as if utterly satisfied.

'That was an incredible dinner.'

It was.

'This is my dream.'

'To eat pistachio ice cream?'

'To own a restaurant like this. To create dishes like these.'

'A law student who wants to be a chef.'

'And a law professor who wants to be a hero.' She regarded him. 'Who *needs* to be a hero.'

His intern was getting too close to the truth for his comfort.

'How old are you?'

She smiled and sipped her coffee. She seemed at home, as Book was on the Harley.

'I want to cook all day and make people happy,' she said.

'You want to make people happy so you went to law school?'

'I went to law school to make my dad happy.'

'That's his dream, Ms. Honeywell. Chase your own dream. Live your own life.'

'I'm too afraid.'

'Of what?'

'Everything. Germs. Heights. Mosquitoes. Melanoma. Cavities. Gum disease. Failure. My dad.'

'You want to live life with a net.'

'What net?'

'Like acrobats in a circus. They have a net beneath them, so they don't get hurt if they fall.'

'What's wrong with that?'

211

'Nothing . . . if you're in a circus. In life, it's fatal.'

'But I won't get hurt.'

'You won't live. Life hurts, Ms. Honeywell. That's the price of admission.'

'You're not afraid of getting hurt?'

'I'm living without a net.'

'That's dangerous.'

'I don't live with fear—of failing, getting hurt, dying. I live every day as if it's my last, because it might be.'

'You're not afraid of dying?'

'I'm afraid of not living.'

'What's the difference?'

'Not living is worse than dying. Death is inevitable. So I'm going out on my own terms, while I can still make the choice. But I can't accept not doing something with my life. With the time I have. I'm going to matter. Not just be matter.'

'My therapist says I'm afraid of life because my sister died, and I don't want to die.' She studied her coffee. 'Do you know why?'

'Why you don't want to die?'

'Why you need to be a hero.'

'I don't have a therapist.'

'What do you have?'

'Regrets.'

John Bookman had always wanted to be a cop like his dad. Wear the uniform. Carry a gun. Ben Bookman had left home that morning in his blue uniform with his holster on his waist and his gun on his hip. He wore a bulletproof vest that protected him against a gunshot to the chest.

But not to his head.

Book rode his bike to school that day, as he did every day. And he rode it home, past Mary Elizabeth's house; she was practicing her cheers in her front yard, so he stopped and flirted a bit. She was cute and perky and acted interested in him. He felt manly when he pedaled away. He didn't know that he was about to become a man in the worst way possible. He turned the corner onto his street and saw the police cars out front of his house. He saw the officers at the front door talking to his mother. He saw her hands go to her face. He saw her collapse on the porch.

He was fourteen years old, and life as he knew it ended that day.

'Professor?'

Book returned to the moment.

'My dad was a cop. He died in the line of duty. Shot in the head by the man he was trying to help.'

'OMG. How old were you?'

'Fourteen.'

'Not fair.'

'No. Not fair at all. As you well know.'

They pondered their losses—his father, her sister—for a quiet moment in the elegant restaurant in Marfa, Texas. Book knew from her expression that she was wondering what her life would have been like if her sister had survived the cancer, just as he always wondered what his life would have been like if his father had survived the bullet. The moment ended, and their eyes met.

'So you're helping people because he can't?'

'He made me proud, being a cop. I want to make him proud, being a lawyer.'

'Professor, your dad would be proud of you.'

Book fought back his emotions and stuck a finger in the air to attract their waiter's attention. When he arrived, Book asked for the bill.

'Your bill's already been paid, sir.'

'By whom?'

'Him.'

The waiter nodded toward the back of the restaurant. Book turned in his chair and saw Billy Bob smiling and holding up a beer bottle as if saluting Book. A young woman kept him company. Book gave Billy Bob Barnett a gesture of thanks; as he turned back, he noticed Carla at the bar. She had observed his interplay with Billy Bob; she shook her head with utter disgust, as if Book had betrayed her.

He turned back to his intern. Nadine Honeywell's eyes drifted down to her dessert plate. She ran her index finger through the remains of the Belgian chocolate then licked her finger as if she would never again taste chocolate. She spoke softly, as if to herself.

'Living without a net.'

Chapter 18

"The Fourth Amendment to the Constitution states that, quote, "The right of the people to be secure in their persons, houses, papers, and effects, against unreasonable searches and seizures, shall not be violated, and no Warrants shall issue, but upon probable cause, supported by Oath or affirmation, and particularly describing the place to be searched, and the persons or things to be seized.""

It was ten that night, and they were sitting on the sofa in Elizabeth Taylor's room on the second floor of the Paisano Hotel. Book was dictating the Welch brief to Nadine; she was a faster typist than Book. They were trying to get the brief finished before returning to Austin the next morning. His cell phone rang. He checked the caller ID.

'Shit.'

'Is shit capitalized?'

'No.'

'It's lower case?'

'No. I forgot I had a date with Carmen tonight.'

'I think you're going to be late.'

He answered the phone. Carmen's voice came over.

'I'm waiting.'

'I'm in Marfa.'

'So I bought a new thong for nothing.'

Carmen Castro worked as a fitness instructor at Book's gym in Austin.

'I'll be home tomorrow.'

Nadine sneezed.

'Are you alone?'

'No, Ms. Honeywell is here.'

'Who's Ms. Honeywell?'

'My intern.'

'Isn't there a law about that sort of thing, a professor and a student?'

'Not in college. It's considered a perk.'

'Still, she is a bit young for you.'

'You're young for me.'

'Not that young.'

'We're working on a brief.'

'Just keep your briefs on.'

'Boxers.'

'Whatever.'

'Sorry to ruin your night.'

'That's okay. I'll just go to the gun range instead.'

He ended the call.

'Is she your girlfriend?' Nadine asked.

'Carmen's a girl and a friend. What about you? You got a boyfriend? Or a girlfriend?'

'I'm straight. I'd know if I weren't. And no.'

'Why not?'

'Guys today, their idea of a date is to go to a sports bar, drink beer, watch a football game, and text their buddies about their fantasy football teams, whatever those are. Sometimes I think it might be good to be a lesbian, I'd have someone to talk to.'

'There's always Billy Bob.'

'Gross. Besides, he's an Aggie.'

'Good point.'

'So your reputation, it's true?'

'What reputation?'

'All your women.'

'Just rumors.'

'I don't think so.'

'Okay, where were we on the brief? Oh, read the search-and-seizure cases—'

'I did. Last year, for your class.'

'I still can't place you.'

'I hid out in the back, behind my laptop. I was too afraid to speak up.'

'I don't know why you guys are so afraid of the other students—'

'We're afraid of you.'

'*Me?*'

'You're, like, a god at the law school.'

'I'm just a teacher. Teaching old cases that don't make a heck of a lot of difference in people's lives. But out here, I can make a difference. Sometimes.'

'But not this time?'

'Apparently not.'

'You ready to tell me the story?'

'What story?'

'How Nathan saved your life?'

Chapter 19

'You got me fired, you sorry son of a bitch.'

'Mr. Koontz, my father was a cop. An honest cop. You're a disgrace to the badge. Hell, you're a disgrace to the human race. But you shouldn't worry about losing your job. You should worry about going to prison. You know what the inmates do to dirty cops in prison?'

Book turned away from Buster Koontz. Turning his back on a dirty cop was a mistake, even in a courthouse. He did not see Buster reach to his leg and draw his backup weapon from a concealed ankle holster.

He pointed the gun at Book and fired.

The first letter had arrived four weeks before, on a Monday, the same day Nathan Jones started his tenure as Book's intern. His first assignment was to read and write responses to incoming mail, typically letters seeking speaking appearances, blurbs for books, recommendations for employment, and comments on important appellate cases—not letters seeking justice.

'Professor,' Nathan had said when Book returned from class, 'you should read this letter.'

Back in the eighties, the bureaucrats running the war on drugs in Washington dreamed up 'regional drug task forces.' The idea was to coordinate law enforcement efforts across jurisdictional boundaries to better combat drug distribution in the U.S. Funded by the Feds, managed by the states, and manned by the locals, the task forces were granted authority to fight the war on drugs across wide swaths of America. But federal funding was 'incentivized': the more arrests you made, the more funds you got, similar to farm subsidies. If you subsidize corn, you'll get more corn; if you subsidize drug arrests, you'll get more drug arrests. The one thousand drug task forces now make two million drug arrests each year in the U.S. And the key to 'making the numbers,' as the arrest game is called, is hiring experienced undercover narcotics agents from outside the locality to come in under fake identities and make the 'buy-bust' arrests. These agents move from task force to task force. They are not the Eliot Nesses of law enforcement; they are 'gypsy cops,' as they've come to be known in the business.

Buster Koontz was one such cop. He saw himself as a Dirty Harry type even though he was short and squat instead of tall and lean like Clint Eastwood. But he was dirty. The badge gave him power, and the power fed his ego. Buster rolled into the small South Texas town in the summer of 2007. In less than a year, he had conducted undercover operations that resulted in the arrest and conviction of fifty-three Hispanics, mostly young Mexican nationals with limited English language skills, all for 'delivery of a controlled substance,' i.e., drug dealing. Fifty-three drug dealers in a town of three thousand. His testimony was the only evidence presented at trial. The prosecution offered no corroborating evidence—no surveillance videotapes, no audiotapes, no wiretaps, no photos—nothing except Agent Koontz's word that he had purchased illegal drugs from the defendants. But his word was enough to secure convictions from juries determined to fight crime in their town and a judge seeking reelection. The mother of one defendant saw

Book on television and wrote him the letter. Book turned to his new intern.

'Mr. Jones, we're going to South Texas.'

'Uh, Professor, I'd rather not.'

'Why?'

'Well, I read it's kind of dangerous down there, with the drug cartels.'

'So?'

'So . . . I'm afraid.'

'Nothing to be ashamed of, Mr. Jones.'

'You're not afraid. Of anything. Even dying.'

'I'm afraid of not living.'

'Me, too.'

'No, you're afraid of dying, Mr. Jones.'

A week later, Book and Nathan Jones rode the Harley to South Texas. Nathan had conducted an Internet search on Buster Koontz and discovered that his past was checkered, to put it mildly. He was a drug task force hired gun, moving from small town to small town, putting up high conviction rates and then moving on. But scandal lingered behind: allegations that he had committed perjury—one convicted defendant was released from prison when his family produced time-stamped videotapes that proved he was at work when the alleged buy went down; another was released because he had been in jail in another county for drunk driving when Buster testified he had made the buy. Their first encounter with Buster Koontz was less than cordial.

'I want to commend Agent Koontz for his courage in wiping out the drug trade in our town. His remarkable work has resulted in twenty-two more arrests . . .'

The local district attorney (up for reelection) was holding a press conference on the steps of the county courthouse to announce the latest victories in the war on drugs. Agent Koontz stood next to him and basked in the glory. Three print reporters and a camera crew from the Laredo TV station captured the moment. When the D.A. paused, Book jumped in.

'Mr. District Attorney, are you aware that Agent Koontz produced the same remarkable results with drug task forces in seven other states over the last eleven years, but that many of the convictions based on his testimony are now being over-turned because Agent Koontz committed perjury and fabricated evidence. That many of his colleagues on those task forces regarded him as a racist, a liar, a bully, a rogue cop, and even mentally unstable. That—'

'Who the hell are you?'

'Professor John Bookman, University of Texas School of Law.'

'And what brings you to our county?'

'Injustice.'

The D.A. cut short the press conference and retreated to his office in the courthouse. Agent Koontz did not retreat. He fought past the reporters asking if Book's claims were true and grabbed Book's arm. Book eyed Buster's hand and then Buster.

'You don't want to do that.'

'What?'

'Grab my arm.'

'Why not?'

'Because I'm going to break yours.'

'You threatening a police officer?'

'I'm threatening a dirty cop.'

Buster released Book's arm and escaped the reporters and camera by driving off in his black pickup truck. Book gave his information to the media. Once the story broke, the D.A. had no choice but to fire Agent Koontz and announce a grand jury to investigate his actions. Buster Koontz would never again carry a badge.

But in Texas, he could still carry a gun.

Book jumped when the gun discharged. He wheeled around and saw Buster running from the courthouse and Nathan Jones slumped to the floor.

'Call an ambulance!'

He dropped down and cradled Nathan's head in his lap then felt his intern's body for the wound. His hand came back bloody.

'Nathan, what the hell were you thinking?'

His intern's eyes blinked open.

'Professor . . . you called me Nathan. Not Mr. Jones.'

He passed out.

Nathan Jones had stepped between Buster's gun and Book's back. The bullet struck his shoulder; surgery saved his life, as he had saved Book's. Buster Koontz was found later that day in his truck, dead of a self-inflicted gunshot to the head. His days as a cop were over, as were Nathan Jones's days as Professor Bookman's intern.

Chapter 20

'Wow,' Nadine said. 'And all I had to do was hit that guy with a beer bottle. What happened to all those people they sent to prison?'

'The governor pardoned them. They're back home with their families. Once that story hit the media, the letters started coming, never stopped.'

'Those drug task forces are scary.'

'They are. Bush tried to defund the task forces, but members of Congress don't get reelected by being soft on crime, so they funded them anyway. After this case and several other scandals, the governor disbanded the task forces in Texas.'

'Professor, I understand now, why we came. Why you had to come. Why you care so much about Nathan Jones.'

'Nathan saved my life, so I wanted his death to be something more than an accident, to have a greater meaning. To make sense. But it was just a senseless accident. Just a coincidence that he died the same day he mailed the letter. No one took the bait. There was no proof of contamination. No evidence of a crime. No murder mystery. That's what we learned today, Ms. Honeywell.'

Book's cell phone rang again. It was Joanie. She again pleaded for him to put their mother in a home. After a moment, he checked out of the conversation.

'Book—don't do that.'

'What?'

'Check out.' She sighed. 'Book, you've been my big brother for thirty-one years. You took Dad's place when I was ten. You rode me to school on your bike, you protected me from bullies—'

His dad had taught Book the basics of self-defense in the backyard. After he died, the anger that consumed Book had given him strength. The school bullies were big and mean; Book was mad at the world. They didn't stand a chance. But the anger threatened to destroy the boy, so his mother had put him in a taekwondo class, her version of anger management for her teenage son. It worked. Taekwondo taught him to control his emotions and to channel his anger into martial arts. He came to each class filled with anger and left with a sense of peace. He now taught the class to other angry young boys.

'—but I'm married now. You need to consider what I think. And what Dennis thinks.'

'I don't care what Dennis thinks.'

'He's a doctor.'

'He's not her son. Or her daughter.'

She again sighed into the phone. 'When are you coming home?'

'Tomorrow morning.'

'What about the dead lawyer?'

'It was just an accident.'

'Good. Because I worry when—'

Book heard the distinctive discharge of a shotgun below their window fronting Texas Street and dove for Nadine just as the glass exploded and buckshot peppered the opposite wall. She screamed. He covered her on the floor and heard a roaring engine and screeching tires outside and Joanie's voice on the phone.

'Book! Book!'

He stayed low and reached for the phone.

'Joanie.'

'Book, what was that?'

'Gunfire.'

'Are you okay?'

'We're okay.'

'We who?'

'Me and Ms. Honeywell.'

'Who's Ms. Honeywell?'

'My new intern.'

'What happened to Renée?'

'She quit.'

'Why?'

'Gunfire.'

He disconnected his sister. Nadine had curled into the fetal position on the floor; her body was shaking uncontrollably. He brushed glass shards off her. She cried.

'You're okay, Ms. Honeywell. They weren't trying to hurt us, not with a shotgun. They're just trying to scare us off.'

'I'm not crying about that.'

'Then what are you crying about?'

'Because we can't go home now. A fish just took the bait.'

Chapter 21

Book opened his eyes, but lay still. It was morning, but something wasn't right. Someone was in the room. Someone was in the bed. Someone's arm was stretched across his bare chest. Someone's face was plastered against his shoulder, covered by a mane of black hair. Someone's drool wet his skin. He turned to the someone.

Nadine Honeywell.

He remembered now. Her window had been blown out by the shotgun blast. So she had slept in his room. He had offered her the bed, but she opted for the couch. She stirred awake and realized her position. She didn't move.

'I got scared on the couch.'

'I said you could sleep in the bed.'

'I did.'

She removed her arm, peeled her face from his shoulder, wiped her drool from his skin—

'Sorry.'

—and rolled over onto her back. They both stared at the ceiling. She finally spoke in a soft voice.

'I've never slept with a man before.'

'We only slept, Ms. Honeywell.'

'I've had sex, once, but it wasn't an overnight thing. It was a back-seat-in-high-school-with-a-jerk thing. I tried a few more times, but like I said, after I got my clothes off, turned out they were gay. Awkward moment.'

'I bet it was.'

'No. This moment.'

She lay silent, which made the moment even more awkward.

'Sorry, Professor. In awkward moments, I tend to over-share.'

He decided to change the subject. 'You want to run with me?'

She groaned. 'Don't tell me it's only dawn?'

'I'm afraid so. So how about it?'

'Please, Professor. My generation does not run at dawn. We stay up late and sleep late.'

'I'll bring you breakfast.'

'That egg, cheese, and ham baguette, waffle with chocolate syrup and whipped cream, Strawberry Banana Cabana smoothie, and a large coffee with real cream.'

'Fear doesn't dampen your appetite.'

'A girl's got to eat.'

'I'll be back in an hour.'

'I'll be here.'

Book got out of bed; he wore long boxers. Nadine pulled the comforter over her head and said, 'Lock the door.'

An hour later, Book had run five miles around town and then stopped off at SqueezeMarfa. He bought breakfast and headed back to the hotel. He turned the corner off Lincoln Street and onto Highland Avenue and saw a Presidio County Sheriff's Department cruiser parked out front of the Paisano one block down. He broke into a run and sprinted past the front desk—

'Another night, Professor?' the desk clerk asked.

'Every night until further notice.'

—and up the stairs and down the corridor to his room. He found Nadine in the shower. Steam filled the bathroom.

'You okay?'

'Professor!'

'Sorry.'

He placed the breakfast on the kitchen counter then went next door to Nadine's room. He found Sheriff Munn standing at the blown-out window and a young female deputy digging with a pocketknife into the sheetrock on the opposite wall. Her blonde hair was pulled back but strands fell into her face; she wore a snug-fitting uniform that emphasized her curves and carried a big gun in a leather holster. She looked like Marilyn Monroe in a deputy's uniform. She smiled.

'Well, hidee there.'

She put a hand on her holstered gun and jutted her hip out. She gave him a once-over and a coy look; he wore only running shorts and shoes. He caught a faint whiff of perfume, not standard equipment on most of the law enforcement personnel he had encountered. She blew hair from her face.

'And who might you be, cowboy?'

'He's the professor,' the sheriff said from the window. 'Dig, Shirley.'

Book walked over to the sheriff, who jabbed his head in Deputy Shirley's direction.

'Niece.'

He had a jaw full of chewing tobacco. He turned back to the window, leaned into the open space, and spit a brown stream outside. Book peeked down to see if the sidewalk below was clear of pedestrians.

'Well, they're damn sure gonna have to replace this window,' the sheriff said.

'That qualify as foul play?'

'Reckon it does. Where's the gal? She okay?'

'She is. She's next door in my room.'

The sheriff's eyebrows rose; he grunted.

'No,' Book said. 'It's not like that. She was too afraid to sleep alone, so she slept with . . . Never mind.'

'Overnight maid downstairs, she heard the gunshot, saw a dark pickup speed away,' the sheriff said.

'Maroon?'

'I asked. She couldn't say. I take it you talked to Billy Bob, know the color of his truck.'

'We talked.'

'You learn anything?'

'I don't like him.'

'That ain't exactly breaking news.'

'Sheriff, Nathan Jones was murdered.'

The sheriff launched another stream of tobacco juice through the broken glass.

'Maybe. Or maybe those boys at Padre's don't appreciate getting their butts kicked by a professor, decided to let you know. And by the way, I figure those boys got what they deserved, but don't you figure you can run around my county playing Rambo—*comprende*, podna?'

'Birdshot, Sheriff,' Deputy Shirley said. She examined a small pellet. 'Number eight, probably from a twelve-gauge shotgun.'

The sheriff grunted then spat again.

'If they wanted to kill you, Professor, they wouldn't have used birdshot. They just wanted to encourage you to go home.'

'When can we go home?'

'When we find out who murdered Nathan Jones.'

They were eating breakfast on Rock's rooftop patio. Nadine finished off the baguette, waffle, and smoothie and then sipped her coffee.

'And how are we going to do that?'

'Someone took the bait last night. I think I know who. Now we've got to reel that big Aggie fish in.'

She sighed.

'I don't like the sound of that.'

Chapter 22

Sam Walker sat behind his desk wearing the same cap but a different Hawaiian shirt when Book and Nadine walked into *The Times of Marfa* office. He looked up and smiled as if an old friend had reentered his life.

'Well, hello, Professor. You've certainly made an impression around town.'

'Not a good one, apparently.'

'Sold out this week's edition, first time ever. Don't reckon the roller derby would've sold out.'

'Sam, you said I could trust you.'

'You can.'

'You ran the story.'

Sam stood and came over to the counter.

'Professor, I figure you're a pretty smart fella, knew what you were doing when you showed me that letter. Figured you wanted me to run the story, stir the pot in Marfa.'

Book fought a smile but failed.

'We talk slow out here in West Texas, Professor, but that doesn't mean we think slow.'

'I expect not.'

'You've been busy, waving that letter all over town, getting shot at. You folks okay?'

'Just a warning shot.'

'Figure you got a murder case?'

'I do.'

'Figure the killer shot your window out?'

'I do.'

'What're you gonna do about it?'

'Send the killer a message.'

Sam removed his cap and scratched his head, a sure sign he was thinking.

'Well, next edition doesn't come out till next week. You want to send a message today, best to use the radio.'

The Marfa Public Radio station operates out of a small studio in a small storefront befitting the smallest public radio station in America. Its audience totals less than fifteen thousand in the sparsely populated Trans-Pecos. The station's 100,000-watt signal spans an area of 20,000 square miles extending north of the Davis Mountains and south to the Rio Grande, west to the Blue Origin spaceport and east to Marathon. Hence the station's tagline: 'Radio for a Wide Range.' Nadine Honeywell sanitized the armrests of a chair with wipes then sat in the small reception area and listened to the professor on the radio.

'A reminder, folks,' the host said. 'It's April, and we don't want a repeat of last April's wildfires, so don't toss those cigarettes out the window. And the burn ban remains in effect. The land is dry, and the wind is up. If you see smoke, there's fire, so call it in. Okay, our *Talk at Ten* interview today was scheduled to be Werner von Stueber discussing existentialism and crushed cars in our continuing series on the works of John Chamberlain, but we're rescheduling Werner for tomorrow morning to make room for a surprise guest, the renowned constitutional law professor from the University of Texas at Austin, John Bookman. We've all seen Professor Bookman on national TV discussing the constitutionality of abortion or Obamacare, but he isn't here to talk about those subjects. He's here to talk about murder. A murder in Marfa. Professor Bookman, welcome to Marfa.'

'Thanks for having me on your show on such short notice.'

'We all know about the terrible death of a local lawyer, Nathan Jones, last week. We thought he died in a tragic automobile accident. But you think otherwise.'

'He was murdered.'

'Why do you believe that?'

'Nathan wrote me a letter and mailed it on April fifth. He died the same day.'

'Coincidence?'

'I don't believe in coincidences.'

'And what did he say in that letter, Professor?'

'Nathan said that his client was committing environmental crimes. That his client was contaminating the groundwater out here with his fracking operations.'

'That's a pretty serious charge.'

'It is.'

'And who is his client?'

'Billy Bob Barnett.'

Across Highland Avenue, Sam Walker howled in his office.

'Hot-damn! That'll sell some papers next week!'

'So, Professor, you received this letter in Austin before you knew Nathan Jones had died. Why'd you come to Marfa?'

'Nathan was a former student and my intern four years ago. He asked for my help.'

'But upon your arrival in Marfa, you learned of his death?'

'Yes.'

'Professor, how do you help a dead person?'

'You find his truth. You give him justice.'

'And how do you do that?'

233

'You learn about his life, who he was. So I spoke with his wife—'

Brenda Jones sat in her house listening to the professor on the radio. She placed her hands on her belly that held Nathan's child. She cried.

'—and his best friend—'

Jimmy John Dale blew blood from his nose onto the handkerchief. He sat among empty beer cans, empty pizza boxes, and loaded guns. Bushmaster AR-15 assault rifle with a thirty-round clip . . . Winchester twelve-gauge pump shotgun . . . Smith & Wesson .357 Magnum handgun with a heavy load—you couldn't own too many weapons in his neighborhood on the Mexican side of town just south of the railroad tracks. He adjusted his position in his ratty recliner in the living room of his mobile home. He was saving for the down payment on a small adobe house on the same side of the railroad tracks; no way could he ever afford a home north of the tracks. The voices of the kids playing outside and chattering in Spanish—he often felt as if he were living in the state of Chihuahua instead of the state of Texas—came through the thin exterior wall as clearly as if they were standing next to him and made the hammer in his head pound even harder. They always left their toys and bikes and skateboards scattered about the open space between their trailers. He finished off the Lone Star beer and tossed the can at the trash basket in the adjoining kitchen but missed and thought, Their mama ought to teach those kids how to pick up after themselves.

Never figured he'd live with the Mexicans, but it was all he could afford; and besides, the Mexicans couldn't even afford to live on the Mexican side of town now, so they were selling out to Anglos who couldn't afford to live on the Anglo side of town, which was now just a suburb of New York City. Goddamn queer artists. But hell, unless he wanted to live the rest of his life alone, he'd probably have to marry a Mexican girl. All the white girls, they get the hell out of town after high school, most for college, the others for a job in the city or a man with a job in the city. They don't come back. That'd be a hell of a thing, having a Mexican mother-in-law.

The mother next door started yelling at the kids in Spanish, so Jimmy John turned up the radio and searched for his Advil.

'—and learned that she had been followed around town—'
'By whom?'
'She didn't know. So I talked to the sheriff—'

Presidio County Sheriff Brady Munn sat in his office with his cowboy boots kicked up on his desk and Deputy Shirley practicing her fast draw against an imaginary gunslinger. He sighed and shook his head. A niece pretending to be a deputy and a professor pretending to be a detective.

'Should've been a cattle rancher,' he said to himself.

'—and went out to the accident scene. I visited Nathan's senior partner in Midland. And I met Billy Bob Barnett.'
'You showed them Nathan's letter?'
'Yes. They all denied any knowledge of Nathan's allegations. I had concluded that his death was just a tragic accident, as you said, until last night.'
'What happened last night?'
'Someone shot out our window at the Paisano.'
'The killer?'
'Who else?'
'Was anyone hurt?'
'No. My intern was scared.'

235

'But not you?'

'I've been through this sort of thing before.'

'I bet you have. So, Professor, why did you want to come on the radio today?'

'Because I have a message for Nathan's killer.'

'Which is?'

'I'm coming for you. I will find you. And I will bring you to justice. For Nathan.'

In the Marfa City Hall, Mayor Ward Weaver sighed as if he had lost a real-estate commission. He might have; he just didn't know it yet.

'Hell's bells, a murder in Marfa. Talk like that, he's gonna scare off all the homosexuals.'

Carla Kent drove her old '96 Ford pickup truck south on Highway 17 from Fort Davis. The windows were down, and the radio was on. The professor, he didn't understand West Texas anymore than those New York artists did. Difference was, they were just insulting the locals with their art and public displays of their sexual preferences; they weren't calling them murderers. Locals out here don't take kindly to such remarks. And they carry guns.

'There's a murderer in Marfa,' the professor said on the radio. 'And I'm going to find him.'

In his office two blocks north on Highland, Billy Bob Barnett grabbed the radio and hurled it against the far wall. He hadn't been that pissed-off since his third ex-wife got the ski lodge in Aspen. His pulled out his little pill box and swallowed a blood pressure pill. He blew his nose into a handkerchief then pointed a finger at the two football-players-turned-bodyguards sitting across the desk from him.

'Follow him. Don't let him out of your sight.'

★ ★ ★

236

'Goddamnit, Roscoe, Bookman's on the radio out here calling my biggest client a murderer!'

Like most successful lawyers who gave lots of money to judges and their alma maters, Tom Dunn demanded preferential treatment at the courthouse and the law school. So, upon hearing the professor on Marfa Public Radio, he picked up the phone and hit the speed dial for the dean of the UT law school.

'You represent a murderer?' Dean Roscoe Chambers said.

'*What?* No. He's in the oil and gas business. But your professor's calling him a murderer.'

'Oh. What do you want me to do about it?'

'Call him back to Austin. Get him off our fuckin' backs out here.'

'He's tenured, Tom. Which means unless he engages in sexual relations with a freshman, there's nothing I can do to him.'

'College freshman?'

'High school. And he's a celebrity. The press loves him. He makes for a good story, that Indiana Jones stuff. What I'm saying is, he's untouchable.'

'Maybe.'

Chapter 23

'I'm thinking you didn't make any friends in Marfa,' Nadine said.

'Wasn't trying to.'

'What were you trying to do?'

'Ratchet up the pressure on the killer.'

'That sounds dangerous.'

'It can be.'

He held the door to The Get Go open for his intern then followed her inside. The Get Go is an organic grocery store started by the woman behind Maiya's restaurant. It's located on the southeast side of Marfa, catty-cornered from a group of crumbling adobes that appear more like a rundown motel. The structures seemed unfit for human occupancy, but Latinos still occupied the homes.

It was past noon, and Nadine hadn't eaten in four hours, so they had stopped at The Get Go on their way to Brenda Jones's house. They didn't have time for a sit-down lunch, and Book refused to eat fast food. The small store's shelves were stocked like the Whole Foods in Austin.

'I'll meet you at the checkout,' Book said.

They split up aisles. There were vegan and ethnic selections, gourmet dog food, and the *New York Times*. Book walked down the wine and beer aisle. There was a wide selection of international wines and beers, and in a cooler, cheeses—Gouda and goat and brie. He ran into Agent Angel Acosta holding cheese in one hand and a bottle of wine in the other.

'Hello, Professor. I enjoyed your radio interview.'

'You're probably the only person in town who did.'

Agent Acosta shook his head. 'A murder in Marfa. You working with the sheriff?'

'Trying to.'

'He's a good man. An honest cop.'

'Good to know.'

'Professor—be careful.'

Book met his intern at the checkout counter. Book had chosen protein bars, granola bars, and bottled water; Nadine had chosen potato chips, an ice cream bar, and a bottle of root beer. At least they were organic.

'Do you have Twinkies or moon pies?' she asked the clerk.

The clerk laughed. 'A Twinkie? No. They stopped making them.'

'*What? When?*'

'Hostess went under a year ago.'

'It wasn't on Twitter. OMG. What about Sno Balls?'

The clerk shook her head. 'Sorry.'

'I thought this is a grocery store.'

'It's an organic grocery store. Means natural foods. There's nothing natural in a Twinkie or a Sno Ball.'

The clerk turned to the cash register; Nadine made a face at her. Book paid, and they stepped outside and to the Harley. Agent Acosta drove off in a late-model convertible. He waved, and Book waved back. Nadine dug into the potato chips; he ate a protein bar.

'I know what the connection is,' his intern said, 'between Nathan, his death, the art, fracking, and Billy Bob.'

'What?'

'Not what. Who.'

'Okay. Who?'

'That Carla girl.'

'Why?'

'She's in the middle of every conflict in Marfa.'

'She's an environmentalist. That's what they do.'

'There's something more.'

'What?'

'I don't know that. But we didn't have this much conflict in San Francisco, and people there fight over everything. Difference is, people there like homosexuals.'

Nadine pointed at the old adobes across the intersection. On one wall graffiti had been painted: *Fuck U ChiNazis*.

'That's what we call the homosexuals,' Jimmy John said. 'The artists. 'Cause of that Chinati deal out there.'

Book and Nadine had ridden over to Nathan Jones's house to meet Brenda. Jimmy John Dale was already there and drinking a beer. Or finishing off a six-pack.

'The Chinati Foundation at the fort? Where Judd's boxes are exhibited?'

'Yeah. At first we called the whole bunch of 'em "Chinatis." Then they took over Marfa, started running the place like they owned it, trying to turn it into another New York City, so we started calling them "ChiNazis." Hell, even the Mexicans hate 'em. First time in the history of Marfa, Anglos and Mexicans are on the same side fighting the same enemy. The homosexuals, they brought us together.'

'Why?'

'They've run up the real-estate prices, locals can't afford homes no more, they got their high-dollar restaurants we can't afford, they got their organic grocery store we can't afford, and now they're starting their own private school we can't afford. They look down their noses at us locals, figure we're all

240

dumb-asses lucky to find our way home at night—hell, least we're not a buncha goddamn queers!'

'Jimmy John!'

Brenda Jones gave him a stern look. His expression eased. 'Sorry.'

'That the friction the mayor mentioned?' Book asked.

Jimmy John laughed. 'Friction? That's funny. More like open warfare, Professor.'

'Over gays in town who pay too much to eat out?'

Jimmy John drank his beer.

'Aw, hell, that stuff just graveled us. But when they started protesting the fracking, they crossed the line with the locals. They're spending a couple hundred bucks to eat French food, but they're happy for us to starve. They come down here and take over our town, now they want to take our jobs. They don't understand, Professor— fracking gave us jobs, and we ain't giving 'em up just 'cause they're worried about a little pollution.'

'Has there been any violence?'

Jimmy John snorted. 'We ain't worried about a buncha queers beating us up, Professor.'

'*Against* the artists?'

'Oh. Not yet. But they keep it up, they're gonna understand why not many folks live in this desert. It can be a hard life.'

'Do you know Carla Kent?'

'Everyone knows Carla. She come down here from Santa Fe, organized the artists to protest the fracking, then they got stories in the New York papers about fracking—they hate it up there. She's a good-looking gal, so the boys are what you call conflicted about her.'

'How?'

'They don't know what they want to do most, screw her or beat the hell outta her.'

Jimmy John grinned. Book didn't.

'Reminds me. Thanks for the help at Padre's the other night.'

241

'Didn't figure you needed any, not with Babe Ruth watching your back.'

'I hit him hard, didn't I?' Nadine said.

'Real hard. You're pretty good with a beer bottle.'

Jimmy John abruptly grimaced as if a bullet had just bored through his brain.

'Are the headaches getting worse?' Book asked.

'Yeah.'

'How are the nosebleeds?'

'Regular.'

'Better see a doctor.'

He turned to Brenda Jones. She sat in her chair; her belly looked as if it might explode. Her expression said it felt that way.

'Nathan was murdered,' he said.

Brenda Jones regarded Book from across the coffee table.

'What are you going to do about it, Professor?'

Book saw in her eyes the desperation of a young woman, pregnant with her first child, whose husband had been taken from her.

'I'm going to find Nathan's truth. Give him justice.'

Brenda pushed herself out of the chair; Jimmy John helped her up. She came to Book; he stood. She hugged him.

'Thank you, Professor. But be careful. They follow us. They know everything. Where we go. What we do. Who we see. Who we talk to. They're always watching.'

Book blew out a breath. This sad young woman needed more help than a law professor could provide. But finding the truth, bringing her husband's killer to justice, that he could do. That he would do. He took her by the shoulders.

'Brenda, listen, I'm going to find out who killed Nathan, I promise you. But you need to stay strong. Mentally strong. Getting paranoid about things, thinking people are following you, watching you, that won't help you. Or your health. Or your baby. Okay?'

The phone rang. Brenda put one hand on the side of her belly as if to hold it in place then walked over to the landline hung on the kitchen wall. She answered. After a moment, she held the phone out to Book.

'It's for you.'

Chapter 24

There was no traffic on Highway 67 north, the road to Midland. Tom Dunn had called Book at Nathan's house and said he had important information that could not wait until tomorrow. So Book and Nadine were riding the Harley to Midland late in the day.

But how did Tom Dunn know that Book was at Nathan's house?

Book glanced in the rearview. A black pickup truck followed behind them a distance. As it had since they had left Marfa. As it still did when they hit Interstate 20 an hour later. The truck exited the highway behind them when they arrived in Midland. Book beat them through a red light and cut around the west side of downtown. He found a spot a block down from the Dunn Building and waited.

'What are we doing?' Nadine asked.

'Waiting.'

'For what?'

'For them.'

The black pickup truck parked in front of the Dunn Building. The two men inside did not get out.

'Stay here.'

Book got off the Harley and walked up to the pickup. He stayed out of their mirror angle—there was an Aggie sticker on the rear bumper—then he went around to the driver's side. The window was down.

'Are you following us?'

The man jumped—'Shit!'—then quickly gathered himself when he saw Book. 'It's a free country.'

Both of the men were shaved bald in the fashion of pro athletes, and both were large enough to have played pro football.

'A week in the hospital isn't. Free.'

'You threatening us?'

'Yes. Don't follow us anymore. And tell Billy Bob I know he killed Nathan Jones. Tell him I'm coming for him.'

'You'll have to come through us.'

'I'd enjoy that.'

The man snorted. 'Fuckin' kung fu Injun . . . that shit don't scare me, Professor.'

'Taekwondo. And I'm part Comanche. You know, the Comanche once roamed this land on horseback—'

'What, and you roam it on a Harley?'

He laughed and shared a fist-bump with his buddy.

'Where's your bow and arrow, Sacagawea?' the buddy said.

'Sack a shit,' the driver said.

They again laughed. They clearly weren't history buffs, so Book stuck his hand into his pants pocket and pulled out his pearl-handled pocketknife.

'I don't have a bow and arrow. All I've got is this little knife.'

He opened the blade and stepped to the rear of the truck. He leaned down and jammed the blade into the tire.

'And you've got a flat tire.'

Book turned away and saw Nadine standing there.

'I was too scared to stay over there by myself,' she said.

'It's broad daylight in downtown Midland.'

The men jumped out of the truck. Book grabbed her arm and pulled her across the street and into the Dunn Building.

'Do you?' she asked.

'Do I what?'

'Know Billy Bob did it?'

'No. But he had the most to lose.'

Once inside, he looked back at the men. They were not happy. The driver held a cell phone to his ear.

Book's cell phone rang. He checked the number. The dean.

'Hello, Roscoe.'

'Book, you're pissing off important people in West Texas.'

'Well, I've pissed off important people in South Texas and East Texas, why not West Texas?'

'True. But Tom Dunn's a donor.'

'He may be an aider and abettor in a criminal conspiracy.'

'Why do you say stuff like that? He pledged five million to the school. Called me up, said he was going to revoke his pledge if you didn't get off his back. And his client's back.'

'Roscoe, I haven't even gotten *on* their backs yet.'

'Book, come home. Teach your Con Law class. Stop calling people murderers on the radio.'

'Dunn's murderer–client is an Aggie.'

'Really?' The dean got a kick out of that. 'He's also Tom's biggest client.'

'I'm in the lobby of his building in Midland right now. I'm heading up to see him.'

'Book, try to have a cordial conversation.'

'I don't think that's going to happen.'

Roscoe exhaled into the phone.

'Well . . . then get a haircut.'

'Hell of a radio interview, Professor,' Tom Dunn said. 'But you might be jumping the gun.'

'How'd you know I was at Nathan's house?'

246

Dunn responded with a wry smile. 'My country club's got more members than Marfa's got people. Small town. Everyone knows everything.'

Book and Nadine sat in Tom Dunn's corner office in Midland again. The sun was setting in the western sky. He held out a small baggie containing a green leafy substance.

'We were cleaning out Nathan's office and found this.'

'Marijuana?'

'It ain't lettuce.'

'You're saying Nathan Jones smoked dope?'

'I'm saying we found this in his office. Maybe he smoked it, maybe he was holding it for a friend. Maybe he was high driving home that night. Maybe he passed out and ran off the road.'

'That's a convenient theory, Mr. Dunn, since the sheriff couldn't have an autopsy performed because his body was so badly burned.'

'I'm just giving you information, Professor.' He tossed the baggie to Book. 'You can take it.'

Perhaps it was because the Koontz case was fresh on his mind, but Book couldn't help but wonder if he were being set up to be pulled over by a county sheriff on a dark road between Midland and Marfa, searched, and found to be carrying marijuana. A drug bust might constitute cause to revoke his tenure; of course, many professors were children of the sixties, so perhaps not. But Book saw no reason to take the chance.

'You keep it.'

'Suit yourself.'

'Where would he get marijuana?'

Dunn laughed. 'Where not? Marfa is only sixty miles from the border, Professor. Marijuana shipments come north as regular as the U.S. mail.'

It was after ten, and the highway was dark and deserted. Book recalled Billy Bob's words: 'You want to live in the light or in the dark?' Driving a country road at night makes you

247

appreciate electricity. When the sun goes down in the city, there's still light. Streetlights and neon lights and store lights and building lights. But night in the country defines dark. They were in a black hole, only the moon offering any light, and the moon that night was only a sliver of white in the black sky. Both sides of the highway lay in pitch black. Book could see only the fifty feet of asphalt illuminated by the Harley's headlight.

So he throttled back.

There was no other traffic to contend with, but a collision with a deer crossing the road could be dangerous. When driving a country road in a three-ton pickup truck or SUV at night and suddenly encountering a deer in your headlights, the rule was simple: hit the deer. Most people veer to miss the deer, lose control of their vehicle, run off the road, and roll over. The deer survives, but the humans often do not. So hit the deer and live to feel bad about it.

But the rule didn't apply to motorcycles.

The night air had turned cool, so Nadine wore Book's leather jacket as well as the goggles and crash helmet. They were about thirty miles outside Marfa when he saw headlights in the side mirrors. The lights came closer, fast. No doubt a local running with his pedal to the metal. Book slowed and steered to the edge of the highway to allow the vehicle clear passage, just in case the driver was working on his second six-pack of the night. The lights were soon on them. And stayed on them, high enough above the road that it had to be a pickup truck. He waved for the truck to pass, but it stayed behind them. Close behind them.

Then it got closer.

'Professor!'

The truck was too close. Book turned the throttle hard, and the Harley shot ahead. They got a distance ahead of the lights. He thought he had outrun the truck, but the lights appeared in the mirrors again. Book gunned the Harley, but

248

the lights came closer. And got brighter; the driver had hit his bright lights. Book didn't know the road well enough to put the Harley wide open, but he was about to take the chance when the lights finally came around to pass. Book steered far to the right, onto the rumble strip. He fought to hold the Harley steady. Then the truck steered to the right— and into them.

Nadine screamed.

Chapter 25

'Someone sure don't like you, Professor.'

Sheriff Brady Munn stood by the door of the hospital room at the Big Bend Regional Medical Center in Alpine just north of the U.S. Courthouse and Detention Center. Alpine is the county seat of Brewster County and twenty-one miles east of Marfa, but there is no hospital in Marfa. They had been run off the road in Presidio County, so Sheriff Munn had jurisdiction over the investigation.

'Billy Bob Barnett.'

'Well, hell, podna, I wouldn't like you either, if you all but called me a murderer on the only radio station in town. That tends to piss people off.'

'Sheriff, Nathan Jones was murdered. By Billy Bob.'

The sheriff grunted. 'I reckon you're right—about the murder. Billy Bob's still an open question.'

'Two of his goons followed us to Midland in a black pickup truck. I confronted them.'

'I take it that didn't go well.'

'It was less than cordial.'

The sheriff chuckled. 'I bet it was. Less than cordial.'

'And a dark pickup truck ran us off the road three hours later. It had to be them.'

The truck had forced Book off the road. He managed to keep the Harley upright through the prairie grass, until they hit a railroad track embankment. The bike stopped; they didn't. They both went flying. Book landed in a barbed-wire fence; he required only a tetanus shot, bandages, and a dozen stitches in his forehead. Nadine flew over the fence, crashed through a mesquite bush, and landed hard in the desert; she broke her left arm and right leg and suffered lacerations on her legs and possibly a concussion. The crash helmet protected her head, the goggles her glasses and eyes, and the leather jacket her arms and torso from further cuts; but Book had not protected her as he had promised. It was just after eight the next morning, and she lay in the bed, medicated and asleep, with casts on her arm and leg and a white bandage wrapped around her head; she looked like a child. A monitor beeped with each beat of her heart. Book sat next to the bed, close enough to touch her face. The Harley now sat in the back of a Presidio County Sheriff's Department four-wheel-drive pickup truck in the parking lot at the sheriff's office.

'Mexican name of Pedro, got a shop south of the tracks, fixes cars,' the sheriff said. 'Knows motorbikes, too. You want Shirley to drop your Harley over there?'

'I'll go with her. Before I leave my Harley with a stranger, I want to check him out.'

The sheriff grunted. 'Way my wife used to be with baby-sitters. So you got nothing on the truck? No make or model?'

'The bright lights blinded me. But it was them.'

'Well, that ain't exactly a positive ID, Professor. I need evidence. I can't go around kung-fu-ing everyone I meet. I'm the law. I gotta play by the rules.'

'It's tae— . . . Never mind.'

Nadine stirred and tried to move. Her eyes blinked open . . . and focused on the white casts covering her arm and

251

leg . . . then moved around the hospital room . . . the IV connected to her good arm . . . the beeping monitors . . . the sheriff . . . and finally settled on Book. The realization came over her face. Tears welled up in her eyes and rolled down her cheeks.

'Oh, Professor.'

Book wiped the tears from her face.

'Where am I?'

'The hospital in Alpine.'

A nurse stuck her head in and said, 'Sheriff, there's a call for you.'

The sheriff stepped outside. Nadine's eyes followed him out then returned to Book.

'You know what we learned last night, Professor?'

'What?'

'A, taekwondo doesn't work against a big truck. And B, they're not trying to scare us off anymore. Now they're trying to kill us.'

'That's not going to happen.'

He wiped her tears again.

'I'm afraid of life, so I'm hiding out in law school. Then you bring me out here on that Harley and now I'm in the hospital with a broken arm, a broken leg, bruises, contusions, assorted scratches, possible brain damage . . . by the way, mesquite hurts.'

'I'm sorry.'

'Professor, has this kind of thing happened before?'

'It has.'

'Is that why Renée quit?'

'It is.'

'Why do you do it?'

'Alzheimer's.'

'You've got Alzheimer's?'

'My mother. Early-onset. She doesn't know who I am.'

She studied him a long moment.

252

'And you're afraid you'll get it early, too? So you take all those supplements and vitamins I saw in your bathroom, you eat organic and run at dawn and hope you don't win that genetic lottery.'

'My mother has one of the mutant genes that guaranteed she'd have Alzheimer's before age sixty-five. She was sixty-two when the symptoms started.'

'I didn't know there was such a gene.'

'There is. Three, actually. All it takes is one.'

Nadine dropped her eyes and did not look up when she asked, 'Professor . . . do you have that mutant gene, too?'

'I do.'

He had been tested. He had never told anyone, not even Joanie. His intern looked up; her eyes were wet.

'I've already lost that genetic lottery, Ms. Honeywell.'

'Maybe they'll find a cure before you . . .'

'Maybe.'

He blew out a breath.

'It's like knowing the day you're going to die. I'm on the clock. So I'm going to make every minute count. I'm going to make my life matter.'

'You're a famous Con Law professor, a best-selling writer, a sure bet for the Supreme Court . . .'

'None of that matters to me.'

'What does?'

'Not what. Who.'

'Who matters? To you.'

'My mother, my sister . . . friends . . . students . . . Nathan . . . Renée . . .' He took her hand. '. . . And you, Nadine. You matter to me.'

'You called me Nadine. Not Ms. Honeywell.'

'I did.'

'I do? Matter to you?'

'You do.'

She pondered that a moment.

'So you live life in the fast lane, no fear of the future because you don't think you'll have a future, not afraid of dying but of not living. I understand now.'

'I try to live every day of my life as if it's my last.'

'Well, Professor, yesterday was almost your last. Mine, too. Only my mom doesn't have Alzheimer's.'

'What does she have?'

'A new husband.'

The sheriff walked back in. 'Miss Honeywell, did you see anything last night?'

'Stars.' She turned her eyes back to Book. 'Professor, I want to go home. I want to sit in a Starbucks and drink a latte and text in relative safety.'

'You can't leave the hospital for a few days. They've got to make sure you don't have a serious head injury. I'll leave the laptop with you. You can work on the Welch brief.'

She blinked back tears. Book felt his blood pressure ratchet up a notch.

'And I've got some unfinished business with Billy Bob Barnett.'

'Hold on there, podna,' the sheriff said. 'If Billy Bob's behind this, I'll find out and then I'll arrest him. But you take the law into your own hands in my county, even if you are a law professor, I'll throw your butt in jail, I don't care how famous you are.'

The professor and the sheriff had left, and Nadine Honeywell lay alone in the hospital room. She started to cry. But just as she was entering the full-scale slobbering and self-pity stage, she thought of Leslie Benedict in *Giant*, the barbecue scene where she passes out from the heat and the sight of the cooked calf's brain, and everyone thinks she's too weak to survive in Texas. She could have run home to her dad in Virginia—just as Nadine now wanted desperately to call her daddy in San Francisco to come and take her home. She didn't. Leslie. Instead, she got up the next morning, determined to be a tough Texan, to work the cattle alongside Bick.

Elizabeth Taylor had been only twenty-three when she came to Marfa to play Leslie Benedict in *Giant*. Nadine was only twenty-three, and she was now in Marfa playing intern to the professor. They had both come from California to Texas. They had both stayed in the same room at the Paisano Hotel. They had both been knocked down to the dirt of this same desert.

Leslie Benedict had gotten up.

Nadine adjusted the bed until she came to a sitting position, wiped the tears from her face, and buzzed the nurse. When she entered, Nadine said, 'Please hand me my glasses and that laptop and take this needle out of my arm.'

The nurse smiled. 'My, we seem to be feeling better now. Are we ready for breakfast?'

'We are. A double order. And a large coffee. With real cream. And we want our own bottle of Purell. We've got work to do.'

'Little tough on your gal back there,' the sheriff said. 'Making her work with a broken arm and leg.'

'That's my job—to make my students tough enough to survive as lawyers.'

'Guess it didn't take with Nathan Jones.'

The sheriff gave Book a ride back to Marfa. He chewed tobacco and spat the juice into a Styrofoam cup; with the wind, spitting out the window could get messy.

'Nathan's senior partner in Midland said they found marijuana in his office.'

The sheriff grunted.

'Of course,' Book said, 'he might've lied.'

'Why would he do that?'

'To get me to go home.'

'I reckon he ain't alone in wanting you to go home.'

'Just about everyone we've met wants us to go home . . . except you.'

'I'm a slow learner.' The sheriff spat into the cup. 'Fact is, I like a change of pace. And we're both in the truth business.'

'You ever find it? The truth.'

'Not as often as I'd prefer. So you figure maybe Nathan Jones got into drugs?'

'Maybe.'

'Wouldn't be the first time. It can take down the best of men. It's the devil, just waiting for a weak soul seeking refuge from this world or a greedy heart wanting to strike it rich. Too much temptation and money for some folks to stay on the good side of the law. Even the law. Sheriff before me, ex-Marine, six-four, wore black boots and a white Stetson, looked like John Wayne on a bad day. Law-and-order sort of guy, worked the West Texas Drug Task Force hard, made a lot of drug busts . . . you ever heard of those task forces?'

'As a matter of fact, I have.'

'Law and order got out of hand there. Anyway, he was a real hard-ass, figured he was twice as smart as anyone else in the county. Half the county loved him, the other half feared him. Which is the way he wanted it. Figured Presidio County was his personal sandbox. Being sheriff for twenty years will do that to a man.'

'How long have you been sheriff?'

'Sixteen years.'

'Take care you don't suffer the same fate.'

'Every day, Professor.'

He slowed the cruiser and drove along the shoulder, eyeing the bare land and grunting now and then. Book had learned that a grunt was a part of speech for the sheriff, but also that it was more rhetorical in nature, so Book did not respond to his grunts.

'Turned out, he was living a double life. Him and a cowboy from Alpine teamed up to run drugs across the border for

256

fifteen years, driving pickup loads of cocaine right across the river—north of Presidio, the Rio Conchos empties into the Rio Grande. Above that, it's usually dry, especially in a drought like this. Stashed the dope in horse trailers at the county fairgrounds. Made a million bucks off each load. Apparently he didn't want to depend on the county pension fund for his retirement. DEA nabbed him bringing a load up one night with twenty armed guards. Now he's retired to the federal prison. Life sentence.'

'Hard way to end your life.'

'I reckon. He's never gonna see another West Texas sunset, eat another steak at Reata, drink another cold Lone Star beer on a hot summer day. Man can live without a lot of things, those would be tough.'

'What about sex?'

The sheriff grunted. 'Hate to break the news to you at such a tender age, Professor, but you're already on the downside of sex.'

'This day just keeps getting worse.'

Which evoked another grunt.

'Anyway, since the artists came to town, recreational use has shot up. Dope's always come through town, just sixty miles from the border. Not much I can do about that, figure that's a job for the Border Patrol and DEA. But now a lot is staying in town. And that is my job.'

He spat.

'We call ourselves Marfans.' He jabbed a thumb behind them. 'Folks in Alpine and Fort Davis, they call us Marfadites. They're jealous of our notoriety. They shouldn't be. 'Cause, damn, we're stocked full up on attorneys, artists, and assholes.'

'Triple As.'

'You been talking to Sam Walker?'

'I have.'

'He's a good man.'

'What about the mayor?'

'He's a real-estate broker.'

'He seems happy to have the artists in Marfa.'

The sheriff spat.

'Reckon he is, making money hand over fist. See, some folks think a town is a place to live. Other folks think it's a place to make money. Mayor, he figures those homosexuals are gonna be struck down by God's wrath one day, but in the meantime he's willing to pocket some real-estate commissions off of them. Me, I don't care what two consenting adults do, long as they do it indoors. They want to get married, I say, Why shouldn't homosexuals have the same right to be miserable like the rest of us?'

The sheriff had amused himself.

'You get along with the artists?'

'I try to get along with everyone. Liking people comes easy for me, just my nature. Guess that's why I'm in the people business. But, those people, I have to confess, they're a hard bunch to like. They segregate themselves, don't want to live in Marfa as much as above Marfa. They don't want to eat with us, live with us, or shop for groceries with us. They don't want their kids sitting next to cowboys and Mexicans in the public schools, so they start their own private school charging more than most folks around here make in a year. They wear those "What Would Donald Judd Do?" caps and shirts, but Judd didn't do that. He put his kids in the public schools like everyone else.'

He spat.

'We've been hoping for a Walmart, but they don't want one here, too working class for their tastes. That's how they view us, a lower class, the little people who don't know modern art from old art. It's like 'cause they're from New York and know art, they got nothing but disdain for us.'

'It's not just you.'

'You try to be friendly, say "howdy" when you walk past them on the sidewalk, even two boys holding hands, but they don't say "hello" or "go to hell," just give you a look like they're telling an inside joke and you're the punch line, got their iPhones and their iPads and their iMentalities.' He exhaled. 'My wife's got one of them.'

'A homosexual?'

'iPad. She reads books on it in bed, you believe that?'

He spat.

'Judd gave us boxes. These young artists, they gave us the finger. They put up that "Hello Meth Lab in the Sun" exhibit and call it art. They paint that "Axis of Evil" sign downtown and call it freedom of speech. I mean, what's the point of getting in people's faces like that? You know, I don't much care for intolerant right-wing Republicans, but these folks taught me I don't much care for intolerant left-wing Democrats either. And these folks are as intolerant as the wind.'

The sheriff pointed.

'Eagle.' He watched the bird soar on the currents a moment then said, 'Sometimes I wish to hell Judd had moved to New Mexico instead of Marfa. I mean, you can't get a goddamn Viagra prescription filled in Marfa, but you sure as hell can buy cheese called Gouda at The Get Go.' He paused. 'You know, if you needed Viagra.'

He spat.

'American cheese ain't good enough for those folks. They got to have cheese from France, so that gal opens an organic store, got all kinds of cheese. Hell, it's just cheese, for Pete's sake. City folks think living out here in this desert's kind of neat at first, then they want what they left behind.'

'Human nature.'

'Reckon so. Course, wanting to eat a special kind of cheese, that's harmless. Trying to take folks' jobs, that can be dangerous.'

'The artists protesting fracking?'

'Put a flame to that gas, someone's gonna get hurt. They don't seem to understand what having a job means to a man.

It ain't just the money or a place to be. It's who he is. It gives value to his life. It means he's worth something in this world. What would I be if they took my badge? Or you, if they took your professorship? Folks would look at me and figure I'm just a dumb cowboy. They'd look at you and figure you're just a hippie biker. But our jobs give us our identity. Tell us who we are. You take that away, and a man's got nothing left. And that's what those artists are trying to do to the locals.'

'What do you know about Carla Kent?'

'Why do you ask?'

'Seems like there's a connection between Nathan's death, the art, the artists, fracking . . . and Ms. Kent's right in the middle of it all.'

The sheriff grunted. 'Hell, she just showed up a year or so ago, comes and goes, stays a few months at a time . . . heard she stays in one of those teepees. I wonder what that's like, sleeping in a teepee? She's a nice-looking gal, but she's always stirring up trouble.'

'And you're in the middle of that conflict.'

'Yep. I'm just refereeing this intramural match between the old Marfa and the new Marfa.'

'What do you figure will happen to Marfa?'

'Sooner or later—hopefully sooner—the artists, they'll get bored and move on . . . to the next Marfa.'

The sheriff braked to a stop. They had returned to the scene of the crime. Where Book and Nadine had been run off the road. They got out and walked to the railroad tracks that paralleled the highway. Book had seen nothing the night before, just the bouncing light from the Harley's headlight until they went airborne. Now he saw everything. Where they had gone off the road, the short distance to the embankment, the barbed-wire fence where he had landed, and the mesquite bush that had broken Nadine's fall—and her arm and leg.

'EMTs, they had a hell of a time cutting you out of that barbed wire,' the sheriff said. 'Said that gash on your forehead was bleeding like a stuck pig.'

Blood stained Book's white T-shirt.

'Lucky your gal was unconscious, or she would've been hurting something bad.'

The heat rose inside Book. He took a deep breath to calm himself.

'Damn,' the sheriff said, 'this land is brittle dry. Nothing but kindling. We get a desert storm, one lightning strike could set the plateau on fire, might not stop till the flames get to Fort Worth. Could be biblical.'

The sheriff knelt and grabbed a handful of prairie grass; it broke off in his hand like twigs instead of grass.

'Year ago this time, the Rock House fire ignited two miles west of town, raced across the grassland. If the wind was blowing east instead of north, it would've taken out most of Marfa—downtown, homes, the art. Instead, it went north and burned a lot of Fort Davis. Burned for a month, scorched three hundred thousand acres, killed a lot of livestock. Horses couldn't outrun the flames.'

He shook his head.

'To see those horses burned to a crisp, make a man cry. We put up the "Burn Ban" notices, but folks from out of town, they flick cigarettes out the window 'cause they never witnessed a wildfire, so they can't imagine what it's like, to see that wall of fire coming your way fast. When the wind's blowing fifty miles an hour, neither man nor horse can outrun the flames.'

'Anything you can do, to prevent a fire?'

'Pray for rain.'

Book walked around the scene. The desert lay silent, and the morning air smelled fresh. The grass crunched under his boots. He spotted something near a yucca plant. He squatted and picked it up: a small plastic bottle of Purell hand sanitizer. He squeezed his hand tight around the bottle as if making a fist.

'I need to see Billy Bob Barnett.'

'Now, Professor, I'm conducting a homicide investigation. I'm compiling a list of suspects—'

'Including Billy Bob?'

'He's at the top of my list.'

'Then arrest him, throw him in jail.'

The sheriff smiled. 'See, you're talking like a man whose gal got hurt, not like a law professor teaching all those constitutional rules we gotta follow—Miranda warning, probable cause, plain sight, incident to an arrest—all those fine points of the law just waiting to trip us up out here in the real world. All that sounds real good in a classroom, but out here when there's a victim in the hospital and a bad guy on the loose laughing at you, it don't feel so good, does it? The rules are meant to slow us down, make sure we get the right bad guy, but now it's personal for you so you want to go fast. 'Cause you *think* he did it.'

'So what are you going to do?'

'I'm gonna investigate, not kick someone's ass—and you are not gonna kick any more ass in my county. I'm gonna build a case, prove he did it. I'm going to go back to my office, call Mr. Barnett, and set up an appointment. Then I'm going to interview him and take a look at the black pickup truck his boys were driving, see if there's any evidence they ran you off the road. Now, we can work together, Professor, or you can go home. *Comprende?*'

'I'll take care of Billy Bob Barnett myself.'

The sheriff spat.

'Oh, I see how it is. The famous law professor, he likes to work alone. Running all over the country, saving folks, righting wrongs, just him and his Harley. He helps everyone, but he don't need help from anyone, is that it? 'Cause he's just so damn smart and tough. Well, first of all, Professor, you playing the Lone Ranger got your little gal back there put in that hospital bed, that's a fact. And you got to live with that fact. And second of all, even the Lone Ranger had Tonto.'

'What's that supposed to mean?'

'Means it's okay for a man to need help. And, podna, you need help.'

Chapter 26

The sheriff dropped Book at the Paisano so he could change before meeting the deputy about the Harley. But as soon as the sheriff's cruiser turned out of sight, Book ran down Highland Avenue to Billy Bob Barnett's office. He thought, I don't need an appointment. I don't need to play by the rules I teach. I don't need help. And he thought of his intern; he had promised to protect her. He had not. The sheriff was right about that: his actions had put Nadine in the hospital. His anger built with each step. His years of taekwondo training to control his emotions failed him. He was mad.

Billy Bob Barnett had hurt his intern.

He arrived at the Barnett Oil and Gas Company office—the black pickup truck was nowhere in sight—and barged through the front door and hurried past Earlene without asking permission—

'Hey! Professor! He's in a meeting!'

—and down the hall past the lunchroom where donuts were piled high on the table—

'Wait!' Earlene yelled from behind.

—and opened the closed door and marched into the office.

Billy Bob sat at the conference table with three other men. They wore maroon shirts and were watching the fracking video.

'Mr. Barnett,' Earlene said, 'he rushed right past me.'

Billy Bob held up a hand. 'It's okay.' To Book: 'You just have something against appointments, don't you?'

He looked Book up and down—the bloodstained shirt and the bandage on his forehead—then stood.

'The hell happened to you?'

'You happened to me. And to Nadine. She's hurt.'

'Honeywell? She's hurt?'

'She's in the hospital. Broken arm and leg. She could've been killed.'

'What the hell are you talking about?'

The same two bald goons who had followed them to Midland entered the office and advanced on him. Book closed the distance and got in the driver's face again. He was a side of beef.

'You ran us off the road, didn't you?'

The man's muscles tensed as if to strike Book.

'Do it.'

Taekwondo is not about kicking someone's ass. It's about self-defense, self-control, physical and mental discipline, about knowing you can but deciding you won't . . . But Book wanted to kick this big Aggie's ass so bad it hurt. And he could.

'Please do it.'

'Don't do it, Jimbo,' Billy Bob said from behind. 'I don't want your blood staining my brand-new Aggie gray carpet.'

He didn't do it. He backed down.

'Where's the black truck you were driving yesterday?' Book asked the goon.

The goon shrugged. 'Butch took it to Hell Paso.'

'Convenient.'

'Beats walking.'

Book turned and pointed a finger at Billy Bob Barnett.

265

'Nathan Jones's son is going to grow up without a father because of you. I'm going to prove that you killed him . . . that these two goons ran us off the road and hurt Nadine . . . and that your fracking is contaminating the groundwater. I'm going to put you out of business, Billy Bob. When you hurt Nadine, you made it personal.'

Book now turned to the men in maroon shirts.

'Don't invest with him. He's going to prison.'

Billy Bob smiled. 'Have a nice day, Professor.'

Carla Kent sat at a table in the courtyard at the Paisano Hotel. She had checked with the front desk; the professor and his intern hadn't returned. The clerk said he'd heard there had been an accident the night before out on the highway. A motorcycle wreck. A man and a woman had been taken to the Alpine hospital. She had called the hospital; the professor was not a registered patient. But Nadine Honeywell was. There was no word on her condition.

God, what had she done?

Book stepped out onto the sidewalk fronting Billy Bob's office and took a deep breath to gather himself. His body teemed with anger and adrenaline. He walked back to the Paisano and cut through the courtyard. He stopped. Carla Kent sat on the other side of the fountain, as if she had been waiting for him. He walked over to her. She stood. Her T-shirt read: *Don't Frack with Mother Nature*.

'Is she okay? Your intern?'

'Word travels fast out here. She'll be okay. Broken arm and leg.'

'I'm so sorry, Professor.'

'Not your fault, Ms. Kent.'

Her eyes went to the blood on his shirt and bandage on his head. 'You okay?'

He nodded. 'Got tangled up in a barbed-wire fence.' He blew out a breath to ease his blood pressure. 'I wanted to ratchet up the pressure on the killer, almost got my intern killed.'

'You taking her home?'

'After I prove that Billy Bob hurt her. And killed Nathan. I'm going to get that son of a bitch.'

Her eyes sparkled. 'Wow, the cool law professor gets mad. I like that side of you.'

'Good. Because you're going to see more of it.'

She was the connection between Nathan's death and everything else. She knew something. So he needed to know her.

'Ms. Kent, I'm ready to work together.'

'Carla. We can start now.'

'I've got to clean up first, and then see a deputy about a Harley.'

A frown.

'Not Deputy Shirley?'

Deputy Shirley blew strands of blond hair from her face then wiped sweat from her brow. She was driving Book in the Sheriff's Department pickup truck with the Harley in the back to the repair shop. He had cleaned up and changed his shirt.

'Pedro,' she said, 'he used to have a gas station and garage in town, but the artists drove him out.'

'How?'

'They ran up rents in downtown, drove the local businesses out. Artists converted Pedro's old garage into a studio. So now he works out of his own garage, on the Mexican side of town.'

'There's a Mexican side of town?'

'This is Marfa, Professor, but it's still Texas. North side of the railroad tracks, that's always been the Anglo side. Now it's the Yankee side, big homes behind walled compounds. South side, that's the Mexican side. Trailers mostly, little homes, crumbling adobes.'

The hot wind blew through the cab. Deputy Shirley blew hair from her face again.

'You know what I like to do on hot days like this?' she said.

'No. What?'

'Get a big ol' snow cone—I like root beer, with cream—and drive up into the mountains where it's cooler, find a nice little spot and spread out a soft blanket . . .'

'Sounds nice.'

'. . . and screw.'

She turned to Book and arched her eyebrows.

'What do you say, Professor?'

She offered a country girl's natural beauty and unabashed sexuality, an excellent combination in Book's experience. But now was neither the time nor the place.

'Well, Deputy—'

'Shirley.'

'Deputy Shirley, I appreciate the offer, but—'

'I've got handcuffs.'

Pedro's Repair Shop was a garage to the side of his house on East Galveston Street past the crumbling adobes with the *Fuck U ChiNazis* graffiti. Latino music played on a small radio and Pedro Martinez sat on a stool on the dirt ground in front of the garage, wearing reading glasses and pondering an engine part. They got out and walked over. Brown-skinned children played barefooted in the street. The voice of a woman singing a Mexican ballad and the smell of Mexican food drifted over from the house.

'Pedro's wife, she makes the best tamales in Marfa,' Deputy Shirley said. 'You can get your car fixed and pick up dinner in one stop.'

Pedro watched them over his glasses as they came toward him.

'Deputy Shirley,' he said.

'Pedro, this is Professor Bookman. He needs his Harley fixed.'

Pedro smiled. 'Ah, the karate professor. I have heard of you.'

'On the public radio?'

'No. We do not listen to that. It is not for us. It is for the rich Anglos from the north. I have heard of you from word of mouth.' He stood. 'Let us look at the bike.'

'I'm gonna get some tamales,' Deputy Shirley said. 'Have a little girl talk with Juanita.'

She headed to the house. Book and Pedro walked to the truck, leaned on the sideboard, and studied the twisted motorcycle. Pedro pondered for a time then nodded.

'I can fix that.'

'You repair Harleys?'

'*Sí.*'

'Have you ever repaired a Harley?'

'No.'

'I don't know. I restored this Harley by hand.'

His father had taught Book how to restore Harleys. It was his dad's hobby. He restored them and then sold them— 'Adopted them out,' as he said—to worthy Harleyites.

'And I will repair it by hand,' Pedro said. He was a white-haired man in his sixties, perhaps seventies. He removed his reading glasses. '*Señor*, I am Pedro Martinez. I am known all over Presidio County as the *hombre* who repairs the vehicles. I can do this.'

Pedro returned to his stool and sat. He replaced the glasses on his face, turned up the radio, and picked up a wrench.

'So, *Señor*, do you want that I fix your Harley?'

Book pulled out his pocket notebook and began jotting down the terms of this repair contract. First, the price.

'How much?'

'Oh, *mucho dinero.*'

Book sighed. *Mucho dinero* was a bit vague. He put the notebook back in his pocket. Perhaps he would rely on an oral contract.

'I need it soon.'

'Okay. I will do that.'

Deputy Shirley returned with a brown bag. She reached inside and came out with a tamale. She handed it to Book. He hadn't eaten that morning, so he was hungry. He ate the tamale.

'That's good.'

'*Sí.*'

They rolled the Harley down from the truck bed and into Pedro's garage. Book felt as if he were leaving his only child at college. Of course, he didn't have a child and would never have a child; he would not pass the mutant gene on to another generation of Bookmans. He hoped Joanie had not.

'Pedro, you sure you can do this?'

'*Señor*, I can repair motorcycles of all makes and models.'

'What kind of bikes have you repaired?'

'Why, just two weeks ago, I repaired a Vespa.'

'A *Vespa*? That's not exactly the same as a vintage Harley softtail classic.'

Pedro shrugged. 'It had only the two wheels, just as your Harley.'

'*Two wheels?*'

Book knew he was leaving his child at the wrong college.

'Vespas, they're for—'

'*La mariposa,*' Pedro said.

'Means homosexual,' Deputy Shirley said.

Pedro smiled. 'The boy, he was the *artista*. And the Vespa, it was purple, and it had the Chinati sticker. And he had the purple hair and that tattoo, on his fingers: wwDJD.'

'Kenni with an "i." We met him at the pizza joint.'

'Yes, that was him. Kenni. He wrote his check in the purple ink.'

Book took one last look at the Harley.

'Take care of my Harley, Pedro.'

'His friend sent him to me,' Pedro said. 'Nice boy. He was the—'

Book took a step away.

'—lawyer.'

Book stopped. 'Lawyer? What lawyer?'

'The lawyer who died, in the accident. His picture was in the paper. He brought the *mariposa* over to pick up the Vespa.'

'Wait. Nathan Jones was here? With Kenni?'

'*Sí*. That was his name. Nathan. I thought he was also the *mariposa*, but the paper said he had a wife and she is pregnant.'

They got back into the pickup truck. Book tried to process the information about Nathan and Kenni, but his thoughts were interrupted when Deputy Shirley leaned his way and revealed a significant portion of her soft breasts.

'How 'bout that snow cone, Professor?'

Chapter 27

Book took a rain check on the snow cone, so Deputy Shirley dropped him at the Pizza Foundation. The purple Vespa was parked outside; inside, Kenni with an 'i' was serving pizzas to a table of roughnecks wearing red *Barnett Oil and Gas* jumpsuits. Kenni waved at Book; the roughnecks gave him hard looks. Book took a table and waited for him. He pulled out the funeral photo and searched the faces. He found Kenni's face near the back.

'The famous professor.' Kenni had arrived wearing a *Don't Frack the Planet* T-shirt. 'I heard you on the radio. You sure got the town talking. What would you like today?'

'Information.'

'About what?'

'Not what. Whom. Nathan Jones.'

'Oh.'

Book gestured at the other chair. 'Sit down, Kenni.'

The waiter looked around as if to escape, then he accepted his fate. He sat.

'Talk.'

Kenni picked purple paint from his fingernails. He shrugged.

'Nathan wanted to be an artist. He had talent. Did you see his photos?'

Book nodded. 'At his house.'

'He loved the art scene. He wanted to move to New York, but his wife didn't. Her folks are ranchers, so she had the locals' attitude toward us.'

'How did you meet?'

'At the bookstore. That's like our clubhouse. The artists. We all congregate there. He started coming to the art events. He loved art . . . even Chamberlain's car wrecks . . . Then he died in a car wreck.'

'Was he gay?'

Kenni picked paint; he finally nodded.

'He had a wife,' Book said.

'He had a double life.'

'Lot of that going on out here.'

'Nathan the lawyer, husband, and father-to-be . . . and Nathan the gay artist. He said he hoped his son didn't turn out gay, too.'

'Were you two in a relationship?'

'We were friends . . . with benefits. God, he was gorgeous. He loved that movie, *Giant,* I don't know why, combed his hair like James Dean . . . See?'

Kenni held up his iPhone to show Book a photo of Nathan Jones with his hair standing tall.

'I guess he was trying to figure out who he was, you know, like when I went through my Madonna stage.'

'Did his wife know?'

'I don't think so . . . Maybe. Not about me, but about him.'

'Does she need to be tested?'

Kenni shook his head. 'Nathan protected her. He loved her. I'm HIV negative, so was he.'

'Did Jimmy John know?'

'Oh, God, no. They were friends, but Nathan would never have told him about us. He calls us queers, Jimmy John. He hates us.'

'Maybe he'd be more tolerant if the artists weren't threatening his job. Trying to stop fracking.'

Kenni shrugged. 'Fracking's ruining our environment.'

'How long have you been here?'

'Eight months.'

'How'd you keep it a secret? Marfa's a small town.'

'We don't talk to the locals, and they don't talk to us.'

'Why not?'

'We're gay, and they're not.'

'Have you ever talked to a local?'

'About what?'

'Anything.'

'No.'

'Why not?'

'Why? What would they have to say that would interest me? They're a bunch of homophobic, anti-Semitic, unintellectual racists. They have no appreciation of art. They know nothing about wine. My God, they'd rather eat barbecue than crepes. They get their news from Fox. They have zero sophistication. They should be thanking us for bringing culture to this awful place, but instead they call us "ChiNazis" and act disgusted because of our sexual orientation. I hate everything about Texas.'

'What about the weather?'

'Especially the weather.'

'Anything you like?'

'All the interesting people in town.'

'I take it you don't mean the locals?'

Kenni snorted. 'I mean other artists from New York.'

'Why do you want to live in Marfa?'

'I don't.'

'Then why are you living here?'

'Fame and fortune.'

'You're working at a pizza joint.'

'This is a temp gig.'

'Pizza?'

'Marfa. See, we're not Marfans or Texans, we're temps. We're all just temping here. We come down here, get discovered, then move back to New York rich and famous artists.'

'Like a reality show.'

'Exactly.'

'That ever work?'

'Not yet. But the buzz here is incredible. I've got a better chance of being discovered in Marfa than in New York. There's maybe a million artists on the make in New York. Here, maybe a hundred. And with the national media all over Marfa, this place is great for networking—it's like Facebook with French food.'

'So what kind of art do you do?'

'What else? Installation.'

'What are you going to install?'

'A plane. Half buried in the ground, as if it flew right into the prairie but stayed intact.'

'What kind of plane?'

'Triple-seven.'

'A jumbo jet? Won't that be expensive?'

'I'm taking donations.'

'How far along are you?'

'Three hundred and sixty-seven dollars.'

'Only forty million to go.'

'I'm not buying a new one.'

'Did Nathan use drugs?'

'No. Never. Just weed at Big Rick's studio. Part of the creative process.'

'Getting stoned and eating Cheetos?'

'I love Cheetos.'

'Who's Big Rick?'

'Rick Fusini. He's rich and famous.'

'I've never heard of him.'

'Because you live in Texas.'

'Marfa's in Texas.'

'No, it's not. It's a suburb of New York City now.'

'Tell me about Big Rick.'

'Oh, he's outrageous. At a gallery opening week before last, he painted "The Real Axis of Evil is the US, UK, and Israel" on the outside wall of the building next door, so everyone would see it.'

'We saw it.'

'The locals went absolutely apeshit! It was fabulous!'

'Did Nathan have any trouble with any of the artists?'

'Trouble? Like what?'

'Anything.'

'You mean, that would make someone kill him?'

'Like that.'

Kenni went back to picking paint. 'Big Rick kicked him out one night.'

'Why?'

'Because Nathan had sued him. For a pipeline.'

'A condemnation suit?'

Kenni nodded. 'Big Rick bought land outside town, for his installation. He's going to stack automobiles to spell out "Bush Sucks" so people flying overhead on their way to L.A. can see it.'

'There's a masterpiece.'

'Big Rick hates that bastard Billy Bob Barnett. We all do.'

'Why?'

'He's an oil man. Artists hate oil companies. They care only about money while they destroy the planet.'

As if reading from a script.

'You do know that oil money funded Judd's art?'

'*What?* No way.'

'Way.'

He pondered that a moment. 'I wonder if an oil company would fund my art?'

'Maybe Billy Bob.'

Kenni shook his head. 'He hates us. But we hate him because he's a fracker.'

'So you're fighting him?'

'With Carla.'

'You know Carla?'

'Everyone knows Carla. She recruited us to fight the fracking. She hates Billy Bob, too. Gave us these T-shirts. I introduced her to Nathan.'

'Why?'

'Because he said Billy Bob was contaminating the groundwater. She got really excited.'

'About what?'

'Said she finally had an inside man.'

'What did Nathan say?'

'That he almost had the puzzle solved.'

'What puzzle?'

'That would prove the contamination.'

'Did he show any proof to you?'

Kenni shook his head. 'Said he'd be breaking the lawyer code of conduct. But I pushed him to go public, to take his proof to the media, change the world. That's what artists do.'

'Really?'

'But Brenda told him to keep quiet about it. That's what wives do. She was scared. So was he.'

'Of losing his law license?'

'Of Billy Bob. And his beasts. We talked about what he could do. That's when he decided to write that letter to you.'

'Did he show it to you? The letter?'

'Sure.'

'But not to his wife.'

Kenni shrugged.

'So Nathan sued this Big Rick on behalf of Billy Bob.'

'Billy Bob wants to put a pipeline under the land, but Big Rick says that would mess up his art. So he said no. Billy Bob is condemning part of it for a pipeline.'

'And Nathan represents Billy Bob. Did he and Big Rick have words?'

'Big Rick has words with everyone—most begin with an "f." He's not gay. Mostly, he's a drunken bully—he's big and he's mean . . . rumor is, he killed someone back East, that's why he moved here. He has guns.'

'What kind of guns?'

'All kinds. He scares me when he gets drunk and starts playing with them. One night he shot his TV with a shotgun.'

'A shotgun?'

Kenni offered a lame shrug. 'But he pays for everything, so we all hang out there.'

'Did he threaten Nathan?'

'You mean, to shoot him?'

'To out him.'

Kenni picked his fingernails for a time. Then he nodded.

Book stood. 'Where's his studio?'

'West El Paso Street, just past Judd's Block. You can't miss it.'

Book tried to imagine his quiet, studious intern living a secret double life in Marfa, Texas, with Brenda at home and Kenni away from home.

'Was Nathan happy?'

'I think so. With both of his lives. But each life had conflict. He loved her, but he didn't belong here. He loved me, but he couldn't leave her. Maybe that was the way he was supposed to go, a bonfire in the sky.'

'Kenni, he didn't die a romantic death. He burned to death.'

Chapter 28

Book walked down West El Paso past 'The Block,' Donald Judd's one-square-block compound that housed his personal residence, two airplane hangars he converted into a studio and a library, and a swimming pool and chicken coop designed by Judd himself, all enclosed behind a tall adobe wall. West of the wall was a steel structure that looked like a warehouse. Outside sat six cars . . . stacked on top of each other. A big black 4x4 pickup truck was parked by the entrance door. Book walked around the truck and examined the glossy black paint for any damage or scratches; he found none. He rang the bell and was soon greeted by a big man in his mid-fifties wearing shorts, flip-flops, and no shirt; his hair was uncombed and his beard a week old. He looked like Nick Nolte in that infamous mug shot, only worse. His entire upper body was one big multi-colored tattoo that seemed as if someone had thrown a palette of paint on him. He took a swig from a half-empty whiskey bottle.

'Big Rick?'

'You the reporter from *Vanity Fair*?'

'I'm the law professor from UT. John Bookman.'

'What do you want?'

'I want to know why Nathan Jones died.'

'What's that got to do with me?'

'I understand he was suing you on behalf of Billy Bob Barnett and you kicked him out of here one night, threatened to out him.'

Big Rick snorted. 'You been talking to that fucking queer, Kenni with an "i"?'

'Queer? That's a little dated, don't you think?'

'I'm a little dated.'

'Being sued, some folks might consider that a motive for murder.'

'Murder? What, you think Nathan's death wasn't an accident?'

'I think someone ran him off the road.'

'What makes you say that?'

'Someone ran us off the road last night.'

'Professor, I stack cars. I don't run cars off the highway. Saw you checking out my truck—you find any evidence of a hit and run?'

'No.'

''Cause I don't murder people.'

'What about the rumor that you killed someone back East?'

Big Rick howled.

'Hell, I started that rumor myself. Image sells, Professor.' He finally took a moment to size Book up. 'You get in a fight?'

'I got in a barbed-wire fence.'

'Ouch.'

Big Rick belched and pushed the screen door open.

'Come on in.'

Book stepped inside to rock music blaring on surround sound. The interior space was a big barnlike structure, a combination home and studio with a kitchen area, a big bed in the far corner, and a living area with a big screen television on the wall with a cable cooking show playing. Big Rick placed the whiskey bottle on a counter, picked up a remote, and pointed it at the stereo; rock was replaced by country, Hank Williams Jr. singing 'Country Boy Can Survive.' He went to the refrigerator, opened it, and retrieved a carton of chocolate milk.

'You want some?'

'No, thanks.'

He poured a glass. He noticed Book eyeing the whiskey bottle.

'Thought you were a reporter.' He shrugged. 'Like I said, I have an image to maintain.'

'You got that hard-drinking artist thing down.'

'It's a living.'

At that moment, a young girl burst out of the bathroom and hurried out the front door with only a finger wave and, 'Later, Big Rick.' She looked like a high school sophomore.

'She part of the image, too?'

'She's Lorraine.'

'She looks a little young for you.'

'At my age, Professor, all the girls are a little young for me.'

'Be careful, Big Rick. I don't imagine the locals would look favorably on a New York artist violating their young girls.'

He laughed. 'Lorraine? Hell, she's laid more cowboys than a Mexican whore in Boys' Town. It's legal down there, prostitution. Man, I've burned up the highway between here and Ojinaga. They got some cute girls down there, young ones. But, hell, fourteen is middle-aged for a Mexican girl.'

'You do know you're a disgusting individual.'

Big Rick shrugged, as if he had heard it before. 'What can I say? I like young girls. We can't all be perfect, Professor.'

'You could try.'

Big Rick downed the chocolate milk then pulled out a joint, lit it, and took a long drag. He held it for a long moment then exhaled. Book tried to stay upwind.

'Medicinal,' Big Rick said.

'Illegal,' Book said.

'You're a law professor, not a cop.'

'So you threatened to out Nathan?'

'Aw, hell, I tend to be a mean drunk. I'm nicer when I'm stoned, like now. Nathan was a nice boy, married with a pregnant wife. His life was fucked up enough, gay and married, no need for me to add to his troubles. I wouldn't ruin his life over a lawsuit. I was mad at Billy Bob, but I took it out on Nathan.' He shook his head. 'Billy Bob Barnett, I'd ruin that bastard's life in a New York minute, trying to fuck up my land.'

'How much do you own?'

'Just a little. Twenty thousand acres.'

'You sound like a real Texan.'

'I wasn't born here, but I got here as soon as I could. I love Texas. Been here twenty years. Started buying land as soon as I got in town. I'm like Judd—I don't want all the land in the county, just what I have, what adjoins me, and what I can see from my land. And I don't want a goddamn gas pipeline under it. God, I'd love to kick Billy Bob's ass. Might could, too. I boxed in college.'

'Where?'

'Princeton.' He waved a hand at his studio. 'Trust fund pays for all this. And my land.'

'Your art doesn't support you?'

'Shit, when I first moved here, early nineties, right before Judd died, I couldn't give my art away. Then this art dealer from Dallas, good-looking woman, she comes down here to check out Judd's boxes. She ended up in my bed. So we made a deal: fifty–fifty on anything she sold. Well, she shipped every-thing I had back to Dallas and talked it up in Highland Park as the next big thing, and damned if she doesn't sell it all to rich folks like her husband. He made a fortune in asbestos.'

'Mining it?'

'Suing over it. Plaintiffs' lawyer. They've got a fifth or sixth home here, fly down in their Gulfstream. He's sixty, she's forty now. Apparently Viagra didn't do the trick for him. Anyway, they brought other rich lawyers to town—'

'Attorneys, artists, and assholes.'

Big Rick grinned. 'I'm an artist and an asshole. Anyway, most of these lawyers wouldn't know art if it dropped on their fucking heads, but they buy my stuff, so I make nice at dinner parties.'

'Must be hard.'

'Very.'

Big Rick finished off the chocolate milk and went back to the refrigerator for a refill. This time he offered Spam. Book again declined.

'I love this stuff. I don't know why.'

'I don't either.'

Big Rick opened the can and took a big bite of Spam.

'You know what you're putting into your body?'

'Do I look like I care?'

He did not.

'Comes in all kinds of flavors: black pepper, hickory smoked, jalapeño, with cheese, with bacon, hot and spicy . . . this is classic, my favorite.'

He let out a loud fart.

'Whoa. Sorry. Stuff does give me gas.'

Book eased back a step.

'I understand there's quite a bit of drug use among the artists?'

'True enough. Part of the culture. Cutting-edge art. Drugs just seem to be a natural part of all that.'

He laughed.

'A *Vanity Fair* article, I've got it somewhere'—he shuffled through a stack of magazines on the table—'reporter wrote that Marfa's an "art cruise ship where you just hope the last stop is a Betty Ford Center." Boy, they got that right.'

He paused.

'Course, we're not the only Marfans partaking in recreational narcotics.'

'What's that mean?'

Big Rick's expression said he was holding aces. He made Book wait for it.

'Billy Bob Barnett is a cokehead.'

Big Rick seemed pleased with himself. That or he really loved Spam.

'How do you know?'

'Let's just say I have it from a reliable source. That head cold, he's had it for two years now.' He took another big bite of the Spam. 'Public company, his board might not be so keen on having a cokehead for a CEO.'

'Even if you got him fired, that wouldn't stop the fracking or the condemnation lawsuits.'

'True. But at least I wouldn't have to see his fat ass at Maiya's every time I go there to drink and eat.'

'Kenni says you have guns.'

Big Rick shrugged, as if feigning modesty.

'Just a few.'

He stepped over and opened a walk-in closet that housed not clothes but weapons. A lot of weapons mounted on both walls. And military gear—flak jackets, meals-ready-to-eat, night-vision goggles . . .

'I like to shoot shit at night.' He pointed out his collection as if he were pointing out fine art in a museum. 'Forty-four Magnum, nine-millimeter Glock, AK-Forty-Seven, sniper's rifle, shotgun . . .'

'What gauge?'

'Twelve.'

'That's a coincidence.'

'What's that?'

'Someone shot out my window at the Paisano Thursday night with a twelve-gauge shotgun.'

'I never heard of you until five minutes ago when you rang my bell.'

'There was an article in the newspaper.'

'Which I don't read.'

'I was on Marfa Public Radio.'

'Which I don't listen to.'

'So why all the guns?'

'An avant-garde artist with an arsenal makes for good copy back East. And I love to go out to my land and shoot the shit out of everything.'

'Why do you hate Bush?'

'What? Oh, the "Bush Sucks" installation. Just part of the image. You want a New York art dealer to sell your stuff, you gotta loathe Bush and vote Obama. Hating Bush is always a big part of any art crowd conversation. But I voted for him. Both times.'

'Kenni said you painted an "Axis of Evil" sign on a building in town.'

'Nah. Everyone blamed it on me, but that was an asshole from Iceland.'

'Big Rick . . . is there any part of you that's real?'

'Everything you see is real, Professor. Everything you read is myth. About me, about the other artists, about Marfa . . . it's all just a myth. A myth that sells.'

'Is everyone in Marfa on the make?'

'Everyone except the cowboys.'

'Get in, podna.'

Book was walking back to the Paisano when the sheriff pulled alongside in his cruiser. He spat brown tobacco juice out his window. Book got in.

'You kinda stubborn, ain't you?'

'I'm kind of mad.'

'Often the last words before someone ends up in my jail.'

'I went to see Billy Bob.'

'I take it that was a less than cordial meeting, too?'

'It was.'

'He didn't confess?'

'He did not.'

'I hate it when that happens.'

'Nathan Jones was gay.'

The sheriff hit the brakes. He slowly turned to Book. He grunted.

'You want to get a cup of coffee?'

Tumbleweeds on Austin Street one block west of Highland Avenue offers washers and dryers by the load and a walk-through to Frama's, which offers home-brewed coffee and Blue Bell ice cream. They walked in just as the mayor of Marfa walked out with a big ice cream cone.

'Heard about your gal, Professor. She gonna be okay?'

'Yes. Thanks for ask—'

'Good. Won't slow you folks getting back to Austin.'

The mayor nodded at the sheriff—'Brady'—and walked away.

The sheriff chuckled. 'The mayor, he's . . .'

'A real-estate broker.'

'Yep.'

Book ordered a small cup of coffee; the sheriff ordered a medium and one scoop of cookies-and-cream ice cream. They went outside and leaned on the hood of the sheriff's cruiser.

'Gay,' Sheriff Munn said. 'And married. Living a double life.' The sheriff grunted then spooned the ice cream past his mustache. 'Seems like that'd be a complicated life.'

'His . . . friend . . . pushed him to go public with his proof.'

'That Billy Bob's contaminating the groundwater, with his fracking?'

Book nodded.

'Who's his friend?'

'Confidential, Sheriff. Nathan had a wife.'

The sheriff grunted; Book took that for a yes.

'Kenni.'

'With an "i"? Over at the pizza joint?'

Book nodded again.

'He's a doper. Damn, sorry the boy got in with that artist crowd.'

'He was an artist.'

'And a doper?'

'Apparently.'

'So the weed they found in his office might've been his?'

'Possibly.'

'Well, that sheds some light on the subject, don't it?'

'An artist named Big Rick threatened to out Nathan because he sued to condemn his land for a pipeline easement.'

'You talk to Big Rick?'

'You know him?'

'Of him.'

'He's a piece of work.'

'He's a pervert. I know about his underage girls. That's stat rape in the state of Texas. Once I get those girls' affidavits, he's gonna be stacking Coke cans in my jail instead of cars.'

'Big Rick said Billy Bob's a cokehead.'

'You getting your information from a pervert?'

'Anywhere I can.'

'Fracking and doping don't add up to murder.'

The sheriff finished off the ice cream then sipped the coffee, which was as good as any coffee in Austin at half the price.

'You figure out the connection between the boy's death and art?'

'I've learned that Nathan was Billy Bob's lawyer and a gay artist living a double life. That art is part of the story.'

The sheriff grunted. 'Art. Why folks would take a plane trip to Hell Paso then drive four hours to look at a bunch of fluorescent lights, I don't figure that. Now, Judd's boxes, I like them. Particularly the concrete ones outside. I go out there and study them from time to time. You know, if you sit on the side of Sixty-seven just south of the boxes, right when the sun's rising, those boxes create some interesting shadows. I reckon that's what Judd was up to.'

287

'Could be.'

'Or I don't have a clue.'

'Do you have a clue who killed Nathan Jones?'

'Well, the boy was Billy Bob's lawyer, so I figure he had access to incriminating evidence, if there was any. And he talked about it with his . . . friend . . . who pressured him to go public with it, that tells me there's evidence out there, waiting to be found. Which makes Billy Bob Barnett the prime suspect in a murder case. But I got no evidence of murder. Except a dead lawyer.'

'What do you need to arrest him?'

'I need that proof, podna.'

Chapter 29

'Kenni introduced Nathan to you.'

Carla glanced over at Book from behind the wheel of her truck. 'Yes. He did.'

'A man inside Billy Bob's operations.'

'A lawyer. The best possible inside man. Privy to his client's secrets.'

'Did you know you were putting his life in danger?'

'Fracking is a dangerous business, Professor.'

'Fighting fracking can be dangerous as well. How'd you get into that business?'

'My dad was a roughneck. I followed him into the industry. Got an environmental engineering degree at Rice, worked at a major in Houston, thought I'd make the industry greener. But the only green they care about is the kind that folds nicely in a wallet. So I quit and went to the other side, joined an environmental group in Santa Fe. Been fighting the industry ever since. When fracking came on line, I knew it had to be stopped.'

'Did you know Nathan was gay?'

The sudden change of subjects didn't throw her.

'I figured.'

'Why?'

'He was friends with Kenni. Gays and straights don't pal around together in West Texas.'

'Did you know Billy Bob is a cokehead?'

'Heard rumors to that effect. Who'd you hear it from?'

'Big Rick.'

'He's a disgusting prick, all those young girls. But he hates Billy Bob almost as much as I do, and he donates to the cause.' Her eyes went to the rearview mirror. 'Aw, fuck.'

Carla had picked Book up at six in an old dark blue Ford pickup with bumper stickers that read *No Fracking Way* and *We Can't Drink Natural Gas*. A shotgun was mounted in a window rack. Book looked in the side mirror. A Border Patrol SUV had pulled them over. Carla braked and steered the pickup truck to the shoulder of the highway.

'Billy Bob said you had a roughneck's vocabulary.'

'Hang around squirrels long enough, you'll start hiding nuts. Hell, I've been around roughnecks since I was a kid.'

She glanced in the rearview again and gestured back.

'They harass me every time, make me get out while they search the entire truck. I think Billy Bob puts them up to it.'

'Maybe that shotgun got their attention.'

'In West Texas?'

Two agents walked up to their windows, one on either side.

'What do you assholes want?' Carla said.

'Nice to see you too, Carla,' the agent said.

Book looked up to a familiar face.

'Whoops,' the agent named Wesley Crum said.

'We meet again,' Book said.

'Hey, Professor.' Agent Angel Acosta leaned down and rested his arms on the driver's side window frame. 'I finished your book. It was brilliant.'

'Thanks.'

Agent Crum was examining the short radio antenna on Book's side.

'Carla, why do you have this big ol' potato stuck on your antenna?'

'Antenna broke off,' she said. 'Potato gives the radio better reception. Don't ask me why.'

'I won't.'

'Well, you folks have a nice day,' Agent Acosta said.

They returned to their SUV and drove off. Carla watched them away then turned to Book.

'You must be really famous.'

Nadine Honeywell sat in her hospital bed running high on caffeine and working on the Welch brief on the laptop when the door opened and the professor and the woman named Carla entered the room. She tried not to look surprised. The professor held an open hand out to her. In his palm was her Purell bottle.

'Where'd you find it?'

'In the desert. You must've dropped it when you went flying off the Harley last night.'

'I was trying to block out that memory.'

She took the Purell. Ooh, there was still some gel left. She squirted it into her palm and rubbed. She loved the smell of ethyl alcohol.

'So, Professor—what did we learn today?'

'A, Nathan Jones was gay.'

'Told you.'

'B, he had a relationship with Kenni.'

'With an "i"?'

The professor nodded. 'C, Nathan told Kenni about the contamination but never showed him any proof.'

'The lost proof.'

'And D, Billy Bob Barnett is a cokehead. Allegedly.'

Nadine felt her mouth fall open.

'Shut the frack up.'

It took her a moment to recover. She looked from the professor to Carla and back.

'So, what, you two are working together now?'

'Looks that way.'

'You think what you're both looking for will lead you to Billy Bob Barnett?'

'I think so.'

'So what are you going to do?'

'Get some proof.'

'Can you get me some food first? I'm starving.'

'Let's get some grub, Jimmy John, before we frack this hole.'

Sonny slapped him on the back. It was after midnight but lunchtime on the well site on the graveyard shift. They both wore red insulated jumpsuits, red *Barnett Oil and Gas* caps, and boots. They walked across the dirt pad toward the mess hall, stepping over pipes and hoses running from the tanker trucks. The pay on the rigs was good; the food not so much. It was like eating at McDonald's three times a day, every day. Jimmy John had had a blood test a few years back, when they had to run him up to the hospital in Alpine after a length of casing had got loose and hit him in the head. Knocked him out cold. Nurse said his cholesterol was high enough to cause two heart attacks. That's what eating rig food would do, hamburgers and hot dogs and sausage and eggs. Roughnecks didn't eat salads.

'Shit,' Jimmy John said. 'I forgot to write down my last pressure reading. I'll catch up. Save some food for me.'

He turned back and headed to the control center. But not to write down readings. He felt the nosebleed coming on, and he didn't want Sonny seeing him bleeding like a stuck pig. Word got back to the boss, Jimmy John Dale might find himself unemployed. And that was a place he didn't want to go. A man without a job ain't no better than a Mexican. He pulled out the handkerchief and ducked behind a tanker truck carrying the frack fluid.

★　　★　　★

292

'They're fixin' to frack.'

After taking a cheeseburger and fries back to Nadine, they had driven out to a Barnett Oil and Gas Company well site that she had been staking out. Book and Carla sat above a low valley in the foothills northeast of Alpine. The five-acre pad down below where the prairie grass had been taken down to the dirt was lit up like Main Street. They were waiting for the crew to take a meal break.

'In the middle of the night?'

'Twenty-four/seven operation.'

'All I see is a lot of trucks and pipes and hoses.'

'The rig's down, and the tanker trucks are here. They're carrying the frack fluid.' She pointed. 'The green tanks surrounding the site, those are the storage tanks. The hoses run to the blender where the proppant is added—those dump trucks carry the sand—then over to the treator manifold and into the pumper trucks—see the red ones?—backed up to the well hole. That equipment next to the trucks, those are compressors to create the pressure they need to crack the rock.'

'What's in those tanks?'

'Diesel fuel to power the equipment. During the day, you can see the black exhaust fumes from the engines, creates ground-level ozone.' She pointed to the sky. 'Way up there, ozone is good. Down here, it's very bad for humans and animals.'

'Smog in West Texas.'

'That trailer, that's the control center.'

'What are those trailers?'

'The man camp. The out-of-town workers live onsite, work twelve hours a day, two-week shifts. They rotate off for a week then back on. It's a hard life.'

'What's that shack over there? Where all the men are heading.'

'Mess hall. They're going to eat first then frack. Odd. Most men like to frack first then eat.'

Carla smiled then dug in her knapsack and came out with beef jerky. She handed him a strip.

'High in protein.'

'You do this often?' Book asked her.

'Actually, I do.'

'Are you afraid?'

'My dad taught me not to be afraid . . . or at least not to show my fear.'

'Good advice. Where is he now?'

'Dead. Well blowout. He went to work one day and didn't come home.'

'When?'

'Six years ago.'

She dug in her knapsack again, but almost as if she were angry this time, and came out with rubber gloves.

'Put these on. This shit is toxic.'

They ran down the rise and to the drill site. They ducked behind the tanker trucks and dodged roughnecks walking past. Male voices came from all around them; the foul smell of the well site was suffocating.

'Well hole gases,' Carla said.

They worked their way to the control center and went inside. She went directly to a large notebook on the desk. She ran her finger down the open page.

'Yep, they're fracking tonight.'

They exited and again ducked behind the tanker trucks, but Carla stopped at one. She pulled out a small plastic container and placed the mouth under a valve at the back of the tank. She turned a knob and filled the container with brown fluid.

'I'm gonna find out what's in Billy Bob's recipe. They claim the recipes are proprietary information, trade secrets, like the formula for Coca-Cola, so they can keep them secret from the Feds. Difference is, you can drink Coca-Cola and not die.'

'You think Billy Bob's using something bad?'

'It's all bad. But legal. Frackers use carcinogens like naphthalene, formaldehyde, sulfuric acid, thiourea, benzyl chloride, benzene, ethylene oxide, even lead. But they don't have to tell us what they're using.'

'The Halliburton Loophole.'

'Yep.'

'Professor!'

They jumped at the voice behind them. They turned and saw Jimmy John Dale holding a handkerchief that was as red as his jumpsuit. He glanced around and came closer. He gestured at Carla.

'You working with her now? She got you trespassing on private property?'

Carla hid the container behind her back.

'Jimmy John—'

He pointed toward the desert. 'Goddamnit, get the hell outta here before someone else sees you, calls the sheriff.'

They ran back up the rise to Carla's truck.

'That was a close call,' Book said.

'I've had closer. But we got a sample.' She held up the container. 'People will soon be drinking this toxic brew in their tap water.'

'I thought the EPA hadn't found any confirmed incidents of groundwater contamination, here or anywhere else?'

'Define "confirmed." Frackers don't have to disclose the chemicals they put down the hole, so how can those chemicals be traced to their wells if they show up in the tap water? They say there's no proof that the benzene or methane was from fracking. Fact is, there's been over a thousand confirmed incidents. The Bureau of Land Management found water wells in Wyoming's shale fields that contained fifteen hundred times the safe level of benzene. And the EPA's now supplying drinking water to people living in the frack fields in Pennsylvania. They found arsenic in their tap water. How'd you like to drink a carcinogen with your morning coffee?'

'Not so much.'

She pointed down at the well site.

'Eighty tons of toxic chemicals are going down that hole tonight—and most of it's going to be left down there to migrate to the aquifer or it's going to come back up and then be injected down disposal wells and allowed to migrate to aquifers. Does that make any sense? But the industry says, "Don't worry, we know what we're doing. It's all safe."'

She blew out a breath.

'They'll start collecting the flow-back in the morning, if the gas flows. I need a sample of what comes up the hole. It's usually worse than what goes down the hole. No sense in heading back to town, we'd have to turn right back to get here in time. I've got camping gear in the truck. A sleeping bag, gets cold out at night.'

'Only one sleeping bag?'

'It's a double.'

Chapter 30

Book woke at dawn wrapped in a double sleeping bag, but he was a single. Carla was already up and at work, perched below the rise and peering through binoculars down at the well site.

'Coffee's made,' she said.

He unzipped the bag and got up then went behind the truck for his restroom duties. He came back and poured coffee into a tin cup. Carla was an experienced camper. He went over and squatted next to her.

'See the open pit? It's filling up with the brown water. That's the flow-back. Frack fluid that comes back up the hole. The frack fluid picks up riders down in the earth, stuff released by the fracking process, like radium, radon, methane. They'll pump it into those tankers and then haul it to the disposal wells, inject it into the earth like an addict injecting heroin. Nearest disposal wells are north of here, in Pecos County. I need a sample.'

'How?'

'I'm thinking.'

★   ★   ★

She thought most of the morning. When the last tanker truck left, Carla jumped up.

'Come on. I've got an idea.'

She went to the truck and rummaged through her belongings then pulled out a pair of shorts. She took off her jeans and put on the shorts. They drove the pickup back to the highway and pulled over. Carla got out and lifted the hood. She then rolled the legs of her shorts up until they were short-shorts. She reached inside the pickup and retrieved a jar with a lid.

'That last tanker truck will be along in a minute. Hide in the brush. When he stops, get a sample from the back of the tank. And wear the gloves.'

'What if other cars come by?'

She held her arms out to the vacant highway. 'We got rush hour, Professor.'

'How do you know he'll stop?'

'He'll stop.'

Book hid in the brush next to the highway and wondered if Carla knew what she was doing. He soon learned that she did. He heard the truck and ducked down. Carla stuck her head under the hood and her butt out toward the highway, her long lean legs serving as a stop sign.

The truck stopped.

The Hispanic driver climbed out and walked over to Carla. Book heard him say, '*Señorita.*' When the driver ducked his head under the hood, Book came out of the brush and ran to the rear of the tanker. He found a drain valve and filled the jar with foul-smelling brown water. He screwed the top on, peeked around the tanker, and ran back into the brush. Carla got into the driver's seat of the pickup and started the engine. She squealed like a teenage girl and thanked the driver profusely in Spanish.

'*Gracias, gracias, hombre.*'

The driver returned to the truck packing more than a set of

keys in his pocket. He fired up the big tanker and drove off. Book came out of the brush with the sample.

'You're good.'

A black-and-white videotape played on the big screen in Billy Bob's office. Security cameras had caught Carla and the professor the night before, sneaking onto well site number 356 and collecting a sample of the frack fluid. Billy Bob stuffed a donut into his mouth then said, 'How many times is this with Carla?'

'Ten, twelve,' Willie said.

Willie Freeman was ex-military police turned security director for Barnett Oil and Gas.

'Now she's got a partner in crime.'

'That's the professor,' Billy Bob said. 'He's from Austin, came out here 'cause Nathan Jones wrote him a letter, said I was contaminating the groundwater.'

'We ain't contaminating the groundwater.'

'Nope.' He pointed at the screen. 'Who's that?'

One of his workers had caught the professor and Carla on the well site behind a tanker truck. The video showed him pointing toward the desert. The professor and Carla ran off the site.

'Jimmy John Dale,' Willie said.

'He working with Carla?'

'No.'

'Why'd he let them go?'

'The professor's been to Nathan's house, talking to his wife, couple times. Jimmy John was there each time. He and Nathan grew up here together. Best friends.'

'Boyfriends?'

'No. Jimmy John's a cowboy, straighter than an iron rebar.'

'Good. 'Cause I don't want queers on my rigs. Or wets. Or Longhorns. Or Democrats. Or—'

'I know the list, boss. You want me to do anything with this tape? Take it to the sheriff? Call Tom Dunn, tell him to get another restraining order against her?'

Billy Bob shook his head. 'We got nothing to worry about with Carla. She's chasing shadows. She ain't gonna find nothing in my slick water.'

'Standard slick water, Carla,' the lab tech named Randy said. 'No arsenic, no diesel fuel, just typical ingredients. It's all legal.'

'Shit.'

They had driven to Sul Ross State University on the east side of Alpine. Sul Ross was known for its ranch horse competition team, but the university had a quality chemistry department as well. Randy was an assistant professor and a friend of Carla; he didn't hesitate when she called and asked him to come in on a Sunday afternoon.

'What about the flow-back?'

'Contains methane and benzene, but that's injected down disposal wells, also legal. Shouldn't be, but the EPA signed off on it. Heck, the government puts radioactive waste down disposal wells, why not frack fluid?' Randy shrugged his shoulders as if apologizing. 'Billy Bob's going by the book, Carla. I know you hate him, but he's no worse than any other fracker.'

'William Robert Barnett Jr., aka Billy Bob Barnett, was accused of tax fraud in two thousand one—he settled that case—securities fraud in two thousand four—he agreed to a cease-and-desist order—and got arrested in college for smoking dope.'

Book and Carla had stopped at the Alpine hospital to check on Nadine and found her propped up in bed, her left arm and right leg in slings, Book's laptop on her tray, and a long bendable straw in her mouth leading to a large soda water. She'd been investigating Billy Bob Barnett on the Internet.

'Hospital's got WiFi,' Nadine said.

'What else?'

'Food's okay, not so much the coffee.'

'About Billy Bob.'

'He's worth a hundred million dollars.'

'Lot of money.'

'He was worth five. His entire net worth is in company stock. Took the company public in oh-four, he got ten million shares. Stock opened at twenty, peaked at fifty in oh-eight, now it's down to ten.'

'What happened?'

'Gas prices plunged, from a high of eleven dollars per thousand cubic feet in oh-eight to under two dollars today.'

'Quite a drop.'

'Glut of gas on the market. His company's all in on shale gas, so the stock price rises and falls with the natural gas futures market.'

'So if the government shut the company down because its fracking was contaminating the groundwater—'

'Billy Bob Barnett wouldn't have a pot to piss in, to use the West Texas vernacular,' Carla said.

'Might be a motive for murder.'

'Actually, it's worse,' Nadine said. 'Billy Bob pledged his stock for a one-hundred-million-dollar personal loan when the stock price was worth twenty. If it drops below ten, the bank can foreclose on its collateral—his stock. He'll lose everything.'

'Big loan.'

'He likes the good life—private jet out at the Marfa airport, homes in River Oaks and Santa Barbara, three ex-wives and five kids to support. So he's heavily in debt personally and his company's revenues are down and fracking expenses are up. He's being squeezed from both ends. And his board deferred his bonus—ten million dollars.'

'That would put a dent in my cash flow,' Carla said.

'He can't raise the price of gas, the market sets that. So his only course of action would be to cut expenses.'

'By cutting corners,' Carla said.

'And his shareholders are putting a lot of pressure on him to boost the stock price.'

'He's a desperate man.'

'That's good work, Nadine. How'd you find all that information on the Internet?'

'Professor, I'm twenty-three. My generation might not know current events, but we know our way around the Internet.'

'Call Henry. Professor Lawson. Explain the situation to him, ask him what Billy Bob might do to cut corners.'

'Other than murder Nathan Jones?'

Book nodded. 'Other than that.'

Book's phone rang. He checked the caller ID. Joanie. He answered.

'Book, Mom wandered off again. The police found her at a strip joint.'

'They're open on Sundays?'

'Book, she walked all morning.'

He blew out a breath. 'We'll talk when I get back.'

'When?'

'Soon as we find the killer.'

'Be careful, Book.'

He hung up. Carla averted her eyes. It was an awkward moment until Nadine looked past him and said, '*Daddy?*'

Nadine closed her eyes and shook her head to clear her vision. She thought she had seen her father standing in the doorway. Perhaps she had in fact suffered a closed-head injury causing blood to seep into her brain and resulting in hallucinations— oh, God. But when she opened her eyes, he was still there.

'OMG—Daddy, what are you doing here?'

'Well, young lady, I was about to ask you the same question. I'm here because my health insurance company called me, said a hospital in Alpine, Texas, submitted big bills for a patient named Nadine Honeywell. MRIs, X-rays, ER, OR . . . They wanted to make sure someone wasn't engaged in fraud. Obviously, they weren't. What the hell is going on?'

'I'm fine, Daddy. Thanks for asking.'

'Oh. Are you okay, honey?'

'Just a broken arm and leg. Bruises. Minor contusions. Possible brain damage. I'm fine.'

Her father wore his standard Sunday attire: a suit and tie. He was a lawyer from birth, destined to a life lived in suits and ties with a briefcase attached to his hand. Mother had left him because he loved the law more than he loved her. Harsh, but true. After her sister died, he found solace in his work; her mother never found any solace. Her father now turned his attention to the professor.

'Who are you?'

'Professor John Bookman.'

'He's famous, Daddy.'

'Never heard of him.'

'And this is Carla Kent.'

'Are you famous?'

'Infamous.'

'I'm the professor's intern,' Nadine said.

'His intern?' He turned on the professor. 'So, Professor, why is my daughter, who was in law school in Austin, Texas, the last time I talked to her, now lying in a hospital bed in Alpine, Texas, with a broken arm and leg?'

'Well, Mr. Honeywell, that's a really interesting story.'

'I'm all ears.'

'We're solving a murder case, Daddy.'

'A murder case?' Back to the professor. 'You got her involved in a murder case?'

'Well, I—'

'I sent her to UT to get a law degree, not to get herself killed. All right, let's go. I'm going to check you out, get you back to Austin where you belong.'

'No, Daddy.'

'What?'

'I said, no. I'm not leaving. We're trying to find a murderer. The professor needs my help.'

Her father frowned. He gave her that familiar suspicious squint then turned it on the professor. He gestured back and forth between her and the professor with his hand.

'You two got one of those professor–student romances going on?'

She laughed. 'Me and the professor? He's trying to get me killed, Daddy, not get in my thong.'

Daddy rolled his eyes. 'Why do you say stuff like that? Now listen, young lady—'

'No, Daddy, you listen. For once, listen to me. What I want to do. I want to stay here and finish this. For once in my life, I am not going to run home scared of life.'

Her father stared hard at her; then he exhaled and all the fight went out of him.

'Have you talked to your mother recently?'

Nadine's father had kissed her on the forehead, secured a commitment from Book to ensure that his daughter got home to Austin safely, and then left to drive to El Paso and catch a flight back to San Francisco.

'Nadine,' Book said, 'I'm sorry I—'

'Don't be. That was a breakthrough moment for Daddy and me. And I don't really wear thongs, I just say that kind of stuff to get him worked up.'

'You know he cares about you?'

'I know. Oh, I finished the Welch brief and emailed it to the D.A., like you said.'

'Reminds me, Scotty Raines called and left a message. Said the D.A. called him this morning, wasn't real happy after he read the brief. Wanted me to call him. On Sunday.'

Book stepped out into the hall and called the number Scotty Raines had left; it was the Travis County D.A.'s cell phone. He answered on the second ring.

'Professor.'

'Mr. Anderson.'

'Don.'

'Book.'

'The hell you doing in Marfa?'

'Murder.'

'You're killing people in Marfa?'

'Trying to find a murderer.'

'Lot more fun than teaching Con Law, isn't it?'

'It has its moments.'

'Your secretary's husband murder any more armadillos? I'm still not happy with that verdict.'

'It's been a year, Don.'

'So, Professor, why are you working for a guy like Welch? He's one of the Republicans ruining Texas.'

'It's not political for me.'

'So what, you're doing it for the money?'

'He's not paying me.'

'Then why? Because he's the chairman of the Board of Regents? What, you want to be president of the university?'

'He promised to put the boy in rehab, for six months.'

'That's it?'

'There's more. But not money.'

The D.A. exhaled. 'You gonna file this brief?'

'If I have to.'

'I can beat you.'

'It isn't about me.'

'Then why isn't Scotty Raines arguing the con law issues? Why'd Welch hire you?'

'He loves his son.'

'Who's a smart-ass punk.'

'Maybe. But just because a college kid gets drunk—'

'And stoned on coke.'

'—and mouths off to a cop doesn't give the police probable cause to search his vehicle, which he was not driving at the time, and to seize his blood without his consent. Thus, that evidence is inadmissible in court, which means you have no case.'

'So you say.'

'So the court will rule. And, Don, the Supreme Court will likely rule this term that the taking of blood without a warrant is an unconstitutional search and seizure under the Fourth Amendment. So even if you go forward with this case and obtain a conviction, it'll be overturned once the Court rules.'

'We'll see. File your fucking brief, Professor. I'll see you in court.'

The D.A. hung up. Book sighed. Another less than cordial conversation. Perhaps it was him. He returned to the room and found Nadine and Carla giggling like girls on a sleepover.

'Daddy wants me to be a lawyer,' Nadine said.

'My dad wanted me to be a boy,' Carla said.

'Okay, you're right. That is worse.'

They laughed again.

'Female bonding?' Book asked.

'We're BFFs,' Nadine said.

'You want some dinner, Carla?'

'I'm game.'

'Where are you guys going?' Nadine asked.

Book looked to Carla for an answer.

'Reata,' she said.

Nadine typed on the laptop keyboard with one finger then stared at the screen.

'OMG, what a menu. Okay, bring me back'—she looked up at Book—'write this down in that little notebook.'

He did.

'The tenderloin tamales with pecan mash for an appetizer, the carne asada topped with cheese enchiladas for an entrée, a side of jalapeño and bacon macaroni and cheese, and for dessert a chocolate chunk bread pudding tamale served with dulce de leche. God, that sounds good.'

'You know how to order,' Carla said.

'She knows how to eat,' Book said.

Nadine squirted Purell into her palms and began rubbing as if preparing to eat.

'Oh, Professor, I need some new underwear.'

'Underwear?'

'The ones I had on, they're gone. My others back at the hotel are dirty. And I wore my spare pair I carry in my bag.'

'You carry a change of underwear in your purse?'

'Doesn't everyone?'

Carla shook her head. Nadine grunted as if surprised.

'Well, someone forgot to tell me to pack for a week. And I don't like this commando thing.'

'Over-share.'

'I'll take care of it,' Carla said. 'I know a store open on Sundays. What kind? Thongs?'

'God, no. I don't like a string up my . . . bikinis. All cotton. No lace. Any color.'

'What size?'

'Four.'

'*Four?* You eat like that and wear a four? That's not fair.'

Nadine waved them away. 'Hurry. I'm hungry, and I need those underwear. And before you leave, Professor, would you empty my bedpan? I really gotta pee.'

Book eyed the bedpan. 'Uh . . .'

'I'll get the nurse,' Carla said.

She went outside to find a nurse.

'I like her,' Nadine said.

'I need you to research her dad. He was killed in an oil rig blowout six years ago. Find out what you can—on him and on her.'

'Why?'

'I don't know.'

'That ain't evidence of a murder,' Sheriff Munn said.

Book had called the sheriff with the information about Billy Bob's shady past and his current financial problems.

'Professor, before I can arrest the second-biggest employer in Presidio County after the Border Patrol and charge him with murder, I need a smoking gun.'

Book did not tell the sheriff about his and Carla's unauthorized entry upon Barnett Oil and Gas Company's well site the night before.

'That's good work by your gal, but it's not enough.'

'I'll talk to Carla at dinner, see what we can do.'

'Carla? You working with her?'

'We teamed up.'

'I asked you to team up with me.'

The sheriff grunted.

'Now, don't take it that way, Sheriff, it wasn't personal—'

Damn. Now he was answering the sheriff's grunts.

'Course, she is a mite better looking than me.'

'Just a little.'

'You figure her out yet?'

'I'm working on her.'

'I bet you are. Taking her to dinner, huh?'

'I am.'

'Where?'

'Reata.'

'Good place.'

'A smoking gun? Any advice, Sheriff?'

'First, the most desperate creature on earth is a cornered bear or a man about to lose everything. Be careful, Professor. And second, order the pecan pie for dessert.'

With six thousand residents, Alpine is like a major metropolitan area compared to Marfa. It has a doctor, a pharmacy, a hospital, a country club, and Reata on Fifth Street in downtown.

'My favorite restaurant in the whole world,' Carla said.

They ate on the back patio, which featured a *Giant* mural painted on the exterior wall of the adjacent building and country-western music playing on the sound system. The clientele was not a hipster artist crowd; it was a cowboy crowd. Deputy Shirley sat at one table wearing her uniform and gun across from a strapping young cowboy. She gave Book a smile and a wink as they walked past. When they sat down, Carla glanced over at Deputy Shirley then back at Book.

'You didn't go for the snow cone, did you?'

'Not yet.'

She sighed. 'Men.'

Their waitress was an authentic cowgirl attending Sul Ross on a ranch horse team scholarship. She wore a belt buckle the size of Montana.

'I won that at a cutting horse competition,' she said.

Carla ordered the jalapeño and cilantro soup and fried poblano chile rellenos stuffed with cream cheese, corn, and pepper served with a corn chowder; Book went for the tortilla soup and grilled salmon with Boursin cream sauce. Book took the sheriff's advice and ordered the West Texas pecan pie for dessert; Carla had the Dutch Oven apple crisp with cajeta. And he placed Nadine's to go order. They had already stopped and picked up her underwear.

'So what brought you to Marfa?' Book asked.

'Fracking. That's my mission in life, to stop fracking.'

'Well, good to have something to do each day.'

'Are you mocking me?'

'No.'

'Aren't you passionate about your work?'

'I am.'

'Me, too. I'm a very passionate person.' She gave him a coy look. 'Who knows, if you play your cards right, you might find out how passionate.'

'You want a beer? Or six?'

She smiled. 'It'll take more than that, cowboy.'

'Beers?'

'Charm.'

The waitress brought glasses of water and buttermilk biscuits with pecans and soft butter. Carla held up the water glass.

'That water,' she said, 'it's from the Igneous Aquifer. That's the aquifer Billy Bob's punching through to frack.'

'The aquifer Nathan thought he was contaminating?'

'Yep.'

'How do we prove it? The samples came back clean.'

'They came back legal. The shocking thing about fracking isn't what the industry does—shit, they thought it was brilliant to put diesel fuel down a well hole—but what's legal. Between the trillions of gallons of drinking water used to frack the wells and the billions of gallons of toxic chemicals put down into the earth, ten years from now we'll end up with lots of natural gas but no drinking water. Lots of jobs, but more people with cancer. Lots of energy, but more global warming . . .'

The waitress brought their dinners, but Carla was on a fracking roll.

'Which is so stupid when the answer is staring at us: green energy. Solar, wind, hydro. Over time, green energy would create a lot of jobs, too, and no cancer, no carbon footprint, no global warming, no groundwater contamination, no earthquakes. If the people knew the truth about fracking, they'd rise up against it. But the industry hires New York PR firms to run disinformation campaigns to confuse the public, same thing they did with cigarettes. They say steel-and-cement casing prevents groundwater contamination, but they don't mention that the failure rate for casing is six percent immediately upon construction and fifty percent over thirty years. They say gases released into the air like benzene are safe, but they don't mention that breast cancer rates spike among women living above frack fields. They say fracking's been around for sixty years, but they don't mention that the amount of chemicals and pressure down hole for horizontal fracking is way more than for those vertical wells drilled back then. They learned from the tobacco companies: lying works. And the media says,

"Well, there's a big debate about fracking." And the people hear that and believe it. And as long as there's a debate, the fracking continues . . .'

Which continued into dessert.

'. . . And the industry touts the jobs. That's the big sales pitch. Jobs. Jobs to keep the masses pacified. Politicians need to create jobs to get reelected, so they take the billion dollars a year the industry spends to lobby them and give the industry free rein to destroy the environment. Because politicians are inherently corrupt and evil. Like the goddamn oil and gas industry.'

Book listened attentively and ate the pecan pie then sipped his coffee throughout her impassioned plea. He had sat through many such pleas from environmental groups in Austin trying to save the springs, the river, the wilderness . . . but no one had brought more passion to the table than Carla Kent. She finally paused to take a breath; he waited to see if the lull were temporary or permanent. Her eyes danced with passion, which made her even more attractive. She drank her beer and smiled.

'I'm done ranting.'

'Good.'

'I feel better now.'

'Good.'

'So, Professor, how do you feel about sex after dinner?'

'Good.'

Chapter 31

'Being gay in West Texas, that wasn't an easy thing for Nathan. It's a hard land with hard people.'

Brenda Jones knew about her husband's double life. It was the next morning, and Book and Carla had stopped off at Brenda's house to bring her up to date. They had called ahead; she had called Jimmy John. He wore his red jumpsuit; he had just gotten off the night shift. He recoiled when he saw Carla on the front porch.

'We were more like brother and sister. Best friends. But I loved him, and he loved me, I know that. And we had been together since grade school, I couldn't imagine living without him. He was a sweet man, Professor. He took good care of me. He would've been a great dad. He saw on TV that babies in the womb could hear voices, so every night at bedtime he'd put his head close to my belly and read children's books to our baby.'

She looked down at her belly; when she looked up, her eyes were wet. She seemed to have aged ten years since Book had last seen her.

'Brenda, are you taking care of yourself?'

'I can't sleep without Nathan next to me.'

She wiped her eyes and blew her nose.

'After law school, he wanted to live in Austin, but I knew he'd have to face it every day, fighting his demons with so many gays there. Out here, there was no temptation. Until the artists came to town. I saw him weakening, and I knew he had given in to his demons.'

She paused.

'Why would he choose them over me, Professor?'

'Nathan didn't choose to be gay any more than you chose not to be. That's who he was. It's hardwired, like your blue eyes. Brenda, he tried not to be himself for you. But he didn't choose to be gay over you.'

She jerked and grabbed her belly.

'Whoa, he kicked me hard. He must want out.'

She blew out a breath and pondered her belly a moment then looked up at him.

'Professor, you don't think he'll be gay, too, do you?'

'Brenda, he's your son. You'll love him no matter what he is.'

Book turned to Jimmy John.

'Did you know?'

Jimmy John drank his beer then nodded. 'I figured. He never said nothing, but he was different. I mean, he tried to be a regular guy, even played six-man football. But he wasn't big, strong or fast.'

'Not a good combination for football.'

'Nope. And he was so damn pretty . . . not that I was attracted to him that way, I'm just saying. And those pictures he drew, never going to Boys' Town down in Mexico with us, never went for the sheep—'

'*Sheep?*'

'Cowboy joke, Professor.'

'It didn't matter to you?'

Jimmy John shrugged his broad shoulders. 'He was the

brother I never had. And he was the only person I could talk to.'

He paused, and his expression said his thoughts had gone to the past.

'Back in high school, my mom cheated on my dad. With a Mexican. Everyone in town knew except my dad. All the other boys laughed at me. Except Nathan. He cried with me.'

'He must've been a good friend.'

'My best friend.'

Jimmy John Dale referred to gays as 'queers,' but his best friend was gay, and he knew it. Human beings were complicated creatures. And his former intern had led a complicated life. A complicated, short, double life. Book gazed at the wedding portrait on the wall and wondered about Nathan Jones's life.

'Heard about your intern,' Jimmy John said. 'She okay?'

'A few broken bones, but she'll mend. Jimmy John, you ever heard any rumors that Billy Bob uses cocaine?'

He thought a moment then nodded. 'But no one on the rigs talks about it. We're too scared.'

'Of Billy Bob?'

'That it might be true. It's like you're on a pro football team and the star quarterback's a cokehead. He could take the whole team down with him. Is it true?'

'I don't know.' Book turned to Brenda. 'Did you find anything in the house that might be the proof Nathan said he had?'

'Nothing.'

'Anywhere else he might have put it?'

She turned her palms up. Book turned to Jimmy John.

'Any idea?'

'Sorry, Professor.'

'I always gave my important stuff to my dad,' Carla said.

'His obituary said his parents survived him. Where do they live?'

'On a ranch west of Valentine.'

'How far out?'

'Forty-five miles.'

'Thirty minutes by pickup,' Jimmy John said. 'Just past Prada Marfa.'

'Back in oh-five,' Carla said, 'these two German artists named'—she read their names on the plaque—'Elmgreen and Dragset, they thought this would be just about the funniest thing in the whole world, a Prada boutique in a ghost town. Locals never got the joke. Hence, the bullet holes.'

Valentine, Texas, qualifies as a ghost town. Only two hundred and seventeen lives play out there; the only thing the town has going for it is its name: every February, thousands of envelopes holding Valentine's cards arrive at the tiny post office to be postmarked 'Valentine, Texas.' One mile west of town on Highway 90, sitting on the south side against a backdrop of cattle grazing on the yellow prairie grass, yucca plants, mesquite bushes, and a distant ridgeline silhouetted against the blue sky was a small white stucco building with plate glass windows (sporting several small bullet holes) under awnings and *Prada Marfa* printed across the front façade. Arranged on shelves and display stands inside were high heels and purses from the Prada Milano 2005 collection.

'A fake Prada store,' Book said. 'In the middle of nowhere.'

'The Jones ranch is a ways out,' Book said.

'Everything in West Texas is a ways out. You think we'll learn anything from them? Nathan's parents.'

'Doubtful. But we've run down every other rabbit trail.'

A rocket suddenly rose into the sky in front of them.

'Look at that,' Book said.

'Bezos, the Amazon guy, he bought a couple hundred thousand acres over there, built a spaceport. Calls it "Blue Origin." They're testing rockets.'

315

'You're kidding?'

'Hey, we're high-tech out here, Professor. We've got the Air Force's Tethered Aerostat Radar site on Ninety—it's a blimp-type craft, they put it up to detect drug planes and ground transports in the desert. We've got the Predator drones flying the river—they operate those out of the Corpus Christi Naval Air Station. And we've got Bezos's rockets.'

'And modern art masterpieces.'

'Is West Texas one crazy-ass place or what?'

'In *Giant*, Bick Benedict puts his boy on a pony when he's four, maybe five, kid starts wailing. That was Nathan. Hated horses and cows and manure. But I still loved him.'

Bill Jones blinked back tears.

'He was your son.'

'I wanted him to be a rancher, take over the spread. He wanted to be an artist. At least he became a lawyer. Reckon I'll sell out to some rich Yankee like everyone else, move over to Fort Davis with all the other old folks. Play bingo.'

'Maybe your grandson will want to be a rancher.'

'You think?'

Nathan's parents, Bill and Edna, had welcomed Book and Carla into their home on a cattle ranch outside Valentine. Their land comprised twenty sections—12,800 acres—of prairie grassland. The Joneses had ranched that land since after the Mexican–American War. On the wall of their living room were framed photos of Nathan as a boy, a young man, a new lawyer, and a new husband. Book wondered if they knew Nathan's truth: his double life, his secrets, his art, his dreams. His unfulfilled life.

'Professor, why do you care so much about my son?'

'He saved my life, Mr. Jones.'

'Nathan? He saved your life?'

'Yes, sir. He stepped between me and a bullet intended for me.'

'His shoulder?'

Book nodded.

'He told us that scar was because he tore his rotator cuff playing basketball.'

'No, sir. That was because of a bullet.'

Mr. Jones seemed to stand a bit taller.

'Mr. and Mrs. Jones, Nathan interned for me at UT law school four years ago. A week ago, he sent me this letter.'

Book handed the letter to Nathan's parents and gave them time to read it. Edna cried; Bill handed the letter back to Book.

'So you're the professor?'

'Yes, sir.'

'He said you'd come.'

'Nathan told you I'd come to see him?'

'No. To see us.'

'You? Why?'

'Because you'd want this.'

Bill Jones held out a key.

Chapter 32

Fort Davis is the county seat of Jeff Davis County, twenty-one miles north of Marfa. It's a cute little mountain town filled with senior citizens, as if the American Association of Retired People had invaded the community. The key opened a safe deposit box in the First National Bank of Fort Davis. Inside was a clasp folder with a stack of papers six inches thick. Carla flipped through the papers.

'Well logs,' Carla said. 'And Barnett Oil and Gas tax returns. This is it. Nathan's proof.'

'Of what?'

She shrugged. 'It's just numbers. I never was good with numbers.'

'I know someone who is.'

Book and Carla walked into his intern's hospital room and found her sitting up in bed and Jimmy John Dale in his red jumpsuit standing next to the bed. He had rolled up the right sleeve as if showing off his biceps.

'Jimmy John?' Book said. 'What are you doing here?'

'He's showing me where the horse bit him,' Nadine said.

'You drove to Alpine to show my intern a horse bite?'

'Oh, uh, no, Professor. I drove Brenda over here. Her water broke right after you left this morning. She had the baby.'

'Are they both okay?'

'Yep.'

Book dropped the papers from the safe deposit box on Nadine's bed tray.

'What's this?'

'Nathan's proof.'

'Proof of what?' Jimmy John said.

'We don't know.'

Nadine thumbed the pages like a card sharp. 'Numbers. Looks like a job for the geeky intern. All right, Professor, I'm on it. And thanks for the underwear. I love the feel of cotton.'

'Over-share.'

'Where's the nursery?' Carla said. 'I want to see the baby.'

'I'll show you,' Jimmy John said.

He led Carla outside. Nadine turned to Book.

'Carla's dad, Wayne Kent, fifty-four, died in an oil rig blow-out outside Odessa six years ago.'

'I know that.'

'He worked for Billy Bob Barnett.'

'I didn't know that.'

'Carla and her mother sued Billy Bob and his company for negligence. They lost. Carla's been after Billy Bob ever since. He's gotten restraining orders against her in four Texas counties. She apparently snuck onto his well sites trying to get incriminating evidence. Tom Dunn represented Billy Bob and the company in court, said she had a vendetta. Said she was mentally unstable.'

'You're a handsome little boy, aren't you? Yes, you are.'

Carla Kent made faces and baby talk to Nathan Jones Jr. wrapped up like a papoose in the crib on the other side of the glass. Book stood next to her.

'So, Professor, you want to make a baby?'

319

'Right now?'

'One day.'

He had always thought that he would be a father one day. Until he got the test results back. There would never be a John Bookman Jr. It didn't seem fair. But life was not fair. Not for Nathan Jones Jr. who would never know his father, or for Nathan Jones who would never know his son. Not for Nadine's sister. Or Book's father. Or his mother. Not for anyone.

'Wave to Aunt Carla.'

They stopped by Brenda Jones's room and told her what they had found and that as soon as they knew what it meant, she would know. She cried.

'I wish Nathan was here,' she said.

'I know you do,' Book said.

They then drove back to Marfa and had a late lunch at the Food Shark under the shed in downtown. They sat at a long picnic table where artists had gathered like moths to a flame, fitting since the Food Shark proprietor was himself an artist; his medium was old television sets, which he arranged in various patterns with an image on each screen.

'Kids need a dad,' Carla said. 'Especially boys.'

They did.

'At least he'll have his grandpa.'

At least.

'You still here?'

Book looked up to the mayor of Marfa. He wasn't smiling.

'I'm afraid so.'

'Well, I hope you're happy.'

'About what?'

'I lost a sale today. A New York couple—two boys—they backed out 'cause they heard about the murder, that we got a murderer running the streets of Marfa, killing homosexuals. Said other artists are worried they might be next, figure the locals are targeting them.'

'Well, look at the bright side, Mayor. If we find the killer, the *New York Times* might write another story about Marfa.'

His expression brightened.

'You really think so?'

Carla sat inside one of Donald Judd's concrete boxes at the old fort and dangled her legs.

'I love these things,' she said. 'My teepee is right over there'— El Cosmico occupied the adjacent tract—'so I come over here and contemplate life on concrete. You know they're big enough to see on Google Earth? Like God looking down on us. What was he thinking?'

'God?'

'Judd.'

They had driven out to the Chinati Foundation then walked over to the field where Judd had aligned sixty concrete boxes— each exactly 2.5 × 2.5 × 5 meters—into fifteen groupings. Carla climbed through the boxes like a kid on a playscape. A tomboy.

'If I was a boy, my dad was going to name me Clark. He always called me his Supergirl.'

'You miss him?'

'Every day. Hard on my mom. She lives with me.'

'You take care of her?'

'More like she takes care of me. She gave me my passion. He made me tough. Taught me to fight boys—not as good as you—and to never back down. And to use guns. He said men respect a woman who carries a gun.'

She pondered her words a moment then pointed past Book.

'There's a tough man who carries a gun.'

Book turned and saw the sheriff standing in the parking lot between his cruiser and Carla's truck. He waved Book over.

'I'll wait here,' Carla said.

Book walked through the prairie grass and over to the sheriff. A Hispanic woman sat in the back seat of the cruiser.

He shook hands with the sheriff who nodded toward Carla and the concrete boxes.

'You figure her out?'

'I did.'

'Anything I need to know?'

'No.'

The sheriff grunted. 'Well, podna, there's something you need to know about her.' He opened the back door of the cruiser. 'This here's Lupe. She's the overnight maid at the Paisano. Lupe, this is the professor.'

Book said hello. She just smiled in response.

'She's a little shy around Anglos,' the sheriff said. 'Anyway, she remembered something about the truck that sped off the night your window got shot out.'

'It was maroon?'

'Uh, no.'

The sheriff turned to the woman.

'Lupe, tell the professor what you saw.'

'The truck, it had the bumper sticker with that funny word.'

'What funny word?'

'The F-word.'

'The uh, f-u-c-k word?'

Lupe giggled. 'No, not that F-word. The other one.'

'The other F-word . . . *Fracking?*'

'*Sí.* That F-word.'

Lupe pointed at the bumper sticker on Carla's truck that read *No Fracking Way*.

'That is the bumper sticker. And that is the truck I saw.'

'And that's a twelve-gauge shotgun in her window rack,' the sheriff said.

Book took a moment to process that information. He turned to Carla. She lay stretched out on top of a concrete box, as if sunning herself on a beach.

'Sorry to have to break that news to you, Professor. You want to press charges?'

Book slowly shook his head. 'No. I want to know why.'

The sheriff nodded at Carla in the field. 'Answer's right out there.'

The sheriff and Lupe left. Book walked back to Carla.

'What'd the sheriff have to say?'

'That you shot out our window at the Paisano.'

Her expression served as a confession.

'Why, Carla?'

'I had to keep you in town. So we could learn the truth about Nathan.'

'So you could have your revenge against Billy Bob.'

'Professor, you've been checking up on me.'

'I have.'

'What's wrong with revenge?'

'It's the wrong motive. I'm here for justice.'

'Billy Bob murdered my dad.'

'You lost your civil trial. The jury said he didn't.'

'In Odessa. Billy Bob cut corners on that rig—on safety, on the environment, on everything and everyone. He doesn't give a damn about the planet or the people. Only his profits.'

'So you're devoting your life to putting him in prison?'

'Or in a grave.' She paused. 'I hate him.'

'Hate's a hard thing to hold onto.'

He knew. He had held onto his hate for a decade.

'It's all I have left to hold.'

'You used me, Carla.'

'No, I didn't. I helped you. You were wrong, Professor. Nathan's death wasn't an accident. It wasn't a coincidence. If you had left town, you would never have learned the truth. And his killer would have gone free. You wouldn't have had your justice. You should thank me, for keeping you in town.'

'For shooting out our window? You could've hurt someone.'

'With number-eight birdshot? Please. Nobody likes a whiner, Professor.'

'You lied to me.'

'Not guilty. I didn't lie. I just didn't tell you the whole truth. That doesn't constitute perjury, they said so on *Law and Order*.'

Book sighed. 'Everyone's a lawyer.'

He stared at Cathedral Rock to the east. That was Carla's connection: she blamed Billy Bob Barnett for her father's death, and she wanted revenge. Book felt no anger toward her; he had had his revenge. The man who had killed his father had been sentenced to death; Book rode the Harley to Huntsville to witness his execution in the death chamber at the state penitentiary. He had looked into the man's eyes from the other side of the glass partition and had seen nothing. Only emptiness. Watching that man die, the man who had stuck a gun to his father's head and pulled the trigger, all desire for revenge had drained from his body. All his hate had dissipated. He found no satisfaction in another human's death. An eye for an eye could not bring his father back. But he felt for Carla; she did not yet know that revenge would not fill the void.

'You mad?'

'I should be.'

'That means you're not. Good.'

'Why?'

She pointed at the teepees on the adjacent El Cosmico tract.

'Because I've never fucked in a teepee.'

Chapter 33

Book woke in a teepee to a ringing phone. He reached down and grabbed his jeans then dug the cell phone out of a pocket.

'Professor.'

Nadine.

'Why aren't you out running?'

She giggled.

'I was up late.'

'I bet. Well, wake up Carla and come over.'

'Why?'

'I figured it out.'

'I did the math. The numbers don't add up.'

An hour later, they all sat in Nadine's hospital room in Alpine. Stacks of paper surrounded her in the bed.

'I talked to Professor Lawson. He said the fastest way to cut expenses is on disposal costs, said they've skyrocketed to about nine dollars per barrel of flow-back. So, if five million barrels of frack fluid go down the hole and fifty percent comes back up, that's two and a half million gallons of flow-back that's got to be injected down disposal wells. A barrel—that's how they measure everything in the business—is forty-two gallons, so two and a half million gallons is roughly sixty thousand barrels. Times nine dollars per barrel, that's half a million dollars in disposal costs per well. That's a lot of money, so I started looking at the disposal numbers.'

She held up a piece of paper from her left side.

'Well number three-twenty-four. Fracked last November seventeenth. The well log says they injected right at three million gallons of frack fluid down the hole.'

She held up another paper, this one from her right side.

'But the expense worksheets—these are the work papers the accountants generate from the actual receipts, bank statements, that sort of thing—for last year's tax return shows Barnett paid for six hundred twenty-five tanker trucks to deliver frack fluid to well number three-twenty-four on November seventeenth.'

'And?'

'And each tanker carries eight thousand gallons. Do the math, that comes to five million gallons.'

'So he's either cheating on his taxes or he's cheating on the amount of fluid used to frack that well. I understand the taxes, but why the frack fluid?'

'I'm getting there.'

She held up another piece of paper.

'After fracking, fifteen to fifty percent of the fluid comes back up the hole—remember, Billy Bob told us that?'

Book nodded.

'That's the flow-back. It's collected in an open pit then pumped into the tanker trucks to haul off to the disposal wells.'

'Okay.'

Back to the second piece of paper.

'The expense worksheet says Barnett paid for three hundred tanker loads to the disposal wells. Do the math, that's two-point-four million gallons. Which is eighty percent of three million—that's too much flow-back—but only forty-eight percent of five million. Which fits.'

'Which leads us to conclude that—'

'They used five million gallons to frack that well and recovered two-point-four million gallons of flow-back.'

'I agree.'

Another paper.

'But, this expense sheet lists all the disposal costs, but by date, not well. On November nineteenth, Barnett paid one hundred seventy thousand dollars to dispose of nineteen thousand barrels of flow-back in the Pecos County disposal well.'

'Which means?'

'He's short.'

'How?'

'Like I said, one barrel equals forty-two gallons. So they disposed of only eight hundred thousand gallons of flow-back from that well.'

'So two-point-four million gallons came back up the hole, but only eight hundred thousand gallons were trucked to the disposal wells?'

'Looks that way.'

'What happened to the other one-point-six million gallons?'

'Never made it to the disposal wells.'

'Where'd it go?'

'He dumped it,' Carla said.

'Why?'

'To save money.'

'About three hundred and forty thousand dollars,' Nadine said.

'On one well,' Carla said. 'Times a hundred wells a year, that's—'

'Thirty-four million dollars,' Nadine said.

'That's real money,' Carla said, 'even in Texas.'

'And especially if you've got three ex-wives to support,' Book said.

'And five children,' Nadine said.

'And a cocaine habit,' Carla said.

'So Nathan was wrong. Billy Bob isn't contaminating the groundwater; he's contaminating the land and surface water.'

'I've gone through the numbers on twenty wells so far,' Nadine said. 'Same deal.'

'But for him to dump that much frack fluid,' Book said, 'the trucking company would have to be a co-conspirator in a criminal enterprise.'

'Wouldn't be the first time,' Carla said. 'The trade treaty with Mexico allowed cross-border trucking, so the cartels bought up a bunch of Mexican trucking companies. They know a little something about criminal enterprises.'

'That's another piece of the puzzle, Professor,' Nadine said.

'What?'

'Apparently someone at the trucking company had a conscience. Wade Chandler, shipping supervisor. Nathan had several manifests signed by Chandler.'

'How?'

She shrugged. 'Who knows? Maybe Nathan figured it out, asked Chandler for the records.'

'Where's this Wade Chandler?'

'Dead. Died in a car accident, two days before Nathan.'

'Why didn't the sheriff mention that?'

'Probably didn't know. Happened in Pecos County. That's two counties north of Marfa.'

'Looks like Billy Bob partnered up with some bad guys, Professor, maybe a cartel,' Carla said.

'Where would he meet cartel people?'

'Cokehead needs a supplier. Maybe he's killing two birds with one stone—buying his cocaine and dumping his flow-back.'

'We need proof.'

'These papers,' Nadine said.

'Too complicated. We need a smoking gun.'

'Don't guns smoke *after* they've been fired?'

'So where would he dump the fluid?'

Carla spread her arms.

'It's a big desert.'

Chapter 34

At three the next morning, Book and Carla sat in her pickup truck parked out of sight off Highway 67 northeast of Alpine, just outside Barnett Oil and Gas Company Well Site 356. They had the high ground; down below, more flow-back fluid in the open pit was being pumped into a long line of tanker trucks. Book was in the driver's seat; Carla was in the passenger's. They ate beef jerky. The evening air had now turned cool, and the breeze brought the smell of distant rain. That night Book would learn Nathan Jones's truth.

'Boo!'

Carla screamed; Book jumped then recovered and saw a face behind night-vision goggles peering in through Carla's window. A hand yanked the goggles off to reveal a familiar face.

'*Big Rick?* What the hell are you doing out here?'

'Scaring the shit out of you two.' He laughed. 'My reliable source said something big is going down at this well site tonight. Thought I'd check it out myself. You know what it is?'

'We think they're dumping frack fluid out in the desert.'

Big Rick opened Carla's door. 'Scoot over.'

She did, and he climbed in with a backpack and an AR-15 assault rifle.

'Is that loaded?' Book asked.

'Why would I carry an unloaded weapon?'

'Point it out the window.'

He did.

'So what's the plan, Professor?'

'We wait. See where those trucks go.'

Carla held up her camcorder. 'We're going to follow them and videotape the dumping. A smoking gun.'

'Well, I've got my gun and I've got my smokes.'

Big Rick pulled out a joint and lit it. He inhaled deeply then offered the joint to Book and Carla; they declined.

'Don't exhale in here,' Book said.

Big Rick stuck his head out the window and exhaled smoke. 'Aah.'

He pulled his head back inside and a big bag of Cheetos from his backpack. He stuffed Cheetos into his mouth then held the bag out; Book declined, but Carla shrugged and took a handful.

'I do like Cheetos.'

Book shook his head. 'Heck of a team. A law professor, an environmentalist with a grudge, and a stoned artist with a loaded weapon and a bag of Cheetos.'

'And ready to kick some ass,' Big Rick said.

Carla pointed. 'Look.'

The tanker trucks carrying the flow-back fluid began exiting the site. They counted fifty trucks that turned north on 67, the road to the disposal wells in Pecos County. But fifty turned south on 67, the road to—

'Mexico,' Big Rick said.

After the final truck had passed, Book started the engine and shifted into gear but did not turn on the lights. He turned south and followed the red taillights. Carla videotaped and narrated. Big Rick smoked pot. Highway 67 turned east and led them through Alpine and toward Marfa. In the distant sky to the south lightning strikes flashed above the mountains. The faint sound of thunder broke the silence of the night.

'Desert storm over Mexico,' Carla said. 'It'll lightning and thunder, but it never rains.'

They passed through Alpine; the streets sat vacant.

'Can we stop and get some potato chips?' Big Rick asked.

'No.'

They cleared the town and wound through the Chisos Mountains then descended onto the Marfa Plateau. Eight miles further, just before the Marfa Mystery Lights Viewing Center, the trucks abruptly turned south on an unmarked dirt road that cut through the desert.

Deputy Shirley liked to come out to the viewing center late at night when she worked the midnight shift. The center was an open rock structure with a cement floor and a low rock wall; people gathered at night in hopes of seeing the mystery lights. But not at three-thirty in the morning. That's when she liked to come out; not to watch the mystery lights, but to screw on the low rock wall under the stars. And tonight the distant lightning made the moment even more romantic. She wore her uniform shirt with the Presidio County Sheriff's Department badge and her leather holster, but her uniform trousers lay on the cement floor. She sat bare-bottomed on the wall with her legs up high and spread for the cowboy named Cody; he was working hard and doing a very good job. The night was cool, but her thick white boot socks and Cowboy Cody's body heat kept her toasty. Shirley felt the heat building down below, and her body began rumbling—

—but not with the throes of an orgasm. The rumbling came from the line of tanker trucks barreling past not a hundred feet away down the Old Army Air Field Road. Cowboy Cody continued his hard work as she watched the tankers—ten, twenty, thirty . . . must be fifty trucks—heading deep into the dark desert. Odd. But then, sculptures made out of crushed cars were pretty odd, too. She turned back to Cody and tried to get her mind and body refocused on the moment before he ran out of gas when another vehicle turned off Highway 67 and headed down the dirt road into the desert. It was a pickup truck, a familiar-looking one, with a driver she recognized in the flash of the next lightning strike: the professor. He was driving with no headlights.

'What the hell?'

Cowboy Cody panted hard.

'Sorry. I held it as long as I could.'

'Not you. The trucks.'

Cowboy Cody backed away to police himself—Shirley insisted her beaus practice safe sex—and she drew the cell phone from her holster.

Presidio County Sheriff Brady Munn slept peacefully in his bed next to his wife of twenty-seven years. With the kids grown and gone, there were no more sleeps interrupted for bottle duty or diaper duty or chaperone duty; and Presidio County was not exactly a hotbed of criminal activity. Consequently, he was startled awake by the ringing phone. He reached out, found the phone, and put the receiver to his ear.

'This better be good.'

'It is.'

Shirley.

'What time is it?'

'Three-thirty.'

His niece told him what she had just witnessed out by the viewing center.

'Goddamn amateurs. They're gonna get themselves killed playing detective. He can't kung fu the cartels. What the hell are you doing out there, anyway?'

'Keeping Presidio County safe.'

'Well, put your pants on and get the hell back to town.'

She giggled and disconnected. He replaced the receiver and rubbed his face. Relatives. If it was just the tankers, he'd call Border Patrol and let them handle the situation. But Carla and the professor made him sit up and say to his wife, 'Honey, I'm gonna run down to the border,' like many a husband might say he was running to the neighborhood convenience store. She grunted and rolled over.

They drove over old runways.

'They're taking a shortcut through the old Marfa Army Air Field,' Carla said. 'Skirting town, to avoid a curious Border Patrol agent wondering what all these trucks are doing heading toward Mexico in the middle of the night. They'll pick up the highway again south of town.'

Rumbles of thunder rolled over the Marfa Plateau. Book's cell phone rang. He answered.

'Hi. I couldn't sleep. Alone.'

Carmen Castro.

'Uh, Carmen, I'm going to have to call you back. I'm right in the middle of something.'

'Does it involve a woman?'

'It's not quite that dangerous.'

Carmen sighed. 'You said you were coming back.'

'I've been delayed.'

'I've gone to the gun range every night, to get over my sexual frustrations.'

'Well, uh, whatever works.'

'It's getting expensive. I've gone through two thousand rounds of ammo. You want to have phone sex?'

'Uh, not a good time.'

A groan from Carmen. 'Call me.'

Book disconnected.

'Carmen?' Carla said.

'How old is she?' Big Rick said.

'Can we focus here?'

Big Rick took a long drag on his joint then hung his head out the window.

Border Patrol Agent Wesley Crum chased the wets into the desert just off Highway 67 about forty miles south of Marfa and twenty miles north of the border. Through the night-vision goggles, he counted five males and five females. No doubt a family reunion. An odd sound broke the silence of the night and caused him to stop and turn back to the highway. He observed an equally odd sight: a long line of tanker trucks heading south like ducks migrating for the winter. Only it was late spring, so they should be migrating north. The ducks, not the tanker trucks.

'Where the hell are they going?'

'Come on,' Angel said, 'let's get these folks.'

'You're always wanting to let them go. Tonight you want to chase them? Look.'

Wesley pointed, and Angel turned and looked. A ways behind the last tanker truck, a pickup truck followed with its lights off. But with the goggles, Wesley recognized the big potato embedded on the antenna.

'I know that potato. That's Carla's truck. And the professor. Maybe he ain't a good guy after all. Let's find out.'

'Come on, Wesley, let's take care of these people.'

Just then another pickup truck with its lights off passed. It was following Carla's truck.

'Who the hell is that? Come on, Angel, they're up to some-thing, and at four in the morning, it ain't no good.'

'They're just tanker trucks, Wesley. Going south, not north. They're not smuggling dope *into* Mexico. Let's do our job.'

'I am.'

Wesley took off running toward the highway and their Border Patrol SUV parked off the road. Angel shook his head then dropped the jug of water he was carrying and yelled to the Mexicans in the desert.

'*¡Agua! ¡Agua!*'

Angel Acosta ran after Wesley Crum.

Twenty minutes later, just outside the town of Presidio, the tankers turned west on Farm-to-Market 170, the river road. Book steered the pickup after them. The Rio Grande was visible to their left in the illumination of the lightning strikes, which came more often now.

'I'm hungry,' Big Rick said. 'You kids hungry?'

'They're going to cross the river,' Carla said.

'How?' Book said. 'The river's full.'

'The Rio Conchos from Mexico joins up just a few miles upriver. Beyond that, the riverbed is dry because of all the dams upstream of El Paso. If not for Mexican water in the Conchos, the Rio Grande would be dry all the way to the Gulf of Mexico.'

'I know an all-night café in Presidio,' Big Rick said. 'We could stop off and—'

Book looked over at Big Rick and put a finger to his lips. 'Shh.'

Border Patrol Agent Wesley Crum drove the SUV. The tanker trucks were leading this caravan south. Carla and the professor were following the tankers with their lights out. The second pickup truck was following Carla and the professor with its lights out. Wesley and Angel were following the whole goddamned bunch of them with their lights out. And Wesley was thinking, Who are the good guys and who are the bad guys? On the border, it was often difficult to tell.

'Am I right, Angel?'

'Yeah, you're right.'

'I figure they're gonna head west on One-seventy, cross the river above the Conchos.'

'Looks that way.'

'We could hit the lights and siren, speed to the front of the line, and try to stop the tankers.'

'That would be one option. How many guns we got?'

'Not enough.'

'Exactly.'

'So we follow?'

'We follow.'

Chapter 35

Six hundred miles southeast of Presidio in the Predator Ops command center on the second floor of an airplane hangar at the Corpus Christi Naval Air Station, U.S. Customs and Border Protection Air Interdiction Agent Dwight Ford watched the live video feed from the infrared camera aboard the Predator B drone as the unmanned aircraft banked left and right with the course of the Rio Grande. The drone's camera gave them 'eyes in the sky' above the 1,254-mile Mexico–Texas border. The images on the flat screen were sharp; from twenty thousand feet up, the camera could identify vehicles and humans, but not faces. But all it was identifying at the moment was the bare desert on either side of the river.

Dwight 'liaised'—a word he had never even heard before he was assigned to the drone—between the drone pilots and the Border Patrol agents on the ground. They had gotten a call-in tip that a big drug shipment was coming across the river below Nuevo Laredo, so the Predator had flown over that location most of the night; but it turned out to be another bullshit call. Dwight figured it might be a decoy, so he had the pilot fly the drone west of Nuevo Laredo. They found no activity, so they flew further west. They were now over Presidio.

Dwight wore his military-style tan jumpsuit and brown cap. He was leaned back in his captain's chair, and his feet were kicked up on the desk where the computers and keyboards and phones were situated; his hands were clasped behind his head. He glanced up at the black digital strip on the wall showing military times in red numerals: *Pacific, 02:31 . . . Costa Rica, 03:31 . . . Panama, 04:31 . . . Eastern, 05:31 . . . Zulu, 09:31 . . . Local, 04:31.* He was having a hell of a time keeping his eyes open.

'Dwight—wake up!'

Dwight snapped forward in his chair. The drone pilot was on the radio. Dwight clicked on his radio headset that connected him to the flight trailer parked outside where Lance and Grady, the pilot and co-pilot, flew the drone with a joystick like the kind his sons used to play their video games.

'What?'

'Look.'

On the screen were images of tanker trucks, a long line of tanker trucks. He checked the other flat screen displaying a Google Earth map that tracked the drone's path.

'They're driving west on FM One-seventy,' Lance the drone pilot said.

The drone had cleared Presidio and now flew west over the river road past the point where the big Rio Conchos flowed into the Rio Grande. The trucks seemed to be slowing—yes, they were definitely slowing—and turning south. The line of trucks drove across the dry riverbed and crossed into Mexico as if they were UPS trucks making deliveries in the neighborhood. But what were those tanker trucks delivering to Mexico?

'Follow those tankers,' Dwight said.

'They're in Mexico,' Lance said.

'So?'

'So we're supposed to respect Mexico's sovereign immunity.'

They all enjoyed a good laugh.

'Who the hell is that?'

On the screen, a pickup truck followed the last tanker across the riverbed, far enough back that it was obviously following with the intent of not being spotted.

'Someone with a death wish,' Grady the co-pilot said, 'following a cartel shipment into Mexico.'

Book hit the speed dial on his cell phone. After a few rings, a groggy voice came over.

'Book?'

'Henry, it's me.'

'This is early even for you, Book.'

'Sorry. I'm about to lose cell service.'

'Why? Low battery?'

'Because I'm crossing into Mexico.'

'That doesn't sound good.'

'Henry, listen. Nadine Honeywell, my intern, is in the Alpine hospital.'

'Why?'

'Long story. If you don't hear from me by eight, I need you to drive to Alpine and take her home to Austin. Will you do that for me?'

'Sure, Book. But where will you be?'

'Dead.'

Nadine Honeywell woke with a fright. Sweat matted her body; her heart beat rapidly. Fortunately, she was no longer hooked up to the machines, or the entire nursing staff would be on top of her by now and putting those paddles on her chest and screaming, 'Clear!' She gathered herself. It was just a nightmare. She checked the clock: 4:33.

'It was just a dream,' she said to the empty room.

The professor and Carla were running from a wall of fire—she had been running with them in spirit, hence the sweat—but they weren't fast enough. The fire had taken them. She shook her head. A wall of fire. How silly. Right now the professor and Carla were probably doing the dirty in that El Cosmico teepee. That's where they were. She felt better now. She breathed out all the tension she had awakened with. But still—

It had seemed so real.

Dwight Ford stared at the screen as if watching an action-thriller movie. His pulse had ratcheted up a notch and not because of the cold coffee he was drinking; because something bad was fixing to go down in the desert. People would die. Real people, not actors playing dead. South of the Rio Grande was a killing field. The drone banked south and the camera followed the tankers. They drove on a dirt road along the Rio Conchos deep into the Chihuahuan Desert.

Book steered the pickup carefully due to the dust kicked up by the tanker trucks. Through the dust cloud he saw the trucks' brake lights come on just as they crested a low rise in the desert. Book pulled over on the north side of the rise. They got out. The wind had picked up and carried the scent of smoke; the distant sky now glowed orange.

'Wildfire,' Carla said. 'Ignited by the lightning.'

'Wind's blowing our way.'

'Yep.'

'Let's get this on tape and get out of here.'

Carla took her camera; Big Rick donned his night-vision goggles and grabbed the AR-15. They snuck through the brush and crawled up the low rise. They lay flat on their bellies and observed the scene below. The trucks had backed up to a wide gulch. A group of armed men—'Cartel soldiers,' Carla said—had apparently been waiting for the trucks. They greeted the drivers as if they were *compadres*. The men opened the drain valves on the tankers and dumped the flow-back fluid into the gulch. The men then drank and laughed as if they were at a party.

341

'Lot of bad guys down there,' Big Rick said.

Carla captured the event on tape. The scene was lit up by the lightning strikes, which were almost nonstop, and the glowing sky from the wildfire. It was closer now.

'Arroyos,' Carla said. 'They lead to the Conchos and then to the Rio Grande. And down to the Gulf of Mexico.'

'I do believe that's an environmental crime.'

'Yep.'

'You got it on tape?'

'Yep.'

'Let's get out of here.'

Big Rick aimed his rifle at the Mexicans.

'What are you doing?' Book said.

'I'm going to take out a few Mexicans before we leave.'

'Don't.'

'Why not?'

'They have a lot more guns than we do.'

'True. But, damn, this sure is fun.'

A shot rang out. Big Rick fell back to the ground with a bullet hole in his forehead. They turned and came face to face with two Mexican men wielding AK-47s.

'*¡No se mueven!*'

'They shot him.'

Air Interdiction Agent Dwight Ford stood in front of the flat screen. He talked to the pilots.

'Zoom in on those figures.'

On the infrared camera, the figures appeared white against the dark background. Three individuals had exited the pickup and run to a spot in the desert and lain down. One held a rifle; another appeared to be aiming a camera at the scene below where the drivers crowded around the tankers. Fluid was flowing from the back of the tankers.

'They're dumping something,' Dwight said.

'Something they're not supposed to dump,' Lance said.

342

The individual holding the rifle had been shot; the other two had been captured by two men holding weapons.

'Got to be a cartel deal going down,' Dwight said. 'Damn, I wish that Predator had some missiles. We could light up the sky.'

'Something else is,' Lance said. 'Another wildfire.'

The screen was now noticeably brighter. The camera panned south and picked up what appeared to be flames in the distance. Then it panned back as the two individuals were brought into the crowd of men around the trucks.

'*Mis amigos*, look what we have found in the desert,' one of the men yelled.

The other men were grouped together by the trucks with handguns in their waistbands and rifles slung over their shoulders. One man stepped forward; he carried an assault weapon. From the respect he was given by the other men, he was obviously the leader. The men spoke in Spanish, but Book did make out 'kung fu.'

'Ah,' the leader said. 'Then we must have a fight.'

The men whooped and hollered as if they were at a bullfight. And Book soon realized that he was the bull. The drivers went to their trucks and turned on the headlights, illuminating an open area, although the sky glowed bright all around them; the men then formed a wide circle. They pushed Book and Carla into the center. The leader stepped over to them.

'So you are the kung fu professor. Word has spread how you beat up the *gringos*. I would very much like to see you fight.'

'How about Padre's tomorrow night?'

The leader laughed. 'No, I think tonight will be better.'

'And whom will I fight?'

'Ramon.'

The leader called out, and a man stepped into the ring. He removed his shirt; he was thicker and more muscular than

Book, but that did not concern him. What did concern him were the two nunchucks he unbuckled from his belt; he swung them around in the fashion of an experienced martial artist. The scene reminded Book of the first Indiana Jones movie when the crowd parts to reveal a bad guy swinging a sword, but instead of fighting him, Indiana pulls a gun and shoots him. But Book had no gun. He had only his hands and his feet and a certain skill set.

'What happens if I lose?' Book said.

The leader shrugged. 'You die.'

'What if I win?'

'You still die.'

'Then why should I fight?'

'So the *señorita* does not die.'

'If I win, you'll let her go? You promise?'

'Oh, sure, I promise.'

Book did not gain much comfort with his promise. But fighting would gain him time and perhaps provide a distraction that might allow Carla to escape. He stuck up his index finger.

'*Un momento.*'

Book stepped close to Carla and lowered his voice.

'I'm going to fight this guy, create a distraction. When I do, you get to the truck and get back to Texas.'

'Book—'

'Do it, Carla. Or we'll both die. And Nathan will have died for nothing.'

He turned away from Carla. The wind blew strong in his face, and the orange sky seemed much closer now. He breathed smoke. He stepped to the center of the ring and took a fighting stance. He extended his left arm and gestured with the fingers of his hand to Ramon to come closer. Ramon grinned; his *compadres* shouted as if they were at a sporting event. Perhaps they were.

Ramon stepped forward swinging the nunchucks.

★   ★   ★

'Shit,' Dwight Ford said, 'they're staging some kind of fucking fight, in the middle of the fucking night in the middle of the fucking desert.'

'Well,' Lance said, 'it's not like they have fucking jobs to go to tomorrow morning.'

Dwight watched the fight on the screen. Unlike a movie, in Mexico the bad guys always win.

The *nunchaku* is an ancient Chinese martial arts weapon, but the Westernized name for the weapon is nunchucks. The weapon consists of two short wood or metal sticks connected by a cord or chain. The martial artist holds one stick and swings the other; when wielded by an expert martial artist, the force generated by swinging the stick can inflict serious and often fatal injuries. Consequently, possession of nunchucks is a crime in a number of countries and in some states in the United States. Book wasn't sure about Mexican law; but then, there was no applicable law in the Chihuahuan Desert at five in the morning when surrounded by armed cartel soldiers. There was only life and death.

Ramon swung the nunchucks—side-to-side wrist spins and around his body with L-strikes and then around his neck and underarm switch-ups and helicopter spins—either to demonstrate his skill level or to intimidate Book. Ramon was experienced with nunchucks. Disarming him would not be easy. He advanced on Book; his *compadres* shouted in Spanish.

Book had two options: waiting for Ramon or attacking Ramon.

He decided on door number two. He abruptly broke and ran at Ramon . . . Ramon's face registered his surprise but he quickly recovered and took his fighting stance . . . Book closed the fifty feet between them . . . but ten feet before he reached Ramon, he dove to the ground as if a swimmer diving into a pool . . . he tucked his body and rolled and then launched himself up into Ramon, too close for the nunchucks to be useful . . . he tucked his right fist and executed an upper elbow strike, driving his right elbow into Ramon's jaw, knocking him unconscious. Ramon's hands dropped, and he fell over backwards. Book grabbed the nunchucks then spun around into a fighting stance. The men turned to the leader for instructions.

The leader's face showed his shock at the unexpected turn of events. He stared at the inert body of Ramon then at Book. His face turned angry. He yelled in Spanish and five men advanced on Book. He maneuvered into striking position and swung the nunchucks. Five swings, five seconds, five more men on the ground.

'Wow, he's good,' Dwight Ford said.

'Not good enough,' Lance the pilot said.

The leader yelled again, and all the men came after Book. He dispatched a few more with the nunchucks, but they over-whelmed him and beat him until several shots were fired into the air. Book lay on the ground bleeding from his nose and mouth; he hoped Carla had made her escape. The men parted for their leader; he straddled Book and pointed his weapon down at him.

'You are a good fighter, Professor. It is too bad you must die.'

From atop the low rise fifty yards out, he saw the Mexican pointing the AK-47 at the professor lying on the ground. He aimed the rifle fitted with the silencer and sighted in through the optic. He pulled the trigger.

The fire was near enough that Book could see the Mexican's eyes; and in his eyes he saw only hardness. He had killed many men. He would pull that trigger and kill Book and then have a beer with his *compadres*. That was the life he knew. The life he was born into. And now their lives had intersected in the Chihuahuan Desert.

Book's last thought was of his mother: who would take care of her?

Lightning illuminated the sky, and a crack of thunder followed quickly—and the Mexican's body jerked and his face registered shock, as if the thunder had frightened him. His hand that held the gun dropped. He looked down at his chest. His shirt turned red. With his blood. He fell to the ground, dead. Bullets sprayed the men; more went down. The others fired their guns wildly into the desert and then disappeared into the darkness. Book looked for Carla; she was gone.

'Holy shit,' Dwight said, 'the bad guys are going down. Someone's shooting them. Pan north.'

The Predator's sixty-six-foot wingspan allowed it to fly slowly above a location. Its camera moved north of the fight scene until it showed a shooter pointing a rifle at the cartel men.

'He's hammering them,' Lance said.

'He's rescuing the two hostages,' Dwight said.

'Hell of a firefight.'

'Literally,' Lance said. 'Look.'

He panned the camera south, but not very far. Flames from the wildfire were coming closer.

'Fixin' to be some fried Mexican food for the coyotes.'

'Oh, man,' Grady the co-pilot said. 'I love flautas.'

'Shut up, Grady.'

Carla crawled up the rise; the truck was parked on the other side. She did not want to leave Book, but she knew he was right. They would both die.

★ ★ ★

347

'That's a female,' Dwight said.

She was trying to escape. She ran hard through the desert brush, stumbled several times, got up and ran again . . .

Carla ran hard until a hand came out of the darkness and grabbed her arm.

Chapter 36

Book crawled through the chaos then got to his feet and ran low to the ground and into the desert. He scrambled up the rise; on the other side, he stopped and called out to Carla. A voice answered, but not her voice. A male voice.

'Hey, Professor.'

Two figures walked out of the darkness and into the light provided by the wildfire. One was Carla; the other was—

'Jimmy John?'

He wore a red jumpsuit and carried an assault rifle over his shoulder.

'What the hell are you doing out here?'

'Shooting a few Mexicans.' He chuckled. 'I spotted your truck outside the well site, figured you two were gonna get yourself in a mess of trouble, so I followed you. But why'd you follow the tankers?'

'To get it on tape,' Carla said. 'So we can shut Billy Bob down.'

'Let's get out of here,' Book said. 'Before that fire reaches us.'

'So Billy Bob's contaminating the groundwater with the frack fluid?' Jimmy John asked. 'That's what those papers proved?'

'No.'

'Then what?'

'He's dumping the flow-back out here in the desert,' Carla said. 'To cut costs. That's illegal. It'll flow into the Conchos, then the Rio Grande. We can put Billy Bob in prison and shut down his frack wells.'

'She right, Professor?'

'Yes.'

Jimmy John sighed then pulled the rifle off his shoulder and pointed it at Book.

'I'm sorry, Professor, but I can't let that happen.'

'Is he pointing the weapon at them?' Dwight said.

'Looks that way,' Lance said.

'For Christ's sake. He rescued them, now he's taken them hostage? What the fuck is going on?'

'Welcome to Mexico.'

'You ran Nathan off the road,' Book said.

'I wasn't trying to kill him. I was trying to get him to pull over, so I could talk some sense into him. He was gonna take his proof to the media, like that queer Kenni with an "i" wanted him to. Kenni got him into that queer stuff, thinking he could be an artist, live in New York, smoking dope. Got him thinking like the ChiNazis. Turned him against frack-ing. Against us. Against me. Like he didn't care about us no more. Like he found better friends. He knew going public would've cost me my job. I begged him, Professor. But he didn't care.'

'Nathan died for your job?'

'You ever not had a job, Professor? You ever go to the store and have to count your pennies to see if you can buy food? You ever live in a dump trailer on the Mexican side of town? You ever look in the mirror every morning and see a loser? Well, I have. Most of my life. But not since I got a job. You

350

shut down fracking, I lose my job. I can't go back to that life, Professor. A life without a job.'

Jimmy John swiped a sleeve across his nose. It was bleeding.

'You drive a big black pickup. You ran us off the road.'

'You wouldn't go home and mind your own goddamn business.'

'You hurt Nadine.'

'Well, what the hell were you doing, putting her on the back of that Harley? That ain't responsible.' He paused. 'Did she ask about me?'

Carla pointed south. 'The wildfire, it's closer.'

'What are you going to do, Jimmy John? Kill us, then go back and ask Nadine out?'

'Well . . . not right away.'

'You figure the sheriff will blame it on the Mexicans?'

Jimmy John pulled a baggie out of his back pocket and tossed it on the ground.

'Mexican black tar heroin. Drug deal gone bad. It happens. I'm sorry, Professor. I like you. Not so much Carla, but you're a good guy, came out here for Nathan just 'cause he was your student back then. I wish it didn't have to end this way.'

'Jimmy John, the sheriff will figure this out.'

'We're in Mexico, Professor. Two more dead bodies don't mean nothin' this side of the river.'

An explosion south of their location sent a fireball into the sky. Jimmy John flinched and glanced that way. Book grabbed Carla, and they ran a few steps into the dark desert then dove into the brush. Bullets zipped through the air over their heads.

'Nowhere to go, Professor. Only coyotes and wolves out there, and they'll eat you both for breakfast.'

Book picked up a rock and threw it at Jimmy John. He twirled and fired but missed.

'Give it up, Jimmy John.'

Book peppered Jimmy John with more rocks.

'I pitched in high school.'

He hit him in his back, his leg, and his face. Jimmy John clamped a hand against his head.

'You got a headache? You want an Advil?'

'You're pissing me off, Professor.'

Screams sounded from the other side of the rise where the sky burned bright orange.

'The wildfire!' Carla said.

More explosions sent more fireballs into the sky.

'The fire's reached the tanker trucks,' Book said.

'We've got to get out of here, make a run for the truck,' Carla said. 'The wind's pushing that fire our way, fast.'

Book threw another rock to the east of Jimmy John—he spun that way—then ran to the west; Book attacked Jimmy John from his rear. Jimmy John heard his footsteps and swung the rifle around, but Book launched himself feet first and struck Jimmy John before he could fire. The rifle went flying, and they went sprawling into the dirt. Book jumped to his feet; Jimmy John did not. He lay in a heap. Then he started crying. Sobbing uncontrollably. After a moment, he pushed himself up; his nose was bleeding. He grabbed his head with both hands.

'Come on, Jimmy John! We've got to outrun the fire!'

'I can't go back to that life. No job and nobody.'

'You want to burn to death?'

Book helped Jimmy John to his feet.

'Come on!' Book yelled.

'I'm sorry, Professor.'

Jimmy John Dale turned and ran up the rise toward the fire. Just as he crested the rise, the flames came over and engulfed him. He fell down the other side.

'Jesus!' Dwight Ford yelled at the video screen. 'He ran into the fire!'

'They better get out of there!' Lance said.

The Predator's camera caught the flames of the wildfire as it

352

engulfed the tanker trucks and set them afire, causing several to explode in fireballs. Cartel men tried to outrun the flames but failed.

'Wind's blowing at forty-three knots,' Lance said. 'I'm having a hell of a time controlling this bird.'

The flames ran across the desert toward the two figures.

'Run!'

Book grabbed Carla's arm; they sprinted to the truck. He jumped into the driver's seat and she into the passenger's. He fired up the engine, shifted into gear, and floored the accelerator. They sped down the dirt road. He saw the flames in the outside rearview; the fire was chasing them to the border.

'Follow them,' Dwight said.

The Predator's camera followed the pickup racing north to the river, fishtailing around curves but staying on the road. The camera panned north to the river.

'Look,' Lance said. 'That's a Border Patrol SUV.'

On the north side of the river was a large vehicle. Two men stood facing south.

'Thank God,' Dwight said. 'Those are the good guys. My guys.'

Border Patrol Agent Wesley Crum peered through the night-vision binoculars into Mexico.

'Man, look at that fucking wildfire. And explosions. I'm telling you, Angel, something big is going down in the desert. Let's call in the Predator.'

'Can't. It's over Nuevo Laredo.'

'How do you know?'

'Daily ops bulletin.'

'Then let's call in the cavalry, set a trap for those tanker trucks when they come back to this side.'

Wesley spotted something.

'Look! One of the pickup trucks is coming back. I think it's Carla and the professor.'

Angel sighed. 'I'm sorry, Wesley.'

His partner still had the binoculars pressed against his eyes. 'For what?'

'This.'

Angel reached down to his ankle, pulled up his trouser leg, and retrieved his backup weapon. He stuck the barrel to his partner's head and pulled the trigger.

'Fuck!' Dwight yelled. 'He just shot him! One of the good guys shot the other good guy! What the hell is going on?'

The shooter flung the weapon far downriver then took the dead agent's binoculars and put them to his face. Then he put something to his ear. A phone.

Billy Bob Barnett inhaled the line of white powder then leaned back in his leather chair and waited for the drug to take effect. To take his mind off the pressures that threatened to push him over the edge.

He had always lived life on the edge.

And if a man lived in Texas and wanted to live life on the edge, he played the oil and gas game. He wildcatted. He punched holes in the earth. He hoped he hit oil or gas or both. When that drill bit is digging deep and nearing the producing zone—what you *prayed* would be the producing zone—man, your heart is pounding and your adrenaline is pumping and your nerves are firing and you've never been so alive. If your geology and your hunch play out, life is good. And you are rich. If not . . .

The thrill of victory or the agony of defeat.

He had enjoyed many thrills and a few defeats. But no defeat like this one. His frack wells had hit gas, a mother lode of gas; but so had everyone else's. Consequently, the market had glutted and natural gas prices had plummeted. As had Billy Bob's emotions. He now wallowed in the depths of depression. And as each time before, he had turned to drugs for respite and relief. Marijuana in college, cocaine in business. It was a daily dose now.

First, the glut of gas. Then, the plunge in prices. Followed by the collapse of the stock value. And the pressure—the constant, pounding pressure—from the analysts, the board, the shareholders . . . and then his own lawyer. Nathan Jones had learned the truth and had threatened to go public with company documents. That would have been the end of Billy Bob Barnett.

The cartel had taken care of Wade Chandler. He would take care of Nathan Jones. But a car wreck did it for him. A stroke of luck. A sign that his luck was changing. He would hold out for the futures market to move back up, as it surely would. Drill more, frack more, stockpile more gas for the inevitable rise in prices. He was saved. Until a law professor rode into town on a Harley.

His cell phone rang.

Angel waited for Billy Bob Barnett to answer. When he did, Angel said, 'They're coming, the professor and Carla. What do you want me to do?'

'Don't let them back on this side of the river. It's like Vegas, Angel. What happens in Mexico stays in Mexico.'

'You're the boss.'

Angel disconnected, replaced his cell phone, and returned to the vehicle. He got the AR-15, snapped in a full clip, and grabbed the night-vision goggles. He walked across the dry Rio Grande and waited for the professor and Carla to arrive. And arrive they would. There was no place for them to go but north to the river. The wall of fire would chase them right into his kill zone. All he had to do was wait.

★   ★   ★

355

Dwight could see the pickup truck speeding directly at the Border Patrol agent.

'He's gonna kill those two people in the pickup truck,' Lance said.

'I know.'

A Border Patrol agent had gone over to the dark side. It wasn't the first time, or even the thousandth time. There was just too much easy money to be made. Look the other way and collect a million bucks. That was bad enough. But killing a fellow agent, that crossed a law enforcement line that no officer can cross. Ever.

The agent Dwight was now staring at on the video screen had to die.

He had to die that night.

On that river.

Before he killed those two people.

While there was still time to control the story.

But who could he call? Other Border Patrol agents would be in Presidio County, maybe near enough to arrive in time, but what if they had been corrupted, too? He needed a law enforcer in Presidio County who was incapable of being corrupted.

He grabbed a phone and dialed.

Chapter 37

Sheriff Brady Munn had the Presidio County SUV running eighty miles an hour with the lights flashing but no siren on Highway 67 just north of Presidio when his cell phone rang. Better not be Shirley telling him she was seeing the Marfa Mystery Lights. He answered.

'Sheriff Munn?'

'Yep.'

'This is Air Interdiction Agent Dwight Ford, at the Predator Ops center in Corpus Christi.'

The Predator boys must've spotted some Mexicans coming across the river.

'Agent, I don't have time to chase wets for you—'

'Sheriff, I'm sorry to wake you up but—'

'I'm already awake. I'm hauling ass to the border. We got something strange going on—'

'With tanker trucks?'

'How'd you know?'

'We've been tracking them with the Predator. They drove into Mexico and dumped some kind of liquid.'

'Frack fluid.'

'Frack? Like from gas wells?'

'Yeah. Like from gas wells.'

'Anyway, there was a shootout. We're following two individuals, a male and a female—'

'The professor and Carla.'

'You know them?'

'If that's them, I know them.'

'Well, they're heading north now.'

'Good.'

'Not so good. We got a man on this side of the river, Border Patrol agent.'

'And?'

'He's rogue. Just killed his partner. Gotta be on the cartel payroll.'

'Who?'

'Can't tell.'

'Where?'

'West on FM One-seventy, just past where the Conchos joins up. A Border Patrol SUV is parked on the river road. Can't miss it.'

Dwight paused.

'He's gonna kill those two people, unless you stop him. Sheriff, they need your help.'

Angel Acosta stepped onto Mexican soil. For the last two years, he had been on the cartel's payroll; all he had to do was turn a blind eye to drug shipments coming north. But while profitable, the job carried significant personal risk. So he had approached Billy Bob Barnett about employment in the oil and gas business; Aggies helped Aggies. Billy Bob had a job for him, but it required that he continue his employment with the Border Patrol. Billy Bob had made an arrangement with his trucking company, which had close ties to the cartel, to dump his frack fluid in the desert; but, there was always the risk of a Border Patrol agent spotting the caravan and getting curious. So Angel's job was to make sure no one was watching Highway 67 when the tanker trucks made their run into the desert. To evade the Predator's 'eyes in the sky,' he called in bogus tips of drug deals going down, way downriver, as he had that night. So he would collect two paychecks for that night's work, one from the cartel and one from Billy Bob. What federal employees call 'double dipping.'

A hundred trips, and all had worked just fine. He had remained partners with Wesley Crum because he was the dumbest Anglo Angel had ever met. But Wesley chose that night to become smart.

What had brought Angel Acosta, son of Carlos and Consuelo Acosta, devout Catholics both, to where he now stood in life, on the bank above the great Rio Conchos waiting to kill two more innocents? He had grown up in Marfa and lived as all Latinos lived in Marfa: out of sight and out of trouble. The old sheriff, he had put the fear into every Mexican's heart with his harsh law and order; but it turned out he was a drug runner, in the law for the money. Angel wanted to believe that he did what he did for some noble cause, but in the end, it was just about the money for him, too. He wanted to have something in life. A life. With things. Everything. He wanted the finer things in life, just as the Anglos from New York enjoyed. Good wine and Gouda cheese. A sports car. A fine home behind tall walls on the north side of the railroad tracks. On the Anglo side of town.

And why should he not have what they had, the Triple As? Were they smarter, better, worthier than he? Every attorney he had met was a borderline criminal, out of jail just because his form of criminal activity had been deemed legal by lawyers who write the laws. Every artist he had met was a queer stoner trying to win the Marfa art lottery and become rich and famous. And every asshole he had met was . . . an asshole. Why were the attorneys, artists, and assholes entitled to more than he? He did not feel that what he did was morally wrong . . . well, perhaps killing his partner was wrong. He would say a rosary for Wesley's soul, such as it was. But his other illegal activities were no worse than rich people's legal activities. How many rich people earned their fortunes through shady dealings on Wall Street and political favors? Through favorable laws gained by legal bribes called campaign contributions? Through legalized corruption? Joe Blow goes to prison for trading stock on insider information, but senators and congressmen go to the bank for doing exactly the same thing. How can that be constitutional, for members of Congress to exempt themselves from the very laws they impose on the people? Perhaps he would ask the professor before he killed him.

He fixed the night-vision goggles to his face. He could now see into the night. He could see the pickup truck driving fast toward him, the wall of fire behind it. Smoke filled the air. He aimed the AR-15 and fired.

The windshield blew out.

'Get down!' Book yelled.

Bullets peppered the truck. The shooter had a perfect line on them. There was only one place to go.

'Hold on.'

'They're between a rock and a hard place,' Lance the pilot said. 'Wildfire's chasing them straight at the shooter. No place for them to go.'

Or so Lance thought. Dwight Ford watched the screen as the pickup truck drove straight off the road and flew into the Rio Conchos.

'Shit, they drove into the Conchos!' Lance yelled. 'They're fuckin' crazy!'

'They're fucking alive!' Dwight said.

Two figures were visible on the screen emerging from the

pickup truck as it sank into the river. Above on the bank, the Border Patrol agent fired more shots at them.

'Not for long,' Lance said.

Angel had them dead in his sights. He would not be able to get an answer to his constitutional law question from the professor. Oh, well.

'*Adiós*, Professor.'

But he could not pull the trigger. He could not move his body. He could not hold the rifle. It fell from his hands. His eyes turned down to his chest. A large hole now gaped in his uniform shirt and his insides hung out. Blood gushed forth. He turned and saw the big sheriff standing there, smoke from the barrel of his handgun hanging in the air.

'*Adiós* yourself, podna,' the sheriff said.

Angel Acosta fell over dead.

Sheriff Brady Munn holstered his .44 Magnum and searched the Conchos for the professor and Carla in the moonlight and the light from the fires. He spotted them; they were being swept downriver toward the point a mile east where the Conchos joined the Rio Grande. Which was just as well since the wildfire was coming Brady's way fast. He turned and ran north and crossed over the dry Rio Grande riverbed. The Conchos turned hard east so he lost sight of the professor and Carla.

He jumped into his SUV, fired up the engine, and stomped on the accelerator. He drove east on the river road a mile past where the Conchos merged in, then slammed on the brakes. He cut the engine and got out. He opened the back liftgate and retrieved his rope. He ran down to the river.

The current was strong with the Conchos's water. He searched the river for the professor and Carla, but he couldn't find them. He yelled for them, but got no response. Just when he was about to run back to the SUV and drive farther downriver, he spotted them.

'There!'

He yelled to them, and they saw him. He fashioned a loop with the rope then twirled the loop above his head as if he were about to rope a calf in a rodeo competition and flung the loop at the professor. He missed. He reeled in the rope and flung the loop again. The professor grabbed the rope this time. He hung onto the rope with one hand and Carla with the other. Brady dug the heels of his cowboy boots into the earth, leaned his two hundred twenty pounds back, and pulled with all his strength against the current that tried to take them downriver. The rope burned his bare hands, but Brady felt no pain. His hands bled by the time he pulled them to dry land.

Dwight Ford threw his fists in the air. 'Yes!'

The professor and Carla lay there coughing and spitting water, but alive and unhurt. Finally, the professor knelt up and stuck a hand out to Brady. He grabbed the professor's hand and yanked him to his feet. The professor then helped Carla up. They stood there on the bank of the Rio Grande and gathered themselves as one does after having barely escaped death. To the southeast, the sky brightened with the breaking dawn; to the southwest, the sky burned bright with fire. The wildfire came to the river, but did not cross. No doubt it had scorched everything and everyone in its path. Just as well. What happens in Mexico stays in Mexico. After a moment, the professor turned back to Brady.

'Sheriff—thanks for the help.'

'Now that wasn't so hard, was it, Professor?'

Sheriff Brady Munn stretched his big body and gazed upon Presidio County and Mexico beyond. The border carried a harsh beauty and a harsher justice. He shook his head and exhaled at the grandeur of it all. Damn, but he loved the desert at dawn. He grunted.

'You folks want to get a cup of coffee?'

Chapter 38

The desert had changed John Bookman. He had come to this harsh land and paid off an overdue debt. And while he would never be a father, he would now be a godfather. To Nathan Jones Jr. Brenda had asked Book when they had said their goodbyes.

'Final exam, Nadine. What did you learn in Marfa, Texas?'

'A, I like to hit bad guys in the head with beer bottles. B, I'm a lot tougher than I thought. And C, I matter. To you. To my dad. To myself.'

'Very good. You made an A on this field trip.'

'Can we go home now?'

'Yes. We can go home now.'

It was Friday morning. Book had brought Nadine back to the Paisano the day before. He and Carla had given written statements to the sheriff and the FBI, DEA, and Border Patrol and an exclusive interview to Sam Walker for his next edition. Nathan Jones had not been killed by an evil oil company or a greedy fracker, but by his best friend who needed a job. But Billy Bob Barnett sat in the Presidio County Jail pending transfer to federal court in El Paso on criminal environmental charges. And his lawyer, Tom Dunn, was under investigation for aiding and abetting his client. But the videotape had been lost, and the tankers burned, and there were jurisdictional issues since the dumping occurred in Mexico. Hence, conviction of either man was doubtful. They were innocent until proven guilty beyond a reasonable doubt. That was constitutional law in America.

Book sat astride the repaired Harley outside the courtyard of the Paisano Hotel; Pedro had done a good job. Nadine sat behind him with her right leg in the cast secured to one side and her left arm in the cast secured to the other. Sheriff Brady Munn and Carla Kent stood next to them.

'Official line is, those two Border Patrol agents died in the line of duty,' the sheriff said. 'Drug bust gone bad.'

'Figures. Thanks again, Sheriff. For your help.'

'It's what we do out here in this desert, Professor.'

Carla bent down and kissed Book on the cheek.

'What are you going to do now?' he asked.

'Make sure Billy Bob's convicted. And fight fracking.'

'It's good to be busy.'

'You ever get up to Santa Fe, look me up, cowboy.'

'Comanche.'

Book, Carla, and Nadine had eaten take-out from Maiya's on Rock's outdoor patio the night before. They drank too much wine and beer. Nadine had fallen asleep, so he had carried her to Liz's bed and tucked her in. Then Carla had collected on her rain check. They had danced under the stars to music drifting over from Padre's Marfa. And they had spent one last night together. Book fired up the Harley and pulled on the doo-rag.

'You know,' Carla said, 'you really should wear a helmet. You're lucky you didn't get brain damage in that crash.'

'It's already damaged.'

'Well, you are a half-crazy Comanche, but you can still find your way home.'

'So far.'

She stared at him then abruptly took his face and kissed him full on the lips. A long kiss.

'There would be romance,' his intern said.

Carla finally released Book and stepped back. The sheriff stepped forward and stuck a hand out.

'I ain't kissing you.'

They shook.

'You take care, podna. You too, little lady.'

Book turned his head to his back-seat passenger. 'You ready to roll?'

Nadine strapped the goggles on over her black glasses. 'Yep. Got on my last pair of new underwear. I'm good.'

'Over-share.'

Book slid on the sunglasses. The sheriff touched his finger to his cowboy hat.

'*Adiós*, podna.'

Book shifted into gear and gunned the Harley south on Highland Avenue. Nadine raised her good arm into the air. Sheriff Munn and Carla Kent smiled at the bumper sticker on the back of Nadine's seat that read: I ■ JUDD.

ONE MONTH LATER

Epilogue

'Mr. Stanton, if the federal government can force an American citizen to buy health insurance, can it also force you to buy a Chevrolet vehicle since the government now owns twenty-seven percent of General Motors?'

'Of course not.'

'Why not?'

'That would be unconstitutional.'

'Why?'

'Because I drive a Beemer.'

The class laughed. But not Ms. Garza. Her T-shirt read *I ♥ OBAMACARE* in honor of that day's Con Law topic.

'Let's turn to the majority opinion of Chief Justice Roberts in *National Federation of Independent Business v. Sebelius, Secretary of Health and Human Services*. It was a five-to-four decision—actually, it was two five-to-four decisions—with Roberts being the deciding vote both times. The law under the Court's review was the Patient Protection and Affordable Care Act, also known as Obamacare, the key provision of which is the so-called "individual mandate." Essentially, that provision requires all citizens not covered by a government or employer plan to buy private health insurance. If they fail to do so, they must pay a penalty to the government. What was the idea behind the law?'

Ms. Garza's hand shot into the air.

'Ms. Garza.'

'The individual mandate requires everyone to pay into the health insurance system in order to prevent cost-shifting. If you go uninsured, my insurance premiums will increase to subsidize your care. You will be shifting the cost of your medical care to me. We must force everyone into the system. That's the only way Obamacare works. That's the only way to make the healthcare system fair.'

'Ms. Garza, is fairness the issue before the Supreme Court?'

'It should be.'

'Not my question.'

'No.'

'What is the issue before the Supreme Court, in this or any other case, when the Court reviews a Congressional act?'

'Whether Congress acted within its constitutional authority.'

'Correct. Mr. Stanton, what was the plaintiffs' main argument in that regard?'

Mr. Stanton's head was down. He was texting on the back row.

'Mr. Stanton, if you please.'

'Sorry, Professor, I'm selling my Whole Foods stock. Bought it at seven after the crash, selling it at ninety-four.'

'The appellant's main argument, please.'

'That the individual mandate exceeded Congress's power under the Commerce Clause.'

'And the Commerce Clause authorizes Congress to do what?'

'Regulate foreign and interstate commerce.'

'But the business of health insurance is clearly interstate commerce—commerce that crosses state lines. Why did the plaintiffs think the individual mandate exceeded Congress's authority?'

'Because the Commerce Clause authorizes Congress to *regulate* commerce, not to *create* commerce. Congress can't compel citizens to engage in commerce in order to then regulate that commerce.'

'Congress can regulate what we do, but they can't regulate what we don't do.'

'Exactly. As Scalia wrote, saying the Commerce Clause allows the government to regulate the failure to act "is to make mere breathing in and out the basis for federal prescription and to extend federal power to virtually all human activities."'

'And the individual mandate orders citizens to act, to engage in commerce, to buy a product, in this case health insurance.'

'Yes. Congress said, we've decided it's a good thing for all Americans to have health insurance, so we order all Americans to buy health insurance, and any American who refuses to buy health insurance will suffer a monetary penalty. We are forced to act at the direction of the government.'

'And what did Chief Justice Roberts have to say about that?'

'He said that was a bit much, even under the Commerce Clause. A government order to purchase insurance, enforced with a monetary penalty, is unconstitutional.'

'Who agreed with him?'

'The other four conservative justices. The four liberals thought that was an okay thing for Congress to do. They said Congress was just regulating our future commercial activity today, what they called "regulating in advance." But no one ever accused them of higher intelligence.'

Mr. Stanton shared a fist-bump with his buddies on the back row.

'So, on a five-to-four vote—five conservative justices to four liberal justices—the Court invalidated the individual mandate?'

'Yes.'

'And thus Obamacare?'

'Uh . . . no.'

'But you just said the Court invalidated the individual mandate as an unconstitutional exercise of Congress's power under the Commerce Clause.'

'That's correct, but the Court then validated the individual mandate under the Taxing Clause.'

'Please explain, Mr. Stanton.'

'The government made a backup argument, that the individual mandate could instead be upheld as a tax, and there's almost nothing or no one Congress can't tax.'

'What tax? The nine-hundred-page Obamacare law never once mentions the word "tax." It provides for a penalty for refusal to buy insurance, not a tax.'

'The government lawyers made it up after the fact. They realized that they might lose on the Commerce Clause argument, so they said, "Oh, that 'penalty' is really a 'tax,'" because the Taxing Clause gives Congress essentially unlimited power to lay and collect taxes for just about any purpose—why not to finance healthcare?'

'But Roberts and the four conservative justices saw through that ploy, didn't they, and disagreed with that contention?'

'They did. He didn't. Roberts joined with the four liberal justices to uphold the individual mandate as a tax and not a penalty.'

'Even though the law says it's a penalty and not a tax? Even though the Court had never before held that a penalty under a law was also a tax?'

'I'm afraid so, Professor.'

'So Chief Justice Roberts was the deciding vote to hold the individual mandate unconstitutional under the Commerce Clause and also to hold the individual mandate constitutional under the Taxing Clause?'

'Yep.'

'So the individual mandate is the law in America?'

'Yep.'

'And Obamacare?'

'Yep.'

Mr. Stanton leaned down then held up a T-shirt that read: OBAMACARE: YOU CAN'T CURE STUPID.

The class shared a laugh.

'Thank you for the levity, Mr. Stanton.'

'My pleasure, Professor.'

'But, Mr. Stanton, what's the difference between A, Congress ordering a citizen to buy health insurance and enforcing that with a monetary penalty, which the Court said is unconstitutional, and B, Congress taxing a citizen for refusing to buy health insurance, which the Court said was constitutional?'

'Nothing. It's exactly the same result. Congress is using its power to force citizens to do something they don't want to do and taking your money if you refuse to do it. Roberts engaged in constitutional sophistry.'

'Why would he do that?'

'Because Roberts wants the *New York Times* to like him. The liberal media destroyed the legal reputations of conservative justices like Rehnquist and Scalia, and Roberts doesn't want to suffer the same fate. Problem is, he doesn't understand that the liberals might like him now since he upheld the biggest government takeover of American life in history, but the first time he goes against them, they'll crucify him. That's what they do. So he cratered. He betrayed the Constitution.'

Ms. Garza stood and faced Mr. Stanton. The debate was on.

'Roberts grew a conscience, that's why he voted with the liberals.'

'Funny how it's always a conservative justice who crosses over to vote with the liberals, but no liberal justice ever crosses over to vote with the conservatives. Why is that?'

'Because we're always right.'

'And therein lies the problem: self-righteous liberals in America who want the government to make an unfair life fair, unsuccessful people successful, stupid people smart, and everyone ride a bike.'

'Ride this.'

Ms. Garza stuck her middle finger in the air at Mr. Stanton. He turned his eyes to Book and his hands up.

'Holster that finger, Ms. Garza. And please sit down. We're here to discuss con law, not social policy.'

'Con law is social policy.'

'Yeah,' Mr. Stanton said, 'because liberal justices believe government should control our economic lives.'

'And conservative white male justices believe government should control our personal lives,' Ms. Garza said.

'I don't want some uneducated minimum-wage government bureaucrat who wasn't smart enough to get a job in the private sector deciding whether my children get life-saving treatments.'

'You'd rather have a greedy profit-driven insurance company deciding?'

'Yes. You know why, Ms. Garza?'

'Because your daddy owns stock in those insurance companies?'

'Besides that?'

'No.'

'Sovereign immunity.'

'What?'

'If the insurance company denies treatment and my son dies, I can sue them for a billion dollars. That keeps them honest. If a government bureaucrat denies treatment and my son dies, I can't sue the federal government for a penny. It's called sovereign immunity.'

Ms. Garza shrugged. 'That's the price we pay to solve social problems.'

'Name one social problem the federal government has ever solved, Ms. Garza. Education? Drugs? Energy? Poverty? Now they're going to *solve* our healthcare.'

'The forty million poor people who can't afford health insurance deserve medical care, too.'

'They've got free healthcare. It's called the public hospital. And how many of those so-called "poor" people have tricked-out trucks with thousand-dollar wheels and iPhones and tickets to every pro football game, but they just can't afford healthcare? Those "poor" people know they can still get free medical care, so why pay for it? Why not suck off everyone else? We don't have forty million people who can't afford healthcare insurance. We have ten million who can't and thirty million who won't. Who'd rather let the rest of us pay their way.'

Mr. Stanton leaned down again and held up another T-shirt that read: OBAMA-MART: WHEN EVERYTHING IS FREE BECAUSE THE GUY BEHIND YOU PAYS.

The class enjoyed the T-shirt.

'Mr. Stanton, did you go shopping this weekend?'

'Yep. In honor of our last class with Ms. Garza and her T-shirts.'

'Ah.'

Ms. Garza was not yet ready to surrender.

'We do too have forty million people who can't afford health insurance—they said so on the evening news.'

Mr. Stanton laughed. 'You shouldn't be so gullible, Ms. Garza. The poverty industry puts out that misinformation so the government will keep sending trillions their way. And the liberal media repeats it without investigation because it fits their political bias.'

'Let's get back to Obamacare,' Book said. 'Under the rationale of this case, is there any human activity or non-activity that Congress may not regulate under the Constitution?'

'Nope,' Mr. Stanton said. 'They've got it all now. In fact, in oral arguments, the justices asked the government lawyer that exact question, and he couldn't think of a single human act that would be free from government control. So now five justices—five lawyers—have given Congress the absolute authority to tell us to do something, to tell us how to do it, and to fine us—I'm sorry, tax us—if we refuse to do it. I think that's what they call communism.'

'It's called social justice,' Ms. Garza said.

'Only if you're a communist.'

'All right,' Book said, 'today's Supreme Court decisions are precedents for tomorrow's decisions. When the Court decided Obamacare, the justices searched for precedents to support their positions. Now that Obamacare has been ruled constitutional—now that the Supreme Court has given its stamp of approval to Congress passing laws that tax citizens if they refuse to engage in a specified commercial activity— what might be the next law that climbs on top of this precedent?'

'Taxing us if we refuse to buy that Chevy to protect the domestic auto industry?'

'Yes. But I'm thinking of something bigger.'

'Taxing us if we refuse to eat vegetables?'

'Come on, people. This requires thought. Think about the Court's prior cases, big precedents that made law, like this case. Put those precedents together and what do you have? If the government can force the citizens to do something they don't want to do by taxing them if they refuse to do it, where might that precedent lead us?'

'To Russia and Comrade Putin,' Mr. Stanton said.

He held up another T-shirt: OBAMACARE: HEALTHCARE YOU CAN'T REFUSE. Which evoked more laughter.

Book scanned the class. Mr. Brennan was dutifully transcribing his every word, other students were texting or tweeting or zoning out. His eyes landed on a head hiding behind her laptop.

'Ms. Roberts.'

She peeked above the laptop.

'You know, don't you?'

She nodded as if confessing to a crime.

'Please, tell the class.'

She pushed hair from her face and spoke in her soft voice. The class seemed to lean toward her as one.

'Well, under the Obamacare ruling, the government can't order a woman to have an abortion even though medical care is commerce because that would exceed Congress's authority under the Commerce Clause; but, under the same Obamacare ruling, the government can tax a woman if she refuses to have an abortion.'

'But the Bill of Rights would prohibit the government from doing that.'

'No, it wouldn't. The Court in *Roe v. Wade* ruled that the, quote, "developing organism" inside the woman has no constitutional rights or protections whatsoever under the Bill of Rights because it is not a, quote, "person" prior to birth. Under the precedents of *Roe* and Obamacare, the Court would uphold such a law. And the circle would be complete: we are nothing more than rocks.'

'But why would our government ever do such a thing?'

'Perhaps the sonogram shows the baby has a genetic defect that would require expensive medical care for life. Or the woman is unmarried with no means of support for the child, and public support would add to the deficit. They would do it to save money.'

'But that's just wild speculation, isn't it? I mean, we don't have anything to really worry about, do we? We're an advanced civilization. What civilized nation on earth would ever pass such a law?'

'China.'

'Thank you, Ms. Roberts.'

Mr. Stanton held up another T-shirt: OBAMACARE: BEND OVER, THIS IS GONNA HURT.

'Mr. Stanton, how many of those do you have?'

'Just one more.'

'But, Professor,' Ms. Garza said, 'if the government can't force people to do the right thing, how can the government solve big problems like healthcare?'

'Ms. Garza, the Framers did not create a federal government that possesses all powers except those denied in the Constitution, but rather a government that possesses only those powers granted in the Constitution. Perhaps the federal government isn't supposed to solve—or try to solve—every social problem in America. To solve the problem of obesity, the federal government is now telling every school district in America what to feed their students for lunch. Is that what Madison, Hamilton, Jefferson, and Washington intended the national government to do when they created this country? Perhaps that responsibility resides in the fifty states.'

'But we have an obesity problem in America,' Ms. Garza said.

Ms. Roberts raised her hand. Book nodded at her.

'The dissent wrote, "The Constitution enumerates not federally soluble *problems*, but federally available *powers* . . . Article One contains no whatever-it-takes-to-solve-a-problem power." I like that.'

Ms. Garza glared at her. 'Like this, Liz.'

Another middle finger. Book couldn't help but hope that Ms. Garza was put in another professor's Con Law II class next year. Mr. Stanton stood on the back row.

'Professor, in honor of our last class with Ms. Garza and her T-shirts, I offer this final rebuttal.'

Mr. Stanton yanked open his button-down shirt to reveal a white T-shirt underneath that read: F#CK OBAMACARE, I'M MOVING TO CANADA.

The class laughed.

'And with that, ladies and gentlemen, Con Law One is adjourned for the year.'

The students applauded. The males slapped backs and exchanged fist-bumps; the females embraced. Classes were finished; final exams awaited. Some students left, others gathered around Book. He signed books; they took photos.

The Marfa story had hit the national media.

★　★　★

378

Book returned to his office to find Myrna on the phone.

'Here he is.' She held the phone out to him. 'The police.'

'Hello.'

'Professor, it's Sergeant Taylor again. Your mother wandered off, we found her at the Condoms to Go store. Took her back home, I'm waiting for your sister.'

'Thank you, Sergeant.'

'Professor . . .'

'Yes?'

'It's time.'

He handed the phone to Myrna then rubbed his forehead. The stitches had come out, but the scar itched.

Myrna smiled. 'All the girls think that scar makes you look sexy.'

'Oh, good. What time is the Welch hearing?'

'Canceled.'

'Why?'

'Scotty Raines called, said the D.A. dropped all charges against Bobby Welch. And his dad called from the Betty Ford Clinic in Palm Springs. Said he checked the boy in for six months. Said thank you and that he had fulfilled both promises.' She looked up from her notes. 'Promises?'

'Personal.'

She leaned down and came back up with a plastic container. She held it out to Book.

'Fried chicken. And don't worry, I fried it in peanut oil. You won't die if you eat it.'

'Thanks.'

She went back to her notes. 'TV shows want you on next Sunday.'

'I can't.'

She regarded him. 'You okay?'

'No. Mail?'

She aimed a thumb at his office. He turned to his office, but—

'You don't have time. You're late for the big faculty meeting. The new assistant dean.'

Book entered the faculty meeting and found an open seat between Henry Lawson and Professors Sheila Manfried and Jonah Goldman. Professor Manfried whispered to Jonah, 'I wonder if we can make more money at the new Texas A&M law school?'

The school had settled her sex discrimination claim by paying her $25,000 more in salary, giving her a $250,000 forgivable loan, and granting her a contractual right to see every other professor's compensation numbers.

'Admin admitted a hundred fewer tuition-payers for next year's one-L class,' Professor Goldman said. 'That's three million in lost tuition. They've got to cut our salaries.'

'I'll go to A&M for more money,' Professor Manfried said.

Professor Goldman grimaced. 'And be an Aggie? Just the thought of it makes me shudder.'

Book popped the top on the plastic container and offered fried chicken to Henry. He grabbed a drumstick and bit into it. Dean Roscoe Chambers stepped to the head of the conference table. The faculty fell silent. Roscoe looked like a senior U.S. senator. And he had the voice to match.

'I have a big announcement to make. Professor Lawson, would you please step to the front?'

Henry turned to Book with a puzzled look; Book shrugged. Henry stood and walked over to the dean, who put an arm around Henry's shoulders. Henry continued his assault on the drumstick.

'Oh, my God,' Professor Goldman said, 'Roscoe's appointing Henry our new assistant dean.'

'But he's not a lesbian,' Professor Manfried said.

'He's married with two children.'

'I want to be the first to welcome Henry Lawson to the club,' Roscoe said.

'Tenure?' Henry said.

Roscoe laughed. 'Tenure? No, the dean's club.'

'I'm the new assistant dean?'

'No. The new dean.'

Book thought Professor Manfried might faint.

'You're retiring?'

'What? Hell, no, I'm not retiring. You're not the new dean here at UT, Henry. You're the new dean at the new Texas A&M law school.'

Henry almost choked on the chicken. 'I am?'

Roscoe laughed again. 'Listen to him playing coy with us. Now, Henry, you're going to be sitting on a pile of money with the two hundred million James Welch donated to the A&M law school—'

James Welch had earned his MBA from UT, but he had earned his B.S. from A&M. He supported both of his alma maters generously. And he kept his promises.

'—so promise you won't steal all my professors.'

Henry gazed upon the assembled faculty, at the Harvard–Yale cartel.

'Oh, don't worry, Roscoe. I would never do that.'

Dean Roscoe Chambers applauded Henry, and the faculty joined in.

Book waited for Henry to accept congratulations from the other faculty members. Then Henry came over to Book; he arrived with the drumstick in his hand and a suspicious look on his face.

'I think I owe you big time,' he said.

'For what?'

'This.'

'Congratulations, Henry. That's where you belong. Just make your law school the best in Texas, or at least as good as the football team.'

'The football team's got more money.'

'It is Texas.'

Professor Manfried walked past and said, 'Henry, I'll email you my CV.'

After she was out of earshot, Henry said, 'I've got to remember to block her email address.'

They shared a chuckle. Roscoe called to Henry, so they shook hands. Henry took a step away but stopped.

'Book, anytime you want to move to College Station, there's a tenured job waiting for you.'

'Thanks, Henry. But this is where I belong.'

Henry walked over to the dean, and Book walked out. Before he got to the door, Dean Roscoe Chambers yelled to him.

'Bookman . . . get a haircut.'

Book returned to his office and found Myrna on the phone again. She held the receiver out to him and whispered, 'Your sister.'

He took the phone and put it to his ear. 'Joanie.'

'Book—'

'I'm going to move Mom in this weekend.'

'Good. You want to say hi to her?'

'Sure.'

'Hold on. I'll put her on.'

A small voice came over. 'Hello.'

'Mom, it's Book.'

'What book?'

'No . . . it's John. Your son.'

'My son?'

'You want to live with me?'

'Who?'

Joanie came back on. 'Sorry, Book, it's a cloudy day for her.'

'I'll take care of her.'

He would take care of her, but who would take care of him?

★   ★   ★

382

He walked into his office where he found a young woman sitting at his work table and reading his mail. She had a sucker in her mouth.

'Who are you?'

She removed the sucker. It was a red Tootsie Roll Pop.

'Veronica Cross. I'm your new intern. But I don't work nights or weekends, I don't do—'

'Where's Nadine?'

'She quit.'

'*Why?*'

Veronica shrugged her shoulders. 'All she said was she didn't go to law school to get shot at and run off the road and put into the hospital and drink lousy coffee in West Texas. She was just joking, right, Professor?'

Book walked over and stared out the window at the campus. Sooner or later they all quit.

'Right, Professor?'

He sighed. 'Yes, Ms. Cross. She was just joking.'

'I thought so.'

'The coffee wasn't that bad.'

He turned to his new intern. She was not dressed like a student, but like a lawyer in a high-collared white blouse, long black skirt, and shiny black heels. Her short black hair was neatly done, and her makeup perfect. She sat with erect posture.

'Oh, she did say one more thing.'

'What's that?'

'Something about living without a net, whatever that means. I heard she quit law school and is moving to France to become a chef. Is that crazy or what?'

Book smiled. 'Or what.'

'And she said to tell you that you're her hero.'

'She said that?'

'Uh, yeah.'

Veronica gestured with the Tootsie Roll Pop at the stack of mail on the table in front of her.

'So let me get this straight: pathetic people from all over the country write these letters to you and expect you to drop everything and run off and help them? Like you've got nothing better to do? I mean, seriously?'

'Seriously.'

'So I've got to read about all their pitiful lives every week?'

'Every week.'

She exhaled. 'These people should stop whining about injustice and go out and get a job and make something of themselves.'

'A little compassion-challenged, are we, Ms. Cross?'

Veronica Cross groaned. 'Oh, God. My dad was right. He watches you on TV, said you were a liberal Democrat.'

Book smiled again. Perhaps the internship would prove helpful to Ms. Cross.

'Let me know if you find any letters I should read.'

Veronica held out an envelope, almost reluctantly.

'Well . . . this one is sort of interesting.'

About the author

Born and educated in Texas, Mark Gimenez attended law school at Notre Dame, Indiana, and practiced with a large Dallas law firm. He lives in Texas. He has written six previous novels: *The Colour of Law*, *The Abduction*, *The Perk*, *The Common Lawyer*, *Accused*, and *The Governor's Wife*.